BRENTFORD F.C.

THE COMPLETE HISTORY
1889 - 2008

By Graham Haynes & Dave Twydell

Published by:
Yore Publications
12 The Furrows, Harefield,
Middx. UB9 6AT.

British Library Cataloguing-in-Publication Data.
A catalogue record for this book
is available from the British Library.

ISBN 978 0 9557889 5 6

Printed and bound by:
The Cromwell Press, Trowbridge

Foreword

I first called on Graham's shop, Clare's Pantry, as a Sales Rep, in January 1995 and over the course of the next few years we built up a good, friendly business relationship. (Unbeknown to either of us at that time we each thought the other was married and therefore did not want to take things any further). For the first 18 months or so when I visited Clare's we always did the order standing by the till, however, one day I was invited to his "office" a shack tacked on to the back of the shop behind the stock room - no desk, no chair, no heating, no phone, just a load of old shelving and a couple of chest freezers for storing spare frozen goods. You get the picture, I hope. Over the course of a couple of years I got to know his office very well! One day, whilst we were doing the business, Graham was called away to the phone and being nosey, I looked at all the paperwork strewn across the tops of the freezers which seemed to have nothing to do with the grocery trade, just football. When Graham returned I asked *"Are you interested in football, then?"* which looking back seems the most ludicrous question to ask of him but then it seemed quite sane. That was the start of our budding relationship.

Unbeknown to me Graham had been trying to find a catalyst, other than work, in order to get to know me more and now he had found it. What was spread over those freezer tops was workings for the book he was writing at the time and later published.... *"A-Z of Bees"*. He was a Brentford supporter and I a Chelsea fan and the first time we went out as friends was to the 1997 FA Cup Final at Wembley, Chelsea v Middlesbrough, when Di Matteo scored the quickest ever Cup Final goal. After the game we had the ticket and a photograph of the goal framed, as the tickets for this game had Brentford F C on them, from where they had been obtained. During our courtship, which began in February 1998, we attended both Brentford and Chelsea matches, although if they clashed we would travel up to London together and each go to our own team's matches. During this time and over the following ten years I came to love Brentford and its supporters many of whom have become good friends. I have been to many away games with Graham, in England and Europe, including the Millennium Stadium supporting both teams, where we also went to watch the Speedway Grand Prix, another of Graham's sporting interests. Graham took a great interest in the Wightlink Islanders having shares in the team and where, during the season, we would travel every Tuesday night.

During the course of his life Graham had owned and bred many racing greyhounds. When I came to know him he had three retired racers living at home. We bought our first dog together in about 2002 and we named her "Griffin Parkbee" (AKA Daisy) – I wonder why? We also have other dogs in our ownership with names such as Nightingale Bee and Braemar Bee. I wasn't allowed to name any of them after my other team!!

Throughout our blossoming relationship and eventual marriage in 2001 I knew Graham to be a fervent writer of articles for the Brentford matchday programme and he was delighted when he was appointed Brentford's official club historian (not before time I said). What would turn out to be his penultimate book *"Timeless Bees"*, which he co-wrote with Frank Coumbe, was published in 2006. Earlier this year after discussions with Dave Twydell, the pair embarked on another book, Graham planning to finish his contribution before we set off on holiday in July. Although well ahead of schedule, he had not quite finished before his untimely death, en route to Brentford's last game of the season. Thanks to Ian Westbrook and Rob Jex for continuing much of the work where Graham had left off .

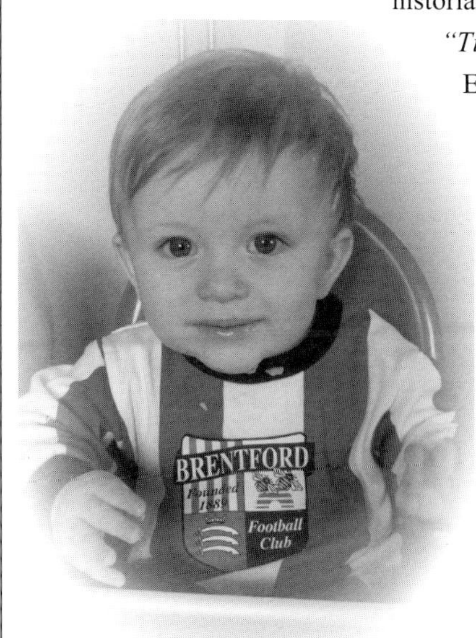

This book is a fitting tribute to Graham and he wanted a dedication to his second grandson, Nathan Graham Haynes, who sadly will not know how great his Grandad was. A great family man, proud of his sons, their respective partners and greatly missed by all whose paths he crossed

Janet Haynes
September 2008

Acknowledgements:

In a book of this nature there are many contributors, major to minor. In the unique circumstances in which this book has been published, with the tragic death of Graham during the writing and compilation period, there are a number of people that immediately offered their assistance and also provided material willingly. Special thanks are especially due to two long time and knowledgeable Brentford supporters; Rob Jex for the use of his statistical work and checking plus other material he provided, together with Ian Westbrook for his help on both proof-reading and his providing a section of the written work. Janet Haynes was pleased to contribute with some checking and other proof-reading was undertaken by my wife Fay. At the club, acting C.E.O. David Heath in particular has assisted and thanks also to Mark Chapman for his design and work on the dust jacket.

I believe that one of the strengths of this books is the diversity and quality of the many illustrations (over 300 in total) - many of which I believe have not been published before. In this respect I offer my special thanks to current Brentford F.C. Official Photographer Mark Fuller for not only permission to use many of his superb photos but also for his assistance in tracing those required and forwarding same. Also of great help and with permission to use various photographs were Tim Street of the Hounslow Chronicle, Mark Chapman, former Brentford F.C. Photographer Ian Stratton and Brentford F.C. who gave permission to use their copyright items. In addition for giving their time and allowing me to select items for inclusion from their private collections, special thanks go to David Harrison, secretary of the Brentford Programme Collectors Club (plus Steve Smith and Lindsay Harverson), and Geoff Buckingham. In addition a number of items have come from both my own memorabilia collection and that of Graham's.

Note: All statements are to the best of the authors' knowledge, unless indicated or suggested otherwise, factual. Views and opinions, where included, are those generally expressed at the time or thereafter. Therefore the views and opinions expressed within this book are not attributable to any individuals or organisations including, without limitation, Brentford Football Club.

The bulk of the photographs from the 2005/06 season and onwards were provided by *©Mark D Fuller: www.markdfuller.co.uk at Official Brentford Pictures: www.officialbfcpics.co.uk* Finally thanks to Tony Brown of Soccerdata Publications for providing sections of the statistical work.

Dave Twydell
(September 2008)

PER ASPERA AD ASTRA!
Through difficulties to the stars!

Dedication:

This book is principally dedicated to Graham Haynes (1945 - 2008), late, official historian of Brentford F.C......

.....In addition all the, often long-suffering, Bees fans', particularly my 'away' game companions, Bill, Rob, Rik and Sarah, plus my regular Griffin Park companion, grandson, Arran Matthews.

CONTENTS

			Page
Chapter	1	In The Beginning	5
	2	The Southern League Years	7
	3	The War Years	15
	4	The Turbulent Twenties	17
	5	The Glory Years	27
	6	The Second World War	39
	7	The Austerity Years	44
	8	The Dark Clouds Gather	50
	9	Ups But Mostly Downs	64
	10	Promotion Then Stability In The Eighties	82
	11	Up, Down Then Turn Around	100
	12	Out With The Old, In With The New	123

The 90's and Onwards... A Colourful History	145
A History In Programmes	157
Grounds For A Change	161
Supporters Through Thick and Thin	168
Brentford Players: Who's Who	170
Appearances - Top Ten	173
Goalscorers - Top Ten	174
International Players	175
Brentford versus The Rest	176
Statistics: Notes	178
Attendances and Seasonal Summary	179
Seasonal Statistics and Team Groups	
1889/90 - 1919/20	180
1920/21 - 1938/39	198
1939/40 - 1945/46	225
1946-47 - 1999/00	228
2000/01 - 2007/08	306
Dedications	319
Yore Publications	320

Chapter 1: IN THE BEGINNING

On Wednesday, October 2nd, 1889, an article appeared in the "Thames Valley Times" decrying the fact that in contrast to many urban areas in the location Brentford, the County Town of Middlesex, didn't have a football team to keep the younger element occupied during the winter months.

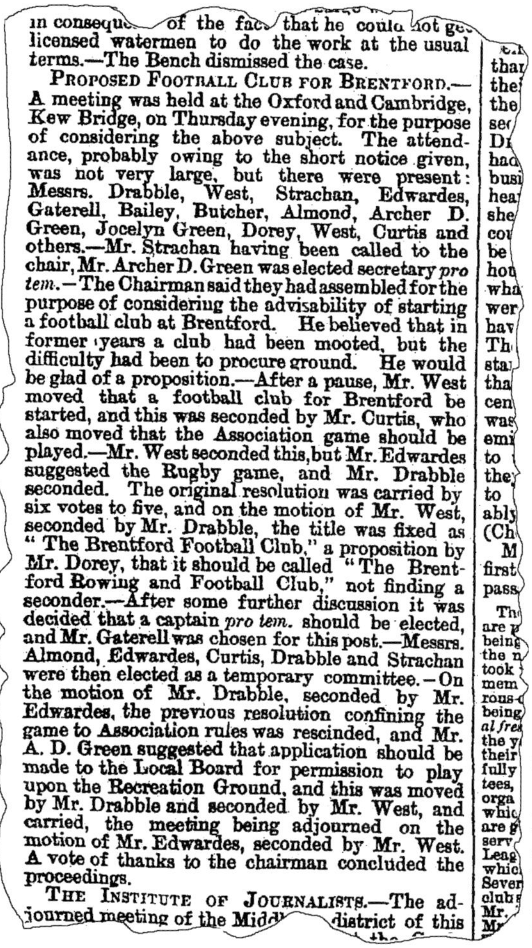

As a direct result Archer Green, the secretary of the Brentford Rowing Club, called a meeting at their headquarters, the Oxford and Cambridge Hotel at Kew Bridge, with a view to forming a football offshoot. Held on Thursday, October 10th, it attracted more than 30 interested parties who, in a mood of high excitement, duly formed " The Brentford Football Club "

in consequ... of the fac... that he coula not ge... licensed watermen to do the work at the usual terms.—The Bench dismissed the case.

PROPOSED FOOTBALL CLUB FOR BRENTFORD.—A meeting was held at the Oxford and Cambridge, Kew Bridge, on Thursday evening, for the purpose of considering the above subject. The attendance, probably owing to the short notice given, was not very large, but there were present: Messrs. Drabble, West, Strachan, Edwardes, Gaterell, Bailey, Butcher, Almond, Archer D. Green, Jocelyn Green, Dorey, West, Curtis and others.—Mr. Strachan having been called to the chair, Mr. Archer D. Green was elected secretary *pro tem*.—The Chairman said they had assembled for the purpose of considering the advisability of starting a football club at Brentford. He believed that in former years a club had been mooted, but the difficulty had been to procure ground. He would be glad of a proposition.—After a pause, Mr. West moved that a football club for Brentford be started, and this was seconded by Mr. Curtis, who also moved that the Association game should be played.—Mr. West seconded this, but Mr. Edwardes suggested the Rugby game, and Mr. Drabble seconded. The original resolution was carried by six votes to five, and on the motion of Mr. West, seconded by Mr. Drabble, the title was fixed as " The Brentford Football Club," a proposition by Mr. Dorey, that it should be called "The Brentford Rowing and Football Club," not finding a seconder.—After some further discussion it was decided that a captain *pro tem.* should be elected, and Mr. Gaterell was chosen for this post.—Messrs. Almond, Edwardes, Curtis, Drabble and Strachan were then elected as a temporary committee.—On the motion of Mr. Drabble, seconded by Mr. Edwardes, the previous resolution confining the game to Association rules was rescinded, and Mr. A. D. Green suggested that application should be made to the Local Board for permission to play upon the Recreation Ground, and this was moved by Mr. Drabble and seconded by Mr. West, and carried, the meeting being adjourned on the motion of Mr. Edwardes, seconded by Mr. West. A vote of thanks to the chairman concluded the proceedings.

THE INSTITUTE OF JOURNALISTS.—The adjourned meeting of the Midd... district of this

Which code was to be adopted, association or rugby, was left to a meeting six days later. Bill Dodge, who ironically was to serve Brentford for the best part of 72 years, initially as a player and later as club President, championed the case for rugby but it was the association game that won the day by eight votes to five.

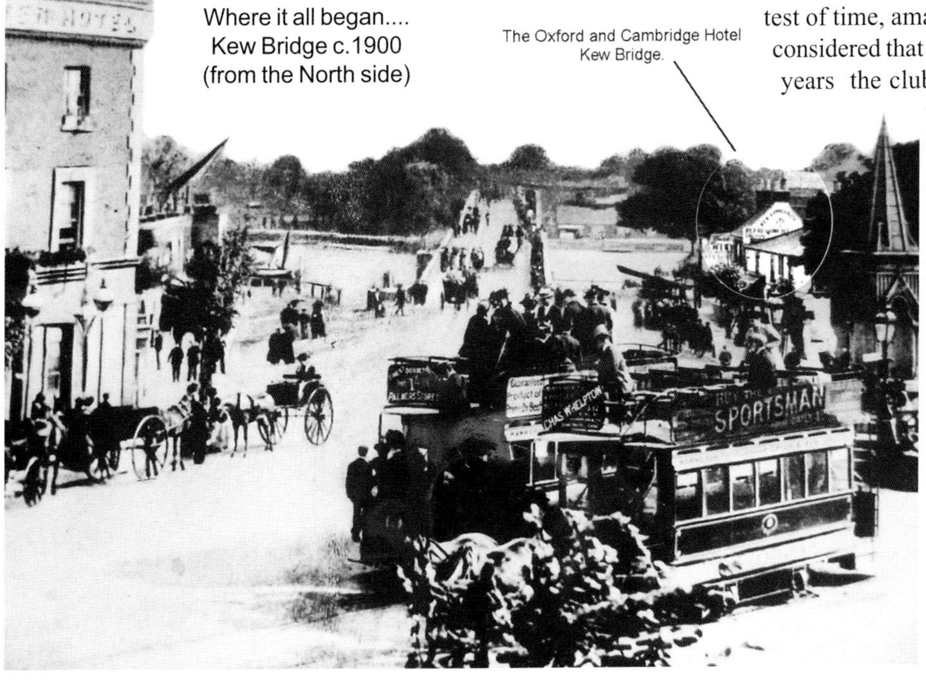

Where it all began.... Kew Bridge c.1900 (from the North side)

The Oxford and Cambridge Hotel Kew Bridge.

Salmon, claret and light blue, the same as the rowing clubs, were adopted as the team's colours, although the salmon was never incorporated in the shirt, and JJK Curtis appointed captain simply on the basis that he was the only one present with more than a passing knowledge of how the game was played!

The problem of a pitch to play on was settled when local businessman Edwin Underwood had his offer of a piece of land behind the old Wesleyan Chapel at the top of Clifden Road gratefully accepted . Underwood, for his part, became the Club's first President.

Brentford Football Club was open for business, the curtain raiser coming on November 23rd when Kew provided the opposition in a friendly. The game ended 1-1 and gate receipts amounted to the mammoth sum of half-a-crown .

Fourteen games, all friendlies, took place in that first season as the club made a tentative start to its life. Apart from Brentford not one of those teams have stood the test of time, amazing when it is considered that for the next few years the club was seen as a very small fish in a large local pond. Hounslow Town, Southall, Hanwell, Stanley and Chiswick Park were the teams most likely to move on to greater things. In fact in 1892, when an abortive attempt was made to form a Southern

League, Chiswick Park were given the nod in preference to Tottenham Hotspur.

Undoubtedly a major reason why Brentford succeeded while others faded into obscurity was the calibre of men running the club in those formative years, men such as the Dorey brothers, Underwood, Bill Stephenson Henry Strachan and Hinton-Bailey, businessmen responsible for supporting such innovations as a library, swimming bath and public market to Brentford and who saw in the football club another means of bringing honour and recognition to the town

Brentford continued to exist on a diet of friendlies for the next two seasons during which attendances began to move upwards into three figures and led the club's committee to sound out the possibility of joining a league.

In the summer of 1892 an application to join the newly formed West London League fell on stony ground, but Brentford had better luck when the West London Alliance smiled on them favourably. This came at a time when the club had been made homeless after the ground in Clifden road was sold for a housing development which meant that the first five games, all won, were played away while the search went on for new premises. The club breathed a sigh of relief when a piece of land became available behind the Plough Inn in Little Ealing which the Committee jumped at like a shot.

The first game on the new ground took place on October 15th against Clarence in the London Junior Cup and resulted in a 2-1 victory. The team now had the bit between its teeth and took the winning run to nine before suffering a 5-0 defeat away to Uxbridge Reserves in the Middlesex Junior Cup. In the league though the "Bonny Boys", as Brentford were known, continued to power forward, and finished as unbeaten champions. Unfortunately no trophy or medals were issued through what the league management described as "lack of funds", as a direct result of which Brentford rescinded their membership and joined the more senior West London League.

The earliest known team group from the 1892/93 season.
Players and Officials include: J.H.Bailey (Senior), J.H.Bailey (Junior), Charlton, Beaver, J.Butcher, Turner, Pring, Bloomer, Ward, Saunders, Foster, James, F.Butcher, HeyPhillips, Pratley, Edwards, Steers, Stevenson, Becket, Davis and

The new alliance lasted for one game, a 5-0 home defeat, and Brentford then pulled the plug following a row with the league over the transfer of Archie Williams from Hounslow.

Brentford were now confined to friendlies and local cup competitions and managed to hold supporters interest by reaching the final of the Middlesex Junior Cup, beating Westminster Ponsonby 2-1 on Crouch Ends' ground. It was a red letter day in the club's short history and around 5,000 people crowded Kew Bridge station and its surrounds to welcome the team home on their way to a civic reception at the Castle Hotel.

Twelve months later the polish came out again when the West Middlesex Cup finished up in the clubs possession after the 8th King's Royal Hussars were defeated 4-2 in the final at Southall. To reach the final Brentford had to overcome Hounslow 2-0 in the semi's, a feisty encounter marred by crowd trouble which led to a temporary halt while the local constabulary restored order.

The diet of friendlies and cup competitions had remained the same and the 1895-96 campaign made it three years on the trot when Brentford did not play a game with points at stake. Before the season got underway the club moved its headquarters to Shotters Field in Windmill Road, a ground more central to the town. Again it was one of the cups that held supporters attention, but this time the team fell at the final hurdle, beaten 2-1 by Southall in a bid for the West Middlesex Trophy.

Brentford's performances gave them leverage into becoming one of the founder members of the London League, Second Division in 1896-97, the team underlining that they were becoming a force to be reckoned with by chasing home Bromley in the race for the title, with QPR and Fulham struggling in their wake. Friendlies apart, the team went unbeaten until March and even then it took the Amateur Cup holders Old Carthusians to lower their colours in the semi-finals of the London Senior Cup.

A measure of Brentford's rising status came in October when crack Scottish First Division side St. Bernards , Cup winners in 1895, were held 0-0 in what may have been a record attendance at Shotters Field ; certainly it more than covered the £10 appearance money the Scots asked for.

1897-98 saw Brentford take their place in the First Division of the London League and such had been the club's progress they didn't feel out of place by entering the FA Cup for the first time either. Here Ward scored a hat trick as the 1st Coldstream Guards were swept aside 6-1 before succumbing 4-1 to the 3rd Grenadier Guards in a replay. The other Cup competitions again brought the best out of the team and both the London and Middlesex Senior Cups ended up in the club's trophy cupboard. The London version was a particular feather in the club's cap and attracted huge interest in the town witnessed by the fact that over a thousand supporters journeyed by special train from Brentford Central to the final against Ilford at the Essex cricket ground in Leyton. Brentford's 5-1 success was telegrammed back to base, leaving the townsfolk to make hasty preparations for a heroes' reception on their return.

By then a welcoming committee of thousands ringed the s tation. A procession was formed, the team were perched on the town's new fire engine and with the Feltham Brass Band leading playing "lively selections" the players paraded through Brentford to a raucous reception from the crowds lining the streets.

There was more excitement to come, as on the final day of the season Brentford only needed to beat Barking Woodville to leapfrog Thames Ironworks (now West Ham United) and be crowned London League Champions.

However, events conspired against them, some of their own making. Two days earlier Brentford beat 2nd Scots Guards to lift the Middlesex Senior Cup, after which it is probable a few sherbets were downed and the next night the team attended a celebration at St. James Hall, Piccadilly, at which the London Senior Cup was presented to captain Harry Edney. Again the beer flowed freely, as the following afternoon they gave a jaded display and could only draw 0-0, a result which handed the Championship to the Hammers.

Chapter 2: THE SOUTHERN LEAGUE YEARS

1898-99

Brentford were now established as one of the better teams in West London and it came as no surprise when they gained election to the Second Division of the Southern League. Although this was another big step forward the club remained amateur, a decision that was to have far reaching consequences.

For a start it meant that some of the best players were spirited away by professional clubs. "Okay" Field left for Sheffield United, Dave Lloyd was signed by Thames Ironworks and by the turn of the year Booth, Pennington and Ward had all turned professional elsewhere.

To make matters worse the club lost the use of Shotters Field when the owner Mr. Beldham decided to increase the rent to an unacceptable level. To get out of a sticky situation the club amalgamated with a junior organisation, Brentford Celtic, whose pitch was out of town at Cross Road, near South Ealing station. Conditions were spartan to say the least, as there were no facilities for spectators and to make matters worse the pitch had a heavy slope.

In 1898, Students from nearby Borough Road College supported fellow pupil Joe Gettins, by crying the college's war-cry 'Buck Up B's', and that nickname for the Brentford football team stuck. Yet Gettins only played one first team match for 'The Bees'!

For all these problems the season began well and St.Albans (6-1), Fulham (4-1) and Wycombe Wanderers (9-2) all succumbed to big defeats in the early stages. It didn't last, however, and the loss of the better players, and no adequate replacements, had a detrimental affect on results. It also became difficult to raise a team each week and matters came to a head when Brentford were forced to scratch from an FA Amateur cup tie at Grimsby All Saints due to a supposed lack of manpower.

The loss of Booth in March was the catalyst for Brentford to adopt the stance "if you can't beat them, join them", but instead of openly turning professional the club began making illegal, under the counter, payments to players. This led to a resurgence in form and a final position of fourth in the table.

However, the FA, who had been keeping a watching brief at the club's indiscretions, were getting ready to pounce with shattering consequences for the committee running the club.

1899-1900

The desirability of turning professional was top of the agenda at the AGM in May. The answer should have been an emphatic "Yes" but instead the committee decided to put off a decision until the following week. It was patently obvious to one and all that players had been paid for their services, some under the heading of travelling expenses or board and lodgings, and one in whisky from a local off license.

However, when the meeting reconvened it was decided to remain amateur as the club was heavily in debt and therefore felt it was a step too far. By coming to this conclusion they laid both the club's and their own head on the chopping block as in October the FA, aware of what was going on, called upon Brentford to produce their books. After managing to evade passing them over for a few weeks the FA lost patience and ordered Brentford to resign. A charge of professionalism was laid against the club and a committee of inquiry set up. The picture it painted when it reported back on November 13th left the FA with no option but to take action. Among the findings were that £20 had been paid to obtain goalkeeper Penningtons' release from the army and books destroyed to hinder the inquiry.

As a result Hinton-Bailey, the secretary, was suspended sine-die; Stevenson, Dodge, Baker, Challis and Dorey, the finance committee, were suspended until the end of April 1900; the club was fined £10 and suspended for one month; and two players, Bert Lane and Nick Mattocks were declared professional.

It could have been worse and in many respects was a blessing in disguise as the club management, or what remained of it, made the decision to carry on as a professional outfit, after it had served its time.

Brentford were not out of the woods yet, though, as results on the field had been abysmal and crowds at Cross Road in the same category, so that by the end of February bankruptcy reared its ugly head. Step forward Edwin Underwood. Almost single handed he went about the business of saving the club by getting many local businesses to write off money owed them and of equal importance persuaded the Boston Park Cricket Club to allow use of their pitch in York Road during the football season.

Meanwhile, Brentford saw out their stay at Cross Road with three successive wins which lifted them to third from bottom and killed the spectre of perhaps needing to seek re-election, which with the club's recent track record might not have been a formality.

1900-01

Brentford began their first full season as professionals with high hopes for the future, especially as thanks to Underwood they now had no significant debt to weigh them down. The only drawback was the refusal of the cricket club to allow the building of stands or terraces which severely restricted the number of spectators it could accommodate.

The Southern League, Second Division, having shrunk to nine teams, meant that Brentford needed another outlet, so they joined the London League as well, a competition in which during the early weeks Barnet were hammered 12-1. A fortnight later Brentford were on the wrong end of a 6-1 defeat by Millwall Reserves, a hiding that persuaded the club's committee to seek out a better class of player for the forthcoming Southern League campaign.

Winger Roddy McLeod was signed from WBA, where he won an FA Cup medal in 1892; centre half Jack Graham won back to back Southern League titles at Millwall in the mid-nineties and made the move across London in the company of goalkeeper Clear and wing half Hainsworth; and Peter Turnbull had been a top notch goalscorer with a number of clubs, latterly QPR.

Brentford, their new signings in tow, proved a cut above the rest and went though the season unbeaten, a sequence that included an 11-1 defeat of Wycombe Wanderers and a 9-1 victory at Southall. It didn't stop there as in the London League, in which Brentford finished 8th, Wandsworth were crushed 10-0 and Lower Clapton Imperial torn apart 11-2.

It was a tremendous achievement, one in which the newcomers played a significant role. Clear conceded few goals, Graham was an inspiration at the heart of the defence and McLeod and Turnbull netted almost 60 goals between them. The team's success rekindled latent support in the town and crowds of up to 3,000 squeezed into the York Road enclosure. As one local scribe eloquently put it: "The Busy Bees of Brentford are filling their hive with the honey of success".

Unfortunately there was no automatic promotion or relegation so Brentford were required to contest a play off with the First Divisions' bottom side Swindon Town. The game, at Reading's Elm Park, ended goal less, so under the rules Swindon retained their status.

Disappointed, but far from despondent, Brentford along with Northampton Town and Wellingborough, applied for a place in an enlarged First Division for the following season. On form Brentford should have won the day, but instead it was Northampton who were voted in. That should have been it, but soon afterwards it became known that Bristol City had surrendered their membership and joined the Football League so Brentford and Wellingborough were given the chance to state their case once more. Due largely to their poor ground facilities Brentford missed out again. However, just as Brentford were resigned to another stint in the lower division, came news that Gravesend had gone to the wall. The Bees were offered the vacancy which was duly accepted.

1901-02

Election to the top strata of the Southern League caused tremendous excitement in the town. The competition was at its zenith with the top clubs drawing the equal, if not better crowds than those in the Football League. It had strength in depth as witnessed by the fact that Tottenham Hotspur lifted the FA Cup in 1901, yet finished only fifth in the Southern League.

It was obvious then that to be competitive Brentford would need to sharpen up, both on and off the pitch. To raise capital for team and ground improvements, to which the cricket club had reluctantly agreed, it was felt desirable to form the club into a Limited Liability Company. A prospectus was issued and in August "The Brentford Football & Sports Club" came into being with a share capital of £2,000 consisting of 4,000 ten shilling shares.

The first board under Chairman Charlie Dorey consisted entirely of local men: Bill Dodge, Tom Dorey, W. Adams, Harry Blundell, William Brown, FH. Knight, H. Jason Saunders, Bill Stephenson and I. Ward. Dodge, who played in the club's very first game, and Blundell were to complete 50 years on the board and see the club rise from parks football to the very pinnacle of the English game by the mid 1930's.

Back in the early days of the Century that seemed a distant pipe dream. Brentford, although now professional, remained amateur in outlook. There was no team manager, everything from player signings to team selection being the responsibility of Honorary Secretary Will Lewis and his board of directors. Although their hearts were in the right place it soon became obvious this was not a sufficient reason to be able to run a professional football club.

Relations with the cricket club were tense, as they gave the distinct impression that Brentford were there under sufferance by refusing to allow an upgrade in facilities. So it was against a background of poor amenities and little tactical knowledge on the part of management that Brentford kicked off their first campaign in the top division. It was November before the team won its first game and one of the few high spots came late in the campaign when Cup holders Spurs were beaten 2-1 in front of the season's best crowd of 3,834.

Away from home the team made very few waves and failed to win once. This left only Swindon Town beneath them, a situation that led to the club being required to play a Test Match against Grays United, the runners up in Division Two. A tense struggle at neutral Canning Town resulted in a 1-1 draw. The rules then called for extra time but Grays refused and, in so doing, forfeited their chance of promotion. Brentford could breathe a sigh of relief as had they lost their First Division status there was little room for manoeuvre elsewhere, especially as the Second Division had become unviable with just six clubs in contention in the season that followed.

1902-03

Quiet simply one of the worst seasons in Brentford's history. Just two wins in the league tells its own story as uniquely the team scored more goals in the FA Cup (17) than they did with points at stake (16). And to underline how outclassed the Bees were they took their winless sequence on the road to thirty and finished the season with just five points to their name.

Record of Matches Played, 1901—1902.

AUTUMN & WINTER SEASON, 1901—2.

THE BEST SELECTION WE HAVE EVER SHOWN.

FOOTBALL KNICKERS, HOSE, SHIRTS, AND TIES.

E. T. COOMBES, 737, High Rd., Tottenham

SPECIALIST IN

GENTLEMEN'S HATS & CAPS, HOSIERY, SHIRTS & GLOVES.

WILSON'S for General Ironmongery.
WILSON'S for Garden Requisites.
WILSON'S for Oil and Colors.
WILSON'S for Stoves and Ranges.
WILSON'S for Lead and Glass.
WILSON'S for Wall Papers.
WILSON'S for Doors, Mouldings and Timber.
WILSON'S for Lime, Cement, Plaster.
WILSON'S for Drain Pipes, latest options.
WILSON'S for Sanitary Appliances.

WILSON'S FOR EVERYTHING!

WILSON'S Celebrated Burning Oil delivered in sealed gall. Cans only. Write for Pamphlet, "How to use and burn our Oil."

WILSON'S LAMPS,
WILSON'S WICKS,
WILSON'S STOVES,
WILSON'S CHIMNEYS.

Our Coupons issued with the Oil, will keep the House in Wicks and Chimneys free of charge.

ON MONDAY, APRIL 28th, SPURS v. PRESTON NORTH END. (Friendly.)
TUESDAY, APRIL 29, SPURS v. WOOLWICH ARSENAL (Southern Charity Cup)

Tottenham Hotspur Football and Athletic Company, Limited.
PROGRAMME.

PIANOS.

PIANOS Tuned and Repaired by best Workmen.
PIANOS PACKED, REMOVED OR WAREHOUSED.
W. SAVILLE & CO., BRUCE GROVE.

SOUTHERN LEAGUE.

TOTTENHAM HOTSPUR.

RIGHT WING. GOAL CLAWLEY LEFT WING.
BACKS
ERENTZ TAIT
HALF BACKS
MORRIS McNAUGHT JONES
FORWARDS
SMITH CAMERON BROWN COPELAND KIRWAN

Referee:—Mr. A. MILLWARD.

ANDREWS SHANKS LOGAN GRIEVE JURY
FORWARDS
STORMONT REGAN McELENY
HALF BACKS
ROBSON McELHANEY
BACKS
GREEN
LEFT WING. GOAL RIGHT WING.

BRENTFORD.

Any alteration taking place in the Players' names, a Board will be sent round the ground corresponding with Nos. on the Programme.

PIANOS.

300 PIANOS to select from. TUNINGS FREE. Delivery Free. Send for Price List Free.

W. SAVILLE & Co.,
TOTTENHAM, WOOD GREEN, WALTHAMSTOW, PLUMSTEAD, &c.

The Public are warned against buying any other Programmes but this, as they are NOT Official.

Inside pages from the 'Spurs programme versus Brentford, April 1902 (which was lost 3-0) - The oldest surviving programme featuring The Bees.

Fortunately there was no automatic promotion or relegation so Brentford were required to take their chance in a winner takes all test match against Second Division Champions Fulham. The game tended to highlight the gulf in class between the two divisions as Fulham were thrashed 7-2 at neutral Shepherds Bush and Brentford once again survived on the outcome of a single game.

The FA Cup was the only joy the club's supporters could take from a desperate campaign, the Bees progressing through three qualifying rounds at the expense of Oxford City, Southall and Shepherds Bush before meeting their match in Football League, Second Division side Woolwich Arsenal in a replay at Plumstead after a record crowd for York Road of almost 7,000 had seen a 1-1 draw in the first attempt to settle the tie.

Brentford's star player had been Tommy Shanks and a few weeks later he moved to the Gunners in exchange for Maurice Connor and a cheque for £200. Connor was an instant success in a struggling side and on March 23rd he became Brentford's first International when capped by Ireland in their 2-0 defeat of Scotland in Glasgow. His partner at inside left was Shanks.

1903-04

Brentford had struggled badly in the last two seasons so to put the club on a firmer footing the board decided to advertise for a man with the expertise to show the way forward. Their choice in Richard Molyneux could hardly have been better. His pedigree was impeccable having been a founder member of Everton in 1878 and later their secretary. In 1892 he was one of the instigators behind Everton's move from Anfield to Goodison, which led to the formation of Liverpool FC. And between 1893-99 he sat on the Football League Management Committee.

His main priority was to sort the wheat from the chaff on the playing strength which resulted in wholesale movement in and out of the club. He managed to sign a number of players with Football League experience including the likes of George Parsonage and Jimmy Jay who were to give sterling service down the years.

The decision was also taken to change the team strip from claret and light blue stripes to blue and gold stripes, the racing colours of one of the club's patrons Lord Rothschilds, who had property locally.

The season kicked off in a mood of optimism and for a time this seemed well founded as the new look Brentford side led the table. The flags were out at the beginning of November when the Bees beat West Ham United 1-0 to chalk up the first away win in 35 attempts. This came a week after an 8-0 defeat of Uxbridge in the FA Cup (Brentford's record win in the competition).

This was the prelude to a decent run until knocked out in a replay at Plymouth Argyle. That game came soon after a new record crowd for York Road of 12,000 had attended the 1-1 draw with Fulham.

From then on though, it became an uphill struggle, not helped by thc enforced absence of Molyneux. Trouble began when goalkeeper Frail was sacked for "insubordination". There was no adequate cover so Molyneux and Bill Dodge approached a promising young keeper named Bishop, a serving soldier, with an offer to buy him out of the Army if he would sign for Brentford. This illegal approach reached the ears of authority and led to Dodge being suspended from football for two years and Molyneux until the end of April. Without their talisman the team went to pieces and eventually finished 13th.

Molyneux remained active during his enforced period of absence, however, as he began finalising details for the new ground at what was to become Griffin Park.

1904-05

The first game to take place at Griffin Park was a Western League encounter against Plymouth Argyle on September 1st. It ended 1-1 with Tommy Shanks netting for the Bees in front of a crowd of 5,000. The main stand was not in use as the Borough Surveyor deemed it unsafe, words of wisdom as it transpired, as during a storm in January the roof collapsed.

Whilst Brentford made a decent fist of their games in the Western League, a mid –week competition to supplement the Southern League engagements, and finished runners-up to Plymouth Argyle, a poor start to the main competition wrote off the campaign almost before it began. Fourteenth was hardly the final position Brentford's management had hoped for, although with gate receipts rising from £3,308 to £4,171 the move to Griffin Park was certainly justified.

There were a couple of other things to chew on: George Parsonage proved a tower of strength at the heart of the defence and was rewarded by a trial for the England side, while the FA Cup tie against Reading saw more that 16,000 fill the new ground, the highest to date at a Brentford game.

1905-06

Brentford's steady, if unspectacular, progress continued, as did the support base since the move to Griffin Park, and a special train carrying a thousand fans journeyed to Southampton for the opening game. A 1-0 victory got the campaign off on the right foot, but it soon became apparent that the Bees were not championship material yet. A final position of 11th was the best to date and the team again gave a good account of itself in the FA Cup, a 4-0 defeat of Wycombe Wanderers being followed by a tremendous win against Bristol City who were in the middle of a run of 14

Griffin Park (looking towards New Road), action versus Fulham, October 1905. The visitors won 2-0 before a crowd of 15,000.

consecutive league wins which underpinned their successful chase for the Football League, Second Division title. Their league compatriots Lincoln City fell victim to another giant killing in the next round, the Bees exceeding expectations with a comfortable 3-0 victory against a team that had just hammered Burnley 5-0 and followed up by crushing Burton United 5-1. Brentford had the toughest possible draw at the next stage away to the reigning Second Division champions Liverpool who were now setting a fierce pace at the top of Division One. Again the Bees rose to the challenge, but in the end found the team heading for the First Division title too hot to handle and lost 2-0.

Not long afterwards another Brentford player was invited for an England trial when Tom Riley represented the South versus the North. He acquitted himself well catching the eye of Aston Villa who made an offer Brentford couldn't refuse.

It was at this stage of the season that Molyneux was laid low by a serious illness, one that claimed his life in June. His loss to the club was inestimable. Not only had he been the driving force behind the move to Griffin Park, and an accompanying huge increase in attendances, but he had also signed the quality of player needed for Brentford to become an established name in Southern League circles. He would be sorely missed.

Players and Officials from 1905

First row: Oliver, Parsonage, Boag, Shanks, Hobson.

Second row: Bellingham, Davidson, Dullroy, Whittaker (goal), Watson, Tomlinson.

Third row: Ward (Director), Stevenson (Director), Lewis (Director), Crone (Trainer), Knight (Director), Harvey (Director), Howarth, Campbell (Ground man).

Fourth row: Brown (Director), Lamb (Director), R. Molyneux (Manager), C. Dorey (Chairman, sitting at table), Blundell (Vice-Chairman), Power (Direct Adams (Director).

Fifth row: Jay, Gates, Warrington, Underwood, Walker, Swarbrick.

1906-07

Instead of appointing a man of similar experience as Molyneux's successor the directors looked to their own ranks and gave the managers job to WG Brown, a local merchant's clerk. He had served the club well in a number of capacities and was secretary at the time of the London Senior Cup success in 1898. However, football had moved on since and, as time would tell, Brown just didn't have the necessary expertise to capitalise on the improvements instigated by Molyneux.

Initially all went well and 10th position in a field of twenty was the best yet. It was in the FA Cup that Brentford enhanced their burgeoning reputation most though. Second Division Glossop North End were first to come under the cosh , beaten 2-1 thanks to Pentland who made up for an earlier miss to net with his second attempt from the penalty spot. The Griffin Park crowd around this time had gained a name for being extremely partisan, a viewpoint challenged by the reporter covering the game for "Sportsman" newspaper. He wrote: "The Bees have an excellent following and Saturday's gate was variously estimated at from twelve to fourteen thousand. To their credit be it recorded that their demeanour during some exciting play was that of sportsmen and we have the greatest pleasure in stating the fact in as much as charges of excessive partisanship have here this season been levelled at the habitués of Griffin Park."Indeed Justin was loudly cheered for saving a penalty by Pentland awarded for a bad foul upon McCallister"

The draw then brought First Division Middlesbrough to Griffin Park, a tie which fired the imagination of the locals. All ground records were shattered as 21,296 crammed in eager to see Brentford do battle with a visiting side boasting five Internationals including the legendary Steve Bloomer, lanky winger Bill Brawn, later to show his paces down the wing at Brentford and Alf Common, who commanded the first £1,000 transfer fee when signed from Sunderland the previous year. The crowd was so large that three times in moments of high excitement fencing around the pitch collapsed spilling spectators on to the playing area. Fortunately there were no casualties.

From this it can be gathered the game lived up to expectations, the home teams' enthusiasm proving the perfect foil for the cultured skills of the Ironsides. The only goal came after the break when Pat Hagan went on a solo run and planted the ball wide of the keeper. All hell broke loose as twenty thousand Brentonians did a dance of joy on the ashbank terraces. Brentford held on to win and at the final whistle little Hagan was carried shoulder high to the dressing room by ecstatic supporters. Middlesbrough's cup of woe was filled to overflowing when as they commenced the long journey home their charabanc shed a wheel in the High Street. Happily none of their party was injured but the incident was the icing on the cake to jubilant Brentford supporters about to paint the town red in celebration of their teams' memorable victory.

Fellow Southern League side Crystal Palace, whose ground at the time was the venue for the final, were next in line. The first game ended 1-1 and the scene then switched to Griffin Park the following Wednesday afternoon when a record number of sick notes must have been issued locally as another new high of 21,478 packed in for the replay. It was nip and tuck for the first 70 minutes but then an incident which resulted in Bees full back Archie Taylor receiving his marching orders swung the pendulum Palace's way. Down to ten men, Brentford were forced to defend desperately and with extra time looming looked to have weathered the storm. But it was not to be and a late, late goal settled the issue in the visitors favour. Out of the Cup and secure in mid table the season ended in anti climax.

1907-08

A poor away record - the team won just one game on their travels - meant that Brentford were again soon out of contention for honours. This, after a relatively successful few years, combined with the loss of Fulham on the fixture list, QPR's surge into prominence as successors to the Cottagers as Southern League Champions and Chelsea now pulling in mammoth crowds, hit Brentford where it hurt most: in the pocket.

The club had always lived a hand- to- mouth existence and the three West London neighbours doing well only exacerbated the situation. Budgets went out of the window as attendances slipped dramatically and when the Bees were knocked out of the FA Cup by Carlisle United and a long barren spell saw crowds dip below 3,000, Brown tendered his resignation. The financial situation became acute and in April the directors called a crisis meeting. Chairman Charlie Dorey explained to a packed audience that he and his fellow directors had been dipping into their own pockets to keep the club from going to the wall, a situation that couldn't go on for ever. Supporters now rallied to the cause and collection boxes were passed around at the few remaining home games to help pay the players summer wages.

It seemed that the club would ride out the storm, but the directors were then hit by a bombshell when the players demanded that before another ball was kicked they wanted their wages up front. Faced with this ultimatum the directors paid in full and then fired back by releasing the whole playing staff, which included George Parsonage, a veteran of 176 games for the Bees and temporary manager while a successor for Brown was sought, Tosh Underwood (175), Jack Watson (169), Jimmy Tomlinson (98) and Freddy Corbett (93) , all of whom had given sterling service.

1908-09

In May Fred Halliday was appointed secretary/manager, an association that was to last for the best part of 18 years. He was just 28, but could already boast a wealth of experience. He played for Everton, Bolton and Bradford City, and spent the previous season as manager of the new Bradford Park Avenue club. His first task was to sign a complete new set of players and, job more or less finalised, he and new trainer Tom Cowper set about moulding them into a viable force. It was easier said than done, and although the team performed its usual party piece and knocked Football League, Second Division side Gainsborough Trinity out of the FA Cup, when the curtain came down the Bees were bottom and facing the possibility of relegation to Division Two.

The club was not too worried, as back in January QPR had put forward a proposition that would have seen the top 16 Southern League clubs form a new Third Division of the Football League. Initially Brentford were not among them, which caused great consternation at Griffin Park. However, at a subsequent meeting it was decided to offer two more places and Brentford and Coventry City were the lucky recipients. It was all to no avail though, as when it came down to making a decision the Football League clubs dismissed the motion by 27 votes to 13.

This left Brentford's fate in the balance once more. The prospect of relegation was hardly worth contemplating as the majority of clubs in the lower division could barely scrape a decent crowd between them and would certainly have not been an attraction in West London.

Salvation came when at the Southern League's AGM there was an overwhelming vote in favour of increasing the First Division by two clubs to accommodate Brentford and also allow for the promotion of Croydon Common. It was a close call but Brentford could breathe again, just!

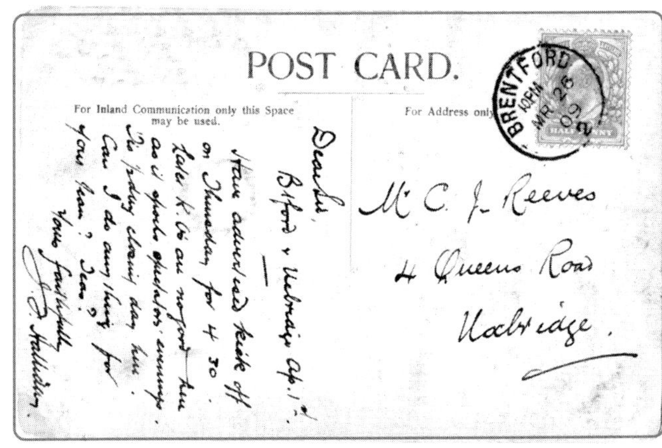

POST CARD.

For Inland Communication only this Space may be used.

For Address only

Dear Sir,

Mr C. J. Reeves
4 Queens Road
Uxbridge.

Postcard sent to Uxbridge F.C., from Fred Halliday. Reference a Friendly match to be played at Griffin Park on 27 March 1909.

1909-10

Brentford went into the season in such a poor state financially that they couldn't even afford new kit for the players. This was remedied when Dick Boxall, a long term supporter, purchased a new set, the proviso being that the colours were of his own choice. So the Bees kicked off in a predominately gold shirt which bore the Middlesex coat of arms, and white shorts.

Eph Rhodes 1909-10 season team captain. Rhodes was to be the club's near ever-present right back from 1908 to1918.

There was yet again a big turn round in players and the customary poor start to the campaign which meant that with a third of the season gone another battle to avoid relegation was in prospect. A 5-1 defeat away to fellow strugglers Norwich City in early February seemed to seal Brentford's fate but astonishingly, and for no apparent reason, things took a dramatic turn for the better, the last thirteen games realising 19 points as the Bees rocketed clear of trouble.

1910-11

The Bees began the season in the sort of form they enjoyed at the back end of the previous one. A good reason was that for the most part the team was largely unchanged, although a notable exception was the absence of Jimmy Jay who retired after making a club record 206 Southern League appearances.

The opening three games yielded a win, two draws and two goals, both of which were penalties converted by goalkeeper Archie Ling, which must be a very rare occasion when a team's goalkeeper has been a team's leading scorer.

Christmas arrived with Brentford hot on the heels of the leaders, thoughts of relegation banished for once. A sign of the club's growing stature came as three of the team were chosen for representative honours; George Reid, the leading scorer for the previous two seasons and destined to score 21 of the sides 41 goals in the Southern League this term, filled the centre forward berth in the Southern's games against the Football League and Scottish XI's.

Whilst Steve Buxton represented London in the annual match against Birmingham, and Christie played for London against Paris.

The New Year began with a 3-0 defeat away to the eventual champions Swindon Town and from thereon matters went from bad to worse. Defeat followed defeat and the Bees drifted out of contention, the only consolation being the red hot form of Reid who finished the season with separate hat tricks to his name on three occasions against Millwall Athletic, Exeter City and Southend United. One man doesn't make a team, however, as Brentford were about to find out.

1911-12

Brentford's financial situation once more dominated the news and the close season was spent looking to increase income. The newly formed Supporters League tried their best to assist, but they were swimming against the tide and when Oldham Athletic bid £425 for Steve Buxton and Clyde offered £500 for Reid, a record for a Brentford player, the club was in no position to turn them down.

It was obvious the team would struggle. Supporters sensed it too, and stayed away in droves. Brentford had never been good travellers, but this campaign was to see them plumb new depths as following a 7-4 defeat at West Ham United came a club record defeat for the professional era when murdered 9-0 at Coventry City. The worst was over, but Northampton Town later secured a 6-3 win and Brentford finished with just two away victories and a goal difference of 17- 43.

At home the team were a tougher nut to crack, highlighted by a 7-1 victory against New Brompton (Gillingham) , a scoreline that was to remain Brentford's best in the First Division of the Southern League. That win helped the Bees stay out of trouble and a final placing of fourteenth was not too bad considering the restraints the club worked under.

1912-13

Trouble and strife had become Brentford's second name and this season was to be no different. Early results did nothing to allay that opinion Halliday came under mounting pressure to stand down and following a string of eight straight defeats he resigned to concentrate on his secretarial duties. Full back Dusty Rhodes was appointed player/ manager and results initially took a turn for the better.

It was only short term, however, and a sequence of seven defeats as Easter approached left the Bees in dire straights. Brentford could have eased their problems as they were then due to face fellow companions in distress, Southampton home and away, but when they lost both the writing was on the wall.

A 2-1 defeat at Merthyr Town confirmed Brentford's position as relegation fodder along with Stoke City.

There was no escape this time and the Football World fully expected Brentford to throw in the towel and fold. The Southern League, Second Division consisted of thirteen clubs in 1912-13, of whom only Southend United (promoted), Croydon Common and Luton Town were English based. The rest were Welsh, many of them little more than village teams, and it was felt that for Brentford, now £7,000 in the red, to enter this environment would be throwing good money after bad.

All the players were paid off and a meeting was called by the directors for the end of May at which it was fully expected Brentford Football Club would be wound up. However, the club's directors showed they were made of sterner stuff and following a lengthy meeting, emerged with the news that the club would carry on.

A number of other clubs, admiring Brentford's pluck, sent donations and altogether £225 was received in " luck money " from amongst others QPR and Millwall. The Southern Leagues' management committee chipped in with a further £100 to offset the high cost of travelling to deepest Wales and the show was back on the road.

1913-14

Now back in business, Dusty Rhodes was re-appointed player/manager. The former Sunderland man had little to work with on the player front and immediately set off in search of new recruits. He was limited to just 16 professionals, of whom Middlesex cricketer Patsy Hendren and goalkeeper Ted Price had been on the books the previous season, but even so managed to sign what on paper looked a half decent squad.

It was imperative that the team got off to a flyer as the local populace had demonstrated in the past that they would only support a winning team. And a good start was just what Brentford made, with victories in all the first nine games and attendances the best for a number of years. By the time Christmas arrived Brentford shared with Croydon Common an unbeaten tag. The two clashed at Griffin Park on Christmas Day , a bumper crowd of 12,000 witnessing a 1-0 away win and from then on Croydon stretched away to become champions while the Bees chased them home, albeit at a distance, in third spot.

Brentford's limited playing resources had been the root cause of the failure to sustain a promotion challenge, as in the New Year injuries took their toll and led to Rhodes blooding two local youngsters of whom much would be heard later: Jack Cock and Bert White.

Chapter 3: THE WAR YEARS

1914-15

The summer of 1914 saw Brentford's fate again hang in the balance, as with Croydon Common and Luton Town promoted and Merthyr Town and Coventry City dropping down, the Bees found themselves out on a limb. Five of the Welsh sides in the division resigned and their only replacement was northern based Stalybridge Celtic, while to make matters worse the Southern League Management Committee withdrew the subsidy for Brentford's still numerous trips to the Principality.

The club's directors gritted their teeth and carried on, now in even more chastened circumstances. As the season approached there were just seven professionals on the books whose total weekly wage amounted to the princely sum of £18. The squad increased by two from the proceeds of a professional athletics meeting at Griffin Park and a boxing tournament in the Princess Hall. The rest was made up of a hotchpotch of locals.

But before a ball was kicked in earnest Britain and its Allies found themselves at war with Germany, as General Von Kluck set forth on a great sweep across Northern Europe. Six weeks is all it would last, was the general opinion, but instead four years of carnage lay in waiting. Many of the players joined the cause, so the season got off to a low key start. Gates were terrible and those who did turn up were likely to be harangued by a Colonel Bott to join the crusade against the Kaiser.

As time drew on there was agitation to get professional football closed down for the war's duration, but with most clubs working on borrowed money this would have been a last resort. Eventually, in December, the War Office came out in favour of allowing the game to continue on the basis that it offered entertainment for off duty servicemen. Not every club lasted the distance though. Abertillery, for example. The previous month Brentford recorded a record victory by thrashing them 10-0 but soon afterwards the Welsh club resigned from the competition and the result was expunged from records.

When the season ground to a halt Brentford were well down the table. Dusty Rhodes then joined the Army Pay Corps leaving Fred Halliday to combine his duties as secretary with management of the team. Total receipts amounted to less than £500, which spelt financial disaster in anyone's language. Most other clubs were in the same boat and it came as salvation to many, especially Brentford, when the FA decreed that the maximum wage should be cut to £3 and summer wages stopped altogether.

1915-19

When it became apparent in the summer of 1915 that there was no end to the war in sight the FA abandoned normal football in favour of regionalised leagues. Brentford joined the London Combination, which meant that instead of the likes of Mid-Rhonda, Pontypridd and Ebbw Vale, Griffin Park would stage games against Chelsea, FA Cup finalists in 1915, and Tottenham Hotspur from Division One; Arsenal, Clapton Orient and Fulham from the second; and top flight Southern League teams QPR, West Ham United, Crystal Palace, Millwall and Croydon Common. (It is worth noting that had the leagues carried on as normal, London would have been devoid of a team in the First Division as the bottom two clubs due for relegation were Chelsea and Spurs).

You would have thought that Brentford were on a hiding to nothing but, with guests allowed, the close proximity of army training camps at Feltham, Hounslow and Wimbledon gave the club a large pool of talent to draw on. It was no easy task though, and Brentford had to thank Halliday for his powers of persuasion in getting commanding officers to issue extra passes for the footballers in their ranks.

Brentford held their own in the first three years of the Emergency Competition and then in 1918-19 surprised the football world by winning the Championship. Stars of the show were Cardiff's Welsh International Fred Keenor, England amateur International Ted Hanney (Manchester City), Brentford's own Patsy Hendren and Alf Amos and most of all the strike pairing of Jack Cock and Bert White.

Between them they accumulated fifty one goals, local discovery White top scoring with 26 and Huddersfield's Cock chipping in 25. This coincided with the end of the war. Returning members of the forces looked to find entertainment outlets and football enjoyed a boom period as attendances rose to unprecedented heights. Brentford enjoyed their share of the market and gates at Griffin Park topped an average of 12,000 with receipts of £5,476 setting a new high as the club enjoyed the fruits of its success.

1919-20

After the glory days of the previous season Brentford toyed with the idea of seeking election to the Football League but in the end decided to accept an offer from the Southern League to join an enlarged First Division. Time would tell that it was the right choice, as beside not really being equipped to move up that far in grade, the prospect of the Southern League's top division being absorbed as a new Third Division was on the drawing board.

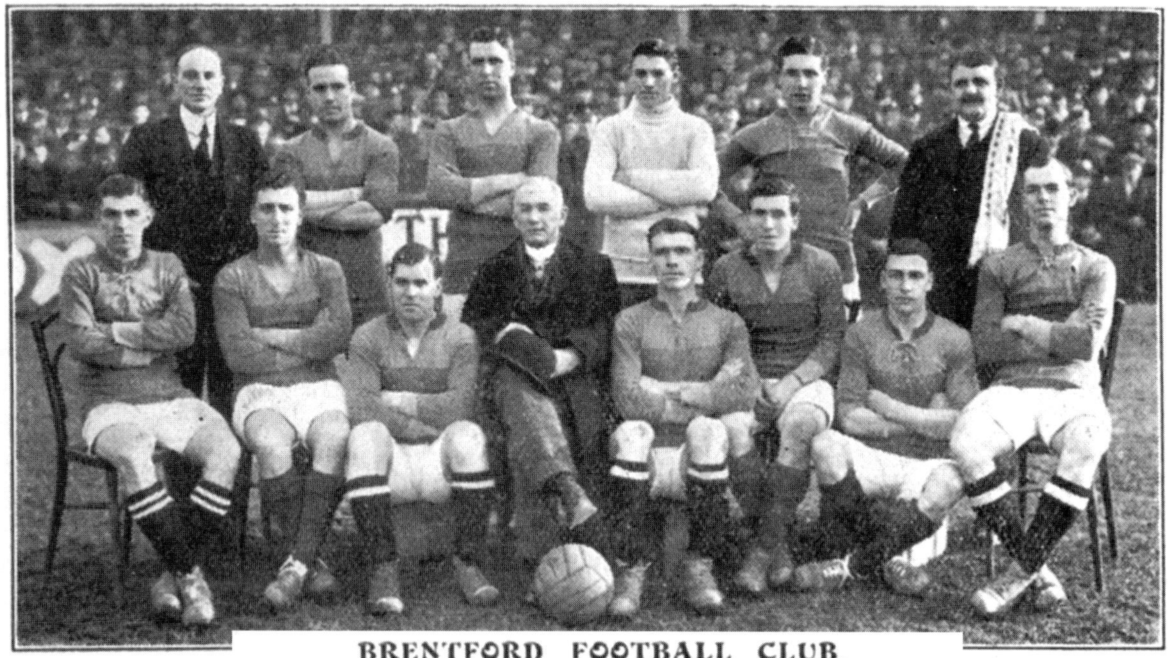

BRENTFORD FOOTBALL CLUB.
(Last Season's Champions of the London Combination).

Three of the better equipped Welsh clubs, Swansea Town, Newport County and Merthyr Town were also fast tracked into the senior division of the Southern League, while Croydon Common were the only major casualty among the Capital's professional clubs and failed to reappear. Crystal Palace moved to their ground at the Nest.

BRENTFORD

Football Club

(Winners London Combination, 1918-19).

Official Handbook

1919-1920.

COMPILED BY "BYSTANDER."

PRICE TWOPENCE.

Richmond:

F. W. DIMBLEBY AND SONS, "TIMES" OFFICE.

Few of the players who won the London Combination were available, leaving Halliday with the task of searching out almost a complete new team, which in the end saw 27 different players given the chance of first team action. This failure to field a settled side led to Brentford finishing down the field in 15th position, but unlike in previous years attendances did not tail off and the average held steady at around the seven thousand mark.

Reginald Boyne -the club's top goalscorer in 1919/20 and scored their first goal in the Football League

After the heady success of 1918-19 it was a season of consolidation. Beyond a shadow of doubt the most important event occurred off the field on May 18th when at a meeting in Sheffield it was proposed that the Southern League, First Division be elected en-bloc to form a Third Division of the Football League. 19 clubs voted in favour, one against and there was one abstention. The outcome was that eleven days later at the Football League's AGM the decision was rubber stamped and Brentford became one of twenty two new members of the Football League.

Chapter 4: THE TURBULENT TWENTIES

1920-21

Brentford's first season in the Football League started fairly well with two wins, two draws and a defeat from the first five games but then got progressively worse as the new set of players found it difficult to gel. Eleven players were signed of whom only goalkeeper William Young, who like a lot of the squad hailed from the north east, Tottenham Hotspur's James Elliott and centre forward Harry King (Leicester City) made an impression. The rest were of the here today, gone tomorrow variety.

Brentford kicked off their first campaign as members of the Football League with a 3-0 defeat at Exeter City, the Bees lining up: Young, Hodson, Rosier, Elliott, Levitt, Amos, Smith, Thompson, Spreadbury, Morley, Henery. Absent were Jack Durston and Patsy Hendren who were required by Middlesex for the crucial County Cricket match against Surrey at Lords. With their assistance Middlesex secured the victory that gave them their first Championship since 1903. It was a busy few days for Durston as at close of play on Monday he dashed over to Griffin Park to take his place in goal as the Bees beat Millwall 1-0. The match winner was Reg Boyne who two days earlier scored a hat-trick for the reserves in a 5-3 victory against Clapton Orient.

As autumn turned to winter and results began to go against the Bees on a regular basis early season optimism was replaced by doom and gloom. A bumper crowd of 16,379, the best for a number of years, was present for the local derby against QPR on Christmas Day.

The two captains when Brentford entertained Huddersfield Town, their first F.A.Cup match as a FootballLeague team.

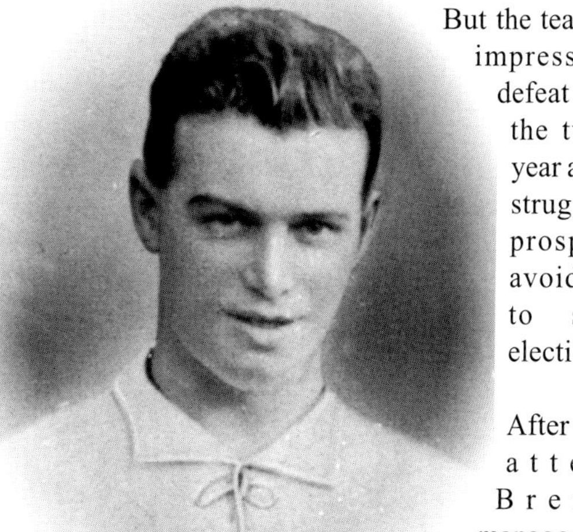

James Elliott (right-half) played in the first League match.

But the team failed to impress in a 2-0 defeat so that by the turn of the year an almighty struggle was in prospect to avoid the need to seek re-election.

After nine failed attempts, Brentford managed their first away win against fellow companions in distress Gillingham but just three more victories left the team second from bottom when the season ended. One of those successes came completely against the grain as at the end of March Grimsby Town were thumped 5-0 at Griffin Park, King recording the first hat trick by a Brentford player in League football.

Brentford now joined Gillingham in the re-election process. Fears that the division would be cut by two teams proved groundless as a new Northern section of the Third Division was given the green light. This paved the way for Grimsby's departure, while Third Division champions Crystal Palace were promoted. Brentford and Gillingham were re-elected unopposed and the division remained at 22 clubs by the election of Aberdare Athletic and Charlton Athletic.

Brentford breathed a sigh of relief, but that still didn't mean all was well at Griffin Park. A hefty loss of £1,555 on the season which brought the total deficit to almost £6,000 precipitated the resignation of three directors, Messrs Adams, Knight and Gomm. This left just the Chairman Jason Saunders, and Board members Pauling, Blundell and Dodge to run the show. After much discussion one of the group's main priorities was seen as the appointment of a team manager. Since the end of the war Secretary manager Fred Halliday had concentrated on the administrative side of the game and team matters were left to the Board, which in their case had obviously not worked. So the decision was taken to seek as team manager someone with a track record in the game. The outcome was that QPR centre half Archie Mitchell , a veteran of almost 500 games during which Rangers had twice been Champions of the Southern League, was handed the task of putting Brentford on its feet.

1921-22

Quality rather than quantity was the order of the day as generally speaking the Bees gave a much better account of themselves to finish 9th. Yet this came after the team initially struggled to find its feet and picked up only two wins in the first eleven games, one of those to Southend United, the team destined to finish last by a street. The turning point came against Mitchell's old club, QPR, at the back end of October when a Dave Morris hat-trick led the charge to a comprehensive 5-1 victory.

Confidence boosted, the team moved steadily up the table, helped by a purple patch that included straight wins against Norwich City 2-1, Reading 3-0, Bristol Rovers 4-2 and Aberdare Athletic 2-1. Interspersed were victories in the FA Cup against Dulwich Hamlet 3-1 and Shildon 1-0, which led to a plum home tie against the holders Tottenham Hotspur. The game was billed as the biggest in the club's history and with Brentford on a roll and Spurs chasing Liverpool hard for the First Division title the directors were optimistic of a new record crowd of around the thirty thousand mark. Unfortunately they let the prospect go to their heads and in hope of a bumper pay day doubled the entrance money to one shilling. Many stayed away in protest and the official attendance of 12,964 was way below expectations; indeed it was lower than the crowd for Aberdare Athletics' visit on Boxing Day. However, it did provide record receipts of £1,488. Spurs won 2-0 but the Bees jumped straight back to winning ways by beating the champions-in-waiting, Southampton 1-0, and Plymouth Argyle, the team destined to finish runners up, 3-1.

Brentford were enjoying their best season in many years and overall were attracting gates to match, the average pre-Christmas standing at 10,106. An indifferent spell followed the Argyle game which killed stone dead an outside chance of challenging for honours.

The team's away form didn't help as a 3-0 victory at Reading in December was all they had to show from their travels. One of those defeats, at Newport County in February, saw Alf Capper become the first Brentford player dismissed in League football. He disputed a throw-in decision by a linesman rather too vigorously and was sent for an early bath by the referee, Harry Curtis. Recognise the name? Yes, the same Harry Curtis who later took over as manager of Brentford and piloted them to the top flight!

The team finished on a high at home with successive wins against Millwall 1-0, Brighton & Hove Albion 4-0, Reading 2-0, Exeter5-2 and Swansea Town 3-0, while the away games ended in farce when Brentford started the fixture at Swansea with only nine men. It came about when three of the team, Young, Capper and Anstiss, missed the train to South Wales. When they did arrive at Paddington they were re-routed via Bristol and Cardiff where a fast car was waiting to whisk them off to Vetch Field. If all had gone to plan they would still have arrived in time for kick-off, but fate decreed otherwise, a burst tyre delaying their arrival until the game was ten minutes old. Brentford, meanwhile, took the field shorthanded and with Archie Mitchell taking Young's place in goal. It was an expensive gamble as the game's only goal came in the third minute when Mitchell misjudged a weak shot and it landed in the net behind him. Hardly the end to his playing career he would have wished for!

1922-23

The question was, could Brentford capitalise on the step forward they made the previous season? Sadly, the answer came before a ball was kicked when three of the side's mainstays, Alf Amos, Harry Anstiss and George Pither, were transferred to Millwall Athletic. Unusually for Brentford, all three were London born and as time was to show, the club would have been best served by holding on to them as they each went on to enjoy long productive careers. Amos won a Third Division (South) Championship medal at the Den in 1927-28; Anstiss did likewise in the Third (North) at Port Vale in 1929-30; and Pither played First Division football for Liverpool.

1922: A pre-season, happy group of players (The new road side in the background)

With the money received, Mitchell waded into the transfer market and signed eleven new men, most of whom had at best only featured in the reserve teams of northern Football League clubs. Why Brentford should have persisted in a policy that had been so singularly unsuccessful over the previous twenty years only the directors could answer. There was no rhyme or reason why many of the northern based players were signed, other than the fact they were cheap. Certainly very few lasted more than one season at Griffin Park before returning from whence they came.

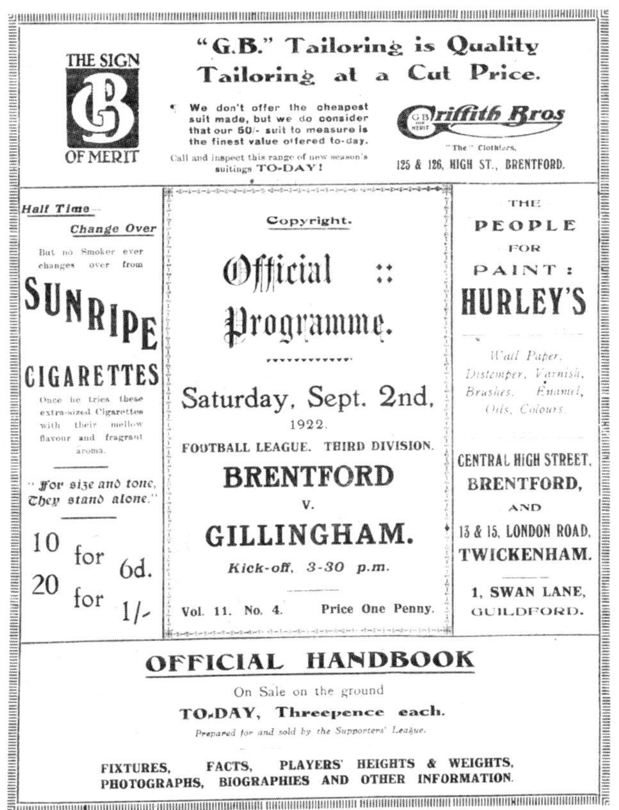

The second home match of the season was won 2-0 over Gillingham.

The season opened with a 2-0 defeat at perennial strugglers Gillingham, where the crowd of 9,000 was boosted by an excursion train run by the recently reformed Brentford Supporters League. The previous campaign's leading scorer, Abe Morris, showed that he had lost none of his prowess in front of goal by scoring a hat-trick as Luton Town were downed 3-2 in the opening home game. It was a case of "so far, so good" when Gillingham were beaten 2-0 in the return but as time marched on it became obvious that Brentford would again feature amongst the also-rans.

The only salvation both on and off the pitch would have been a good run in the FA Cup. Here again the team pulled up short. Kent League side Maidstone United were beaten 4-0 in a replay at Griffin Park, as a result of which the Bees were faced with what seemed a straight forward assignment against Merthyr Town who they had beaten 3-1 at home the previous month. It turned out to be one of those days, as after dominating for most of the game without converting their chances, they paid the penalty seven minutes from time when Young made a hash of a goal kick and presented the winner on a plate to the opposition.

To Brentford's long suffering supporters it was the straw that broke the camel's back and Young felt the full force of their derision over the next few weeks. Another to suffer in the same way was Abe Morris, the side's leading goal getter the previous season but who tended to miss more than he converted.

Young won the fans round, but that was not the case with Morris and at the beginning of February he joined the exodus to Millwall . The fee of £750 was one that Brentford were in no position to refuse. At the time the player had scored 13 goals and was the Bees leading marksman, a position he held to the end of the season He didn't take long to get cracking at the Den either and finished as their top man as well.

Over the next few years Abe blossomed into one of the most prolific goalscorers in the game's history, his 433 League appearances yielding 285 goals. His best days were at Swindon Town where he led the charts for seven seasons, setting an unsurpassed record of 216 goals in the League and a season high of 46 in 1926-27.

Abe was not the only decent player to leave Griffin Park, as the same month skipper Bert Rosier left for Clapton Orient. A veteran of almost 150 games for the Bees and a P.O.W. during the war, Bert went on to play almost another 250 League games in the colours of Orient, Southend United and Fulham. Brentford now began to really struggle and in the wake of Morris's departure went seven games during which they scored just a single goal and that by stand in centre forward Roland James, in a 1-0 win against the bottom team Newport County.

Next on the fixture list was a home game versus the runaway leaders Bristol City. An away banker if ever there was one. But in one of the turn-ups of the season Brentford not only won, they absolutely whitewashed the opposition to the tune of four goals to nil. The Bees showed it was no fluke by holding City to a draw in the return a week later and next beating high flying Portsmouth.

That was as good as it got, however, and the team failed to muster a win in the remaining five games. This left Brentford in 14th position, a disappointing finish to the campaign, although there was a ray of hope from the reserves who after three seasons propping up the London Combination managed to improve their situation to one off the bottom, above QPR.

1923-24

Anstiss, Amos, Morris, Pither, Rosier. The basis of a good team, but players all sold by Brentford since they joined the league in 1920 to help keep the club solvent. It is easy to understand where Brentford were going wrong and another season of struggle and strife was to see the average attendance at Griffin Park dip significantly from 8350 to 6825.

Botwell Mission (later Hayes F.C.) were eventually beaten in the Griffin Park replay.

A lack of money meant that Brentford went into the season with basically the same squad of players of whom only Hendren and Young survived from the club's initial campaign in the Football League. The team found it difficult from the outset and home and away defeats by QPR, who were destined to finish bottom, and a single point from two encounters against Plymouth Argyle, did little for morale. The Bees then got off the mark with a 2-1 defeat of Luton Town, a match that coincided with goalkeeper Young's 100th league appearance, the first Brentford player to reach three figures. It was only a brief respite from a series of poor results and a 3-0 defeat away to the eventual champions Portsmouth, at the beginning of November, left Brentford propping up the table. They continued to court disaster and a crushing 6-0 hammering away to lowly Gillingham set the team firmly on course for a place in the bottom two.

QPR had already booked the wooden spoon and Brentford approached the final weeks of the season requiring maximum points from two games against Northampton Town if they were to stand any chance of avoiding the need to share a trip, with West London neighbours, when the time came to go cap-in-hand to the League's AGM in June. Supporters, long troubled by a poor team and an on-going bus strike, had become indifferent to Brentford's fate and a crowd below 5,000 assembled for the game at Griffin Park that was crucial to the club's prospects of staying in the Lague. Northampton, although they had little but pride to play for, were the form horse having recently slammed Southend United 8-0 and surprised Portsmouth 3-1 at Fratton Park.

Score Card

American Legion Baseball Season

GRIFFIN PARK, BRENTFORD.

BASEBALL

SUNDAY, OCTOBER 7th, 1923.

ALL STAR LEGIONNAIRES

v.

U.S.S. PITTSBURGH

Under the auspices of LONDON POST No. 1 of THE AMERICAN LEGION 13, Hertford Street, W.1. Phone: - Grosvenor 2315.

PROGRAMME - TWOPENCE.

A different sport at Griffin Park!

Central to Brentford's hopes was that of far wing man Patsy Hendren, who was free of cricketing duties for Middlesex, but on the debit side the Bees played for much of the second half with only ten men, after Johnstone was carried off with a broken leg. However, in Hendren the Bees had the trump card as beside running rings round the opposition defence all afternoon it was his ball from which Clayson headed home the game's only goal. The final whistle was greeted with a sigh of relief and when news filtered through that fellow strugglers Southend and Watford had lost, Brentford were safe in the knowledge that they would live to fight another day.

Seven days later the Bees rounded off the campaign with a 3-2 victory at the County Ground, Northampton. Hendren was an absentee due to cricketing commitments with Middlesex and his replacement Bert Hughes scored a hat-trick to earn himself a contract for the following season. He was one of the few to survive a purge by manager Mitchell, and not one member of the reserve side that finished bottom of the London Combination for the third time in four years was retained.

This followed an article in the programme for the match against Northampton in which the Board laid their cards on the table.

"The season's football has not been to everybody's liking, there being periods when we were all very downhearted. But fortune has favoured us a little more during the last few weeks and a win today will save further worry.

"Important changes have taken place in the directorate. Mr. Dovey and Mr. Buck have resigned and gentlemen of influence and stability in Mr. Bradford and Mr. Louis P. Simon co-opted to fill their places.

"The directorate now consists of a body of men all successful in their own businesses and they are determined that the Brentford club shall also be successful if business brains combined with a love of sport and football can make it so"

So while Brentford beat Northampton that afternoon, the arrival of Bradford, appointed chairman a few years later, and Simon , who held the position throughout the thirties as Brentford stormed through to the top flight , can be seen in retrospect as one of the defining times in the club's history. However, it was to get worse before it got better. A lot worse.

Top left: John Kerr (1921-24)
Top right: Charles Alton (1921-25)

Bottom Elias ('Patsy') Hendren. Played for Brentford in two periods between 1907 and 1927and represented Middlesex and England at cricket.

1924-25

Quiet simply the most miserable season in all the years Brentford have been in the Football League. A club record 7-0 defeat at Swansea Town preceded weeks earlier by a 7-1 hiding at Plymouth Argyle and followed by heavy defeats to Exeter City 2-5, non-League St. Albans 3-5 in the FA Cup and Southend United 1-6, tells its own sad story. All this occurred before Christmas, and following the reverse at Southend, the 8th on the trot, Mitchell stood down and Fred Halliday took the helm for his third shot at the job.

The Board recognised that to even contemplate getting out of the mire an injection of fresh blood was needed, so they dug deep into their own pockets to sign Scottish International centre half Alec Graham and full back Jack Steel from Arsenal, winger Harold Young(Aberdare Athletic) and inside forward Jack Lane(Chesterfield). Lane's signing was the most significant as it came at a time when Brentford had suffered a run of nine games without a win and were already booked for the re-election process.

The opposition for his debut was provided by Champions-elect Swansea Town, who since beating Brentford 7-0 at Vetch Field had gone 16 games unbeaten. All things considered then, an away certainty. But in a turn up for the books, new look Brentford won 3-1 with Lane netting the first of his 86 goals in the club's colours.

Brentford not only turned the tables on Swansea, they did the same to the other top Division Three sides, Plymouth Argyle and Bristol City. Following a 7-1 defeat at Home Park, the Bees won 1-0 at Griffin Park. Similarly, Bristol City won 3-0 at Ashton Gate but were beaten 1-0 in the return. These are statistics that are difficult to explain, especially when lined up alongside Brentford's overall record. For starters the team conceded 91 goals, the worst defensive record in the entire League.

Then, away from home they won 2-0 at Northampton Town and lost the other twenty games on their travels, which included a 5-1 thrashing at Exeter City a week after the victory against Swansea. And yet with so little to shout about the average attendance breached the seven thousand mark, the 13th best in the division

It is probably true to say that given their track record, had there been another worthy candidate, Brentford would have been out on their ear when it came to seeking re-election. As it happened there wasn't a likely replacement and Brentford were re-elected unopposed. It was only a temporary reprieve, as everyone realised that any further applications would almost certainly bring an end to League football at Griffin Park. Given this, the Board announced that in a determined bid to secure the club's future they were going to make available a significant sum of money in an effort to attract a better class of footballer to Griffin Park.

The decks were cleared in anticipation of their arrival. Of the players who started the season only Jack Allen and Richard Parker survived the cull and they were added to the recent signings Steel, Graham, Lane, Young and Jimmy Walton who had been transferred from Bristol Rovers, while it was hoped Hendren would be available after spending the previous winter on tour with England.

1925-26

Throughout the ages a player capable of hitting the target on a regular basis has been worth his weight in gold. You can field the most watertight defence in Christendom but you won't win a thing if there is nobody up front with the ability to regularly send opposition goalkeepers on a back bending exercise.

Brentford's early years in the League had been a double edged sword; a lousy defence coupled with a shot shy attack, the outcome of which had been two forced applications for re-election and a struggle to steer clear its stranglehold in most other years.

A disastrous day, a 6-1 record home defeat!

After the latest visit the League's Management spelled out in no uncertain terms that they didn't want to see Brentford in those circumstances again, so the club's brief was simple: Don't turn up cap-in-hand at the Football League's AGM in 1926 expecting any more favours.

With this in mind Fred Halliday went in search of the men necessary to prevent that threat. And to add to the team's new look, the now familiar red and white stripes were adopted as the club colours, replacing the, by comparison, drab white shirts and black shorts.

Unfortunately, it soon became apparent that the latest crop, harvested mainly in the summer, was again not up to scratch as the Bees made a dreadful start by collecting a single point from the first ten games and shipping 32 goals to leave themselves anchored to the bottom. Included was an appalling 6-1 home defeat by Brighton & Hove Albion, the worst in the club's history, which saw Jack Allen receive his marching orders, sections of the home crowd baying for the referees blood and attempts made to attack some of the opposition players. Brentford were subsequently hauled over the coals by the FA and had the ground closed for fourteen days, while Allen spent a period of time on the sidelines.

By the turn of the year the team had at least managed to chalk up a few wins but were still in dire straights following successive 6-1 drubbings away to Exeter City and Northampton town. Meanwhile, Brentford had been scouting around for a new centre forward and found just the man when Ernie Watkins was transfer listed by Southend United. The goal getter had impressed the Bees management by scoring a hat-trick in Southend's 3-1 win at the Kuursal back in September and were quickly on the ball when it came to light he was available. The big drawback was the price of £1,000, but to the World and his brother's amazement, Brentford stumped up the cash, the first four figure transfer fee in the club's history.

To say Brentford had gone for broke is an understatement and in this instance his signing proved money well spent. A goal minutes into his debut in a 3-1 victory at Gillingham gave the team a big lift and Ernie was to the forefront as the Bees went on a morale boosting run of six wins in eight, the new centre forward accounting for six of the sides 20 goals in this period.

Brentford subsequently drifted back into the danger zone and it became imperative that they managed a decent points haul from the three games in quick succession over Easter. So when Norwich City were thrashed 5-1 on Good Friday, Watkins leading the way with a hat trick, and Charlton Athletic were beaten 2-0 at the Valley the following day, the Bees were as good as home and dry. Just a single win in the last six games meant it was a close shave, especially as the goal average took a pounding with a 6-0 defeat at Merthyr Town, where Allen was sent off for a second time, and a 7-1 pounding at Reading which handed the Championship to the Biscuitmen on a plate.

The beating at Elm Park again left Brentford with the worst defensive record in the Third Division (South) and the 94 goals conceded represents the highest total ever in the League by a Brentford team. But on the credit side the average gate hit a new high of 9,146, while Ernie Watkins paid a huge instalment off his transfer fee by leading the club's goal charts with eleven in just 19 appearances.

1926-27

There were many changes at Griffin Park during the close season, the most significant being the arrival of Harry Curtis as manager in place of Fred Halliday. Curtis spent the previous three years as secretary/manager of Gillingham, prior to which he played football for Walthamstow Grange in the London League, earned his spurs in management at senior amateur club Gnome Athletic and, to complete an impressive CV, spent twelve years as a referee on the Southern and Football League lists. It was through his friendship with Brentford director Frank Barton, another former referee, that Curtis was offered the position and in the light of subsequent events, it can be classed as Brentford's most significant appointment ever.

He inherited only nine of the previous seasons' squad so returned to Priestfield to sign Bill Berry, Wally Barnard, Charlie Reddock, Joe Butler, Claude Craddock and Frank Marshall, a £750 buy who tragically succumbed to a fatal illness twelve months later. The same fate awaited another of his early signings, Ted Winship, who died of yellow jaundice in November 1929. In addition, goalkeeper Jim Ferguson (St.Rochs) and centre forward George Anderson (Airdrie) journeyed south from Scotland, and later attracted substantial transfer fees when they moved on. The new look Bees made a flying start by beating Brighton & Hove Albion 4-0 and continued in much the same vein by winning four of the first five games including a 4-2 victory against QPR, which attracted a record high in the League at Griffin Park of 19,380. Brentford continued to keep pace with the frontrunners and in October beat Coventry City 7-3 to chalk up their best win since joining the League. Patsy Hendren, who once played for Coventry, became the first Brentford player to net four goals in a League game in the process.

The team continued merrily on its way, but then got sidetracked by the FA Cup. Brentford had not made any waves in the competition for many years, a situation that changed for the better this season as the team battled through to the fourth round and a tie against West Ham United. Brentford took the long way round to reach this stage, having been drawn away in the previous three rounds in all of which a replay or re-staging was required. In round one Isthmian League Clapton held the Bees 1-1 at their Spotted Dog ground before getting collared 7-3 in the replay, Watkins notching a hat-trick. A Steve Dearn goal paved the way to victory against Gillingham in round two following a 1-1 draw at Priestfield.

The first attempt to settle the issue at Oldham Athletic in round three was fogged off after 70 minutes with the Bees losing 2-1. Sensing it might only be a temporary reprieve, Curtis had the presence of mind to order the players straight into the bath. Low and behold, the referee put his head around the door minutes later to say the fog was lifting and play would resume shortly.

Curtis then persuaded him that the players were in the tub and to do so could be detrimental to their health. The referee took note and called the game off. With the restaging set for two days later it was hardly worth returning south, so the Brentford party booked into a Manchester hotel with strict instructions from the management to lay off the booze. Bellamy couldn't resist the temptation but was caught out, as a result of which he was dropped in favour of 12th man Jack Allen, who then proceeded to score a hat-trick as Brentford turned the tables to win 4-1.

Allen, not a popular figure amongst supporters, "clumsy" and "awkward" were two of the descriptions he attracted, held his place for the tie against West Ham. The Bees held the Hammers 1-1 at Upton Park, and then caused a major upset by beating the First Division high flyers 2-0 in the replay. Allen scored the opener in front of a post-war record crowd of 20,799. Brentford departed from the competition, at the next stage, losing 1-0 to Second Division Reading watched by Elm Park's all-time record attendance of 33,042.

In the summer, Allen was sold to Sheffield Wednesday, for whom he top scored in their back-to-back League Championship successes in 1929 and 1930. He went on to net both Newcastle United goals in the FA Cup final win against Arsenal in 1932 and finished his career with 148

Penalty Ref! Fortunately for The Bees, this handball was missed, but they still lost 1-0 at Elm Park (before a record attendance) in the F A Cup.

League goals to his credit. Beauty, as they say, is in the eye of the beholder! While Brentford gave an excellent account of themselves in the Cup, performances in the League suffered and just one win in the final ten games condemned them to mid-table mediocrity. This didn't prevent Ernie Watkins setting a club record by finishing the season with 20 League goals in his locker.

There was also a major financial kick-back. Almost 150,000 people attended the nine Cup games which generated further interest in the League, pushing the average to 9,713, the best to date. The money this pulled in, added to the fruits of the cup run, enabled the Board to invest in ground improvements by replacing the "cow shed" on the Braemar Road side, with a posh new stand. Brentford at last were moving forward.

1927-28

Griffin Park was a hive of activity during the close season as builders set about erecting the new stand, the opening ceremony of which was performed by FA secretary Fred Wall before the game against Bournemouth & Boscombe Athletic on September 3rd. On the playing side, too, Curtis was a busy man, selling Allen to Sheffield Wednesday, Archie Clark (Arsenal) and George Anderson(Chelsea). His war chest replenished, the manager set about improving the squad and he signed eight new men. The most significant was John Phillips, the top scorer with 29 goals for Merthyr Town the previous season, a record, incidentally, that stood the test of time until they lost their place in the League in 1930.

Phillips soon won the hearts of the fans by scoring a hat-trick on his home debut in a 3-0 victory against Northampton Town and in the early months formed a powerful partnership up front with Watkins and Lane. Included in this spell, which enabled the Bees to keep tabs on the leading teams, was a 6-1 hiding dished out to Millwall Athletic, who were destined to finish as champions by a country mile, popping home a Divisional record of 127 goals in the process.

All was going well, but prospects took a dive when Phillips was sidelined by injury for 15 games during which the Bees slid out of contention for honours, by recording just four wins. Included in that sequence was a 7-1 thrashing by Manchester United in the FA Cup. With memories of the fog scenario at Oldham, this time it was Walsall's turn to pull a similar stroke. With just seven minutes remaining of the home game on November 19th, and the Bees leading 4-1, the referee called the teams off.

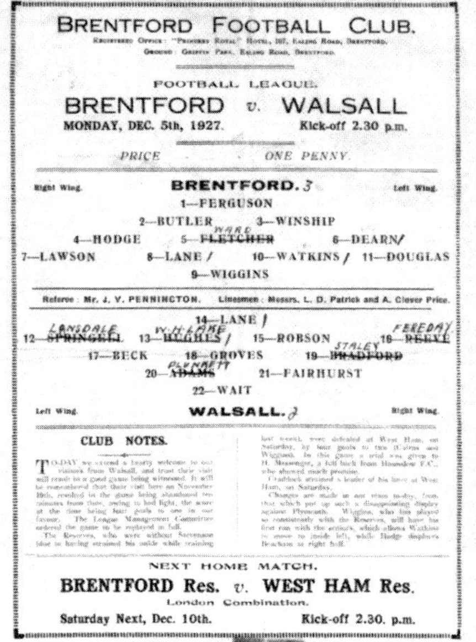

BRENTFORD FOOTBALL CLUB.

FOOTBALL LEAGUE.

BRENTFORD v. WALSALL

MONDAY, DEC. 5th, 1927. Kick-off 2.30 p.m.

PRICE - ONE PENNY.

Right Wing. BRENTFORD. 3 Left Wing.

1—FERGUSON

2—BUTLER 3—WINSHIP

4—HODGE 5—~~FLETCHER~~ WARD 6—DEARN/

7—LAWSON 8—LANE / 10—WATKINS / 11—DOUGLAS

9—WIGGINS

Referee: Mr. J. V. PENNINGTON. Linesmen: Messrs. L. D. Patrick and A. Clever Price.

14—LANE /

12—LANSDALE 13—W. H. LAKE / 15—ROBSON 16—FEREDAY

17—BECK 18—GROVES 19—STALEY

20—PLUNKETT 21—FAIRHURST

22—WAIT

Left Wing. WALSALL. 2 Right Wing.

CLUB NOTES.

NEXT HOME MATCH.

BRENTFORD Res. v. WEST HAM Res.

London Combination.

Saturday Next, Dec. 10th. Kick-off 2.30. p.m.

The programme for the smallest crowd.

Initially everyone thought he had blown early and when it was realised bad light was the cause all hell broke loose. He was persuaded to change his mind by the indignant Brentford camp but by then the Walsall team were sitting in the bath. Ernie Watkins, in particular, had cause to blow his top at the outcome as his hat-trick that afternoon was obviously wiped from the records. The restaging took place on a murky mid-week afternoon on December 5th and justice was served by Brentford's 3-2 success. However, on the debit side the attendance of 2,024 represents the smallest of all time at Griffin Park in the League and was lower even than for a reserve game against Portsmouth (4,120) three months later.

By the time Brentford got back to something resembling full strength it was too late to be thinking of promotion, so Curtis channelled his energy into preparing for the following campaign. In a flourish of activity before the close of play, centre forward Joe Wiggins was sold to Leicester City for £1,400, a record for Brentford and an enormous sum by any standards, let alone for a player with only four first team appearances; Claude Craddock signed for Dundee; and Joe Ferguson reaped another large fee when moving to Notts

County. The new arrivals included former England International goalkeeper Freddy Fox from Halifax and Teddy Ware from Chatham, both of whom were to play their part over the next few seasons.

Meanwhile, Brentford finished with a number of decent results beating, amongst others, Bristol Rovers 5-1 and Merthyr Town 4-0, Phillips netting twice against his former club to help lift his season's tally to 17 in twenty-three appearances. With Lane (11), Bert Lawson (10), and Watkins (10) also in double figures the Bees ended with 76 goals to their credit, the best yet.

1928-29

If there is a lesson to be learned from the 1928-29 campaign it is that you are courting trouble by selling your main goalscorer. Since Harry Curtis took over as manager Brentford's stock had risen considerably and, although never looking serious contenders for the one promotion place, the team was no longer a chopping block for the rest. Indeed, the opposite was true and following a couple of quality signings in Charlton Athletic full back Baden Herod, whose fee of £1,500 was a new club record, and wing half Reg Davies, a key man in Portsmouth's spectacular rise from the Third, South, to the First Division, Brentford were seen as a dark horse for promotion as the season got underway.

With six games gone it appeared the Bees would give their backers a run for their money as they headed the table unbeaten. Next, a bumper Griffin Park crowd in the region of twenty-one thousand saw a 1-1 draw with fellow challengers QPR and all seemed tickety-boo.

Unfortunately Curtis then dropped a bombshell by selling leading scorer John Phillips to Bristol Rovers. His record since joining Brentford was second to none and he left for a large fee, even though it was a recognised fact that you sold the team's main goalscorer at your peril. With a record of 22 goals in twenty nine appearances Brentford needed a ready made replacement fast and took a chance on Charlton Athletic's leading marksman the previous season, Dave Sherlaw. He was on a hiding to nothing as over the next few months the goals dried up and the next twelve games produced a single point leaving the Bees to plummet from top to bottom.

Towards the end of that demoralising sequence Curtis bolstered his defence by paying Manchester United £500 for Jimmy Bain. It proved an inspirational signing as he took over as skipper and led the team out of trouble. Later Jimmy spent 22 years as the club's assistant manager and when he retired from the game in 1956 was presented with the Football League's Long Service Medal for his contribution at Brentford. A player with a lot less mileage on the clock at the club was Baden Herod.

The record buy the previous summer now moved to Tottenham Hotspur six months later for a fee of £4,000, easily the highest to date for a Brentford player.

The team's roller coaster ride continued after Christmas, moving up the table before settling down in 13th. Even so the Bees still had a say in the destination of the title which in the closing weeks boiled down to a close run affair between Charlton Athletic and Crystal Palace .Brentford visited the Valley in the penultimate away game and with time running out a draw seemed the most likely outcome. But this changed when Wyper appeared to handle as he was about to centre. Bees' full back Alex Stevenson, expecting the referee's whistle, caught the ball as it reached him in the box and was mortified when the official pointed to the spot for a penalty. Heated protests followed, to no avail, and Pugsly slotted home the decisive goal. Decisive is the right word, as Charlton finished top above Palace on goal average.

1929-30

This was the season when the team's extraordinary feat of winning all twenty-one home games put Brentford Football Club on the map in a big way. It was a stupendous achievement, underlined by the fact that since the League expanded to four divisions in 1921 no other team has managed to go through a campaign without dropping a point at home.

Curtis was again busy in the transfer market pre-season and pulled off a number of astute signings, the best of which proved to be Bill Lane from Reading and the Bristol City pair, Jackie Foster and Cyril Blakemore. The Bees sent out a message that they were now a force to be reckoned with by winning seven of the opening ten games to keep themselves hanging on the coat tails of Plymouth Argyle. The contest between the two continued until the final weeks of the season, Brentford blowing their chances by then losing in successive away games at Luton Town and QPR.

At this stage Plymouth pulled clear to finish top by seven points. Brentford, in second, were a full ten points ahead of next in line QPR and a measure of how well the Bees had done can be measured by the fact that in all but one season since the Third Division was formed, the team's 61 points would have been sufficient to take the title.

It was a campaign in which virtually every club record went out of the window: Bill Lane scored 33 of the team's 94 goals, both new highs; the average gate of 12,123 smashed the previous best of 9,713 in 1926-27; the visit of Fulham in February attracted a new record attendance of 21,966; and only nineteen players were used of whom Davies, Fox, Bakemore and Bill Lane were ever-present and Bain, Payne and Foster were absent just once. Brentford Football Club, led by the dynamic duo of manager Harry Curtis and Chairman Louis P Simon, was on the march!

Aug.31st Swindon Town W3-2 Att: 11,084
Brentford's new look side, including the complete front line of Jackie Foster, Percy Whipp, Bill Lane, Cyril Blakeman and John Payne, went into action not even road tested and lit the touch paper to success through goals by Blakemore and Payne(2).

Sept. 4th Clapton Orient W3-1 Att: 9,345
Orient held the aces in the early exchanges and it was against the run of play when Blakemore opened the scoring. Galbraith put through his own net for number two and Bill Lane got off the mark with a third before Jack netted a late consolation.

Sept. 14th Merthyr Town W6-0 Att: 11,040
The Bees failed to make inroads early but after Whipp scored in the 55th minute the floodgates opened. Lane stole the show with a four timer and Blakemore also featured on the scoresheet as Brentford took a stranglehold on affairs.

Sept. 26th Bristol Rovers W2-1 Att: 6,265
Brentford were anything but shipshape and Bristol fashion as they struggled to get going and it came as no surprise when ex-Bee, Phillips, gave the visitors the lead. This spurred the Bees into action and late goals by Foster(80) and Lane(86) secured a rather fortuitous success.

Sept. 28th Newport County W1-0 Att: 11,073
Who scored the goal that gave Brentford another last gasp victory ? The press were hopelessly divided and in the gathering gloom credited it to either Lane, Watkins, Blakemore or Foster before Harry Curtis had the final say and awarded it to Payne.

Oct. 12th Coventry City W3-1 Att: 11,957
Buoyed by the return from injury of Jack Lane for his first game of the season, Brentford were always in command to the extent that skipper and centre half Jimmy Bain made a rare excursion over the half way line to complement two earlier goals by Blakemore and Jack Lane.

Oct.26th Norwich City W3-0 Att 11,052
A victory overshadowed by the death the previous Saturday through Yellow Jaundice of Bees full back Ted Winship. As a measure of respect, before the game, the crowd and two teams stood to attention as the band played " Abide With Me" The Bees again took time to get into their stride and a purple patch of three goals inside fifteen minutes around the hour mark by Bill Lane(2) and Blakemore settled the issue.

Nov.9th Gillingham W2-1 Att: 9,603
Brentford made heavy weather of beating the tail-enders but hit the front when it matters most after trailing to Cheesemuir's early strike. Bill Lane again showed what an excellent buy he was by scoring both goals, the latter with five minutes left on the clock.

Nov.23rd Exeter City W2-0 Att: 6,502
The Bees continued their disconcerting habit of notching a late winner, and the referee was looking at his watch when the points were finally secured. Blakemore, who specialised in scoring from distance, was on target for the first after Bill Lane missed from the spot. His namesake Jack wrapped things up almost on time.

Dec.7th Luton Town W 2-0 Att: 7,167
A stroll in the park as goals either side of the break gave Brentford a comfortable win.

Dec.21st Walsall W6-2 Att: 5,041
The lowest gate of the season as the Bees equalled their best score. The team, celebrating the news that Curtis had turned down the vacant manager's job at Tottenham, were soon ahead through Jack Lane and turned the screw further with goals by Bill Lane(2), Blakemore(penalty) and Payne.

Dec.25th Brighton & H.A. W5-2 Att: 14,612
A Christmas treat for the home fans. The visitors were soon on the back foot as Jack Lane(2), Payne, Bill Lane and Blakemore left their 'keeper clutching thin air.

Jan. 4th Plymouth Argyle W3-0 Att: 20,571.
The Big One. Brentford put on their best bib and tucker and beat their main rivals for the title out of sight. Individually and collectively the Bees were much the better side and after Foster scored on 20 seconds there was only one team in it. A brace from Jack Lane completed a fine afternoon's work.

Jan. 25th Torquay United W 5-0 Att: 10,997.
The team served up a masterclass to totally outplay the opposition and overhaul Plymouth into top spot. Jack Lane and Foster were on target but were outdone by hat-trick hero Bill Lane.

Feb. 8th Watford W 5-0 Att. 11,356.
Brentford were now on fire as they recorded straight (home) win number 15 to surpass the record set by Tottenham Hotspur in 1919-20. All five goals came in the last twenty minutes as the opposition capitulated to the firepower of Blakemore, Payne, Bill Lane (2) and Jack Lane.

Feb. 22nd Fulham W 5-1 Att: 21,966.
A memorable day all round as near neighbours Fulham were trounced 5-1in front of a new record crowd. The Bees won with the minimum of fuss through Blakemore, Jack Lane and another hat-trick by Bill Lane to go two points clear at the top.

Mar. 8th Crystal Palace W2-0 Att:19,555.
Once again the Bees emerge triumphant, early goals by Bill Lane and Payne ensuring the team kept up the pressure at the head of affairs.

Mar. 22nd Northampton T. W2-0 Att: 16,460.
After 20 successive games without a change, an injury to Stevenson meant that Dumbrell got a rare call up. The line up during this period was Fox, Stevenson, Adamson, Davies, Bain, Salt, Foster, Lane J., Lane B., Blakemore, Payne. It made no difference and two Bill Lane crackers continued Brentford's quest for honours.

Apr. 5th Southend United W2-1 Att. 13,255.
A close call if ever there was one as the Bees came literally within seconds of failing to win. With 13 minutes remaining they trailed 1-0 but then Payne equalised and after Bill Lane rattled the cross bar, Payne scored the winner with almost the last kick of the game.

Apr. 19th Bournemouth & Bos. Ath. W 1-0 Att.7,694.
Successive away defeats at Luton and QPR killed off Championship hopes and the one promotion place but victory over Bournemouth courtesy of Jack Lane kept alive the dream of winning all 21 home games.

Apr. 21st QPR W3-0 Att. 18,549.
Mission Accomplished and what a way to do it! A comprehensive hammering of local rivals QPR and all three goals by Bill Lane on the way to a total for the season of 33.

Chapter 5: THE GLORY YEARS

1930-31

With basically the same group of players to choose from for once, Brentford approached the campaign as serious contenders for honours. The only departure of note was reserve full back George Dumbrell and this was due to the eye catching transfer fee of £1,750 he commanded from Leicester City. Increased attendances meant that the Board felt it prudent to make improvements to the ground, the most notable of which was to concrete the open terrace behind the Ealing road goal.

With just the Champions moving up, a good start was always of paramount importance. Unfortunately it didn't happen. The 21 game winning streak at Griffin Park was not extended, as in the opening home game the team crashed 4-0 to Northampton Town and by the end of October the Bees were playing catch up, eight points behind the unbeaten leaders Notts County.

On November 22nd Brentford were part of a little piece of football history when they went down 3-0 to Clapton Orient in the first League game to be played at Wembley. Orient's new ground at Lea Bridge had been deemed unfit until it was brought up to specification, so for a short period they rented Wembley stadium. In the weeks prior to this Brentford beat QPR 5-3 and Thames 6-1, excellent results sandwiched in between by a 3-0 defeat at Norwich City, the side destined to finish bottom, as the team continued its erratic course.

Good one minute and bad the next became a feature of the campaign, highlighted by the Christmas encounters against Crystal Palace, who eventually finished second in the table. On Christmas morning the Bees slaughtered them 8-2 to record the best win since joining the League, yet the following day crashed 5-1 at Selhurst Park. Brentford continued to blow hot and cold, Bristol Rovers (5-2) - Bill Lane notching his third hat trick in five weeks - Walsall (6-1) and Swindon Town (5-2) meeting an on-song Bees side, while struggling Thames won 2-0 at their West Ham Stadium home. The horse had bolted and Brentford finished third, nine points adrift of Notts County. It says much about the Bees rise in status that this was met by disappointment, where a few years earlier the flags would have been out for such an exalted position.

Supporters did have a decent run in the FA Cup to look back on, though. In round one Ilford were overturned 6-1 away, and while it was a bloodless victory on the pitch, rival supporters on the terraces fought a running battle off it. At the final whistle a three hundred strong mob surrounded the Brentford team coach stoning and jostling the players and it took the intervention of the police to make good their escape. Norwich were the victims at the next stage, followed by a win in a replay at Ninian Park against Cardiff City, who four years earlier became the only non English team to lift the Trophy. The draw then paired Brentford with First Division high flyers Portsmouth. Griffin Park welcomed a new record attendance of 23,544 for the tie, a blood and thunder encounter which the visitors scraped 1-0.

Now out of contention in both the league and FA Cup, Curtis took the opportunity to freshen up his squad. All was not to everyone's liking though, especially when he split the prolific Lane partnership, who would be responsible for 48 of the side's 101 goals in cup and League, by transferring Jack to Crystal Palace.

Action from the F.A.Cup match versus Portsmouth

It caused a greater stir than Phillip's move to Bristol Rovers a few years earlier. However, Curtis felt he had a ready made replacement in Freddy Gamble, the club's reserve centre forward, who had scored 71 goals in two years in the London Combination. Fred didn't last long as in only his sixth game he scored a 22 minute hat-trick against Walsall and moved to top flight West Ham United in exchange for Leslie Wilkins four days later. Wilkins followed in the footsteps of fellow Hammer George Robson, later described by Curtis as his best ever signing, and Fulham's Ralph Allen who was to replace Gamble as a prolific marksman for the reserves before going on to set a seasonal goalscoring record for Charlton Athletic in 1934-35, which stands to this day.

1931-32

The side had undergone huge changes over the last twelve months as Curtis sought a promotion winning team, and only Adamson, Bain and Foster survived from the team that kicked off the campaign against Luton Town twelve months earlier.

A bumper crowd, not far short of the record, welcomed the new season with a 1-0 defeat of QPR. Despite failing to win the next two games, the Bees soon regained their stride and five straight victories in September had them jostling Southend United on the leader board.

The team now enjoyed a large vociferous away following and six coach loads travelled down to Kent for the visit to Gillingham. They left Isleworth in convey shortly after one o'clock, but owing to the leader losing his way attempting a short cut they failed to arrive until the game was thirty minutes old and according to the local newspaper "they let Gillingham have it hot and strong when 200 Bees supporters dashed on the terraces with colours flying and bells and rattles clanging ".

Crompton scores his second goal for the club against his former one, but Southend won 3-2 at Griffin Park in March.

Although the sequence of wins was broken by a 3-2 reverse at Cardiff City, the team soon returned to winning ways and a 3-1 win at Bournemouth & Boscombe, set up nicely the two Christmas holiday encounters with nearest challengers for top spot Fulham. The match at Griffin Park on Christmas morning had the ground groaning under the weight of a record attendance of 26,139, indeed so great was the crush that ten minutes into the game a section of railings at the Ealing road end collapsed under the strain and spectators were forced onto the playing area. Happily, there were no injuries and the game finished nil-nil.

The return next day, in front of a crowd of 25,000, ended 2-1 in Fulham's favour but with QPR, under former Brentford manager Archie Mitchell, then lowering the Cottager's colours the Bees went into the New Year well on terms with themselves. The first team led Division Three (South), the reserves held a five point advantage over Arsenal in the London Combination and for good measure a Third round tie against Bath City beckoned in the FA Cup...... Heaven!

Sadly Hell was just around the corner, but not before the Bees extended their lead at the top by winning 2-1 at the White City against QPR. The crowd of 33,553 represented not only the best in England that day but was also a record for the Third Division. Seven days later Bath City were eased aside in the FA Cup to set up a money spinning tie away to Manchester City. The game fired the imagination of the sporting fraternity and besides being filmed for posterity on Movietone News and piped into cinemas it attracted a huge attendance to Maine Road of 56,190.

Brentford were never at the races and City cruised to a 6-1 success, the Bees one consolation being their share of the gate which amounted to £3,361. In the ensuing months Championship hopes went for a Burton as the team's form dipped alarmingly, a dismal Easter of three defeats in four days finally calling time on thoughts of Second Division football at Griffin Park later in the year.

Unrest on the terraces now called into question Curtis's tenure as manager and in the wake of Brentford's slide it was freely rumoured that he tendered his resignation. Fortunately, Chairman Louis P. Simon and his board of directors persuaded him to stay, convinced it was only a blip on the way to greater things for the club.

Fifth place was not the end of the world and there was also the sweetener that the reserves had kept right on to the end of the road and won the London Combination to become the first side in seven years to deprive all conquering Arsenal of the trophy.

Curtis, the full backing of the board behind him, set about the task in hand with renewed vigour, and in May pulled off the transfer deal that in years to come would be described as one of the coups of the era by signing Middlesbrough reserves Jack Holliday, scorer of 78 goals for Boro's second string in the just finished season, Billy Scott and Bert Watson for a combined fee of £1,500. Not exactly flush for money Brentford sold Bill Lane to Watford to finance the deal, a gamble which over the next few years was to pay a rich dividend.

1932-33

Brentford were now established as one of the teams to keep an eye on in the division, this despite the fact that Curtis generally made wholesale changes to the normal line-up each season. There were six alterations to the team that finished the campaign and only Tom Adamson, England Amateur International JackieBurns, skipper Jimmy Bain, Jackie Foster and George Robson survived the cull. Of the squad of 25, eight were newcomers.
Besides the trio from Middlesbrough another to make a telling contribution was Southport goalkeeper Tommy Baker.

Brentford started the season on fire by winning their first seven games and thereafter kept up a blistering pace to finish as champions with something to spare. The opening game saw old rivals QPR beaten 3-2 at the White City, Holliday giving notice of intent by scoring twice. Coventry were next brushed aside 3-1, Allen, in for the indisposed Holliday, netting twice. Wins against Torquay United, Coventry, again, Luton Town and Exeter City followed as the team worked up a head of steam. Holliday then scored the first of his many hat tricks for the club as Newport County were pulverised 6-1 at Somerton Park. The Bees now had a great chance to set a new post war record by winning their opening eight games, but Bournemouth & Boscombe Athletic threw a spanner in the works by holding on for a 1-1 draw on a mud heap of a Griffin Park pitch.

The balance in the team was now just about right. The skills of JC Burns and Watson at wing half, and inside forwards Scott and Robson were a match for any team in the division and dovetailed perfectly with the robust style of centre forward Holliday, whose first ten games yielded 13 goals. The defence, too, was playing its part. Baker, at 5ft. 9ins. one of the shortest 'keepers around, conceded only eight goals and was kept well protected by a trio of Scots in Stevenson, Adamson and Bain. The only cause for concern was down the flanks which Curtis remedied by returning to Middlesbrough and paying a four figure sum for Ernie Muttitt, to be followed a fortnight later by Crystal Palace winger Idris Hopkins in exchange for the veteran Bill Berry. Both were at Griffin Park for the long haul as everything Curtis touched in the transfer market at this time turned to gold.

FOOTBALL

BRENTFORD F.C.

Playing.	At Home.	Playing.	At Home.
Torquay United	Sept. 3rd	Reading	Jan. 14th
Luton Town	,, 17th	Exeter City	,, 21st
Bournemouth	Oct. 1st	Newport County	Feb. 4th
Clapton Orient	,, 15th	Swindon Town	,, 18th
Crystal Palace	,, 29th	Southend United	Mar. 4th
Watford	Nov. 12th	Gillingham	,, 18th
Brighton and Hove	Dec. 10th	Cardiff City	April 1st
Aldershot Town	,, 24th	Norwich City	,, 15th
Queen's Park Rangers	,, 31st	Bristol Rovers	,, 29th

SATURDAYS

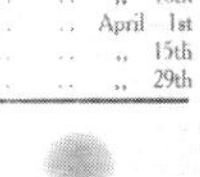

Aug. 27th, 1932, to May 6th, 1933

CHEAP TICKETS

WILL BE ISSUED TO

BRENTFORD

FROM	Return Fares, Third Class. s. d.	FROM	Return Fares, Third Class. s. d.
WINDSOR AND ETON	2 0	COLNBROOK	1 3
SLOUGH	1 9	UXBRIDGE (Vine Street)	1 3
LANGLEY	1 6	COWLEY	1 3
IVER	1 3	WEST DRAYTON	1 0
STAINES	1 3	HAYES AND HARLINGTON	0 9
POYLE (For STANWELL MOOR) HALT	1 3	SOUTHALL	0 6

These Tickets will be available on the forward journey by any Ordinary Train between 12.0 noon and 3.30 p.m., and for the return journey on day of issue only, by any Train having a connection.

Special Trips will run from Brentford to Southall as may be necessary.

In the event of these Matches being postponed or abandoned, the special facilities announced on this bill will not be given.

Children under Three years of age, Free; Three and under 14, Half Fares.

NO LUGGAGE ALLOWED.

Paddington.
July, 1932.

JAMES MILNE,
General Manager.

L.D. 474 D.S.{30 / 5750 C.R. 250. (T4/78018). B/236060.

Meanwhile, the Brentford express roared on. Crystal Palace, expected to be one of the main contenders, were given short shrift at Griffin Park, beaten 2-0 in front of a crowd of almost 20,000 packed so tight, that "whenever play approached either goal the masses rolled like a huge concertina" Word was getting around about Brentford and Gillingham welcomed a record crowd to Priestfield of 12,698, to marvel as Holliday mopped up all the goals in a 3-0 victory.

The Bees unbeaten certificate eventually went away to bottom team Cardiff City and the team wobbled after losing the next two games against Reading in the FA Cup and Norwich City. Fears that the bubble had burst proved unfounded and the team was soon back on track, so that by the halfway stage the rest, led by Reading, were chasing the Bees' shadow, five points in arrears.

Barring a collapse of the first magnitude the title was in Brentford's pocket already. That reckoned without a five star show by Exeter City who went on a ten match unbeaten run, including a 2-0 victory at Griffin Park, which edged them into poll position, albeit the Bees had a game in hand.

Exeter continued at the head of affairs for the next few weeks but with Brentford breathing down their neck they went through a sticky patch which the Bees took full advantage of to shoot clear once more. During this time the Bees showed character to come from 4-1 down to hold Luton Town 5-5 at Kenilworth Road, Holliday becoming the first Brentford player in League football to score five goals in a game, thrash Newport County 6-0 and win 5-1 at Clapton Orient.

Match action from the 2-0 victory overBristol City, watched by over 20,000. Promotion to the Second Division was coming ever closer.

Entering the home straight Cardiff City were given a going over by 7-3 and five points out of six at the busy Easter period, more or less tied matters up. One of those games was against Norwich City who were making a late bid for honours. It ended 2-2 in front of Griffin Park's best crowd of the season, 22,000.

Brentford had earlier shown their mettle by winning the Good Friday encounter against Bristol City 2-1 despite having Holliday and Crompton stretchered off and finishing the game with nine men. A 2-1 victory at Brighton & Hove Albion with three games remaining sealed the title in Brentford's favour, Holliday netting the winner to take his tally for the season to 38, an unsurpassed club record.

The spotlight now switched to the reserves and what was dubbed a record home crowd for the club's second team of around 9,000 saw them beat Aldershot 3-0 to clinch the London Combination Championship for the second year running, a fabulous achievement for a Third Division club in what at the time was the preserve of Arsenal. Brentford's success was built on a mind boggling home record which was to see the junior Bees eventually chalk up 43 home wins on the trot between November 1931 and November 1933.

1933-34

Brentford's stock was now at an unprecedented high, both on and off the pitch. The average attendance the prev-ious season was an unmatched 13,300, and with a higher standard of football in the offing, plans were set in motion to increase the capacity to accommodate the expected extra faces by building a covered stand at the Brook Road end. Curtis only tinkered with the playing staff, convinced in his own mind that he could already field a team capable of holding its own at the very least. He did though, sign three experienced campaigners in Charlie Fletcher from Clapton Orient, Jack Astley (Shelbourne) and Jack Clough (Mansfield Town).

To celebrate Brentford's success, the two Davis brothers on the board, Frank and Harry, presented the club with a Championship flag which was unfurled by FA secretary Sir Frederick Wall and Chairman Louis Simon before the start of the home game against West Ham United. The Bees then went out and won 4-1 to take their tally to five points out of six.

Brentford could not maintain that start and the team went five games without a win which included a 5-2 defeat at Bradford Park Avenue and 4-3 home beating by bottom of the table Manchester United. It was time for changes, especially in defence, so for the home game against Burnley, out went Clough, Hodge and Bain to be replaced by Baker, old campaigner Tom Adamson and young Joe James and with the indefatigable Muttitt called back into the attack, the Bees went on the rampage to win 5-2.

James, a whole hearted centre half who in four years at Griffin Park had played second fiddle to Bain, now grabbed his chance and in the years leading up to the war missed only a handful of games and became known as the best uncapped centre half in the game. Brentford followed the win against Burnley by beating Oldham Athletic 4-1, James netting one of only two goals he scored in 255 appearances, and next drew 1-1 at Fulham in front of a crowd of 36,189 to keep in touch with the front runners.

By the turn of the year the line-up had a settled look about it and while the defence on occasions gave cause for concern the front five of Hopkins, Scott, Holliday, Muttitt and Fletcher could generally be relied upon for a goal or two; indeed they failed to hit the target just three times in a League game all season.

Brentford stumbled in the early weeks of 1933, losing at West Ham and making an early exit from the FA Cup at Hull, where another defensive blunder settled the issue. To Curtis it was the final straw and he produced the cheque book to sign Southend United full back Arthur Bateman. The fee was very reasonable, especially for a player destined in May 1938 to be selected as travelling reserve for England's game against Germany in Berlin.

Brentford Football Club.

Season 1933--34

Directors:

Chairman: L. P. Simon, Esq.
Vice-Chairman: J. R. Hughes, Esq.
H. J. Saunders, Esq., W. Adams, Esq.
H. F. Davis, Esq., H. N. Blundell, Esq.
W. Flewitt, Esq., W. Barton, Esq.
F. A. Davis, Esq., H. W. Dodge, Esq.
C. L. Simon, Esq.

Secretary-Manager: H. C. Curtis

TRAINING RULES AND REGULATIONS.

(Above) Player's employment 'requirements' and match card.
(Right) Receipt for the share of the gate taken at Bury in the 1933/34 season - under £64.

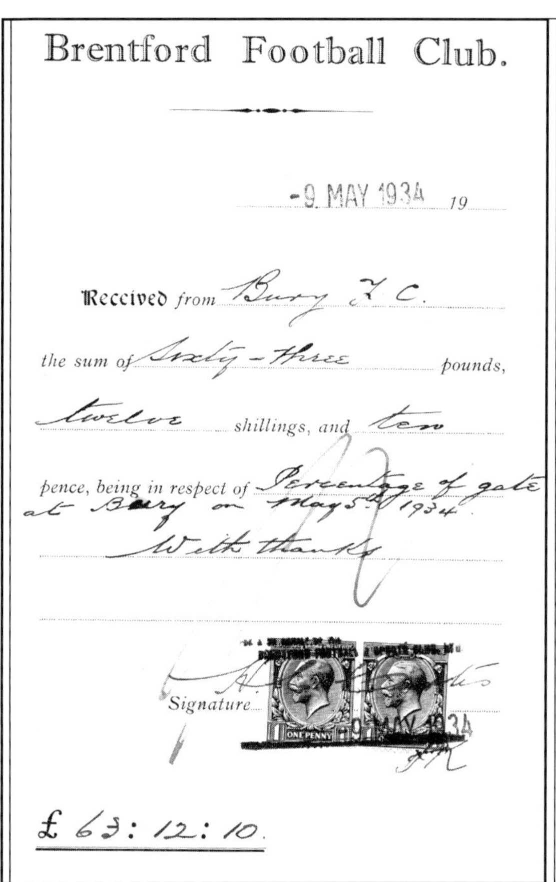

Brentford Football Club.

-9 MAY 1934 19

Received from Bury F. C.

the sum of Sixty-three pounds,

twelve shillings, and ten

pence, being in respect of Percentage of gate at Bury on May 5th 1934.

With thanks

Signature

£63: 12: 10.

The "Iron Man", as he became known, made his debut in a 3-0 home win against Plymouth Argyle and coincidence, or not, from that point on the Bees moved steadily upwards to the situation where with three quarters of the season gone the possibility of becoming the first side to rise from the Third to the First Division in successive seasons was very much within the team's scope Six teams were in the shake up for promotion. Grimsby Town had shot clear and were more or less home and dry, which left Brentford, Bolton Wanderers, Preston North End, Port Vale and Blackpool to fight it out for second place.

Brentford did themselves no favours by dropping a point at Southampton and losing to Bradford City, leaving themselves little room for manoeuvre in the crucial Easter Holiday games against Grimsby, twice, and Port Vale. The Bees made an excellent start on Good Friday by holding Grimsby 2-2 at Blundell Park and again rose to the occasion the following day to dispose of another of the contenders, Port Vale, 2-0.

A lot now rested on the Easter Monday encounter at Griffin Park in the return against Grimsby. A record crowd of 26,934 flooded in hoping the team would extend its good run but alas it was not to be as despite having the edge on play the Bees failed to capitalize on their chances and went down 2-1. As a result of those games Brentford slipped to fourth place, one point behind Preston and Bolton. All was not lost though as by recording their sixth away win of the season, at Notts County, and then beating Swansea Town while the other two contenders dropped points, the Bees moved into the second promotion place on goal average. And with relatively easy fixtures to round off the campaign the odds were that Brentford would stay there.

It was not to be, however, as in a turn-up for the books the team proceeded to lose 2-0 at relegated Millwall where a goalkeeping error helped cause the Bees downfall. This allowed Preston and Bolton to nip past and despite winning the final two matches against the Lion's companions in distress Lincoln City and Bury, it was too late, as the damage had already been done.

The defence which had served the club so well in recent times was found wanting in this grade of football, the Millwall game proving just the tip of the iceberg, so Curtis, never one to let the grass grow under his feet, initiated a mass clearout.

Both goalkeepers, Baker and Clough, were given free transfers, as were full backs Hodge, Adamson, Stevenson and French. The forward line which had been responsible for the vast majority of the team's 85 goals remained intact.

Brentford had come within a whisker of promotion with what can be termed a suspect defence so during the summer the manager set about remedying the situation.

1934-35

The management concentrated their energies during the close season rebuilding the defence. There was little wrong elsewhere, especially in attack where only Grimsby Town and Bradford Park Avenue scored more than the Bees' 85 goals. Top priority was a goalkeeper and here Curtis came up trumps with the signature of Middlesbrough's Jimmy Mathieson, the fifth player to tread the path from Ayresome Park in recent years. A veteran of more than 250 games, Jimmy already had two Second Division Championship medals and was now set for a third at Brentford. The vacant position at left back was filled by George Poyser, a club record £1,550 buy from Mansfield Town who again was to prove his worth over the passage of time. A significant appointment was Jimmy Bain as assistant manager, and it says much for the confidence felt in the club's future that an extra 5,000 terracing spaces were added to the New Road side.

Brentford served notice that this confidence was not misplaced by going unbeaten until the end of September. Muttitt scored a hat trick as Newcastle were swept aside 5-2 on their own pitch and Holliday repeated the feat in a 4-1 romp against West Ham United. One point from the next three games saw the Bees slip five points behind leaders Bolton Wanderers so in an effort to reverse the situation Burns moved up front and Duncan McKenzie was given his head at wing half. Like James he had been champing at the bit for a few years for a chance and now it had come he grabbed it with both hands. Burns showed that he was an ideal utility man by scoring three times as Notts County were swept aside 4-1 and the show was back on the road especially when leaders Bolton were defeated 1-0 at Griffin Park in front of the division's highest crowd of the day, 26,000. Later in the month Dai Hopkins became the first Brentford player capped by his country since joining the League when he took his place on the right wing in Wales' 3-2 defeat by Scotland at Aberdeen.

Brentford now had in place the side that was to take them to the title. Apart from injuries, International calls and when Watson replaced Burns for eleven games, the following blossomed into a force to be reckoned with: Mathieson, Bateman, Poyser, McKenzie, James, Burns, Hopkins, Robson, Holliday, Scott and Fletcher.

Brentford confirmed the good impression they made against Bolton by going on a ten match unbeaten run that encompassed a 6-1 hiding dished out to Burnley and a new club record victory as Barnsley were sunk without trace 8-1. Scott captured the lions share of the headlines by netting five times and set the seal on a blockbusting team performance by scoring the goal two minutes from time which gave Brentford the leadership of the division on goal average. The Bees goals record read 51-25, challengers Bolton 50-25 and both had 28 points from nineteen games.

The rags to riches story at Griffin Park was epitomised by George Robson. He had spent eighteen months languishing in the reserves and after almost moving to Heart of Midlothian had now forged a place as the side's main playmaker. Before Brentford got too carried away they had a nasty spell over December and January during which the team collected just six points from seven games. They remained in touch with the leaders though, almost incredibly the sixth successive campaign that Brentford were in line to capture the promotion prize come the half way stage.

The natives were getting restless as their expectations had risen accordingly and the call went out from the terraces to sign new players. Curtis turned his back on the doubting Thomas's and refused to panic. He stuck by his guns and was rewarded by a sequence of results that shot the Bees back to the top. Five straight wins against Notts County, Southampton, Oldham Athletic, Burnley and Swansea Town left the rest puffing and panting to keep up, and in between the latter two games Hopkins was again on International duty, scoring in Wales 3-1 victory against Ireland. A lot now rested on the crucial Easter period of three games in four days. The Bees were on the crest of a wave and had gone almost two months without defeat to open a three point lead over nearest challengers Bolton; they made the perfect start by beating Bradford Park Avenue 1-0 on Good Friday. The following day they touched the heights of brilliance to trounce Port Vale 8-0, a new club record set in motion by a hat-trick apiece by Holliday and Robson, and when Hopkins notched the winning goal seven minutes from time at Bradford on Easter Monday the Championship was in Brentford's pocket.

It was a dramatic victory as with 25 minutes remaining the Bees trailed two nil. The revival started when Bateman scored with a pot shot from fully 40 yards, his only goal in 153 appearances for the club. Hopkins equalised and then scored a spectacular winner from a mazy run that began on the half way line. Bolton, meanwhile, blew their chances by losing at Swansea but joined Brentford in the top flight by beating the Bees 2-0 at Burnden Park in the penultimate game. In between Scott set another club record by scoring a hat trick in a 3-3 draw at Barnsley to take his tally in the two games against them to eight.

The Second Division Championship Shield was presented by Mr. Rinder of the Football League management committee in front of a crowd of 21,017 at the final game against Sheffield United The Bees celebrated by winning 3-0 and not to be outdone the reserves beat Millwall 2-1 on Jubilee Monday in the final of the London Challenge Cup. The honours did finish there as two days later Holliday played at centre forward for England in the Jubilee Fund game at Highbury against the Anglo Scots, and Scott acted as twelfth man.

The Chairman, Mr, Simon, presents silver tea sets to each of the players, in recognition of the wonderful 1933-34 season that brought First Division football to Griffin Park

A 3-1 win at Portsmouth relieved the pressure, but the Bees continued their erratic course by securing a single victory in the next ten games, that at home to the reigning League champions Arsenal. Also included was a 6-1 defeat at Grimsby Town, that was to become the worst Brentford result in the top flight, and a game that attracted the lowest attendance in which the Bees were involved at this level of 5,276.

1935-36

Progress on the pitch had been matched by significant improvements to the ground which from little better than a glorified tip now rated with the best. Even then Louis Simon did not rest on his laurels and during the summer the New Road side was roofed and the capacity increased to around the forty thousand mark. On the playing side it said much for Curtis's eye for a footballer that all, apart from James, had been bought in the transfer market. Although with a higher grade of football in prospect, he kept his powder dry in the hope that the squad would be strong enough to hold its own. If not, he was poised ready to act.

The campaign opened at Bolton Wanderers who, despite finishing five points behind Brentford, it was felt were better equipped to stay the course in Division One. That opinion received an early knockback as the Bees won 2-0 with seven of the team -Watson, McKenzie, James, Hopkins, Robson, Holliday and Scott - survivors of the Third Division South championship year. The scene now switched to Griffin Park and a crowd of 25,047 against Blackburn Rovers in the first top flight game held at Griffin Park. The Bees didn't have too much difficulty winning 3-1 to set the stage for the visit of Huddersfield Town, and although beaten 2-1 the attendance of 33,481, with many more locked out, smashed the previous best.

Next in line was a visit to Middlesbrough, a game that attracted a lot of media attention due to the number of ex-Boro players Brentford now housed. Mathieson, Watson, Scott and Holliday all took their place in the Bees line-up, the absentee was Muttitt, as Ayresome Parks' best crowd of the season of 38,107 turned out curious, no doubt, to see what they were missing. It ended scoreless and by the beginning of October Brentford were starting to feel the pinch following a run of two draws and four defeats which left them perilously close to the bottom.

The team was in dire need of a transfusion of fresh blood and at a board meeting Curtis was given the funds to do just that. He didn't waste any time and for £10,000, way above what the club had previously spent on players, Scottish International centre forward Dave McCulloch was signed from Heart of Midlothian and Welsh International wing half Dave Richards moved south from Wolverhampton Wanderers. The McCulloch transfer was completed at two o'clock in the morning and the same afternoon he scored on his debut in a 2-2 draw with Leeds United.

Dave McCulloch signs for Brentford on the 30th November.

The new signings took time to settle as Brentford sat propping up the table but came good over the busy Christmas holiday from whence the Bees hardly looked back. On Christmas morning Preston North End were crushed 5-2 at Griffin Park, the Bees following this by winning the return next day 4-2, Hopkins firing the first hat trick by a Brentford player in Division One. McCulloch repeated the feat as Bolton were seen off 4-0 and everything in the garden looked rosy again.

One point from the next three games furrowed a few brows but it was only a temporary setback and with another new signing in harness, Hamilton Academical's winger Bobby Reid, Brentford were soon back on the straight and narrow. A number of clubs were angling for Reid and he chose Brentford in favour of them because of his friendship with McCulloch. They were born and brought up in the same street in Hamilton and went to school together before setting out on a career in football.

Harry Curtis
Brentford's Manager

Pitch-forked straight into battle against high flying Middlesbrough, Reid soon showed why he was so highly rated north of the border and was key to the goal by Scott that secured victory. February got off to an excellent start when Wolverhampton Wanderers were hammered 5-0 while events off the field gave cause also for Brentford to celebrate.

First Harry Curtis put his signature on a new five year contract and then Hopkins and Richards were in the Wales team that beat England 2-1 at Molyneux. Slowly but surely the three newcomers made their presence felt and the 2-1 home defeat against Birmingham City at the back end of February was the last the Bees suffered as they set out on a twelve match unbeaten run that sent them scurrying up the League to finish fifth, ten points behind the champions Sunderland and with the accolade of being London's top side.

It was well earned as against Chelsea on March 28th, Griffin Park was filled by a new record crowd of 33,486 to see the Bees win 2-1 and the following week the team drew 1-1 at Arsenal where both sides were depleted by International calls. This included Brentford's man of the moment McCulloch who was centre forward in the Scots side that held England 1-1at Wembley. Six goals in three games the previous week, 18 since he arrived at Brentford and 17 for Hearts before that gave Big Dave an automatic right to the dark blue jersey.

A measure of the improvement shown can be gathered from some of the wins during this period. Sunderland were beaten 3-1 at Roker Park; Everton were sliced open 4-1; and to cap a marvellous end to the season runners up Derby County lost 6-0 on their visit to Griffin Park, with McCulloch poaching four goals in the first 37 minutes to end the campaign averaging a goal a game in his twenty six League appearances. Judged on New Year performances Brentford had the best record in the division included in which was a run of nine away games without defeat.

And to cap a happy story Brentford were the only team to beat both the Champions Sunderland and FA Cup winners Arsenal. "Little Brentford"? No more!

The season over Brentford took advantage of their new found fame by accepting an invitation to play in Portugal. McCulloch couldn't make the trip so fellow Scot Billy Dunn, the reserves leading scorer took his place, earning most of the plaudits by netting eight goals as the Bees drew 4-4 with a Lisbon XI, defeated League champions Benfica 5-0 and the Cup holders Sporting Lisbon by 2-1.

1936-37

Compared with most other First Division sides Brentford had no real stars apart from McCulloch and relied instead on a combination of dash and enthusiasm, a trait epitomised by Billy Scott who never gave less than 100% and was equally at home in defence or attack. Team spirit was also a factor, something engendered by manager Curtis, whose main attribute was man management rather than coaching the game's finer points. The mix had served Brentford well so far and Curtis was not about to change tack now. There was little of note to report on the transfer front and Brentford went into the campaign confident of carrying on from where they left off. The only dark cloud was the loss of Reid who spent the opening month recuperating from an appendicitis operation. Even then the Gods smiled, as waiting in the wings was teenager Leslie Smith. As a 16 year old he had been loaned to Wimbledon and played for them in the 1936 FA Amateur Cup Final before turning professional for Brentford on his 17th birthday. The Boy Wonder was to translate his immense promise into a situation where he became recognised as Brentford's finest ever discovery. This was put to an early test due to Reid's absence and he did not disappoint as Brentford set out to disprove the theory of 'Second Season Syndrome'.

Brentford were pitched twice against the mighty Arsenal in the early weeks and like his team mates Smith came through with flying colours. A crowd of 31,056 crammed in for the home game, with thousands reported to be locked outside, as the Bees continued to get the better of the Gunners with a 2-0 success. The return ended 1-1, Brentford's goal coming from the spot after Hapgood handled Smith's shot on the line.

The month of October saw Brentford's rating in the football world rise to unprecedented heights as they took over at the head of affairs after beating the previous leaders Derby

County 3-2 at the Baseball Ground, Manchester United 4-0 and Liverpool 5-2. Against United Billy Scott was at his usual razor sharp best and so impressed the watching England selectors that he was chosen for England in the game against Wales the following Saturday. Scott thereby became Brentford's first full England International. It was a fitting tribute as in his five years at Griffin Park he had never gone missing in action and during this time missed only four of the team's 178 games and scored 62 goals. Marking Scott in the Welsh side was Dave Richards while a third player from the Club's ranks was Dai Hopkins. Wales won 2-1 and although Richards and Hopkins continued as fixtures in the side, it proved to be Scott's sole International call up. Brentford, meanwhile, were forced to field three reserves that afternoon and went down to a disappointing 2-0 defeat at Grimsby Town.

'Dai' (Idris) Hopkins the diminutive winger.

Yet again though they failed to come up with the goods on their travels and a 2-1 defeat at Chelsea in front of a crowd of 51,079 left them treading water. Christmas had generally been a fruitful period for Curtis's Bees and 1936 was no exception as five points from the three games kept them in the hunt. One competition in which Brentford had not really achieved much in recent years was the FA Cup, but after thrashing Huddersfield Town 5-0 in round three, hopes were high of a change of fortune. They were soon dashed as at the next stage the team gave a lacklustre display and went out 3-0 at Derby County.

It was a busy month on the International front and following the win against Liverpool in which McCulloch scored a hat trick, the Scottish selectors gave in to pressure and chose him for the match against Ireland. Duncan McKenzie continued to knock on the door and was named as reserve. McCulloch had continued where he left off in the goalscoring stakes by netting 11 in the first twelve games and was again on target as the Irish were beaten 3-1. International calls were good for Brentford's prestige but did little to aid the chase for First Division honours as with McCulloch absent the Bees lost 3-1 away to bottom side Leeds United.

The Bees got back on track with a 2-0 defeat of Birmingham City but then fell victim to an ale house brawl at Middlesbrough where James was forced to take cover following an incident with Boro's England International Camsell, which led to a few spectators invading the pitch looking for retribution. It took police intervention to calm things down and to cap an unfortunate episode the Bees lost 3-0.

For the second time in three weeks, three Brentford players were called up for International duty, Richards and Hopkins for Wales and McCulloch for Scotland. The Welsh came off best winning 2-1. On the home front Brentford continued their near invincible form by beating table toppers Portsmouth 4-0, all the goals coming from the heads of McCulloch(2) and Holliday(2).

The Bees underlined their Jekyll and Hyde home and away form by thrashing Derby 6-2 in the League encounter at Griffin Park seven days later to keep their hopes alive. There was a cloud on the horizon though. Richards' family had failed to settle in London and a move back to the Midlands looked on the cards. Curtis asked him to give it more time but in early March bowed to the inevitable and accepted an offer from Birmingham City for the wing half's signature. He made his debut for his new club against Brentford and was instrumental in a 4-0 victory which didn't do the Bees prospects much good. A 3-2 defeat by Grimsby Town, the first at home in 23 games, had already dimmed those chances and the loss of Richards was almost certainly a major factor as to why the Bees slid out of contention.

There were a few brief respites, like a 4-1 defeat of Middlesbrough in which McCulloch netted his second hat-trick of the campaign, but to counter balance this the champions elect Manchester City took them to the cleaners in a 6-2 walkover at Griffin Park. Brentford eventually finished sixth, not as high as at one time expected but never the less a very respectable position.

The season over Brentford accepted an invitation to play a number of friendlies in Germany. It was a welcome diversion from the rigours of a long First Division campaign but ended in controversy when before the start of the game against Schalke 04, the team gave the Nazi salute out of courtesy to their hosts when the German anthem was played. A photographer from the London Evening Star was in attendance and his picture of the event caused a lot of adverse comment about the club when it was published. Brentford lost that game 6-2 but fared better in the others, beating SV Hamburg 3-0, Hertha Berlin 4-0 and drawing 2-2 with 1st. FC Nuremberg.

	HOME				Goals		AWAY			Goals		
	P	W	D	L	F	A	W	D	L	F	A	Pts
Brentford ..	28..	8	4	2	30	17..	6	3	6	18	18..	35
Wolves ..	25..	8	4	0	27	8..	6	2	5	18	20..	34
Leeds Utd ..	28..	9	5	1	28	16..	2	6	6	18	24..	33
Arsenal	27..	10	2	1	33	11..	3	4	7	18	21..	32
Preston	27..	7	6	1	25	12..	3	5	5	20	19..	31
Charlton....	26..	8	3	2	25	11..	2	7	3	13	18..	30
Bolton......	28..	7	3	4	27	18..	3	7	4	19	23..	30
Sunderland.	27..	8	3	2	23	14..	1	7	6	14	26..	28
Derby C	28..	7	4	4	33	27..	3	4	6	13	31..	28
Stoke	27..	7	5	1	30	9..	3	2	9	12	23..	27
Chelsea	27..	8	4	2	29	15..	2	3	8	20	34..	27
Middlesbro..	26..	8	3	2	28	16..	3	2	8	18	28..	27
Man. City ..	25..	8	2	3	26	16..	2	3	7	23	28..	25
Everton	27..	7	2	3	31	17..	4	0	11	16	30..	24
W.B.A.......	26..	5	3	6	22	22..	4	3	6	20	26..	24
Grimsby	28..	5	5	4	17	18..	1	7	6	16	26..	24
Leicester....	28..	7	3	4	22	15..	2	3	9	14	33..	24
Huddersfield	27..	7	2	4	18	16..	3	2	9	14	27..	24
Birmingham	27..	4	8	2	22	17..	1	6	7	10	20..	23
Liverpool ..	28	4	4	6	24	23..	3	4	5	12	23..	22
Portsmouth.	28..	4	5	4	23	20..	2	4	9	15	33..	21
Blackpool ..	29..	3	6	6	15	20..	4	2	9	18	28..	21

F.A. CUP—Fifth Round

ARSENAL - - - -	0	PRESTON N. END	
72,1[illegible] (£[illegible])		Dougal	H.T.
BRENTFORD - -	2	MANCHESTER UTD.	-
[illegible] (£[illegible])—Holliday, Reid			H.T.
CHARLTON - - -	1	ASTON VILLA -	-
78,031 (£3,920)—Robinson		Shell	H.T.
CHESTERFIELD - -	2	TOTTENHAM- -	-
30,516 (£2,627)—Clifton, Sliman		Gibbons, Miller	H.T.
LIVERPOOL - - -	0	HUDDERSFIELD T.	-
57,882 (£4,107)		Barclay	H.T.
LUTON TOWN - -	1	MANCHESTER CITY	-
21,099 (£2,873)—Payne		Heale, Doherty, Nelson (og)	H.T.
SUNDERLAND - -	1	BRADFORD - -	-
59,326 (£3,032)—Duns			H.T.
YORK CITY - - -	1	MIDDLESBROUGH-	-
23,860 (£2,193)—Spooner			H.T.

February 1938: Brentford are top of the First Division and on February 12th, they beat Manchester United in the F.A.Cup.

1937-38

The greatest season in Brentford's history bar none. Not for the silverware, there wasn't any, but for the sustained pleasure the team gave by leading the top flight for three months and battling through to the sixth round of the FA Cup. To a club like Brentford it could hardly have got better, especially when the illusive League and Cup double loomed on the horizon for a time.

Curtis spent heavily in the close season paying £4,000 for Bolton playmaker and England International George Eastham, £1,000 for Falkirk wing half Bill Sneddon and a similar sum to East Fife for a goalkeeper destined to be feted as the club's best ever last line of defence, Joe Crozier.

Sneddon and Eastham went straight into the team that made a relatively tame start by taking just five points from the first six games, at which point Curtis rang the changes and for the match against Wolverhampton Wanderers gave Crozier his debut in place of grand old servant Mathieson, and reintroduced Bateman and Holliday. It had an encouraging effect on performances as the team rattled off a string of excellent results. Crozier, especially, proved a positive influence and in the lead up to the war was absent just once in the next 85 games. Back in the autumn of 1937 the team's run of five wins and a draw, lifted them into top spot. Included in that sequence were excellent wins against Sunderland(4-0), the attendance of 35,584 was a new high for Griffin Park, and Charlton Athletic(5-2), in which McCulloch netted four to take his tally for the season to 14 in twelve games, the best in the division.

'Keeper Crozier grabs the ball off a Charlton foward's feet in October. A 5-2 victory before 35,000 spectators.

Seven days after outclassing the South Londoners Brentford sustained an unfortunate setback when James badly twisted an ankle during the 2-1 defeat at Chelsea, an injury that sidelined him for six weeks. The attendance at Stamford Bridge of 56,810 was to be getting on for the highest to attend a League game in which Brentford have been involved. James was missed, although Buster Brown did an excellent holding job as Brentford continued to keep one step ahead of the field.

Curtis now had an embarrassment of riches to choose from in the forward line - current or future Internationals Reid, Eastham, Hopkins, Smith, Scott and McCulloch were all in the mix, not to mention old war horse Holliday who a couple of years earlier played for England in an unofficial International against the Anglo-Scots. This was underlined when Reid was selected to play for Scotland against Ireland. Wing half Mckenzie was also in the team, reward at

This time the ball eludes Crozier, as Bolton score their goal in the 1-1 draw on New Year's Day

last for a couple of years of sustained brilliance. The minds of the Scottish selectors worked in mysterious ways though, as absent was McCulloch, the most prolific goalscorer in Britain. It obviously escaped their attention that in 122 top flight games either side of the Border, Big Dave had notched 113 goals and with 15 in fourteen outings was again the English First Division's leading marksman!

Reid celebrated news of his selection by potting the only hat-trick of his career in a 4-3 win at Liverpool. Inevitably McCulloch scored the other. It was now Hopkins turn to grab the spotlight when he played for Wales in a 2-1 defeat by England. Brentford, meanwhile, continued to set a hot pace at the top. They were the talk of football as in a short space of time they had risen from the Third Division (South) to the very pinnacle of the English game and could boast eight current or future Internationals in their ranks.

The rest continued to dance to Brentford's tune for the next few weeks until the side hit a dodgy spell of two points from four games. During this period ace marksman McCulloch scored twice on his return to the Scotland side in a 5-0 defeat of Czechoslovakia in Glasgow, but Reid was dropped, another strange decision in light of the tremendous partnership they had forged at Brentford.
Despite this poor spell the Bees continued to keep a tenuous hold on their lead at the top and moved clear once more

following a run that saw them complete the double over reigning League champions Manchester City and also deprive Huddersfield Town and Everton of the spoils.

The FA Cup now came into focus, a competition in which the Bees at last made their mark. Brentford joined the race to Wembley with a comfortable 3-1 success against Second Division bottom dogs Fulham and continued by seeing off Portsmouth 2-1, watched by another new record home crowd of 36,718. It was all systems go, as beside holding a four point lead over their nearest challengers the Bees were favoured with a relatively easy home draw in the fifth round of the cup against Second Division Manchester United. Meanwhile things were not going to plan in the League. Results began to go against the Bees which enabled the chasing pack to move within striking distance. Brentford were now caught like a pigeon between two stools. Should they concentrate on winning the League or the Cup as attempting to succeed in both was starting to prove beyond them?

Manchester United were beaten 2-0 and in the ensuing weeks, before the home quarter-final against Preston North End, three straights defeats answered the question. So the Cup it was. For the third time that season Griffin Park welcomed a record crowd (37,586) but the majority left disappointed as the visitors won easily 3-0 and powered on to beat Huddersfield Town in the final.

It seemed the season would peter out in frustration as with seven games remaining the Bees were struggling to keep up. But wait! Just as all hope of winning the First Division looked lost, the team found its feet once more. First came a 1-0 win at Middlesbrough, then Grimsby were steamrollered 6-1, young reserves Maurice Edelston and Gerry McAloon featuring on the scoresheet. A 4-3 defeat at relegation threatened WBA did the Bees no favours but they were still in with a squeak of a chance, if Arsenal could be overcome in the two encounters at Easter. At Highbury, Reid returned from International duty in Scotland's 1-0 defeat of the Auld Enemy in Glasgow, a game

The Team!

from which surprisingly McCulloch was dropped. A mammoth crowd of 55,299 congregated looking to see Arsenal cement their place at the top, but it was Brentford who called the shots and won 2-0. Stoke City held the Bees 0-0 the next day and on Easter Monday Brentford brought the house down to win the return against the Gunners 3-0 in front of 34,495 enthralled spectators. Those two results put the whole season back in the melting pot as quite a few teams now lined up looking to knock Arsenal off their perch.

If Brentford won their last two games and Arsenal lost theirs and other results went the Bees way there was still a chance. Sadly, it was not to be and defeats to Leeds United and Birmingham City closed the door on that notion as Arsenal beat Preston North End, Liverpool and Bolton Wanderers to streak seven points clear of Brentford in sixth position.

1938/39

After the season just completed, it was little surprise that Curtis stuck with the same players that had previously served the club so well. More with an eye for the future two notable youngsters were signed, 17 year-old full back Harry Oliver from Hartlepool (for a near record fee for a player of that age) and RAF and England Amateur International 'Jackie' Gibbons, who was not only was to serve the club as a player but later as manager.

Brentford started the season in fine form, beating F A Cup Finalists Huddersfield Town at Griffin Park by 2-1 before a 29,000 crowd. The next match was lost by the same score at Everton, then the journey to London became something of a farce. With little time to spare to catch their train, the coach from the ground was slow in starting, the driver lost his way and the party was directed to the wrong platform. Fin-ally McCulloch in the final rush fell down some stairs and fractured his finger which led to his missing the next game, the big one. Arsenal were the visitors, and with no Mc-Culloch, Gibbons was given his debut.

By now Brentford had become a bogey side to Arsenal, having never been beaten by the Gunners, and a late McAloon goal was sufficient for the record to remain intact.

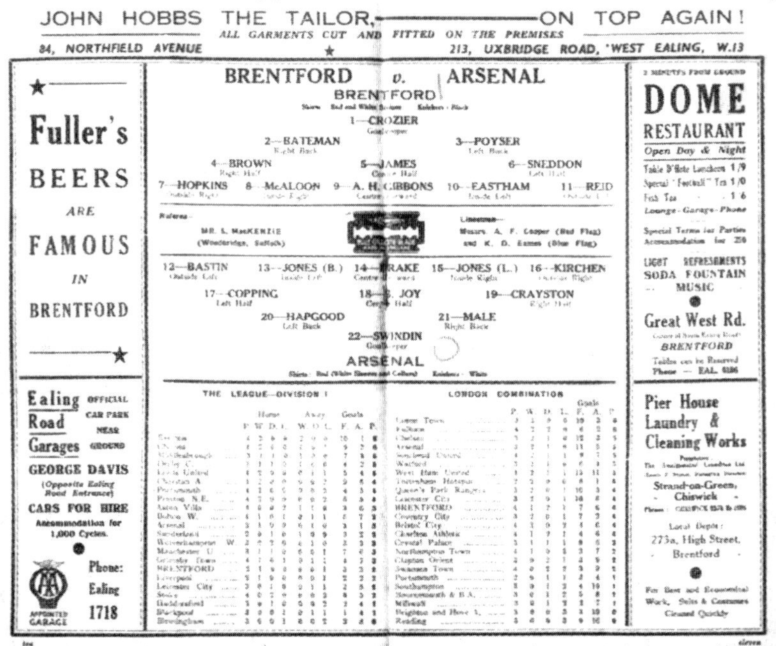

The big one: Line-ups pages from the Arsenal Programme

The attendance of 38,523 was the biggest crowd at Griffin Park for a Football League match. A good start led the supporters to believe that perhaps they could improve on their exploits the previous season. But it was not to be for three defeats followed - when just one goal was scored and ten conceded - then another reverse at home versus Sunderland after leading 2-0. Just one point was picked up in the next three games and rather than prospective champions, now lying in bottom place in the table, The Bees looked more likely relegation fodder.

Moves were attempted to strengthen the team, but just the reverse happened with the transfers of McCulloch to Derby County, for an irresistible £9,500, and later when Eastham left to join Blackpool for about half this sum. Two star players leaving certainly helped to balance the books but not enhance the team's chances. Even so efforts were made to obtain replacements but were frustrated by other clubs.

The home record was improved, including victories over Chelsea and Liverpool, and then a turbulent end of the year followed. Heavy defeats at Birmingham and at home to Manchester United, when the attendance plunged to less than 15,000, were balanced with three unbeaten games and five valuable points. The 5-1 thrashing at struggling Birmingham was especially hard to bear, as the midlanders played for much of the game with only ten men. This match also was the final one for club captain Arthur Batemen who retired. Just prior to the Manchester game, Bill Gorman - the prematurely bald defender - was signed from Bury.

Any hopes of success elsewhere were soon dashed with a third round cup defeat to Newcastle. It was now left to concentrate on the team's League position, and the introduction of three youngsters, Mc-Aloon, Townsend and Briddon, paid off for a while, with the rest of the season finishing in see-saw fashion, as the club eventually edged their way to safety.

Brentford was struggling financially amongst the 'big boys' in the First Division, and high offers for players just couldn't be ignored.

Reid moved to Sheffield United for £6,000 and McAloon to Wolves for £5,000.

Losing several players for big money was counteracted to a degree with the earlier acquisitions of Tommy Cheetham from Q.P.R. and Leslie Boulter of Charlton, and at least the 'new' team was able to eventually guarantee top division football for the 1939-40 season.

The club in fact was still able to continue to field several international players, with Gorman appearing for Ireland, Boulter and Hopkins for Wales, plus both Edelston and Gibbons representing England at amateur level.

The final game of the season was symbolic, for at last the team lost to Arsenal, by 2-0 at Highbury. The match indirectly became something of a famous one for it was filmed and used as background footage for the film 'The Arsenal Stadium Mystery'; Brentford, in the production, portrayed Arsenal's opponents, the amateur Trojan team.

Another enormous crowd for the local derby versus Chelsea in the 1938-39 season.

18th of 22 teams in the final League table perhaps was not so bad after all, but plans to spend much of their money during the close season, to improve the club's lot on the field, was to prove unwise, with war looming on the horizon.

Chapter 6: THE SECOND WORLD WAR

1939-40

When war broke out in September 1939 all normal football came to a halt. From a purely sporting point of view it was a big blow to Brentford, for in the summer, as planned, they spent heavily bolstering the squad so that there was no repeat of the previous campaign's relegation battle. Curtis spent £13,000 on goalkeeper Frank Clack (Birmingham City), defender James Anderson (Queen of the South), wing half Tom Manley (Manchester United) and forward Percy Saunders (Sunderland),much of the money surplus from the previous season's sale of Internationals McCulloch, Reid, Eastham and young McAloon.

With three of the big money purchases, Anderson, Manley and Saunders, in place the Bees made a promising start by holding League champions Everton 1-1 at Goodison , the goal scored by Saunders (the only first team player to lose his life on active service during the war). A 2-1 defeat at Blackpool followed and with war now inevitable the team chalked up a win by beating Huddersfield Town 1-0 in front of Griffin Park's lowest ever top flight attendance of 12,079. The goal was scored by Jack Holliday, his 119th and what transpired to be his last in League football.

The following day, at lunchtime, Prime Minister Neville Chamberlain went on the radio to announce that following the invasion of Poland a state of war now existed between Britain and her Allies and Nazi Germany. The Football League programme was abandoned and the players' contracts cancelled. Harry Curtis also missed out as he had only recently signed a new five year contract.

The Football Association and The Home Office met to decide what course of action the game should take and in the meantime 23 of Brentford's thirty man squad joined either the Police War Reserve or signed up for work in local munitions factories. Others such as Cheetham, a former regular soldier, received their call up papers. A couple of weeks into the war the government sanctioned a tentative return to action. The threat of an air raid resulted in attendances to be limited to 8,000 and to ensure this was strictly adhered to each spectator was given a free marked programme with admission.

A number of regional leagues were set up, Brentford now finding themselves on a par with the likes of Aldershot, Reading and QPR. But with more important things to worry about it was very low key and crowds were generally a lot lower than the permitted maximum. Brentford, as a good example, were lucky to pull in a couple of thousand on many occasions which did nothing to help the cash flow even though the players were on little more than appearance money.

The first season under war restrictions came to a stuttering end at the beginning of June when a crowd of little more than 500 was present for a game at Fulham. Times were desperate and it coincided with an armada of small ships heading for France to rescue the remnants of the British Expeditionary Force trapped on the beaches of Dunkirk.

1940-41

It was a wonder the new season even started as with the Battle of Britain in full swing football was very low on the Nation's list of priorities. London, especially, took a battering from the Luftwaffe, a situation highlighted by the fact that between September and November six Brentford games were either abandoned or interrupted by enemy action. The game at Chelsea on September 7th was abandoned in the 78th minute. Seven days later an air raid during the Charlton Athletic match had spectators and players alike heading for the shelters, although when the all clear sounded the game continued.

On the 28th0, a time bomb in Braemar Road caused the visit of Chelsea to be called off. The sirens then brought a premature end to proceedings at Charlton Athletic and the match at West Ham on November 9th fell victim to bomb damage. To complete a sorry chapter the visit to Norwich City on the 30th was cancelled with the transport system in disarray.

Players, even if they could obtain leave, often found difficulty reaching the ground and sometimes it was a case of not being able to name the line up until the last possible moment. Many would have thrown in the towel under such conditions, but the show somehow carried on. Gate receipts in the early part of the season in the newly constituted Football League (South) were in the region of £30-£40 which with the players paid a token thirty shillings (£1.50) left Brentford struggling to make ends meet. A dramatic fall-off in crowds from November onwards, there was just 400 in attendance for the visit of West Ham United, pushed Brentford close to the brink financially and there were real doubts about the club's ability to carry on. Fortunately Curtis and his board of directors rallied to the cause and, with the eternal optimism which had been their trademark in years gone by, they pressed on regardless.

This unquenchable spirit was rewarded when the League instigated a London Cup and at the same time Hitler began back peddling in his attempt to blitz the country into submission.

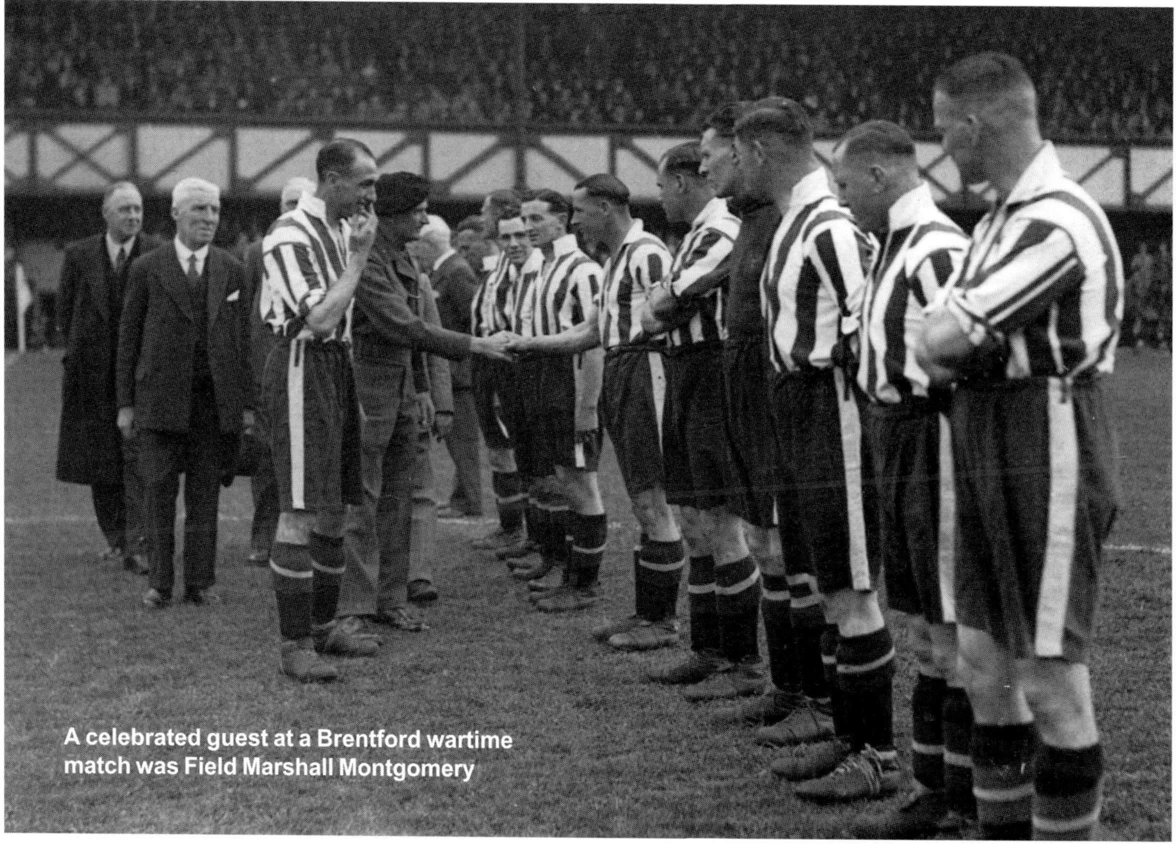

A celebrated guest at a Brentford wartime match was Field Marshall Montgomery

The cup competition consisted of two groups of six from which the Bees emerged on top above Crystal Palace, who also progressed to the semi finals. A lot of that success was attributed to the two guest forwards Doug Hunt, a Sheffield Wednesday player in peacetime, and Doncaster Rovers' Eddie Perry who between them accounted for ten of the sides 26 goals. A 2-0 win against Tottenham Hotspur paved the way to a date with Reading in the final at Stamford Bridge. A crowd of 9,000, one of the highest anywhere all season, saw the underdogs, Reading, win 3-2. Hard lines on Brentford but at this stage of the game a situation where the size of the share of the gate takings was of equal importance to winning.

With a war raging you might have thought football would have been played in a more sedate manner. Far from it! Leslie Smith had his jaw broken when he received a right hander from QPR's Reay, which led to the Rangers man serving a seven month suspension. Hunt let his temper get the better of him and was sent off twice in two months in games against Crystal Palace and Chelsea. And in another match against Palace, Brentford were trailing 4-0 when the referee awarded a penalty. The Bees players were up in arms and tried to get him to change his mind. The official obviously refused at which point the Bees walked off. Following a heated debate order was restored and the game continued, but without the original referee. Mob Rules OK!

1941-42

The Football League (South) had been a big drain on resources for many London clubs who now lobbied the FA to sanction a league competition that consisted only of teams within easy travelling distance of the capitol. The FA's management committee wouldn't play ball and went so far as to say that either the club's involved agreed to fulfil the fixtures allocated to them or they would be expelled from the League. The London clubs stood their ground and refused, as a result of which the London War League was formed.

Sixteen sides contested the breakaway league which was dominated by Arsenal from start to finish, the only team to lower their colours at their adopted home, Tottenham's White Hart Lane, being Brentford with a 3-1 success the week before Christmas. The Bees went on to finish down the field. By March the fixture list had more or less been completed so the sixteen teams formed into groups of four for the London War Cup, from which Arsenal, Brentford, Charlton Athletic and Portsmouth emerged to contest the semi finals. The Bees were paired with Arsenal, a game that aroused enormous interest as witnessed by the crowd at neutral Stamford Bridge of 41,253, easily the country's best attended match to then, apart from the England/Scotland Internationals.

The game ended without a goal, the Bees then causing an upset by winning the replay at Tottenham seven days later 2-1. Wilkins gave Brentford the lead which was wiped out when Poyser put through his own net. Hunt restored the Bees advantage and it took a save from Bastin's penalty by Jackson to keep Brentford ahead until the final whistle. The crowd was again above forty thousand, the receipts from the two encounters touching £5,350.

The scene now switched to Wembley on May 30th where the largest attendance ever to watch Brentford in action of 69,792 saw another penalty save by Jackson help Brentford on the way to a 2-0 victory, both goals courtesy of Leslie Smith. The Bees, with the guests' normal club (other than Brentford) in brackets, lined up: Jackson (Chelsea), Brown, Poyser, McKenzie (Middlesbrough), James, Sneddon (Swansea Town), Hopkins, Wilkins, Perry (Doncaster Rovers), Hunt (Sheffield Wednesday), Smith. A week later Brentford's Cup winning team, with Arsenal's Ernie Collett replacing the injured Sneddon, drew 1-1 in a showdown against the League's cup winners Wolverhampton Wanderers at Stamford Bridge in a charity game in aid of King Georges Fund for sailors.

The three games against Arsenal and Portsmouth were very important to Brentford's wellbeing as the share of the gate receipts amounted to more than £6,000, cash that helped put the club back on a firm financial footing.

This had been Brentford's second visit to Wembley during which it came to light that back in 1933 it could easily been a more permanent arrangement. Talks were held between the stadium's chief Sir Arthur Elvin and a deputation from Brentford of Harry Curtis, plus directors Frank and Harry Davis with a view to the club leaving Griffin Park for a regular trip down Wembley Way. Elvin liked the idea of housing a League team but was worried about Brentford's status. *"If they were in the top division I'd have them like a shot and build them into the best team in the land"*, he confided in the stadium's press officer Harold Hastings. Two years later he would have got his wish.

The story does not end there as on the outbreak of war the idea was given another airing. The Brentford & Chiswick Times reported: *"Brentford are hoping to recommence football, but the games will not be staged at Griffin Park, although it will remain their headquarters. Plans have been made for matches to be staged on the cup final pitch at Wembley and on Wednesday morning Mr. Harry Curtis, the Secretary/manager with other club officials, was at the Football Association's headquarters discussing possibilities"*. For reasons unknown, the idea was not pursued.

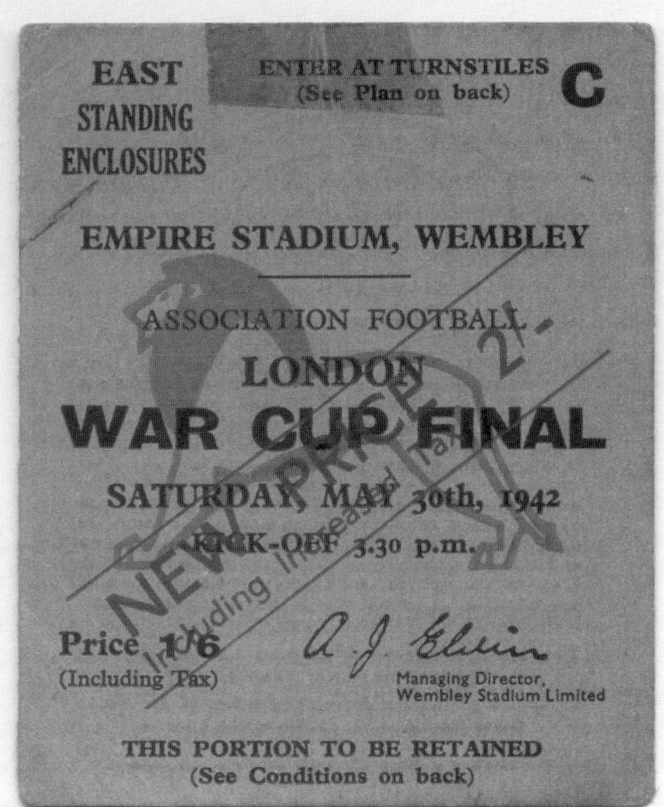

The 1942 War Cup Final programme is a valuable collectors' item. Not worth so much, but not normally seen is the 'Pirate' programme - with little content - an unofficial publication. The (genuine) match ticket is now also valuable.

1942-43

Thanks in no small measure to success in the London War Cup, the club was now on a much firmer financial footing, added to which during the summer the London clubs returned from their one year, self imposed, exile and with the addition of Southampton and Luton Town reformed the Football League (South).

Arsenal again showed they were a cut above the rest and finished well clear, while Brentford had their moments before finishing 9th of the eighteen clubs. The games against Arsenal were the highlight and in October one of the best crowds to that date of 16,700 was present for the Bees 2-0 win at White Hart Lane. A measure of the competitive nature between the two sides can be gathered from the attendance for the return in January which at 23,180 was one of the highest anywhere all season and way above Griffin Park's average of around six thousand. The visitors won 1-0 on their march to the title. The Bees' hopes of a return to Wembley in the final of the League (South) Cup took an early hit and while Arsenal completed the double by hammering Charlton Athletic 7-1, Brentford departed after finishing bottom at the group stage.

A feature of the campaign was the goalscoring exploits of Len Townsend, who netted 19 in just twenty appearances, including six as Brighton & Hove Albion were swept aside 9-4. Altogether Len scored 103 in his 150 games for Brentford during the war; twenty four of them against the Seasiders. On the International front, Dai Hopkins added to his list of games for Wales in the 2-1 victory against England at Molyneux and the subsequent 5-3 defeat at Wembley, while in December Griffin Park was the setting for a game between Holland and Belgium. Whether it is classed as a proper International is open to question as with mainland Europe under the heel of the Nazis the teams could only be drawn from personnel based in the British Isles.

1943-44

As the conflict turned slowly but surely in the Allies favour, the war effort required all the manpower the forces could muster. Servicemen were transferred here, there and everywhere as a result of which it became impossible for football teams to predict their line-ups from one week to the next. Brentford, for example, played 38 matches during the season and used fifty-two different players of whom thirty-six were guests and no fewer than twenty-three made just a single appearance.

Some were youngsters pressed into service at the last minute to make up the numbers. Brentford's predicament was highlighted by the goalkeeper's jersey, as with Crozier not always available and no adequate reserve, ten players filled the role including five for the group games in the League (South) Cup - Houldsworth, Roxburgh, Bentley (the only one to play twice), Saunders and Crozier. Not surprisingly the Bees did not make the next round. It was a similar story in the League where Brentford finished 7th, eleven points behind the champions Tottenham Hotspur.

Brentford were not helped by a number of International calls on their players. Wales were beaten 2-0 by England in Cardiff, a game for which Brentford provided Hopkins on the right wing for the home team and Leslie Smith on the opposite flank for the visitors.

Sandwiched in between were three near England walkovers against Scotland, 8-0, 6-2 and 3-2, the latter at Hampden Park attracting a crowd of 133,000. The Scots unfortunate goalkeeper all three times was Brentford's Crozier. His debut in an 8-0 thrashing at Manchester City's Maine Road had the press searching for superlatives to describe the England performance, while at the same time offering warm congratulations to Crozier, without whom, they felt, the Scots would have conceded double figures. England gave him a little respite at Wembley and the third defeat came in a return to Hampden where Leslie Smith made the second of his three appearances of the season for England.

Overshadowing completely the season's happenings was the death on November 3rd of the club's President Louis P Simon following a long illness. He was Chairman for fifteen years during which he forged a tremendous working relationship with manager Harry Curtis as the Bees rose post haste to previously unprecedented heights. The proprietor of Pier House Laundry in Chiswick, his son succeeded him on the Board of which he was a member for the best part of the next 25 years.

1944-45

The Bees made an excellent start to the campaign and went top of the Football League (South) after dropping only three points in the first eleven games. Len Townsend, especially, was in fine fettle and led the way in the goalscoring stakes on ten. Up to that point Curtis had been able to field a fairly settled side but as war duties took some of the mainstays away, so Brentford's form dipped and eventually they finished third behind runaway champions Tottenham Hotspur and West Ham United.

Along the way the Bees recorded some fine wins which included home and away successes against Brighton & Hove Albion 6-2 and 7-2, and crushing victories at Griffin Park against Portsmouth 7-1, Luton Town 6-0 and Reading 7-2. Altogether 87 goals were scored in the thirty League games, the lions share coming from the deadly duo of Townsend (24) and fellow local find Bob Thomas (22). Next in line was Leslie Smith who despite being a regular in the England team still managed seven goals in his 21 appearances.

England again dominated on the football field, winning four and drawing the other two of their six internationals. Smith was an integral part of a forward line which featured all time greats Tommy Lawton, Stanley Matthews, Raich Carter and Stan Mortenson and played in the victories against Scotland 6-2, 3-2 and 6-1, defeat of Wales 3-2 and 2-2 draw with France. He was chosen for the early season game against Wales as well but was forced to cry off because of a freak accident on his bike that hospitalised him for a few days. A further medal came his way when he guested for Chelsea in their 2-0 defeat of Millwall in the final of the Football League (South) Cup at Wembley.

1945-46

Although the war in Europe reached a satisfactory conclusion in May, it was August before Japan surrendered so it was felt prudent for the 1945-46 season to continue on basically the same lines as before. The Bees made few waves in the League (South) campaign and finished out of contention with thirty-eight points from 42 games. However, they did give a good account of themselves in the FA Cup which had been mothballed since 1939. As an experiment ties were settled over two legs , Brentford progressing to the sixth round at the expense of Tottenham Hotspur (2-2;2-0), Bristol City (1-2;5-0) and QPR (3-1;3-0). Charlton Athletic then ensured there would be no further progress by winning 6-3 at the Valley and completing the job 3-1 at Griffin Park.

With servicemen returning from Overseas seeking entertainment, attendances at sports events went through the roof. The Cup, especially, drew in monster crowds, the aggregate for Brentford's eight games in the competition reaching 231,754 (225,411), an average of 28,969 (28,176), the different figures shown depending on the source, but most impressive, whichever. The home game against Charlton Athletic attracted a full house of some 36,000 paying record receipts of £3,065-11s-9d, with an estimated two thousand locked out, but there was no cash bonanza for the club as this breakdown reveals.

The eight games attracted gross receipts of £18,939, of which £7,685 went on entertainment tax, leaving Brentford 's share at £3,538 which equates to less than £500 per game This, as Curtis pointed out, was little more than a drop in the bucket. He said; " the wage bill at Griffin Park is £300 and any profit on the season is taxed at a rate of 10s (50p) in the £pound, which begs the question has the Government already Nationalised professional football?"

Brentford did have the coffers replenished to a greater degree when in October 1945 Leslie Smith was sold to Aston Villa for £6,500. In a perfect world the club would not have chosen to cash in on their prize asset. However, he was newly married and with housing at a premium in war torn London, the promise of a new bungalow in the Midlands swayed Smith into making the move.

With a return to First Division football on the cards later in 1946 Brentford could ill afford to lose Smith. The money did allow the club to begin planning ahead by signing Charlton Athletics' war time England International centre half George Smith and Wolverhampton Wanderers former Brentford starlet Gerry McAloon One by one Brentford's expected squad for the first post war season were demobbed and as they adjusted to life back on civvy street Curtis dusted off the drawing board in preparation for the brave new world ahead .

Chapter 7: THE AUSTERITY YEARS

1946-47

The war over, football returned to normal and rather than start from scratch with a new fixture list the League programme was a carbon copy of the aborted 1939-40 campaign. However, before getting underway stock needs to taken of the effect six years of hostilities had on the game.

Football's finances were in disarray with almost all the League's 88 clubs on the breadline. Many of the grounds suffered through war damage or a lack of funds to keep them in reasonable condition, and of equal importance players who completed the last pre-war season were obviously getting on for seven years older and in a number of instances their best days were well behind them.

In Brentford's case the backbone of the side were now thirty at least. Crozier (33), Gorman (35), Brown (34), Manley (33), Muttitt (32), and Boulter (34), were all what under normal circumstances could be termed veterans, while the two aged war horses Hopkins and Scott were close to their 40th birthday.

It was no easy task finding replacements, the reason being two-fold. Players in reserve occupations such as the mines or engineering were loath to move as it invariably meant they would be called up for National Service and, even if they were prepared, the thorny subject of accommodation raised its head. There was an acute shortage of housing, thanks to the attentions of the Luftwaffe, so that all things considered managers like Harry Curtis were left banging their heads against a brick wall when it came to upgrading.

Curtis was left under no illusion about the strength of his squad following a brief pre-season tour to Denmark in which the Bees lost three times to a representative Copenhagen side 3-1, 5-2 and 5-1 so it was with mixed feelings that the first game of the New Era kicked off away to the reigning League champions (1938-39 style) Everton. Those misgivings were given a swipe as Brentford won 2-0. George Wilkins gave the Bees an early boost by scoring from the penalty spot and McAloon sealed matters on the hour mark. A 4-2 defeat at Blackpool followed but successive wins against Huddersfield Town 2-0, Wolverhampton Wanderers 2-1 and Blackpool 2-1 placed them in a challenging position near the top of the table. That was as good as it got, though, and in the ensuing weeks and months there was very little to lift spirits as the Bees drifted into the drop zone.

Curtis moved heaven and earth in his attempts to beef up the team and sold Fred Durrant to QPR for £4,500 to raise funds. With a reasonable amount to spend, the manager secured the signature of Malcolm McDonald from Kilmarnock as player/coach and Archie Macaulay from West Ham United, neither of whom were in the first flush of youth. Then following George Wilkins' sale to Second Division Bradford Park Avenue for £6,000 the Crystal Palace wing pairing of Bill Naylor and Dickie Girling made the short trip from South London to Griffin Park. And in another throw of the dice McAloon moved to Celtic in exchange for George Paterson. It was to no avail and by the turn of the year relegation beckoned

Brentford and a Copenhagen X1 take to the field in a pre-season Friendly.

The team did have its moments. The last point the Bees picked up was against the Champions Liverpool while runners up Manchester United also had to settle for a draw at Griffin Park. Meanwhile, Wolves were left to count the cost of losing twice to Brentford as they finished just a single point off Liverpool. Indeed that 4-1 victory on January 18th proved to be the last time the home fans celebrated a top flight win at Griffin Park as the team collected only three points from the last nine games on home turf. A 2-1 victory away to Leeds United was the only win the Bees recorded in the second half of the season and the fate of both teams was settled way before the curtain came down. Brentford's eventful five season adventure in the game's top flight came to an end on May 26th when Arsenal won 1-0 in front of the lowest home crowd of the season, 17,599. This left the average at 25,768 ironically, for a campaign that ended in relegation, the best in the club's history Brentford's last season mixing it with the Big Boys was a big disappointment and saw a number of club records of the wrong sort set: least home wins (5), least wins in total (9), most home defeats (11), most overall defeats (26), and fewest home goals (19).

Despite Blakeman scoring two goals, The Bees went down 3-2 to Preston in October.

Brentford could take some small consolation in that two players were capped by three different countries during the season. Gorman was in the Northern Ireland side beaten 7-2 by England in Belfast on September 28th and three days later represented the Republic of Ireland in their single goal defeat by the same opposition. Archie Macaulay was in the Scotland side which drew 1-1 with England at Wembley in April 1946 and the following month lined up for Great Britain as the Rest of Europe XI was thrashed 6-1 at Hampden Park.

1947-48

For Brentford, 1947 was a year you wouldn't wish on your worst enemy. It began with the team fighting a losing battle to avoid relegation and following a surprise 2-1 victory at Leicester City at the back end of the year, the Bees were left with a sorry looking record which read:

P 48 W 9 D 13 L 26 F 42 A 88 PTS 31.

The team had undergone wholesale changes, as witnessed by that game against Leicester City with only Frank Latimer, Tom Manley, Jackie Gibbons and Tommy Dawson surviving from the opening day of the campaign. To say that Harry Curtis was finding life tough is an understatement. Some of it was of the club's own making, however.

The board reasoned that the team's demise was due in part to the fact that many of the squad the previous season had been working part time elsewhere. This, they felt, interfered with performances on match day. So in the close season they decreed that from now on the players would be required to concentrate on nothing else but football. This caused uproar and at one time sixteen of the squad refused to sign a new contract. In the end common sense prevailed, although three of the better players did leave because of the board's decision. The previous season's top marksman Len Townsend moved to Bristol City and was the leading scorer in the Third Division (South) in 1947-48; George Smith accepted the terms offered by QPR and skippered them to the Championship of the same division; and Archie Macaulay was sold to Arsenal with whom he won a League championship medal in his first season.

Brentford were active in the transfer market, the most significant signing pre-season being Jackie Gibbons who cost a new club record fee of £8,000 from Bradford Park Avenue. Gibbons played for Brentford before the war as an amateur and would later be groomed as Harry Curtis's successor as manager. Two early season additions were the Fulham pair Peter Buchanan and Dave Nelson. Both had been operational in the game pre-war and were no spring chickens. Their arrival did little to buck up performances and with five games gone the Bees were propping up the table without a point to their name.

A win against Nottingham Forest temporarily alleviated the situation but it was hard graft and even the appointment of the World renowned coach Jimmy Hogan failed to harvest more than a smattering of extra points.

Hogan, who coached Austria to the semi-finals of the World Cup in 1934 and the final of the Olympic Games in Germany two years later, found the task at Brentford beyond him and lasted only to the end of the season.

Tom Manley

Brentford, meanwhile, continued to search for the players that could get them out of the mess they were in and avoid becoming the first team to slide from the First to the Third Division in successive seasons. This hunt bore fruit when Jack Chisholm was signed from Tottenham Hotspur in a deal that involved reserve player Cyril Toulouse moving in the opposite direction. The tough tackling centre half made his debut on Christmas day against Leicester City and from the New Year onwards was an ever present as the Bees inched away from the relegation zone. His arrival put new heart into the team, a measure of which came in January when Newcastle United, who were to finish second, were beaten 1-0 and Birmingham City, the eventual Champions, were held 0-0.

Brentford were back in business and the fans responded by turning out in force, with a season's best of 34,500 for the FA Cup, 4th round tie against Middlesbrough, which resulted in the Brentford team sending a strongly worded protest to the Players Union with regard to the referee's handling of the game. The scores were level at one apiece, and time was running out when Gibbons broke free in the penalty box only to be sent sprawling by a wayward tackle. "Penalty" cried the crowd and Bees players in unison.. The referee rejected the heated pleas and play switched quickly to the other end where McCormack was left with all the time in the world to fire home the winner. It was aggravating but there was no doubting that on the credit side Brentford were now a very different proposition. Chisholm was a rock in the centre of defence and this helped inspire his team mates, to the extent that by the end of the season the Bees finished eleven points clear of the drop.

1948-49

In the early stages Brentford relied on the old guard to steer them clear of trouble and to start with all went reasonably well. The team went unbeaten in the first five away games and overall held the opposition to 0-0 five times up to the beginning of October as the Bees settled down on the heels of the front runners.

It remained obvious that reinforcements were needed up front if Brentford were to mount a serious challenge for a promotion slot, so Curtis moved swiftly for the signature of Leicester City inside forward Peter McKennan. The fee of £8,000 was hefty for a player turned thirty and it was some time before he started to repay it as goals remained hard to come by. The defence, mean-while, continued to hold firm and apart from the game with Southampton at the back end of October, when Roddy Munro replaced MacDonald at right back, the defence line-up of Crozier, MacDonald, Gorman, Nelson, Chisholm and Manley remained intact until March, a run of 33 games in League and Cup. Brentford's achilles heal was the attack and meant that at the turn of the year another relegation dog fight was in prospect.

Then totally out of the blue the forwards clicked and Bury were swept aside 8-2. It was a shock scoreline of the first magnitude. At the time the Bees had the worst goalscoring record in the Second Division, having beaten the 'keeper just 24 times in twenty seven prior games and with one win in nine were courting disaster near the foot of the table. Bury, on the other hand, were making a decent fist of their season and actually led the field at one stage. So all things considered, a high scoring win for Brentford was the least likely outcome. For the game there was a new man at the helm as following a board meeting the previous Tuesday it was announced that this was to be Harry Curtis' last season at Griffin Park, thus ending a reign which spanned the best part of 23 years. The person charged with taking over from the great man was Bees' current inside forward Jackie Gibbons.

Can a manager have ever made a better start? Almost every shot found the target as the Bees rampaged forward, the goals arriving at regular intervals as McKennan became the third player, after Holliday against Luton Town in 1933 and Scott against Barnsley the following year, to score five goals in a single game for Brentford. Monk scored twice and to round off the perfect day Gibbons also featured on the score sheet.

It was an exciting period for the club as the following week Leicester City were the visitors in the sixth round of the FA Cup.

Bury Football Club Company Limited.

REFEREE AND LINESMENS' EXPENSES.

BURY v. *Brentford Saturday 25th September* 1948

	£	s	d.
Fare from .... to BURY (Return)		12	6
FEE	2	12	6
OTHER EXPENSES—			
Details			
TOTAL	3	5	0

Received this *25th* day of *September*, 1948, the sum of £ *3 : 5 : 0*

Signature *J.K. Collinson*

The expenses details for the officials at the Bury v Brentford match

Brentford had already disposed of First Division sides Middlesbrough 3-2, the winner in extra time coming from McKennan, his first after a barren spell of sixteen games since he joined, and Burnley 4-2, as well as Torquay United 1-0 and now welcomed an all time record crowd of 38,678 to Griffin Park. Leicester, like Brentford , were at the wrong end of the Second Division so with home advantage and the boost of the Bury result seven days earlier, hopes were high of progress to the semi-finals. Alas, it was not to be. Leicester won 2-0 and went on to reach the final where they lost 3-1 to Wolverhampton Wanderers.

The Bees subsequently went to pieces and won just two more games to finish above relegated Nottingham Forest by a single point It was a narrow squeak as Forest were the last team Brentford managed to beat, and defeat that day would have left the Bees high and dry instead.

Gibbons soon set about dismantling the side and five of the players against Bury had departed before the start of the next season. First to go was skipper and defensive lynch pin Chisholm, who in March was sold to Sheffield United for a club record fee of £16,000. It was good business on Brentford's part as to replace him Gibbons signed his former Bradford Park Avenue team mate Ron Greenwood for a fee half the sum Sheffield United paid for Chisholm.

McKennan's Bury bonanza was a flash in the pan and he moved to Middlesbrough for £9,000. Crozier, a virtual ever-present since he arrived from East Fife in 1937, joined Chelmsford City. MacDonald hung up his boots but remained on the coaching side. And Buchanan retired to take over a pub in Guildford. The departure of Harry Curtis precipitated the resignation of Bob Kane, his right hand man for twenty mainly productive years. Kane followed Curtis from Gillingham previous to which he served in the Royal Navy for 26 years and at one time held the middleweight championship of New Zealand at both boxing (1908) and wrestling (1909).

1949-50

Once Harry Curtis bowed out for good, Gibbons set about the task in hand and in a team bonding exercise went on a five match tour of Sweden. A 2-2 draw with Boras Elfsborg was followed by wins against Norkopping 5-1, Halmstad Bellklubben 2-0, Elskilstuna Verdandi 2-0 and Sliepner, who were coached by former Brentford superstar Dai Hopkins, 1-0. Billy Dare and Freddy Monk gave cause to believe that Brentford had found a strike force worthy of the name by scoring seven goals between them. It was in this department, more than any other, that Brentford had been lacking since the war and only Gibbons (13) and Dawson (10) in 1947-48 and Monk (11) in the season that followed had reached double figures. With some of the other newcomers like Dennis Rampling (ex-Bournemouth & Boscombe Athletic), and the Birmingham City pair Jackie Goodwin and Wally Quinton, showing promise, the squad returned home in good spirits confident that after the summer recess the team would give a good account of itself in the season ahead.

They were in for a rude awakening as in the opener the Bees were given the run around by Tottenham Hotspur, the team destined to romp to the title. A crowd of 32,793, the highest first day attendance ever at Griffin Park, saw their new look side put to the sword as the visitors won 4-1 in a game notable for the debut of Ken Coote at inside left, the first of a club record 514 League appearances for Brentford. In contrast, for Rampling out on the right wing, it proved to be his only first team game.

The unmistakeable Bill Gorman.

Four days later QPR were held 3-3 at Loftus Road, with Dare (2) and Monk getting off the mark. A 2-1 win at Bury followed, before the aggregate for the two early home games reached almost fifty nine thousand when 25,762 piled in for the return against QPR. It ended 2-0 in the visitors' favour which incredibly, when added to Spurs four, would account for exactly half the goals Brentford conceded at home all season!

Brentford's new look side had been found wanting, but Gibbons retained his faith in youth by blooding Jimmy Hill and Jimmy Anders in the 1-0 defeat at home to Leicester City. It was a sign of the times that only Nelson, Manley and Girling bridged the gap between that defeat and the FA Cup-tie six months earlier. Despite teething problems Gibbons determined to carry on with his youth policy but added more bite and experience with the arrival of winger Johnny Paton from Celtic for £5,000. He scored on his debut, a 2-0 win at Bradford Park Avenue, and again four days later as Blackburn Rovers were beaten by the same scoreline, but a depressing sequence of four points from the next nine games left the Bees again staring relegation in the face.

Amateur, Doctor Kevin O'Flanagan, only played seven games for Brentford, but was arguably the most talented all-round sportsman of his time.

Another dip into the transfer market brought Arsenal's Kevin O'Flanagan to Griffin Park. Famous for playing one week at wing three-quarters for Ireland against France and football for his country against Scotland the next, the "Flying Doctor" stayed only briefly as the Bees continued to flounder at the wrong end of the table. The Christmas period shed a ray of light as maximum points were taken from home games against Bury and Hull City, the Christmas day encounter against the latter being notable for the attendance of 33,836. It helped boost the Football League aggregate to 1.22 million, a new record for a single day, and with 48,587 at Boothferry Park for the return twenty-four hours later, the record increased to1.26 million.

The FA Cup saw Brentford drawn at home to Chelsea, a game that because of the interest it aroused was made all ticket. More than thirty eight thousand were tightly packed in but there was no joy for the Brentford contingent as Chelsea squeezed home by a single goal. Brentford now needed to concentrate on Second Division survival, a task that for a few more weeks looked beyond them. But then came the transfer deal that made the world of difference, with Bill Pointon arriving from QPR in exchange for Nelson. When announced it seemed that Brentford were making a mistake as Nelson had performed well alongside Greenwood and Manley. However, time soon showed that the Bees got the best end of the deal. Pointon scored on his debut, a 3-3 draw away to Sheffield Wednesday, who eventually accompanied Tottenham Hotspur into the top flight, and was key to Brentford' shift upwards by the winning of half of the final twelve games in which he was involved at inside forward.

By then Gibbons had moulded the team into one to be reckoned with, especially at home, where with Greenwood outstanding as the centre piece the Bees defence didn't concede in eight games from the turn of the year. The average age of the team had dropped dramatically. The likes of goalkeeper Reg Newton and centre forward Tom Garneys were bloodied late, as would have been 16 year old Peter Broadbent, had injury not prevented it at the last minute, while the more established newcomers, Coote, Monk, Hill and leading scorer Dare, all had their best days ahead of them. Fans showed their support for" Gibbon's Babes" by turning up in greater numbers, the average attendance of 23,468 representing the highest since the first post war campaign. So after three years juggling with relegation and its associated ills, Gibbons had ultimately been successful in taking Brentford into calmer waters in his first season at the helm.

1950-51

Gibbons policy of placing a reliance on the younger element continued, underlined by the fact that none of the eight additions to the squad had experience of League football elsewhere. Two of the newcomers, Blackpool reserve Ken Horne and youth team graduate George Bristow, were to make a telling contribution over the next decade, both making more than 200 League appearances before moving on, but they were defenders and the immediate problem facing the Bees was the lack of a proven goalscorer as back up for Dare. The little centre forward led the way the previous season with fourteen, but next in line with a mere six was Goodwin while Monk, top scorer in 1948/49 was now the preferred right back.

This lack of bite was the reason why Brentford were given little chance of challenging for promotion, indeed, most pundits had them down as relegation fodder. For a time this seemed the most likely outcome. Three straight defeats to begin with led to a tiny crowd of around 12,000 for the visit of Blackburn Rovers, the effervescent Hill scoring twice to complement Manley's spot kick conversion in a 3-1 victory.

Away wins at West Ham United and Barnsley followed and when Swansea Town became the fourth victims on the trot, a period during which Hill was on target five times, it was a case of "fingers crossed", the corner had been turned. Optimism and pessimism are long term stable mates at Griffin Park and this was shown once again when the team collected a single point from the next six games.

Greenwood had now taken over as skipper from Manley, who made his last appearance in a 4-2 defeat at Preston North End and Gorman, another of the old guard, departed to manage Deal Town in the Kent League. This meant the average age of the team was amongst the lowest in the League and, as a consequence experience in some departments was thin on the ground.

A shocking 4-0 home defeat by surprise leaders Coventry City prompted Gibbons to throw caution to the wind and only Monk, Latimer, Greenwood, Hill, Dare and Sinclair retained their places for the visit to Manchester City. Among those drafted in were teenagers Bristow and Peter Broadbent. The pair were not overawed by the occasion, but it was hardly the starting point to their careers they would have wished for, as the Bees crashed 4-0.

Gibbons had by now given almost every recognised player on the books a game and failed to find a winning formula. It didn't get any better in the weeks that followed, either, and a 7-2 hiding away to relegation doomed Grimsby Town set the seal on a very disappointing few months. Gibbons was absent from the game as he was confined to bed with sciatica, but he was aware of the situation and more changes were forthcoming as Leicester City and Chesterfield were held to a draw and QPR came off second best in the quest for local bragging rights.

The lowest crowd since before the war of 9,773 witnessed the 1-0 home win against Luton Town, just before Christmas, and Dare showed a welcome return to form by scoring all four as Southampton were swept aside on Boxing Day.

Brentford player Ron Greenwood - and future England manager.

Freddie Monk - over 200 games in his six years at Griffin Park.

All was still not well though and the New Year started with an early exit from the FA Cup at the hands of Third Division (North) Stockport County and a 2-1 defeat away to fellow strugglers Swansea Town.

Gibbons decided the time was right to wave the big stick again, and for the visit of Hull City only Jefferies, Greenwood and Sperrin retained the same shirt they wore at Vetch Field. What transpired as the most significant alteration was Horne returning at right back, leaving Monk free to switch to centre forward for the first time in over a year. And as luck would have it, an injury to Latimer left the way clear for Tony Harper to team up at half back for the first time in what became a winning combination with Greenwood and Hill. More by chance than design, it would appear, Gibbons had been dealt a winning hand at last.

Monk, back in the position that reaped a rich harvest of goals at his previous club Guildford City, soon made up for lost time and set a club record by scoring in ten consecutive games as Brentford won ten and drew three of the last sixteen to shoot into mid-table respectability. Champions Preston North End were one of the few teams to get the better of the new look Brentford, and it was a case of revenge is sweet as Grimsby Town were crushed 5-1, a victory that condemned them to become the first team since the war to crash from the First to the Third Division. Following the defeat by Preston, Brentford accepted an offer from Wolverhampton Wanderers for Broadbent, the fee of £10,000 representing at that time one of the highest ever paid for a seventeen year old. He went on to earn three League Championship medals at Molyneux and play seven times for England. His departure meant a recall for Dare and with Monk taking some of the weight off his shoulders the confidence (and goals) came flowing back. Dare finished the season as top scorer on 16 , Monk was close behind, on 13, and Brentford's tally of 75 was at least thirty more than in the four previous post-war campaigns.

Chapter 8: THE DARK CLOUDS GATHER

1951-52

A campaign which for a number of reasons fell into the category of what might have been, and in the end the only consolation was that for once the issue of relegation didn't raise its ugly head. The main protagonists in the saga that was ultimately to cost Brentford dear were Ron Greenwood and Jimmy Hill, who in later years emerged as two of the best coaching brains in football. Greenwood took West Ham United to glory in the FA Cup and European Cup Winners Cup and managed England with distinction, while Hill was the inspiration behind Coventry's rise to the top flight. Both cut their teeth at Brentford where they were pioneers on the new fangled coaching courses run by the FA at Lilleshall in the summer of 1951, under the direction of Bees' goalkeeper Ted Gaskell. They returned to Griffin Park for pre-season training bubbling with ideas and, with Jackie Gibbons' permission, Greenwood devised a cunning plan which it was hoped would turn Brentford into world beaters.

Like many of the best plans it was basically very simple and in this case years ahead of its time. If Brentford were on the attack and the opposition gained possession, the players would retreat into preset positions in their own half and block every avenue to goal. The opposition just couldn't fathom it out and the scheme became especially successful at Griffin Park where, on a pitch that had been well watered beforehand, Brentford conceded just four goals and a single point in the first ten games. Having to run 20-30 yards with one of the old fashioned leather footballs on a pitch that became progressively heavier had many teams on their knees and it seemed for a time that the Bees had discovered the key that would unlock the door back to the top tier.

Just consider some of the early results at home and the timing of the goals. Rotherham were beaten 2-0 and conceded both goals in the second half; the winner against Everton came in the 86th minute; the game's only goal against Birmingham City arrived with minutes to spare. Nottingham Forest were pegged back in the 88th minute; and the Notts County defence was finally breached seven minutes from time. The Bees continued merrily on their way with wins against Bury (4-0) and Coventry City (1-0).

A visit from League leaders Sheffield United followed and this time there was no need to bring out the hosepipes as torrential rain reduced the pitch to a soggy mess. Indeed, the fire brigade was called to pump off gallons of water before the referee gave the game the green light. The conditions were right up Brentford's street and the visitors were humbled 4-0.

Victory lifted Brentford to third and they remained in contention for the next six weeks, thanks in no small measure to a home record which read: P10 W9 D1 F19 A 4. All then went horribly wrong as the Bees pushed the self destruct button during the two Christmas games against Southampton. It seemed business as usual when Billy Dare scored after ten minutes of the Christmas morning encounter at Griffin Park. However, just before the break a mix up between Gaskell and Greenwood led to a soft equaliser. Gibbons laid into them back in the dressing room and when Hill tried to mediate he was drawn into the argument. A very unhappy Brentford team returned to the pitch and when Southampton scored a freak goal to claim the points there was another almighty row at full time. Gibbons hadn't cooled down by the return the next day and when the Saints came from behind to repeat the scoreline, he again blew his top.

Hill and Greenwood were the targets, the outcome of which resulted in the plan they devised being abandoned and both demanding a transfer. Hill moved to Fulham and Greenwood stayed for a time before joining Chelsea. The damage had been done and a disappointing run of six games without a win killed off any chance of promotion.

Brentford were in desperate need of a lift and it came from an unlikely source, when the club surprised the football world by signing Tommy Lawton from Notts County for a club record fee of £16,000. Lawton was one of the biggest names in the game and although at 32 his best days were behind him, he still had an awful lot to offer. He had previously played for Burnley, Everton and Chelsea and was an England regular for a number of years, including his time in the Third Division at Notts County. So, boasting a pedigree almost second to none, Brentford hoped he would have the same effect at Griffin Park as he had at Meadow Lane, where he was a huge draw card when they won the Third Division (South) title in 1949-50 on gates which averaged more than thirty five thousand.

Initially it did the trick and his debut at home to Swansea Town attracted thirty-one thousand, a nine thousand increase on the previous match at Griffin Park. Lawton's magnetism continued to pull in the punters and the win at Sheffield United was watched by the Football League's highest attendance of the day of more than twenty eight thousand. The Good Friday encounter with the eventual champions Sheffield Wednesday welcomed a crowd of 35,800 through the turnstiles, one not matched at Griffin Park since, and although attendances dropped off in the remaining weeks, this was due more to a poor sequence of results, and the average for the season was a highly respectable 23,022.

1952-53

If supporters were given a pleasant surprise by the arrival of Tommy Lawton, the opposite was true of the sudden departure of manager Gibbons before the new season got underway. For some time problems between himself and the board had been simmering beneath the surface. Eventually relations reached breaking point and Gibbons handed in his notice. By no stretch of the imagination can his term in office be labelled a failure, as in three seasons the Bees never finished lower than tenth, a remarkable achievement given that the Lawton deal apart, any other transfer where money was involved had to be self financing, and there weren't many of them.

PROGRAM

May 27th Tuesday.
Arrival and Dinner at Hotel Skjaldbreið At 9 p.m.

May 28th Wednesday.
Brentford v. Reykjavík Selection. 8.30 p.m.

May 29th Thursday
Trip to Keflavík Airport on invitation from The Anglo Icelandic Society and The U. S. Base Command.

May 30th Friday.
Brentford v. Fram & Víkingur (Combined) 8.30 p.m.

May 31st Saturday.
Tour to Thingvellir, Ljósafoss, and Reykir on the invitations of the Reykjavik Municipal Council

June 1st Sunday.
Sight seeing in Reykjavík.

June 2nd Monday.
Brentford v. Akranes (The last year's champions).

June 3rd Tuesday.
Brentford v. K.R. & Valur (Combined).

June 4th Wednesday.
At own disposal.

June 5th Thursday.
Brentford v. Southern Iceland Selection 8.30 p.m.

June 6th Friday.
Cocktail party at the British Legation and Dance at Tjarnar Café.

June 7th.
Day of departure

1952 Close season tour programme to Iceland.

The timing of his departure could have been better chosen as the squad had just returned for pre-season training. Assistant manager Jimmy Bain, a Brentford man since 1928, stepped into the breach on a temporary basis while Leslie Smith returned after six years at Aston Villa, although this was tempered by the fact that the former England winger was now 33 and in the twilight of his career. A major plus was that relations were patched up with Ron Greenwood, who was reinstated as skipper. Unfortunately it soon became apparent that he and Bain were on a different wave length as regards to the duties of a centre half. A sledgehammer to crack a nut was Bain's viewpoint, while Greenwood preferred a more cultured approach. The two were poles apart and it didn't come as a surprise when Greenwood moved to Chelsea at the back end of September in exchange for Northern Ireland International Jimmy D'Arcy and a cash adjustment in Brentford's favour.

With 15 points in the locker from the first twenty-one games, it became obvious that the two games over the Christmas holiday against the division's whipping boys, Barnsley, would have a major say in the outcome of Brentford's season. So when both games ended in victory, 4-0 at Griffin Park and 2-0 at Oakwell, the Bees at least bought themselves a bit of breathing space. Not so Bain, who was replaced by Tommy Lawton at the turn of the year. In a shuffling of the managerial pack, Lawton became player/manager, Bain stayed on as his assistant and Dennis Piggott was promoted to secretary, a task that had been Bain's alongside his moniker as manager.

Lawton's first game in charge saw fellow strugglers Hull City beaten 1-0 and after a brief flirt with the FA Cup, which ended in a replay defeat to Aston Villa in round four following a 2-1 victory against Leeds United, Brentford continued in the relegation mix by crashing 5-0 at Everton. The season had reached another crucial stage as the next four games were against tailenders Bury, Doncaster Rovers, Southampton and Notts County. The obvious conclusion was that the Bees needed to harvest the majority of points at stake if they were to remain in the Second Division. On paper it was a tall order as the team had now gone five games without a win. However, they buckled down to the task in hand and a point from a 2-2 draw at Gigg Lane, where teenage debutant Jimmy Bloomfield, a future England Under-23 International, netted the crucial second goal, and wins against Doncaster (1-0),

Tommy Lawton scores in the 3-0 victory over Southampton in October

Southampton (2-0) and Notts County (5-0) set the Bees on the road to salvation.

The victory at home to County, his previous club, was especially sweet for Lawton, but also marked a turning point in Ken Coote's career. Hitherto Coote had been a bit player, nominally an inside forward and yet to establish himself as a first team regular. Against County he played at wing half where his performance was a real eye opener and from an occasional first-teame he blossomed into a star performer as he carried on the road that was to lead him to making a club record 514 League appearances. Brentford's purple patch continued with a 3-2 victory away to Leicester City and all seamed fine and dandy as the team cruised nine points clear of the drop. But for some reason the Bees then reverted to their sad, bad ways and of the final ten games only one ended with two points in the locker, a 1-0 victory away to Luton Town in the penultimate fixture. For Luton it was the end of their promotion dreams, while Brentford, on the other hand breathed a huge sigh of relief that the two points now made them safe.

It became abundantly clear during this period that unless seasoned recruits were signed, Brentford's immediate future looked bleak especially after the retained list was announced. Of the thirty-one no fewer than 23 numbered Brentford as their only League club and most of them – youngsters - would need a few years to mature before stepping up to the plate as Second Division standard footballers. Included were George Francis and Jim Towers, "the Terrible Twins", who were destined to become the club's all time leading goalscorers, and similar future long servants like goalkeeper Gerry Cakebread and winger Dennis Heath.

Printed by The Brentford Printing & Publishing Co., Ltd.

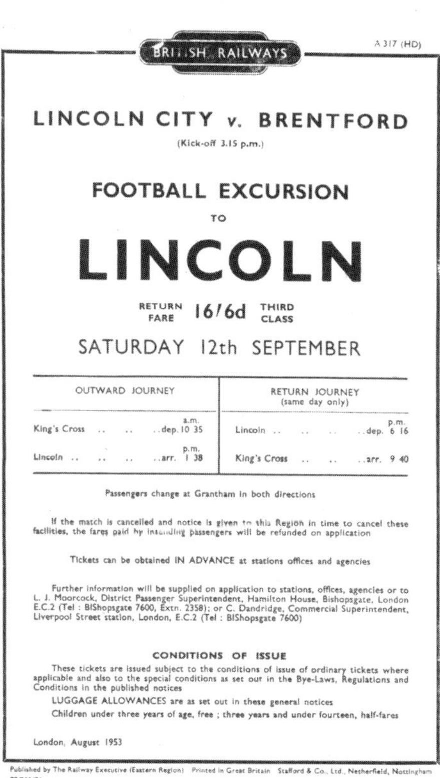
BRITISH RAILWAYS

A 317 (HD)

LINCOLN CITY v. BRENTFORD

(Kick-off 3.15 p.m.)

FOOTBALL EXCURSION

TO

LINCOLN

RETURN FARE 16/6d THIRD CLASS

SATURDAY 12th SEPTEMBER

OUTWARD JOURNEY		RETURN JOURNEY (same day only)	
King's Cross .. .. ..dep.	a.m. 10 35	Lincoln .. ..dep.	p.m. 6 16
Lincoln .. ..arr.	p.m. 1 38	King's Cross .. .. ..arr.	9 40

Passengers change at Grantham in both directions

If the match is cancelled and notice is given to this Region in time to cancel these facilities, the fares paid by intending passengers will be refunded on application

Tickets can be obtained IN ADVANCE at stations offices and agencies

Further information will be supplied on application to stations, offices, agencies or to L. J. Moorcock, District Passenger Superintendent, Hamilton House, Bishopsgate, London E.C.2 (Tel : BIShopsgate 7600, Extn. 2358); or C. Dandridge, Commercial Superintendent, Liverpool Street station, London, E.C.2 (Tel : BIShopsgate 7600)

CONDITIONS OF ISSUE

These tickets are issued subject to the conditions of issue of ordinary tickets where applicable and also to the special conditions as set out in the Bye-Laws, Regulations and Conditions in the published notices

LUGGAGE ALLOWANCES are as set out in these general notices

Children under three years of age, free ; three years and under fourteen, half-fares

London, August 1953

Published by The Railway Executive (Eastern Region) Printed in Great Britain Stafford & Co., Ltd., Netherfield, Nottingham PP/203/76

While the first team and reserves gave supporters little to shout about, Alf Bew's junior team showed promise by reaching the semi finals of the inaugural FA Youth Cup where they gave a good account of themselves before losing over two legs to a Manchester United side containing eight full time professionals, including Duncan Edwards, David Pegg and Eddie Colman all of whom were to perish in the Munich air disaster. Of the young Bees only Cakebread, Vernon Avis and John Pearson progressed to the first team although Paul Bates went on to play for England Amateurs and John Murray kept wicket for Middlesex and England for many years.

1953/54

Brentford had a role call of 31 players to call upon at the end of the previous season, of which over two-thirds could name The Bees as their only League club. Of these Heath, Francis and Towers were to well and truly make their mark at Griffin Park in the years ahead. But Lawton knew that he had to reinforce the squad if a serious challenge to regain First Division status could be made. Two veterans were signed from the manager's previous club, Notts County, with Frank Broome and Ian McPherson arriving at Griffin Park. But no other players were signed and so the pair were the only newcomers in the team that faced Stoke City at the Victoria Ground for the first game of the season. The match on a Wednesday was the first time a Football League season had started midweek. A 1-1 draw was a satisfactory start, but things then immediately took a turn for the worse.

Two 4-1 defeats followed, at Derby and at home to Blackburn Rovers, and the prospects for the season already looked grim.

Fortunately a Griffin Park victory over neighbours Fulham gave some hope, but the next few weeks were to confirm that the season was going to be a struggle. With the crowd becoming ever more agitated at the poor performances, the situation came to a head when Bristol Rovers walked off with the two points in early September, Lawton had had enough. Used to adulation rather than aggravation, a few days later he handed in his resignation. As a player he remained for three more games, all of which were lost, as the team struggled in the wilderness.

Lawton was sold to Arsenal in part exchange for Jimmy Robertson, whilst Freddy Monk took over as captain. But it was all to no avail for although a point was obtained at Notts County another defeat, versus Hull City, found the team rock bottom of the pile.

Finally, on October 1st, the directors appointed Bill Dodgin as the new manager. Ironically, just eight days earlier Dodgin had been leading Fulham, who at the time were bottom of the table, and hence he moved to the new occupants of this position! He had been at the helm at Southampton from 1945, where he had reasonable success before taking over at Fulham for three years.

Success for the new man was immediate, when unbeaten leaders Everton at Goodison Park were overcome by a Dare goal early in the second half, and two home wins followed. New signing Johnny Rainford from Cardiff City made his debut in the latter match, and over the years was to become another firm favourite at Griffin Park. The short 'honeymoon period' came to an end with an embarrassing 5-1 (5-0 at half-time) defeat at Birmingham City.

Once again hopes were raised when two draws followed before a 1-0 home victory over Plymouth Argyle.

Two Brentford stalwarts of the 1950's.
Above: Ken Horne was to be a mainstay in the defence for 11 years.
Below: Billy Dare, after nearly 300 appearances his Brentford career came to an end in 1955.

It was by now mid-November and upto Christmas five more matches were played, when no goals were scored, just two points were won whilst the defeats included a 6-0 hammering at divisional leaders Leicester (where The Bees had not lost in the previous ten matches). Frank Dudley was signed from Cardiff City and made his debut in the Christmas Day victory over Oldham Athletic. But yet again this was only a very brief respite in a season which was increasingly looking like a relegation one for Brentford.

The two Christmas matches (the return at fellow-strugglers Oldham's Boundary Park was lost 2-0) had one absentee, the legendary George Sands. The sports editor of the Middlesex Chronicle incredibly missed only this pair of games (apart from the war years) between 1935 and his retirement in 1976. Hospitalised over Christmas the reporter had enjoyed a run of 723 consecutive League and cup matches and returned for another 1,126 without a break!

The financial break-even average attendance was 20,000, but gates had by now slumped to under 15,000, and with the team struggling on the pitch the future looked bleak. A second replay F A Cup defeat to Hull City didn't boost the balance and with only three victories in the last 14 games, relegation was the final result. Money had to be found and players had to be sold. Peter Broadbent realised £10,000 and together with Bill Slater moved to Wolves, were the two were highly successful and were capped by England. Former Brentford supporter and later player Ron Greenwood – a future England manager – joined Chelsea, and Jimmy Hill moved over to Fulham. The lesser known Tom Garneys became a prominent goalscorer at Ipswich and during the close season, Jimmy Bloomfield was sold to Arsenal, and became another ex-Bee to play for his country.

1954-55

Back in the Third Division. The two captains before the first match at Southampton - a near disastrous start!

Despite two demotions since the war attendances at Griffin Park held up remarkably well and the club couldn't really grumble at an average of 15,626 on the way to relegation in 1954. Despite this encouraging level of support Brentford still struggled financially. With little money in the kitty to buy players, the club decided on a change of emphasis and now put most of its energy into bringing on its own talent This was highlighted when Dodgin made only two pre-season signings from outside, Millwall's George Stobbart in exchange for Terry Ledgerton and Northampton Town reserve goalkeeper Sonny Feehan.

Dodgin rarely fielded the same team from week to week and was not adverse to giving youth a shot of first team action, so when amateur goalkeeper Gerry Cakebread made his debut in a 1-0 defeat at Norwich City, it took the number of home produced players in the team to eight, the most number to that date: Lowden, Bristow, Heath and Towers progressed from the junior ranks, Dargie and Coote were recruited from non-League teams, while also making his debut was amateur wing half Terry Robinson, a schoolmaster at Greenford Grammar School, with no previous Football League experience.

With only one team promoted from each of the two sections of the Third Division, it was imperative that to challenge for honours a team realistically needed to be on the pace from the outset. In this respect Brentford soon knew their fate as the first victory wasn't forthcoming until match number seven. The opening game was at Southampton, where after conceding a goal on 15 seconds, the visitors trailed 6-1 at half time. It remains the quickest goal in Southampton's history and although the Bees fought back to lose 4-6 it was a severe blow to the camp's confidence.

The defence again made a hash of the opening exchanges against Shrewsbury Town five days later, conceding a goal after 30 seconds before going on to draw 2-2. Stobbart then found the net inside half a minute in a 3-2 defeat at Coventry City, and the winless sequence continued in the return at Shrewsbury, where Jim Towers scored on his debut in another stalemate.

Games against QPR and Reading ended in the spoils being shared and at this stage the number of drawn matches was getting monotonous. The Bees at last got off the mark by beating Brighton& Hove Albion 4-3 at the Goldstone. Fifteen coach loads of Bees supporters travelled to the south coast and were rewarded by their team's first away victory in almost a year. Brentford moved ging-erly forward in the ensuing weeks, generally picking up points at home but struggling on the journeys away.

Jim Towers

The next away trip was to Aldershot who at the time were nursing an unbeaten home run of seventeen games. Given Brentford's away form it was a no-hoper but buoyed by a goal in the 10th second the Bees kept a firm grip on matters and emerged with a 3-2 victory. Stobbart's goal is recognised as the quickest ever by a Brentford player and was described thus by George Sands in his match report for the Middlesex Chronicle: "There was no settling down stage to this game for Brentford began with their quickest goal of the season. Only four of the 22 players touched the ball before it came to rest in the Aldershot net. I do not time goals by the stopwatch, other writers apparently do, and they declared that 10 seconds elapsed between Stobbart starting the move with his foot and finishing with his head. From Stobbart the ball went to Rainford, then back to the kicker off who had run a dozen yards upfield. Stobbart next put it out to Heath and moving into position to meet the young winger's centre, he glided the ball home with one of those half backward headers which have brought him quite a few goals in recent weeks".

The Bees continued to plod along, some way off the front rank and by November had little to look forward to apart from the FA Cup. Here they had the benefit of a relatively easy passage to round three with wins against Nuneaten Borough and Amateur Cup holders Crook Town before being taken to three games by Bradford City. The Yorkshiremen were eventually overcome 1-0 at Highbury.

That set up an away tie against Newcastle United, the scene of one of the best individual goals ever by a Brentford player, when Rainford took on the bulk of the home defence in a mazy dribble from the half way line before chipping the 'keeper. It failed to secure a win though and Newcastle went on to claim the trophy in the final. Absent from the Bees line-up was Billy Dare who two days earlier had his name inscribed in the record books as the first player to be transferred live on television when he signed for West Ham United in a £5,000 deal.

It would be wrong to say that Brentford had nothing left to play for as a subsequent 4-2 defeat at Torquay United left the Bees on twenty-two points, just three points clear of the re election zone. Happily, that was as bad as it got and the team suffered only three more defeats, all away, to bottom side Colchester United 2-3, Newport County1-3, who didn't finish far above them, and Southend United 2-3 in the final game at the Greyhound Stadium before the move in the summer to Roots Hall. During this time Dodgin continued to give youth its head and George Francis emulated Towers by scoring on his debut in a 2-2 draw at Walsall.

All things considered it wasn't the awful season as had once seemed likely. Brentford shared 11th position with Norwich City, as both had identical records, three players Frank Dudley (20), Stobbart (19) and Towers (16), in his first season, reached double figures in the goalscoring stakes and Rainford again showed he was a class act by scoring for the Third Division (South) in the inter-League encounter with their opposite number from the North. The final score was 2-0.

A feature of the season was the number of games played under the new floodlights. League fixtures were banned, but Brentford still made a handy profit on their investment. They cost just £5,345 and were primitive to say the least, stretching the length of the roofs on the New Road and Braemar Road stands.

Chelsea, heading for their first Championship success, did the honours on opening night, October 5th, winning 4-0 in front of an audience of 11,300. Impressed by the financial benefits, the management set about arranging a number of Friendlies which included a 1-1 draw with Malcolm McDonald's Kilmarnock, a 4-1 defeat of Dundee, an 8-0 hiding dished out to WAC Vienna and the 7-0 victory against their fellow Austrians Grazer Sportklub. Attendances averaged around ten thousand but were put in the shade by the visit of an International Managers XI who were thumped 7-2 in front of a bumper 21,600. To put that crowd into perspective it almost doubled the figure for the Third Division fixture at home to Bournemouth & Boscombe Athletic three days earlier.

1955-56

A season in which Brentford's young bloods charted an erratic course as they continued to learn the ropes. Following Bill Dodgin's appointment as manager, and subsequent relegation to Division Three (South), Brentford had become more and more reliant on home produced players, a situation forced on the club by the dictates of its less than favourable financial circumstance. In nine seasons since the war Brentford dropped two divisions and the average gate plummeted from 25,768 to 11,077. Although a number of quality players had been sold, little of the money was made available to compete in the transfer market which left the management to seek a solution in Alf Bew's junior squad.

The production line moving youngsters through the ranks was working at full tilt and of the previous season's retained list of twenty-six only Sonny Feehan, Frank Dudley, Reg Newton, Jim Robertson, Jeff Taylor, George Stobbart and Johnny Rainford had experience of first team action elsewhere. Of those, Taylor and Rainford were the only ones to make a telling contribution over the course of the new campaign along with the solitary outside addition to the roster of Chelsea full back Sid Tickridge

At times the average age of the first team fell to 23, low for the period, and although packed with potential it was some way short of promotion material. Catch them in the right mood and the young Bees were a match for the best as the teams destined to fill the top four places could testify, with Champions Leyton Orient (1-0), runners-up Brighton & Hove Albion (4-2), and next in line Ipswich Town (3-2) and Southend United (2-1) all coming unstuck at Griffin Park. In contrast, on other occasions the team could be a nightmare as highlighted by the 1-0 home defeat by bottom of the table Swindon Town; although one excuse could have been that as this was the first League game played under the Griffin Park floodlights, it finished after many of the Baby Bees would normally be tucked up in bed!! That blot on the copybook showed how unpredictable performances could be, as Swindon failed to win another game and were forced to seek re-election. It was a result that came hot on the heels of the win against Brighton, a defeat Albion lived to regret as they missed out on the title by a single point.

Brentford eventually finished sixth, fourteen points behind Leyton Orient. Although generally is was a campaign to forget, especially on the crowd front with a plethora of sub five figure audiences at Griffin Park in the latter stages, bottoming out at 5,563 for the visit of Newport County, it did throw up a few pointers to the future, top of which was the blossoming partnership enjoyed by Jim Towers and George Francis; "the Terrible Twins" as they would become universally known. Locals, like many of their team mates, the pair were born within ten months of each other, Jim in Shepherds Bush on April 15th, 1933, George in Acton on February 4th the following year.

Eleven men of Brentford. They are Ken Coote, Jim Towers, George Francis, Dennis Heath, Bill Livingstone, George McLeod, John Rainford, Sid Russell, Vernon Avi Bill Goundry and George Bristow.

They lined up in the same Acton, Brentford and Chiswick Schools team, did their National Service together in the Royal Irish Fusiliers and featured in the same Brentford junior squad. Jim, of the cannonball shot, had already made his mark and was now the team's leading scorer, having hit the target 12 times in ten games as the season built to a climax, which helped him set a post war record of 22 goals. George, of the never-say-die profile, was on the verge of cementing a regular first team slot having netted eight times in his eighteen appearances. Another to show he was made of the right material was part time professional Gerry Cakebread, who after an unsteady start went on to make the goalkeeper's jersey his own for many years

And there was more in the pipeline as witnessed by the record of the reserves who finished a respectable 7th in the Football Combination having beaten Aldershot 6-0 in the final game to chalk up one hundred goals over the season. It was a fitting finale to Jimmy Bain's 27 years of service before he retired as it was he who guided the reserves' fortunes.

Bain had more than 200 games for the Bees before being appointed assistant manager and stood in briefly as manager following Gibbons departure in August 1952. His contribution was rewarded by a Testimonial against an All Star XI and also noted by the Football League who presented him with their Long Service Medal.

Mention should also be made of the floodlight friendlies that took place as they helped greatly to swell the coffers. Fears that the novelty would soon wear off proved unfounded as games against Arsenal (2-3), Fulham (1-1) and Chelsea (0-4) attracted attendances almost the equal of the Bees home League games, while the 3-3 draw with Argentine's San Lorenzo pulled in 16,300, almost the highest crowd of the season. Brentford also battled through to the final of the London Challenge Cup in which they lost 2-1 in front of a crowd of 10,400, a record for a game in the competition at Griffin Park, thanks in no small measure to the floodlight facility.

Match action during the 1955-56 season, note the first set of floodlights on the roof, from 1954.

1956-57

Brentford opened the campaign in a style that raised hopes they were now genuine contenders for honours. Four straight wins against Plymouth Argyle 4-1, Swindon Town 4-1, Aldershot 2-0, and Swindon, again - 3-1 - sent the Bees clear at the top and rekindled memories of 1932-33 when the team won their first seven games to lay the foundations for a successful tilt at the Third Division (South) title. With matches against slow starters Watford and Brighton & Hove Albion next it was not beyond the realms of possibility that the lead at the top would be extended. Unfortunately the Watford game ended in a crushing 5-1 defeat in front of a crowd of 19,000, the best since the Second Division days, to be followed swiftly by a demoralising 5-2 beating by Albion. Absent from the Bees' line up for the only time all season was Francis, who arrived at the ground late after oversleeping. Before the game he had an afternoon nap, but a relative asked to give him a call forgot and by the time he awoke from the land of nod manager Dodgin had already handed in the team sheet to the referee.

It seemed Brentford were back to square one, especially as the team travelled to Shrewsbury Town next and lost 3-2. Brentford's young bucks under Dodgin had gained a reputation for the unexpected and just as supporters were about to throw in the towel on another season Brighton were beaten 2-1 at the Goldstone and Walsall walloped 6-2 at Griffin Park. That result underlined how unpredictable Brentford could be, as in the return at Walsall four months later they ran the Bees off their feet to win 7-0 and equal the club record defeat suffered at Swansea Town back in November 1924. The visit of Walsall saw Jeff Taylor hit a hat trick to take his tally to nine in as many outings, followed by Towers and Francis on five apiece as Brentford led the country's goal charts by a mile. Three days later Francis followed suit and notched the first of six hat tricks he recorded for Brentford, a feat only Jack Holliday (9) and Bill Lane (7) have bettered, and Towers equalled, as Gillingham were overcome 3-2.

It soon became apparent that the Bees were not yet capable of sustaining a promotion challenge, as a sequence of one win in seven showed. Included was a 4-0 defeat away to the eventual champions Ipswich Town, two of the goals arriving in the first 120 seconds. Early in November Francis had a field day against Southampton when he hit the target four times in a 4-0 victory to lift spirits.

Subsequent to the Saints game, however, Brentford's fortunes took another turn for the worse and the next thirteen games produced a single victory. A run of four straight wins in twelve days early in March against Crystal Palace 2-0, Millwall 5-0, a ninety minutes sequence significant as one of the few times five different players have featured on the scoresheet - Taylor, Francis, Towers, Coote and Goundry - Reading 4-0 and Southend United 3-2, lifted the team above the halfway mark. To counter balance this run, problems surfaced behind the scenes between Dodgin and the Board. Rumours were rife that his job was on the line and despite the usual denials it became apparent at the Southend match that something was in the wind. And following a board meeting that began earlier in the evening and reconvened at the final whistle, Chairman Frank Davis emerged with the news that that Dodgin was leaving at the end of the season.

It was a harsh decision allowing for the constraints he worked under. Although Dodgin could not prevent relegation in 1954, his record since of 11th and 6th was no disgrace considering the financial situation, which apart from the signing of Chelsea's veteran winger Eric "Rabbit" Parsons, meant the rest of the squad was made up of bargain basement signings and home produced players. Of these 19 of the twenty-eight to get a game in 1956-57 had played first team football for Brentford only. Ironically, after the decision was made to dispense with the manager's services the team lost just two of the last eleven games to finish 8th. This led to speculation that Dodgin might stay on, but there was no going back and the season over he moved to Italy as manager of Sampdoria.

One of the legacy's he left behind was a front three of Francis (24), Taylor (17) and Towers (13), who between them accounted for fifty four of the side's 84 goals in Cup and League. But Brentford had a surprise in store when Taylor asked for his release so he could join the Yorkshire Opera Company. Taylor was just 26 and had shown his worth since following Dodgin from Fulham in March 1954 by scoring 37 goals in just ninety eight appearances. The Yorkshire man performed under his stage name of Neilson Taylor and his bass baritone voice was a feature at Covent Garden and Glynebourne for many years.

1957-58

A campaign in which Brentford's almost total reliance on growing their own came close to bearing fruit. Indeed it took a bit of underhand dealing by certain Brighton & Hove Albion players to upset the apple cart and led to the South Coast side, not Brentford, being crowned champions; but more of that later.

The club's number one priority during the summer was the appointment of a new manager and considering the restrictions he would have to work under, the board pulled off a major coup by signing Kilmarnock manager Malcolm McDonald. He was no stranger to Griffin Park having made almost one hundred senior appearances for the Bees at the tail end of a career that saw him win many of the game's top honours in his thirteen years at Celtic and play three times for Scotland in war time Internationals. After retiring, Malky became trainer/coach under Harry Curtis before turning to management at Division "B" strugglers Kilmarnock. In his seven years at the helm he inspired them to previously

George Francis in aerial action at Millwall in the F.A.Cup.

undreamed of heights. Killie reached the final of the League Cup in 1953, in his last season finished third in the top division, behind Rangers and Hearts and were finalists in the Cup.

With no money in the kitty McDonald was forced to mend and make do, although on the credit side he had a major plus in a strike force featuring Francis and Towers. Complicating the issue though, was the decision to abandon the Northern and Southern sections in favour of a Third and Fourth Division. It was long overdue as with only the Champions of each section winning promotion previously, it meant that for many clubs the season was over by Christmas. The top half of each section would form Division Three, the bottom half Division Four, and it was an indication of the task McDonald faced that many people felt quite happy for Brentford to forget about promotion and concentrate on keeping out of Division Four. The new manager set his sights a lot higher than that and at the end of the day took his new charges tantalisingly close to the Championship.

For up-to-the-minute Sport news, I always buy "The Star". A favourite of mine is "The Star" Sportsman's Diary (particularly on Saturdays with it's 'Round the Clubs' gossip). This well informed feature will be in "The Star" tonight with a special article by Bernard Joy.

Geoff Taylor

Geoff Taylor endorses 'The Star' newspaper - and no doubt earns some extra money!

The campaign opened with a 1-0 defeat at QPR but the Bees were soon off the mark, winning 1-0 at Exeter City before throwing away a three goal lead to draw 3-3 at home to Colchester United. In Dodgin's day the outcome of losing a lead like that would have been wholesale changes at the back. McDonald's management style dictated otherwise and the players were given a vote of confidence for the next game away to Exeter. With fifty minutes gone, and trailing 3-1, it seemed that faith had been misplaced but the Bees came charging back to win 5-3, the best away from home since the 5-2 defeat of Newcastle United in September 1934. A tasty victory against Northampton Town, 7-1, followed soon afterwards as the Bees continued on the right track although they needed to be continually on their toes to ensure they remained in the top half of the table.

One win and three defeats at the back end of September saw the Bees drop to 13th and remind them how easy it was to slip below the dreaded cut-off line. However, the defence then proved its worth by not conceding a goal in the next seven games, five of which were won, as the Bees cruised up alongside the front runners. That position remained steady into December but a sequence of poor results leading up to the New Year did nothing for confidence both on and off the park. Promotion at this stage seemed out of the question although a 7-1 hiding dished out to Norwich City, who at the time were third, early in January showed the team's potential.

Over the next few months that potential was realised and a string of excellent results drew the Bees ever closer to the leaders. As Easter approached there was still much work to be done, but the Bees at least remained in with a shout. On Good Friday Towers was on target to settle the issue at Tor-quay United. The next day it was back along the coast and a goalless draw at Plymouth Argyle. So with other results going their way Brent-ford were now jockeying for position at the top with Reading, Brighton and Plymouth and on Easter Monday were set to face

Torquay whose fate as founder-members of Division Four had already been sealed.

The largest crowd of the season to date, 15,690, flooded into Griffin Park confident of a home win, which crucially didn't materialise. It started to go wrong when Bernard Newcombe broke a collarbone early on and got worse two minutes later when the visitors scored. Try as they might Brentford couldn't get back into the game and the shock result of the day left Brentford fifth with 50 points from 41 games. Brighton led the way with 54 points but had played one game less and nearest challengers Plymouth had 53 from 41 games.

On paper the odds weighed heavily in Brighton's favour. All was not lost though, as Brentford still had to face Brighton twice, as well as promotion outsiders Reading. First in line was a visit to the Goldstone where a season's best crowd of 25,597 witnessed a1-1 draw. The Bees carried on the good work and won 2-1 at Reading and continued to keep the pressure on by beating Port Vale 4-1 in the penultimate fixture, Towers notching a hat-trick to take his total for the season to 29. A lot now hinged on the final game at home to Brighton. The highest attendance for six years of 25,720 packed into Griffin Park, the majority of whom left delighted by Bill Goundry's match winning goal. Brentford were now top, leaving Brighton with the task of beating Watford at home to regain the lead and with it the title of champions.

Brighton duly won 6-0, but the outcome left a sour taste in many people's mouth. Concerns were voiced about the manner of Brighton's success, the spotlight falling on the two late season clashes with Watford. Brighton were an odds-on chance for the title at the beginning of April but faltered badly losing to Northampton Town and Torquay United and being held by Millwall and Port Vale, all of whom, like Watford, were destined for Division Four. Brighton were set to finish with three games in six days, the visit to Brentford sandwiched between the two Watford matches.

They won 1-0 at Vicarage Road after which the referee reported his suspicions about the game being rigged to the League. Although no concrete evidence emerged at the time, whisper had it that both games were fixed. This was confirmed in October 1960, when a Daily Mail expose confirmed that some of the Watford team accepted an inducement to let Brighton win. It came too late to put matters right, although Brighton didn't get away totally scot-free as the first game they played at the start of 1958-59 ended in a club record 9-0 defeat at Middlesbrough!

Despite missing out on promotion Brentford showed they were becoming a force to be reckoned with at this level. A close knit squad of which Ian Dargie was an ever-present at the heart of the defence and Gerry Cakebread, Ken Coote, George Francis, Johnny Rainford and George Bristow, all of whom had progressed through the ranks, made at least forty appearances, added to the goalscoring power of Towers and Francis who shared 51 goals between them, augered well for the future.

1958-59.

McDonald's second term in office was to see his team narrowly fail to land the spoils, with a game at Easter, that on paper looked a nailed-on certainty, again proving a major stumbling block. An indifferent start didn't help either and a 0-0 draw at Bournemouth & Boscombe Athletic early in November left the Bees 10th , eleven points adrift of the leaders Plymouth Argyle It was hard to put a finger on what was wrong.

The Terrible Twins remained as prolific as ever, indeed Towers was on his way to a score of 37 for the season, while defensively the team was generally sound. The problem stemmed from an inability to polish off the lesser lights, three of whom Stockport County, Notts County and Doncaster Rovers, all of whose days at this level were numbered, took points off the Bees. Doncaster's win at Griffin Park represented their sole away win of the campaign.

Despite this, McDonald continued to keep faith with the players at his disposal and this is reflected in a comparison between the line-up that kicked off the season and the one that finished it. Newcombe apart, the other ten, aside from injury, more or less remained intact. The total League appearances were: Cakebread(45), Wilson (46), Horne 45), Bristow (37), Dargie (37), Coote (44), Heath (25), Rainford (46), Francis (45), Towers (46).

McDonald was convinced this policy of sticking by his men would tell eventually. He did well to stick by his guns as everything started to fall into place following a 2-1 victory at QPR, a day on which Ken Coote equalled Billy Scott's record of 298 League appearances for the club. Victory triggered a series of results that shot Brentford into a challenging position behind pacesetters Plymouth Argyle and Hull City. A draw at Stockport set a post war record of nine games without defeat and the Bees then whitewashed Southampton 6-0 at the Dell.

The Saints were a formidable proposition at home, as testified by their achievement of bagging 44 goals in just sixteen matches to date. However, the management made the mistake of announcing their retained list on the morning of the game and a number of the team to play Brentford were not on it. Hardly an incentive to give of your best! The rampant Bees took full advantage, Towers especially as he added four more goals to his catch. The result was further reason for merrymaking as it marked Dargie's one hundredth consecutive appearance.

F.A.Cup action in the 1958-59 season. Top: Brentford's goal under pressure in the 3-2 win over Exeter. Below: Through to the 4th round, and thousands of Bees fans arrive at Snowhill station, Birmingham. The Bees lost 2-0 before a near 42,000 West Bromwich crowd.

The team now had the bit between its teeth and ended Reading (3-1) and Colchester United's(4-0) hopes of promotion while greatly increasing their own chances. This meant that with Easter around the corner promotion boiled down to a three way fight between Plymouth (played 37, 51 points), Hull (played 36, 50 points) and Brentford (played 35, 45 points). Who should provide the opposition in two of the three holiday encounters, but Plymouth! With the gates locked and 29,000 inside Griffin Park the Bees gave their prospects a mighty boost by beating Argyle 3-0 on Good Friday and on Easter Monday held them1-1 at Home Park.

Three points out of four against the League leaders would under normal circumstances have been a cause for celebration, but in this case it was muted as in between the team suffered a body blow when defensive linchpin Ian Dargie was carried off with a broken shinbone against Bournemouth. The ten men carried on as best they could and held firm for a point but with its main man absent the defence crumbled to a 4-1 defeat at Norwich City, to be swiftly followed by a 2-0 loss at Southend United. To all intents and purposes the promotion challenge was over. A 6-1 beating dished out to Southend United and a 4-0 victory against relegated Notts County came too late, although Brentford could take some consolation in that Towers finished as the Third Division's leading scorer and the team boasted the best defensive record having been breached just 49 times, thirteen of those in the absence of Dargie.

1959-60.

"Third time lucky" was the optimistic cry from Griffin Park as the season got underway. Following two near misses Brentford could put forward a strong case for success this time around. The jewel in the crown, the inside forward trio of Rainford, Francis and Towers remained intact and apart from broken leg victim Dargie, who was sidelined until the New Year, the rest of the team was pretty much as you were.

For the first time in a number of years, Brentford fielded a team in four different league competitions, the latest being the newly formed Seanglian league. It was designed for the reserve teams of interested Southern League clubs and the Third XI's of lower division Football League sides. Although this competition was shortlived, Brentford couldn't complain about its usefulness. The opening game was against Crystal Palace "A" and the line up featured three youngsters making their debut who went on to play more than 1,100 League games for Brentford:

Peter Gelson (471), Tommy Higginson (388) and John Docherty (255); Higgy scored one of the goals in a 2-0 victory.

A tardy start cost Brentford dear in the two previous campaigns, so when the team set off like a scalded cat and won the opening games against Barnsley and Wrexham, everything seemed to be purring along nicely. Unfortunately one win in ten brought everyone down to earth. All was not lost, however, and the picture changed again as the team notched up a sequence of six wins in seven to make contact with the leading pack once more. Towers (11) and Francis(14) were at their rampant best during this period and with nineteen matches gone accounted for 25 of the Bees thirty-seven goals. Midfield maestro Rainford chipped in with another seven. The match at home to Accrington Stanley on October 24th was a red letter day for Towers as in scoring a hat trick he surpassed Jack Holliday's club record haul of 119 league goals. He achieved that figure in 194 games while "Olly Olly" took 213 appearances spread over divisions Three (South), Two and One.

Winger Johnny Rainford.
A great favourite at Brentford
between 1953 and 1962

Big Jim was not the only player to write himself into the club's record books that day, as young Jimmy Gitsham was called upon to play for the Juniors in the morning, a cup-tie against Fulham that went to extra time, and then dashed across to Craven Cottage as a last minute replacement for the injured Wilson. Not to be outdone by his strike partner, Francis helped himself to a hat-trick in the 4-2 away win at QPR seven days later, an afternoon that saw Rainford celebrate his 100th game on the trot. He went on to surpass Ron Greenwood's straight run of 123 games and made it to 135 before it came to a halt. Victory over Rangers took Brentford to within four points of the leaders Bury before yet another indifferent spell scuppered plans, terminally this time, as although the Bees finished with a flourish, a place in the top two proved beyond them.

John Docherty.
Incredibly signed for
Brentford on five occasions!
Three as a player and twice
in management.

McDonald's three seasons at the helm had seen Brentford finish 2nd, 3rd and now 6th, with a team that showed few changes and apart from the £6,000 paid to Luton Town for winger George McLeod in October 1958, no newcomers that cost more than a signing-on fee. This is highlighted by the appearances during this period. Of the 138 League games played, no fewer than eight topped the hundred mark: Rainford (137), Cakebread (136), Francis (136), Coote (131), Towers (126), Bristow (113), Dargie (103) and Horne (102). And five more had in excess of fifty games: Wilson (92), Parsons (89), Goundry (64), Heath (53), and McLeod (65). Great servants that these players were, Brentford's failure to improve the team when necessary by loosening the purse strings cost them dear. Poor attendances couldn't be blamed as the average over those three seasons was 12,973, a figure few other clubs in the division could match. Brentford were now set to struggle both on and off the pitch.

1960-61

Brentford kept faith with the policy that up until now had served them reasonably well and continued with a squad of mainly home produced players. While the team was to show few changes there was a major difference to the kit. Out went red and white stripes to be replaced by amber shirts and a blue "V"neck. The reasoning behind the switch was the number of times Brentford had been forced to wear the change strip of white shirts on their travels. But with

Watford, Hull City and Torquay additions to the fixture list and further visits to Shrewsbury Town, Newport County and Port Vale, the team would still be required to forsake the new colours six times and the change became a shortlived affair as the shirt reverted to the much loved red and white stripes twelve months later.

The Bees in their new blue and yellow colours. Front row (left to right): Johnny Rainford, George Bristow, Dennis Heath, Ken Coote, Jimmy Towers, George Francis, George McLeod. Middle row: Tom Wilson, Eric Parsons, Ron Peplow, Ian Dargie, Bill Goundry, Terry Curran, Tom Higginson, George Summers. Back row: John Docherty, Peter Gelson, Fred Ryecraft, Gerry Cakebread, Jimmy Gitsham, Vernon Avis, Ken Horne. Not included in the picture are Sid Russell, on cricket duty with Middlesex, and John Hales and Danny O'Donnell, who were both in Scotland when the photograph was taken.

Brentford christened the new colours in style by hammering Tranmere Rovers 4-1 and beating Watford 2-1 to feature at the top of the first published League table. Successive defeats at Halifax Town (0-1) and Watford (1-6) followed and as the weeks went by it soon became apparent that reinforcements would be required if Brentford had any chance of surpassing the efforts of the three previous seasons. None were forthcoming, the management instead preferring to take a chance on some of the club's young reserves. It was a policy doomed to failure especially in the light of a 5-1 home defeat by the eventual champions Bury.

At the back end of October the club and its ever dwindling band of supporters had a brief respite from the trials and tribulation of the Third Division in the shape of a new competition, the Football League Cup. After receiving a bye in the first round the Bees were drawn at home to Second Division Sunderland. They, too, were struggling to make headway, but on name alone presented a formidable stumbling block.

Brentford v League Champions in the new League Cup.

Rainford scores The Bees goal, in the 1-1 draw.

An era was coming to an end, andwith two players coming near the end of their Brentford careers.

George McLeod with The Bees from 1958 to 1964

Ken Coote the club's all-time record appearance maker.

The game ran true to form in the early stages as the visitors built a 3-1 (Towers) lead, but with young Scot George Summers, on his debut, playing out of his skin as replacement for the injured Francis, the Bees clawed their way back into contention. Goals by McCleod and Rainford (2) secured an unlikely 4-3 success which prompted a pitch invasion at full time. The mood was euphoric and hit even greater heights when Brentford came out of the hat with the League Champions Burnley in the next round.

A bumper crowd was in prospect, but in the event as the opposition were involved in a European Cup-tie against French side Rheims, it was a reserve team a disappointed Brentford public faced. Brentford protested about the line-up, to no avail, and a lower than could have been expected turn-out of 9,900 witnessed a 1-1 draw. The Clarets took no chances in the replay and fielded their first XI. Brentford lost 2-1 and Burnley went into the record books as the only team to use 22 different players in a major two match cup-tie.

Meanwhile, Brentford's poor showing in the League was giving cause for concern and relegation became a very real threat.

It was a particularly bad time for the club as at the AGM Chairman Frank Davis announced a loss on the year of £7,000, taking the total deficit to more than £50,000, and for the visit of Swindon Town the crowd of 4,857 represented the lowest in almost thirty years. To add to the gloom, on January 24th, Bill Dodge died. The 95 year old was the club's President at the time and the last remaining survivor of the first year in operation back in 1889.

The team continued its downward spiral and just when it was thought matters couldn't get any worse the club was hit by a bombshell when both Towers and Francis asked to go on the transfer list. Brentford, eager to ease their cash problems agreed, but surprisingly had no takers. Instead, an injection of money came from an unlikely source when John Docherty was sold to Sheffield United for £17,000. The young Scot had only made seventeen first team appearances and the fee set a new record for a Brentford player. Docherty's departure and the impending loss of the "Twins", who again accounted for more than half the team's goals, gave out little hope for the remainder of the season. The Bees did in the end manage to steer clear of trouble but that didn't impress the fans and a crowd of just 3,500 was present for the penultimate home fixture against Port Vale, leaving the average at 7,392, the lowest since 1928.

Chapter 9: UPS BUT MOSTLY DOWNS

1961-62

Storm clouds had been gathering over Griffin Park for the best part of a year and now broke with a vengeance in a season that provided conclusive proof that a strategy which involves setting out with just nine full time professionals, padded out by a few part-timers, is asking for trouble. The removal of the maximum wage in the summer had the Brentford management reaching for the self destruct button and ten seasoned professionals were given a free transfer, including Bristow, Heath, Parsons, Goundry and Horne, all of whom had given sterling service and in the majority of cases still had some more mileage in them.

Mick Block joined The Bees from Chelsea in January 1962.

To top everything the most prolific goalscorers in the club's history, George Francis and Jim Towers were sold for peanuts to arch rivals QPR. As per usual the pair accounted for more than half the side's goals in 1960-61, leaving an enormous void, filled only by Brian Edgeley from Cardiff City. The excuse that so many players had been turned out to grass because of their age didn't wash when it is taken into account that the only other signings, Jim Belcher (Crystal Palace) and Ray Reeves (Reading), were older than many of those they replaced! In another economy measure Jack Holliday was sacked as assistant trainer after nearly thirty years at the club, meaning that within the space of a few days the three most prolific marksmen in the club's history departed the scene.

Bearing all this in mind everyone in the whole wide world forecast that Brentford would end up relegated. The Bees rarely gave the pundits much cause for concern. The writing was on the wall from an early stage after the team collected a single point from the first ten games, included in which was a 6-1 thrashing away to Newport County who then went on to win once in the next 24 outings! The signing of England International playmaker Johnny Brooks from Chelsea for £6,000 and the return of Francis from his brief sojourn at Loftus Road, helped improve Brentford's shocking goalscoring record - four in nine and one of those was an own goal - but with a third of the season gone the Bees had the weight of the other twenty-three teams on their shoulders. The prospect of improvement was not helped by the fact that the next home games were against the top two, Portsmouth and Bournemouth & Boscombe Athletic.

Portsmouth, under former Brentford centre half George Smith, had sustained only one defeat to date but were caught cold at Griffin Park as the Bees coming from behind to win 3-2. Two weeks later a last gasp equaliser earned a point against Bournemouth and for the first time the Bees had a glimmer of hope. It was soon extinguished and some fearsome away defeats, which left Brentford with the worst record in the division apart from Newport County, had the team struggling to keep its head above water as the season built to a climax. Desperate times called for desperate measures and with judgement day approaching McDonald tried to buy Towers back from QPR. Terms were settled, with Rangers due to make a thousand pound profit on their investment. The parties agreed to meet in Brentford Market but McDonald got his wires crossed and drove to Acton Market and when they did finally catch up with each other, the deal, for one reason or another fell through.

This did nothing to help Brentford's cause and they continued to struggle, so that with three matches remaining, and all at home, they entered the last chance saloon seeking a football miracle. Northampton Town were dispatched 3-0 to give a glimmer of hope, something recognised by the fans who came out in droves for Grimsby Town's visit, an amazing 18,126 of them to be precise. There was a lot riding on the game as on top of Brentford's desperate need for points, Grimsby required a win to stave of QPR's bid to oust them from second spot. Despite a brave effort it was the visitors who prevailed and won promotion, leaving the last rites to be read on Brentford's season two nights later, following a 2-0 defeat by Hull City.

1962-63

Who said money can't buy success? Brentford certainly showed otherwise in winning the Fourth Division title in 1962-63. Almost from the time Jack Dunnett succeeded long serving Frank Davis as Chairman in October 1961, money became no object and although his big spending almost led Brentford down the road to oblivion, in the short term it did pay a rich dividend. Dunnett, a Mayfair solicitor, future Member of Parliament for Nottingham Central and later President of the Football League, joined the Brentford Board in the summer of 1961 and soon made his financial presence felt as the struggling Bees paid £6,000 for Johnny Brooks and £4,000 to secure the return of George Francis from QPR.

Soon after Brentford wrote out a cheque for £6,000 to buy Chelsea winger Micky Block, but with relegation staring the club in the face the purse strings were pulled tight until the close season when the management could regroup and look at the options open to them in the transfer market.

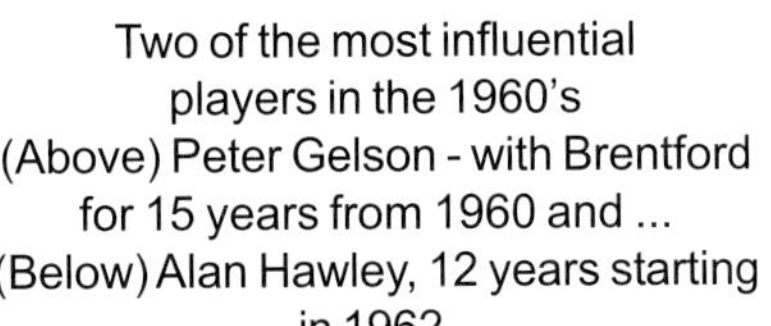

Two of the most influential players in the 1960's (Above) Peter Gelson - with Brentford for 15 years from 1960 and ... (Below) Alan Hawley, 12 years starting in 1962.

The ambitious Dunnett, at 39 one of the youngest chairman in the League, was not at Griffin Park for the fun of it and laid out his stall when he told fans: "my directors and I have guaranteed a large sum of money which will bring at least one high quality player to Griffin Park during the close season. When I say high quality I do not mean around £3,000. We mean to buy the best available." It was not empty rhetoric, as over the course of the next eight months five players were signed for an outlay of around £52,000. Today that sounds like chicken feed, but at the time the reaction involved a deep intake of breath.

First through the door was classy wing half Matt Crowe. The thirty year old cost £5,000 from Norwich for whom he played more than two hundred games and served under former Bee Archie Macaulay when as a Third Division club they reached the semi-finals of the FA Cup. Next to sign was current Northern Ireland International Billy McAdams who cost £10,000 from Leeds United. That made two Internationals in the front line and in September it became three when Brentford broke the existing Fourth Division transfer record by paying £17,500 for West Ham United's Scot John Dick. By March promotion, if not the title, looked a formality but just to make sure Chelsea's England Under-23 centre half depleted the bank balance by a further £12,500. Brentford were obviously at full stretch to overhaul long time leaders Oldham Athletic and beefed up their armoury further by paying Southport £7,000 for winger John Fielding.

Despite a stuttering start there was never much doubt that Brentford wouldn't hang around long in Division Four. The team was a cut above anyone else and even when loss of form or injury looked like throwing a spanner in the works, manager Malcolm McDonald could always seek a remedy in the cheque book. The fans recognised this, too, and the average attendance of 11,418 represented a significant increase on the relegation year (8,483).

As the season drew to a climax promotion had become a formality and the big question was, could Brentford go up as champions? With the finishing line in sight the main contenders were Brentford, Oldham Athletic and Crewe Alexandra, with Mansfield Town lively outsiders. Brentford took on the mantle of favourites by beating re-election bound Lincoln City to ease past Oldham who the same afternoon crashed 5-2 at York City. The Bees next game against a Hartlepool United side cast adrift at the bottom without a win in 18 games, should have been a stroll in the park. It was anything but as the Bees, beaten just once in the previous thirteen games, lost 2-1. Five days later one of the highest Fourth Division crowds of the season, 17,771, crammed into Boundary Park for the clash of the Titans. This time the Bees gave a much better account of themselves and were denied a point when the referee blew for time just before McAdams header crossed the line for a goal. Victory took Oldham back to the top and Brentford now faced the daunting prospect of a home game against Crewe. With the stakes high, a bumper crowd of 15,820 made their way to Griffin Park and were rewarded by a classic encounter which the Bees won 3-1 to regain top spot. It was a lead they did not relinquish again.

The title as good as in the bag, attention focused on whether the Bees could score the six goals necessary in the final game at home to Workington to hit three figures for the first time. Leading 4-0 at half time the odds favoured the Bees achieving their target. However, in a turn round of fortunes the visitors set about testing Fred Rycraft in the Brentford goal and at the final whistle the score was 4-3. Failure to secure the extra two goals was soon forgotten as the fans invaded the pitch to cheer off their heroes and celebrate Brentford becoming the first team in history to win the Champ-ionship's of Divisions Two, Three(South) and Four. Brentford's liberal use of the cheque book paid off handsomely, especially in regard to the forward line as Dick (24), McAdams (23) and Brooks (22) accounted for sixty nine-goals between them.

Johnny Brooks a member of the classy and expensive forward line of the period, with (above) his Fourth Division Champions medal.

1963-64

The impressive way the team motored to top honours the previous season left the impression that there was plenty more in the tank. The management obviously felt so as the only major signings were the returning England International Bill Slater - the game's "Player of the Year" in 1960 - from Wolverhampton Wanderers and Liverpool full back Allan Jones. High on the club's list of priorities off the pitch was a new set of floodlights as the old rickety one's had served their purpose and now reached their sell by date.

A steady, if unspectacular, start kept the Bees in line with the early pacesetters, the highlights of which were a hat-trick within eighteen minutes, by John Dick as Reading were swept aside 4-2, and Ken Coote's 500th League game. The team's form was erratic to say the least and that there was trouble in the camp became apparent when midfield maestro Johnny Brooks asked for a transfer. There were murmurings that other members of the squad were unhappy with their lot and matters came to a head when Bristol Rovers beat a lacklustre Brentford side 5-2 at Griffin Park. Manager McDonald, normally a placid, mild tempered man, felt it was time to wave the big stick and he rang the changes with a vengeance for the visit of Wrexham three nights later. Cakebread, Coote, Higginson and Brooks returned to the fray, and newcomer Dai Ward signed just in time to take his place in the side. For Ward it was the culmination of a busy few days, which began on Monday after Watford accepted an offer of £8,000 for his signature. This left the player to agree terms, but as Millwall, too, were on the Welsh International's case, McDonald took him on a tour of London to keep them off the scent. After much haggling Ward signed and rushed home to collect his boots.

The way that Brentford threw in the towel against Rovers determined many supporters to give the Wrexham game the cold shoulder and the attendance of 10,500 was three thousand down. The absentees must have kicked themselves when they saw the scoreline of 9-0, which totally vindicated McDonald's whole-sale team changes. The goalchart for Brentford's record win in the Football League reads:

2 minutes: Ward forces a corner on the right and Summers' cross is volleyed home by McAdams.

6 minutes: Hales corner is flicked on by McAdams, and Ward, lurking, nets with a brilliant overhead kick.

15 minutes: Seconds after, Summers rattles the crossbar, Ward forces a corner from which Brooks' first time shot is deflected off the prostrate McAdams into an empty net.

35 minutes: With Brooks and McAdams in close attendance, the visitor's centre half Fox loses his bearings and puts through his own net.

44 minutes: Brooks takes a corner and little Johnny Hales meets it with a flying header.

52 minutes: No let up for Wrexham as Brooks lets fly from twenty yards and the 'keeper can only stand and stare in disbelief as the net behind him bulges.

60 minutes: Hales splits the defence with a superb ball and Ward thunders in a shot which goalkeeper Fleet can only parry. Summers nips in first to tuck the ball home and as Wrexham continue to sink all five Brentford forwards are now on the score sheet.

75 minutes: Tommy Higginson, Mr. Perpetual Motion, finds Brooks fifteen yards out, and the former England man chips the keeper in the style of Brazil's finest.

88 minutes: Ward rounds off a good evenings' work by leaving his markers for dead and walloping home number nine.

F A Cup action versus Middlesbrough. Brodie clears a Boro' attack while Thomson and Scott guard the goal.

The 9-0 victory surpassed the previous record set in April 1935 when Port Vale were hammered 8-0. Buoyed by the Wrexham result Brentford went undefeated in the next five games to haul themselves up to fourth. Included in this sequence was an unusual first in the 1-1 draw at Barnsley as the forward line included an International from each of the home countries: Brooks (England), Dick (Scotland), McAdams (Northern Ireland) and Ward (Wales). The goals continued to flow freely and when Dick beat Pat Jennings in the Watford goal in the 23rd minute of the encounter at Griffin Park on November 9th it was the quickest half century in the club's history. While on the subject of records the line up for the 4-1 defeat at Oldham Athletic a few weeks later contained seven Scots: Recent recruits Chic Brodie and George Thomson, who between them cost £20,000 from Northampton Town and Everton respectively, Willie Smith, Tommy Higginson, George Summers, John Dick and George McLeod.

Brentford's star was now on the wane and failure to win in the next twelve games, including a 6-2 hiding at home to bottom side Luton Town which prompted a demonstration from disgruntled fans on the Braemar Road forecourt, sent them plummeting down the table. A decent run in the FA Cup offered a brief respite. It took in a 2-1 win against Middlesbrough in round three, but reached a disappointing conclusion at the next stage in front of a packed Griffin Park (26,000) as Fourth Division promotion contenders Oxford United won 2-1 after the first attempt to settle the issue finished 2-2.

The team was struggling against the tide and as the weeks went by the unthinkable started to look like it could become a reality and the Bees would go straight back down. In the event a late season rally pulled Brentford clear, although it was a close call and they were separated from relegation by just six points when the curtain came down.

1964-65

The management continued to flourish the cheque book with uninhibited abandon and the season, still in its infancy, had made three more relatively expensive signings to come. Ex- Bee and England Under-23 International Jimmy Bloomfield cost £12,000 from Birmingham City; journeyman centre forward Joe Bonson, already past the century mark of goals for his five previous clubs, set Brentford back £6,000 from Newport County and Billy Cobb was signed from Plymouth Argyle for another £12,000. Missing from the squad was Ken Coote, who after a club record 559 senior appearances, in not one of which did he receive a booking, decided to call it a day.

Following a slow start the team was soon into its stride and a 3-1 win away to arch rivals QPR early in October lifted Brentford to the top of the table. Bloomfield, especially, was playing out of his skin and deservedly won the prestigious "Evening Standard" Player of the Month award. The same month saw a Brentford player sent off for the first time (the war years apart) since a bout of fisticuffs between Duncan McKenzie and Manchester City's Eric Brook forced the referee's hand in October 1935. Now, after a gap of twenty nine years, Higginson and Shrewsbury Town's Eric Brodie incurred the arbiter's wrath and took an early bath.

Most other things in Brentford's garden looked rosy especially as Chairman Jack Dunnett, gave the impression that even if the wheels looked like coming off there was money available to plug the gaps. This became apparent when to replace McAdams, who was sold to QPR for £5,000, Brentford tabled a bid of £40,000 for England centre forward Gerry Hitchens, at the time peddling his wares for Torino in Italy. This was rejected and the management turned its attention instead to Mansfield Town's Tony Wagstaff and Hull City striker Chris Chilton. An astronomical figure of £30,000 each was mentioned but neither club would play ball and they eventually teamed up at Boothferry Park, scoring fifty-three goals between them, as Hull finished champions of Division Three the following season. McDonald plugged on in his search for a new centre forward and signed Scunthorpe's Northern Ireland International Ian Lawther for £17,000, the deal being struck in the Houses of Parliament where Dunnett had recently been signed in as MP for Nottingham Central.

Two very capable goalkeepers in the early 60s and into the 70's 'Chick' Brodie (left) tended to be the first choice, but in Gordon Phillips (right) he had an able deputy.

The Irishman made his debut in the 5-1 defeat of Watford as Brentford continued to show promotion form into the New Year. Brentford's front runners were full of themselves at this stage and a magical spell of five games reaped eleven goals. Cobb claimed the lions share with seven including a hat-trick as leaders Carlisle were crushed 6-1. The Bees now turned their attention to the FA Cup. Easy wins against Wisbech Town (2-0) and Notts County (4-0) paved the way for a visit to top flight Burnley in round three. It was nip and tuck through-out and a draw was a fair result. The scene then switched to West London where a tremendous turn out of 30,448 saw the visitors progress to the next round 2-0.

The Cup exit apart, everything seemed sweetness and light at the club. Within weeks there was evidence that all was not well, however, when McDonald tendered his resignation, effective from the end of the season when he would take over as manager of Kilmarnock.

Dunnett was not best pleased and gave him leave of absence with immediate affect. Coach Tommy Cavanagh, who had been McDonald's right hand man for three years, was appointed manager in his place and Jimmy Sirrel was brought in from Aldershot as trainer. Cavanagh's first game at the helm was away to League leaders Bristol Rovers from which the team emerged with flying colours by winning 2-1. Soon afterwards QPR were slammed 5-2 as the Bees continued to track the leaders, but just two wins in seven appeared to put the kibosh on achieving promotion. Then, just as all looked lost, the Bees made a dramatic return to form and won four, drew two and lost just once, a crucial defeat away to fellow contenders Hull City, as promotion eluded them by two points. Brentford's failings on their travels cost them dear as at home only bogey team Hull City left with all the spoils. Away, Brentford were beaten by three of the relegated teams, Luton Town, Port Vale and Barnsley, points lost that in the final analysis proved crucial.

Lazarus (on the ball) with Bonson and Dick close by during the 1964-65 season.

1965-66

A strong candidate for the most disappointing Brentford season ever.

After narrowly missing out on promotion at the end of the previous campaign, Brentford's talented squad appeared a good bet to make amends this time around. New manager Tommy Cavanagh had an embarrassment of riches at his disposal although in the end that description took on a very different meaning as the team stumbled to relegation and the manager out of a job. Yet the season got off to a flyer as QPR were slaughtered 6-1. A game against the nearest neighbours is always looked upon with relish and their big money transfer deals in the summer gave this one added spice. They had lived in Brentford's shadow for years and their chairman, the ebullient Jim Gregory, decided it was time for a change to which end they spent heavily in the transfer market. Brentford, in contrast to the previous few years, kept the till closed.

The Bees were in no mood to relinquish their crown as Third Division Kings of West London and gave the upstarts from Shepherds Bush a roasting. So with the first ninety minutes of the season gone it appeared the status quo remained unaltered. How wrong could you be!! One swallow doesn't make a summer and as autumn turned to winter and results went from bad to worse, the Bees' status in the Third Division was in grave danger.

There was a brief ray of hope when Brentford's ten men came from behind to beat Oxford United 5-1 and followed up with a 2-0 success against Southend United. It was a false dawn though and following a 5-0 thrashing away to fellow relegation candidates Exeter City in mid-April the axe fell on Cavanagh's fourteen month stay in office.

Billy Gray, who was in the process of leading Millwall to a second successive promotion, was surprisingly prised away from the Den to take his place. It was too late to do anything about Brentford's plight and relegation was a certainty still with games remaining. The rug had been well and truly pulled from beneath the club's feet and the final Third Division game for some years saw the Bees beaten 2-0 at home by Gillingham, which bizarrely was chosen by the BBC for televising as "Match of the Day".

1966-67

Everything had gone badly wrong at Griffin Park over the previous twelve months. Championship favourites at the start of 1965-66, the bottom dropped out of the club's world when instead of promotion, relegation became their fate. To say it was a shock to the system is an understatement. Dunnett had invested heavily in buying the best available and relegation was something he hadn't bargained for. A quick return up the ladder was of paramount importance if Brentford were to hold on to the crowd numbers, and when the team struggled to make much early headway and attendances dropped well below the club's break even figure, alarm bells started to sound.

Few could have foreseen what was just around the corner though. Early in December QPR Chairman Jim Gregory approached Dunnett, with a suggestion that to save running costs the two clubs should share Griffin Park. This was discussed at length and eventually Gregory made an offer to buy Brentford out, lock, stock and barrel. Dunnett, looking to get shot of his involvement at Griffin Park so that he could take up the offer of a seat on the board at Notts County, near to his Parliamentary constituency of Nottingham Central, jumped at the idea. The news broke nationally on Thursday January 19th, leaving everyone at Brentford from fans to players to board members aghast, especially as there had been no consultation.

Two mainstays in the early to mid-60s team (left) right winger Mark Lazarus and (right), right half Mel Scott.

It was a classic fait accompli, or so the bad guys thought. However, the fact that everything had been done behind people's backs helped galvanise the three factions into joint action. It soon became apparent that the Dunnett/ Gregory axis was not in for an easy ride, and when the call to arms came everyone responded magnificently, leaving Dunnett and Gregory in no doubt whatsoever that they faced World War III if they sought to consummate the proposed marriage.

Brodie in action, with Gelson in close attendance.

The first hurdle to overcome was the match against Southend United two days after Dunnett's thunderbolt. Attendances for the two previous home league games against Barnsley (4,250) and Hartlepool United (5,770) had given cause for concern and a five figure crowd was required as a show of strength that enough people cared about the club's fate. As it happened, when the teams came out a highly charged audience of 10,650 were waiting to throw their weight behind Brentford's bid for salvation. The players, none of whom knew what was in the wind until it broke in the press, went at the visitors with all guns blazing although the score of 1-1 came second to everyone's reaction, which with emotions running high on the terraces made it obvious to Dunnett that he had bitten off more than he could chew. Even then it only needed long serving secretary Dennis Piggott to sign on the dotted line and the game, so far as Brentford would be concerned, was up. That he refused, when he had nothing to lose personally having already been promised a job in the new organisation, bought Brentford time in a bid to save the club from going under.

A nice pay cheque from the FA Cup tie at Sunderland a week later, where a crowd of 37,000 saw the Bees lead for a time before losing 5-2, helped finances and when within days Ron Blindell rode, metaphorically speaking, into Griffin Park on his shining white charger (in this case it could have been true as he owned the mag-nificent grey Stalbridge Colonist, winner of the Hen-nessy Gold Cup and one of the few racehorses to finish in front of the great Arkle) Brentford were back in business. Just!

The team continued to give a good account of itself and equalled a club record by going 16 League games undefeated, and in the meantime a new board headed by Blindell assumed control of the club's affairs. Dunnett, his days at Brentford over, departed for Notts County taking manager Billy Gray with him. Trainer Jimmy Sirrel was put in charge of team affairs and as the season built to a climax it seemed for a time as if Brentford were set to achieve an unlikely promotion, until a string of five straight defeats put an end to those thoughts. Brentford finished ninth, but of more importance the club lived to fight another day.

So how was the takeover recorded at the time by the club's trustees? This was their diary of events as published in the following season's handbook.

JANUARY

19th The Evening News headline reported "London Soccer Bomshell! QPR to take over Brentford" At a routine meeting that evening Peter Pond-Jones, George Hutchinson and Lionel Green decided that Brentford must not die!

20th Early morning telephone call from former director Walter Wheatley, who said that Les Davey and he would put forward £20,000. Mid-afternoon, an action committee was formed in the office of script-writer Alan Simpson. At an evening board meeting held in the House of Commons, directors Radley-Smith Davis and Rogers voted against the takeover.

21st 10,650 people attended the home match against Southend United. Both national press and television reported thousands of fans parading on the terraces, before and after the match chanting - "Rangers leave us alone!"

"Hands off Griffin Park!" and "Brentford must live!" Mr. Michael Barnes, MP for Brentford & Chiswick, offered his help in the fight.

22nd Director Frank Geraghty resigned

23rd Mr. Ron Blindell met Mr. Jack Dunnett in the House of Commons. Mr. Blindell stated he was shocked at a figure of £262,000. 3,500 fans who attended an evening meeting at Griffin Park heard director Eric Radley-Smith say "we do not want any more power politics, this situation happens when too many shares get into one hand." Peter Pond Jones, chairman of the supporters club, stated "We want every man on the terraces to be a shareholder." Michael Barnes, MP said, "these past few days have taught us that soccer is big business." George Hutchison, Supporters Club secretary said, "this has always been your club morally, now make it your club in fact." Alan Simpson said, "In a few years time we will be able to take over Fulham, Chelsea and QPR." The managers and terrace supporters also made speeches.

24th At a shareholders' meeting Mr. Dunnett said, "I have had enough, I want to get out!"

25th The bank agreed to extend the club's overdraft for two weeks. The "Save Brentford Trust Fund" was created, the trustees being Peter Pond-Jones, George Hutchison and Lionel Green.

26th A seven man syndicate consisting of Mr. Ron Blindell, Mr. David Brooks, three existing directors and two former directors, was formed to purchase Mr. Dunnett's interests in Brentford FC.

29th Mr. Wheatley stated, "After two long meetings our group are prepared to take over from Mr. Dunnett.

30th Trust Fund reached £1,000.

FEBRUARY

2nd Trust Fund reached £4,000.

3rd Mr. Wheatley made an offer to Mr. Dunnett on behalf of the syndicate; it was rejected. Mr. Dunnett stated that he would guarantee Brentford FC's existence for one more season, as tenants of a QPR owned Griffin Park.

4th Under chairmanship of David Coleman, Peter Pond-Jones challenged Mr. Dunnett on BBC TV's "Grandstand" to re-open negotiations.

6th Peter Pond-Jones met Mr. Dunnett in his Park Lane office, and handed him a letter offering him complete release from his responsibilities at Brentford.

8th In search of funds, Walter Wheatley, Peter Pond-Jones and George Hutchison addressed the Brentford Chamber of Commerce.

14th Mr. Dunnett said he would accept syndicate's offer.

15th Mr. Dunnett demanded certain conditions.

21st Mr. Dunnett agreed to sign unconditionally.

22nd It was announced that Mr. David Brooks was no longer a member of the syndicate.

23rd On behalf of the syndicate, Mr. Blindell bought Mr. Dunnett's £41,000 worth of shares and guaranteed the bank overdraft; he also personally arranged a 12 month bridging loan of £104,000.

24th 36 days after the beginning of the crisis, a new board, headed by Mr. Ron Blindell, assumed control at Griffin Park.

MARCH

14th Mr Blindell announced at a shareholders' meeting that Mr Walter Wheatley would not stand as a director. The Trust Fund closed at £8,589 10s. It was agreed that all future moneys go direct to Brentford FC.

And how did the watching world react to the proposed take over, or "Pop Gun Wedding" as the esteemed Daily Mail sports columnist JL Manning described it? Well for a week or two Brentford were front page news in the National Press. There was regular updates on television stations, while QPR fans looked on in bemusement, their views mirroring the thoughts of their Brentford counterparts: QPR belonged at Loftus Road and Brentford could keep their Griffin Park!!

1967-68

Brentford lived in the fast lane under the Dunnett regime and when he applied the brakes and decamped to Notts County it was those left behind who had to pick up the pieces. Despite Ron Blindell's timely intervention with a loan, Brentford remained in a financial straight jacket in the knowledge that £104,000 needed repaying to creditors by June 30th 1968. Nobody was under any illusion about the task ahead if Brentford were to survive let alone prosper and "Economy with Efficiency" became the club's motto as it struggled to keep on an even keel.

First to go was the reserve and junior teams and manager Jimmy Sirrel was given a budget that would allow for no more than seventeen professionals at any given time. Sirrel had been the driving force behind the 16 match unbeaten run at the back end of the previous season and despite the restraints he worked under, given a bit of luck he felt capable of moulding the players at his disposal into a force to be reckoned with. Initially all went well, although attendances were some way short of the 9,000 break even figure. By the end of November the Bees were handily placed, four points off the lead having just beaten Exeter City 5-1, York City 3-1 and Darlington 3-2. At this stage there was reason to believe that quality would triumph over quantity but fate then took a hand and blasted Brentford's wafer thin squad with both barrels.

Lack of a reserve team was a handicap to John Richardson as he recovered from a broken leg, so a friendly was arranged against Southern League Bedford to help speed his recovery. He came through with flying colours but unfortunately George Dobson, one of the finds of the season, sustained a broken leg in the game and was sidelined for two months. Brentford failed to win in his absence and drifted down the table. To make matters worse, chances of a boost to the exchequer in the FA Cup were cut short by a morale sapping defeat by Guildford City in the FA Cup.

1967-68 was the first season the loan system was taken on board with two per club the maximum allowed. Hoping to take advantage on a short term basis the management sent out a circular asking for likely candidates. Portsmouth manager George Smith, a Brentford player back in the First Division days, responded and inside forward Dennis Edwards made his way to Griffin Park. The move was a success and Brentford tried to make the deal permanent. £4,000 was scraped together, to no avail as Aldershot upped the bid to £5,000, a sum outside Brentford's scope.

By March the race for promotion was over, attendances dipped below four thousand and as a result another crisis loomed. Brentford's days at Griffin Park looked numbered when Blindell announced that the ground was about to be sold to QPR for £250,000 and the Bees would relocate to Hillingdon Borough. Blindell explained: *"Financially we are in a tremendous jam. Moving to Hillingdon for the start of next season might help us survive as a league club. Hillingdon have good facilities and a ground capacity of twenty thousand and the prospects of development. Our debts are running at about £135K, including a loan of £70K, which must be paid by the end of June. The position must get worse because between now and next August we have only five home matches to meet expenses. I have had meetings with Hillingdon chairman Alfred Whittit. He agrees the transfer might suit both clubs".* Peter Pond-Jones, chairman of the outlawed Brentford Supporters Club, thought it was a positive move, but only if Brentford could be kept alive. He said: *"The move might even help Brentford. A lot of the club's fans come from that area".*

All that was needed now was for the FA to apply the rubber stamp and Brentford would have been off to Hillingdon, eight miles to the west. But just as the deal seemed done and dusted, in stepped former director Walter Wheatley with an offer of a £68K interest free loan, sufficient to keep the wolf from the door for another twelve months. The club's hierarchy couldn't wait to snap his hand off and the Brentford born businessman again became the hero of the hour.

1968-69

Brentford's ongoing financial problems dictated that the playing staff was again kept to the bare minimum, just 15 full time professionals. Manager Jimmy Sirrel could give you chapter and verse on running a football club on a shoestring. The original head cook and bottle washer, he coached the players, washed their kit and for good measure swept the dressing rooms. As Sirrel was to show time and time again, he was a shrewd cookie when it came to getting the best out of his players and soon had the team at concert pitch. Undefeated in the first eight games, which included a tremendous 3-0 victory against Second Division Hull City in the League Cup, all appeared well.

However, the threat of injury hung like the Sword of Damacles above the team's head and when it struck it did so with a vengeance. One by one the side's mainstays fell by the wayside, including both goalkeepers Chic Brodie and Gordon Phillips at one stage.

Brentford get the season off to a good start with a 4-0 win at home to Colchester. Number 8 Deakin, on his debut, scores one of the goals, whilst Dobson celebrates.

Matters came to a head when for the visit to Bradford City Sirrel was forced to borrow 'keeper Ron Willis from Charlton Athletic. Then against Rochdale he required the assistance of Brian Caterer, an Amateur Cup finalist for Chesham the previous season, and named George Dobson as substitute purely on the basis that he was the least unfit of the professional staff. In between the club nervously opened its war chest and paid £10,000 for Arsenal winger Gordon Neilson and signed prolific goalscorer George Kirby following his return to these shores from New York Generals. To make way for the newcomers and retain the wage bill at a manageable level, Peter Deakin and Keith Hooker were released.

This didn't help in the event of injuries, which continued to feature prominently and forced Sirrel into a position where he had to cobble together a team struggling for fitness most weeks. Results suffered as a consequence and by December thoughts of promotion had gone out of the window. Attendances, which averaged almost 8,500 in the early stages, fell alarmingly as the threat of the re-election process raised its ugly head and just 3,361 turned up for the visit of Notts County, less than half the figure for Tom Higginson's benefit game against QPR soon after.

Problems continued to blight Brentford's season and a policy of keeping a limited playing staff left them in the embarrassing situation of being unable to raise a team for the Easter home games against Chester and Bradford City, as flu confined a number of players to bed. To rub salt into the wound, the team's disciplinary record was giving cause for concern. Pat Terry, sent off against Colchester United, was suspended for twenty-eight days to add to the fourteen day ban he was given back in October; and against York City three names went into the book - Brodie, Jones and Mansley - the first time this had ever happened to a Brentford side.

All this, at a time Brentford was still coming to terms with the loss of its main benefactor Ron Blindell, with the club on its knees. The 63 year old Ascot businessman, a leading light behind the effort which averted the takeover by QPR, died after a short illness and left Brentford in limbo as the other major shareholder Les Davey was unwilling to take the chair. Another of Brentford's savours, Walter Wheatley, stepped in.

A 5-0 defeat by the eventual champions Doncaster Rovers at the beginning of April left Brentford in dire straights just three points clear of the bottom four. Rovers, in contrast were at the top and unbeaten in 20 games. Everything taken into consideration Brentford were on a hiding to nothing for the return the following week, but in the event turned the tables and emerged victors thanks to an early goal by John Richardson. Judged on the results that followed, the win put new heart into the team and they pulled well clear of trouble thanks to winning six of the last seven games.

1969-70

Another season in which Brentford's lack of resources on the park was to cost them dear. The management failed to take on board the lessons of the previous season when injuries to a tiny squad meant that from early promotion contenders the Bees slid down the table and for a time looked to have a fight on their hand to stay out of the bottom four. Brentford were in trouble on the injury front from the outset as for the opener away to Hartlepool United, Sirrel was forced to choose from fourteen fit players. Skipper Ronnie Foster, Allan Jones and Portsmouth signing Bill Brown were all on the treatment table and the squad numbers fell still further when John Richardson was sold to Fulham for £10,000. No more early signings were forthcoming yet despite this obvious drawback the Bees made a promising start and following a 1-1 draw with Oldham Athletic, in the middle of October were third, having suffered just two defeats in 15 games.

Running with such small numbers had Jimmy Sirrel holding his breath every time the trainer was called on the pitch to administer first aid, hoping against hope that it was only a minor knock. He could see there was no future in the policy Brentford were pursuing and when the opportunity arose to manage Notts County he was off like a shot. Brentford at the time were fourth, County down the field in twelfth. The situation soon changed as the following season County were Fourth Division champions, and by 1981 Sirrel had led them back to the top flight after an absence of fifty-five years.

After Sirrel's departure, Ron Fenton, a qualified FA coach, took the reins on a temporary basis while Brentford advertised for a new man and one month later Chelsea youth coach Frank Blunstone made the appointment his. With the new man in charge, the Bees continued to keep pace with the leaders and probably not wishing to rock the boat, the board released funds to underpin the team's challenge. For an outlay in the region of £25,000 Blunstone signed New Zealand International Brian Turner from Portsmouth, winger Brian Tawse (Arsenal), striker Roger Cross (West Ham United) and John Docherty (Reading), the third of five entrances to Griffin Park he was to make as a player, manager and assistant manager.

Ironically, Brentford's challenge for honours began to falter following their arrival and four straight drawn games in March against York City, Colchester United, Port Vale and Aldershot, during which the only Bees goal was scored at Layer Road by Bobby Ross, left the team in a spot of bother. The visit of Aldershot attracted a bumper crowd of 12,261 and there was another five figure assembly for the game against Exeter City seven days later. Brentford won 2-0 leaving them still in with a squeak with seven games remaining.

The side's strength had been a watertight defence, breached just 26 times in thirty-nine matches, and subsequent visits to lowly York City and Oldham Athletic were not seen as a problem. Unfortunately they chose the wrong time to have a couple of off days and leaked eight goals, as the bubble burst on Brentford's season following a 4-2 defeat at York and the 4-1 hiding at Oldham. There was no way back from these two shockers and the Bees had to settle for fifth, three points off a promotion place.

The results at York and Oldham proved critical and accounted for eight of the 39 goals the defence conceded all season, a total that set an unsurpassed club record. Equally, Brentford sailed close to the wind on many occasions and a 5-2 win against Peterborough apart, in a number of other games it was a case of the issue not being settled until the fat lady burst into song.

1970-71

To say that Brentford were slow off the starting blocks is the understatement of the year. The campaign got underway with six straight defeats and with the season a third gone you would have laid money on the Bees being required to go through the re-election process. The team was well adrift of safety and shared its sorrows with Barrow and Newport County, who had a miserable two points apiece. It was the worst start since joining the league in 1920 and showed, yet again, that the board's policy of keeping the playing staff to a bare minimum and operating without a reserve team was courting trouble.

The peril of running a League club on a shoestring was perfectly illustrated by the visit to Crewe Alexandra. An injury to Alan Hawley sustained away to the leaders Notts County four days earlier put the cat among the pigeons as it left Frank Blunstone with just twelve fit men to choose from and one of those was second choice goalkeeper Gordon Phillips. He was named as substitute. Other players were forced to play out of position and with thirty minutes gone the Bees were 4-0 down. A second half recovery pulled the final score back to 3-5 but the damage had been done.

Soon afterwards winger Alan Mansley moved on loan to Fulham, giving Blunstone the opportunity to make an addition to his armoury. He chose wisely when Brighton & Hove Albion made Alec Dawson available, as he was just the fillip Brentford's shot-shy attack needed.

Tommy Higginson comes to the end of an illustrious Brentfordcareer.

Dawson was a battering ram type centre forward and took the weight off the shoulders of his fellow forward partners John Docherty, Bobby Ross, Roger Cross and Jackie Graham, a pre-season signing from Guildford City destined to become a key figure at Griffin Park throughout the 1970's, who all relied on the skill factor to make progress.

After a settling in period the mixture turned into a heady cocktail as promotion chasing Exeter City were crushed 5-0, to be swiftly followed by four straight wins, which included an incredible 6-4 success against York City, another side giving its best shot in the promotion race. With seventy-two minutes on the clock the Bees led 5-1 and seemed home and hosed. The visitors thought otherwise and three goals in ninety seconds hauled the score back to 5-4, before Docherty put Brentford out of reach by completing his hat trick, all scored within the space of twenty-one minutes. The team now had the bit between its teeth and despite the loss of Dawson, who returned to Brighton after he failed to agree terms, the Bees roared up the table taking some notable scalps in the process including three games in early March when Southend United (4-2), Crewe Alexandra(3-1) and Grimsby Town(5-1, away) felt the full force of an in-form Brentford side.

Dawson's brief sojourn at Griffin Park was the catalyst for Brentford's upward surge in form and the lesson learned probably entered Blunstone's thoughts at the tail end of the season, when with the Bees clear of problems, he took a gamble by paying £1,500 for John O'Mara, a tall, lanky 6'4" centre forward from Southern League Wimbledon. He was to have a profound effect on the club's fortunes the following season.

Dawson, a FA Cup finalist at Manchester United (in 1958) and Preston North End (in 1964), left behind a legacy in the competition at Brentford by scoring the last gasp winner in the first round tie at home to Gillingham which paved the way for the best run since 1949. With a couple of minutes remaining the Bees trailed 1-0 and another early exit was on the cards. But then in a complete turn round in fortunes Docherty slammed an equaliser and with the referee about to blow for time Dawson scored a last gasp winner, as the success starved Brentford fans celebrated in style. Walsall and Workington, both 1-0, were the next victims before the team was saddled with a tough looking task away to Cardiff City, who at the time were chasing a place in the top flight.

Incessant rain over the previous two days turned the Ninian Park pitch into a quagmire to which Brentford, the underdogs, responded best. A suicidal back pass in the conditions let in Graham for the opening goal and Docherty settled the issue by scoring from a trademark free kick. Next station along the line was Hull City as the Bees attempted to become only the second Fourth Division team to reach the sixth round (the first was Oxford United who beat Brentford along the way in January 1964).

The massive debt is paid off at last!

Unfortunately the Bees failed to join them in that particular section of the record book, but it was a close call. Ross gave the Bees an early lead and they were denied a second when Turner's shot cannoned off a post. The home team scored a fortuitous equaliser when the referee failed to spot a foul by Chilton on Bees 'keeper Phillips and wrapped things up through a late goal by Houghton. It was a sad ending to a marvellous cup run, but Brentford could at least take solace in the cash it generated leading to a profit on the season of £20,000 as the final instalment of the £104,000 borrowed in the dark days of 1967 was paid off.

1971-72

It is said that one man doesn't make a team. Mention this to a Brentford supporter of a certain vintage and he will spend the next few hours singing the praises of a player who blasted that theory to smithereens. Need I say more than John O'Mara, or"Ted" as he was known in the dressing room? He played at few games at the back end of 1970-71 without pulling up any trees, indeed not to put to fine a point on it he looked out of his depth. Blunstone was convinced that he had signed an uncut diamond and in the close season set about knocking off the rough edges. As the season got underway the big fellow showed some improvement but nothing to get excited about. The turning point came in match number five when he opened the scoring with what became his trademark, a header, as Barrow were beaten 4-0.

Three nights later he underlined his potential by scoring a second half hat-trick when Hartlepool United were demolished 6-0, a win that took Brentford to the top of the table.

Brentford supporters were on cloud nine but were brought back down to earth within twenty-four hours, when Roger Cross was sold to Fulham for £30,000, a new club record. The "Sun" newspaper alleged that the sale was to help clear Brentford's over-draft. In fact Cross had written into his contract when he joined that if a higher division club made an offer for his services the Bees were duty bound to accept. Brentford took the newspaper to court for libel and were awarded £1,000 damages. The loss of Cross, a class act at Fourth Division level, left Blunstone with just twelve fit players to choose from for the top of the table clash at Grimsby Town, where a 3-1 defeat knocked the Bees off their perch.

The management now held their breath hoping there would be no backlash against the sale of Cross and subsequent set back at Grimsby. So there was a collective sigh of relief when the next home game pulled in almost 9,000 for the visit of Peterborough United. O'Mara, fast approaching cult status, rewarded the fans with another blinding goal, Neilson, Docherty, Ross and Graham also featuring on the score sheet.

A draw at Chester and a 2-0 victory against Stockport County, Big John giving their defence all manner of problems but leaving the goalscoring to Ross, lifted the Bees back into top spot. Next on the agenda came Northampton Town, a match that confirmed O'Mara as one of the most lethal strikers around. Word was getting round about this giant in the number nine shirt and the crowd of 11,004 was the best for some years. Many of them were still queuing at the turnstiles when the visitors took the lead after 38 seconds, but the Bees were not to be denied and lifted by a twenty four minute, second half hat-trick by 'you-know-who' they eventually cruised to a 6-1 victory. Blunstone's strategy of all out attack at home and defence in depth away was paying off and 27 goals in just ten games had the team on a high, clear at the top of the division.

The Bees continued to mix it into the New Year. Mix it was the right expression in O'Mara's case. Visiting teams, especially, had problems containing the rangy striker and often resorted to breaking the rules to stop him. O'Mara gave as good as he got and often went into the referee's note book for his trouble. Eventually he was called in to explain himself by an FA commission. Legend has it that he read them their fortune, as a result of which they suspended him for six weeks.

The team went to pieces in their talisman's absence, failed to win in the five games he missed and for the first time dropped out of the top four. His comeback against Lincoln City was eagerly awaited and although the weight of expectation hung heavily on his shoulders he did not disappoint his legion of fans.

The pay-off came when he headed home from distance a free kick taken by Brian Turner to score the side's first goal in 325 minutes. Terry Scales netted a second and the bid for promotion was up and running once more. A measure of his popularity was that the crowd of 12,070 represented a three thousand increase on the previous home game, a disappointing 2-0 defeat by Colchester United.

(Above) Defender Alan Nelmes went on to make over 300 League appearances for The Bees. (Below) Action in the Darlington home match. Bobby Ross (number 10) scored (from the penalty spot) in the highly entertaining 6-2 win.

John O'Mara receives the Player of the Year trophy, Peter Gelson looks on

After Lincoln the Bees won the next four games against Aldershot 2-0, Doncaster Rovers 3-0, leaders Grimsby Town 2-0 and Workington 2-0. The Grimsby encounter was the second time a game at Griffin Park took top billing on London Weekend Television's "The Big Match" following the encounter back in August against Aldershot.

Promotion was eventually achieved with games to spare, O'Mara accounting for 25 of the team's goals in the League. He was also voted as the Fourth Division's "Player of the Year" in a poll of the managers. The awards did not end there as Frank Blunstone was the division's "Manager of the Month" for September and again in April and in so doing laid to rest the old chestnut that it was the kiss of death to subsequent results.

For good measure Brentford were the best supported team in the division with an average of 11,738. At the time a visiting club was entitled to a share of the gate money, so Crewe Alexandra (average 2,104) were onto a winner when 18,237 flooded into Griffin Park on Boxing Day, from which they later received a cheque for £840. Likewise Chester who banked £860 from their visit on Good Friday, when the attendance reached 18,521.

No League game at Griffin Park, to date, has seen a crowd of those proportions since, or for that matter attracted an average attendance anywhere near 11,738.

1972-73

Goalscoring virtuoso, John O'Mara' scored another at Aldershot in March 1972, but much to the fans disgust he was soon to move on.

One of football's golden rules should be never to sell your main goalscorer without having a replacement waiting in the wings. It is a lesson that obviously went over Brentford's head in 1972. Promotion had been achieved on the back of John O'Mara's firepower, his 27 goals in all competitions representing the highest since Towers and Francis were at their glorious best back in the 1950's. He enjoyed cult status among Brentford fans, yet when struggling Blackburn Rovers came in with a £50,000 bid for his services in mid-September, the board couldn't act quickly enough to cash in their main asset. It was an incredible act of tomfoolery and did not go down well with supporters. The fact that Brentford were second to Wrexham at the time and Blackburn were propping up the table having already been thrashed 4-0 at Griffin Park, O'Mara scoring one of the goals, didn't help their mood. It wasn't even as if the club was desperate for money. General manager Dennis Piggott had already predicted a £30,000 profit on the promotion year and since the dark days of 1967 the club had virtually wiped out its debts.

The departures did not end there as soon afterwards Bobby Ross, scorer of 15 goals from midfield the previous season, a total second to O'Mara's, moved to Cambridge United. Their replacements were untried Bognor Regis Town amateur Andy Woon and Stan Webb, the latter a £10,000 buy from Carlisle United, neither of whom made a lasting impact. As time passed and the Bees slid into the relegation zone, the board woke up to the fact that unless Blunstone was given the money to buy ready made reinforcements, Brentford would be in trouble.

A decent marksman was of paramount importance and at the turn of the year Roger Cross made the short trip back from Craven Cottage. The fee of £15,000 was half that paid by Fulham just over a year earlier. Although he scored in his first game, a 1-1 draw with Rotherham United, the Bees continued to struggle and went on a run of seven games without a win which culminated in a 6-2 beating away to Tranmere Rovers. Needing to upgrade his squad Blunstone paid £9,000 for QPR winger Barry Salvage. He went straight into the side for the visit of Port Vale and although he scored, the goal was overshadowed by a hat trick on his home debut by Woon, as Vale were beaten out of sight 5-0. The way that Woon, Cross and Salvage gelled raised confidence levels, but alas it was a false dawn. Woon never hit the same heights again and failure to win one of the last six games condemned the Bees to relegation.

A lack of firepower was a major reason for the team's demise, midfielder Alan Murray leading the way with just seven League goals, while a dreadful away record didn't help as after winning 1-0 at Plymouth Argyle at the beginning of September the team failed to return with another two points from its travels until a 1-0 success at Rochdale in March. Crowds held up remarkably well as can be gathered from an average of 8,742 which included a near twelve thousand assembly for the last home game against Notts County when there remained an outside chance of avoiding the drop. This is more than could be said about the late season away game at Halifax Town when the lowest authenticated crowd since joining the League of 970 turned up.

1973-74

Brentford now entered one of the darkest periods in the club's time in the Football League. The team's one season back in the third tier was obviously a grave disappointment and had supporters tearing their hair out in frustration. By and large Blunstone assembled a more than adequate squad which, with a few additions, could have done Brentford proud. Unfortunately the board's motto might well have been "Prudence in the Extreme" as they were loath to sanction sufficient funds to upgrade and arguably save the club from the drop. When they did, the expression "locking the stable door after the horse has bolted" springs to mind. The board was split into two camps.

Mike Allen, with the club for most of the 1970's, scores a rare goal, while Stewart Houston looks on..

On the one hand the Les Davey group wanted to press on with the scheme to build a new stadium on the Brentford Market site, "a modern stadium designed with the comfort of spectators in mind would help to attract bigger crowds", he forecast. On the opposite side was Walter Wheatley & Co. "I do not think, using hindsight, we did enough to stay in the Third Division. We have made a £25,000 profit, but it would have been better to have made none and stayed up", was his forthright opinion, and one shared by the fans.

One of the most popular post-War players, 'Jackie' Graham made over 400 appearances during a similar period as Allen.

Brentford had a strong, loyal support, the eighth best in the division despite relegation, and one which only Hereford United matched in the Fourth Division in 1972-73. Now, though, disenchanted by the team's poor performance, the crowds drifted away and fell to their lowest levels in sixty years. It is easy to see why Blunstone became disillusioned at the board's perceived penny pinching. He had shown at Brentford and with the youngsters at Chelsea that he was a coach out of the top drawer. But without the tools to work with he felt he was flogging a dead horse and it led to him resigning his post at Griffin Park and moving to Manchester United as youth team coach. In a telegram to the board he said: *"I was never allowed to manage in the way I'd hoped and under the present system have no alternative but to resign".*

This occurred on the eve of the season and three weeks later Wimbledon player/manager Mike Everitt was selected from thirty-six applicants to take the reins. He inherited a squad of just fourteen and was on a hiding to nothing. A number of loan players came in, to little effect, and it soon became clear that promotion was out of the question and survival was the name of the game. Apart from a 5-1 victory against Barnsley, supporters had little to cheer and spirits sank to a new low on October 27th after the Bees crashed 4-1 at Scun-thorpe United to end the day bottom of the League. Thirty-six years earlier Brentford sat proudly on top of the Football League and now they became the first club in history to go from number one to number ninety -two. Like the song goes, "things can only get better" In this instance, merc-ifully, they did when a week later high flying Man-sfield Town were the visitors. After picking up a single point from six games, confidence was at a low ebb.

The first half went true to form and the Bees trooped off at the break trailing 1-0 and seemingly down for the count. The second half was a very different story and thanks largely to a twenty-four minute hat trick by Roger Cross, the Bees emerged victorious by four goals to one. A win at Workington, 2-0, and a draw away to Stockport County 1-1 kept the pot boiling before Cross scored his second hat-trick in successive home games as Chester were downed 3-0. It meant that the classy attacker had scored six goals in just 95 minutes of action at Griffin Park

Brentford failed to match those performances over the next few months and it was the middle of January before the team recorded another win by beating Doncaster Rovers 2-0 away. Absent was Stuart Houston for whom Manchester United paid Brentford a new record fee of £50,000. He went on to be capped by Scotland and was later assistant manager under George Graham at Arsenal. Little of the money was recycled in the transfer market and Brentford continued to flirt with a place in the bottom four until the points taken from a 2-0 win against Bradford City in the penultimate game ensured safety. Brentford managed to wriggle off the hook by just two points for which they can be thankful that none of the five teams below managed to lower their colours. Indeed take them out of the equation and Brentford's record was pretty appalling: won 7, drawn 11, lost 18.

1974-75

There was little to look forward to as the season approached, as Chelsea reserve centre half Keith Lawrence was the only signing. Behind the scenes the board was in disarray and at the sharp end rookie manager Mike Everitt was running on empty with a squad of fifteen plus five juniors, who were there to make up the numbers now that Brentford entered a reserve side in the London Midweek League. Little was expected and little was achieved in the opening part of the campaign, although the Bees did give Liverpool a run for their money in the League Cup at Anfield where Roger Cross found the net early, only for the home team to strike back and win 2-1. That game was Peter Gelson's swan song as he left for Hillingdon Borough soon after, having worn the shirt 517 times in all competitions, at the time a total surpassed by only Ken Coote (559).

Gordon Sweetzer
had two periods at GriffinPark.

Results at home kept the Bees afloat and during one period, stretching back to the previous March, Chelsea's on loan goalkeeper Steve Sherwood went 792 minutes spread over ten games without conceding. It was a whole new ball game on their travels and a masochistic streak was required to follow the team around the country, as the 1-0 victory at re-election regulars Workington in late November represented the first success in twenty attempts. The goalscorer was Willie Brown, a recent recruit from Newport County at the same time as his alter ego Terry Johnson arrived from Southend United. The total fee was £20,000 and their inclusion led to slightly improved results. This did not appease new chairman Dan Tana, a Hollywood film producer and former professional footballer with Red Star Belgrade, and following the 2-1 defeat at Darlington in January, Everitt was relieved of his duties. It was the manager's 34th birthday. In the climate that prevailed at Griffin Park at the time, Everitt faced an impossible challenge and he later proved his worth as coach to Egyptian side Arab Contractors when they lifted the African Cup Winners cup in 1982 and 1983 and the League in 1984.

John Docherty, who since retiring as a player the previous summer had been coaching at QPR, was drafted in as manager (his fourth entrance at Griffin Park) and Eddie Lyons followed him as second in command.

Results took an instant turn for the better as the Bees strode clear of trouble and by taking eleven of the 16 points at stake in April, Docherty earned the Fourth Division's Manager of the Month award To finish ninth after at one time berthing just three points clear of fourth from bottom was no mean feat and for the first time in a few years Brentford had a team worthy of the name.

There had to be a downside though, and this manifested itself at the turnstiles. Football at the League's lowest level was going through a particularly grim spell and for the first time since regionalisation was abandoned in 1958 the aggregate attendance slumped below two million (it was 2.3 million the previous season). Brentford was not exempt from this downward spiral and the average of 5,172 was only marginally better than the previous season's shocker on the field of play. Even so, only the champions Mansfield Town (7,204), Lincoln City, Rotherham United and Reading could boast a better average than the Griffin Park figure and seven games on the Bees travels were watched by less than two thousand including Southport(1285), Scunthorpe United(1439) and Swansea City(1706).

1975-76

The season kicked off with Brentford again in the ridiculous situation of having a threadbare squad of just fifteen players, the only addition of note being goalkeeper Bill Glazier,a veteran of almost 400 games for Coventry City. So it came as a pleasant surprise when the team got off to a flyer and by mid-September they were good value for third spot. In tandem with this promising start, higher division Brighton & Hove Albion were outwitted in the League Cup, in the next round of which the Bees led Manchester United before letting in two soft goals. The first was a howler by Glazier which rattled his confidence and was part of the reason why soon afterwards he decided to call it a day.

This left Brentford short-handed but by a stroke of luck a couple of weeks earlier Paul Priddy was given a second chance to make good following a couple of years away at Wimbledon and latterly Walton & Hersham. He was one of four young signings that week, all of whom were to make a contribution. The others were Gordon Sweetzer, England Schoolboy International Paul Walker and Danis Salman.

Priddy made his comeback in a 2-1 defeat away to Huddersfield Town, Sweetzer coming on as a substitute and scoring the Bees goal. A depressing run of one win in seven saw the team slide out of contention, only halted by two wins in as many days against Scunthorpe United by 5-2 and Workington 4-0. The pendulum quickly swung the other way with a 6-2 defeat at Tranmere Rovers. A 1-0 victory against Watford followed, a match significant in that when Salman came on as substitute in the 84th minute he became at 15 years 8 months 3days the youngest player to appear in League football for Brentford. The Cyprus born defender was at Griffin Park for the long haul and over the next eleven years made 361 senior appearances.

Sweetzer, just eighteen and later to play in the World Cup for Canada, had become a great crowd pleaser for his never-say-die attitude to the game and he was to the forefront as Brentford beat Fourth Division leaders Northampton Town in the first round of the FA Cup. The Bees next showed their mettle by beating Southern League champions Wimbledon 2-0 at fortress Plough Lane before losing to Second Division high flyers Bolton Wanderers in a replay. The first attempt to settle the tie attracted a crowd of 12,450 to Griffin Park, paying record receipts of £8,032

Danis Salman, the youngest ever debutant in the first team.

The Bees finished three points clear of a place in the bottom four and in the final analysis the results against the top two proved crucial, as had they gone to form, the Bees would have been up a creek without a paddle.

In some ways the cup was an unwelcome distraction, as in the League the team coughed and sputtered its way to two wins in sixteen. Almost unbelievably those victories were against the two clubs miles clear at the top, Northampton Town and Lincoln City. Bill Dodgin's Northampton, boasting many players destined for Brentford in a couple of years, were to finish with 68 points, which exchanged into 'new money' represents a 97 point haul. Lincoln, meanwhile, smashed a number of Fourth Division records, notably by recording twenty one home successes, to finish on 74 points or 106 if three for a win had been in vogue. Northampton lost 2-1 at Griffin Park and Lincoln 1-0, a game that marked Andy McCulloch's home debut following a club record £25,000 move from Oxford United.

Following the Lincoln game Brentford visited bottom side Southport and in true Jekyll and Hyde fashion lost 2-0. The season petered out in disappointment, the visit to Rochdale attracting only 894 spectators, the lowest ever at a League game in which Brentford have been involved to date.

1976-77

Brentford were deep in the doldrums when the campaign set off. The squad showed few changes from the one that limped to 18th the previous season and, with the new signings failing to inspire, it came as no surprise when the defeat by Barnsley attracted just 3,903, the lowest opening day League attendance at Griffin Park in sixty years. Brentford had already made an early exit from the League Cup by losing 3-1 on aggregate to Watford, the away leg featuring Paul Walker, skipper of the England Schoolboy team that had just whacked France 6-1, who at 15 years 7 months 28 days edged out Salman to become the youngest player ever to pull on a Brentford shirt.

Worse was to follow and just two points from five games prompted manager John Docherty to resign. His replacement was Bill Dodgin (Junior), who surprisingly left Northampton Town in the summer just months after taking them to promotion. Dodgin, whose father managed Brentford back in the fifties, had a reputation as a football purist, no kick and rush for him, and it didn't take long to realise that many of the players he inherited didn't meet his requirements. However, with little money in the kitty for fresh faces he was forced to soldier on to begin with.

Dodgin was in the unenviable position of trying to make a silk purse out of a sow's ear as Brentford continued to keep company with perennial strugglers Hartlepool United, Newport County, Workington and Southport. Decent results were few and far between, a 5-0 defeat of Workington, in their last season in the league, momentarily lifting spirits, although to balance this the crowd of 3,160 was the lowest at Griffin Park since the game against Walsall in December 1927. Dodgin tried a number of permutations in a bid to rectify the situation, to no avail, and even gave youth its head for the visit of Colchester United at the beginning of January. A mixture of youth and experience failed to pay off and the youngest side to date was outclassed 4-1 by a team destined for promotion.

The Bees side that miserable afternoon, with their ages was: Cox (17), Salman (16), Smith (19), Riddick (33), Allen (28), Walker (16), Fraser (25), Graham (31), McCulloch (27), Rolph (16), Sweetzer (19), sub: Scrivens (19).

By the middle of January the Bees were short odds to finish in the bottom four, especially as Dodgin shocked all and sundry by selling leading scorer Roger Cross to Millwall for £9,500. As will be seen, there was method in his madness, although over the next few weeks the team plunged to new depths and following a 1-0 home defeat by Aldershot on February 19th it looked as if the game was up so far as Brentford were concerned. With twenty eight games gone the Bees were cut adrift, seven points from safety, and had one of the worst away records in the League and with no sign of improvement.

Andy McCulloch, like his namesake of 40 years earlier, a prollific goalscorer.

Dodgin felt it was time he got busy in the transfer market. Earlier he returned to Northampton for midfield maestro Dave Carlton, and now armed with the Cross transfer money, he raided the County ground for goal machine Steve Phillips; took skilful John Bain on loan from Bristol City; Paul Shrubb(ex-Fulham) on trial from Cape Town Hellenic; and paid a mammoth (by Brentford standards), £20,000, for Torquay United centre half Pat Kruse. The skill factor all five possessed meant they soon gelled as a team and with youngster Sweetzer a revelation in attack, the Bees started to claw their way back.

Four straight wins, with Sweetzer netting a hat trick against Torquay, set the ball rolling and the Bees continued to improve in leaps and bounds to finish 15th. This upsurge in form caught some of the top teams on the hop and promoted Bradford City and Exeter City were rolled over as were fifth placed Swansea City, while Brentford became the only team to win at Watford, which helped end their chances of promotion.

The record in the final eighteen games showed true promotion form and read: won 13, drawn 3 lost 2 (one of those was to the champions Cambridge United). Just about every department played its part with a special mention for Sweetzer whose 22 goals in 25 games since the turn of the year deservedly won him the accolade of "Player of the Year". Brentford were on the march, at last.

French scores one of the goals in the 2-0 hiome win over Chesham United in the F.A.Cup.

Chapter 10: PROMOTION THEN STABILITY IN THE EIGHTIES

1977-78

The era had become notorious for its reliance on defensive football. Teams played cat and mouse with each other and many games were one long yawn. This, rampant hooliganism, and the lack of protection for the skilled practitioner, was reflected in attendances which in 1977-78 totalled 25 million, when the previous season, by way of comparison, they reached getting on for five million more. And this was during a period when English clubs dominated the European Cup, Liverpool (3), Nottingham Forest (2) and Aston Villa (1) making sure the trophy remained within these shores for six years on the trot. For the most part football was not a pretty sight and "Cloggers Rule OK" became the in-phrase. Well, in Brentford manager Bill Dodgin's opinion it was definitely not OK! He was a graduate of the school of thought which believed implicitly in bold attacking football to keep the fans entertained and despite problems in the early part of his tenure at the club, he was determined to send out a team that would be a delight to the eye.

Expectation soon turned to reality. First his old team Northampton Town were outplayed 4-0 and the Bees continued to hit the right notes when in front of 11,001, the highest crowd at Griffin Park in five years, League newcomers Wimbledon were given a lesson in the game's finer points and beaten 4-1. The television cameras then made a rare appearance at the ground as Reading held the Bees 1-1. The first away game the following Saturday at Crewe Alexandra epitomised Dodgin's ideals. There was a mere 1,837 present and for a time it looked as if they were to witness as many goals as there were faces at Gresty road that afternoon. Following a slow start, the action hotted up and after Crewe took the lead on 22 minutes the goals rained in from all directions. At the final whistle Brentford were on the right end of a 6-4 score line and sat proudly on top of the table. Many managers would have reached for the smelling salts after a game like that. Not Dodgin, who commented: "We are playing great football and the fans went home happy, so who was I to complain about letting a few goals in."

Brentford's stay at the top was brief but the fans were treated to some exhilarating football and promotion was always within the team's grasp. A 4-1 victory against Halifax Town at the beginning of October took the goal tally to 25 in ten games and in Sweetzer and Phillips, Brentford could boast the division's top scorers, each having netted eight times.

The fans warmed to Dodgin's style of football and a bumper 14,496, paying new record receipts of £11,160, turned out for the battle between Brentford and Watford, the main challengers for top position. The visitors won 3-0 but the Bees took some consolation in that attendances at the first seven home games showed a 50% increase on the corresponding number of matches twelve months earlier.

A subsequent indifferent spell and the loss of Sweetzer through injury sent Dodgin off in search of reinforcements, resulting in a peach of a signing when winger Doug Allder put pen to paper. A veteran of more than 250 games for Millwall and Orient, yet still not twenty-six, Doug had been wasting away in the reserves at Watford. The move to Griffin Park revitalised his career and as the season progressed he supplied much of the ammunition for the McCulloch/Phillips strike force. For a time, on his return, Sweetzer featured in an all singing, all dancing Bees front line that accounted for Crewe Alexandra 5-1, Torquay United 3-0 and Rochdale 4-0.

But Dodgin then surprised everyone by selling the bulldozer of a striker, Sweetzer, to John Docherty's Second Division bound Cambridge United for £30,000, the fee representing a new high for them. It was by no means a popular decision as in seventy-five games the effervescent Sweetzer notched 44 goals. Dodgin's argument was that with midfield dynamo Jackie Graham back from injury, Phillips, scorer of 16 goals already, could take more of the weight off McCulloch's shoulders. His assessment proved spot on as Phillips couldn't stop scoring and finished the season as the Football League's leading marksman with 36 goals in all competitions meaning he fell just three short of the club record set by Jack Holliday in 1932-33. McCulloch enjoyed the extra freedom and finished with 22 goals, the Francis/Towers era apart, one of the rare occasions when two Brentford forwards have shared more than fifty goals between them.

Tracking back to early spring, weeks before the Sweetzer deal, Dodgin signed full back Barry Tucker, who thereby became the fourth member of Northampton Town's promotion team the previous year to follow him to Griffin Park. It was a timely capture as Brentford had slipped to seventh and the defence, especially, was beginning to feel the heat. Watford had gone beyond recall and a whole gaggle of clubs set off in vain pursuit, Brentford included. By winning 3-1 at Southport the Bees soon regained their long held position in the top four and with the team now

Steve Phillips scores his 31st League goal of the season - from the penalty spot - against Darlington in April - which confirmed The Bees promotion.... at last!

firing on all cylinders eventually achieved promotion by beating Darlington 2-0 at Griffin Park with two games to spare. Fittingly McCulloch, voted the club's "Player of the Year", and Phillips, were the marksmen.

It had been less than two years since Dodgin's appointment. In that time he completely revitalised the club's fortunes, mainly with bargain basement signings like Phillips, Kruse and Allder, while balancing the books through the sale of Sweetzer, Cross, French and Pritchett, the latter encapsulating Dodgin's ability to maximise profits as he played just thirteen games after arriving on a free before being sold to Watford for £4,000, nice money in Brentford terms.

1978-79

It is hard to believe from the final League position of 10th, that for a major part of the season relegation was very much an issue. In the early stages the team was found wanting as Dodgin refused to compromise his principals and accept kick and rush in favour of pass-ball. Some of the players treated it like a hot potato and results suffered accordingly. Three wins in thirteen in the opening phase left the Bees with only Lincoln City beneath them and a repeat of the early seventies, when the side came up and went straight back down, became a distinct possibility. Dodgin had been very loyal to his troops up until now, but his patience snapped and for match number fourteen at home to fellow strugglers Tranmere Rovers he introduced two new signings; Jim McNichol , a club record buy from Luton Town for £30,000 and striker Dean Smith, who cost £20,000 from Leicester City. They were typical Dodgin players and soon settled into the scheme of things as a 2-0 victory gave the Bees a welcome breathing space. McNichol, especially, was money well spent. "Player of the Year" in his first season, he became famed for his cannonball free kicks, and stood in for Jackie Graham as skipper later in the season, the youngest ever at Brentford, not to mention his seven Scotland Under-21 caps.

There was still some leeway to make up but with their input and the introduction of Allan Glover from Orient to pep up the supply of goodies from midfield it was a very different Brentford over the ensuing weeks and months. A long unbeaten spell between Christmas and March looked to have given the Bees an edge over the other teams seeking salvation, but it was dog-eat-dog at the bottom and following a 6-0 hiding meted out to Chester which seemed to give Brentford the all clear, four games without a win plunged them back into trouble. It led to a defining game in the club's season when promotion chasing Blackpool came to town. Two down at the break, the outlook was bleak, but in a surprising turn round in fortunes, three goals in twelve minutes by McNichol (2) and Phillips, celebrating his 100th consecutive League appearance, led to an unlikely victory.

Defender Pat Kruse proudly displays the 'Player of the season' award that was presented to him before the last home game.

Those two points took the pressure off to some extent and from then on results improved in leaps and bounds as the Bees finished the season on a high of eight wins in eleven.

The season had already featured a 3-3 draw with Watford for a game that attracted a crowd of 13,873 paying record receipts of £12,809, and such was the team's improved form another five figure crowd of 13,320 presented itself for the final home game, a 2-1 defeat by promotion contenders Swindon Town. This took the average crowd to a respectable 7,455, the sixth best in the division. Dodgin was as pleased as punch with the upturn, while local neighbours Chelsea had been keeping a watching brief on the Bee's progress, with particular reference to the way the game under Dodgin was played. It led to their manager Danny Blanchflower, like the Bees manager an advocate of flowing, entertaining, football, offering Dodgin the position of assistant manager at Stamford Bridge, a role he turned down much to the delight of all at Griffin Park.

1979-80.
A season in which the sale of ace striker Andy McCulloch to Sheffield Wednesday for a club record fee of £60,000 before a ball had been kicked in anger was to have repercussions for Dodgin's term in office. The break-up of the Phillips/ McCulloch strike force, who between them were responsible for 86 of Brentford's 146 goals over the previous two seasons, was not felt too badly initially and by the middle of October The Bees had wormed their way into fourth position.

Danis Salman, in the home match against Mansfield, keeps a close tag on his man.

During this period it was the defence that came up trumps as Len Bond & Co. went four away games at Sheffield Wednesday (2-0), Wimbledon (0-0), Exeter City (0-0) and Oxford United (2-0) without conceding a goal, and when Pashley netted for Blackpool on the stroke of half time in the fixture at Bloomfield Road, the clock stopped on a club record run lasting 423 minutes. Incredibly, this was the signal for the floodgates to open and in total the Bees conceded five in forty three minutes to crash land 5-4.

It proved only a temporary set-back as Blackburn Rovers were then beaten 2-0 to set up a game two days later against table-toppers Sheffield United. A crowd of 13,764, the gate receipts of £16,183 represented a new high, witnessed a stormy affair, the catalyst for which was a twice taken penalty by the visitors on the hour mark.

Bond saved the first attempt, but the referee deemed he moved too early and ordered a retake. The 'keeper and John Fraser were booked for contesting the decision before Bourne stepped up to drill home what transpired the winner.

The gloves came off and a fiercely contested battle erupted with ten minutes remaining when Doug Allder and Speight clashed on the halfway line and sent each other sprawling into the dug-out. The referee made sure it was the last piece of action the pair saw that evening! Brentford had their revenge a fortnight later by winning the return 2-0, a 1-0 victory against fellow contenders Colchester United which followed keeping them just two points behind the leaders Millwall.

Subsequently results started to go against them and three heavy defeats to Rotherham United (1-4), Swindon Town (1-4) in the FA Cup, and Carlisle United (1-3), prompted Dodgin into making changes. He felt the side lacked a cutting edge since McCulloch's departure and as Bob Booker had been performing well on loan at Barnet he recalled the big central striker for the visit of Hull City. He showed his worth by netting a hat trick in a 7-2 massacre, and with Phillips (2), Kruse and Fear also on target Brentford seemed to have turned the corner. However, this proved not to be the case as the Hull win was the only success the Bees enjoyed in fourteen attempts, As a result the slide towards the relegation zone gathered pace and at the time of Blackpool's visit at the back end of February the Bees were only four points clear of the bottom four.

To show how bad things had become, the two previous games had seen two of the teams destined for the drop, Wimbledon (0-1) and Southend United (2-3), take both points. Blackpool were seen off by two late goals but relegation still beckoned following a 3-0 defeat in the next game to Blackburn Rovers.

To try and save the situation Dodgin paid £60,000, a new club record, for Gillingham striker Tony Funnell. In the short term it made little difference and the team continued its decline which culminated in a 6-1 defeat at Colchester and a 1-0 setback at home to Rotherham. With just seven games remaining and Brentford in free fall the board took the decision to change managers. So Dodgin was given "leave of absence" and replaced by taxi driver Fred Callaghan, who had been guiding Woking's fortunes.

The new man did the trick, although it was a close call as it took a late solo effort by Tony Funnell, in the final match against Millwall to secure the two points which enabled the Bees to stave off another taste of life in the Fourth Division. Dodgin's departure showed how quickly fortunes can change, as within the space of four months he went from a position of job security with a side challenging for promotion to being relieved of his duties. On the evening of December 8th he was in charge of a team that had just beaten Hull 7-2, yet by early April he was gone, a victim of the side's failure to win only one game since.

1980-81

The 1980/81 season started with Fred Callaghan being confirmed as the new permanent manager after saving the side from relegation at the end of the previous campaign. He had a busy summer - bringing in Chelsea legend Ron Harris as his assistant and making sweeping changes to the squad. Legendary striker Steve Phillips returned to Northampton for £40,000 and seven other players, including long-serving Jackie Graham, also left while four more would not sign new deals.

This upheaval meant that there were five players making their Brentford debuts in the first game against Charlton in the League Cup and they got off to a great start, winning 3-1. However the 5-0 second leg defeat and then another 3-1 defeat at The Valley in the opening League game were more representative of how the season was to pan out. The Bees did win three out of the next four games, which included a televised 3-2 victory at Walsall featuring the debut of Terry Hurlock, signed from Leytonstone and Ilford, and an impressive 2-0 triumph at Portsmouth's Fratton Park, but they only picked up maximum points in another 11 League matches during the season. Hurlock was in a team which included fellow non-Leaguer David Crown, signed from Walthamstow Avenue, and much-travelled midfielder Barry Silkman.

The 3-0 win at Blackpool in late September saw the debut of on-loan Derby goalkeeper David McKellar who became a permanent signing the following month. The away form was impressive, with a fourth successive win on the road, 1-0, coming at Barnsley, and a draw at Exeter and a further vicotry at Carlisle, where new signing from Wembley, Gary Roberts, made his debut, taking the unbeaten run outside west London to six games. However the fourth home defeat of the season, 1-0 to Chester, persuaded Callaghan to make changes for Gillingham's visit two days later. He dropped two of the side's six ever-presents, Bob Booker and Silkman, with the latter responding by immediately asking for a transfer. He was sold to QPR for £20,000 shortly afterwards.

Another home win still proved elusive, although Dean Smith did snatch a late goal for a 3-3 draw against the Gills, and even the away record was dented when Brentford went down 2-0 at Burnley. But as October ended and November started there was finally some good news for Callaghan's men as they pulled off back-to-back wins at Plymouth and finally at home, to Oxford.

The Bees failed to win any of their other five League games in November and almost suffered a shock FA Cup exit against non-League Addlestone & Weybridge. Although the Bees were drawn away, the match was switched to Griffin Park where Brentford let slip a 2-0 lead and were held to a draw by the Southern Leaguers who fielded Jackie Graham in their ranks. There was no mistake in the replay, which Brentford won 2-0 to earn a second round tie at near neighbours Fulham.

More than 11,000 fans flocked to Craven Cottage, including a sizeable Brentford contingent hoping for some relief from the wretched League form. However it was not their day as Fulham won 1-0, despite controversy when Dean Smith's shot which bounced down off the bar was ruled not to have crossed the line by the officials. To complete Smith's misery he never played for the club again.

Callaghan, still desperate to improve the scoring rate paid Chelsea £30,000 for strikers Lee Frost and Gary Johnson and although Johnson scored on his debut, it was in a 4-1 defeat at Rotherham. Boxing Day brought a first win in eight League games - 2-1 against Colchester - but eight draws in the next nine matches, six of them goalless, provided little excitement for the fans. The only highlight in this period came in late January with a 4-0 hammering of Walsall, the best win of the season, which saw Frost finally break his duck and Johnson score twice. Four wins and five draws finished off the season and saw Brentford finish in ninth with a slightly better record away than at home. Meanwhile off the field a significant event occurred when Martin Lange joined the board.

Chris Kamara joined The Bees in October 1981.....

Despite an encouraging 2-1 win at neighbours Fulham on the opening day of the campaign, in which three points were awarded for a win for the first time, things overall did not start well. A winless run of seven games saw the Bees only score in one match, a 2-2 draw at Portsmouth, and also go out of the League Cup, 3-0 on aggregate to Oxford.

The supporters wanted changes but rather than manager Callaghan losing his job, Dan Tana was replaced as chairman by Martin Lange - and as often happens in these situations, the next game produced a victory, 1-0 at Newport.

The first five League matches in October saw two more wins, one a 2-0 triumph at leaders Chesterfield, but three more defeats before Brentford made one of their biggest signings for years. At the same time as the Bees surprisingly swapped winger David Crown for Portsmouth midfielder Chris Kamara, they also paid Orient £25,000 for the colourful Stan Bowles. The excitement generated by the news added 1,500 fans to the gate for their first game against Burnley. Although that match finished goalless, the pair inspired the side to a 3-0 win at Swindon three nights later, with Kamara on target against his former club.

1981-82

The 1981 close-season was much quieter than the equivalent period 12 months previously. Two signings were made with Fred Callaghan smashing the club's transfer record to sign centre-half Alan Whitehead from Bury for £65,000 and goalkeeper Paul Priddy returning for his third spell at Griffin Park, but striker Lee Frost left after barely six months on the books. Whitehead's fee beat the £55,000 paid to Gillingham the previous year for Tony Funnell, who left the club early in the new season.

Things were looking up and five victories followed in the next seven games, among them a 2-0 FA Cup first round win over Exeter. A rearranged 1-0 second round replay defeat at Colchester ended the run after the weather had played havoc with the Bees' December fixtures. That match started another depressing sequence of nine games without a win. The most significant moment in that run came with the return of Gordon Sweetzer, who was brought back from Canadian side Toronto Blizzard.

....As did the enigmatic Stan Bowles, seen here, both players made their debuts in this match at home to Burnley.

A lot of behind-the-scenes work saw him registered in time to make his debut in a midweek game at Reading and he responded with a sixth-minute goal, only for Brentford to go on and lose 4-1.

Bowles got on the scoresheet for the first time in a 2-2 draw with Portsmouth and the first wins for two months finally arrived at the end of February as Newport and Exeter were each beaten 2-0 in successive home games and the goals started to come a bit more freely. The closing stages of the season saw both Millwall and Swindon concede four goals at Griffin Park while the side won 2-1 away at Wimbledon, Chester and Bristol Rovers. Those victories were part of an incredible seven-game away run to the end of the season which saw Brentford end the campaign with 11 wins and five draws on the road - and a better away than home record for the second successive season.

The Bees finished the campaign one place higher than in 1980-81, in eighth place, and with some encouraging signs for the future. Record signing Whitehead had played a significant part in the season, making more appearances than anyone else, and goalkeeper David McKellar, Barry Tucker, Danis Salman, Terry Hurlock, Gary Roberts, Bob Booker and Keith Bowen had also played over 40 games, while Kamara and Bowles had been regulars since their arrivals.

1982-83

Fred Callaghan prepared for his third full season in charge of the club by trying to solve the goalscoring problems of previous seasons by signing strikers Francis Joseph from Wimbledon and Tony Mahoney from Fulham. He also brought in experienced Manchester United goalkeeper Paddy Roche to replace David McKellar and Chelsea full-back Graham Wilkins.

The season got off to a sensational start with Mahoney and Joseph both on target in a 5-1 rout of Bristol Rovers which set the tone for a season full of goals. By the end of October, The Bees had also beaten both Southend and Chesterfield 4-2, drawn 3-3 at Orient and shared an amazing 4-4 draw at Doncaster, with Mahoney and Joseph scoring 10 goals apiece. In that time The Bees only lost two of their opening 12 League games winning five, but with five draws costing vital points. The side were also on the way to recording the club's best-ever run in the League Cup, known as the Milk Cup that season.

Wimbledon were beaten 3-1 on aggregate in round one, with Joseph failing to score against his old side, before Second Division Blackburn went down 3-2 at Griffin Park in the first leg of the second round and a second leg goalless draw sealed Brentford's victory. Two defeats in the subsequent three League games were hardly the ideal preparation for the visit of First Division Swansea in round three, but the fans were not put off and the best Griffin Park crowd since Boxing Day 1971, of 15,262, turned up to see Gary Roberts earn a 1-1 draw. The replay the following week followed a 2-0 defeat at Huddersfield, but another goal from Roberts, this one after 19 seconds, and an 82nd minute strike from Mahoney earned a famous 2-1 victory and a place in round four for the first time.

The excitement continued with Mahoney hitting a hat-trick in a 7-0 thrashing of Windsor & Eton in the FA Cup first round and then a 2-1 League win at Sheffield United before the Milk Cup dream finally went sour in a 2-0 defeat at Nottingham Forest. The team gave a good account of themselves for this was one of the best Brentford sides in ages, with Joseph and Mahoney playing in front of a midfield of Terry Hurlock, Chris Kamara and Stan Bowles and Roberts shining on the left wing.

Anything seemed possible but a second round FA Cup tie with Swindon proved a cruel turning point. Roberts snatched a 90th minute equaliser to earn a 2-2 draw at the County Ground but Brentford fans wished he had not, for three nights later Mahoney suffered a horrific broken leg in the first half of the replay, which eventually sidelined him for nearly 10 months.

An amazing game at Wrexham. 'Keeper Roche, Rowe (no.2) and Casells can't prevent King levelling the score at 2-2 - after just four minutes! Later Bowles missed a penalty, but Brentford eventually won 4-3...... then....

.....The next 'away' match produced another incredible game - a joint record away win, by 7-1, at Exeter. Here, Joseph scores the sixth goal, his second.

The 3-1 defeat was insignificant compared to the loss of the striker who had scored 15 goals in 28 League and Cup appearances.

Although Exeter were beaten 4-0 in the next game, the side then endured their worst run of the season of five defeats and a draw in six games. A 5-2 win over Orient stopped the rot but three nights after a 4-2 defeat at Southend, the club suffered another huge blow when a fire destroyed half the main stand on Braemar Road one night. Only the swift action of Stan Bowles' wife Jane saved the maintenance man who was asleep at Griffin Park at the time.

The next match was a rare Sunday fixture - away at Newport which ended goalless - following which Callaghan splashed out £25,000 on Southampton striker Keith Cassells. The newcomer scored in his second and fourth games, which were respectively 2-1 defeats at Chesterfield and Lincoln but after that Brentford ended the season strongly. The last 13 games featured just three defeats but seven victories, which included in successive away games a 4-3 win at Wrexham and then a remarkable 7-1 triumph at Exeter - a joint record away victory for the club.

The last game of the season against Bournemouth was supposed to bring down the curtain on Bowles' incredible career and he fittingly scored from a penalty, while Roche saved one as he completed an ever-present season, in a 2-1 success.

The campaign was a case of what might have been with Joseph (26 goals), Roberts (17), Mahoney (15), Kamara (11) and Bowles (11) all having double figure goal tallies and the injury to Mahoney costing Brentford dear.

1983-84

The main change at Brentford over the summer of 1983 was the decision to change the colour of the club's shorts from the traditional black to white. The Football League also acquired its first sponsor so Brentford kicked off the campaign with a 2-2 draw against Millwall in the Canon League Division Three.

The team that day featured the club's only summer signings goalkeeper Trevor Swinburne, who cost £12,000 from Carlisle, and midfielder Terry Bullivant from Charlton. They helped the Bees impressively beat Bullivant's old team, a division above Brentford, 4-2 on aggregate in the first round of the Milk Cup, and earn the reward of a two-legged second round tie against Liverpool.

However between the first leg win over Charlton and the Anfield side's visit, the Bees' League form slumped. A 3-0 win over Lincoln was their only victory in six games while the side suffered three defeats, including a 4-2 defeat at Gillingham just four days before the big game. Nearly 18,000 fans packed into Griffin Park to see a star-studded Liverpool team with Bruce Grobbelaar, Mark Lawrenson, Alan Hansen, Kenny Dalglish, Ian Rush and Graeme Souness in the line-up. After Michael Robinson gave the visitors a controversial lead, Gary Roberts equalised, but although Danis Salman hit the post, Liverpool stepped up a gear to romp to a 4-1 win.

The poor League form continued with one win in four matches before the 4-0 second leg cup defeat in a game which saw Brentford wear an unfamiliar all-white kit and which attracted less than 10,000 fans to Anfield. The eight League games between that game and Christmas yielded not a single win and led to calls from the terraces, for manager Fred Callaghan's dismissal. There were some embarrassing defeats, including a 6-0 hammering at Southend, a 4-1 home loss to a Bradford City side - who had not won in nine matches beforehand - and a 4-3 stuffing by Wimbledon on Christmas Eve, in a match which was originally scheduled to take place 24 hours later.

Again the only respite was in a Cup competition, with the Bees managing to reach the third round of the FA Cup for the first time in eight seasons. Non-League Dagenham were beaten 2-1 in a first round replay following a 2-2 draw and then Wimbledon were despatched 2-1, but the reward was disappointing - Gillingham away in round three.

By this time, there had been some additions to the squad with Stan Bowles making a welcome but unexpected return to the club, Tony Mahoney returning after his long injury lay-off, defender Paul Roberts signing from Millwall following a loan spell and fellow centre-half Ian Bolton arriving from Watford for £15,000 and promptly being made club captain. The winless run finally ended in the final two matches of 1983, when back-to-back victories were earned at Exeter and against Newport before a bizarre 4-4 draw at Scunthorpe preceded the Cup game at Priestfield. Brentford had not been in the fourth round since 1971 and looked set to end this run as they led 3-1 with just 10 minutes remaining, but somehow contrived to lose the game 5-3 and miss out on a fourth round clash with Everton.

The writing was on the wall for Callaghan now and despite a 2-1 win at Millwall the following Sunday, in which fans invaded the pitch to try to reach ex-Lion Roberts after an incident following the winning goal, two more defeats saw the manager shown the door after nearly four years at the helm.

Assistant and former boss Frank Blunstone was in charge for one game, another defeat at Gillingham, before Frank McLintock was appointed manager with assistant John Docherty, returning for his fifth spell with the club. Two draws and a 3-0 win at Bournemouth gave them a good start but two points from the next five games left the club in real danger of relegation.

After Griffin Park wins over Rotherham and Preston, the black shorts returned for the visit of Bolton and superstitious fans at the time thought that made the difference as two early goals set up a 3-0 win. The next two home games were also won 3-0, including a crucial battle with relegation rivals Scunthorpe. Two 1-1 draws, at Newport and then at home to Walsall finally proved decisive as the Bees stayed up ahead of the Iron by just three points.

(Above) The first game of the season, at home to Millwall. Talented but frustrating at times winger Gary Roberts (facing) and dependable striker Cassells.
(Below) At the much lamented Brook Road/Royal Oak end, Joseph nets his first goal of two in the 3-0 win over Bolton in April.

1984-85

After the previous season's relegation battle Frank McLintock cleared the decks in the summer of 1984. Out went Jim McNichol, Paddy Roche, Tony Mahoney and Ian Bolton on free transfers while through the Griffin Park gates came just two players - Cambridge left-back Jamie Murray for £27,500 and centre-half Steve Wignall from Colchester for £18,000.

Despite an opening day defeat at home to Orient, the side made a good start to the season, with four wins from the next five League games and progression to the second round of the Milk Cup. The results came at a cost though with prolific striker Francis Joseph breaking his leg in Brentford's first-ever win over Wigan in early September. The injury put the popular player on the sidelines for a year.

Tenacious Terry Hurlock.

The 2-1 aggregate Cup win over Cambridge set up a tie with First Division opposition for the second season in a row - this time in the shape of McLintock's old club Leicester City.

New signing Rowan Alexander made a sensational debut in the first leg at Filbert Street by scoring after just 90 seconds and then having a goal disallowed. Chris Kamara doubled the Bees' lead after the interval but Leicester dashed the giant-killing dreams with four goals in the last nine minutes, the last scored by Gary Lineker and finished off the tie with a 2-0 win at Griffin Park.

League results became disappointing with only two wins in nine games, a 5-2 victory over Gillingham thanks to a hat-trick from Gary Roberts and a 2-1 defeat of York with Roberts again on target. However more interest came in the Cup competitions and also the weather. Non-League Bishop's Stortford were swept aside 4-0 in the first round of the FA Cup and then the Bees were held 2-2 at Griffin Park in round two by Northampton, who were at the time bottom of the League.

The replay at the County Ground started in foggy conditions and was abandoned after two attempts at playing the game totalling 26 minutes, strangely less than two months after the midweek League match at Newport had also been called off because of fog. The first half of the game in south Wales was played in clear conditions but the gloom descended at half-time and was abandoned around the hour mark.

The F A Cup replay was finally restaged and Brentford won 2-0 with late goals from Keith Cassells and Terry Hurlock, to earn a third round tie at Second Division Oldham.

After the replay McLintock bought striker Steve Butler and midfielder George Torrance out of the Army but they suffered disastrous debuts in a 4-0 hammering at Hull. Undeterred, McLintock continued spending, signing Barnet's goalkeeper Gary Phillips for £5,000 and Cambridge striker Robbie Cooke, initially on loan, but then permanently for £20,000.

The Cup run ended 2-1 at Boundary Park, with wonderboy Wayne Harrison hitting Oldham's first, and the League results continued to be patchy into the new year, a 5-2 home defeat by Newport County being the worst. Things finally began to improve in February, which was also the start of what happened to be the most important event of the season - the Freight Rover Trophy.

The competition for lower division clubs was in its second season and offered a Wembley final for the first time - a rare opportunity for Third and Fourth Division clubs to maybe play underneath the famous Twin Towers. Brentford's run started by hitting back from a goal down to win a first round, first leg game 3-1 at Reading and wrapped up the tie with a 2-0 second leg victory.

The Bees met Cambridge United for the fifth time that season in round two and a second half Cooke goal against his former club was enough to beat them for the fourth time and progress on to the next round. Two Bob Booker goals saw off Swansea in round three at the Vetch Field and set up a southern area semi-final away to holders Bournemouth.

Cooke and Kamara put the Bees 2-0 up after the break but the Cherries quickly levelled before Cooke snatched a dramatic winner. With the League season petering out into mid-table safety, all eyes were on the southern area final against Newport County and over 8,000 turned up for an unforgettable night. A Cassells double, one a penalty, put Brentford in charge before Gary Roberts hit a four-minute hat-trick either side of half-time to put the game beyond reach. Cassells then missed a second penalty before Roberts hit his fourth - and Brentford were at Wembley!

This was a dream come true for the club's fans, most of whom thought they would never see such a day.

Nice day, shame about the result!

But on June 1, 1985, in front of at least 25,000 Bees supporters the team walked out alongside Wigan. But it wasn't to be Brentford's day and after they fell behind to a controversial opening goal and then conceded again, the highlight came when Cooke hooked in Murray's cross to halve the deficit. Wigan scored again to make the game safe but it was still an unforgettable experience.

1985-86

The euphoria of the day out at Wembley quickly evaporated during the summer when captain Chris Kamara, striker Keith Cassells and winger Gary Roberts all demanded transfers. Kamara and Cassells moved to Swindon and Mansfield respectively and although Roberts decided to stay, he missed the start of the season because of injury.

But despite all that the side made a tremendous start and were joint top of the table after winning their first three games against relegated Wolves and Bournemouth at home and at Bristol Rovers. They also progressed to the second round of the Milk Cup after beating Cambridge yet again.

The celebrations ended with a 4-0 defeat at bogey team Wigan which started a run of six League games without a win. In the Milk Cup a Rowan Alexander double earned a 2-2 draw with Sheffield Wednesday but the First Division side reached round three by winning the second leg 2-0. Summer signing Terry Evans made his first appearances for the club in the early matches while Francis Joseph made his long-awaited comeback from injury only to hobble off in his second game.

Popular Gary Phillips who took over in goal midway through the season.

The topsy-turvy season continued with three consecutive wins at the start of October - the best of them a 5-3 triumph at Darlington in which Alexander scored a hat-trick. The mixed bag of results continued and there were certainly plenty of goals flying about, although not always at the right end. The Bees lost 4-0 at Blackpool but bounced back in consecutive home games to beat Cardiff 3-0 with three goals in the first 15 minutes and then draw 3-3 against Derby by equalising three times.

There was disappointment in the FA Cup with a 3-1 first round defeat at home to Bristol Rovers which was significant only for Evans' first goal for the club. In mid-December Brentford beat Bury 1-0 in a notable game for two players. The winner that day was a penalty from new signing Andy Sinton, following his arrival from Cambridge, but the day also marked the final appearance of Roberts, who was forced to retire from the game because of injury. Bristol Rovers were then beaten 1-0 on the Sunday before Christmas and Brentford went into the festive period in the top six and in the hunt for one of the three promotion places.

However it proved to be a false dawn as a shocking home record for the rest of the season put paid to any dreams of a place in the Second Division for the first time in 32 years.

The Bees failed to win another League game at Griffin Park until the last one of the season against Darlington in early May - a run of 10 winless matches. At the same time they were proving unstoppable away - winning six games on the road in the second half of the season. Included in this run were memorable victories at Wolves - 4-1 in front of a crowd of less than 3,500 and at Notts County by 4-0.

The team even failed to make any progress towards a repeat of the Wembley final of the previous season - failing to emerge from the new group stage of the Freight Rover Trophy where they drew with Derby and Gillingham.

A certain air of depression at Griffin Park was not helped by the demolition of the much-loved Brook Road terrace, the club record sale of captain Terry Hurlock to Third Division rivals Reading for £92,500 in February and an injury which ruled Evans out for the rest of the season at this same time. However, on the positive side Francis Joseph returned to the side once again and lined up alongside brother Roger, a full-back, with both scoring in a 3-3 draw against York. Brentford ended the season with a much better away record than that at home once again were looking at what might have been.

1986-87

The disappointment of the 1985/86 season continued into the summer when assistant manager John Docherty left the club to become manager of Millwall. Furious Brentford accused the Lions of an illegal approach for Docherty for which they were fined £1,000. As if losing Docherty was not bad enough, long-serving defender Danis Salman followed him to south-east London for a tribunal-decided fee of just £20,000.

George Torrance, Steve Butler, Rowan Alexander and Terry Bullivant also left, but Frank McLintock did bring in two midfielders in Ian Holloway for £25,000 from Wimbledon, following a loan spell the previous season, and Hereford's Paul Maddy for £8,000, with two players coming on free transfers - defender Phil Bater from Bristol Rovers and Shrewsbury striker Gary Stevens.

The Bees made a dreadful start to the season, in which clubs were allowed to use two substitutes for the first time. They picked up just one point from the first three games and suffered a rare first round exit in the League (now Littlewoods) Cup by 4-2 on aggregate to Southend. The versatile Bob Booker suffered an injury in the home leg which sidelined him for the rest of the season. To make matters worse, captain Steve Wignall was then sold to Aldershot for £8,000, but the season finally got going as The Bees claimed their first win of the season down the road at Fulham, a 3-1 success, after going a goal behind.

Another 5-3 win over Darlington followed a draw at Carlisle and things looked brighter although as autumn became winter the results were still inconsistent. In mid-November McLintock signed two famous names in the game in former England and Tottenham midfielder Steve Perryman as player/assistant manager and ex-Chelsea centre-half Micky Droy. Both made their debuts in a 1-1 draw at Chester.

The FA Cup was next on Brentford's radar and this turned into a marathon of epic and damp proportions. The Bees were drawn away to Bristol Rovers, who were groundsharing at Bath's Twerton Park. The original tie was moved to the Sunday but when the players and fans turned up they found the pitch waterlogged and the game was postponed. Staggeringly it was called off a further five times before finally being played and almost inevitably resulting in a goalless draw. The replay three days later, on second round Saturday, saw the Bees win 2-0 and they then had to play their second round tie at Cardiff three nights later. Brentford lost 2-0 and so their FA Cup campaign eventually had been decided by three games in just six days!

That was just the start of McLintock's problems as in the next 10 matches, the Bees only recorded two wins - both in the Freight Rover Trophy. In their first group game they won 5-1 at Orient with four goals from Robbie Cooke and one from on-loan striker David Geddis before a crowd of just 749, following this Swindon were beaten 4-2 in the second match. It was the League form which was more significant though and after a 4-1 defeat at Port Vale, which included a League debut for young on-loan Arsenal striker Paul Merson, McLintock left the club.

Perryman was put in temporary charge and made an immediate impact as player-manager with a 4-2 Trophy win over Walsall in his first game. Two more home matches followed with a 3-3 Sunday morning draw with Fulham and then finally another League victory as Carlisle were beaten 3-1. Bristol City ended the Trophy run with a 3-0 quarter-final win at Ashton Gate but Brentford had turned the corner and the League form continued to improve.

Perryman was appointed full-time manager and brought in his old Spurs team-mate Phil Holder as his assistant after which the team embarked on an eight-match unbeaten run. The manager also made a significant move into the transfer market with Crewe Alexandra striker Gary Blissett arriving for £60,000 to replace Stevens who was sold to Hereford United, while Oxford United striker Lee Nogan and Chelsea's Philip Priest joined on loan. After losing at soon-to-be promoted Middlesbrough they won three games in a row before suffering their usual defeat to Wigan on the last day of the season. It was another mid-table finish but given the way the Bees had tumbled down the table at one stage respectability was gratefully received.

1987-88

Steve Perryman marked his first full close-season at the helm by reshuffling the squad. Leaving Griffin Park were five players including Francis Joseph and Micky Droy while he signed the experienced Colin Lee in the dual role of player and youth development officer and four other players including Leicester's Andy Feeley.

For the second time in three seasons Brentford started their campaign against a relegated big-name club as Sunderland came to Griffin Park, but unlike the Wolves game in 1985 this time the Bees lost - 1-0. This set the tone for a disappointing start with defeat against Bristol City and for the second season in a row, elimination in the first round of the Littlewoods Cup to Southend. They finally got on the board with a win at Grimsby where Gary Blissett scored the only goal, but was then sent off, and followed that with a 1-1 draw against Rotherham with a goal from Keith Jones - a new £40,000 signing from Chelsea.

Losing 2-1 at Northampton left the Bees in the relegation zone but the team suddenly came good and won five of the next six games to charge up the table. Notable in this run was the return of Bob Booker from his long-term injury and a goal in each of the last four victories from Andy Sinton, who scored in his fifth consecutive game as the winning run ended in a 2-2 draw at Bury. By this stage left back Roger Stanislaus had joined from Arsenal and trialist Steve Thorne had also arrived, scoring his only goal for the club in a 1-0 win at Gillingham and being immortalised in the name of the fanzine *"Thorne In the Side"*, which is still going strong to date. That game also saw Terry Evans chosen and the centre-half only missed one game for the rest of the season.

Robbie Cooke ,was signed by John Docherty for Brentford and joined him again at Millwall.

Eddie Lyons, former professional footballerwho joined the Brentford staff, becoming the Trainer/ Physio for many years, and even came on as a sub. in his 1984 testimonial, aged 63 years!

Brentford's inconsistency was proving frustrating and after the winning run which had taken them up to seventh, a sequence of seven League games with only one victory, that at Priestfield, saw them slip out of promotion contention once again.

The other two Cup competitions were also under way by now and although Brentford suffered a disappointing first round exit in the FA Cup - 2-0 at home to Brighton - they made progress in the Freight Rover Trophy thanks to a Paul Williams hat-trick in the second group game against Notts County.

As December emerged on the calendar, the popular Robbie Cooke moved on - joining Millwall for £30,000 - which meant he missed one of the most explosive games at Griffin Park for many years when Mansfield came visiting. Brentford trailed 2-1 at half-time and little of note happened until the 80th minute when an almighty brawl occurred in the Brook Road penalty area. When the officials had calmed the situation, referee Mr James made history by sending off four players - the Bees' Jamie Bates and Colin Lee and then Town's George Foster and goalkeeper Kevin Hitchcock. Former Bees striker Keith Cassells took over in goal for the last 10 minutes and made a couple of great saves, although he did concede an equaliser to Blissett.

It was the only fifth time that four players had been sent off in an English League or Cup game, and the second time that season, and stood as a joint record until five players were dismissed in one match in February 1997. The festive period was profitable with Aldershot beaten 3-0 on Boxing Day, with former England winger Graham Rix making his debut on loan from Arsenal, before a 2-2 draw at Fulham and 3-2 New Year's Day win at Bristol

City, at which a post-match warm-down annoyed the home fans. These results gave hope of reaching the play-offs, which were in their second season of operation. However the campaign took a downturn after that.

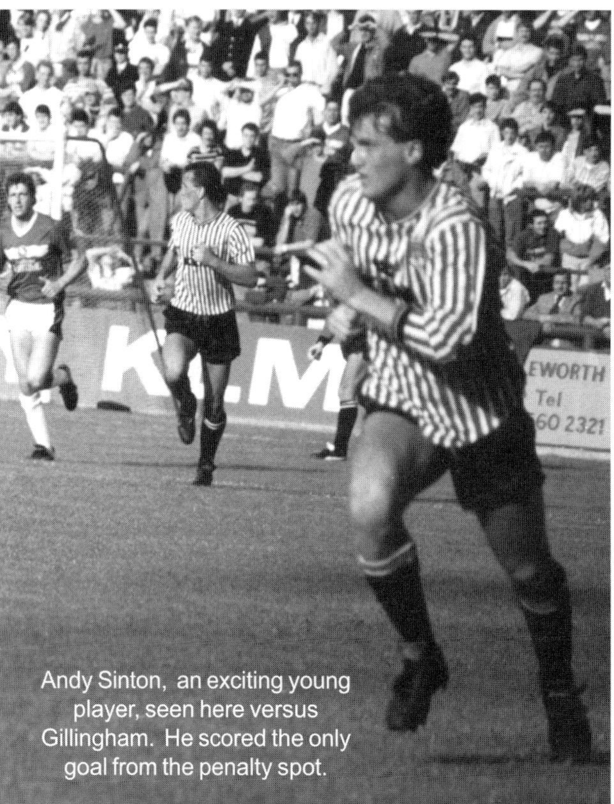

Andy Sinton, an exciting young player, seen here versus Gillingham. He scored the only goal from the penalty spot.

The Freight Rover Trophy campaign ended in a 4-0 defeat at Wolves and of the final 18 League games, only three finished as victories and none of these came in the last seven matches. Yet again Brentford finished in mid-table, this time in 12th, and it was now 10 years since they had been promoted from Division Four.

1988-89
Anyone supporting the Bees 20 years ago will look back at the 1988-89 season as one of the most exciting - but ultimately frustrating - of their lives following the club. The mood was boosted during the close-season when Steve Perryman smashed the club transfer record to buy Sheffield United striker Richard Cadette for £130,000. Perryman also paid his old club, Tottenham Hotspur, £60,000 for goalkeeper Tony Parks, while Reading winger Neil Smillie also arrived, on a free, for his second spell at the club, following a brief time on loan in 1977.

Neil Smillie,anexcellent addition to the squad.

Some of this money was recouped with another club record as Roger Joseph joined Wimbledon for £150,000 just months after becoming the first Brentford player to be voted into the PFA team, while Gary Phillips and Wayne Turner also moved on. To cap it all the club were building towards their centenary in 1989 and sported a new red and white pinstripe home kit - with revamped club badge to boot.

By the end of September the League had thrown up two wins, two draws and two defeats but the excitement had started in the Cups. Fulham were despatched 3-2 on aggregate, after extra-time in the second leg, in the first round of the Littlewoods Cup and the Bees came close to upsetting Second Division Blackburn in round two before losing 6-5 on aggregate. League results continued to be mixed as the season moved into November and movement continued on the player front with long-serving Bob Booker joining Sheffield United but three new faces arriving - striker Dean Holdsworth on loan from Watford, and former Leyton Orient front man Kevin Godfrey plus Maltese International sweeper John Buttigieg, both coming on trial.

The month also saw the start of two more Cup competitions. In the FA Cup first round Brentford beat non-League Halesowen 2-0, then both Fulham and Gillingham were beaten by the same score in the group games of the Sherpa Van (former Freight Rover) Trophy. The FA Cup second round took the Bees to Fourth Division Peter-borough where they drew 0-0. The most significant moment of the game was when Andy Sinton suffered concussion, forcing him out of the replay, which Brentford won 3-2, thus ending his run of 161 consecutive appearances.

Brentford were establishing a nice unbeaten League run as they travelled to Second Division Walsall in the third round and drew 1-1 before winning the replay 1-0. The big tie arrived in round four - Manchester City, then in the Second Division, at home.

The City fans with their inflatable bananas took their places in a sell-out crowd of 12,100 but could only look on as an inspired performance saw two goals from Gary Blissett and one from captain Keith Jones seal a famous 3-1 win - the club biggest giant-killing for many years. Earlier in the month Notts County had been beaten 2-0 in the Sherpa Van and February arrived with two big Cup games in prospect.

A 1-0 home defeat by Chester ended an unbeaten League and Cup run of 14 games the week before Brentford travelled to their Littlewoods Cup conquerors Blackburn for their first fifth round FA Cup tie since 1971.

The packed away end at Anfield.

With an estimated 3,000 travelling fans, two late second half goals from Blissett at the away end gave the Bees a 2-0 win and earned a dream quarter-final tie at Liverpool - only Brentford fourth-ever appearance at this stage. Blissett also scored the only goal of the Sherpa Vans quarter-final against Chesterfield and the club was buzzing.

The trip to Anfield saw no fewer than 7,000 Bees fans journey up the motorways, most carrying inflatable bees, but although they enjoyed the experience they saw their side outclassed as Liverpool, led by John Barnes, ran out 4-0 winners after Cadette had missed a glorious early chance. That was the start of a pivotal week for the club as three nights later, Torquay won 1-0 at Griffin Park in the Sherpa Van semis.

Two days after, on transfer deadline day, Sinton was sold to QPR for a club record £350,000 and the next day Fulham also earned a 1-0 Griffin Park win. Brentford had to play 13 League games in April and May and although they won six of them, including a 3-0 defeat of Bristol City in which Tony Sealy scored after 13 seconds, they finished four points outside the play-offs in seventh place.

Alongside all this the Juniors reached the FA Youth Cup semi-finals, beating Manchester United 2-1 in the last eight, before losing to Watford. In all, the first team played 63 games during the season, 17 of them cup-ties, but despite all the thrills along the way, they ended up with only memories to show for it.

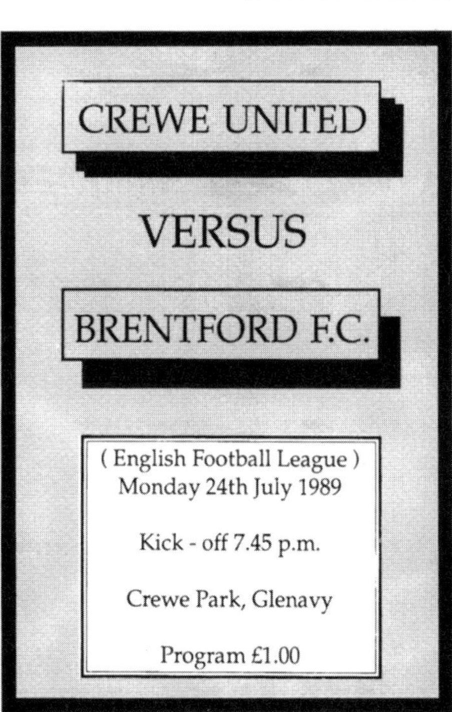
CREWE UNITED

VERSUS

BRENTFORD F.C.

(English Football League)
Monday 24th July 1989

Kick - off 7.45 p.m.

Crewe Park, Glenavy

Program £1.00

1989-90

Celebrations for the club's centenary season were to come in October, and after what could be regarded as a reasonably successful season, optimism was high amongst the supporters, in the hope that perhaps they could follow on with a serious promotion push from the Third Division, which had become their 'home' for so many years. Included amongst the usual set of pre-season friendlies was a game against Crewe, in Ireland not versus the Railway-men, and a visit to Switzerland.

The campaign hardly got off to a flying start with a single goal defeat at Bristol Rovers, but was followed four days later with an encouraging surprise victory at the Goldstone Ground when Second Division Brighton were beaten 3-0, in the first leg, first round, of the Littlewoods (League) Cup. The goalscorers were Keith Millen, after just two minutes, Kevin Godfrey and new record £167,000 signing Eddie May from Hibernian. A 1-1 draw in the second leg, with fans' favourite Gary Blissett netting for the Bees, was enough to send the team through to the next round and a tie against Manchester

Another pair that were to terrorise opposition defences, Gary Blissett and Dean Holdsworth.

City, with memories of the FA Cup victory against the then Second Division side (now First) just a few months earlier.

In the home leg, Brentford overcame the visitors 2-1 before a disappointing crowd of under 7,000. In the second leg, despite equalising an earlier effort by City and controlling much of the first half they finally succumbed to a 4-1 defeat. The Maine Road side's scoreline was somewhat flattering, the Bees, outplayed in only the first 15 minutes of the second period, causing the damage. Back in the bread and butter world of League football, all was not well. The first victory didn't come until late September, after two draws and four 1-0 defeats, with a 3-2 victory over the 'other' Crewe, Alexandra, at Gresty Road. When bogey side Wigan Athletic were beaten 3-1 at home, it was hoped that the corner had finally been turned, but the four defeats that followed showed that it was going to be a further uphill road to success. A total of nearly £700,000 on transfer fees was reached assembling the squad, when Watford's 20 year old Dean Holdsworth was signed, after earlier appearing on loan the previous season. £125,000 was paid in a bid to increase the goalscoring which had been the biggest problem at this time. An earlier signing had included midfielder Simon Ratcliffe, for an outlay of £100,000, from Norwich City.

More was expected of the squad, but it wasn't until the 28th of October that the next win came, 2-0 over neighbours Fulham at Griffin Park. But with just three victories in the first 13 League games, the Bees were anxiously looking more towards the foot of the table rather than the top. After losing 2-0 at home to Bristol City, this latest defeat could have subdued the 600 supporters, players, management and guests that assembled at the Hilton Hotel in London.

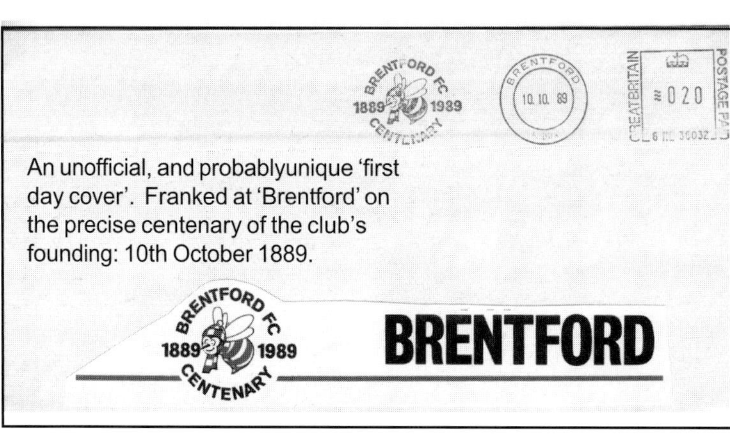

An unofficial, and probablyunique 'first day cover'. Franked at 'Brentford' on the precise centenary of the club's founding: 10th October 1889.

The occasion was for the eagerly anticipated Centenary Dinner the next day. But the celebration was for the past century of the club, rather than a shaky start to the current season and one of the highlights of the evening was the launching of the book *'100 Years of Brentford'* which had been compiled by a team of knowledgeable Brentford supporters, under the stewardship of long time programme editor Eric White. This massive 400 page volume was to quickly sell out, as did the reprint, and become a much sort after reference, which years later would fetch up to £200 per copy!

On the pitch, another defeat the following Saturday, on Preston's unpopular plastic pitch was to follow. Before the Fulham victory the Bees had plunged into deep relegation territory, at third from bottom, yet amazingly the supporters kept faith, even though worse was to come. Much of the optimism rested with manager Steve Perryman who insisted on playing attractive football and it was felt that with the undoubted talent at his disposal the results would come right - but when?

Perryman himself had come out of semi-retirement early in the season, and went on to make his final five playing appearances, his last in the FA Cup. Other players who were tried but never really made it included Kelly Haag, midfielder John Moncur a loan signing from 'Spurs and perhaps most disappointing of all John Buttigieg.

The Maltese International (ironically Brentford's all-time most capped player) had been an unusual signing for £40,000 from Sliema Wanderers, by Perryman a year earlier. Undoubtably a stylish player, he was a sweeper, a surprising acquisition since Brentford never adopted this system and although he made a number of early season appearances, he was used as a right back and was never able to display his talents to the full. He later moved to Swindon for a spell on

The authors of the Centenary book (Left to right) Ian Westbrook, the late Eric White, Dave Twydell, Graham Haynes and Rob Jex.

Fittingly, apart from Eric White, the others have all made their contribution to this publication.

loan before returning to Malta, and the resumption of his international career.

A heavy defeat at Blackpool was not helped with the sending off of Jamie Bates. His dismissal was undefendable after he fouled a player in the box whilst play was some distance away. At this time the Bees were only losing 2-0, but the resultant penalty goal and another late in the game added to the team's woes.

By Christmas 22 different players had been tried, and only Eddie May had been an ever-present, although Terry Evans, who formed a successful partnership with Keith Millen, had missed just one game and dynamic winger Neil Smillie, two. But the situation had hardly improved by the 1st of January, when only a mini-run of three consecutive victories a month earlier had relieved the gloom. At this point Brentford were fifth from bottom of the table, just goal difference separating them from a relegation position. But the visit of fellow strugglers Walsall on New Year's Day was to prove to be the turning point of the season.

A highly entertaining and skilful display by the Bees produced a 4-0 win, with goals from Blissett, Smillie, Holdsworth and Jones at last showed what the team was capable of. The six unbeaten League matches that followed (including just a single draw), had propelled the team into the top half of the table, and a possible play-off place was not out their reach, for they now trailed the coveted sixth place by just eight points. Just when everything was going right another poor spell followed, which saw just one win in the next five games.

The rest of the season was to become something of an anti-climax for another winning run couldn't be duplicated and just below halfway in the table was the final outcome. But at least the signs looked good for the future, with Holdsworth proving his worth with his 24 goals in 39 League games, and Blissett adding 11 in 36. Perhaps more should have been expected from expensive signing May, who only managed eight goals from his 30 appearances, although he missed much of the latter part of the season through a recurring injury problem. Whilst Holdsworth was undeniably the star player with his goals, the diminutive Smillie will especially be remembered for two of his six goals. Against both Shrewsbury and Bristol Rovers (in the Leyland Daf Cup), he took the ball from his own half and dizzying runs into enemy territory ended in goals which could be contenders for 'goals of the season'.

There was no success in the FA Cup, for defeat came in the first round at Colchester, and only a modest run in the Leyland Cup to the regional quarter-final stage, when defeat came at home to Bristol Rovers in a penalty shoot-out.

With their insistence on attractive football and the early year revival the final outcome was a big disappointment overall. Yet to add to the team's credentials several players had won accolades, notably Holdsworth (the *Evening Standard* Player of the month in February), Stanislaus who was the *'Match Magazine'* Third Division player during the same period, with Ratcliffe and Evans also up with the leaders. In fact at this time it was felt that manager Perryman should have been the Third Division Manager of the Month, but he was just pipped by Bristol City's Joe Jordan. Injuries and a poor disciplinary record played their part in the club's late season mediocrity. Bates missed many games, after he had re-established himself in the side following the Blackpool fiasco (the return match ended in a season's best, 5-0 victory). Alan Cochran who had earned himself a regular midfield slot was also missing. Meanwhile Ratcliffe and Jones, two of the most influential players in the side, were absent due to suspensions.

1990-91

There was only one major transfer during the close season when Roger Stanislaus opted to move to unfashionable Bury, a fellow Third Division club, for a tribunal fixed fee of £90,000. He made 111 League appearances in his three years with Brentford and was a favourite with the crowd, but later, by then with Leyton Orient, he blemished his career after being tested positive for drug taking. Kelly Haag, a free goalscorer with the Juniors was unable to repeat this in the first team and was released, as was ex-'Spurs goalkeeper Tony Parks. Graham Benstead was the replacement between the sticks, a £60,000 (plus appearances) buy from Sheffield United, who became a popular figure during his four years at Griffin Park.

Manager Holder holds aloft the December 'Third Division Manager Of The Month Award'.

The Bees progressed on to the second round of the cup, despite losing the return match with The Bulls by 1-0 and were unlucky to go down 2-1 at Second Division Sheffield Wednesday. A crowd of over 8,000 for the second leg saw the homesters lose by the same scoreline. But the League was the main target where good progress was being made.

The loss of Perryman had little effect on the team as overall they made a very encouraging start to the season and by late September the Brentford Board rewarded Phil Holder with a two year contract. By the time Elm Park, Reading, was visited in late October, the team were undefeated on their travels, albeit having lost two home matches. They lay sixth from top, seven points behind the leaders Grimsby who had only lost one League game - at Griffin Park! After another victory (a milestone for the Bees in obtaining their 3000th point in League football) by 2-1 in Berkshire, a poor run followed which fortunately lasted for only four matches, before getting back on song again with a single goal win in the local derby at home to Leyton Orient in early December.

With a settled and talented squad, the start of the season was keenly anticipated and the hope that the team could recapture the form of six months earlier. Then completely out of the blue, manager Perryman resigned just one week before the League fixtures commenced. Although popular with the fans and it was thought with the Board, a row with the Chairman over the signing of Fulham's Elkins led to his departure. The former Tottenham man had built up a strong squad that was allowed to play football and who had the respect of the players. Fortunately Assistant Manager Phil 'Noddy' Holder was able to step into his shoes at short notice, and whilst under his stewardship the club had two very successful seasons, it was really seen as Perryman's team that did it.

Despite a handy placing, still at sixth, Holder did not field a settled team. Godfrey and Smillie were the only ever-presents to this time, although Benstead only missed one match (through injury), when ironically Tony Parks came back on loan for a single game at Tranmere. Right back Jason Cousins stepped in for a few matches, but later faded out of the Brentford scene, although he was to achieve great success at Wycombe Wanderers. Gary Brooke came on loan from Wimbledon but didn't impress and other infrequent appearances were made by Alan Cockram (who later established a regular slot) plus strikers Gary Blissett and Dean Holdsworth whose outings were limited due to injuries. If the pair had only been fit throughout the season, automatic promotion would quite likely have been the outcome!

In view of the managerial turmoil, a scoreless home draw with Bournemouth, then victory in the Littlewoods Cup at Hereford (the first competitive meeting between the pair) and a 2-0 victory at Mansfield which followed could be considered a very satisfactory start.

Holdsworth scores the winning goal, in a 2-1 victory at Leyton Orient in March.

Freezing conditions prevailed in mid-December, and the second round FA Cup tie at Birmingham City was initially postponed before the re-match, which Brentford comfortably won 3-2. The Midland team were on a downward spiral at this time, and were placed at mid-table in the Third Division with home gates that often only just topped 7,000. To rub salt in the wound, The Bees returned to St. Andrews two weeks later on League action, and before only 6,612 won 2-0. Earlier in the Cup, Brentford had overcome a potential banana skin when they entertained famed giant-killers, non-League Yeovil Town, but a comprehensive 5-0 home win ensued. The third round of the Cup at Oldham Athletic was best forgotten. A 3-1 reverse, once again on a highly controversial plastic pitch, in gale force conditions - located in what many consider to be the coldest ground in the Football League (especially in January) - saw The Latics score from two penalties (one highly controversial), and Brentford denied a 'goal' from an 'over the line' situation.

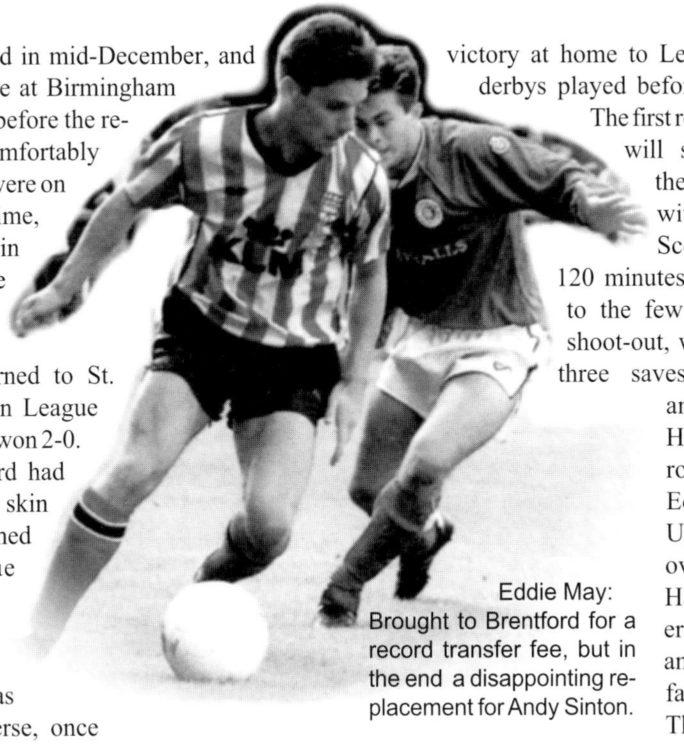

Eddie May: Brought to Brentford for a record transfer fee, but in the end a disappointing replacement for Andy Sinton.

By now the club had parted company with Eddie May. The Scot's family was unable to settle in the south and after a transfer request in September he moved on to Falkirk. Many considered that May was poor value for money (47 League games and only 10 goals), but he made his mark with a highly successful resumption of his career in Scotland. On a happier front, Holder received the Third Division 'Manager of the month' award for December, but this did not lead to the usual immediate defeat, for Shrewsbury Town were overcome by 3-0 at Griffin Park on New Year's Day. This lifted the team into third place in the table and an automatic promotion place.

Then an indifferent spell over the next few weeks, which produced three victories, two draws and four defeats, culminating in a 4-0 thrashing at home to mid-table Stoke City, saw a slump to sixth. During this period, Wilf Rostron signed up from Sheffield United, as player/assistant manager. Although well into the twilight of his career, his experience and strong tackling saw him play in most of the remaining games that season.

But a diversion of interest was enjoyed in the fairly unlikely setting of the Leyland/DAF Cup. Despite its general lack of attraction, there was always the lure of a Wembley final, and Brentford made good progress in this direction. They overcame the mini table first round stage with a goalless draw at Fulham (in which Benstead excelled) and a 2-0 victory at home to Leyton Orient - both local derbys played before sub-3000 attendances. The first round match with Wrexham will surely go down as one of the most boring games ever witnessed at Griffin Park! Scoreless, and shotless for 120 minutes, excitement was limited to the few minutes of the penalty shoot-out, when three successes and three saves by Benstead, earned another encounter with Hereford United in the next round. After the 2-0 win at Edgar Street, Southend United were comfortably overcome by 3-0 at Roots Hall, leading to the Southern Area Final, versus yet another frequent set of faces - Birmingham City. The encounter at St. Andrews produced a narrow 2-1 defeat, and the second leg watched by less than 9,000, ended in a disappointing 1-0 reverse; the saga with Birmingham City thus came to a end after five matches that season. A number of team changes with injuries to Smillie, Godfrey and captain, Jones, plus the absence of Evans, who was suspended, led to a weakened eleven.

But there was still the real prospect of promotion to look forward to, and after the Stoke disaster the team recovered, the highlight being a 6-0 drubbing of Bradford City on the 23rd of March. A customary defeat at Wigan (1-0) then a 1-0 victory over Crewe Alexandra kept the Bees just outside a play-off place. The next home game saw a blood and thunder game against local rivals Fulham. The two clubs' situations were very different, with Brentford clamouring for promotion and The Cottagers looking likely to drop with their third from bottom placing. But form was not respected, and despite a rare goal from Rostron, The Bees slumped to a 2-1 defeat. Rostron's only other goal was also against Fulham, when the return at Craven Cottage was won 1-0.

Despite this victory, a play-off place was looking less likely by the time Reading were entertained, as the team had slipped to 10th, although only two points behind 7th place Huddersfield Town. But the remaining four games produced three victories and only one defeat, ominously the latter at home to Tranmere Rovers in the penultimate League match. By this time the Bees had secured their play-off place, as had the visitors, but by virtue of their victory, the latter finished one place above Brentford, and hence gained the marginal advantage of playing the second leg of the play-off matches at home.

The play-offs were an innovation introduced a year earlier, which had been largely envisaged by Brentford Chairman Martin Lange. Whilst these matches have proved to be well merited over the years, it is ironic that they have tended to work against Brentford, who on two occasions would have been promoted automatically rather than appearing as top play-off contender, and losing out on both occasions!

The home leg versus Tranmere Rovers was a tense affair and Brentford fielding their strongest team took a first half lead through Evans.

Rovers came back strongly in the second period and deservedly equalised before taking the lead in the 73rd minute. The Brentford fans wouldn't give up and their continual urging was rewarded with a last minute equaliser from Godfrey, to give some hope for the return.

Brentford was well supported on the Wirral with around 2,000 fans who made the long midweek trek, but in truth the team was never at the races, and in fairness the Rovers were probably better value than their one goal victory suggested. So it was Tranmere who would appear, and win, at Wembley, whilst Brentford had to wait for promotion, but not for long!

Chapter 11: UP, DOWN, THEN TURN AROUND

1991/92

Several players left Griffin Park during the close season including Jason Cousins, a former Junior who had made 21 League appearances, goalkeeper Laurence Batty who never made it in the first team but went on to a successful career in senior non-League football, and surprisingly Alan Cockram. Although nearing the end of his career, the midfielder had become a popular figure with the fans and had notched up 14 goals (many from distance) in his 90 League appearances. Initially permanent terms couldn't be agreed with captain Keith Jones (*'The People'* newspaper's Third Division player of the season) and Gary Blissett. The only money signing was £60,000 Billy Manuel from Gillingham.

The other Bees had started their career at this level in bizarre fashion, losing at home to Crewe Alexandra by 7-4, and then followed this up a few days later with another 10 goals at Underhill in the Rumbelows (League) Cup. This saw a see-saw match with the homesters 5-3 ahead and only 12 minutes remaining.

But another brace of goals from Holdsworth, secured an unlikely 5-5 high-scoring draw. Brentford won 3-1 in the second leg to earn a second round match with Brighton. A modest set of results led up to the cup match, with four victories and three defeats, the latter coming from a home reverse to Huddersfield and likewise at Hartlepool (managed by former player Alan Murray) plus Shrewsbury.

Graham Benstead's unfortunate pulled hamstring gave youngster Ashley Bayes a run-out in the first team, the first match being won 4-3 over Leyton Orient. Dean Holdsworth scored a hat-trick, providing a taste of what was to come from his lethal goalscoring foot. Whilst this was the first opening day hat-trick marksman since 1965, and the ninth consecutive victory in various competitions over the East London side, the unexpected continued on to the next game, when another local derby saw Brentford visit new boys to the League Barnet.

Summer signing, Billy Manuel.

Regular 'keeper Graham Benstead.

Smillie nets one of the goals in the 2-1 win over Peterborough in October.

Brentford had fluctuated between third and sixteenth during the early season matches, and lay in a useful 6th place at the time of Second Division Brighton's visit. Brentford provided one of the shocks of the round as they crushed their higher division opponents, taking a three goal lead at half-time, which was increased to four (and could have been five), before the Albion slotted in a consolation. Two more League victories then followed, taking the Bees to the top of the Third Division, before the second leg of the cup-tie. The expectation of needing to just hold their opponents at bay was soon dispelled when Brighton tore into the Bees and were two goals up on the night after just 13 minutes. This caused concern in the Brentford camp, but they allayed the fears when they pulled back one goal, only for the home team to restore their two goal lead before half-time.

The situation looked grim when the tie was equalled at 4-4 and the game went into extra time. But far from deflated, the Bees finished as the stronger team and a Holdsworth goal sealed the game. After this exciting match, the third round game was an anti-climax, but was also controversial. Whilst Brentford had no complaints on losing at Carrow Road to First Division Norwich City, the 4-1 scoreline was unjust. Scoreless at half-time, the Bees were rocked when they conceded two goals in 44 seconds (probably an unwanted record), with the second looking suspiciously offside.

The City then added two more goals, which were unquestionably following the result of a player in an offside position. The complaints that followed were such that the 'offending' linesman, Mr.Hair, realising his terrible mistakes asked to be removed from the Football League lists a week later. Manuel netted a consolation, his debut goal for the club, in the dying minutes.

Sandwiched between the cup-ties, two victories and a defeat (2-1 at West Bromwich Albion) kept the team more or less on their promotion course. Following another victory and a draw, a comprehensive 4-0 win followed over Wigan Athletic at Griffin Park, after which the Bees led the table by two points over Birmingham City. To this time they had scored no fewer than 49 goals, 32 in their 16 League games, and 17 in just five cup matches. Dean Holdsworth was far and away the top marksman with 17 already to his credit. It was now time for the FA Cup, but this competition did little to divert the team from their League ambitions. A 3-3 draw was first played out at home to Gillingham, the Bees winning the replay 3-1, before losing to Bournemouth, 2-1, in the second round.

Evans celebrates after scoring against Shrewsbury, his eighth goal of the season.

The 2-0 April victory put The Bees well on course for promotion.

An eight game undefeated sequence was brought to a halt with a 2-1 Boxing Day defeat at fellow promotion aspirants Huddersfield Town. The only, fairly insignificant, blemish between times was the 6-3 defeat at home to Barnet in the Autoglass Trophy. Therefore, in three cup matches, the pair of Bees' had amassed 23 goals (Brentford 11-12). Having previously beaten Aldershot (their last ever encounter with The Shots) in the two match 'Round Robin', Brentford went on to lose by 3-2 at Leyton Orient in the first round.

The team faltered slightly in the early New Year games, losing to Stockport, West Bromwich and Bury, although balancing this up with victories over Hartlepool, Stoke and Preston (plus two drawn games). Of some concern was the necessary shake-up in the line-ups before and around this time. The biggest loss had been the transfer of inspirational captain Keith Jones to Second Division Southend United for a tribunal fixed fee of £175,000 in November. Benstead, due to a further injury, was replaced with loan signing Perry Suckling for nine matches. Holdsworth missed the occasional match due to injury, whilst Tony Sealy, who returned from a spell in Finland, deputised. A surprise return to Griffin Park, a favourite player to many, was Bob Booker. A former 'Player of the Year' and later a 'super-sub', he had subsequently made a surprise move to Sheffield United where during his three year spell he became a true cult hero,.

The core of the team picked itself, with Blissett, Holdsworth, Smillie and Gayle (who was destined for greater things but frustratingly never really realised his full potential at Brentford), providing and scoring most of the goals, whilst behind them the ever reliable Ratcliffe (who alternated between midfield and right back), was aided by Bates, Evans, Millen and Manuel. Rostron faded from the playing side mid-season and Godfrey more or less disappeared from that time on. Cadette was another absentee latterly, whilst several different players made occasional appearances to bring the total number for the season to 27.

Promotion looked less likely when a poor run continued after the Preston defeat and was followed with a 1-0 reversal at other title contenders Birmingham City, a shock 4-3 home defeat to struggling Bradford City and another at lowly Wigan Athletic. By the time of the visit of Bournemouth on the 29th of March, the Bees had slipped to 4th, and six points behind the leaders Stoke City. But the match with the seaside club was to prove to be the start of the turning point for the team. Although only a 2-2 draw was achieved, followed with a scoreless encounter at Reading, Brentford finished the season in fine fashion winning all their final six games. But not before the manager, Holder, and his team was loudly criticised after the lacklustre match at Elm Park, although perhaps it was this outburst that really woke them up.

Those last few games were exciting ones, and with the addition of Detsi Krusynski, a Polish player from Wimbledon F.C. to bolster the midfield, the ultimate goal was reached. Notable amongst the six last ditch victories was the 3-0 win at another struggling club, Hull City - the first away win surprisingly for five months - and the last two games. The visit of Fulham, the final home match, was played on Sunday the 26th of April with Brentford lying in 3rd place, one point behind Stoke City and two from leaders Birmingham City, who also had a game in hand. With only two games to play, second looked marginally possible, and first close to impossible. 12,071 packed into Griffin Park, with the visitors having an outside chance of reaching the play-offs themselves.

The Bees put on a superb show, and aided by a brilliant goal from Gayle, took a four goal half-time lead which had shattered any hopes for the visitors. However, typically, the second half was a case of, 'after the Lord Mayors Show', with no further goals. This left everything to play for at Peterborough the following Saturday. Things had already swung somewhat in Brentford's favour, with Birmingham only picking up three points from their two matches, and Stoke surprisingly earlier losing their single one (at home to lowly Chester). The team needed to win to claim the Championship, and at least draw to finish second and ensure promotion. Meanwhile, Peterborough were sitting comfortably, having all but ensured a play-off place come what may.

DIVISION 3

As at 16.4.92

	P	W	D	L	F	A	Ps.
Birmingham	45	23	12	10	69	50	81
Brentford	45	24	7	14	80	55	79
Stoke	45	21	14	10	68	46	77
Huddersfield	45	21	12	12	55	38	75
POSH	45	20	14	11	65	57	74
Stockport	45	21	10	14	73	51	73
Bournemouth	45	20	11	14	52	47	71
West Brom.	45	18	14	13	61	48	68
Fulham	45	18	14	13	55	52	67
L. Orient	45	18	11	16	62	51	65
Hartlepool	45	17	11	17	56	57	62
Wigan	45	15	14	16	56	61	59
Bradford	45	13	19	13	61	59	58
Reading	45	15	13	17	56	60	58
Bolton	45	13	17	15	54	55	56
Hull	45	15	11	19	51	54	56
Swansea	45	14	14	17	55	62	56
Preston	45	14	12	19	59	72	54
Chester	45	13	14	18	55	59	53
Exeter	45	14	11	20	55	75	53
Bury	45	13	12	20	55	72	51
Shrewsbury	45	12	11	22	52	65	47
Torquay	45	13	8	24	42	64	47
Darlington	45	9	7	29	51	88	34

How the table looked, before the crucial Peterborough match.

Around 5,000 Bees fans made the journey up the A1 to swell the crowd to 14,539, and a tense atmosphere ensured the game would never be a classic display of good football. But midway through the first half, the event at the far end, sent the visiting supporters into ecstasy, when Gary Blissett scored the all important goal with a header after the ball had rebounded off the crossbar following Terry Evans' shot. A goal that will be remembered by those 5,000 for the rest of their lives. The second half was 45 minutes of shear hell, that seemed more like 45 hours, but with no more goals, the final whistle was greeted with rapturous applause from one end of the ground.

Brentford were promoted, but more good news soon followed. Birmingham City had lost at Stockport County, therefore Brentford were the Champions! Even the Posh fans joined in the celebrations, for despite their defeat they were in the play-offs, and were also subsequently promoted. The irony of the final day was that the Championship Trophy had been taken to Stockport for the expected presentation to Birmingham City, and no doubt the embarrassed officials had to smuggle it away from Edgeley Park under cover, for its subsequent receipt at Griffin Park.

Terry Evans, in the opening First Division game versus Woves.

At times the situation was far from cut and dried, but after 38 long years Brentford would grace the second tier of English football once more. During the season it would be unfair to heap all the accolades on one player, for everybody had played their part, right down to Andy Driscoll and his single substitute appearance plus Anthony Finnigan's three outings (remember him?), but if there was a star, it had to be Dean Holdsworth. The previous season he had shown promise, but this season, and now free of his long term injury, he piled up 37 competitive goals (just one short of the alltime record - albeit in more games) held by Jack Holliday in 1933). It had truly been a memorable season for many reasons, not least of course, The Championship!

1992/93

Due to the re-naming of the different sections, not only were Brentford promoted, but numerically they jumped up by two divisions! From the old Third Division (now Second) they moved to the new First Division (formerly the Second); the First became the Premier Division. Naturally Griffin Park was buzzing with anticipation, and advanced season ticket sales increased by over double to well over 2,000.

But it was recognised that the task ahead would not be easy. There was not the finance to go on a squad-building spending spree, a factor which was considered not really necessary anyway. Based largely on the players accrued two years earlier by Steve Perryman, who championed a more skilful approach to play, but through necessity manager Phil Holder had adapted to the hustle and bustle of lower division football in order to escape from its confines. A more measured approach had now to be adopted and by and large it was felt that Brentford had the players to do it.

One major change was the transfer of the club's greatest asset, Dean Holdsworth. Finance was the obvious reason and Brentford have invariably adopted the policy that they would not stand in the way of a player who was able to better himself at a higher level. What proved to be a bargain buy at £125,000 was transferred into a move valued at £720,000 to Premiership club Wimbledon F.C. The deal included the acquisition of former on-loan player Detsi Krusynski and Mickey Bennett. Holdsworth later moved to Bolton Wanderers for £3.5m. The so called replacement, Murray Jones, was later considered to be one of the worst deals the club have ever made! For a fee of £75,000 from Grimsby Town (supposedly on the recommendation of Keith Millen), Jones was not, and never claimed to be, a goalscorer. This he proved in his one season at Griffin Park, when in 21 appearances he did not hit the target once (although he was unlucky in one home match when his shot hit the post). The criticism by the fans was somewhat unfair since his commitment and outfield play could not be faulted, and despite a wretched time at Brentford he left with no animosity felt towards the club. He later moved and played in China, and his claim to fame was appearing whilst there in a TV Documentary.

Two Junior players moved up to the senior ranks, but never made a mark, whilst a number of others who had only made occasional first team appearances were released, including Guernsey born Lee Luscombe. Off the field the biggest move was Chairman Martin Lange who relocated to the USA for business reasons, and long time supporter Jerry Potter took over the reins. At the ground itself, the 'away' end was changed with home fans moving to the open Ealing Road terrace from the much maligned Brook Road covered standing and seating area.

The season kicked off with a home match when Wolverhampton Wanderers were the visitors. With much the same line-up as a few months earlier the visitors spoiled the party, in front of a crowd exceeding nine thousand, for they won 2-0. In the first round of the Coca-Cola Cup, the

Brentford in Europe!

Bees recorded two 2-0 victories over Fulham, when Booker made another comeback in place of Rostron who had also made a brief re-appearance in the Wolves game. Of great concern was the long term injury of Terry Evans whose knee injury would sideline him for many months. Another defeat, at Bristol Rovers, left the team pointless after two matches.

However, it was not all clouds on the horizon, for home victories over Southend and Portsmouth - an excellent, but somewhat flattering 4-1 thrashing of the latter who had first taken the lead - lifted the team to an early season eighth in the table. This transpired to be their highest. Brentford's promotion entitled them to take part in the Anglo/Italian competition; the club had made it to Europe. An all English 'round robin' produced two victories, over Swindon Town and Oxford United, which opened the gates to Italy.

More importantly things were not looking good in the League as the team went on a win-less run of eight games, four of which were drawn. These matches included meeting the likes of Newcastle United (a Griffin Park all ticket match which was shown live on TV) and Leicester City for the first time on League duty for many years. The team was showing it was somewhat out of its depth, but much could be attributed to injuries that were piling up. Benstead in goal was sidelined for a long period and with Ashley Bayes not really fulfilling the role, Gerry Peyton was loaned from Everton. Players were being asked to play whilst not fully fit, and the only real hope lay with Blissett who at least was scoring goals, which overall the team were unable to do. Blissett was the only ever-present and with 21 League goals to his credit at the end.

In the Coca-Cola Cup, the team performed well at Premiership side Tottenham Hotspur, and although trailing 3-1 there was a slight hope for the second leg. Another all ticket match produced an attendance of 11,445, produced record gate receipts, and another defeat. The tie was all but finished after eight minutes, with the visitors adding two more goals to their total. New signing Grant Chalmers (another Channel Islander) had a good debut and he followed this with a further encouraging performance, a scoreless, dour, draw at Peterborough.

The 3-2 defeat at Barnsley was particularly hard to take, as the Bees had first taken a two goal lead (both scored by Blissett), and four games later this scenario was repeated at Tranmere, when Gayle assisted Blissett with the brace of goals. Between times a very encouraging run of three straight wins was enjoyed, the most impressive being a 5-1 home game thrashing of Bristol City, when most of the damage was done in a devastating 16 minute spell; a week later the 2-0 lead at Swindon was not surrendered. Having slipped to fourth from bottom, only goals scored keeping them above a relegation position, this mini-run lifted the club five places.

Their improved fortunes were due in part to the first major signing for some time, Shane Westley, who made a £100,000 move from Wolverhampton.

Progress in the Anglo/Italian Cup was a rare success in a relegation season.
Joe Allon scores one of his three in the home match versus Derby County.

On the 11th of November, the pressure in the League was turned off, when the team and around 200 supporters made the journey to Ascoli, Italy, in a chartered plane, after a very early morning start from Gatwick. The Bees were in Europe! A long coach ride after the flight took the followers to the Stadio Cino e Lillo Del Duce, the Ascoli stadium. A midweek afternoon game hardly set the Italian emotions alight, and the attendance of just 880 rose to well over 1,000 if the police presence was counted. The setting was more exciting for the supporters rather than the match, but the team coasted through to an easy 3-1 victory, the last goal - from a free kick - being credited to Blissett, but evidence from a supporters' video refutes this one.

A good crowd of over 4,000 was on hand to see Brentford top their cup group, after a 1-0 win over Lucchese, a match best remembered for an over exuberant Italian referee and a second goal from Joe Allon. The Geordie had been a record £275,000 buy from Chelsea, and after scoring four goals (albeit two penalties) in his first five games, it was hoped that coupled with Blissett this would cure the club's low scoring rate. But it was not to be, for after 23 appearances this season, he only netted three more League goals.

Whilst success came in the Anglo/Italian Cup, with further group matches won at Cesena and at home to Bari, the League results were more important, and a six match unbeaten run up to the end of the year gave hope. But this was no more than false hope as events transpired, for after overcoming Derby County at Griffin Park on Boxing Day, only four more win bonuses came their way in the remaining 24 League matches. The worst defeat was an embarrassing 6-1 televised match at Millwall on Sunday the 17th January. One tiny crumb of comfort came from this game, for being the only First Division game played that day and by virtue of their solitary goal, the team rose one place in the table (goals scored rather than goals difference being the league positioning factor)!

Back in the Italian extravaganza the Bees finished top of their group and were pitched against Derby County to contest the English final (the winners to play their Italian counterparts at Wembley). An entertaining home leg was undeservedly lost 4-3, despite a hat-trick from Allon, and further disappointment came at the Baseball Ground for despite winning 2-1 the Bees lost out on the 'away goals count double' rule. Another exit had already come at home to Grimsby Town in the FA Cup competition.

As the team plunged down the table little was done to halt the slump. Several players after encouraging starts failed to impress, and few measures were taken to stem the tide. Paul Mortimer briefly appeared, on loan from Crystal Palace and Paul Stephenson was obtained for a modest fee from Millwall. The latter came to replace the injured Smillie and although an exciting and skilful player at times, during his period at Brentford he tended to flatter to deceive. For two months the team were unable to score a goal in the eight matches played, for even the result at St James' Park, a 5-1 thrashing, saw the Brentford consolation coming from an own goal.

The spell was broken with a 1-0 home victory over Grimsby, and the match saw the welcome return of Terry Evans. This briefly lifted the team to sixth from bottom, but just one point above the safety zone. However, the management refused to panic, despite the club's precarious situation and with few games left for salvation just two largely ineffectual signings were made with the introduction of freebie Alan Dickens from Chelsea, and Everton's veteran Kenny Samson. But it was all too little too late. The home match with Swindon was something of a farce, for despite playing against only nine men for all of the second half, only a scoreless draw was the result.

There was still hope when Notts County were the visitors on the 12th of April. Now lying 8th from bottom and two points clear of relegation, a win against their fellow strugglers was all important. The match should have been won by 2-1, except that after an uneventful second half, referee Mr Bigger, in his wisdom decided to add on eight minutes of extra time; Notts County equalised seven minutes into this period. Just one more win was gained, at home to Barnsley, but a draw in the last match, at Bristol City would have saved the club (and condemned Sunderland as it panned out). But a lacklustre display, which suggested that the team had already considered themselves doomed, produced a 4-1 defeat.

It had taken many years to reach the higher level, but just ten months to drop back again.

1993-94

Relegation was a bitter pill to swallow but the club and the supporters just had to grin and bare it and hope for the best with a return to better times. But for this season that was not meant to be.

Perhaps inevitably manager Phil Holder paid the price and he was sacked in June, whilst Chairman Gerry Potter stood down, and Martin Lange took over again. Potter was a genuine supporter, and although he accepted the vice-Chairman position, he resigned at the year end. Whilst the incumbent pair took all the criticism, injuries, some long term, during the campaign had taken their toll.

David Webb, on the face of it was a good choice to take over the managerial hot spot. In a temporary capacity he had guided Chelsea to safety and previously had managed Southend United well.

Three YTS players were given contracts, but of these only Carl Hutchings was to fulfill his promise to any degree. A sad, but not unexpected departure was that of Bob Booker, who decided to hang up his boots. In all he had been involved with Brentford for 15 years and whilst not being one of the Bees most outstanding of players it would be difficult to find a better clubman, or to criticise him for his lack of wholehearted enthusiasm. But the greatest playing loss was that of Gary Blissett. His 105 goals for Brentford in all competitions ranks amongst the most for the club, and now losing your top goalscorer again, after Holdsworth a year earlier, was difficult to accept.

David Webb.

Ex-Bees favourite Gary Phillips - then with Barnet.

Promotion and then relegation had cost the club dear, for lucrative contracts had been given, and now with less income to look forward to, inevitably the purse strings had to be tightened. A tribunal figure of £350,000 from Premiership Wimbledon for Blissett was far below Brentford's valuation, but at least this popular player had been a good investment at the £60,000 paid to Crewe around six years earlier. Smillie was also coming to the end of his playing career and he moved to Gillingham as player/coach, Kruszynski, moved back to Germany - a player who promised much but never really delivered - and Evans made a surprise move to Wycombe Wanderers on loan.

In a major clear-out most of the fringe players moved on to give new manager Webb a reduced slate from which to build upon. Yet alarmingly few signings were initially made, the most notable being the two Dean Williams' - goalkeeper Dean P. came from non-League Tamworth for a £2,000 fee, whilst Dean A. was bought for £14,000 from St. Albans. Two players formerly under the manager's charge were signed in Paul Smith (Southend United) and Denny Mundee (Bournemouth). The later, self-named, 'Flying Pig' from 'Spurs (and with wide experience on loan at countless clubs), Kevin Dearden, soon became a favourite at Griffin Park, such that he later became the fans 'Player of the Year'.

A fair start was made on the pitch with a 2-1 home win over Exeter City and a 1-1 draw at Blackpool. Between times the Bees made an early exit from the Coca-Cola Cup, Watford winning and drawing in the two first round legs. When Reading were beaten in the third League match, it really looked as if the team may immediately bounce back up. But from a play-off place in the table to 22nd (a relegation spot) soon put paid to that optimistic idea. Seven matches were ground out and just two points were obtained, therefore the victory at Hartlepool United in early October came as a welcome relief.

Inevitably team selections were changed, with 24 players used in the first 11 games and in particular goals were hard to come by, Allon being the only forward to make any impact with just three during this period. He moved on to Southend on loan and on his recall added another seven to his tally in the next few games, before a broken jaw sidelined him, an injury sustained not in a game but in an incident with Mickey Bennett in training! At Brighton the two Williams' made the starting line-up together, but this was never repeated, for neither really made their mark in the team.

Two loan players from Southend - midfielder Steve Tilson and wide player John Cornwall arrived but soon departed, whilst non-League signing, prolific goalscorer, Matthew Metcalfe (from Braintree Town) obviously left his shooting boots in Essex for he recorded no goals in his nine games for Brentford. Fortunately the core of the team, namely Statham, Ratcliffe, Bates, Westley (an earlier Holder signing who was initially a disappointment) and Gayle, prevented any complete disasters. In his first season with the Bees, Denny Mundee made a big impression, turning out in 39 League games and scoring 11 goals.

On the playing front things now started to look up, with seven wins and six draws in a 13 match unbeaten run into the New Year, which lifted the team to 6th in the table. During this time a remarkable transformation came about when midlfielder Mundee was pushed up front and netted, amazingly, nine goals in eight games, including a memorable hat-trick at home to Bristol Rovers (which, perversely, was lost 4-3). Another factor in the Bees upwards surge was the signing of left back Martin Grainger for £60,000 from Colchester United. This tough tackling, no nonsense player soon became a favourite with the fans and frequent name writing, in referees books. Another influential signing, in late November, was Lee Harvey, an experienced attacking midfielder from Nottingham Forest. He became a regular during the season, but injuries were to later blemish his career at Griffin Park. In the other direction, centre half Terry Evans made a permanent move to Wycombe for £40,000. 'Big Tel' had become a favourite with the fans in his eight years at Brentford, during which he amassed 285 first team games, and he was another regrettable missing face.

Simon Ratcliffe coming near to the end of his Brentford career.

The FA Cup produced little joy. A rare trip to a non-League ground, that of V.S. Rugby (formerly 'Valley Sports'), saw a not surprising victory (3-0) but a defeat in the second round at home to Cardiff City. The (Associate Members) Autoglass Trophy paired Brentford with Barnet and Football League newcomers Wycombe Wanderers, from which two clubs would proceed. A 2-2 draw with the other Bees transpired, Wycombe beat the same team 1-0, and consequently in the home match with the Wanderers, the team only had to score a goal to move on. Eventually the Bees achieved their goal and although the game was lost 3-2, the team left the field to loud applause from the three thousand plus crowd, despite the defeat; through to the next round without winning a game! The run ended at Leyton Orient after a 2-0 victory over Hereford United.

After a 4-1 victory at home to Bristol Rovers, in which Allon netted a hat-trick, the Bees had climbed to 5th from top, but this was to be their highpoint of the season. Inexplicably, at this crucial stage, the team crashed out of the running, and in the long final run-in of 16 games (over one third of the total fixtures), not one win was recorded. Half of the games each produced one point, and the club slumped to a final 16th in the table.

Without any real highlights to the season, the principal memory was the incoming and outgoings of players, plus absences due to injury.

After the New Year Ian Benjamin (an earlier signing from Luton Town) who made a promising start, albeit with very few goals, was laid off due to injury, popular 'keeper Benstead moved down to non-League, and previously the third 'B' - Bennett, had been discarded for disciplinary reasons. Long serving Keith Millen moved to Watford for a below par value £100,000 plus new incomer Barry Ashby, and Paul Buckle moved on to Torquay. David Thomspon (from Bristol City) joined the troops in February, but the greatest acquisition for some time was that of Robert Taylor from Leyton Orient, when all the Millen money was well spent.

Feelings regarding Webb the manager were difficult to assess at the time. On occasions he appeared to have put together a promotion team, at others he had obviously recruited some unsuitable players and let others go too easily. Without doubt what was to prove the best move was that of Taylor's from East to West London. Early thoughts were that Webb was going to take the club places as he had at his other clubs and he received strong support in January from the fans to stay put rather than take over at Southampton. As events were later to prove, in fact the majority would wish that he had gone!

1994-95

Whilst the 1993-94 had its moments, this season was to have its highs and could definitely be considered a successful one, but equally a campaign that was to end in heartbreak.

Webb had built up a reasonable squad that at times had shown it was capable of greater things. The main area for reinforcement was on the goalscoring front, for the 57 scored in the League the previous season needed to be improved upon. In this respect the manager unearthed two gems. Nicky Forster was signed for an initial £100,000 (to double dependant on appearances) from Gillingham and Carl Asaba was snatched for a song from non-League Dulwich Hamlet, although he had to wait a year before he made his presence felt.

Gus Hurdle who joined the previous season (having the initiative to turn up at the training ground and boldly ask for a trial) was to feature this season, whilst several former Juniors made the grade, although of these only David McGhee was to make any real impression.

Allon had already departed for Port Vale on a free transfer despite being the club's leading goalscorer with a moderate 13 in League games. George Parris came on loan from Birmingham City but failed to impress in the first few games, and Bob Booker re-signed yet again! This time as Youth team coach.

To say the first League match result was a shock would be putting it mildly. Plymouth Argyle had just missed promotion the previous season, yet were beaten 5-1, with a debut brace from Forster, by the rampaging Bees on the 13th of August; top after one game! This was a Brentford record score for a first of the season away match (and the record opening home defeat for the Devon side) and this after the homesters had initially taken the lead. For once this was a good omen for the task that lay ahead, although a 1-0 first home game defeat to Peterborough produced an unwanted hiccup. But two more victories put the team on the route to a recovery, albeit before three successes defeats left them languishing 15th in the table. But this transpired to be the lowest all season.

Meanwhile, as usual, the Coca-Cola Cup produced no riches. Colchester were first overcome in two legs before defeat to First Division Tranmere Rovers. The fans were not impressed and only 4,157 showed up for the League home game with Blackpool which was won 3-2. The team then began to reassert themselves, for five more victories came their way and lifted them to fourth in the table. Whilst most of these wins were low-scoring, the so-called 'F.T.' partnership was beginning to produce the goods. Forster had already netted eight League goals in 12 games, whilst Taylor had added the same number.

Most notable amongst the victories was that at Crewe, where the team played with only ten men after 30 minutes - Westley being despatched for a second yellow card - but won by 2-0. A generally settled team was not upset by long term injuries, although occasional niggles and hence absentees by now saw only three ever-presents. By the season's end, Forster was left to carry the appearance flag and he became ever-present for the whole season. A 2-1 home defeat to Birmingham City in late October was particularly unfortunate since it was the Midlanders who were destined to take the title and this was also the start of a five match run without a Bees win, with just one point obtained. Then the form book was once again turned upside down when the team went nearly three full months without a League defeat. Most of these successes were moderate affairs, but there were two exceptions. After their poor run, a home victory (Brighton) and a draw at London Road, Peterborough, were recorded, before Plymouth Argyle were welcome visitors to Griffin Park. With memories of the scoreline in the earlier fixture, the Pilgrims must have come with some trepidation, and this proved to be not misguided. A bumper 7-0 victory to the Bees (with six goalscorers on the list) was the result. The overall score against the Devonians thus being 12-1, a Brentford record goal bonanza in any seasonal pairing.

The team gradually climbed the table, from a low of 13th in mid-November, to 2nd, and finally the top spot on the 28th of January, after Cambridge United were severely thrashed at Griffin Park. The second highest home crowd of the season to date, 6,390, were hardly impressed with their favourite's half time performance with the score goalless against their low mid-table opponents. But in the second half the floodgates opened, which commenced with Forster after 63 minutes and finished with the score at 6-0 when Bailey (his second goalscoring header within four minutes) after 90. This was Dennis Bailey's debut, having signed from Q.P.R., and although he scored again in the next match, he was only to play a total of six games for Brentford.

A week earlier, Brentford celebrated their 3,000th Football League match with a 2-1 victory at Hull City, and a week later manager Webb received the Second Division Manager of the Month (January) award. This did not become the typical 'poison chalice', for it was only after 14 League games without defeat that the Bees finally succumbed, on the 25th of February, at Shrewsbury. But the team held on to top spot, on goal difference, with both Birmingham City and Huddersfield Town hot on their heals, all three having recorded 59 points. During the next two months the Bees only occasionally relinquished the top place in the division, as they surged towards the much sought after promotion, albeit with the Midlanders and the Yorkshire team always in close attendance.

Forster nets the winner in the exciting 4-3 home victory over Bradford City.

On the playing front there had been a few earlier changes. Manuel was unable to agree terms with the club and left in September but reappeared at Griffin Park with Cambridge, when to add to that club's misery he was - somewhat harshly - sent off. Yet another Southend player drove around the M25 to Griffin Park on loan, former Bee Andy Ansah, but his stay was shortlived, and John Hooker who had signed from Hertford Town in December, came on as a substitute in just one game. In February winger Paul Abrahams joined the Bees from Colchester for £30,000, and initially he fitted in well, but soon disappointed and moved back to Essex a year or so later.

Injuries were not a major problem, although an horrific one was sustained by Stevenson at Bradford City in early November. The skilful winger, was stretchered off after an hour and was taken to hospital where it was diagnosed that he had a double fracture to the skull, yet he made an amazingly quick recovery and was back in the team three months later. The dependable Smith missed 11 mid-season matches due to a stomach injury, and the ever popular Dearden was absent for just two matches all season, and appeared in 56 first team games. His willing substitute, Tamer Fernandes, was amazingly named in the squad for every game, yet played in only five (including three as substitute).

The three leading teams continued to generally win their games, and Brentford's final trio of matches were destined to become the crunch encounters of the season. The virtual Championship decider was held at St. Andrews on the 26th of April, with Brentford in pole position, three points ahead of Birmingham City, who had a game in hand.

Brentford's goal difference at this time was 78-33, whilst the Brummies was 77-33! The team's opponents were on a high for they had just won the Autoglass Trophy at Wembley, and it was an emotionally charged game played before a 25,581 crowd.

Brentford defended well in the first half, but were unable to hold the home team in the second, who won the match 2-0. The 3,000 or so Bees fans present more or less acknowledged that the Championship was not to be theirs as they slipped into second place, by virtue of just one goal. But there was still a chance (remembering the defeat at the end by Birmingham two years earlier), and the penultimate game of the League season brought Bournemouth to Griffin Park. A victory was vital to both teams, for the Cherries in order to avoid relegation, and a season's best home crowd of 10,079 packed in to what should have been an easy win. Brentford lost 2-1, Bournemouth were saved, and Brentford were shattered.

Lee Harvey scores one of the seven against Plymouth Argyle in December.

The last game saw a 2-2 draw recorded at Twerton Park, versus Bristol Rovers, but even a win would have denied the Bees the Championship, for they finished second trailing Birmingham by four points. Any other season the runners-up slot would have been sufficient cause for celebration but due to re-organisation within the divisions, for the first time in 37 years, only one team was to be automatically promoted. The last occasion in this situation was that of the old Third Division South at the end of the 1957/58 season, Brentford were also runners-up, and the following season two clubs were promoted!

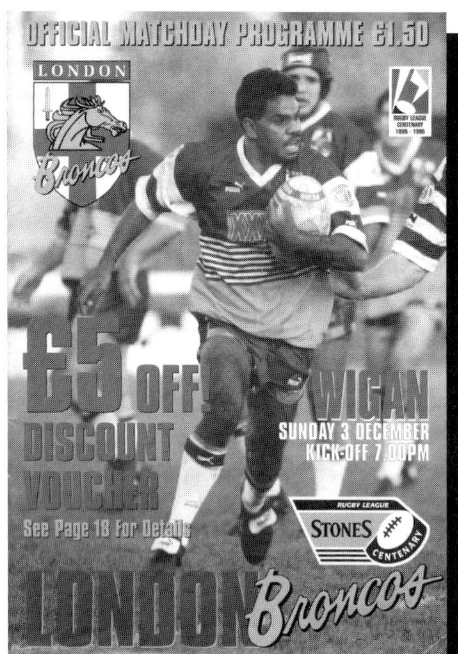

The last ground-sharing season at Griffin

In the play-off semi-final, Brentford travelled to play fifth place Huddersfield Town. The team played well and earned a well merited 1-1 draw, although arguably they deserved to win the game had it not been for two uncharacteristic easy chances missed by Taylor. Hopes were high for the second leg and a capacity 11,161 packed into Griffin Park. But it was not to be, for another 1-1 draw could only be gained after Brentford first took the lead. Extra time produced no more goals, and so agonisingly the game moved on to the penalty shoot-out lottery. It was even in goals until Bates missed his effort, and the Bees had to look forward to another year of Second Division football.

1995-96

Despite the great disappointment of a few months earlier the close season soon passed by, and club and fans alike felt reasonably confident that another promotion push was on the cards - how wrong can you be!

Having a strong squad in all departments, there were few departures or arrivals. The only real surprise was that of Simon Ratcliffe who had performed soundly for Brentford for six years and the fans were displeased with the popular defender or midfield player's move to Gillingham. Paul Stevenson, a very 'hot and cold' player moved North to York City and the big 30 year-old centre-half Shane Wesley travelled to Colchester. New signing Ijah Anderson became yet another player from Webb's old club Southend United to move across London, and after moving to the left back position soon became a crowd favourite. Dean Martin the ex-West Ham player signed on, started well, faded at Christmas and was released at the season's end.

Other moves were not directly football related when the team reverted back to the old one to eleven numbering system (rather than the squad method), whilst in the backroom Keith Loring who had turned around the club's commercial activities resigned, and his role was taken over by Peter Gilham.

The season got off to a modest start which saw the team win three, draw two and lose three of their opening League fixtures (including a single goal defeat at Burnley, when incredibly no fewer than five Brentford shots which found the back of the net were disallowed), placing the team exactly halfway up the Divisional table at 12th. Although they reached the second round of the Coca-Cola Cup, by drawing at Walsall and winning the second leg 3-2, the end came versus Bolton Wanderers. The away leg was narrowly lost 1-0 and the Bees acquitted themselves well, but lost to the Premier League side in the return match at Griffin Park by only 3-2, the goalscorers being Forster and Grainger from the penalty spot. A good start was made in the Auto Windscreens Trophy, with a victory at Bournemouth before a paltry 1,092 and a 1-1 draw at home to Exeter City when just 1,431 turned up, but defeat later came at Griffin Park in the first round when neighbours Fulham snatched a one goal victory (attendance 3,760).

Nothing of special note could be reported in the League except Brentford finding it difficult to score goals, until the 30th of September, when a disappointing 2-1 home defeat to Chesterfield, signalled the start of a terrible run. From a modest mid-table place the team slumped to 22nd (third from bottom) by Christmas, during which time in the League seven defeats were endured, with a single win and three draws. Although the one win was a good 3-0 defeat of Peterborough, just 10 days later a 4-0 thrashing at Notts County was experienced.

The big name signing of Paul Davis from Arsenal, in the twilight of his career, was arguably manager Webb's worst signing! He persevered with the player for seven consecutive first team games, during which the ex-Gunner was a great disappointment and later he was unable to even retain a reserve eleven place. Initially the club fielded a fairly settled team, with dependable Robert Taylor rarely missing a game - leading goalscorer by the New Year but with only five in the poor 16 in total (from 20 games) - whilst midfielder Paul Smith was an ever-present to the season's end. Captain at this time was Jamie Bates and other regulars included Nicky Forster, although he had a generally disappointing season not helped by injuries, Kevin Dearden (whose form never allowed Fernandes a look in), and centre back Barry Ashby who proved that he was well worth his nominal value in the earlier Millen deal.

Brentford heroes Terry Evans and Jamie Bates, both captains for different teams - a 2-1 defeat at Wycombe Wanderers was the result.

The final score was 2-1, which to a degree compensated for the unfair thrashing experienced four seasons earlier. The home fans, already unhappy with their Chairman, sportingly clapped the Brentford team off and the 2,000 Bees supporters who, vocally, had made their presence felt. For their victory the team received the third round 'Littlewoods Giant Killers Award'.

David McGhee had his best season with the Bees, but the handful of goals he scored were insufficient to cause much excitement and Denny Mundee played few games, appearing to be out of favour with the management. Other players that flitted in an out of the team were Carl Hutchings, and two that were later to make their mark, Carl Asaba and Marcus Bent.

Without doubt the club had a talented squad, but coupled with injuries they were all developing and peaking at different times. By the dawn of the New Year, a real danger of relegation had not been on the agenda. At least the FA Cup produced some excitement, although the omens were not good after Conference side Farnborough Town held the Bees to a 1-1 Griffin Park draw. Sensing a giant-killing, the TV cameras were at Cherrywood Road for the replay. The non-Leaguers welcomed Brentford to their somewhat humble home, the match attracting a record attendance of 3,581. The Boro' could not recapture their form of a few days earlier, and the Bees coasted to a 4-0 victory.

On December the 2nd , a third visit of the season was made to Dean Court, Bournemouth, where the Bees Cup form proved better than that in the League. After an early Taylor goal gave the visitors the lead, Ashby was harshly given his marching orders in the second period, then tragedy struck with Statham being stretchered off with a broken leg. Substitute Anderson came on to fill the full back position, and from an indifferent midfielder, his new role was the making of him. By holding their slender lead the team reached the third round for the first time for five years.

Norwich City were visited for the Cup match, the Norfolk team now playing in the First (second tier) Division. Casting League form to the wind once again, the Bees took the lead through an own goal and made it two after 60 minutes through Bent.

Yet another away journey had to be made in the Cup, this time across London to The Valley, Charlton. The ground had by now had its capacity very much reduced, but the 15,000 represented a new record for the completely revamped enclosure; of these 3,000 were from Brentford (transport included 18 coaches). Postponed due to freezing weather, the match was played on the 7th of February, by which time the next round had been drawn, the reward for the London cup-tie winners, being a trip to Anfield. Another stunning display rocked the high flying First Division team, yet the Bees were 2-1 down into the second period. Smith equalised and another shock result was well on the cards, before the homesters scored a very late and undeserved winner from a shot that went in off the post.

Buoyed by the Cup run, the second half of the season was fortunately a big improvement on the first, although goalscoring was still a problem. The team very gradually moved away from the relegation zone to safety and by the season's end they finished 15th in the table. Hardly cause for celebration in view of the hoped for success back in August, but at least relief from the dire position a few months earlier.

A few late additions to the team had differing experiences. Loan signing Scott Canham from West Ham initially impressed in midfield and although later becoming a permanent move to Brentford, he arguably was never given a real chance under three successive Griffin Park managers. Another loan signing, from Luton Town, David Greene played in most of the later games, whilst the ever willing Joe Omigie made the occasional appearance.

But a big disappointment was the late season move of tenacious Martin Grainger, who for £400,000 moved to Birmingham City where he also became a crowd pleaser.

As the season petered out, Eric White, matchday programme editor for a near record 37 years (surpassed at the time only by the Crewe Alexandra scribe) died in early April. A fierce defender of Brentford whatever, he had been elected as Deputy President of the club, a well earned position that he was proud to hold.

1996-97

Every club has its ups and downs, some more than others, and all Bees fans would class themselves as belonging to the 'more than others' group. On the verge of promotion, then at one time on the precipice ready for relegation. What next? The 1996/97 season certainly had its thrills!

Confident of having built up a solid squad, there were few player movements and none of any great significance. Three players were given free transfers, viz. Hooker - a low key buy from non-League who only managed a handful of appearances, Ravenscroft - local born he too only played occasionally in the first team during his three years before moving on to Woking, and Martin - a good start in his only season at Griffin Park, but his form slipped dramatically. Conversely Bates was given a Testimonial for his ten years service, his initial first team appearance being made in September 1986. Incoming were four players who never got the pulse racing - Malcolm McPherson, Kevin Dennis, Richard Goddard and Stuart Myall.

The first League match produced a 1-1 draw at Bury, the Gigg Lane outfit becoming surprise champions at the season's end. The line-up showed no drastic changes from that of the previous season, Hurdle replacing Statham who was still recovering from a long term injury, and two less familiar faces in Bent and Asaba. Two victories followed, including a very entertaining 3-2 home victory over Luton. The other match (2-0) was rather like meeting an ex-Brentford club, with no fewer than five ex-Bees in the Gillingham squad.

The next game was at Shrewsbury and the true worth of Asaba shone through as he scored a record-breaking League hat-trick for Brentford, netting the trio in an incredible seven minutes first half blitz before a 400 band of delighted Bees fans. There were other goalworthy efforts, not least two Asaba shots cleared off the line in the second period. The defence was strong, and although only early in the season the team really looked as if it meant business.

By the end of September the Bees topped the Second Division table by a clear four points from second placed Millwall, having won six and drawn three of the nine League games. Webb was therefore deservedly awarded the divisional manager of the month award. This excellent form was based on a sturdy resilient defence and goalscoring players. Asaba leading the way with ten, aided by Taylor (five) and Forster (four) after the 2-1 victory at Bristol City on the 1st of October. These feats included goals scored in the 3-2 home leg win over Plymouth in the Coca-Cola (League) Cup, which, after a scoreless draw in Devon, pitched the club into battle with familiar higher division opponents Premier League Blackburn Rovers in the next round. Two defeats put the Bees out of this competition at this stage.

The first defeat in the Second Division finally came at Crewe on the 12th October, after 11 matches, but then, following a 1-0 victory at Peterborough, the team still led the table, now by six points ahead of Bury. Perhaps inevitably a lean period followed during which only three points (from draws) were picked up in five matches, which was sufficient to allow Millwall to sneak in above The Bees in the table.

One of the defeats was against Bristol Rovers who had now moved to their new home, the Memorial Ground, the home of Bristol Rugby Club. Arguably little better than their former Twerton Park (Bath City F.C.) Ground this venue was still poor by League standards. One goal down at half-time a second was conceded in very dubious circumstances. Hearing a whistle, presumably for offside, Dearden placed the ball outside his area, withdrew to take the kick, whereupon a Rovers player nipped in and scored. The whistle had come, not from the referee, but from an unidentifiable person behind the goal. A similar incident had happened in the past at this venue it was claimed, when again the whistler was, surprisingly, never heard by the home manager and his players!

The FA Cup sortie this season produced a 2-0 home victory over Second Division rivals Bournemouth and then an intriguing game against non-League Sudbury Town from Suffolk. The match was played at Layer Road Colchester when two David Webbs came face to face (respective managers), before a crowd of 3,973 overcharged fans - tickets costing more than the incumbent Football League club charged for their home matches. The hosts had notably despatched Brighton in the first round and took a shock first half lead in this game. The Bees even then never really looked troubled and two early goals in the second period plus a second from Taylor in the 74th minute clinched an eventual comfortable victory. The third round in January required another encounter with Manchester City, but this time the Bees lost 1-0 at home.

The club's early season good form was undoubtably due to an almost unchanged starting eleven. Forster through injury missed four matches and it was debatable who should take over.

Marcus Bent, not unlike his namesake - Gayle - was an unquestionably talented player who never really made his mark at Griffin Park, yet his later move proved his true value. Scott Canham, although by now a permanent Brentford man never displayed the skills he had shown whilst on loan, while Paul Abrahams it was felt was never given a real chance and his transfer back to Colchester United in October was seen by many as premature.

Four days after the Bournemouth cup match, the team and fans were back at Dean Court for League action. Although the game was lost 3-1, it was little short of a farce. Torrential rain all day left the pitch a quagmire and the away terrace flooded and uninhabitable with a further downpour during the match. Brentford might have been playing well and up with the best of them, but luck was certainly not in their favour when they were required to play in conditions such as these. Despite such an overall encouraging first half of the season, the Brentford public were slow to respond. Until Christmas the best home attendance was only 7,691, for the top of the table local derby with Millwall (a scoreless draw) in late October and little over a month later a lowly turn out of 3,675 were there for Notts County's visit, the 2-0 victory lifting the team back into top place.

Although, in context it was seen as of little importance, the Auto Windscreens Shield produced a 2-0 victory at Bristol Rovers, providing some consolation for the earlier defeat, a 2-1 victory over Barnet and exit at the southern quarter final stage when the team lost 1-0 at Colchester. Poor weather over the Christmas and New Year period resulted in postponed matches (the FA Cup tie on two occasions), but a magnificent run of 14 undefeated games from mid-November into early March kept the team well in line, if not for the Championship, at least the runners-up spot.

There were few comprehensive victories, save for Plymouth Argyle, who were battered again on their home ground, 4-1, on Boxing Day. In fact, despite the potential firing power in the squad, matches in which more than two goals were scored were rare, and the successes were mainly down to a resolute defence which had eight clean sheets during the winning sequence. But it all came to an end on March the 8th, for after heading the table from late November, the team lost to middle of the table Preston North End. A week later the team crashed 3-0 at home to promotion chasing Burnley before a crowd of nearly 9,500, the best to date at home in the League. Bad luck comes in threes so the say, and so it was with Brentford, for they then proceeded to lose 1-0 at Luton, and consequently slipped to second in the table.

Kevin Raply
An exciting prospect who came up from the Juniors but never made the big-time.

This was not the right time (is there ever?) to suffer a string of defeats, and although they did recover slightly the team were never able to recall their earlier dominance in the division. The end of the season was heartbreaking for the fans, as the team completed the normal League fixtures with four consecutive defeats, each by 1-0. This dropped them to fourth, and so the dreaded play-offs again, whereas their position little more than a month before would have meant automatic promotion.

But one factor responsible for the team's apparent lack of form, that far from being contributory was in most supporters' eyes the actual cause. Under no pressure to sell and hopefully heading towards a higher division, the bombshell was dropped when Nicky Forster was sold to Birmingham City for a bargain fee of £700,000. It was unbelievable that in all the circumstances such a situation could have happened. But such was the action at the club at this time, and incredibly the first of a quartet of arguably the most talented and lethal strikers in the Second Division was allowed to move on (the others were soon to follow).

But surprisingly the loss of Forster initially didn't appear to affect the team, and the next match was won at fellow promotion chasing Stockport County. But disharmony was becoming apparent, and this no doubt led to the caving in at the end. To balance the loss, the manager in his wisdom had signed Q.P.R. striker Steven Slade on loan; he played in four matches without scoring. Then the top marksman of the team, Asaba was unbelievably switched to the wing soon after Forster's departure, this resulted in the last 18 games with just six goals to his credit; in total that season he scored 23 in the League in 44 outings. It was questioned by many, did Brentford, or more pointedly, did the manager, want promotion?

A visit to Ashton Gate for the first leg of the play-off semi-finals was hardly relished, as in the recent form table (for the last six games), Bristol City were top (with one defeat), whilst the Bees were fifth from bottom with no victories and only four draws. But the form book didn't count, for as early as the 13th minute Smith put the Bees ahead. City came back strongly and equalised before half time, yet in a highly entertaining match, Brentford refused to play for the away draw and they scored the winning goal through Taylor just two minutes later.

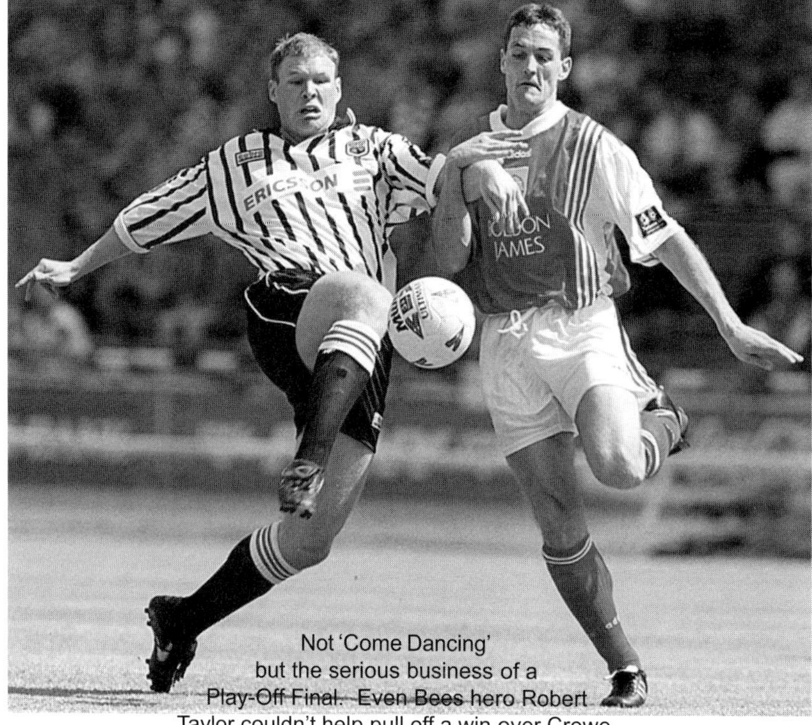

Not 'Come Dancing' but the serious business of a Play-Off Final. Even Bees hero Robert Taylor couldn't help pull off a win over Crewe.

Suddenly the confidence was back and the second leg was keenly anticipated, with a real chance of competing in the final at Wembley. The game was played before 9,946 supporters from both teams, and perhaps the loudest and longest rendering of the Bees 'anthem' *Hey Jude* was sung with enthusiasm. It was a very nervy game and when Bristol City took the lead the worst was feared. But once again the team didn't sit back, but instead equalised in the second half and then for good measure also won this second leg 2-1. So a Wembley final it was on May 25th.

Now, the ever optimistic supporters really thought that this would be their day after coming back to form at such a crucial time. But their opponents Crewe Alexandra, who had already completed the double over the Bees, were not going to be a pushover. From a Brentford standpoint the game was awful! For about the first ten minutes the Bees looked the better team, but Crewe slowly edged into the match, playing fluent football and it came as no surprise when they took a first half lead. Brentford looked ever more ragged as the game wore on, the defence having lost the confidence they had displayed all season and the attack becoming ever more desperate to get the equaliser.

As their play got worse Statham made a reckless and unnecessary challenge for which he received a red card. The fans knew then that this was it, and almost thankfully the whistle signalled the end of the match. Another opportunity was lost, a season wasted, could it get more depressing. Well, yes, actually it could!

1997/98

The summer of 1997 was one of gloom for those involved with the Griffin Park club. Many clubs would have envied the performances of The Bees the previous season and would expect greater things in the months to come. However, football history often produces just the opposite effect, and so it was for Brentford.

Chairman Martin Lange made no secret that he no longer wanted a controlling interest in the club and wished to sell his shares in the club. However, it came as something of a surprise when a consortium of manager David Webb, director John Herting and an 'unknown' man, Tony Swaisland, took over. Swaisland, claimed to have been a long time supporter of the club, and referred to his dog named 'Griffin Park', but his affection for The Bees appeared to have been a well kept secret! Webb's undoubted ability as a manager wasn't questioned, but the earlier selling of Forster (seen by most Brentford fans as being at the cost of promotion), followed by the offloading of other star performers meant that his improving the lot of Brentford certainly was open to conjecture.

Any expected hopes of promotion were soon dashed when a trio of the team departed just prior to the start of the season. Barry Ashby was the first to go, for a tribunal bargain fee of £140,000, to Gillingham. Part of a player swap with Watford, he had become a major influence in the Brentford defence during the previous three years. Brian Statham also moved to Priestfield, but for an undervalued £10,000 fee, then immediately after the most telling transfer occurred. Leading goalscorer Carl Asaba was signed by Reading manager, ex-Brentford player Terry Bullivant, for £800,000. Whilst this was a record fee for both clubs, it wasn't until his move to the new high-spending Gillingham a year later, that he proved his real worth.

With a depleted team, the Chairman recognised that the remaining squad needed strengthening, and efforts were being made to bring in new players. But little of the near £1m was spent in this way. Two free transfers - a pair of Simons' - Wormull and Spencer, both midfielders from 'Spurs, barely featured in the Brentford first team before they moved on and a step up from the Juniors of Ryan Denys hardly set the team alight.

The new consortium: Herting, Swaisland and Webb.

£60,000 was spent on Stevenage Borough's Paul Barrowcliff, but he went back to his old club on loan after a fairly short period and 34 year old former favourite Graham Benstead returned principally as goalkeeping coach, which was seen as a somewhat unnecessary expense. Dennis, Omigie, McPherson and Bent were all on the transfer list, the latter being the only player to later make a real mark elsewhere.

The expectation of doom amongst the supporters was soon confirmed when the team of eleven individuals were comprehensively beaten 3-0 at Millwall and the next game, at home to Third Division Shrewsbury in the Coca-Cola cup - a 1-1 draw - hardly set the pulses racing. That day the club announced the new management team at Griffin Park, but this was hardly greeted with enthusiasm. The new manager was 'unknown' Eddie May, one time in charge at Cardiff City, and after touring Europe, latterly in part-time management in Northern Ireland, who was assisted by the highly experienced former player Clive Walker. The new manager was quick to repeat the earlier words of the Chairman Swaisland, that new players were being sought and would be signed. This announcement produced Charlie Oatway, a £10,000 buy from Torquay. Hardly a move to set the pulses racing, but the likeable Londoner proved to be a reasonable acquisition, although he became more famously known for his eleven first names - those of the QPR stars of the 1970's

A reasonable goallesss home draw with Chesterfield, preceded another poor performance, this time at Watford. Therefore few Bees fans would have forecast one of the very few highlights of an overall disastrous season that unfolded at Shrewsbury's Gay Meadow a few days later. Just 109 supporters made the trip to Shropshire, but they were entertained by a dazzling display.

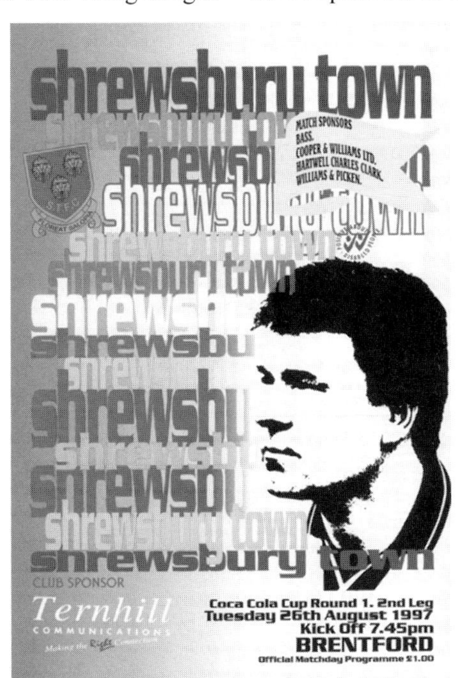

A determined team led 3-0 at half-time, then allowed their opponents to pull two goals back, before Taylor (arguably the only quality player left on the books) netted a second. Man of the match Kevin Rapley made it 5-2 before the Shrews scored a third in the 81st minute.

But this was only a cup match, and in the League, the team were lying bottom of the divisional table. But two good results followed, a 3-1 win over eventual promotion winners Grimsby, then another home game, versus 'ex-Brentford' in the shape of Gillingham, who could display over half a team of ex-Bees. Statham was made to feel most unwelcome, since it was felt that he had deserted Brentford after the club had earlier retained him during his long injury. The crowd were 'rewarded' when he was sent off. A unique and unwanted hat-trick, for he also received his marching orders in his first match against The Bees, playing for Reading plus in his last appearance for Brentford (at Wembley).

The crowd barracked the directors asking *"where's the money gone"*, however, it became apparent that this was not to be spent on new players, but rather set aside for the inevitable end of season losses, the board not having the personal capital to bail the club out. Derek Bryan was a modest purchase from Hampton - but he only made infrequent appearances, hampered as he was with frequent injuries - and worse still was Ricky Reina who arrived with an undisclosed knee injury which led to his retirement a few months later.

With the team lying third from bottom in early November, manager May was given his marching orders. Although criticised by the majority, apart from his lack of recent knowledge of the English game he more or less inherited a by now overall indifferent squad and was not allowed to spend any real money to improve it. The new manager was Mickey Adams from Fulham, whose reward for promotion for The

Cottagers had been the sack, in favour of Kevin Keegan. Such is football!

No longer a hero to the fans!

Adams' number two, and still a player, was Glenn Cockerill, whose leadership qualities lifted the players and fans, but, as it transpired, not sufficiently. At this time Webb stood down as Chief Executive, a move greatly appreciated by the supporters who by now were displaying the 'Red Card' for the former manager, in direct contrast to three years earlier when he was urged to stay! He had in any event been rarely seen at Griffin Park, and was retained as a 'consultant', which ensured he was paid out on his contract. Webb's actions over the previous eight months or so (which started with the sale of Forster) reinforced the feelings of many supporters - was he really looking after the best interests of Brentford F.C.

Adams was able to attract a few reasonable players to the club, including veteran Nigel Gleghorn (from Burnley on loan), much travelled Warren Aspinall from Carlisle, plus Sheffield United's Andy Scott. The latter made little impact initially (despite scoring on his debut), but he went on to become a popular player at Brentford for four years, before his return to Griffin Park ten years later in a completely different role. One necessary replacememt was at left back, for Ijah Anderson had sustained a long term injury and Adams moved quickly to sign experienced Paul Watson from Fulham; the manager once described the player as having *'a sweet left foot'*, unfortunately The Bees fans were rarely to witness this! A late season £75,000 signing from Fulham was Danny Cullip, who was worthy of a greater stay than two years.

Despite the changes and additions, as the season progressed wins continued to be a rare commodity, and by the New Year just five victories had been recorded in the League, leaving the club still perilously close to relegation, at fourth from bottom. Much earlier, in the Coca-Cola Cup second round, the team lost over the two legs to Premiership Southampton - the first time the two clubs had met for nearly 40 years, whilst in the FA Cup they succumbed, in a replay, to Colchester United after a penalty shoot-out.

Just six more wins were recorded in the second part of the season and with only 50 points, the team's fourth from bottom final placing ensured relegation to the basement division. There had been little of note achieved during this period, apart from Micky Adams' move out of retirement for his only Bees appearance, when he came on as a substitute at Luton in the Auto Windscreens Shield match (a 2-1 defeat) and the only five figure home gate of the season. For the latter, promotion bound Fulham were the visitors, and victors, in mid-April, when the home fans were almost the minority. The final nail in the coffin came at the Memorial Ground, Bristol, when over 700 faithful fans did their best to urge the team to victory, but despite Rapley's second half goal, this did not prevent a 2-1 defeat. As the Bees went down, their opponents confirmed a play-off place for themselves.

A dreadful season that started and ended with despair, in which there had been no real highlights of substance. But things were soon to change dramatically, for the far better, at least initially.

1998/99

Every football club has its ups and downs; it's the name of the game. In this respect, Brentford were no exception, particularly over the previous decade. But coupled with the changing face of football, those ups and downs during the next ten years turned to mountains and valleys for the club and the supporters.

With no money to spend, a manager, who despite his credentials was unable to save Brentford from relegation, a board who effectively had done nothing to improve the lot of the club over the previous twelve months, although there were by now were only a few debts. Now, there was the prospect of playing football in the lowest League tier for the first time in twenty years. If twelve months earlier there had been an air of gloom around Griffin Park, now there was the real prospect of struggling at the lowest level, or even worse.

A knight in shining armour was needed, and he arrived, or did he? This was left for the fans to decide for themselves.

In the Auto Windscreens Shield, Wycombe were beaten 4-1 at Adam's Park. Quinn (seen here getting the third), Scott (2) and Fortune-West, his only one for the club, were the goalscorers.

Ron Noades, although with a non-football background, first took a real interest in the game in 1974 when he took over at non-League Southall, and during his time there the club were promoted to the Second Division of the Isthmian (now Ryman) League. In 1976 he bought Wimbledon F.C., and a year later helped guide them into the Football League. He soon became the owner of Crystal Palace and over a long period of time the club rose from a mediocre second tier club to the Premier League and a first FA Cup Final appearance.

Before leaving the South London club in 1998 he had overseen the transformation of Selhurst Park and put the club on a stable financial footing. He obtained a coaching certificate and in his unofficial scouting role he discovered a number of high-profile players. On paper his credentials were a good omen for the future. Whilst in hindsight the majority of fans would say that a new owner with more the welfare of Brentford at heart should have been sought, none was forthcoming, and Noades' arrival was the immediate answer to the club's salvation. For around £850,000 he bought out Webb's majority shareholding in the club.

One of Noades' first tasks was to install himself as team manager. This initially alienated the fans for this meant the departure of Micky Adams, who had built up respect with the supporters, but it has to be remembered that he hardly improved the lot of the club during his few months at Griffin Park.

Frustrating at times -Tony Folan.

Noades immediately acquired a highly experienced coaching team in Ray Lewington (Palace coach), Terry Bullivant (former Brentford player and Reading manager), plus Brian Sparrow whose last association was also at Selhurst Park. It was made clear that the coaches would coach, and the manager would manage!

Money for new players was soon made available, albeit after a few departures. Carl Hutchings had become a worthy squad member and he moved to Bristol City for a bargain price, Glenn Cockerill inevitably moved on as did Scott Canham who disappointingly never reached his expected potential. Paul Barrowcliffe was another departee and despite looking useful in the pre-season friendlies, Niall Thompson wasn't taken on. In their place, Noades made some shrewd and worthwhile signings.

Darren Powell from Hampton cost little, and Martin Rowlands from Farnborough at £45,000 was an excellent purchase, as was Slough Town's Lloyd Owusu - at various times this trio were to become firm favourites at Griffin Park and later they each moved on to higher levels. Goalkeeper Jason Pearcey was unlucky. Signed from Grimsby he was first choice for the first few months of the season before breaking a finger.

He was unable to regularly regain his place in the team, and in 2001 was forced to retire with a serious leg injury. Defenders Robert Quinn (£40,000) and Danny Boxall (free transfer) were useful additions from Crystal Palace, and Fulham's Darren Freeman also joined. With an emphasis on youth, the new look team at this stage did not cost a fortune.

There was some scepticism about the lack of money spent on these mostly unknowns, but whatever the criticisms levelled at the new manager, he and chief scout John Griffin were to prove that they had chosen wisely. The one real disappointment was the transfer of fans' favourite Robert Taylor who moved to, almost inevitably, Gillingham at a bargain price of £400,000. Whilst this could have been seen as a money making exercise, the fact remained that Taylor was determined to better himself, albeit only up one division, but to a team that was determined to buy themselves promotion.

A much changed side from the previous season, had just six players from before in the starting line-up for the first match. Mansfield were easily overcome by 3-0, and for the crowd of nearly 5,000 this was an encouraging start this basement season. The next match required a visit to The Hawthorns and First Division West Bromwich in the Worthington (League) Cup. Being two goals down at half-time - and it could have been more - despite a bright start, it looked all up for the visitors, yet they fought back strongly and scored with an 89th minute Rapley goal.

The second leg of the tie was a revelation. Playing cultured football not seen for a long time at Griffin Park, The Bees overwhelmed The Baggies, and thoroughly deserved their 3-0 victory. There was no further progress, for Brentford narrowly lost to Tottenham Hotspur by 3-2 in both legs of the second round, but the gates of nearly 12,000 and 23,000 were welcome financial bonuses.

Two of the season's signings: Top - Darren Freeman, and below - Martin Rowlands.

Meanwhile the team had lost at Halifax Town, newly promoted from the Conference, but redeemed themselves with four consecutive League victories, which took the team to second in the table, and after winning 3-2 at Hull City on the 5th of September they topped it. But three defeats followed by which time they had slipped to seventh.

The last of these, proved to be the first and last, visit to Seamer Road the home of Scarborough F.C. Cullip sustained a bad injury in the Tottenham cup game which kept him out for the rest of the season and Chris Coyne from West Ham was brought in on loan but after seven games a more substantial replacement was considered necessary.

And the latest signing could hardly have been more substantial. A figure of £750,000 was generally quoted for the transfer of Hermann Hreidarsson from Crystal Palace, although it is believed the true figure was nearer one half a million. In any event the fee was by far a new club record and also one for a Third Division club. A colossus of a central defender, the Icelandic International was way above the standards found in Third Division football. The 'Iceman' soon became a favourite with the crowd, noted for his accurate passing and converting defensive moves to attacking ones with a calm assurance. He was without doubt one of the best players to wear a Brentford shirt in modern days. This signing rather overshadowed that of Tony Folan who cost £100,000, the Irishman also coming from Palace.

Folan could well have become a top class player if it hadn't have been for his inconsistent performances which prevented him from becoming a regular first choice in the team. But he scored an amazing goal at Peterborough (a 3-2 Bees victory) when he came on as a late substitute. Initially a clever acute angle lob evaded the 'keeper, but hit the bar, yet within a minute Folan appeared on the other side of the goal. From near the corner flag he beat a defender jinked into the penalty area where he beat a second man, then the first player again - Dean Hooper an ex-Hayes man - before sending in an accurate lob which this time sailed over the goalkeeper and into the net. An amazing debut goal and what proved to be the match winner.

The match at Plymouth on the 10th of September was postponed due to three Brentford players on International duty (Folan, Hreidersson and Boxall) - a double record since this was first time that Brentford had been 'honoured' in this way, and also the first such cancelled match for a Third Division club. The Bees had little trouble in home matches, winning all but one of the first seven, but often failing in their away fixtures, including a heavy 3-0 defeat at the match re-arranged at Plymouth (albeit finishing with only ten men after Bates was harshly sent off) and by 2-0 at Shrewsbury. One of the strangest of transfers was that of Drew Broughton just prior to the latter game. Brentford won the race with Peterborough to sign the striker from Norwich for £15,000, and he played at Gay Meadow for 56 minutes before being substituted. Then a few days later was sold on to the Posh for the same fee!

A bargain buy and a terrific sale - Hermann Hreidarsson.

There was then a break from League action with the visit to Griffin Park of little non-Leaguers Camberley Town in the F A Cup. Both teams normally wore red and white shirts, and both changed, The Bees opting for their blue and yellow away strip. Probably uniquely the matchday programme recognised the occasion with it being predominantly blue instead of the usual red. The Surrey team were comfortably dispatched by 5-0, but Brentford progressed no further losing in a penalty shoot-out to Oldham Athletic, in a home replay. A victory would have produced a very rare visit by a top division team, that of Chelsea in the third round - a money spinning tie.

The Oldham replay featured on Sky TV and three days later the Bees were on the 'box' again when Cambridge United came to Griffin Park; the first time a Third Division team had been twice featured live within a week. On a rain drenched pitch the Bees won again, thanks to the enigmatic Folan, who produced a wonder 40 yard lobbed goal. He tried this feat again in the second half, but on this occasion the by now wary goalkeeper tipped the shot over the bar.

The Bees earlier suffered an outrageous 2-1 defeat at Brisbane Road, Leyton Orient, due principally to several unfathomable decisions by one of the referee assistants (shades of the cup match at Norwich few years earlier). The far distant assistant signalled an infringement and a penalty for the homesters, despite the much closer referee who saw no such incident. Then several lesser, but none the less incomprehensible, decisions were given in favour of the East London side. A rumour was spread after the match that the assistant was a friend of a member of the Orient board! The person in question was one Wendy Toms who had made a rare female inroad into officialdom at this level of football, but won no support from the visitors. The referee did not escape criticism for after making a gesture (bowing to the Brentford fans), following chants of *'Two-one to the referee'*, he was censured by the League for his action.

A Boxing Day defeat came at Gillingham, versus Brighton, who had made Priestfield their temporary home. But when table-toppers Cardiff City came to Griffin Park, The Bees were still well in contention, just one place below the Welshmen. The match was not an all ticket affair, for the Cardiff officials had predicted around just 2,000 travelling supporters, but on the day an estimated 5,000 besieged the ground (their home attendances earlier in the season never matched this figure). In order to avoid more criminal damage (several cars had been vandalised by those who were unable to gain entry to the ground), the police allowed many in free of charge. Once again the bad reputation of this club's 'fans' was exposed. The official crowd numbered 9,535, and a satisfying 1-0 victory to Brentford ensued.

Whilst the supporters were enjoying the overall success of the team, Noades recognised there were shortcomings, and moved to bolster the team. Once again a very shrewd move brought non-League Hereford's Gavin Mahon to Griffin Park back in November, for a bargain £50,000 (rising to £90,000 on appearances), which was well repaid in his performances and subsequent move to Watford. Other occasional members of the team were the German, Dirk Hebel, from Tranmere Rovers, who after some appearances went missing due to injury and never made it back, plus striker Scott Partridge, who was a late addition to the squad, in February. One of the more expensive signings (£100,000) from Torquay, he scored seven goals in the last 14 League games. Finally Paul Evans who signed during transfer deadline week from Shrewsbury Town, for the same fee as Partridge.

Evans immediately took over the captaincy of the team, and whilst he was not always the best player on the pitch, he will be long remembered for some sensational goals and arguably the most inspirational team captain seen at Brentford for many years.

One player in the squad who turned out to be a huge disappointment was Leo Fortune-West. Signed for £60,000 from Lincoln City he wore a Brentford shirt for just three months before moving on to Rotherham at a loss of £15,000. Despite his prolific goalscoring before and after his short Brentford career, he could claim just one goal to his name for The Bees, that being one of the four that were netted at Wycombe in the Auto Windscreens Shield. In this competition, The Bees went out at the Southern quarter-final stage, after a scoreless draw then losing on penalties, at home to Walsall.

Darren Powell (from non-League Hampton) - a dynamo in the Brentford defence.

A capacity crowd at the Abbey Stadium included a packed open end of Bees fans, and their enthusiasm was rewarded when Owusu scored the winner in the second half. Finishing two points ahead of United, Brentford made a quick exit from Division Three after just one season. Noades, not always the best friend of the press, could not be denied the divisional manager of the season award and amongst the fans was acclaimed the hero of the day. But in a few short years this was all to change!

Other players worthy of mention during this exciting season were goalkeeper Andy Woodman (a £75,000 buy from Northampton in January), who took over after Dearden played in goal for a few games, Ijah Anderson who fought back from his long injury and appeared in two thirds of the games plus the enthusiastic Derek Bryan who was used mainly as a substitute.

The second half of the season saw more of the same, with the team winning fairly regularly, but it was the final run-in when they proved their real sustained ability. Fourth from top after losing at Swansea in mid-February, the team remained in the promotion position of third from four days later, when they won 4-2 at Rotherham, until the penultimate game. The highlight during this period was the 4-1 victory at Roots Hall, Southend. Leading goalscorer Lloyd Owuse netted a hat-trick (and frustratingly missed as many others) in the rout. But in March, with some sorrow, the club said goodbye to Jamie Bates who moved to Wycombe. Having made 419 League appearances he stands third in line for the most with the club.

On May 1st, Exeter City were beaten 3-0 at Griffin Park, Partridge being one of the goalscorers - his third in consecutive games - and with this result, The Bees confirmed they would be promoted. After beating Swansea 4-1 three nights later, for the first time since early September the team led the table and the Championship decider was destined to be at Cambridge the following Saturday - for United had also been promoted.

1999/00

Rather appropriately the book *Brentford F.C. 1989 - 1999- Ten Traumatic Years,* was published around the start of the season. It was an apt title, for the club indeed had seen a traumatic period with a procession of players (good and bad), managers (successful, otherwise and controversial), with the joys of promotions (two) and relegation (two), plus a number of interesting cup sorties. Any thought that football at Griffin Park would progress in a dignified, and hopefully successful run was soon dismissed!

After the roller-coaster ride and success of the previous season, it came as no surprise that there were relatively few player movements - in or out - at Griffin Park.. Paul Watson who never became a regular or indeed a favourite with the crowd, moved on to join Micky Adams (now the Brighton manager), as did Charlie Oatway. The often volatile Warren Aspinall had already gone, Mahon having taken over his position, and Kevin Rapley of which so much was expected, moved on to Notts County for £50,000. Sadly, the 'flying pig' (his words) Kevin Dearden at last said farewell when he moved north to Wrexham.

Noades considered that the squad required little strengthening (the departed players being considered no real loss), and his early signings cost little, and indeed produced little.

Gavin Mahon was another excellent buy who after a spell moved up to a higher division.

Philip Warner came on long term loan from Southampton but rarely featured in the first team, likewise full signing David Theobald from Ipswich, although he did prove useful, but only nearly two years later. Richard Kennedy from Wycombe Wanderers played a few games, notably at his old club, where he was sent off, and 18 months later the midfielder drifted into non-League football. Three players came up from the Juniors, but Clement James and Nevin Saroya (although local born he was the first Asian player at Griffin Park) never made the grade. Conversely Michael Dobson (son of former Bee,George Dobson) eventually became a great success at the club, including at one time the role of team captain.

Paul Evans with one his 'specials' was one of the goalscorers in the 2-2 draw at Burnley.

Compared to a year earlier, everything in the garden was rosy, except perhaps for one factor. After a dismal 1997/98 season and relegation, support at the gate was at an average of 5,029 and this was no surprise being about 15% down on a year earlier. Yet this last promotion campaign saw an average rise to only 5,444, a figure which must have severely disappointed Noades who had always considered that if you had a successful and exciting team the crowds would flock back.

The season started reasonably with a scoreless draw at Bristol Rovers, when Hreidarsson received a red card - an inauspicious start. The Worthington (League) Cup exploits ended, more or less as usual, with defeat in the first round, to Ipswich by 2-0 in each leg. The League campaign, however, started strangely, for the first defeat didn't come until the 11th match, by 2-1 at home to Gillingham in mid-October. Before this game The Bees were in an encouraging 5th place, which would have been higher if it had not been for their five draws.

However, working back to, and including, the 1998/99 season, this produced an unbeaten run of 26 League games, a club record. During this run, when Preston were the visitors, a goal was scored that will forever go down in Brentford folklore.

Brentford had chances during the first half but didn't score until just before half-time when Partridge outran a defender and slotted the ball past the goalkeeper. Preston nearly equalised early in the second half but were denied this until the 73rd minute. The resultant kick-off saw the ball played back to captain Paul Evans, who sighting the goalkeeper off his line hit the fiercest of shots (subsequently shown on TV as one of the fastest ever seen) from fully 55 yards for the equaliser. The goal was credited as having being scored in the 73rd minute, the same time as the earlier Preston goal! Unfortunately The Bees were unable to capitalise on the lead, and the visitors scored again nine minutes from time. Whatever was to befall The Bees, that goal will always be remembered as the highlight of the season.

Something that Bees fans would never have dreamed possible - at least in the post-second World War period - was that during September, four Brentford players were on international duty - Hreidersson for the full Iceland squad (his 26th appearance), whilst Boxall, Folan and Rowlands all represented the Irish Under-21 side (and later goalkeeper Alan Julian was also called up for the Northern Ireland Under-16 team).

In early October, disappointingly, albeit not totally unexpected, Hreidarsson left the club. In a very shrewd piece of dealing, Noades had persuaded the genial giant from Iceland that he could better his career when he dropped two divisions a year earlier, at the time being out of favour at Crystal Palace, with the prospect of a later rising again to a higher level.

The plan worked for he moved on to Premiership Wimbledon, but best of all was the whopping £2.5m fee - a new record for Brentford. Hermann had given the Bees excellent service for a year, and now they were around £2m better off. Whilst many fans criticised the decision to sell it had to be recognised that to attract such players in the first place they had to be assured that the club would not stand in their way if they could better themselves at a higher level club. So popular had the player become that 45 Bees fans travelled to see him play for Iceland in France a week after his final game for Brentford.

Ghanian Patrick Agyemang came on a three month loan in early October, and although there were great hopes for this tall striker, after 12 games (nine of which he came on as a substitute) he was unable to score, yet like some others before him, elsewhere he later had more success. Later that month an agreement was made with another Icelander, Ivar Ingimarsson, from home country club IBV, for £150,000; the defender/midfielder proved to be another excellent signing by the manager. Scott Marshall was signed from Southampton for £250,000, to replace Hreidarsson, and he proved to be a reasonable acquisition over the next three years or so. Around this time Cullip also moved, to Brighton, for £50,000.

In the FA Cup, after a poor game, The Bees were unfortunate not to win the replay versus Plymouth Argyle, a 2-1 defeat after extra time. The side had to make some team changes due to injuries, principally that of captain Evans, and the manager was quick to remark that the players chosen to replace the absent ones, after clamouring for a chance in the team, hardly distinguished themselves! But on the more important League front the team were still on the verge of the play-off places, lying seventh after beating lowly Wrexham 1-0, the goal due to a goalkeeping error by former Bees favourite Keven Dearden. Neil Clement came on loan as cover for the injured Anderson, but the Chelsea man failed to impress, although his later transfer to West Bromwich Albion showed that here was a possible opportunity missed.

Two defeats in late November and early December saw the team slip to ninth in the table. For the latter game, at Wycombe, the Chairboys were able to field former Bees favourite Jamie Bates, and cast-off Jason Cousins who was to enjoy a long and successful career at Adams Park. Matches around the Christmas and New Year period were grim. Hampered by injuries and suspensions, eight matches were lost and only four points obtained in the ten games. Amazingly this only saw a slip down the table to ninth, with just a 1-0 victory at Peterborough in the Auto Windscreens Shield on a positive note. In this competition, Oxford United were then overcome before defeat came at Exeter. The Millennium came and went and for Brentford it was best forgotten - a 3-2 defeat at Millwall for the last game in 1999, and a single goal reverse at home to Stoke that started 2000.

Although two League victories were achieved in late January, the following two months produced mostly poor performances, and by early April, lying exactly in a mid-table position, all hopes of even a play-off place had to be abandoned. Is is easy to blame injuries for a loss of form, but for Brentford this was to a large degree a genuine excuse. The absence of their true leader, Evans, had been a hard blow and the late February cruciate ligament injury to Boxall were just two on the list. On the field the results continued poorly and by the season's end the team finished in the bottom half of the table. From possible promotion candidates early on, the end result was very disappointing. The fact was that with a relatively expensive team for this level, overall they had not performed sufficiently well, the average home attendance had dropped to around 5,700, and Ron Noades was not a happy man. In the fans eyes, the manager/owner was moving from hero of the day to villain of the peace.

In total 33 players had been used, a large number brought on principally by injuries. Amongst the late new arrivals had been Italian striker Lorenzo Pinamonte, who did not find his shooting boots with Brentford and could be considered a wasted £75,000. Steve Jones also came from Bristol City, on loan, but he too did not fit the bill. A return, also on loan, was Carl Hutchings, of whom Bees fans had mixed feelings, but whatever these were he passed by without making any impact. Gareth Graham, from Crystal Palace, was expected to do better, especially as he was a current Northern Ireland Under-21 player. Although he remained during the following season he appeared just once, as a two minute substitute!

The famous (or infamous) Jimmy Glass - the goalkeeper who saved Carlisle from relegation to the Conference with his last gasp goal a year earlier - joined Brentford on loan as cover but made only two appearances. One of the biggest losses to the team was Folan who was plagued with injury this season and made few appearances. Yet another injury victim was Derek Bryan who at times showed that he might well have made the grade, but a cruciate ligament injury early in 2000 sidelined him for nearly two years. When the sums were finally added up crowd favourite Lloyd Owusu was the top scorer, but with only 12 League goals, whilst Kevin O'Connor began to appear in the first team, and went on to become one of the Junior team's most successful of players.

The lack of amenities for generating extra income at Griffin Park was realised, and around this time serious talk started with regard to a new home. Initially the development of Feltham Arenas (then being used by Feltham F.C.) was considered which would provide plenty of site area, but access was not ideal, and for only 12 to 15,000 seats this was felt to be insufficient. Serious talk had started with a view to developing the Western International site, for which a stadium up to 40,000 was possible. But this (and Feltham) eventually bit the dust. Another two sites were soon to be taken on board much to the indignation of the club's supporters.

Chapter 12: Out With The Old, In With The New

2000/01

What had ended as only a modest season, after the summer's rest and starting free of injuries, Brentford and the fans could reasonably have hoped that with their newly strengthened squad, more could be expected this campaign. But it wasn't to be. During the season the manager was sacked - by himself, and that same person came in for increasing criticism regarding the running and performance of the club. Yet it had all started so well....

There were a number of major changes during the close season regarding players, the most notable being the acquisition of yet another Icelandic star in Olafur ('Ollie') Gottskalksson, a full and Under-21 International. On a 'Bosman' (free) transfer from Scottish Premier League side Hibernian, he soon became a favourite with the fans. The goalkeeping position had caused problems over the past season or so, not least as a result of injuries. Probably uniquely, Ollie was also a Basketball International for Iceland. Unfortunately, the other major signing did not enjoy much success at Griffin Park. 22 year-old Mark McCammon could have cost the Bees up to £300,000 from Charlton Athletic, but the tall striker never performed well enough to dictate this full fee. Paul Gibbs from Plymouth Argyle eventually became a useful member of the squad as did former non-League man Edie Hutchinson - not the most cultured of players but one who would die for the cause! Another goalkeeper, Paul Smith, joined, he also rose from the non-League scene, at Carshalton Athletic, and signed for The Bees after appearing against them in a pre-season friendly.

With two other 'keepers on the books, Smith was very much regarded as a reserve man, but the tall 21 year-old was to prove to be an excellent recruit. Jay Lovett was a £75,000 signing from Crawley Town, and despite becoming a regular for a time he soon faded from the first team. Mark Williams was an exciting graduate right winger from the Juniors, who never quite made it despite his number of appearances for the first team, albeit mostly as a 'super-sub'. A few players moved on, including Steve Jenkins (just six appearances), and goalkeeper Woodman who after a loan spell at Southend, signed for Colchester.

Ron Noades, the manager who sacked himself!

Any hopes of a generally injury-free season, unlike the last, were immediately quashed, as these soon piled up, and some were long-term; after just three games, out of action were Anderson (cartilage), new signing Paul Gibbs (hairline fracture of the fibula), Boxall who was still absent with two serious injuries to his knee and Powell (hamstring), then Owusu suffered a dislocated shoulder. In these circumstances, the start wasn't too bad, with two draws and an away win at Oxford United, when Folan scored the only goal.

Then disaster struck with a vengeance, for the Bees lost to Bristol Rovers by a record home defeat of 6-2. Three-nil down at half-time, left back Andy Scott was moved up to the front after the Bees had pulled one goal back, in an effort to claw their way back and at least earn a draw. But this turned out to be a disastrous tactic for his vacated flank was dreadfully exposed, and rather than pull two goals back, Brentford conceded three more! Doubtless the defeat was due very much to the injuries in the squad, for it was a very sub-standard performance particularly in the defensive back four, but the detractors were inevitably quick to blame Noades. By now the club were close to £4m. in debt (from less than £1m. two years earlier), and the majority felt that there was now little to show for it. It was said that Noades had contributed little if any of his own money, although the financial clout and business acumen that he could exert at least prevented any question of going into administration, or worse.

The Worthington (League) Cup produced a great deal of drama. In the first round, first leg at Bristol City, a dreadful run of injuries to both sides during the match resulted in two players being stretchered off, the last was Owusu who received treatment on the pitch for 13 minutes, but fortunately it wasn't as serious as first feared. During this break it was announced that there would be 14 minutes of injury time, and this was then finally extended to 22 - all this in the first half - surely a record period in professional football. By now the score stood at 2-1 against Brentford (the brace of goals against coming from two dubious penalty decisions), one goal from each side being obtained in the injury period. The drama continued into the second half, when Gibbs became the third player to be carried off, and then on almost the stroke of time McCammon netted a deserved equaliser.

Brentford, 1-0 down in the second leg went through when Andy Scott struck twice in the last 13 minutes. 'Spurs were once again the opposition in the second round of the cup, and in the first leg at Griffin Park, The Bees gained a very creditable score-less draw. As expected the return encounter was lost (2-0), but there was no disgrace in defeat especially since at the time no less than 11 players were unavailable due to injuries. In League matches there was a five match winless run including a 4-0 defeat at Reading and after eight games the team languished in 18th place. By now some signings had been made to counter the injuries and the defeats. Jason Crowe on loan made a few appearances before being recalled by Portsmouth, Jean-Phillipe Javary a French player signed from Raith Rovers never made the mark and Birmingham City's Simon Marsh helped out for a while in September.

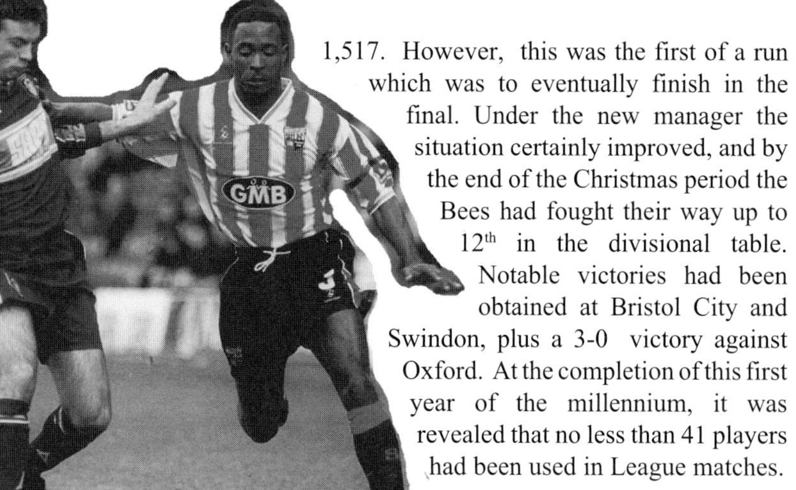

IjahAnderson suffered a season-long injury, and was never quite himself after his return.

Fortunately things began to take a turn for the better and three consecutive home games produced three victories, the second a somewhat fortunate win over Peterborough. Then a 3-1 defeat to struggling Luton Town (only their second win of the season) and just a 1-1 draw at another lowly club, Port Vale, did not produce a great deal of optimism. Things were not particularly smooth behind the scenes, with Noades being vocally criticised, and he giving back as good as he got, whilst there was some disquiet amongst the players, especially Rowlands who showed what a fine player he was, but also demonstrated that he had a volatile side. The second major disaster on the pitch came in the first round of the FA Cup and certainly led directly to the 'sacking' of the manager, this coming after a poor 3-0 home defeat to Rotherham.

Brentford entertained near neighbours Kingstonian, two 'divisions' lower in the Conference. The extravagances at Griffin Park could be seen with the 35 players on their books compared with the opposition's 19 part-timers. But these differences weren't reflected in the result which finished as a 3-1 defeat to The Bees, thus representing one of the most embarrassing results experienced by the club in the Cup. To add insult to injury, Brentford's consolation goal was scored in the 89th minute. This was the final straw for the fans, and Noades bowed to the pressure, although even he would surely have admitted that the way had been lost, and Ray Lewington from the coaching bench stepped up to take over. A better result came on another cup front when Oxford United were easily beaten 4-1 at home in the first round of the LDV Vans Trophy, but only before a paltry crowd of 1,517. However, this was the first of a run which was to eventually finish in the final. Under the new manager the situation certainly improved, and by the end of the Christmas period the Bees had fought their way up to 12th in the divisional table. Notable victories had been obtained at Bristol City and Swindon, plus a 3-0 victory against Oxford. At the completion of this first year of the millennium, it was revealed that no less than 41 players had been used in League matches.

February 10th brought Reading to Griffin Park after a record seven consecutive away matches. Postponements due to bad weather and cup commitments (Brentford beat Brighton in the LDV Vans Trophy after extra time within this period) led to this one-sided situation. Of the five League games there was just one win and two draws , but mid-table was maintained. As usual defeat came at Stoke without the Bees scoring (0-1) - where Brentford over the years had recorded a dismal record.

But once again developments off the pitch began to overshadow the team's improved performances, which could possibly have led to the play-offs. Noades announced, much to the indignation of the majority that led to vociferous protests, that he was considering selling Griffin Park, then buying and developing a new ground whilst playing at either Kingstonian or Woking. Kingston was local enough, but the ground was no better than a reasonable, albeit new, enclosure, with little room for expansion, and a capacity for a paltry 4,000 or so. Woking was way out of the catchment area for fans, and although an improvement, this venue was overall no more suitable than the Kingston-based ground. Noades later insisted that these proposals had been to hopefully shake the 'home' council (Hounslow) into supporting their local team into obtaining a new ground - eventually this appeared to be achieved. The plan was later revealed, with a move to Woking for the 2002/03 season, then sell Griffin Park, and with Hounslow council's co-operation seek a suitable site. Feltham was still the favourite.

By mid-March the dream of promotion was looking unlikely, for with only 46 points the team trailed the last play-off place by seven points. But now another goal was being seriously sought, the LDV Vans Trophy Final to be played at the Millennium Stadium, Cardiff. As things turned out in the League, far from the play-offs there was a downturn in fortunes which saw the team finish in 14th place, just below halfway.

The last embarrassment of a largely forgettable season, apart from the Cardiff visit and the antics off the field, was a 6-0 thrashing at Swansea City.

The Bees continued their route to Cardiff via a 2-1 victory at Barnet, then 3-2 - ironically - at Swansea, plus two wins over Southend United in the southern final. After winning 2-1 at Roots Hall, the team repeated this scoreline in the second leg, in what was only their second home game in the competition. A disappointing crowd numbering just under 6,600 saw a memorable performance, to produce a final showdown against fellow, and much improved, Division Two team Port Vale, who were met just eight days earlier at Griffin Park in League action (when two goals were shared).

The occasion and the lead-in turned out to be better than the game in Cardiff itself. Another somewhat poor crowd (25,654), saw Brentford yet again fall at the final hurdle for the third time, now in Cardiff plus a brace before at Wembley. Yet for a long time things looked good after Dobson had given The Bees a third minute lead. But as the game moved on, with Vale first equalising from the penalty spot it ended as a bitter disappointment. It was felt that the teams should have been evenly matched, but at the finish Brentford were just not at the races. A very sub-standard performance saw the Bees hanging on to a 1-1 draw, when a defensive disaster by Mahon, who was by far the best player in the Brentford team, led to a goal and - it has to be said - a deserved win for the Potteries team.

2001/02

It's probably fair to say that the close season was viewed with mixed feelings. After an overall poor season, but one which had its (few) moments, although not short of disasters, everybody was probably glad to see the back of it. Yet it was generally perceived that far from a squad of losers, the club had players with potential that really could - if injury free - challenge for promotion. And so they did.

Ray Lewington, who had been acting as caretaker manager, had enjoyed a relatively successful few months in charge (the team won more than they lost), therefore it came as no surprise that immediately after confirmation of reaching the LDV Vans Final he was offered, and accepted, the job full time. Then a month or so later he dropped a bombshell when he resigned. He obviously felt his prospects would be better at Watford, but this unexpected loss turned out to be Brentford's gain for Steve Coppell, who had returned to manage Crystal Palace, then left after a dispute with the club's owner and jumped at the chance of coming to Brentford, linking up with his former boss Ron Noades. Coppell brought with him his own coaching staff, including Wally Downs.

Noades' influence and outspoken ways still galled the fans, and to add insult to injury a pre-season friendly was played at Woking, which if Noades had his way would soon be the Bees new home. Demonstrations at Kingfield let it be known the feelings of the majority.

There were few player movements pre- and early in the season. Robert Quinn and Andy Scott had already, surprisingly, moved to Oxford United (for £75,000 each) but there were no significant departures during the close season. New faces included goalkeeper Alan Julian, who moved up from the Juniors. Although very much second choice he was to deputise adequately for four years before moving on to Stevenage Borough. Lee Fieldwick made a similar move up, but played in only a few games before moving on three years later. More significant was another youngster, Matt Somner, but he had a one year wait before playing in the first team. Stephen Hunt from Crystal Palace was a real find, a free-signing from Crystal Palace. The speedy winger made a first team place his own and although sometimes a frustrating player, soon became a favourite with the majority of Bees fans.

Just before the season started Jason Price joined the club on a three month contract from Swansea, and although a useful addition moved on to Tranmere, supposedly for twice the salary! Finally Blackburn's Ben Burgess also came on long term loan. 'Big Ben' scored on his debut, at home to Port Vale (a 2-0 victory which was some sort of revenge for the earlier cup defeat) and formed a lethal partnership with Lloyd Owusu. But after netting 17 goals to the end of February, they suddenly dried up, and thus his leaving after one year at Griffin Park was not really seen as that great a loss.

With the likes of 'Ollie', Dobson, Powell, Ingarmarsson, Anderson, new signing Price, Evans, Mahon, Gibbs, Owusu, and O'Connor - the starting line-up for the first match (a 1-1 draw at Wigan) - and the later services of Burgess, Hunt and Rowlands, The Bees had a formidable Second Division squad to call upon. An excellent start continued in the League, with a 1-0 victory at Chesterfield (in truth a boring match after Evans had scored what transpired to be the winner very early on), and two further home victories. By early September The Bees headed the table.

Meanwhile there was also excitement in the Worthington (League) Cup. A rare win over higher opposition in this competition saw the team oust Norwich City in an exciting Griffin Park match, with a late, late goal from O'Connor. This victory earned an interesting match at Premiership Newcastle United's St. James' Park. This was the club's first visit since 1993, and after a much longer period, the hiring of a special train which saw nearly 1,000 Bees fans head north. High up in the away corner (the home club could have advised that binoculars should be brought) the Bees supporters saw the team put on an excellent display which produced heaps of praise from the likes of the Geordies manager Bobby Robson.

Lloyd Owusu and 'Big Ben' Burgess both scored in the League game at Stoke, but The Bees lost 3-2. They also lost to the Pottery team in the play-off final

Owusu's goal put Brentford ahead ensuring the match ran into extra time, but the final scoreline of 4-1 to the homesters was far from a fair reflection of the play. One thing became clear, that Newcastle's Alan Shearer could always have taken up acting when his football career finished!

In one week in September The Bees faced the sternest of tests when they met at Griffin Park both Oldham Athletic and Bristol City, the two leaders of the division (The Bees were third). Two draws, both of 2-2 was perhaps predictable and satisfactory, but then a 2-0 defeat at Swindon pushed the team down to sixth. In the next home encounter, Brentford took the lead against Colchester, let the opposition back in, but then went on to score three more, the only downside being the later sending off of Anderson. Then a visit to the (supposedly) temporary home at Withdean for Brighton and Hove Albion - arguably the worst football ground in the League - was won 2-1, to take the team back into the runners-up spot, and a mouth-watering encounter with Peterborough United.

With the Posh in sixth place it was always going to be an interesting game, but this was something special for it was a 'first' in the Football League. It was an all-ticket match, but the tickets were free! Always looking for new innovations, Brentford in a tie-up with sponsors GMB and St.George PLC created this free game. One benefit of this idea was to attract 10,000 to the game and hence continue en route for the club's '10,000' Campaign (10,000 names and addresses, a 10,000 crowd, 10,000 average attendance, etc.). It worked for there was a near capacity 11,097 present and the visiting supporters (the Ealing Road end was also full with 'freebies') appreciated the gesture, displaying a large banner thanking the club. Both teams celebrated the occasion with an excellent game, and to top it all, Brentford won 2-1, with Owusu and Evans the goalscorers. At least some revenue came by way of the extended programme which cost £3 instead of £2 - but nobody complained.

A week later and another special occasion when Brentford went to Dorchester to play Bournemouth (The Cherries temporarily sharing with their non-League neighbours), where another three points were gained. More or less injury free for a change the team was fairly constant with several players being ever-presents or missing only one match. After bottom side Bury were thrashed 5-1 at home and then an excellent 2-1 victory at Reading's Madejeski Stadium - before a near 15,000 attendance - The Bees maintained their top of the table spot and promotion was a serious discussion point.

To strengthen the team - an inspired loan signing - 18 year-old Steven Sidwell from Arsenal arrived in time for the Bury massacre, initially to replace injured captain Paul Evans. Whilst at Brentford he became a fans' favourite and won an England Under-20 cap, but rated at £1m plus even then, realistically Brentford knew he would never be theirs. In the run-up to Christmas it was a mixed bag of results.

Three League defeats on their travels, included a remarkable 5-3 reverse at Adams Park, Wycombe. The Bees took a two goal lead before the Wanderers pulled one back following a bizarrely awarded free-kick, which took a wicked deflection off Owusu. Luck was against the visitors again when Ingimarsson was crudely brought down, no free-kick given, and a superb equaliser resulted from 35 yards. Burgess made it 3-2, but the home side came back strongly and by the 67th minute were leading 4-3, before completing this goal feast in injury time.

The Bees also lost to their Buckinghamshire neighbours in the LDV Vans Trophy, but beat non-League Morecambe (who were to be met again six years later in the Football League) in the first round of the FA Cup, before losing 3-2 at Scunthorpe in the next round.

Steve Sidwell came on loan from Arsenal...

......and Brentford made excellent use of the highly talented youngster.

The only other game in this travelling dominated period was the 'big one' when QPR came to Griffin Park for the first time in 36 years. A near 11,000 crowd saw a disappointing and fairly lifeless scoreless draw. By Christmas the club could take stock. Third from top of the division, top goalscorers (45) - with Evans (11), Burgess (9) and Owusu (9) in the 'top ten'. They also held the best goal difference (18) and with the average gate, to date, at 6,523, this was the best since the 1992/93 season; and there had been two 10,000 plus attendances. Following two 3-0 home victories just before Christmas the team were back on top, before a dismal festivities period which produced three away defeats (two games were postponed) and a slump to fifth in the table; and it got worse!

All the earlier good work was undone with two more reverses, one when the undefeated home record was lost to Wigan; amongst the unused substitutes was a young man by the name of Jay Tabb. Now at seventh, this was to be the lowest position in the table all season. But it all looked a lot better when a rip-roaring 4-0 victory, live on TV, completed the double over second placed Brighton. On the 9th March, Castleford beat the home team 19-6 at Griffin Park, but this was in the Rugby League with the return of the London Broncos to the west side of the capital.

As the season ran down the tide turned and The Bees started climbing again. A near excellent run of 14 games produced just one defeat, and by the end of March a football feast was in store for the final chapter. Fourth place Stoke City came to Griffin Park and before a near 9,000 crowd were beaten by a Sidwell goal.

The next match should have been the easiest, at third from bottom Bury. With The Shakers not only on the verge of relegation but also liquidation, they won, of course! However, The Bees were still reasonably comfortable in third place, just two places ahead of the next visitors Huddersfield. Another good performance saw the Yorkshire team easily dealt with by 3-0.

Just two games left, the first the big local derby at Loftus Road and then what became the promotion decider at home to Reading. The QPR encounter was, at the final count, heartbreaking. With over 18,000 present - the home team were also challenging for an outside chance of the play-offs - including of course several thousand Bees fans - the game was goalless, when three points was all but necessary to ensure promotion. Substitute McCammon came on after half-time, and following much Brentford pressure he was presented with a golden opportunity to become a Griffin Park hero. In front of the Bees fans, the big man had already hit the post with one shot, and then in the 74th minute he received the ball a few yards out with the goal at his mercy. Somehow, rather than find the back of the net, he managed to head the ball downward, in fact with too much force, for it hit the ground, bounced up, and was tipped over the bar by the goalkeeper. The draw sealed QPR's fate as they missedthe play-offs but those two extra points could have ensured automatic promotion for The Bees.

It is difficult to remember a more tense match than when Reading came to Griffin Park on the 20th of April; in fact many probably felt that perhaps it would have been far less nerve-racking to not be at the ground at all! A capacity crowd of 11,303 (the third five figure gate of the season) greeted the teams as they ran out from the corner of the ground. The journey had started nearly nine months earlier and for only two days (in January) during that period had the Bees, at 7th, not been in at least a play-off position. And now everything rested in this, the 46th match. Reading were in second position, just one point ahead of Brentford; whatever the outcome both were assured of at least the play-offs.

The first half reflected the nerves felt also by the two teams and remained goalless, with just two chances coming to Brentford, when Burgess forced the 'keeper to push the ball over the bar from his header, and on the stroke of half-time when Hunt was unable to convert a half chance. The second half started in a more positive way, and it was not long before a cross from Owusu was taken by Rowlands and his first time shot gave the Bees the lead. The ground erupted - but could they hang on to this slender advantage? Reading naturally had to fight back strongly and the heartbreak for The Bees came with just 13 minutes left on the clock. A Parkinson pass went to Cureton who lobbed it over Brentford's Smith in goal from a narrow angle, and that was it! It was the turn of the Reading fans to celebrate, and they were promoted, just one point ahead of Brentford. If only......

Joy in the final League match when Martin Rowlands gave Brentford the lead. But Reading equalised and were promoted.

The young Brentford team surprisingly bounced back from this heartbreaking match and eight days later faced Huddersfield at the McAlpine Stadium for the first leg of the play-off matches. Brentford started the stronger and had several chances to take the lead but no goals were scored in the first period, then Brentford hearts, all 1,600 of them, missed a beat when Booth got the ball in the net - but the 'goal' was ruled offside. Both teams had a few chances to score, but at the end of the match Brentford were able to start the second leg all square. For the fifth game running the starting line-up remained the same, and another near capacity crowd (11,191) again greeted the teams at Griffin Park. With memories of previously losing to the same club in the play-offs, there was no penalty shoot-out repeat, for this time the majority of the crowd went home in high spirits. Goals from Powell and Owusu, after the visitors took an early lead, secured a visit to the Millennium Stadium again.

The attendance for the final was 42,523, the majority from their well supported opponents Stoke City (with approximately 12,000 from Brentford). It was ominous that Brentford were allotted the 'lucky' south dressing room - in all 11 past finals at this stadium, every team had won from there; but this run had to end somtime! In an overall scrappy game, the Potters took lead after 16 minutes through Deon Burton (ironically he become a future Brentford player), but the Bees hit back and came close through Burgess and Sidwell. Then disaster when a free-kick was deflected by Burgess into his own net on the stroke of half-time; the last goal he 'scored' as a Brentford player! Two-nil, and there was no way back. Stoke were happy to hang on to their lead and despite a few half chances, it wasn't to be. Brentford had underperformed yet again, just when it counted the most.

Brighton ended as Champions, who to date are still playing, on a two year 'temporary' athletics stadium. Reading were runners-up, who in all truth were well equipped and worthy of promotion, whilst Brentford missed out in third place. It was small consolation that The Bees had the best goal difference (34), scored the most goals (77), and jointly won the most (17) plus were defeated in the least (1) matches at home. But these records meant nothing at the final count.

2002/03

Gutted! That described the feelings of club and supporters alike. For Brentford there had been near misses in the past - perhaps too many - but this had to be one of the most depressing. The club had shown they were the most prolific goalscorers in the division, had a resilient defence and on their day the team could match anyone. They had an excellent squad of players who never seriously faltered during the season, and the attendances had improved significantly. Time is a great healer, and the length of the close season was needed to repair the wounds.

It was inevitable that the worst wasn't over, for the club had to pay for its non-promotion, which resulted in many personnel losses and financial hardships. An additional blow was the loss of the income received from ITV Digital which had gone broke, and no compensation came despite both Carlton and Granada being pursued through the courts. Fortunately for Brentford the income derived from this source was not as great as for some clubs as they had sensibly not budgeted for all the money in advance that never materialised. But despite already playing with a limited wage bill, the fairly large and expensive squad had to be trimmed further, with no prospect of extra income to come from playing in a higher division.

The biggest loss was arguably that of manager Coppell. In his one season at Brentford he was, statistically, one of the most successful at Griffin Park, with 25 wins, 12 draws and only 12 defeats in his League and play-off games in charge. Unable to secure a long term contract at Griffin Park, he saw no future for himself there and the quiet spoken northerner resigned. It was surprisingly another 12 months before he was snapped up again, this time by Brighton (whom he had come close to joining in the summer of 2002

New manager Wally Downes, but his success was shortlived.

Fortunately (or was it!), Wally Downes - former coach under Coppell was there and ready to take over the manager's job when it was offered. He already knew the players, at least those that were left, together with the excellent club scout John Griffin, who between them had the task of obtaining bargain replacements. An excellent pre-season of friendly matches went well, except - ludicrously - two players (including Anderson) were sent off, and therefore the pair started the season under suspension.

But this was the least of the club's worries, for it became known that the finances were in a perilous state, and in fact they could even fold within a couple of months. There is no doubt that since Noades had taken over four years earlier as well as the lows, there had also been the highs, with a promotion, the acquisition of some excellent players and some exciting games. But these had been at a cost. It had always been anticipated (promised some would say), that part of the Chairman's large fortune would be ploughed into the club, but - and he always denied it - this was not to be.

A critical time had come and the sale of the freehold of Griffin Park seemed inevitable. This was the club's only real and substantial asset. The local council had started to be sympathetic towards the club's plight, but they offered nothing positive. A new ground at Feltham had already been all but abandoned, and there were at this time only two realistic alternatives. One was to take out the option to play at Kingstonian's little ground, which would allow the sale of Griffin Park, or to take up another offer which allow the club to play at Griffin Park for three more seasons before it was developed - but what then? Neither choice was acceptable. Fortunately, on the horizon, was Bees United, who perhaps held out some hope for the club's continued existence. In order for survival something had to happen, and quickly.

Some of the prize assets on the pitch had already departed, including Burgess and Sidwell who had come to the end of their loan periods. The two biggest losses were initially those of Ingimarsson, the *'2001/02 Player Of The Season'*, who was allowed to join Wolves, and inspirational captain Evans, to Bradford City, Brentford simply being unable to afford to keep the pair. Owusu was another favourite who was worth a large transfer fee that couldn't be realised and he soon moved on to Sheffield Wednesday. Mahon had already moved to Watford before the end of the previous season, before his contract ran out, and therefore a fee was received, but only £150,000.

Other departures were perhaps not so significant but each had helped formed a strong squad: Boxall joined Bristol Rovers, Bryan had already left in March (ending up in non-League football), as had Gibbs (to Barnsley) to reduce costs, and Theobald, although never a regular also left. Just after the season commenced came another devastating blow with the transfer of Powell to Crystal Palace, but at least this brought in £400,000 to the club, which provided them with liquidity, at least for a while. Icelander Gottskalksson had been displaced by Paul Smith in goal, and by November he retired, before a later comeback at Torquay.

A mixed bunch replaced the outgoings, few of whom ever really made the pulses race. But what could have been a dispirited team managed to win at Huddersfield by 2-0 in the first League match, albeit only 300 or so hardy Bees fans were there. The team included newcomers Ibrahima Sonko, Leo Roget, Rowan Vine, Jamie Fullarton (the latter two each scoring) and Leo Constantine as substitute.

Under-21 Senegal International Sonko, from French club Grenoble, was something of a coup by manager Downes, and the tall defender, although initially raw, turned out to be an excellent and popular player at Griffin Park. Stockport's Roget, as with Sonko, initially only signed a short-term contract, but he was plagued with injuries and may well have become a more useful addition, although his discipline was in question at times. Vine was a loan signing from Portsmouth, and although he scored well to begin with, and stayed all season, his goals soon dried up. Fullarton, from Dundee United only played in around half the games this season, another who was somewhat injury prone.

Constantine came on loan from Millwall, and the striker left after recording no goals for Brentford, but typically became quite prolific elsewhere! Steven Hughes was a youngster who signed professional forms but never made a name in League football.

Ibrahima Sonko from Senegal was a definite asset to the team.

Young Dobson took over as team captain, and finished as the only ever-present during this variable season. The team made an amazing start to the season, by defying all the critics, and after five games were undefeated, headed the table and after drawing 2-2 at Notts County, Downes won the divisional manager of the month award.

But this was as good as it got, and for the rest of the season it was more of a struggle than a success story. Although actions off the pitch involving the long-term future of the club had to be seen as the important issues. Bees United were gaining a foothold in the running of the club, with one board member in place, and the incentive to raise sufficient money to take over Altonwood's (Noades' company) majority shareholding was undertaken.

One small bright spot at this stage was the team overcoming a 3-1 deficit at half time in the Worthington Cup at Bournemouth to force a 3-3 draw. For a change the Bees won the penalty shoot-out (4-2). But Brentford were comfortably beaten 4-1 at home in the second round by Premiership Middlesbrough. A run of three consecutive League away defeats that followed was depressing after such a good start, the worst being the thrashing experienced at Peterborough by 5-1; by now the team had slumped to 9th. But there was something of a recovery, the most memorable being the 5-0 demolition of Blackpool at Griffin Park. By now another name had been added to the squad, that of left back Andy Frampton, who later became a definite asset.

But at least there was better luck in the other cups competitions. Brentford moved on to the southern semi-final of the LDV Vans Trophy, beating Plymouth away and Kidderminster (the first competitive game against the midlanders) at home before losing to Cambridge United by a 'Golden Goal'. In the FA Cup, the third round saw First Division Derby County visit Griffin Park - after both Wycombe Wanderers and York City were overcome away from home. The visitors included the return of Keith Loring.

Not necessarily one of the most popular of staff with the fans at Griffin Park, he joined the club in 1986, and for a few years was a tremendous asset as he transformed the commercial side of Brentford before his 'transfer' to these cup opponents. The underdogs, before a crowd of 8,709, overcame The Rams, with a goal from Hunt, but lost out in the fourth round, when another higher level team, Burnley, comfortably won 3-0 before a near 10,000 Griffin Park crowd. These two acts of mercy, via the turnstiles, at least helped stave off the possible collapse of the club.

After a scoreless draw at Mansfield (with just 129 Bees fans present), the club had slumped to 13th in the table (albeit with games in hand over every other club), but having lost in two cup competitions, in four days, a slight chance of a play-off place, or possibly a relegation battle, was now all that was left to play for.

There were two player movements in March. Anderson, who at one time was the idol of the crowd, later to join Bristol Rovers, with some acrimony (two years on he was tested positive for drug tacking), and in came the French striker Mickael Antoine-Curier on loan. Despite this somewhat romantic sounding appointment, apart from two goals at Chesterfield (which settled any fears of relegation) next month, his short time at Griffin Park was unremarkable.

Before the end of the season, the club finally quashed any prospects of moving from Griffin Park in the short-term, despite the annual large losses incurred, until another site for a new ground was confirmed. At least planning consent for development had been granted, albeit to a lesser value than hoped for, with the requirement to provide a large proportion of social housing. Whilst the house was put in order in the boardroom, it certainly wasn't on the pitch, when an horrendous March saw seven of the eight games played produce just one point. Relegation had become a real threat now, the team languishing at 15th place in the table.

Later that month, Noades announced that he would be resigning as Chairman of the club, much to the delight of the majority of supporters. He explained in detail, in his programme notes, his expectations, strategy and the current situation. It all sounded very plausible and genuine although in most fans' eyes they had expected Noades to literally finance with his own money, the running of the club.

The club were heavily in debt, and even without loan repayment interest they would have been losing around £1/2m a year, despite the latest economies that had been undertaken. Over the previous four plus years the debt had climbed a great deal, albeit the fans had the excitement of a Championship, a near miss play-off promotion, a cup final and the entertainment given by many quality players. Football success is measured by results on the pitch, but in Brentford's case the financial situation was to remain a real worry.

It was more of a relief when the season finished. One that started well, had produced a reasonable cup run, one or two good League results, but which at the end was, although not altogether surprising, yet another disappointing one. A season which, as would be seen in the future, the play off the pitch would have more repercussions than those on it.

2003/04

Being a Brentford supporter is never dull, even if often not very successful. And this season eventually became one of the more interesting, if not the most successful. What looked like relegation to the basement division again was dramatically and rapidly turned around, by one new character in the cast - and arguably the most colourful!

A lot was hoped for from on-loan signing Tommy Wright, but he proved to be a disappointment.

Player movements were relatively few during the close season, although as manager Downes stated, this wasn't from lack of trying. Inevitably the main requirement was for one or preferably two strikers, although such an item is at the head of most clubs' shopping lists come the pre-season period. In Brentford's case, and limited to a very tight budget, it was - and still is - not a simple case of going out and grabbing a few marksmen, as many fans would think. It was hoped that Vine would extend his loan, which his club Portsmouth were happy with, yet suddenly he was snatched away by Colchester United. Darius Henderson of Reading was a target, but once again joined another club - Steve Coppell's Brighton - before a serious loan offer from Brentford could be made. Downes' inexperience or agents greed? Probably a bit of each.

Leicester's Tommy Wright was targeted, but sustained a pre-season injury, although a month later he did in fact join The Bees on loan. Midfielder Fullarton could well have made an impression at Griffin Park. A good ball winner, he was injury prone, and was signed by Southend during the close season, where his fitness problems continued. Previous big-signing Marshall was also out of the team for much of the time due to injuries, but in his four years at Brentford he made nearly 90 appearances. He chose to move on to Wycombe, but was soon to retire from the game as a player. McCammon was something of an enigma, for he never scored the numbers of goals hoped for and expected from him, and it was with mixed feelings when he joined Millwall earlier, in March, where he had modest success.

Mark Williams, a former Junior, showed great potential, and many supporters felt he was discarded too early. A clever right winger, perhaps he was given too few real chances at Griffin Park, albeit he holds the dubious distinction of being the most used 'super-sub', with his 61 record number of such League appearances.

The most notable to move on was Rowlands. An outstanding midfielder who was picked up cheaply from non-League football, and despite some medium to long term injuries, during his five years at the club he made nearly 150 League appearances. He 'defected' to QPR, and his supposed later detrimental remarks about Brentford, turned him from the Bees fans hero to villain overnight. Another great loss during the summer was that of Brentford's record appearance holder, Ken Coote, at the age of 75. A true gentleman player, and later supporter of the club.

There were no new players of note to welcome at the start of the season, but striker Ben May came on loan from Millwall in late August and stayed for the rest of the campaign. He was yet another disappointment, scoring only a handful of goals. Around the same time Tony Rougier was a free signing, from Brighton. He was effective as a winger and became a favourite with the supporters. It soon became apparent that the team required bolstering when the season started in dreadful fashion. 31 year-old Peter Beadle was given a month's trial at Brentford and in the opening game at Tranmere was unbelievably sent off for an innocuous challenge after just 12 minutes.

As suspension and injury followed, he thus recorded the shortest ever playing time for a player with the club. This was a terrible blow for him personally, and the match referee (Boyeson - who was making his debut) was criticised strongly for his action. Fortunately for Beadle, although near, this was not the end of his career, for he carried on for a while with Barnet, when Martin Allen the 'other Bees' manager signed him.

Hat-trick hero Matt Harrold, but disaster in the next round of the cup!

The Tranmere match was lost by 4-1 and a few days later two more notable incidents occurred in Brentford's chequered history. Fielding their youngest ever side for a competitive match, the team battled it out with West Bromwich Albion who had been just relegated from the Premiership. Holding their own and just one goal down, Smith in goal was sent off, but substitute Julian played well, before three more late goals were conceded. Rather than better, things continued badly, with just one victory in the first five League games, which saw the team just one position above the bottom of the table.

Reinforcements were urgently needed and in September there were three signings. Chelsea's Joel Kitamirike came on loan but made no big impression, whilst young Leicester striker Tommy Wright initially wooed the fans, scoring in his first two full matches, then only once more in the next 23! Another youngster, Matt Harrold joined from Harlow Town and apart from a few substitute appearances only came to prominence later, when, with his striking red hair and the hat trick he netted in the 7-1 demolition of Gainsborough Trinity in the first round of the FA Cup. This was one of the few highlights in a generally dismal season, which took another turn for the worse in the next round.

Away to Conference club Telford United, Brentford were highly embarrassed once again by a non-League team, losing heavily by 3-0. The Shropshire team went on to beat Crewe Alexandra before losing at Millwall, then five months later they folded. Their ground had been improved enormously but financially they overstretched themselves. There was no joy for Brentford in the LDV Vans Trophy either, for defeat came at Peterborough.

The gloom continued through to Christmas, by which time the team lay precariously in 18th place, one of the only real triumphs having been a comprehensive beating of Coppell's Brighton by 4-0 in October.

By now there was a deal of unrest building up against manager Downes and after two thirds of the season the situation remained unchanged. The squad was crying out for more personnel, but the finances were not there to get them, and it was fortunate that at least the attendances were holding up (due in no small part to the well supported or local opposition) at just about budgeted levels. It was therefore ironic that one of the club's few stars left in January when goalkeeper Paul Smith was sold The supporters in general realised that such a move was inevitable, for the initial fee of £250,000 from Southampton at least covered a good deal of the losses that would be experienced that season. As a replacement, Stuart Nelson joined the club from non-League Hucknall Town. After sharing the number one slot with Julian, he became the first choice for the job and a popular 'keeper for over three years. Ronnie Bull (from Millwall) also came on loan, and was a near ever-present at left back for the remainder of the season.

In mid-March the situation had become desperate, for with just 11 games to play the team had by now slumped to third from bottom and with the real threat of relegation hanging over them. The removal of Downes was being urged by the supporters before it was too late, or was it already at that stage? By now there had been a couple of new reasonable signings, but the newcomers were largely unable to do anything about Brentford's plight. Rotherham's former captain, 30 year-old midfielder Steward Talbot joined, but it wasn't until his time under a new manager that his ability to stabilise a young team came to the fore. Scott Fitzgerald was Downes' last signing shortly before the manager left, and the 33 year-old centre-half from Colchester proved to be a definite asset for the nerve-wracking finish to the season.

After defeat at home to Stockport on March the 13th, this being the last in a run of five consecutive defeats, the inevitable happened and Downes was asked to leave. He had shown that he was a good coach but obviously not a good manager, thus illustrating that the two posts require different talents. Assistant manager Garry Thompson took charge for just one game, a creditable 1-1 draw at Blackpool, with Hunt scoring from the penalty spot, when there were just 85 Bees fans present at Bloomfield Road. The new manager selected was to bring a great deal of light to the gloom and one of the most colourful periods in Brentford's long history. 38 year-old Martin Allen, on a short term full manager contract with the other Bees - Barnet - came to take charge and attempt the near impossible, that of staving off relegation (four points adrift with nine games to play).

We now enter the realm of fantasyland! Supposedly Allen had not even discussed a salary and was more interested in obtaining a replacement car! At his first press conference after the move, he announced, *"My car is knackered"*, and two Brentford fans in the motor trade came to the rescue with a new Mondeo. On the pitch, Martin's charisma transformed the team. In his first game in charge, Rushden & Diamonds were somewhat fortuously beaten 3-2. To add to the tension the kick-off was delayed 30 minutes due to traffic problems.

The first bizarre episode in Allen's reign was enacted in the north-east. On the eve of the Hartlepool match, one of the players bet another £50 that he wouldn't swim across the river in Darlington, whereupon Allen immediately offered to do it for £40. And he did. The moral of the story, so the manager said was: *"If you say you are going to swim it, swim it."* Despite this apparent nonsensical statement, this was re-quoted to the players the next day before the match and at half-time, and they certainly adopted the attitude if you're going to win it, win it (they won 2-1)!

The 1-1 draw at home to Chesterfield that followed was somewhat disappointing, but another draw at - surprisingly struggling - Sheffield Wednesday provided new hope. This left just five matches, and most, if not all, had to be won to be sure of salvation. The defeat of Colchester at Griffin Park maintained the optimism, and hopes really soared after Barnsley were overcome at Oakwell. But those hopes were all but dashed when two points were dropped to Wycombe Wanderers, and then a real calamity when a close match was lost at fellow strugglers Grimsby Town. Isaiah Rankin scored his last goal (an excellent strike), the winner, for the Mariners in this match, and his next goal in the League came the following season, for Brentford.

The last game was a cliff-hanger and 9,604 were present at Griffin Park to see the final chapter. It wasn't clear cut, other than Brentford had to win to be sure to stay up, any other result and it was likely that the 'drop' would be the result. The tension was there, but so was the determination, and an inspired substitution in the second half of former non-Leaguer Alex Rhodes paid dividends. In the 83rd minute the young striker struck a superb angled volley in front of the packed Brook Road end, and hence The Bees beat Bournemouth 1-0 to ensure safety, at least for another year.

2004/05

The roller-coaster ride started as early as the close season of 2004. Whilst supporters in recent seasons had been broadly kept up to date via the website during the summer, Martin Allen started a trend which was to be a hallmark of his period at the club. With a passion for the job rarely seen in this position, he went to great lengths to inform with regular postings on the club's website and often on a daily basis. Some were useful and informative, some were outright zany, but the point was put over that everybody was part of the Brentford F.C. 'family'. From a fans viewpoint there was a buzz about the place that was a definite pleasant and new experience. After the struggle of the previous season, but with the ultimate uplift at the end, everybody was cautiously upbeat about the prospects for the following months.

After the Bournemouth last match of the season, and the avoidance of relegation, Allen viewed this his *"greatest achievement."* His ramblings and reports started as early as the 9th of May when he informed website viewers of the playing staff's short holiday to Ireland as a reward that had been donated by a Director. But already he was thinking ahead and *"getting ready for next season."* Soon after this trip, Allen announced some early player movements. Stephen Evans was not given a new contract; the central midfielder had played more than 50 games for The Bees over a two year period. Kitamirake, May (although the Millwall man did make a brief but unproductive return for a few games during December) and Wright all returned to their clubs whilst it was hoped that Bull could be retained at Griffin Park, but it was not to be. Frampton later had his contract extended a further year, whilst Julian and Jay Smith were given free transfers further on in the season.

One major decision was that the reserves would be disbanded, and with a smaller squad this gave the opportunity for financial savings and/or the ability to pay more for newcomers. But the Juniors (under-18) would be retained, with the chance for them to be blooded into the first team should the situation arise. On May the 12th, over 500 fans attended a question and answer session, with several of the coaching staff, players, directors and of course Allen present, the latter was inevitably the most entertaining. Lasting two hours this was a terrific success. Two days later and the manager reported that all the players had been given their fitness programme for the following six weeks - no peace for the wicked - as 'next season' started on May 17th! For Tabb there was another match, for later that month he was called up by the Republic of Ireland Under-21 team.

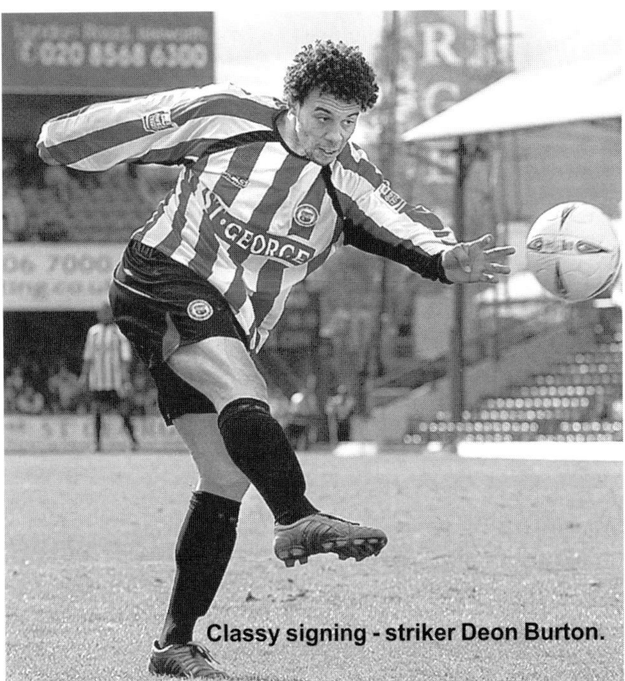
Classy signing - striker Deon Burton.

By now season ticket applications were flooding in, and it was confidently expected they would eventually surpass the previous season numbers; four new ones were those from the manager's sons. Before the end of the month, Allen signed a three year contract, and the team coaches for two, which pleased the club and supporters alike, as the bandwaggon continued to gain momentum. 19 year-old Harrold signed a new contract, but Somner was given the opportunity to join another club if he wished. After a loan spell he was signed by Cambridge United in February, but during his time at Brentford did win two Under-21 caps for Wales and made 84 League appearances. The supporters were certainly getting behind the club, notably one (unnamed) man, presented a cheque to the manager, made out to Brentford F.C., for £5,000.

Sam Sodje was an early and somewhat controversial signing from non-League Margate. One of the family of four footballing brothers, he had a poor disciplinary record (in fact he was banned from playing for the first few Brentford games), but his questionable record resulted more from over-enthusiasm rather than rough play. Another notable signing was Isaiah Rankin who had played such an impressive game for Grimsby against Brentford a few weeks earlier. He was a one time £1.3m player. Feeling that Rankin could up his pace, Allen promised he was going to be made to work morning, noon and night, *"There will be times when Mr Rankin will not like me"*, he said. In June the manager was to attend a short management course at Warwick University, *"my Mum will be so proud that I'm going to University"*, he quipped. Around this time he made the first of many cryptic football statements, whilst making reference to 'his garden': *"...weeding out the rubbish....trying to improve the garden with seedlings for the future... by next year it will be tidy and good to look at."*

There were two new signings in June in Andy Myers and Chris Hargreaves. Hargreaves was a strong attacking midfielder and near ever-present until two injuries put him on the sidelines. Myers was a disappointment and made only a few appearances. Despite a better contract extension offer, Sonko chose to move to Reading, one of many that made this short trip. Later signings included Deon Burton, from Portsmouth, who became the club's top League goalscorer this season with a modest 10, and another 'big' name, John Salako, now aged 35, he saw out his career with a season at Griffin Park. Allen also, *"had a look at what plants are on offer, still with some space in my garden. A couple would have looked nice, but the price was too high."*

An interesting sponsored player, San Lee, an Under-20 International from Korea, was taken on, but never made a competitive appearance. Hunt was desirous of a move - upwards - and was put on the transfer list. He was then given few opportunities during the season, and a year later, at the end of his contract, he moved to Reading for free, where he went on to play in the Premiership and for Ireland.

With all the information emanating from Griffin Park during the close season, particularly from the manager who put many smiles on faces, when the season finally started it already seemed a few months old. An exciting season was ahead, coupled with the celebrations (and book) marking one hundred years at Griffin Park. The many 'happenings' and excitement during this period could fill half a book, but here, there is only room left for the essentials.

Michael Turner came on a three month loan from Charlton and later, after much pestering by Allen of the south-east London side's manager, Alan Curbishley, he was signed permanently for an undisclosed, but for what must have been a bargain fee. The quiet, unassuming, centre half was to give an all but faultless season and proved to be arguably the best bargain around this period in the club's history.

After losing 3-1 at Chesterfield, a modest start was followed with an eight match unbeaten run that took the club to second in the table by early October. Defeat came at the first hurdle in the Carling Cup and also in the LDV Vans Trophy, a minor shock 3-0 home defeat to MK Dons, with The Bees being represented by fringe and junior players. In the League match soon after, in Milton Keynes, Allen endeared himself to the supporters when he deliberately stood unprotected in the pouring rain urging his team on, being conscious of the fact that this was what the travelling fans were having to endure.

Around this time, Jamie Lawrence, on loan from Fulham, made a few unremarkable appearances and 17 year-old Junior, Ryan Peters, made his debut and featured in the team, mostly as a substitute.

(Left) Chris Hargreaves and Ben May (with Sam Sodje looking on) at Hinckley in the F.A.Cup

The fans still couldn't be enticed out of their armchairs, as despite an exciting team and some good results, until late in the season home attendances rarely reached 6,000. Then a fairly poor run until the end of the year saw the team slip to 8th in the table, with the last game of the year producing a depressing 3-0 defeat at Swindon. To boost the team, Steve Claridge joined in December, and promptly left after just four games, whilst Rhodes, with a serious knee injury when he collided with an advertisement board at Griffin Park after a bad tackle by a Walsall defender, was out for the rest of the season and longer.

Jay Tabb wins the ball during the first Southampton game.

If the effervescence had disappeared from the team, at least the manager kept things bubbling and an exciting FA Cup run had already started. At Bristol City a Salako goal earned a replay, and after 120 minutes at Griffin Park the score was 1-1. For once, The Bees actually won a penalty knockout decider, by 4-3. Pastures new were experienced when the team were drawn away to non-League Hinckley United. The game was played live in front of the TV cameras on Sunday the 5th of December, on a rain-sodden ground at a crumbling venue. A scoreless draw (which included a missed Brentford penalty) hardly satisfied the TV viewers but where football was all but impossible to play it sufficed. A few months later and the match could have been played on the Leicestershire club's new, but not at the time completed, impressive stadium up the road.

The replay was no walkover, but as expected Brentford won 2-1. In the third round Luton were comfortably beaten 2-0 at Kenilworth Road, before a rare appearance in the fourth round, and a home game with fellow First Division team Hartlepool. They thought it was all over, after a scoreless draw, but the faithful fans who made the Saturday replay trip, delayed due to poor weather, to the north-east were rewarded with a 1-0 win, aided by a home defender's sending-off. The fifth round was therefore reached and played at Premiership Southampton the following Saturday. Chaos rained when it transpired that many of the thousands of Bees fans (suddenly everybody was a supporter) could not get a ticket. A badly organised situation saw the ground far from full for the all-ticket match, and Brentford's own ticket distribution open to question. Hardly settled in their seats, the travelling fans were dismayed when The Saints scored from an easy tap-in in the fourth minute.

Martin Allen and back-stage team, happy

Luck was against The Bees later for a Nelson innocuous clearance struck the back of a Southampton player's head, and three passes led to another easy goal. But within a few minutes the score was 2-1, when Rankin's run and angle shot beat former Bee - Smith - in goal. The second half was Brentford's, and they deservedly equalised from a Sodje header in the 58th minute. In fact the game could have been won if a justifiable penalty claim had been awarded near the end. So it was back to Brentford nine days later when a capacity 11,720 crowd looked for a giantkilling, with a further reward being a quarter-final match at Old Trafford. But it wasn't to be, for the Premiership side won 3-1. The end of another possible fairytale, but at least the finances were helped with a pot of gold from the cup run.

Earlier, in February, two players with the same two names appeared on the books - Scott Fitzgerald - but this later signing was a frustrating striker, who rarely hit the back of the net. Of course promotion was always the priority and The Bees continued to hover around the play-off placings, with steady if not sensational results. Some were best forgotten such as the 3-1 defeat at Hartlepool - just ten days after the cup match, and a dour scoreless draw at Doncaster, on a bleak and freezing cold terrace for the intrepid travelling fans. But just one defeat in seven up until early April gave reason for hope. A warm reception was given to Marcus Gayle who signed for The Bees at this time and played in a handful of matches. MIdfielder Darren Pratley was another late signing, who arrived from Fulham on loan.

Two victories then three defeats in the final run-in, the worst a poor 4-1 reverse at Bradford, did not enhance their chances. Then the match that sealed cashless Wrexham's fate - relegation - and confirmed the treasured play-off place for Brentford.

Up in North Wales, the homesters took the lead before Rankin equalized and Fitzgerald (the striker) scored a rare goal, in injury time, and hence sealed both teams' fate. The last match, at home to Hull City, was bizarre to say the least. Decided to be an all ticket match earlier, due to an anticipated large attendance as both teams were involved in promotion possibilities, but on the day The Tigers were already promoted and The Bees had sealed their place in the play-offs. Therefore Allen rested most of the leading players. There were nine team changes from that which had played a few days earlier at Wrexham, with three youngsters making their debuts.

Therefore the 9,604 crowd had come to see virtually Brentford Juniors in a match that had nothing hanging on it. Three more debuts were given via the substitutes that came on, including 16 year-old Charlie Ide. It was a boys versus the men match, and when the latter took a first minute lead, an embarrassing slaughter was on the cards. But an entertaining game saw the young Bees equalise just before half-time and in true story book fashion, captain for the day Tabb scored the winner four minutes before the end.

The season had exceeded all expectations, and the supporters were happy just to be there, in the play-offs. But on this occasion there was no repeat fairytale ending. Before a near 29,000 crowd Sheffield Wednesday won 1-0 in the first leg, and in the return, before close to 11,000, The Owls won 2-1 and hence marched on to the Millennium Stadium. Despite the obvious defeat that was looming, the team was lifted with the tremendous support given them to the end. On past occasions it would have been a subdued Brentford crowd, but they had experienced an exciting season, with an exciting manager and a lucrative cup run. Apart from that elusive promotion it had been a good year, and there was always next season. Perhaps!

2005/06

Naturally the season started with high hopes and inevitably players moving in and out, but after the previous good season, these were less than usual. The most notable to move on were Deon Burton, who was top goalscorer in his one season at Griffin Park, Matt Harrold - who many thought perhaps wasn't given sufficient chances - and Chris Hargreaves, who nearing the end of his career joined League Two side Oxford United. John Salako left and was soon to retire, whilst frustrating at times but overall popular Stephen Hunt moved on to join Reading and manager Coppell, where his career blossomed. Scott B. Fitgerald stayed at Brentford as Youth Team Coach.

One-time captain Stewart Talbot left during the close season.

The influx of newcomers proved to be a mixed bag. Ricky Newman's career at Griffin Park started disastrously as injury kept him out of the team until late October. He was named team captain and played in most games from then on. Paul Brooker arrived from Brighton, a most frustrating player, who at times was a brilliant winger and at others a wayward figure who faded in and out of games. High hopes were expected of Icelander Olafur Skulason, from Arsenal, and an Under-21 International. He played in the first two League games and in the latter suffered a cruciate ligament injury and sadly didn't play again this season. Sam Tillen signed from Chelsea and proved to be a reasonable and versatile player. Lloyd Owusu was welcomed back, from Sheffield Wednesday, with open arms (or perhaps more accurately upstretched hands!) by his many fans and proved that his heart was in Brentford. Finally unknown Dudley ('DJ') Campbell was an inspirational bargain buy from Yeading.

Another departure and another captain initially out on loan to Reading, was former Junior Michael Dobson.

As hoped for the team made a good start, winning their first two games, before failing at Port Vale in a lacklustre televised match. Then a 2-0 home victory over Tranmere saw the Bees topping the table, before an unbelievable - and highly embarrassing defeat in the Carling (League) Cup. Clearly manager Allen wanted to concentrate on the League, for a very substandard team, made up with several Junior players, lost 5-0 at Cheltenham, much to the dismay of the 350 loyal supporters in the away stand. But the (first!) team soon hit back and after two draws they visited Nottingham Forest where they won 2-1 before a 17,000 plus crowd, which saw The Bees heading the table again. Darren Pratley came back for a second loan period and appeared in most of the following games, however long-serving former captain Dobson was sidelined due to a knee injury and on his return later in the season then suffered a broken arm.

If Martin Allen showed his disinterest in the League Cup, this was equally apparent in the LDV Vans Trophy, when Oxford United were entertained and the fans also voted it a non-event with only 1,785 turning up. Once again a fringe and Juniors team was fielded, and in fact did well to record a 1-1 draw after extra time, but eventually lost 5-3 on penalties. Ricky Newman's first full League game coincided with an awful display at home to Bournemouth which was lost 2-0 and sent the team down to fourth in the table. Allen was so disgusted that his programme notes at the next home game contained less than 100 words, including, *" I'm afraid there is nothing else to talk about. I never want that feeling again when I leave the ground...."* His subsequent talk to the team must have had the right effect, for the team won the next two matches on their travels - 1-0 at Rochdale in the FA Cup and 2-1 at Hartlepool.

The return to form continued with an unbeaten run of nine games up to Christmas, including a replayed (at Griffin Park) victory over Oldham Athletic in the FA Cup, and an excellent 4-1 victory at Tranmere Rovers. Leading 3-1 at the break, the team went on to dominate the second half - the first win on the Wirral since the 1978/79 season. This took the team back to second, two points behind leaders Swansea City, who provided the Griffin Park opposition on Boxing Day. Meanwhile the Juniors took a little of the limelight when they beat Arsenal in the FA Youth Cup at Barnet's Underhill. An exciting game was finally decided on penalties.

Just under 10,000 were present for the top of the table League One clash with Swansea which was won 2-1, O'Connor and Hutchinson both scoring in the first half, with the Welshmen getting a consolation on 90 minutes, putting Brentford one point clear in pole position. The victory was particularly commendable as a spate of injuries barely gave the manager any choice in his line-up with just about all those that were fit playing or as subs. Despite the excitement in the League games, this season provided another good cup run. In the third round, and for the third time, The Bees were drawn away, and also for the third time to a Lancashire team - Stockport County from League Two.

Stuart Nelson clears, in the cup match versus Sunderland.

Perhaps, unlike the other two, there was too much concentration on the F A Cup, for the promotion aspirations faltered for a while. The fourth round was a near sensation, for not only were The Bees drawn at home, but also to a Premiership side. Amazingly, this was the first time the club - having been drawn at home - had played a top division club since 1950. Yet even then as a Second Division club they had entered at the third round stage, therefore the previous top division opponents for the team having played through from the first round was a staggering 75 years earlier! Don't ever call the Bees a lucky cup team. On this occasion the opponents were struggling Sunderland.

loan signing Calum Willock made his debut (coming on as a substitute) in the Walsall 'demolition'.

The County were going though a terrible period, struggling both in the League and for survival and having to rely on several novice players. Yet the homesters put up strong opposition, and early in the second half took a 2-1 lead. In a highly entertaining and quite skilful game, Brentford fought back to equalise through Campbell and Rankin score the winner six minutes before time. D.J. was beginning to be taken note of, having scored eight goals in his 15 starting appearances, and more were to come.

A neutral would have thought Brentford were the Premiership side (especially as both clubs normally played in the same colours) for they dominated the game and easily beat their illustrious opponents.

"Brentford truly were a team" (Daily Mail), *"Brentford dominated the Premiership team throughout"* (Sunday Mirror), *"Sodje was imperious, Tabb and Newman were tenacious and Campbell and Owusu dominant"*. (The Sunday Times) - were three of the headlines. It was a team effort but the hero of the day was young 'DJ' Campbell. Although Brentford marginally took the edge, Sunderland's millionaires held the workers to a scoreless draw at half time. Then in the 57th minutes the ground erupted when DJ confidently beat a defender and the 'keeper and rolled the ball into the net. Yet, against the run of play, the visitors equalised, but in true story book fashion, that man DJ struck again with a superb left footed shot in the 89th minute.

The Bees had made it to the 5th round in two successive years, but the match versus Charlton Athletic at The Valley was missing one notable team member - DJ.

Campbell had further captured the headlines, his brace of goals making it eight in six games. The manager (and indeed the Brentford policy) has always been not to inhibit a player who is able to better himself at a higher level; the transfer money also comes in handy! On transfer deadline day the player moved to Birmingham City for £½ m., after just £5,000 had passed hands a few months earlier. Calum Willock was a hasty signing from Peterborough, but the big striker failed to impress and left early into the 2006/07 season.

To Charlton (also of The Premiership), Brentford took 5,496 supporters but there was no repeat cup surprise. The Bees never really recovered from a shock 3rd minute goal, and always chasing the game finally succumbed 3-1, recording a late consolation from Rankin. But the purse was far fatter after another lucrative cup run, and so it was back to the League. The Juniors had their day also losing in the 5th round, in the FA Youth Cup, 2-1 to Newcastle United.

The cup run and postponements due to the weather had left the team having played less games than all their opponents, most of them by three matches. Yet now in 5th place they were only trailing second place Colchester by two points. The current leaders, Southend, had been beaten at Griffin Park the week after the Charlton match, and earlier Walsall were thrashed 5-0, each goal being scored by a different player. A home defeat was a setback, but four points from two away games lifted the team to second by mid-March. In playing 'catch-up' with their games, Brentford - typically - faltered and with six left to play they nonetheless were still in contention for automatic promotion, in second place but now six points behind Southend. Crucial defeats had come at Swansea and Gillingham, but a far from impressive 1-0 victory was won at Milton Keynes, where the home team dominated the play but could not score (even from a penalty).

The normally irrepressive Martin Allen was even briefer than before, in his Blackpool home game programme notes, just 45 words were written, ending: *"But now is the time to walk the walk and not talk the talk."* It didn't really work, because the game was drawn, the fourth running, and gradually automatic promotion was slipping away. But whatever happened this season, the 3-1 victory at Swindon will never be forgotten by all The Bees fans there. The 'hot and cold' Brooker from a defensive position around 20 yards from his goal, ran three-quarters the length of the pitch with the ball, outpacing four Swindon players, before coolly slotting the ball past the goalkeeper from an angle just inside the penalty area. This was, without a doubt, a contender for the 'Goal of the season' no matter what division.

The final home game, yet another draw, all but settled the promotion issue leaving Colchester needing just one point in their last match. Brentford needed to win at Bournemouth for this slender lifeline - and they drew! So for the second season running it was the play-offs yet again. However, this season the team had been more consistent, except for the crucial tail-end of the season. Could they regain their form or were they to be the 'Bridesmaid' once more?

Finishing third they played at Swansea in the first semi-final play-off match. A fiercely partisan home crowd urged their team on, but it was The Bees who morally came out on top, having taken the lead through Tabb, but then conceding a goal and having Nelson sent off controversially. A 1-1 draw, and a Griffin Park match to follow a few days later; surely they could do it this time. The home crowd, the majority of the 10,652 present, did their best, but the team failed once more just when it mattered, Swansea won 2-0 on the night. It had been a thrill packed season, a memorable one, but failure at the last hurdle was far more difficult to accept than a year earlier.

2006/07

During the early days of the close season The Bees were - not surprisingly - one of the favourites for promotion. That was until a bombshell was dropped and subsequent events which later made them one of the favourites for a move in the other direction, at least in the eyes of the supporters. In May, manager Martin Allen gave in his notice and left. It had been rumoured before and after his move that he had already been applying for other managerial jobs to higher level clubs. He then supposedly expected during the summer that the Crystal Palace job was his for the taking, then it wasn't and he retracted his resignation.

The manager's post at Tranmere Rovers, it would seem, was seen by him as even more of a formality - hardly an upward move but to a club with theoretically more potential than Brentford. Once again this fell through. But he was now out of a job, and his move to Milton Keynes Dons was hardly an upward progressive move as it was to a club one division lower! Albeit the Dons Chairman Pete Winkelman could offer plenty of money to buy promotion. Unfortunately, at Brentford this wasn't the case and Allen was no doubt frustrated that he couldn't do more. He was very upbeat about the move, but one suspects that perhaps rather than choosing the job, in the final event this was the only suitable one offered. With plenty of money at his disposal he took his new club to the brink of promotion, then lost in the play-offs - his third consecutive experience of this heartbreak. Martin Allan was undoubtably an inspirational manager who soon got the fans batting for him, but he was also no more than a 'nearly' man. However, one tends to think that if there was a club that he would support it would be The (Griffin Park) Bees.

The new manager was Leroy Rosenior who had experienced a long career. A respected player he gained various managerial experiences, most notably during his four years with Torquay United, whom he took to promotion in 2004. His move to Griffin Park was greeted with mixed feelings amongst the fans, and following on from Martin Allan was always going to be a difficult act to follow. Alarmingly, he also had to virtually build a new team, as all the gems, and others, departed in a mass clear-out.

No fewer than a near full team (10) of major players moved on, and effectively broke up a winning squad. The three key players were without doubt Jay Tabb, Sam Sodje, and Michael Turner - a trio of bright talent that had been nurtured at Griffin Park. The diminutive Tabb, who was called up for the Under-21 Irish squad was signed by Coventry, for an 'undisclosed fee', Sodje was another defector to new Premiership club Reading, for an initial £350,000; the enthusiastic defender had cost nothing from Margate two years earlier. The slim and tall defender Turner, whom Allen had patiently enticed away from Charlton Athletic moved to Hull City for a similar fee. The money received was without doubt a lifesaver for the new Brentford owners, the Brentford Supporters Trust, but at what cost! The unlucky Michael Dobson signed for Walsall.

Others movers who, albeit were not so crucial, were: 'George' Bankole (the rarely used stand-in goalkeeper) who joined Allen at Milton Keynes, Marcus Gayle, now past his best, moved on to Conference side Aldershot, as did veteran Ricky Newman who never really made his mark at Griffin Park. Eddie Hutchinson joined now non-League Oxford United, and Rankin rejoined Grimsby Town (where he didn't impress), whilst Pratley ended his loan spell.

To replace the outgoings there was a variety of newcomers. Goalkeeper Clark Masters stepped up from the Juniors, but was initially overshadowed by Nelson, and Charlie Ide gradually made his mark in the squad. Thomas Pinault a French midfielder became a regular in the team and the tall central defender Matt Heywood initially came on loan from Bristol City but later signed permanently. However, experienced but slow, he had a fairly poor season but came good a year later. Adam Griffiths joined from Bournemouth, missing the first game due to his sending-off in the previous season in the last match - against Brentford. Striker Jo Kuffour, who signed from Torquay was a rare success this season, but in contrast Gavin Tomlin, from Staines Town, was tried for a while but never succeeded, and Chris Moore, from then non-League Dagenham and Redbridge, had a similar experience. Young Simon Cox came on loan from Reading in September and initially looked an exciting prospect.

Brentford's famous supporter, Bill Axbey, then aged 102 years, presents a bouquet to 'young' fanr Alice Price, aged just 95!

Despite the end result the following May, it all started so well. A 1-0 home win over Blackpool before a 6000 plus crowd, a 1-0 victory at Northampton, cheered on by 699 travelling fans and a good 2-2 draw at Brighton. This put The Bees in a play-off position at 4th. The Blackpool victory saw young Masters have an excellent display in goal (Nelson was suspended due to his dismissal in the play-offs), whilst Skulason showed what the supporters had missed for a year (although sadly his good form was not often repeated) and he scored the only goal. Moore also netted his debut goal, at Northampton, pouncing on a goalkeeper error, but he too only flattered to deceive. This good run continued with draws at home to Huddersfield and away at Scunthorpe. At Glanford Park, The Bees took a first half lead, and from then on were under constant pressure, yet it was an unlucky headed own goal from Mousinho that settled the draw; Scunthorpe were later to become the division's unlikely runners-up.

After beating Bradford City 2-1, with Kuffour netting his fourth League goal plus one from the evergreen O'Connor, then a 1-1 draw at Leyton Orient, the team retained fourth place and were unbeaten in the first seven games. Despite the grim forebodings, perhaps this really would be promotion at last. But no, this was as good as it got, and from then on it was pretty much all downhill. Diplomatically the least said about the 2006/07 season, the best! There were very few highlights, just a dismal plunge to the depths of the table, where the team stayed, and the only real newsworthy items concerned activities off the field rather than on it. In short it was one of, if not arguably THE worst season in the club's history.

After beating Swindon Town in the first round of the Carling (League) Cup in a dull match at the County Ground, enlivened only by the exciting penalty shoot-out (with a goal saved and a goal scored by Nelson), The Bees failed dismally at home to Luton in the next round.

Likewise, in October, Northampton were again beaten on their own ground, on penalties, in the Johnstone's Paint Trophy, but then defeat came at Nottingham Forest before a paltry attendance of 2,031.

In the League, six matches produced just three points and the team had slumped to below mid-table by the end of September. Although one bright spot to relieve the gloom was the production of *"There'll Always Be A Brentford"* which was written by Bees supporter Duncan Aldrich and performed at the Questors Theatre in Ealing. It related to the ups and downs of a family of Bees supporters, poignant and so true to life.

Scott B. Fittzgerald
(not to be confused with 'Scott P.)
Player, Youth Team Coach and even temporary manager during the 2006-07 season!

A long term injury had kept Owusu out of contention and at Millwall, with Cox suffering a fractured fibula and Griffiths a broken nose, steps were taken to halt the slump when much travelled Clyde Wijnhard came on loan for three months. But a dreadful 1-0 home defeat to Doncaster Rovers in the FA Cup, followed by an even worse 4-0 Griffin Park reverse to Crewe, which resulted in a plunge to second from bottom in the League table, spelt the end for Rosenior.

The manager was a likeable man (perhaps not a good thing for a football manager) although it was said that at times he was unsure of himself and found it difficult to make some tactical decisions. If so, this no doubt found its way down to the players and the morale dipped. By the time of the next home match, on the 5th of December (after yet another defeat and again at Cheltenham), Scott B. Fitzgerald had been elevated from the Juniors to take over the temporary running of the first team. Any hope of a brief 'honeymoon' period for a new manager was dispelled with another home defeat, this time by 4-0 to Doncaster Rovers, again.

Since mid-October, goalkeeper Nelson appeared to have suffered a mysterious injury that was barely referred to, and in his place young Clark Masters was thrown into the deep end in a dispirited losing squad. Charlie Ide started to be featured in the team, yet even Simon Cox's return on loan, after his injury, in early December, and the experience of Wijnhard couldn't halt the disastrous slump. By the year end The Bees were bottom, with a record-breaking run of 18 matches without a win (and only six draws), which stretched back to the 2nd of September.

It was a great testament to the fans that even in these bleak days, the home atendances still topped 4,000, and even 180 brave souls travelled to Carlisle two days before Christmas - the reward being a 2-0 defeat. The blame for the defeats could hardly be attributed to Masters alone, but a third regular 'keeper, Nathan Abbey took over, whilst there was still no news of Nelson.

A 2-1 home win over Chesterfield relieved the gloom, but the team were soon back to their losing ways, and as such rarely had any luck. Five minutes into the game at Yeovil, on-loan defender David Partridge from Bristol City was unbelievably sent off for an alleged attempted head-butt. It was certainly unbelievable to both managers, the home fans and the Bees supporters behind the near goal, who had no idea why the referee had suddenly halted play. To cap a miserable afternoon, despite Brentford fighting gamely on, they conceded an early second half goal, and then with five minutes left, Che Wilson another loan signing making his debut was also shown the red card in debatable circumstances. The sad plight of the team was at least tempered by the fact that Bees United continued to make inroads into their overall running of the club.

The new manager did his best with a few short term loan signings, the most notable being 32 year-old Neil Shipperley, but he had gone before the end of his four month loan period from Sheffield United. Around this time Tomlin and Moore had their contracts cancelled by mutual consent.

With nine games left the team, although not bottom at this time, were seven points clear of safety, and relegation began to look unavoidable. In mid-March both Owusu and Nelson returned to the team, but they could do nothing to halt the slide and with four games left to play The Bees' relegation was confirmed. Just for good measure a new temporary manager also took over, Barry Quin, a long serving member of the Brentford staff and at that time the Head of Youth Development, was placed in charge for the remaining irrelevant matches. Fitzgerald could hardly be criticised, for he had taken over a dispirited losing team, with no chance of buying new players. Three weeks later, on the 7th of May, the Club's fourth manager in 11 months, Terry Butcher, was announced as the new permanent man in charge.

Quin's last game actually ended with a victory, in which The Bees scored four goals, beating mid-table Port Vale 4-3. Butcher notionally began, ominously, with a defeat, by 3-1 in the last game of the season at Tranmere (his contract didn't start until two days later), when Willock scored the Brentford goal, his last for the club. The final and unwanted club record was set, when for the first time ever Brentford finished bottom of their division in the Football League.

In April Brentford lost a supporter legend, Bill Axbey, aged just seven weeks short of his 103rd birthday. Until his death, as well as surely being the oldest football supporter in the country, he was probably the oldest ever. Older than Griffin Park itself, he was born in neighbouring New Road, he was a team mascot aged 95 and until a short time before he died regularly travelled unaccompanied on the bus from his Ealing home. It was fitting that the New Road stand was soon to be renamed the 'Bill Axbey' stand.

2007/08

After the previous 12 month nightmare, it couldn't get any worse. It didn't, but for a time things looked as is if they might!

Yet another manager! But Terry Butcher couldn't find the winning formula.

Manager Butcher was joined by former Brentford player Andy Scott as his assistant. On paper, the two should have made a good partnership. Butcher had managed at the top level in Scotland, guiding Motherwell along during a period of financial problems for this club and as a well known former England International he no doubt would command respect from the players and his contemporaries in the game. Meanwhile Scott had played and assisted in management at the lower League divisions, therefore it could be expected that he would be able to seek out potentially good players at this level.

A new manager, coupled with the previous season's performances meant that many players became part of a mass clear-out. Notably Nelson moved to Leyton Orient, Rhodes (to Bradford City), Kuffour (to Bournemouth) and the most disappointing to most fans, the departure of Owusu to Yeovil Town. Stand-in goalkeepers Abbey joined Milton Keynes Dons and youngster Masters dropped down into non-League midway through the season. Frampton moved over to Millwall, for an undisclosed fee and Skulason did not have his contract renewed. Naturally all the loanees returned, and the somewhat tempestuous career of Brooker finally ended at Griffin Park after two games.

To make up the losses, and with two goalkeepers on the move (and another later on), Simon Brown joined after his variable season at Hibernian, and Ben Hamer came on loan from Reading. Other loanees were Adrian Pettigrew of Chelsea and Charlton's Grant Bassey who each stayed for three months, whilst Sammy Moore from Ipswich was around for six months; all had their chances but didn't over impress. Unattached Ricky Shakes initially signed on a match by match basis, and at times displayed some exciting work on the wing. Probably the biggest disappointment of the newcomers was John Mackie, a mainstay in Orient's promotion side two seasons earlier. Despite starting as team captain, he was later dropped and left before Christmas; in fairness, although he did not make a good impression at Brentford, he left with no hard feelings from either side. Gary Smith proved himself to be a worthwhile free signing from Milton Keynes, but not so the experienced Lee Thorpe, who didn'tt become the hoped for poaching goalscorer and was unable to display the enthusiasm that was expected.

Midfielder Craig Pead from Walsall was a member of the PFA select side of the previous season and became a fairly regular member of the team, as did Glenn Poole, arguably the best of the newcomers, who signed from Grays Athletic. Alan Connell also arrived, having been a regular in Hereford's side but who favoured a move back to London. John Mousinho was unlucky, for on breaking into the team on a regular basis, he missed much of the season through injury. But Heywood was a revelation. A poor season and a highly paid player, it was expected he would move on but he stayed at Griffin Park, later became the team captain and although slow to turn he was dominant in the middle of the back four and was later voted the player of the season. Charlie Ide soon became a favourite with his enthusiasm, but his early promise faded after a few months. The evergreen O'Connor with close on 300 appearances for the club (achieved on December 8th - Butcher's last game in charge), was a very familiar face during the season.

The season started in a subdued fashion with a 1-1 draw at home to Mansfield and the same score at Notts County, after The Bees first took the lead. Between times the team crashed out of the Carling Cup suffering a 3-0 home defeat to Bristol City. 2-1 wins over Barnet and at Bury gave the fans early season false hopes with the team then lying 6th from top. But another 3-0 home defeat, to well-fancied Milton Keynes, soon put things into perspective. The form at home games continued to be a problem and after a somewhat embarrassing, but undeserved 3-2 defeat to newcomers Dagenham and Redbridge, the winner coming from ex-Bee Chris Moore, the record showed just one win in five at Griffin Park. After a very poor performance at Edgar Street, Hereford, where most of the away fans were housed in an antiquated 'shed' in the corner of the ground, the warning signs were there, with the team slipping to below halfway in the table.

New signing Nathan Elder is on the ball, in the home match versus Wrexham.

In November, a 1-0 defeat to Macclesfield, followed a 2-1 victory at surprising fellow-strugglers Bradford City. The attendance at Valley Parade was 13,326, incredible by League Two standards, but the majority of those City supporters had taken up the pre-season ticket option of paying around one third the full price. By now The Bees were around mid-table, and on the 10th of November travelled for a first round FA Cup match, to a candidate for the worst ground in the Football League at Kenilworth Road, Luton. In one of their best games of the season, the visitors took a deserved lead, and were unlucky when the homesters later equalised. Cheats do prosper sometimes, and the over watering of the Brentford end (and surprisingly not contravening FA rules) during halftime ensured that those defenders were liable to slip when turning. There were no excuses though for the 2-0 home defeat in the replay, which was played before a lamentable crowd numbering 2,643.

But bigger disasters befell the team between the cup-ties, with yet another home defeat, 2-0 to Darlington and then the worst result of this and for many seasons.

Unfortunately for them, 480 Brentford supporters had to witness the club's joint record defeat, 7-0, at Peterborough. There was a partial excuse, for goalkeeper Brown was, some would say unfortunate, to be sent off after just three minutes. The resultant penalty put the Bees behind, and the free-scoring Posh just couldn't stop from then on. Two more home defeats, making it four on the trot (including the cup replay), saw The Bees now languishing sixth from bottom and just a few points ahead of the unthinkable - relegation out of the Football League; something drastic had to happen, and it did, for Manager Terry Butcher was given his marching orders.

In fact the cover for the last programme with Butcher's notes included within, on the 8th of December, said 'Merry Christmas' but not for him. Subsequent events showed that he had assembled reasonable players but just was not able to motivate them. Andy Scott stepped up as temporary manager - the sixth man at the helm in 19 months. On this occasion there was the traditional new-man good-start syndrome, for Brentford's former striker steered the team first to a 3-1 win at Wrexham and then a particularly creditable 1-1 draw at Milton Keynes. In the Dons' luxurious surroundings the visitors first took a surprise lead and then showed tremendous character, for despite being under non-stop pressure for the rest of the match, they conceded just one goal.

In just a short time the prospects began to look better, and when The Bees took the lead at home to Wycombe on Boxing Day the future indeed looked even brighter. To add to the shine, Poole's 23rd minute strike had to be the goal of the season. Standing alone well outside the box for a corner, a low perfect pass was driven to Poole's left foot and on the volley he scored; everybody was mesmerised for a few seconds. This was to be one of many impressive strikes from the midfielder, who finished the season as the leading goalscorer. Unfortunately Starosta, a near ever-present in the team, committed a reckless foul in the penalty box and was sent off, just on the stroke of half-time. The penalty was converted and from probable conquerors, Brentford became the conquered, and lost the match in the second half. Fortunately this was only a short blip on the recovery road.

Now playing with a confidence and purpose (yet still with the same pool of players), not shown under Butcher, the team went on to win 2-1 at Dagenham, when the surprise inclusion in the team was the return of popular on loan 'keeper Hamer, and a well deserved victory at Shrewsbury, with the first League goal for Osborne. This was the first visit to The Shrews compact and neat new ground, the only disadvantage, on a very bright winter afternoon was the sun which all but blinded the travelling fans behind the goal. With everybody's agreement Scott by now had been given the manager's spot permanently.

Manager Andy Scott, assistant Terry Bullivant (both former players), staff, players and fans - a time to forget the recent past and looked to the future!

Following two further victories and a draw, after 28 games The Bees had climbed to the top half of the table, nine points off a play-off place; yes even this goal was now being spoken of! However, during this run came a farcical day at Accrington. Heavy rain had ensured that frequent checks were made that the game would proceed, and this was confirmed by Stanley at midday.

The match referee arrived, and at 2.30 p.m. he called the game off. Despite no rain during the morning, the pitch was indeed waterlogged, but there were many hundreds of Brentford fans who were left fuming. For the Tuesday re-match a few weeks later, 187 of those supporters were let in at half price, but this was no consolation for a dismal 1-0 defeat. The Bees were beaten by The Brentford Bees at Barnet, and then won at home by 3-1 - to Accrington Stanley - then the wheels came off the wagon.

Four dismal reverses followed (including the Stanley re-match) after nine undefeated games and only one loss in 12. Relegation fears were all but over, but now so were any outside promotion hopes. Even with 10 matches left there was little to play for, the first time in some years that the club found themselves in this situation. The final matches produced a variety of results, the last home game being a 3-0 home defeat, before the best crowd of the season, to Hereford United, and their large contingent of fans were able to celebrate automatic promotion. Then the last match was also lost, to Stockport, who were eventually promoted via the play-offs.

14th in the lowest division can hardly be seen as a success, no more than an away record that bettered that at home. But Bees fans have had to endure much over the years.... one season in the First Division (second tier) in 54 years, several relegations to the lowest division in that time, a few good cup runs. This time having sunk to (hopefully) the lowest point, but now under a bright young new manager who was able to make his players play for him and play attractively. It is traditional to end a history book on an optimistic note. For Brentford it can't be on a high, but at least it can with hope......

'.....The Only Way Is Up'!

The 90's and onwards....
A Colourful History

Promotion Day 1992

Phil ('Noddy') Holder (Manager 1990 -1993)

The Italian Job (Off to Ascoli - 1992)

Dynamic 'Denny' Mundee (1993-1995)

The popular 'Flying Pig' Kevin Dearden (1993-1999)

We lost!
(1996-97 season Play-off final)

Captain, Paul Evans, 'wears' the Championship Trophy.

Failed saviour Micky Adams, couldn't avoid relegation in 1997-98.

We Won! (1998-99)
Championship winning goalscorer:
Lloyd Owusu....

.....And the celebrations after the goal.

Stylish, but seldom on target - Ben May, versus Wycombe Wanderers 24th April 2004. Also in attendance, Tabb, Hutchinson and Talbot.

Paul Smith - safe hands in the early 2000's before moving up to a higher level.

Martin Rowlnds - a popular player... until his move to QPR!

Stephen Hunt beats the Barnsley defender during the 2003-04 season.

(Left) Matt Somner tries to thwart another Sheffield Wednesday attack - they won 3-0 at Griffin Park in October 2003.

And on to 2004 - 05

(Below) Isiah Rankin (in blue and yellow), surrounded by Saints, scores the first at Southampton in the Cup.

Tense atmosphere... packed house for the Southampton replay.

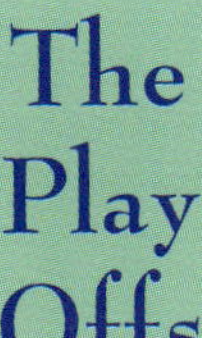

45th game - Brentford through, Wrexham down.

46th game - Tabb scores the dramatic winner, with four minutes left on the clock.

47th game - Nearly a goal at Sheffield Wednesday, in the first leg of the play-off semi-final.

No-nonense Eddie Hutchinson played in the cup game..

The Sunderland Cup-tie 2005 - 06

....as did John Salako (seen here with Stephen Hunt)

'DJ' Campbell nets the opening goal.....

....and the celebrations start - aided by Andy Frampton, Lloyd Owusu and Stephen Hunt.

Sam Sodje's effort hits the post in the 5th round match.

Isiah Rankin scores a consolation goal at Charlton, and the massed Brentford crowd show their appreciation for the team's excellent cup run.

Meanwhile.... in the League, Kevin O'Connor scores a last minute penalty in the 5-0 demolition of Walsall in February.

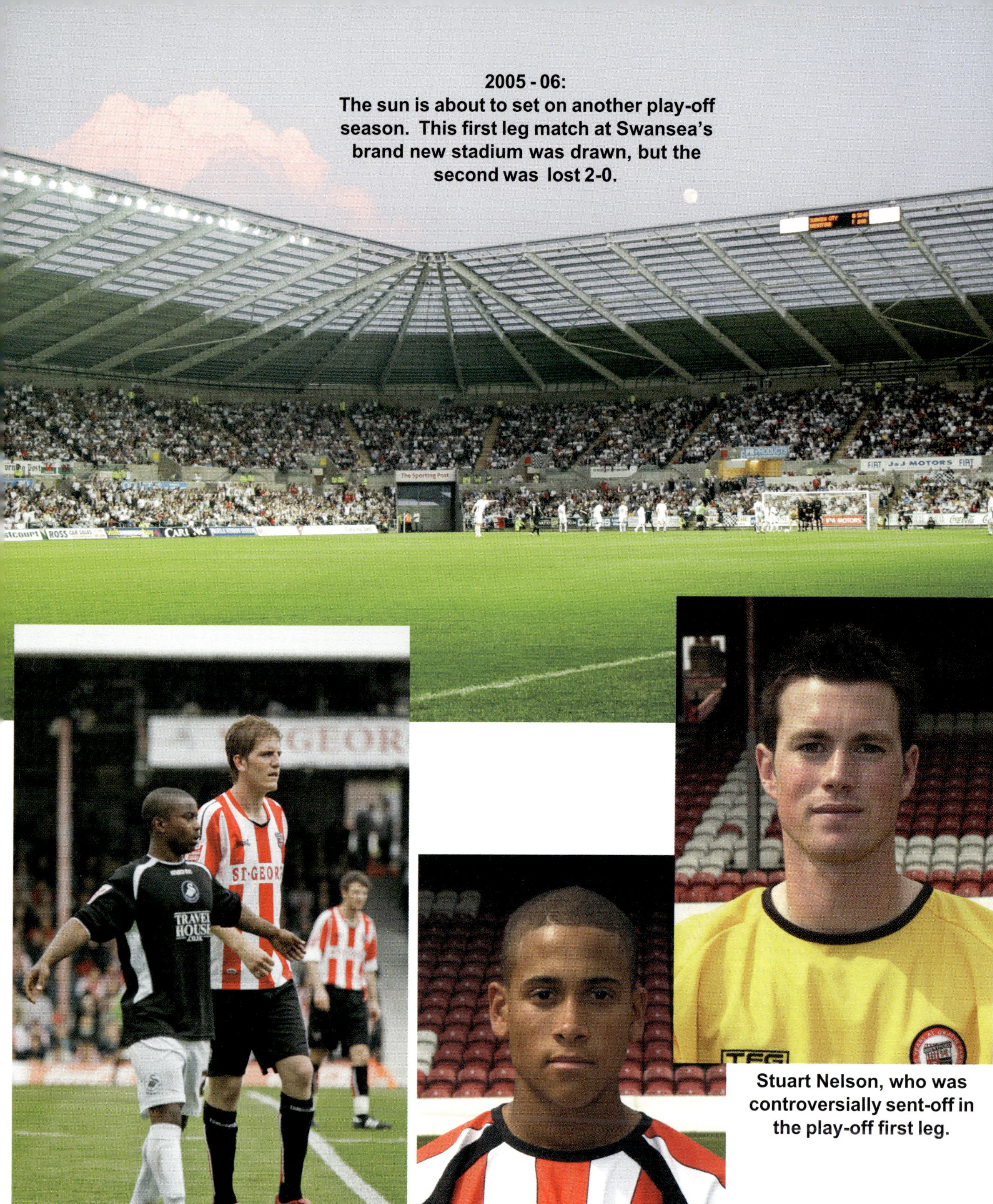

2005 - 06:
The sun is about to set on another play-off season. This first leg match at Swansea's brand new stadium was drawn, but the second was lost 2-0.

The long and short of it. Bargain buy Michael Turner competing with Swansea's Leon Knight in the play-off semi-final second leg.

Stuart Nelson, who was controversially sent-off in the play-off first leg.

Alex Rhodes, recalled to the team for the second leg

There were few happy moments in the 2006-07 season!

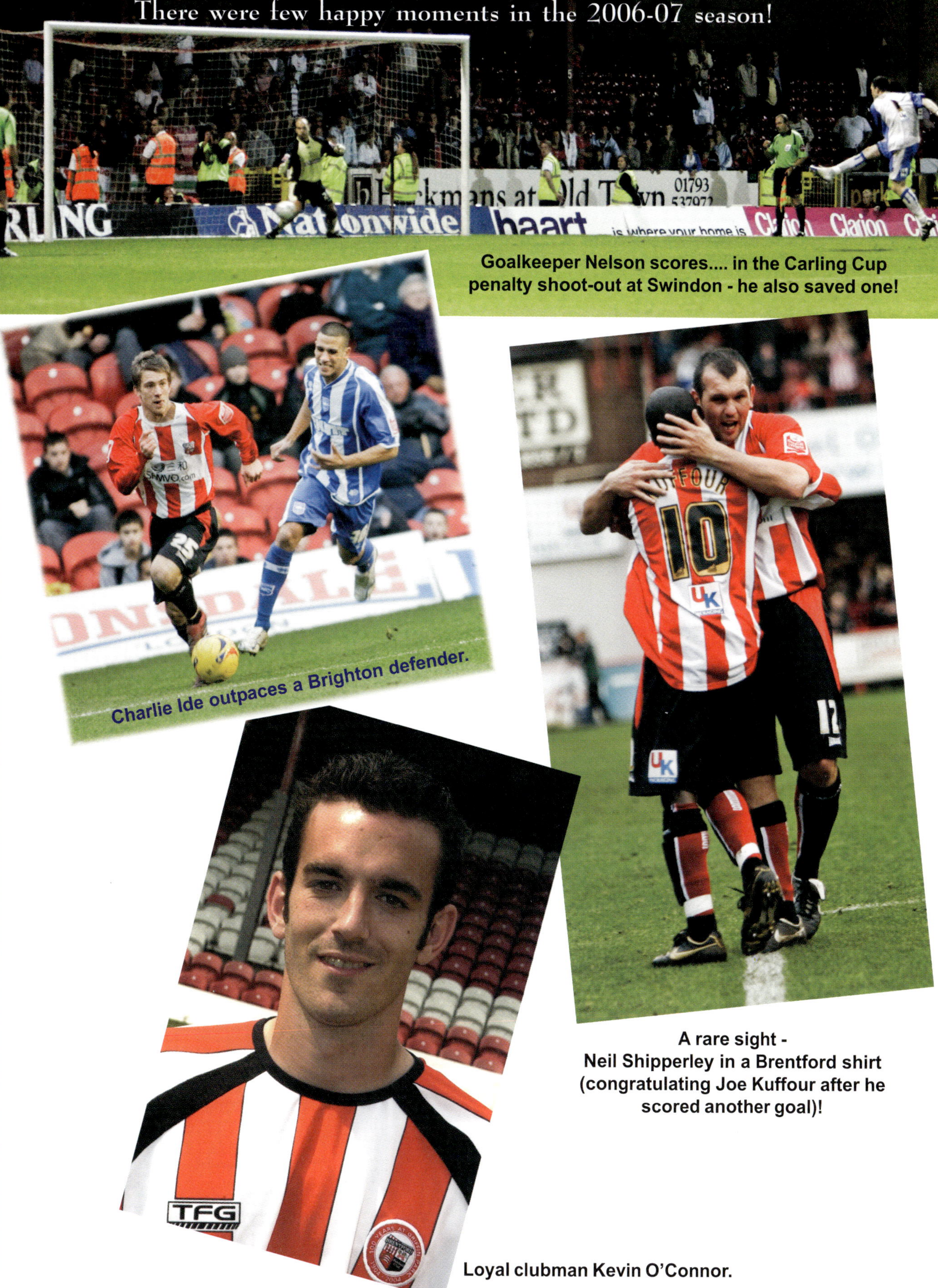

Goalkeeper Nelson scores.... in the Carling Cup penalty shoot-out at Swindon - he also saved one!

Charlie Ide outpaces a Brighton defender.

A rare sight - Neil Shipperley in a Brentford shirt (congratulating Joe Kuffour after he scored another goal)!

Loyal clubman Kevin O'Connor.

Joe Kuffour scores this 'wonder-goal', an overhead volley, versus Bradford City.

Charlie Ide celebrates his goal against Tranmere, with Kevin O'Connor and, on loan, Simon Cox joining in.

Supporters celebrate with the players - Pinault, Tillen, Ide and Wilson - after Frampton (left) scores at Blackpool.

Glenn Poole's 'goal of the season' (from a corner) versus Wycombe.

2007 - 08

'Loyal supporters', at Shrewsbury in the January sunshine.

Paul Brooker promised so much, disappointed so often! Left early in the 2007/08 season.

Not what it looks like; Rickie Shakes didn't try to score against Ben Hamer in the home match versus Notts County!

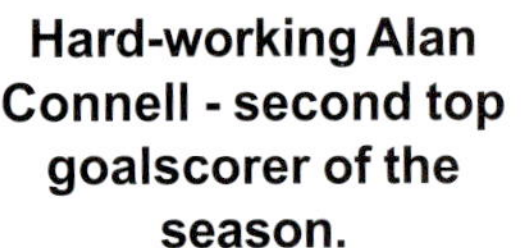

Hard-working Alan Connell - second top goalscorer of the season.

The vocal centre at Griffin Park - the newly covered Ealing Road terrace.

Manager Andy scott surveys the scene at the end of the 2007-08 season. All agreed he had done a good job after a difficult period.

Nathan Elder scored the last Brentford goal of the season at Lincoln.

A History in Programmes

1904-05: The oldest known Brentford programme
1918-19: Versus Arsenal, the Bees won 4-1, and were later Champions, Arsenal were runners-up.

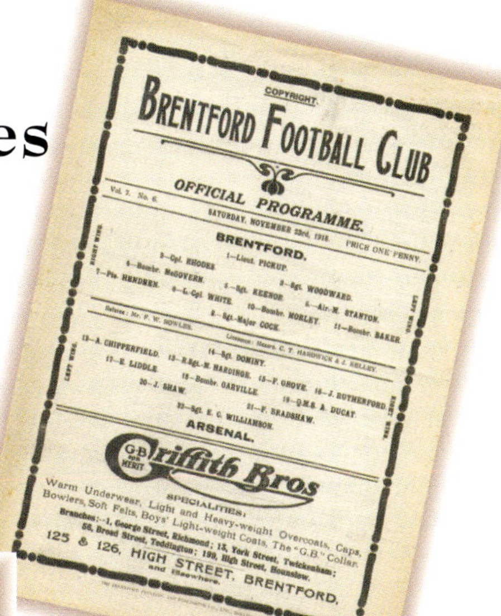

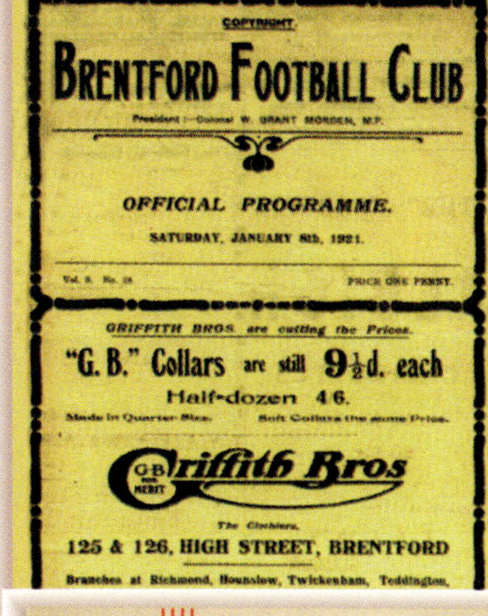

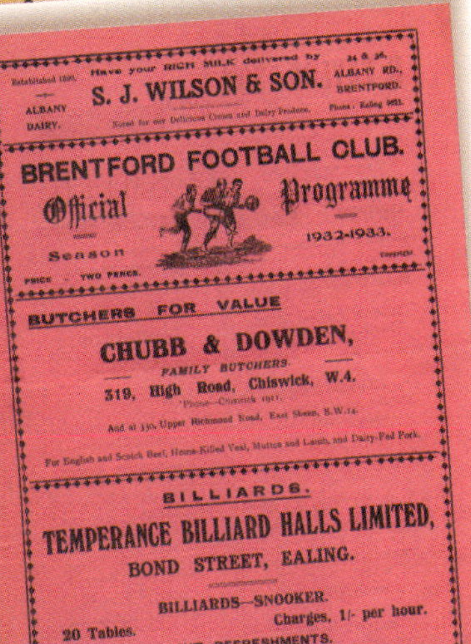

1920-21: The first in the Football League and the local derby v QPR on Christmas Day. A 2-0 defeat before a crowd of 16,379 (a new record at this time).
1920-21. The first FA Cup match as a League club, versus Huddersfield Town, which was lost 2-1, before a 14,892 crowd.
1929-30: All covers were the same this season, when every home match was won (a Football League record).
1932-33: Promotion from the 3rd Division South. Again all covers were the same with no match information on the front.
1934-35: Promotion to the First Division. A special programme for the last match which was watched by 30,000.
1935-36: The first in the First Division.

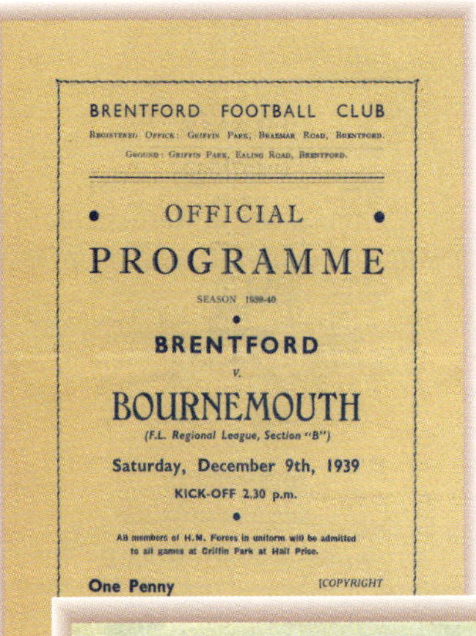

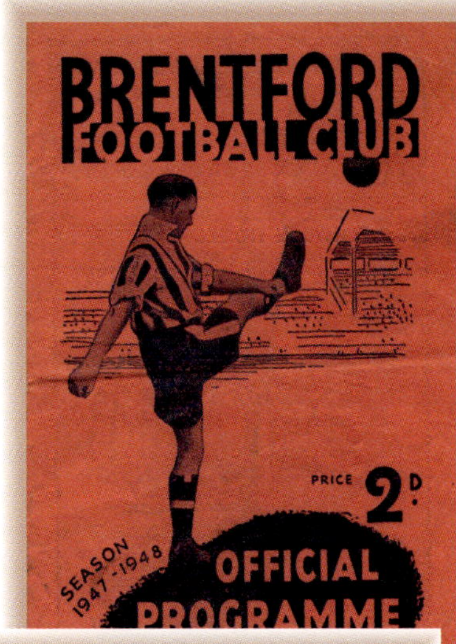

1939-40: League matches were suspended during the War and Brentford played in the Regional League. This match was won 5-2.
1946-47: The Football League fixtures resume. Huddersfield Town were beaten in the first home match by 2-0, before a crowd numbering 31,264.
1947-48: The first home match back in the Second Division gets off to a bad start with a 3-0 defeat to Luton Town.

1948-49: The FA Cup match versus Leicester City produced an all-time record attendance at Griffin Park of 38,678.
1954-55: A 2-2 draw with Shrewsbury Town watched by 12,743 - the first (home) back in the Third Division South.
1957-58: After beating Brighton 1-0 (attendance 25,720) in the last home match, The Bees were top for five days. (Brighton won their last match and were Champions).
1960-61: Sunderland were beaten 4-3 in the club's first ever League Cup match.
1962-63: Brentford bounce straight back into the Third Division as Fourth Division Champions, after beating Workington in the last home match.

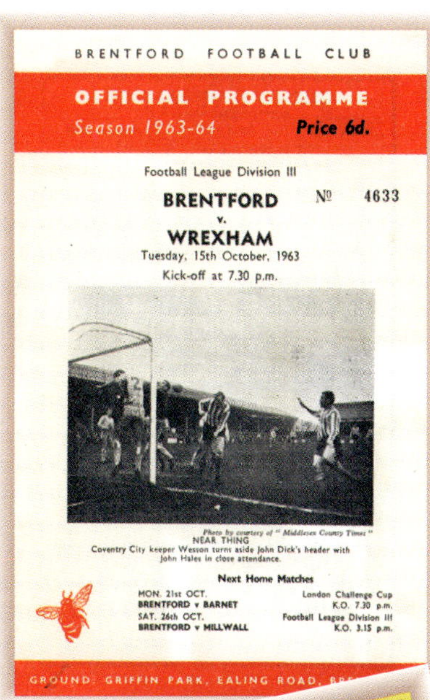

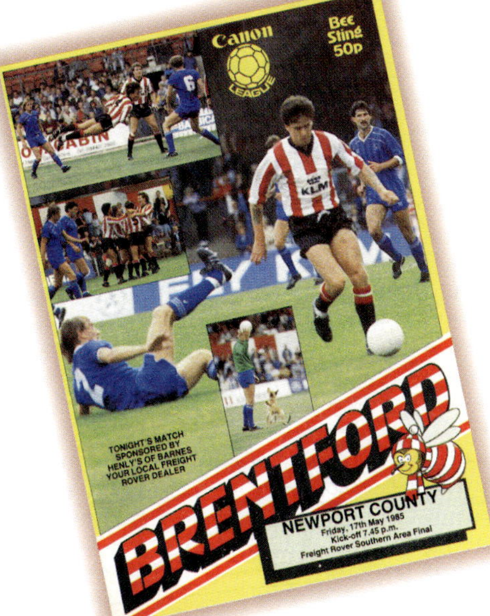

1963-64: Brentford recorded their record Football League victory, 9-0, versus Wrexham.

1971-72: After six seasons in the Fourth Division, The Bees are promoted (but only for one season!) The last home match was watched by 14,520.

1978-79: The first home match back in the Third Division - again.

1984-85: Newport County are beaten 6-0 and The Bees march on to the Freight Rover Trophy at Wembley.

1988-89: Brentford beat Manchester City 3-1 in the FA Cup, en-route to the quarter finals (6th round).

1990-91: Brentford played Tranmere Rovers in the club's first ever promotion play-off match.

1991-92: Fulham are beaten 4-0, the last home match before promotion to the First Division (second tier)

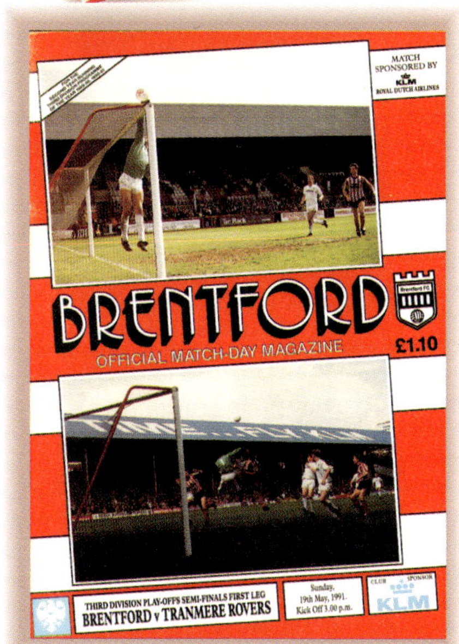

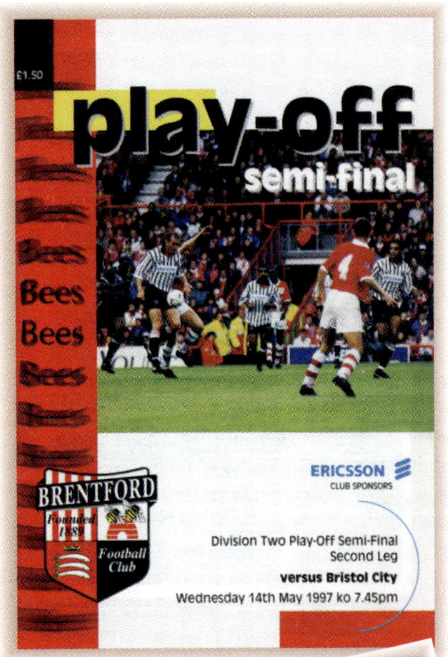

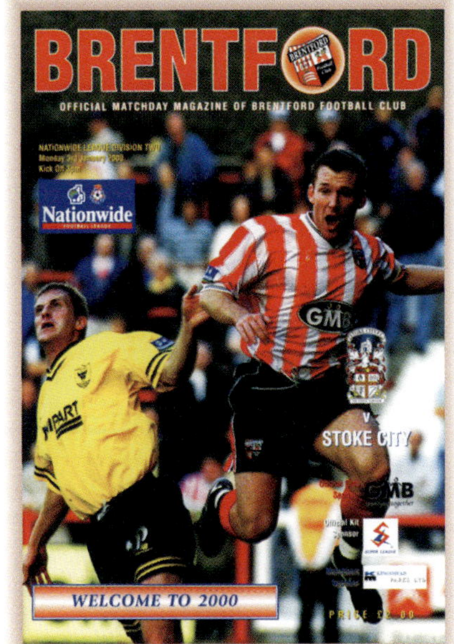

1996-97: Bristol City are beaten 2-1 in the second leg play-off match, but then lose to Crewe Alexandra in the final at Wembley.

1999-00: Stoke City are entertained in the first match of the new millennium (a 1-0 defeat).

2000/01: A one-off special cover, and 'gift wrapped' (protective transparent cover) was produced for the Worthington (League) Cup match versus 'Spurs.

2001-02: Huddersfield Town are beaten in the second leg play-off match, but again lose in the Final, this time at the Millennium Stadium.

2005-06: Premiership Sunderland are beaten in the 4th round FA Cup match.

2007-08: The Bees lose 3-0 in the last home match - the end of an era and the start of a better one?

Grounds For A Change

After the formation of Brentford F.C. on the 10th of October 1889, at the Oxford and Cambridge Hotel, Kew Bridge, the first priority was a ground, or more accurately a patch of grass on which to play. A full account of the various grounds was published in 2004, viz. *'100 years of Griffin Park'*, therefore the following is only a brief summary of the various venues and developments.

The Clifden House Ground, Brentford (October 1889 - March 1892).

Various references fairly accurately pinpoint this location as the open land between the later Lateward and Clifden Roads'.... *"Field at the rear of Clifden House"..."private entrance near to The Griffin".... "at the back of the Weslyan Chapel."* The ground was fenced and The Griffin was used as a clubhouse and dressing rooms, with the entrance to the enclosure via a walkway off Brook Road, opposite the junction with Braemar Road.

The first Brentford match was played at the Clifden House Ground on the 26th of October when neighbours Kew F.C. were entertained. There were few people attracted to the match, the gate takings totalling just 2/6d. (12½p - representing perhaps 20 or so spectators). Bonnell of Brentford scored the first goal, and the match finished in a 1-1 draw. At the end of the 1891/92 season, and against their wishes, the club had to vacate the ground, as Mr Underwood (the owner) had sold the site and the lease was not renewable. There were many open areas in the district but presumably none suitable for enclosing or their owners prepared to allow the, by now successful, football club and its noisy followers occupation.

Benn's Field, Little Ealing (October 1892 - December 1894).

With the season already in progress, the club had little option but to accept the only ground offered them, a very large field, opposite where Northfields Avenue and Little Ealing Lane merge and extending to the railway line to the north. At the south-west corner, The Plough Public House (a rebuilt version still exists today), that was run by the owner of the ground, Charles Benn, served as a reasonable matchday clubhouse and as changing rooms. Adjacent to the pub was an ornate arch which led to the 'Bowling Greens and Pleasure Grounds' (this entrance can still be seen).

These other sporting pursuits were presumably also located with 'Benn's Field'. The football area was big enough for two pitches, and in fact the reserve and first teams occasionally both played there at the same time, although the size of this area must have made an enclosure fence difficult to incorporate. Located some distance from Brentford, support declined to around 400 average.

In the Summer of 1894, St.Paul's Football Club amalgamated with Brentford. Around this time Bill Stephenson became the new chairman and he was able to find the club a new home, but Before the move one match was played at Ealing Park, which was close to The Plough, on the other side of Little Ealing Lane. This was a somewhat undersized ground that had previously been used by the St. Paul's club.

Shotter's Field, Brentford (December 1894 - April 1898).

Shotter's Field had occasionally been used by the club in the early days for reserve matches and one first team Friendly. Then known at Montgomery's Field, off Windmill Road, but previously entitled George Clark's Field. Mr Clark resided in Boston Lodge, alongside The Ride, which formed the northern boundary of the ground. The lodge and the field had changed ownership to Lt.Col. Stracey Clitherow, and he leased the latter to Mr. Shotter and Mr Veysey, who in turn sub-let it to Brentford F.C.

The 1894/95 season started with the ground unenclosed and with no facilities, but perhaps tents being used for changing, etc., although some distance away, the Duke of York pub was later used. By April 1896, the Windmill Road side had hoardings erected and The Ride side may also have had a form of enclosure fence or have been treelined. Despite the ground not being an ideal venue, it was described as being *"One of the best in Middlesex. It is dry very level and quite close to the town"*, and in April 1895 was used for a match between the Middlesex and Surrey F.A.'s. That summer a 'reserved enclosure' (probably uncovered) was incorporated, but also around this time the Lodge and the ground changed hands yet again. The new owner, Mr Beldam, disliked football and later complained about the noise during matches! Being sub-let the ground also attracted a high rent, and this had to be increased in order to persuade Mr Beldam to allow the club's continued use. By now crowds of 1,000 were not uncommon, and 2,000 were present for an F.A.Cup match.

The club's success led to a proposed further rent increase for the 1898/99 season, which was refused and so a new ground had to be found again. A return to Benn's Field was not possible as building on the site was due to start and reluctantly the club moved to an adjacent field.

Cross Roads Ground, Little Ealing. (September 1898 - April 1900)

So named for a marker post known as 'Pope's Cross' at the junction of Little Ealing Lane and South Ealing Road, the field was to the north-west. Far from ideal, this venue had no facilities and was around a 15 minute walk from Brentford. In effect Brentford amalgamated with the occupants - Brentford Celtic F.C. - and at least the ground could be accessed via horse-drawn buses from Ealing and Kew, plus from nearby South Ealing Station. During the summer a corrugated iron structure was erected at one end of the ground, euphemistically called a pavilion, which was used as dressing rooms and a tea bar. An uneven, narrow and sloping pitch left a lot to be desired!

The 1898/99 season was a financial nightmare, with gate takings well down and a large sum spent on players' 'travelling expenses', which brought into question the club's 'amateur' status. This came to a head in October, for the books relating to the club mysteriously went missing when the Middlesex F.A. came to inspect them, and payments to players were revealed. The club was suspended for a month, a new committee was formed and the club formally turned professional. The public initially rallied round, but gates soon slumped to around 200, when the very continuance of the club was in question. But just when the end appeared nigh, Mr Underwood (who owned the first ground), managed to persuade members of the Boston Park Cricket Ground to ground share at their York Road ground.

Boston Park Cricket Ground, York Road, Brentford. September 1900 - April 1904

A few years earlier there had been plans to turn the ground into a general sports ground, but these never came to fruition. However, at least at the new venue there were two small pavilions on the north side of the ground towards the Ealing Road end and after some persuading, the cricketers agreed to the football club raising money for spectator enclosures. A successful season in the Southern League saw crowds of up to 4,000 at York Road, and with their election to the First Division, the club was formed into a limited company in August 1901. Rapidly, temporary covered stands (known as the 'flower pot stands') were installed along the Ealing Road end, earth banked terracing was built on the York Road side opposite, whilst the facilities in the pavilions were upgraded. The following season, Woolwich Arsenal were entertained in the F.A.Cup for which the 'flower pot' stands were extended and extra entrances installed. On Boxing Day 1903, a new record attendance (for any of the club's grounds) was created when Fulham's visit attracted 12,000 to York Road.

Braemar Road, Griffin Park, Brentford. (January 1903 to date)

During the tail end of the 1903/04 season, it was announced that the club had obtained the rights to use a former cherry orchard, owned by the brewers, Fuller Smith and Turner. The site was offered for £5,000, however, this was beyond the club's means, but they were happy to agree a 21 year lease at £40 per acre (about £200 per year in total) with the option to buy at the same price during this time. Over the next 100 years the main changes are briefly listed here:

Summer 1904: The Stands from York Road were re-erected on the New Road and Braemar Road sides at Griffin Park, and entrances were provided on three sides. Earth and some timber terraced banking was installed elsewhere. By 1915 the New Road 'Flower Pot' stand had gone.
1920: Concrete terracing to the New Road side was installed.
1927: A new Braemar Road Stand (substantially as still exists) was built.
1930: Ealing Road end concrete terraced.
1931: Brook Road end concrete terraced, and New Road terracing roofed over.
1933: Brook Road end terracing roofed over.
1935: The close season and into the Autumn saw the most extensive changes undertaken. Brook Road concrete terracing and a roof over was extended to cover virtually the full width of this end. Also the wing ends of the Braemar Road Stand were extended as was a small area of terracing at the Ealing Road end at the New Road side junction. In addition the New Road terracing was extended back several steps and the whole side was re-roofed.
1936: Two houses in New Road were purchased, demolished and a new entrance to this side of the ground was created (now access was possible on all four sides).
1937: The New Road covered terrace was extended further by adding several steps towards the pitch, but was unpopular as part of this area was now below ground level and also caused drainage problems. This now brought the capacity of the ground to around 40,000.

1954: After the intervention of the war, the next change of any significance was the installation of floodlights, which consisted of a series of lights along the roofs of the New Road and Braemar Road sides.
1963: The floodlights were replaced with four pylon towers, whilst the entrance frontage to Braemar Road was rebuilt and various other improvements were undertaken to the offices, etc.
1974: The old floodlight gantries on the New Road side were removed and the roof surface painted in red and white
1982: The airline KLM took over the New Road roof for an advertisement, which was acknowledged in the *'Guinness Book of Records'* as the largest in Europe. During the Summer new seats were installed in the Braemar Road Stand.

1983: In February, 800 seats were lost in the devastating fire which also destroyed a portion of the stand itself and adjacent facilities. A substantial portion of the stand was rebuilt and other improvements in this area were added.
1985: The area between the Ealing Road terracing and the road itself was sold off for housing (named 'Bowles Hall' after Stanley Bowles), leaving just a narrow access strip to the road. After the Bradford City fire tragedy, new regulations required that some crush barriers and fencing had to be strengthened, and the ground capacity was reduced from 37,000 to just 10,600.
1986: The much lamented 'Royal Oak' or Brook Road end stand was demolished and most of the area behind was sold for housing. Meanwhile a new, but much criticised narrow seated stand (the 'Wendy House') with standing below was built to partly replace the enormous terrace that had been lost.
1987: The roof over blocks A, B and C in Braemar Road was replaced and the terraced paddock below rebuilt.
1991: The concrete terracing at the Ealing Road end was replaced (the profile being designed for the possible later installation of seating), and the turnstiles removed making the access to Ealing Road an exit only. The Braemar Road A block (end wing) was refurbished and brought into use again. The ground capacity was now increased to nearly 13,000.
1996: The New Road and Braemar Road standing terraces were made into seating areas.
2007: The last major change at the ground was the roofing of the Ealing Road terrace.
2008: The ground was now seated on three sides (with some terracing at the Brook Road end), all four sides were covered, with a total capacity for around 12,763. Whilst Griffin Park may be considered old fashioned, and in fact in most respects has not visually changed greatly since the late 1930"s, it still retains the feel of a 'real' football ground, generates an atmosphere and has the visual impact and individuality, that cannot be emulated by most new stadiums.

The Future: During the 1940's it was first suggested that Brentford move to Wembley Stadium! However this idea was never progressed, and it wasn't until 1974 that the idea to build a new ground, on the old Brentford Market site (near Kew Bridge), was mooted. This plan did not progress and in the mid-1990's some consideration was given to moving to the Feltham Arenas (then used by Feltham F.C.). During the 'Noades era' the prospects of moving to the Kingstonian F.C. or Woking F.C. grounds was firmly rejected by the supporters, but finally, in November 2002, serious thoughts were given to a move to the industrial site in Lionel Road, adjacent to Kew Bridge Station.

(Above) c. 1900: The Plough - to the left the entrance to Benn's Field (an opening still exists today).
On the extreme right of the photo', the (probable) entrance to Ealing Park.

(Below) The top end of Windmill Lane. Shotter's Field lay behind the current trees in the background.
At the end of this line (on the bend of the road) was one entrance to The Ride.

(Right) 1932: The only known photograph of the Boston Park Cricket Ground. This view looks west towards York Road. The raised perimeter fence indicates an embankment at this end that was constructed during Brentford's occupation.

(Below) 1935: At Griffin Park, major works were underway including extended terracing and new roofing to the New Road side and the enlargement of the terracing plus the extended roof over the Brook Road end.

Above and below: Summer and Autumn 1983. Renewal and repairs are carried out to the Braemar Road stand.

Views from the Ealing Road end:

(Above) Two police teams at Griffin Park in 1915. To the left, a rare view of part of the early Braemar Road stand (that had been moved from the cricket ground). Behind the team is the Brook Road embankment end.....

.....(Below) From a similar viewpoint. c. 1980 a fine view of the south-west corner of Griffin Park, pre-the demolition of the Royal Oak end and the fire.

2002: A unique view taken from the top of the north-east floodlight pylon.

Match action at Griffin Park, March 1938 versus Preston North End. The Bees lost 3-0 before a new record attendance of 37,586

Above: A fine aerial view of Griffin Park taken c.1980.

The last major work undertaken at the ground, The Ealing Road end is roofed over in the summer of 2007.

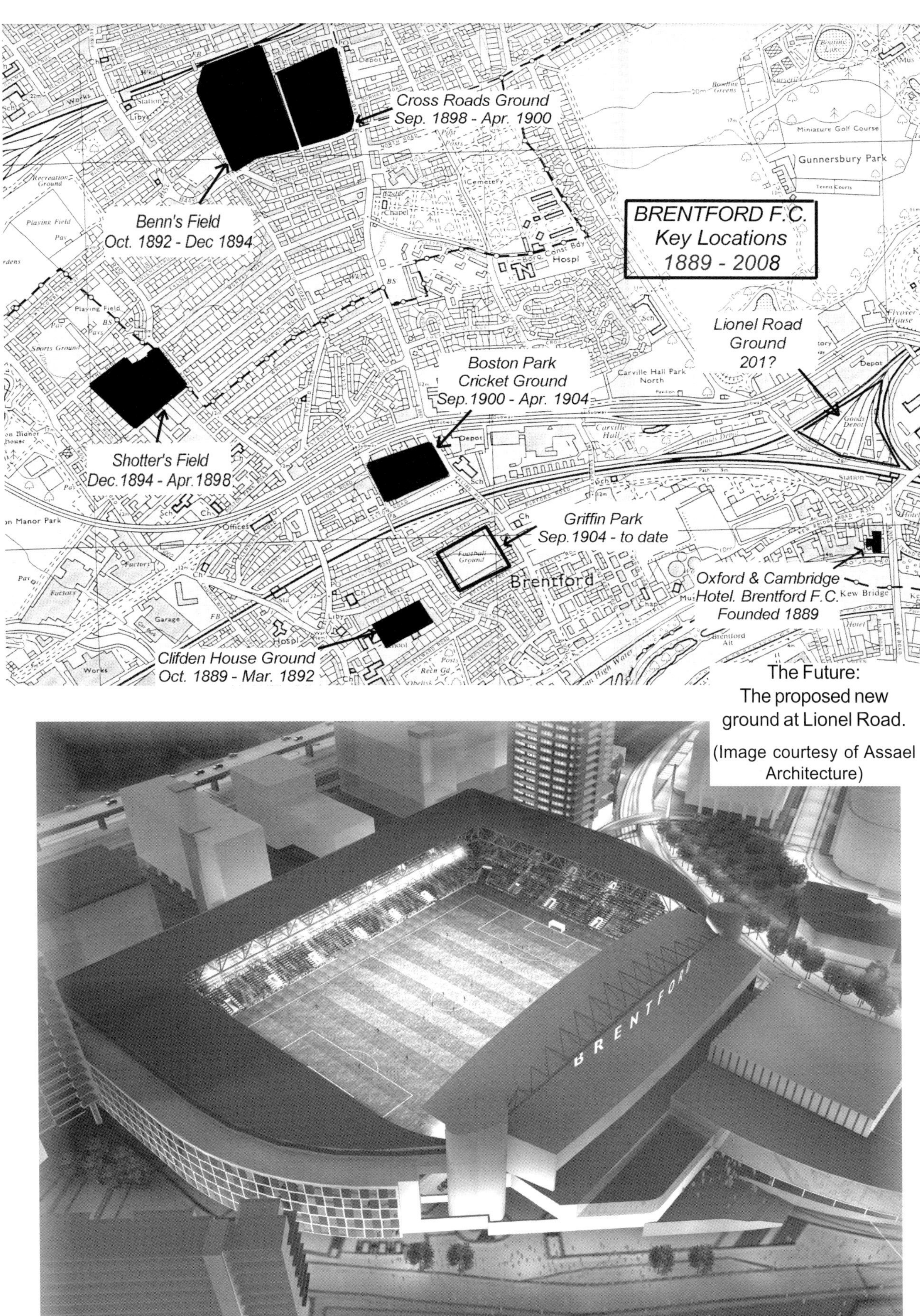

The Future:
The proposed new ground at Lionel Road.
(Image courtesy of Assael Architecture)

Supporters - Through Thick and Thin!

Since the early post-war days it has been increasingly difficult for football clubs to make ends meet. Much of this situation has been brought about by the relatively high wages that the players now earn, and especially the ludicrously high figures enjoyed by those with the elite. Initially supporters organisations within clubs principally functioned in a non-fundraising capacity, literally doing what the title suggests - supporting. However increasingly clubs have relied more on money raised elsewhere other than at the gate.

At Griffin Park, in the early years, there had been supporters' organisations, but in 1948, was born the official ***Brentford Football Supporters Club***. Rather than providing funding for the parent club, initially, the main aims of this organisation was the arranging of transport for 'away' matches, which soon led on to the advent of a more social side and modest money-making schemes such as dances and whist drives. Weekly meetings were held in the old St. Paul's Hall in Brentford and successful Sunday football teams 'Hayesbees' (run from the Hayes Branch) were two of the club's social activities. Another worthy function was the commentaries given to the Blind, which has been running continuously since 1951.

A rival organisation later appeared, ***The Bees Association***, but after a short period the two combined to become the ***Brentford Supporters Association***. The parent club tended to become more involved with away travel in the 1980's and so the activities of the Supporters Association diminished from that time, which in any event had always been a passive group.

Apart from virtual continual financial hardship since the late 1950's, which culminated in the near extinction of the club a few years later (covered elsewhere in this book), the first meaningful effort to provide additional substantial financial support came by way of the ***Brentford Lifeline Society***, which was founded in February 1986 with 600 inaugural members. The aims of the Society was, and still is, to assist the Football Club (principally financially) and over the years the Society has donated, directly or indirectly, nearly £2m. Various projects and innovations have been achieved, and in addition the membership (which at times approaches the 1,000 mark), still pay just £2-00 per week and enjoy frequent draws for many prizes including luxury holidays.

The ***Brentford F.C. Programme Collectors Club*** was inaugurated in November 1990, when 15 founder-members attended the first meeting chaired by Eric White. Although embracing only a small number of enthusiasts, this club, through buying and selling programmes, has managed to support the parent club in several ways, notably occasional matchday sponsorships and in more recent years has supplied articles for the matchday programme.

However, these organisations were run for the benefit of the club and its supporters, and direct involvement in the running of the Football Club had never been sought. This attitude started to change with the vociferous phenomena of the ***Fanzines.*** In general there was an increasing awareness by the mid to late 1980's that some owners (or consortiums) that owned football clubs were often not looking towards the best interests of the supporters (who were providing the bulk of the income). The 'Fanzine', a magazine produced for the fans, by the fans, and usually without editorial restraint, addressed these accusations and other related issues regarding their club. In reality, these magazines were often crude (in production and language), lacking in eloquence and often, arguably, slanderous. However, this somewhat anarchic behaviour made those running the clubs sit up and take notice, and indeed often led to desired actions being taken.

Brentford were represented for over a decade or so by no less than four Fanzines***, 'Voice Of The Beehive', 'Hey Jude', Thorne In The Side'*** and ***'Beesotted'***. Whilst still being critical of various aspects within Brentford F.C. each acted with a fair degree of restraint and for a period the three survivors were even given there own editorial space within the Matchday programme. At the time of writing, only two of the four still publish, but over the ensuing years they too have made financial contributions to the football club.

Following on from the fanzines the ***Griffin Park Grapevine*** came into prominance, a website to which views and opinions can be aired. The site has survived the test of time and continues to be very active in respect of all things Brentford. Naturally it is completely independant of the football club, and being unsponsored it makes the reasonable claim that it is both unbiased and independant. The views and opinions expressed on the site are very varied, although the site does have the caution: 'Warning: May contain nuts'!

Disquiet amongst many supporters due to proposed actions by the football club led to the desire for co-ordinated protest action and so ***BIAS*** (Brentford Independent Association of Supporters) was formed in the late 1990's. In a sense, BIAS became a natural progression from the fanzines. Loosely describing itself as a Trades Union for Brentford fans, being democratically elected, its aim was and still is for grievances to be aired and to protect the football interests of the supporters. This new group's membership, as well as supported by 'the man on the terrace' also included employees of the football club. The organisation became particularly vocal when there were plans to move the club to Kingstonian F.C. (In Kingston) or Woking, around the turn of the last century.

In April 2001, ***'Bees United'*** was formed, in effect out of BIAS, a supporters trust, more properly known as the **Brentford Football Community Society Limited**, an Industrial and Provident Society. The aims being twofold, to give ordinary football supporters greater involvement in the future of Brentford Football Club and to bring the Club closer to the whole community.

By raising sufficient funds to purchase a majority shareholding in the club - a professional club run by its supporters - was the ultimate goal. Such an ambitious scheme required substantial funds and over the next few years many varied events were held to raise them. BIAS and Bees United working together have, and continue to, generate funds principally through members' annual fees, financial pledges, donations and matchday bucket collections. Bees United saw itself as carrying on the work that BIAS had instigated, with a view to a link between the club and the supporters; the first aim was for this new group to be represented on the parent Brentford F.C. board.

In an effort to gain local authority (Hounslow Council) support for the club and to increase the public's awareness, BIAS instigated ***'AbeeC'***,whereby candidates for councillors in many wards for the forthcoming local elections in 2002 were put forward. A history-making election saw one such candidate - ***Luke Kirton*** for the Brentford Ward - win and he was able to champion the cause of the club.

Meanwhile both BIAS and Bees United continued in unison, the former being the more vocal and openly critical, the latter gaining credibility in a more sedate fashion in order to achieve the aims of the members and ultimately Brentford F.C.

Bees United and BIAS both support the proposed move to Lionel Road.

Meanwhile, an earlier proposed new ground scheme, to relocate the club to Feltham Arenas, was ditched and an alternative, a move to Lionel Road that was instigated by Bees United in November 2002, was put forward and gradually gained credibility. The community stadium that was envisaged saw Hounslow Council became far more sympathetic to the cause and moves proceeded in order to secure the site.

The next few years saw Bees United progress, in particular with the securing of seats on the Brentford board. Eventually Bees United were able to take over the majority shareholding in the club, but they agreed that the only way to make the club sustainable in the long term was to move to a new stadium, in a partnership with the local council and possibly another partner, develop Griffin Park for housing and wipe off the club's debt (which by now was considerable).

A move to a new purpose built ground, together with ancillary activities, would enable the football club to diversify and hence generate more income. In January 2006, Bees United's main aim was realised when sufficient funds were accumulated in order to secure the majority shareholding.

There will no doubt be many more hardships, continued frugality, plus monetary requirements from the fans in the future. A tie-up with a developer who would takeover Griffin Park after first providing the funds for the building of a new ground in Lionel Road is hopefully coming to fruition and it would seem that, perhaps, the corner has at last been turned.

Brentford Players: Who's Who

(Every player to have played in a competitive Football League match from 1920-21 to 2007-08)

See also page 178. Players names' are followed with 'first' (first season, e.g. 1995 = 1995-96) and 'last' (season) with Brentford.
The book *'Timeless Bees'* contains the complete Who's Who of Brentford to 2005-06. Brief records of new players (2006-07 and 2007-08) follow.

Name	First	Last
ABBEY, Nathan	2006	
ABRAHAMS, Paul	1995	1996
ADAMS, Micky	1997	1997
ADAMSON, TOM	1929	1934
AGYEMANG, Patrick	1999	
AIKEN, Vic	1937	1939
ALEXANDER, Rowan	1984	1986
ALLDER, Doug	1977	1980
ALLEN. Jack	1924	1927
ALLEN, Mike	1971	1978
ALLEN, Philip	1922	1924
ALLEN, Ralph	1930	1933
ALLEN-PAGE, Danny	2002	
ALLON, Joe	1992	1994
ALTON, Charlie	1921	1925
AMOS, Alf	1913	1923
ANDERS, Jimmy	1948	1951
ANDERSON, Doug	1937	1939
ANDERSON, George	1926	1927
ANDERSON, Ijah	1995	2002
ANDERSON, James	1939	1946
ANNON, Darren	1994	1996
ANSAH, Andy	1989	1990
ANSTISS, Harry	1920	1922
ANTHONY, Tom	1962	1965
ANTOINE-CURIER, Mickael	2003	
ASABA, Carl	1994	1997
ASHBY, Barry	1994	1997
ASPINALL, Warren	1997	1999
ASTLEY, Jack	1933	1935
AUSTIN, Kevin	2000	
AVIS, Vernon	1952	1961
AYLOTT, Steve	1976	1978
BAILEY, Dennis	1995	
BAILEY, Harry	1927	1929
BAIN, Jimmy	1928	1934
BAIN, John	1977	
BAKER, Billy	1918	1921
BAKER, Gerry	1969	1970
BAKER, Kieron	1973	
BAKER, Tommy	1932	1934
BALDWIN, Tommy	1977	1978
BAMFORD, Harry	1945	
BANKOLE, Ademola	2005	
BANN, Billy	1930	1932
BARROWCLIFF, Paul	1997	1998
BASEY, Grant	2007	
BASEY, Phil	1966	1967
BASSHAM, Alan	1951	1958
BATEMAN, Arthur	1933	1939
BATER, Phil	1986	1987
BATES, Jamie	1986	1999
BAYES, Ashley	1990	1993
BEACHAM, Albert	1925	1928
BEADLE, Peter	2003	
BEDFORD, Brian	1966	1967
BELCHER, Jimmy	1961	1962
BELLAMY, Bert	1926	1927
BENCE, Paul	1970	1977
BENJAMIN, Ian	1993	1994
BENNETT, Alan	2007	
BENNETT, Micky	1992	1994
BENSTEAD, Graham	1990	1993
BENT, Marcus	1995	1998
BERRY, Bill	1926	1932
BERTRAM, George	1921	1922
BETHUNE, John	1921	1922
BIRCH, Paul	1987	1988
BLACKMAN, Lloyd	2002	2004
BLAKEMAN, Alec	1946	1948
BLAKEMORE, Cecil	1929	1931
BLANEY, Steven	1998	
BLISSETT, Gary	1987	1993
BLOCK, Mike	1961	1966
BLOOMFIELD, Jimmy	1952	1954
BLOOMFIELD, Billy	1956	1959

Name	First	Las
BOLTON, Ian	1983	1984
BOND, Len	1977	1980
BONSON, Joe	1964	1966
BOOKER, Bob	1978	1988
BOROTA, Petar	1982	
BOULTER, Les	1939	1947
BOWEN, Keith	1981	1983
BOWIE, Jimmy	1952	
BOWLES, Stan	1981	1984
BOXALL, Danny	1998	2002
BOYNE, Reg	1919	1921
BRAGG, Wally	1946	1957
BRANAGAN, Keith	1989	
BRIDDON, Sam	1935	1939
BRISTOW, George	1950	1961
BROADBENT, Peter	1950	1951
BROADBENT, Bill	1924	1925
BRODIE, Chic	1963	1971
BROOKE, Garry	1990	1991
BROOKER, Paul	2005	2007
BROOKS, Johnny	1961	1964
BROOME, Frank	1953	
BROUGHTON, Drewe	1998	
BROWN, Jimmy	1935	1936
BROWN, Micky	1973	
BROWN, Simon	2007	
BROWN, Wayne	2007	
BROWN, Willie	1974	1975
BROWN, Bill	1969	
BROWN, Buster	1937	1946
BRYAN, Derek	1997	2002
BUCHANAN, Peter	1947	1949
BUCKLE, Paul	1988	1994
BULL, Mike	1948	1953
BULL, Ronnie	2004	
BULLIVANT, Terry	1983	1986
BURGESS, Ben	2001	2002
BURKE, Steve	1986	
BURNS, Tony	1977	
BURNS, Jackie	1931	1935
BURTON, Deon	2004	2005
BUTLER, Charlie	1926	1928
BUTLER, Steve	1984	1986
BUTTIGIEG, John	1988	1990
CACERES, Adrian	2001	
CADETTE, Richard	1988	1992
CAESAR, Bill	1929	1931
CAIN, Tommy	1924	1925
CAIRNS, John	1927	1928
CAKEBREAD, Gerry	1955	1964
CAMPBELL, DJ	2005	
CANHAM, Scott	1996	
CAPPER, Alf	1921	1924
CARDER-ANDREWS, Karle	2006	
CARLTON, Dave	1976	1980
CARROLL, Robbie	1986	1988
CARSTAIRS, Jim	1991	
CARTMELL, Jack	1919	1921
CASH, Stuart	1990	
CASSELLS, Keith	1983	1985
CATERER, Brian	1968	1969
CAVEN, John	1957	1959
CHALLINOR, Sammy	1920	1921
CHALMERS, Grant	1992	1993
CHARLES, Julian	1999	2001
CHARLES, Darius	2004	
CHEETHAM, Tommy	1936	1946
CHISHOLM, Jack	1947	1949
CHORLEY, Ben	2002	
CLARIDGE, Steve	2004	
CLARK, Archie	1927	
CLARK, Dean	1997	1998
CLAYSON, Bill	1922	1925
CLEMENT, Neil	1999	
CLOUGH, Jack	1933	1934
COBB, Billy	1964	1966

Name	First	Last
COCK, Herbert	1921	
COCKERILL, Glenn	1997	1998
COCKRAM, Allan	1988	1991
COCKS, Alan	1970	
COLGAN, Nick	1997	
COLLINS, Arthur	1926	1927
CONNELL, Alan	2007	2008
CONSTANTINE, Leon	2002	
COOK, Billy	1931	1932
COOK, Mickey	1969	1970
COOKE, Edwin	1924	1925
COOKE, Robbie	1984	1987
COOPER, Gary	1985	
COOTE, Ken	1949	1964
CORNWELL, John	1993	
COTTON, Roy	1973	1974
COURT, David	1972	1973
COUSINS, Jason	1989	1991
COX, Graham	1975	1978
COX, Simon	2006	
COYNE, Chris	1998	
CRADDOCK, Claude	1926	1928
CRISP, Ron	1965	1967
CROMPTON, Arthur	1932	1933
CROSS, Roger	1970	1971
CROWE, Jason	2000	
CROWE, Matt	1962	1964
CROWN, David	1980	1981
CROZIER, Joe	1937	1949
CULLIP, Danny	1998	2000
CURLEY, Tom	1965	1967
CURRAN, Terry	1957	1961
D'ARCY, Jimmy	1952	1953
DARE, Billy	1948	1955
DARK, Lewis	2006	2007
DARGIE, Ian	1952	1963
DAVIES, Ian	1983	
DAVIES, Reg	1928	1932
DAVIS, Paul	1995	
DAWKINS, Trevor	1971	
DAWSON, Alex	1970	
DAWSON, Tom	1947	1948
DEAKIN, Peter	1968	1969
DEARDEN, Kevin	1993	1999
DEARN, Steve	1926	1929
DENNIS, Kevin	1996	1998
DENYS, Ryan	1997	1998
DICK, John	1962	1965
DICKENS, Alan	1993	
DICKSON, Ryan	2007	
DOBSON, George	1967	1970
DOBSON, Michael	1999	2005
DOCHERTY, John	1959	1961
DONNELLY, Jim	1925	1929
DOUGALL, Tom	1947	1948
DOUGLAS, Alf	1925	1929
DRINNAN, James	1927	1929
DRISCOLL, Andy	1989	1991
DROY, Micky	1986	1987
DUDLEY, Frank	1953	1958
DUMBRELL, George	1928	1930
DUNCAN, Peter	1922	1923
DUNN, Billy	1935	1937
DURNION, Andy	1928	1929
DURRANT, Fred	1938	1946
DURSTON, Jack	1919	1921
EAMES, Billy	1978	
EASTHAM, George	1937	1938
EDELSTON, Maurice	1937	1939
EDGLEY, Brian	1961	1962
EDWARDS, Dennis	1967	
EINARSSON, Gunnar	2000	
ELDER, Nathan	2007	
ELLIOTT, Jimmy	1920	1921
ELLIOTT, Tommy	1921	1923
EMANUEL, Lewis	2007	

Name	First	Last
ENGLAND, Jamie	2006	
ETHERIDGE, Brian	1966	1967
EVANS, Evan	1925	1929
EVANS, Paul	1999	2002
EVANS, Steve	2002	2004
EVANS, Terry	1985	1993
FEAR, Keith	1979	
FEEHAN, Sonny	1954	1959
FEELEY, Andy	1987	1989
FENTON, Ron	1968	1970
FERDINAND, Les	1988	
FERGUSON, Jim	1926	1928
FERNANDES, Tamer	1993	1998
FIELDING, John	1963	1965
FIELDWICK, Lee	2001	2004
FILBY, Ian	1974	
FINLAYSON, Bill	1925	1926
FINNEY, Tom	1984	
FINNIGAN, Tony	1992	
FISHER, Charles	1921	1922
FISHER, Bobby	1984	1986
FITZGERALD, Scott	2004	
FITZGERALD, Scott	2004	2005
FLEMING, Mark	1989	1991
FLETCHER, Bert	1927	1928
FLETCHER, Charlie	1933	1935
FLETCHER, Chris	1957	1959
FOLAN, Tony	1998	2001
FORSTER, Nicky	1994	1997
FORTUNE-WEST, Leo	1998	
FOSTER, Jackie	1929	1933
FOSTER, Ron	1969	
FOX, Freddie	1928	1931
FRAMPTON, Andy	2002	2006
FRANCIS, George	1953	1961
FRASER, John	1976	1980
FREEMAN, Darren	1998	1999
FRENCH, John	1932	1934
FRENCH, Mickey	1975	1977
FROST, Lee	1978	
FRUDE, Roger	1969	
FULLARTON, Jamie	2002	2003
FUNNELL, Tony	1980	1981
GABRIEL, Jimmy	1974	
GALLEGO, Jose	1947	1948
GAMBLE, Freddie	1929	1931
GARNER, Bill	1983	
GARNEYS, Tom	1949	1951
GARNISH, Tom	1923	1925
GASKELL, Ted	1937	1952
GAYLE, Marcus	1988	1994
GAZZARD, Gerry	1954	
GEARD, Len	1953	1956
GEDDIS, David	1986	
GELSON, Peter	1960	1975
GIBBINS, Vivian	1932	
GIBBONS, Jackie	1938	1952
GIBBS, Paul	2000	2002
GILBERT, Albert	1924	1925
GILLIES, John	1946	1947
GIRLING, Dickie	1947	1951
GITSHAM, Jim	1959	1963
GLASS, Jimmy	2000	
GLAZIER, Bill	1975	
GLEESON, Percy	1947	1948
GLEGHORN, Nigel	1997	
GLOVER, Allan	1976	
GLYNN, Terry	1977	
GODDARD-CRAWLEY, Richard	1996	1998
GODFREY, Kevin	1988	1992
GODWIN, Verdi	1952	1954
GOLDTHORPE, Bobby	1976	1977
GOODWIN, Jackie	1949	1954
GOODYEAR, Clive	1991	
GORMAN, Bill	1939	1950
GOTTS, Jim	1945	

Name	First	Last
GOTTSKALKSSON, Oli	2000	2002
GOUNDRY, Bill	1955	1961
GOWER, Herbert	1923	1924
GRAHAM, Gareth	1999	2001
GRAHAM, Alec	1924	1926
GRAHAM, Jackie	1970	1980
GRAHAM, Willie	1977	1981
GRAINGER, Martin	1993	1996
GRAVETTE, Warren	1987	
GRAY, Nigel	1984	
GREENE, David	1996	
GREENWOOD, Ron	1949	1952
GRIFFITHS, Adam	2006	
HAAG, Kelly	1989	1990
HAGGAN, John	1922	1923
HALES, John	1958	1963
HALL, Gareth	1997	
HAMER, Ben	2007	
HARDING, Kevin	1972	1975
HARDING, Kevin	1980	
HARGREAVES, Chris	2004	2005
HARNEY, Dave	1969	
HARPER, Tony	1948	1955
HARRIS, Ron	1980	1984
HARRIS, Paddy	1948	1949
HARROLD, Matt	2003	2005
HART, Roy	1949	1955
HARVEY, Lee	1993	1997
HAWLEY, Alan	1962	1974
HEATH, Dennis	1952	1961
HEATH, Micky	1971	1972
HEBEL, Dirk	1998	1999
HEEPS, Andrew	1928	1929
HAENDERSON, Frank	1924	1925
HENDREN, Patsy	1907	1927
HENDRIE, Dick	1927	1929
HENERY, John	1920	1921
HEROD, Baden	1928	1929
HEYWOOD, Matt	2006	2007
HIGGINSON, Tom	1959	1970
HILL, Jimmy	1949	1952
HILL, Mark	1980	1982
HILLIER, Sean	2004	
HODGE, Bill	1927	1935
HODGSON, John	1926	1927
HODNETT, Joe	1926	1927
HODSON, Jimmy	1919	1921
HOGG, Graeme	1998	
HOLDSWORTH, Dean	1988	
HOLLIDAY, Jack	1932	1944
HOLLOWAY, Ian	1986	1987
HOLMES, Jimmy	1983	
HOLMES, Lee	1979	1980
HOLMES, Billy	1978	1980
HOOKER, Jon	1994	1996
HOOKER, Keith	1966	1969
HOPKINS, Dai	1932	1947
HORN, Graham	1975	
HORN, William	1958	1959
HORNE, Ken	1950	1961
HOUSTON, Stewart	1972	1973
HOWARD, Matthew	1988	
HOWE, Fred	1921	1922
HREIDARSSON, Hermann	1998	1999
HIGHES, Harry	1924	1925
HUGHES, Robert	1923	1924
HUGHES, Stephen	2002	2004
HUGHTON, Chris	1992	
HUGHTON, Henry	1986	
HUNT, Dennis	1968	1969
HUNT, Steve	2001	2005
HUNTER, Cyril	1921	1922
HURDLE, Gus	1993	1998
HURLOCK, Terry	1980	1986
HUTCHINGS, Carl	1993	
HUTCHINSON, Eddie	2000	2006
IDE, Charlie	2004	2007
INGIMARSSON, Ivar	1999	2002
INGLIS, Bill	1922	1925
ISAAC, Arthur	1923	1925
JAMES, Clement	1999	2000
JAMES, Joe	1928	1944
JAMES, Roland	1922	1924
JANNEY, Mark	1997	
JAVARY, Jean-Phillipe	2000	2001
JEFFERIES, Alf	1945	1954
JENKINS, David	1972	1973
JENKINS, Iori	1979	1981
JENKINS, Steve	1999	
JOHNSON, Gary	1980	1981
JOHNSON, Rob	1981	1982
JOHNSON, Terry	1974	1977
JOHNSTONE, Gordon	1922	1925
JONES, Allan	1963	1970
JONES, Eric	1945	1946
JONES, Horace	1922	1925
JONES, Keith	1987	1991
JONES, Murray	1992	1993
JONES, Steve	2000	
JONES, Tecwyn	1950	1953
JOSEPH, Francis	1982	1987
JOSEPH, Roger	1984	1988
JULIAN, Alan	2001	2005
KAMARA, Chris	1981	1985
KEARNEY, Bill	1920	1921
KEENAN, Joe	2005	
KENNE, Doug	1946	1950
KEITH, Joe	2006	
KELL, George	1922	1925
KELLY, Bernard	1950	1952
KEMP, David	1982	
KENNEDY, Richard	1999	2001
KERR, Jock	1921	1924
KEY, Richard	1984	1986
KING, Harry	1920	1921
KIRBY, George	1968	1969
KITAMIRIKE, Joel	2003	
KRUSE, Pat	1977	1982
KRUSZYNSKI, Detsi	1992	1993
LANE, Jack	1925	1931
LANE, Bill	1929	1933
LATIMER, Frank	1945	1956
LAWRENCE, Jamie	2004	2005
LAWRENCE, Keith	1974	1976
LAWSON, Herbert	1927	1933
LAWTHER, Ian	1964	1968
LAWTON, Tommy	1952	1953
LAZARUS, Mark	1963	1966
LEDGERTON, Terry	1950	1954
LEARY, Michael	2006	
LEE, Colin	1987	1989
LENNIE, Josh	2004	
LEVITT, Ernie	1920	
LEWIS, Junior	2005	2006
LINE, Simon	1991	1992
LIVINGSTONE, Bill	1959	1960
LLOYD, Barry	1977	1978
LOVETT, Jay	2000	2003
LOWDEN, George	1951	1959
LUSCOMBE, Lee	1991	1993
LYNCH, Tony	1983	1986
MACAULAY, Archie	1946	1947
MacKENZIE, Hamish	1964	1967
MACKIE, John	2007	
MADDY, Paul	1986	1987
MAHON, Gavin	1998	2002
MAHONEY, Tony	1982	1984
MANLEY, Tom	1939	1952
MANSLEY, Allan	1967	1971
MANUEL, Billy	1991	1994
MARSH, Simon	2000	
MARSHALL, Frank	1927	1928
MARSHALL, Scott	1999	2003
MARTIN, Dean	1995	1996
MASKELL, Micky	1970	
MASTERS, Clark	2006	2007
MATHIESON, Jimmy	1934	1937
MAY, Ben	2003	
MAY, Eddie	1989	1990
McADAMS, Billy	1962	1964
McALOON, Gerry	1934	1938
McCAFFERTY, James	1927	1929
McCAMMON, Mark	2000	2003
McCLENNON, James	1925	1926
McCLURE, Joe	1933	1934
McCREE, James	1925	
McCULLOCH, Andy	1976	1979
McCULLOCH, Dave	1935	1938
McCULLOUGH, Paul	1980	1981
McDONALD, Malcolm	1946	1948
McDONOUGH, Frank	1930	1931
McGHEE, David	1994	1999
McGUIGAN, Charlie	1924	1925
McINALLY, Charlie	1958	1960
McKELLAR, David	1980	1983
McKENNAN, Peter	1948	1949
McKENZIE, Duncan	1932	1938
McKINLEY, Charlie	1928	1929
McLAUGHLIN, Hugh	1961	1966
McLEOD, George	1958	1964
McNICHOL, Jim	1978	1984
McPHERSON, Ian	1953	
McPHERSON, Malcolm	1996	1998
MERSON, Paul	1987	
METCALF, Matthew	1993	1994
METCALF, Walter	1934	1937
METCHICK, Dave	1973	1975
MILLEN, Keith	1984	1992
MILLER, Paul	1989	
MILSOM, Robert	2007	
MITCHELL, Archie	1921	1924
MOLESKI, George	2005	2006
MONCUR, John	1989	
MONK, Fred	1948	1954
MONTAGUE, Ross	2006	
MOORE, Chris	2006	
MOORE, John	1946	1950
MOORE, Sammy	2007	
MORGAN, Scott	1993	1994
MORGAN, Wendell	1954	1957
MORLEY, Fred	1913	1921
MORRAD, Frank	1951	1953
MORRIS, Abe	1921	1923
MORRIS, Sam	1919	1921
MORTIMER, Paul	1993	
MOUSINHO, John	2005	2007
MULDOWNEY, Luke	2004	
MULFORD, Sandy	1922	1924
MUNDEE, Denny	1993	1995
MUNRO, Roddie	1946	1953
MURRAY, Alan	1972	1973
MURRAY, John	1978	
MURRAY, Joker	1936	1938
MURRAY, Jamie	1984	1987
MUTTITT, Ernie	1933	1947
MYALL, Stuart	1996	1998
MYERS, Andy	2004	2005
MYERS, Cliff	1967	1968
NASH, Teddy	1930	1932
NAYLOR, Bilbo	1947	
NEILSON, Gordon	1968	1971
NELMES, Alan	1967	1976
NELSON, Dave	1947	1950
NELSON, Stuart	2003	2006
NEWCOMBE, Len	1956	1960
NEWMAN, Ricky	2005	2006
NEWTON, Reg	1949	1957
NICHOLLS, James	1934	1937
NOBLE, Alan	1925	1927
NOGAN, Lee	1987	
NORTON, Horace	1921	1922
OATWAY, Charlie	1997	1999
OBI, Tony	1986	
O'CONNOR, Kevin	1999	
O'DONNELL, Danny	1960	1962
O'FLANAGAN, Kevin	1949	1950
OGBURN, Mike	1965	1967
OLIVER, Tony	1988	
OLIVER, Harry	1938	1948
OLUGBODI, Jide	2003	
O'MARA, John	1971	1972
OMIGIE, Joe	1994	1998
ONIBUJE, Fola	2006	
OSBORNE, Karleigh	2004	
OSEI-KUFFOUR, Jo	2006	
OWUSU, Lloyd	1998	2002
PACQUETTE, Richard	2004	
PALMER, Jamie	2004	
PARKER, Richard	1922	1925
PARKES, Jordan	2007	
PARKINSON, Henry	1923	1924
PARKINSON, Noel	1980	
PARKS, Tony	1988	1991
PARRIS, George	1994	
PARSONS, Eric	1956	1961
PARTRIDGE, David	2006	
PARTRIDGE, Scott	1999	2001
PATERSON, George	1946	1949
PATON, John	1949	1952
PAYNE, John	1929	1931
PEAD, Craig	2007	
PEARCE, Graham	1988	1989
PEARCEY, Jason	1998	2001
PEARSON, John	1951	1958
PEARSON, John	1923	1924
PEPLOW, Ron	1955	1961
PERRYMAN, Steve	1986	1990
PETERS, Mark	2002	2004
PETERS, Rob	1989	1994
PETERS, Ryan	2004	2007
PETTIGREW, Adrian	2007	
PEYTON, Gerry	1992	
PHILLIPS, Gary	1984	1988
PHILLIPS, Gordon	1962	1973
PHILLIPS, Jack	1927	1928
PHILLIPS, Steve	1977	1980
PINAMONTE, Lorenzo	2000	2001
PINAULT, Thomas	2006	
PITHER, George	1921	1922
POINTON, Bill	1950	1951
POLLITT, Mike	1998	
POOLE, Glenn	2007	
POOLE, Richard	1972	1976
PORTER, Trevor	1978	1980
POWELL, Darren	1998	2002
POWER, John	1987	
POYSER, George	1934	1946
PRATLEY, Darren	2005	
PRICE, Jason	2001	2002
PRICE, Jack	1925	1927
PRICE, Johnny	1928	
PRIDDLE, Sean	1987	1988
PRIDDY, Paul	1972	1974
PRIEST, Phil	1987	
PRITCHETT, Keith	1976	
PURDIE, Jon	1989	
PURDY, Albert	1928	
QUINN, Rob	1998	2001
QUINTON, Wally	1949	1952
RAE, Harry	1925	1927
RAINFORD, John	1953	1962
RAMPLING, Dennis	1949	1950
RANKIN, Isaiah	2004	2006
RAPLEY, Kevin	1996	1999
RATCLIFFE, Simon	1989	1995
RAVEN, Jimmy	1934	1936
RAVENSCROFT, Craig	1993	1996
REDDOCK, Charlie	1926	1930
REDKNAPP, Harry	1976	
REED, Hughie	1973	
REEVE, Eddie	1964	1968
REEVES, Ray	1961	1962
REGAN, John	1966	
REID, Reuben	2007	
REID, Bobby	1936	1939
REINA, Ricky	1997	1998
RELPH, Bill	1924	1926
RENWICK, Dick	1969	1971
RHODES, Alex	2003	2006
RICHARDS, Albert	1928	1929

Name	First	Last
RICHARDS, Dai	1935	1936
RICHARDS, Garry	2006	
RICHARDSON, John	1966	1969
RIDDICK, Gordon	1973	1977
RIX, Graham	1987	
ROBERTS, Charlie	1930	1931
ROBERTS, Gary	1980	1985
ROBERTS, Jeremy	1988	1989
ROBERTS, Maurice	1946	1947
ROBERTS, Paul	1983	1985
ROBERTSON, Jimmy	1953	1956
ROBINSON, Terry	1954	1957
ROBSON, George	1930	1935
ROCHE, Paddy	1982	1984
ROE, Maurice	1952	1958
ROFFEY, Bill	1984	
ROGET, Leo	2002	2003
ROLLINGS, Andy	1983	
ROLPH, Gary	1976	1979
ROSIER, Bert	1913	1923
ROSS, Bobby	1966	1972
ROSTRON, Wilf	1991	1992
ROUGIER, Tony	2003	2004
ROWE, Terry	1981	1984
ROWE, Ron	1924	1925
ROWE, Vivian	1924	1925
ROWLANDS, Martin	1998	2003
RUSSELL, Sid	1956	1961
RYCRAFT, Fred	1959	1964
SALAKO, John	2004	2005
SALMAN, Danis	1975	1986
SALT, Harry	1929	1932
SALVAGE, Barry	1973	1975
SANKOFA, Osei	2007	
SANSOM, Kenny	1993	
SAROYA, Nevin	1999	2000
SAUNDERS, Percy	1939	
SCALES, Terry	1971	1977
SCOTT, Andy	1997	2001
SCOTT, Archie	1934	1937
SCOTT, Colin	1990	
SCOTT, Mel	1963	1967
SCOTT, Billy	1932	1947
SCRIVENS, Steve	1976	
SEALY, Tony	1989	
SHAKES, Ricky	2007	
SHARP, Tom	1976	1977
SHAW, Arthur	1946	1948
SHAW, James	1930	1931
SHEPHERD, Edward	1924	1925
SHERLAW, Dave	1928	1932
SHERWOOD, Steve	1974	1975
SHIELDS, Ralph	1921	1922
SHIPPERLEY, Neil	2006	

Name	First	Last
SHRUBB, Paul	1977	1982
SIDWELL, Steve	2001	2002
SILKMAN, Barry	1980	
SILMAN, Dave	1978	1979
SIMMONS, Dave	1974	1975
SINCLAIR, Emile	2007	
SINCLAIR, Tom	1950	1951
SINTON, Andy	1985	1989
SKULASON, Oli	2005	2006
SLADE, Steve	1997	
SLATER, Bill	1951	1952
SMEULDERS, John	1988	
SMILLIE, Neil	1977	
SMITH, Alan	1946	1949
SMITH, Cecil	1931	1936
SMITH, Dave	1931	1932
SMITH, Dean	1978	1980
SMITH, Gary	1973	1975
SMITH, Gary	2007	
SMITH, George	1945	1947
SMITH, George	1920	1921
SMITH, Graham	1974	1975
SMITH, Jamie	2006	
SMITH, Jay	2000	2004
SMITH, Leslie	1934	1945
SMITH, Nigel	1975	1978
SMITH, Paul	2000	2004
SMITH, Paul	1987	1988
SMITH, Paul	1993	1997
SMITH, Willie	1963	1966
SMITH, Bill	1933	
SNEDDON, Tally	1937	1939
SOBERS, Jerrome	2005	
SODJE, Sam	2004	2006
SOMNER, Matt	2001	2004
SONKO, Ibrahima	2002	2004
SOUTAR, Tim	1961	1966
SOUTH, John	1966	1967
SPARHAM, Sean	1990	
SPENCER, Tony	1982	1984
SPENCER, Simon	1997	1998
SPERRIN, Bill	1949	1956
SPRATT, Walter	1920	1921
SPREADBURY, Bert	1919	1921
STAGG, Billy	1972	1975
STANFORD, Harry	1925	1926
STANISLAUS, Roger	1987	1990
STAROSTA, Ben	2007	
STATHAM, Brian	1992	1997
STEEL, John	1925	
STEELE, Aaron	2005	2006
STEPHENS, Bert	1931	1935
STEPHENSON, Paul	1993	1995
STEVENS, Gary	1986	1987

Name	First	Last
STEVENSON, Alex	1927	1934
STEWART, George	1946	1948
STEWART, Ian	1988	
STILL, Ron	1967	
STOBBART, George	1954	1956
STONE, Craig	2007	
STONE, Norman	1928	1929
STOTT, Harry	1922	1923
STRONG, Les	1982	
SUCKLING, Perry	1991	
SUMMERS, George	1959	1965
SUSSEX, Andy	1995	
SWEETZER, Gordon	1975	1978
SWINBURNE, Trevor	1983	1985
TABB, Jay	2001	2007
TALBOT, Stewart	2004	2005
TAWSE, Brian	1970	1971
TAYLOR, George	1920	1921
TAYLOR, Jeff	1954	1957
TAYLOR, Robert	1994	1998
TAYLOR, Scott	2006	
TEER, Kevin	1981	
TERRY, Pat	1968	1969
THAIN, John	1922	1923
THEOBALD, David	1999	2000
THOMAS, Bob	1944	1946
THOMPSON, Alf	1919	1920
THOMPSON, David	1994	
THOMPSON, Niall	1998	
THOMSON, George	1963	1968
THOMSON, Jack	1925	1926
THOMSON, Norman	1930	1933
THORNE, Steve	1987	
THORNLEY, Barry	1965	1967
THORPE, Lee	2007	
TICKRIDGE, Sid	1955	1957
TILLEN, Sam	2005	2007
TILSON, Steve	1993	
TOM, Steve	1971	1972
TOMLIN, Gavin	2006	
TONGE, Keith	1982	
TORRANCE, George	1984	1986
TOULOUSE, Cyril	1946	1947
TOWERS, Jim	1951	1961
TOIWNLEY, Leon	1997	1999
TOWNSEND, Len	1937	1947
TOWSE, Gary	1973	
TRAYNOR, Robert	2002	2004
TUCKER, Barry	1978	1982
TURNER, Brian	1970	1972
TURNER, Michael	2004	2006
TURNER, Wayne	1986	1988
VENTOM, Eric	1946	1948
VINE, Rowan	2002	2003

Name	First	Last
WALKER, Paul	1976	1983
WALLACE, Ken	1971	
WALSH, Charlie	1933	1935
WALTON, Jimmy	1924	1926
WARD, Dai	1963	1965
WARD, Sam	1927	1928
WARE, Teddy	1928	1933
WARNER, Phil	1999	2000
WATKINS, Ernie	1926	1930
WATSON, Frank	1925	1926
WATSON, Bert	1932	1936
WATSON, Kevin	1994	
WATSON, Paul	1997	1999
WATTS, Ryan	2004	2006
WEBB, Stan	1972	1974
WEEKS, George	1929	1939
WEIGHT, Scott	2004	2006
WELLS, Dean	2003	
WESTLEY, Shane	1992	1995
WHEELER, Alf	1932	1933
WHIPP, Percy	1929	1930
WHITEHEAD, Alan	1981	1984
WHITTAKER, Bill	1941	1946
WHITTON, Percy	1925	1926
WIGGINS, Joe	1927	1928
WIGNALL, Steve	1984	1986
WIJNHARD, Clyde	2006	
WILKINS, George	1938	1947
WILKINS, Graham	1982	1984
WILKINS, Leslie	1931	1932
WILKINS, Steve	1978	
WILLIAMS, Dean A	1993	1994
WILLIAMS, Dean P	1993	1994
WILLIAMS, Harry	1923	1925
WILLIAMS, Mark	2000	2003
WILLIAMS, Paul	1987	
WILLIAMS, Ralph	1924	1925
WILLIS, Ron	1968	
WILLOCK, Calum	2005	2006
WILSON, Che	2006	
WILSON, Joe	1935	1939
WILSON, Bob	1967	
WILSON, Tom	1957	1962
WINSHIP, Ted	1926	1929
WOOD, Alex	1928	1929
WOODMAN, Andy	1999	2000
WOODWARD, Viv	1948	1950
WOON, Andy	1972	1975
WOOSNAM, Martin	1928	1931
WORMULL, Simon	1997	1998
WRIGHT, Edmund	1921	1923
WRIGHT, Tommy	2003	
YOUNG, Bert	1925	1926
YOUNG, Bill	1920	1925

New players (2000-06 and 2007-08 seasons)

2006-07	D.O.B.	Birthplace	Previous	Next	A.	G.
ABBEY, Nathan	11-Jul-1978	Islington	Torquay United	MK Dons	16	
CARDER-ANDREWS, Karle	13 Mar 1989	Feltham	Trainee		6	
COX, Simon	28-Apr-1987	Reading	Reading (loan)		14	
DARK, Lewis	10-Apr-1988	Harlow	Trainee		3	
ENGLAND, Jamie	27-May-1988	Epsom	MK Dons		1	
GRIFFITHS, Adam	21-Aug-1979	Sydney	AFC Bournemouth		39	1
HEYWOOD, Matt	26-Aug-1979	Chatham	Bristol City	Grimsby Town	67	2
KEITH, Joe	1-Oct-1978	Plaistow	Leyton Orient		18	2
LEARY, Michael	17-Apr-1983	Ealing	Luton Town (L)		17	
MASTERS, Clark	31-May-1987	Hastings	Trainee	Southend Utd.	20	
MONTAGUE, Ross	1-Nov-1988	Twickenham	Trainee		15	1
MOORE, Chris	13-Jan-1980	Hammersmith	Dagenham & Red.	Dagenham & Red	26	2
ONIBUJE, Fola	25-Sep-1984	Lagos	Swindon Town (L)		4	
OSEI-KUFFOUR, Jo	17-Nov-1981	Edmonton	Torquay United	AFC Bournemouth	44	14
PARTRIDGE, David	26-Nov-1978	Westminster	Bristol City (loan)		3	
PINAULT, Thomas	4-Dec-1981	Grasse	Free agent	Crawley Town	31	1
RICHARDS, Garry	11-Jun-1986	Romford	Colchester Utd. (L)		10	1
SHIPPERLEY, Neil	30 Oct 1974	Chatham	Sheffield United		11	
TAYLOR, Scott	5-May-1976	Chertsey	MK Dons (L)		6	
TOMLIN, Gavin	13-Jan-1983	Gillingham	Windsor & Eton		15	
WIJNHARD, Clyde	9-Nov-1973	Paramaribo	Macclesfield T.		12	
WILSON, Che	17-Jan-1979	Ely	Southend Utd. (L)		3	

Key: 'D.O.B.' = Date of Birth. 'Previous' and 'Next' (clubs)
'A'=total competitive appearances, 'G' = total goals scored (to end of 2007-08 season)

2007-08	D.O.B.	Birthplace	Previous	Next	A.	G.
BASEY, Grant	30-Nov-1988	Bromley	Charlton Ath. (L)		10	
BENNETT, Alan	4-Oct-1981	Cork	Reading (loan)		11	1
BROWN, Simon	3-Dec-1976	Chelmsford	Hibernian		28	
BROWN, Wayne	6-Aug-1988	Kingston upom T.	Fulham (loan)		11	1
CONNELL, Alan	15 Feb 1983	Enfield	Hereford Utd.	AFCBournemouth	47	12
DICKSON, Ryan	14-Dec-1986	Saltash	Plymouth Arg.		31	
ELDER, Nathan	5-Apr-1985	Hornchurch	Brighton & HA		17	4
EMANUEL, Lewis	14-Oct-1983	Bradford	Luton Town (loan)		3	
HAMFR, Ben	20-Nov-1987	Chard	Reading (loan)		21	
MACKIE, John	5-Jul-1976	Whitechapel	Leyton Orient	AFC Hornchurch	16	
MILSOM, Robert	2-Jan-1987	Redhill	Fulham (loan)		6	
MOORE, Sammy	7-Sep-1987	Deal	Ipswich Town (L)		24	2
PARKES, Jordan	26-Jul-1989	Hemel Hemp.	Watford (loan)		1	
PEAD, Craig	15-Sep-1981	Bromsgrove	Walsall		35	
PETTIGREW, Adrian	12-Nov-1986	Hackney	Chelsea (loan)		14	
POOLE, Glenn	3-Feb-1981	Barking	Grays Athletic		48	14
REID, Reuben	26-Jul-1988	Bristol	Plymouth A. (L)		10	1
SANKOFA, Osei	19-Mar-1985	Streatham	Charlton Ath. (L)		11	
SHAKES, Ricky	26-Jan-1985	Brixton	Swindon Town	Ebbsfleet Utd.	42	4
SINCLAIR, Emile	29-Dec-1987	Leeds	Nottingham F. (L)		4	
SMITH, Gary	30-Jan-1984	Middlesbrough	MK Dons		32	1
STAROSTA, Ben	7-Jan-1987	Sheffield	Sheffield Utd. (L)		23	
STONE, Craig	29-Dec-1988	Strood	Gillingham (loan)		6	
THORPE, Lee	14-Dec-1975	Wolverhampton	Torquay United	Rochdale	21	4

APPEARANCES (MOST - FOOTBALL LEAGUE) - TOP TEN

1. **KEN COOTE** born Paddington (514 games): 1949-1963
Ken holds the record for the greatest number of senior appearance, having made 559 (514 League, 35 FA. Cup, 10 League Cup) and it is a measure of the man that not once was he booked. Brentford was Ken's only League club and he was fast tracked into the Second Division side after signing from Wembley F.C. in the summer of 1949. Initially an inside forward, it wasn't until he switched to a defensive role that his career took off. 'Mr Reliable', Ken was skipper of the Bees Fourth Division Championship side in 1962-63 previous to which he was a member of the London Select XI that reached the final of the European Fairs Cup in 1958.

2. **PETER GELSON** born Hammersmith (471 games): 1961-1974
Peter was part-time in his early days at Griffin Park, combining football with an outside job as a Post Office engineer. A rugged, no-nonsense centre-half, he became the lynch-pin of a defence in which his red-blooded tackling was an outstanding feature for almost 25 years, loyalty which earned him two separate testimonials. During his stay the Bees experienced wildly contrasting fortunes, twice winning promotion from Division Four - as champions in 1963 - and suffered the pain of relegation three times. He left in September 1974 and went on to play for Hillingdon Borough, Hounslow Town and Walton & Hersham.

3. **JAMIE BATES** born Croydon (419 games): 1986-1999
Jamie could be considered a late developer, as in his early days he struggled to make an impact and was third choice central defender behind Keith Millen and Terry Evans. However, Jamie became a key figure in the (old) Third Division in the 1991-92 season when for the most part he played at full back. By the time Millen and Evans moved on he had made the central defender's role his own and won a (new) Third Division championship medal in 1999. That was his swan-song and he moved to Wycombe Wanderers in March that year. He brought his career to an abrupt halt by calling it a day following a superb performance in Wycombe's F A Cup semi-final against Liverpool in 2001.

4. **TOMMY HIGGINSON** born Newtongrange (388 games): 1959-1969
Tom joined Brentford from Kilmarnock ostensibly as cover for record goalscorer Jim Towers. He made little inroads until he switched to wing half where his never-say-die attitude and toughness in the tackle soon made him a cult figure with the home crowd. Tom popped up with the odd goal every once in a while and remarkably his total of 15 was spread over ten seasons, with at least one per a year. When he left Brentford, Tom became one of the many expatriot Bees at Hillingdon Borough and helped them reach the final of the FA Trophy in 1971.

5. **JACKIE GRAHAM** born Glasgow (374 games) - 1970-1979
A Scot who commanded a £15,000 transfer fee when he left Greenock Morton for Dundee United and had his first experience of the game south of the border at Guildford City in the Southern League. He soon caught Brentford's eye with his ability as a playmaker and the touch of steel he added as a full time professional at Griffin Park was instrumental in helping the Bees win promotion from the Fourth Division in 1972 and again six years later. A master in dead-ball situations, Jackie twice scored for Brentford direct from a corner kick. He left for Addlestone & Weybridge Town and later played locally for Hounslow Town, Woking, Burnham & Hillingdon and Farnborough before spells coaching at Staines, Millwall and Cranleigh.

6. **GERRY CAKEBREAD OBE** born Acton (348 games): 1954-1963
Gerry was an amateur when he made his debut and remained part-time throughout a career which saw him twice named as reserve goalkeeper for England U-23's. Gerry won a Fourth Division championship medal in 1963 and holds the record for the most consecutive games in a Bees shirt (187), he was also in goal the night Wrexham were hammered 9-0 to set a club goalscoring record. He shared his duties at Griffin Park with a full-time job at the Admiralty and in 1995 was awarded an OBE for his work on Hydrographics at the Ministry of Defence.

7. **DANIS SALMAN** born Cyprus (325 games): 1975-1985
Danis became Brentford's youngest ever player in League football when he came on a substitute against Watford in November 1975 at the tender age of 15 years 8 months and 3 days. The precocious teenager soon made his mark and besides playing for England Youth against Turkey, Spain and Poland he was a regular in the Fourth Division promotion side of 1977-78. Danis had pace and confidence in abundance and slotted in well in a variety of defensive roles. He left Brentford for Millwall and helped them into the top flight for the first time in their history, later playing for Plymouth, Peterborough and Torquay, where he made the last of his 513 total Football League appearances.

8. ALAN HAWLEY born Woking (319 games): 1962-1973
Alan was Brentford's youngest player, at the time, when he made his first League appearance at home to Barrow in September 1962 at the age of 16 years 3 months 22 days. It was the latter part of the following season before the young right back got a regular game, by replacing Bees legend Ken Coote and from then on there was no looking back as he missed few games over the next ten years. Alan skippered the side for a time and was given a testimonial in May 1974 with Orient providing the opposition.

9. ALAN NELMES born Hackney (316 games):1967-1975
Alan was signed by manager Jimmy Sirrel from Chelsea and when he established himself he became versatility personified, with his ability to make a decent fist of any position in the back line. A good, honest professional Alan was Player of The Year in 1970-71 and ever present in the Fourth Division promotion year which followed. He was, for a number of years, a permanent fixture in the Bees' defence and later played for Hillingdon Borough and Hayes.

10. KEITH MILLEN born Croydon (305 games): 1984-1994
Like fellow South Londoner Jamie Bates, Keith was on schoolboy forms at Southampton and Crystal Palace before joining Brentford where in 1983-84 he was skipper of the junior side which won the South East Counties League Division Two Championship. A cool customer at the heart of the Bees' defence he featured in the Freight Rover Trophy Final at Wembley against Wigan in 1985 and won a Division Four Championship medal seven years later, before joining Watford in part exchange for Barry Ashby. From Watford he moved to Bristol City where he completed his 500th League appearance.

GOALSCORERS - (MOST - FOOTBALL LEAGUE) - TOP TEN

1 JIM TOWERS born Shepherds Bush (153 goals): 1951-1961
Jim, who played 262 League games for The Bees, was the leading goalscorer of the 'Terrible Twins' partnership. Still in his prime, aged 28 he moved on to QPR, then Millwall, Gillingham and Aldershot, before ending his career at Gravesend.

2. GEORGE FRANCIS born Acton (124 goals): 1953-1961 and 1962-1963.
The other 'twin', who between them had the remarkable record of being a club's top two goalscorers, playing at the same time (probably a unique record). George moved with Jim to QPR, before returning to Griffin Park, then on to Gillingham.

3. JACK HOLLIDAY born Cockfield (119 goals): 1932-1944
'Olly Olly' and his goals were one of the main reasons for Brentford's rise from the Third Division to the First. In his first season at Griffin Park he scored 38 goals, still a club record. He continued to play into the early days of the War.

4. DAVE McCULLOCH born Hamilton (85 goals): 1935-1938
Leading Goalscorer for Hearts in 1935, Dave was a shrewd buy at £6,000. His three years at Brentford, saw him net his 85 goals in just 116 League games. He was sold on to Derby County for a near British record fee of £9,500.

5. BILLY SCOTT born Willington Quay (85 goals): 1932 - 1947
Billy joined the club whilst they were still in the Third Division and saw them through the good years, including all those in the First Division, and the war period. He finally hung up his boots in February 1947, just short of his 40th birthday.

6. BILL LANE born Tottenham (79 goals): 1929-1933
Although Bill's playing career spanned a total of 19 years, only four of them were at Brentford. He made just 112 League appearances, and therefore scored around two goals in every three games. He later returned to Griffin Park as coach.

6. GARY BLISSETT born Manchester (79 goals): 1987 - 1983
A £60,000 buy from Crewe, he initially disappointed in front of goal, but his scoring took off after netting a brace versus both Manchester City and Blackburn Rovers in the Cup, plus notably the winner at Peterborough and promotion in 1992.

7. DAI HOPKINS born Merthyr Tidfil (77 goals): 1932 - 1947
Welshman 'Dai' (real name Idris), like Billy Scott he spent 15 years at Brentford and only just misses out in the top ten appearance makers (293). Even so, he scored a good number of goals for a winger (approximately one per four games).

8. LLOYD OWUSU born Slough (76 goals): 1998 - 2002 and 2005 - 2007
One of the most charismatic of players in recent years. A bargain buy from Slough Town for £25,000, noted for his 'pushing the ceiling' celebrations. Frequent top goalscorer, his most important - the match winner at Cambridge in 1999.

9. JACK LANE born Cradley Heath (74 goals): 1925 - 1931
'Two Lane top goalscorers', but not related, although they partnered each other at Brentford for a while. Moved on to Crystal Palace and then Aldershot, before retiring and moving back to Brentford, for 47 years as a pub licensee.

(FULL) INTERNATIONAL PLAYERS
Players whilst with Brentford who have represented their country.

England

Billy Scott (1); v Wales 17 Oct 1936.
Leslie Smith (1) + v Romania 24 May 1939.

Wales

Idris Hopkins (12): v Scotland 5 Oct 1935, v N.Ireland 27 1935 Mar, v N.Ireland 11 Mar 1936, v England 17 October 1936, v N.Ireland 17 Mar 1937, v Scotland 30 Oct 1937, v England 17 Nov 1937, v N.Ireland, 16 Mar 1938 v England 22 Oct 1938, v N.Ireland 15 Mar 1939, v Scotland ? 1939, v England ? 1939.
Dave Richards (4); v N.Ireland 11 Mar 1936, v England 17 October 1936, v Scotland 30 Oct 1937, v England 17 Nov 1937.
Leslie Boulter (1); v N.Ireland 15 Mar 1939
Paul Evans (1 as Sub); v Czech Republic 27 March 2002

Ireland:

Tommy Shanks (1); v 25 Feb England 1905
Maurice Connor (2); v Scotland 21 Mar 1903, 18 April 1903
Bill Gorman (4); v Wales 16 Apr 1947, v Scotland 4 Oct 1947, England 5 Nov. 1947, v Wales 10 Mar 1948
Jimmy D'Arcy (3) v Wales 15 Arp 1953, v Scotland 3 Oct 1953, v France ? 1953

Scotland:

Dave McCulloch (4); v England 4 Apr 1937, v Wales 30 Oct 1937, v N.Ireland 10 Nov 1937, v Czechoslovakia 8 Dec 1937.
Duncan McKenzie (1); v N.Ireland 8 Oct 1938.
Bobby Reid (2); v England 9 Apr 1938, v N.Ireland 8 Oct 1938
Archie Macaulay (1) * v England 12 Apr 1947.

Malta

John Buttigieg (20)

Barbados

Gus Hurdle (4)

Iceland

Hermann Hreidarsson (12) (1 as Sub)
Ivar Ingimarsson (3)
Olafur Ingi Skulason (1) (Sub)

Canada

Niall Thompson (1)

St Vincent & Grenadines

Julian Charles (3) (1 as Sub)

Ghana

Lloyd Owusu (1)

In total, 22 players have gained full 'Caps' for their country whilst with Brentford , from 10 different countries. The first international player for the club was Maurice Connor (for Ireland) in 1903, when he scored a goal in the 2-0 victory over Scotland

The most capped Brentford player is John Buttigieg (for Malta) - with 20 caps.
'Dai' (Idris) Hopkins is the second most capped player and also the most from the home countries, with 12.

* Archie Macauley also played for Great Britain v Rest of Europe Xl in May 1947

+ Leslie Smith also made 13 (unofficial) wartime appearances for England.

On 17 Oct there were three Brentford players in the Wales (Hopkins and Richards) v England (Scott) match and on the the 2 Dec 1937 there were also three players in the Wales (Hopkins and Richards) v Scotland (McCulloch) game.

Arthur Bateman was the travelling reserve for the England v Germany match in May 1938

During the 1938/39 season Brentford were able to field a full forward line of international players: Hopkins, Scott, McCulloch, Eastham (England player formerly with Bolton) and Reid.

Paul Evans came on as a sub for Wales in 2002, in the 73rd minute, hence making his the shortest appearance record in time for a Brentford player, of 17 minutes!

Brentford Versus The Rest

(The complete Football League record: 109 different clubs)

	CLUB	FIRST HOME GAME					COMPLETE RECORD										
		Div.	Season	Date	Score	Attend.	Played	Home					Away				
								W	D	L	F	A	W	D	L	F	A
1	Millwall	3	1920-21	30 Aug	W 1-0	11,000	56	15	9	4	52	28	5	8	15	22	51
2	Exeter City	3	1920-21	4 Sep	D 0-0	10,000	80	28	4	8	82	30	12	12	16	54	69
3	Brighton & H.A.	3	1920-21	11 Sep	W 2-0	8,000	52	15	3	8	59	39	5	5	16	29	53
4	Crystal Palace	3	1920-21	25 Sep	L 0-4	13,000	30	10	2	3	36	21	3	2	10	18	27
5	Norwich City	3	1920-21	16 Oct	W 3-1	8,000	40	12	3	5	48	26	3	5	12	19	34
6	Southampton	3	1920-21	30 Oct	D 1-1	12,000	32	8	5	3	27	14	3	4	9	24	30
7	Bristol Rovers	3	1920-21	13 Nov	D 0-0	9,000	70	14	8	13	57	58	11	8	16	41	52
8	Reading	3	1920-21	27 Nov	W 3-2	5,000	76	17	12	9	63	45	6	10	22	36	72
9	Luton Town	3	1920-21	11 Dec	W 1-0	6,000	64	17	7	8	49	39	5	5	22	33	69
10	Newport County	3	1920-21	18 Dec	D 2-2	6,000	78	18	14	7	64	43	14	11	14	50	55
11	Q.P.R.	3	1920-21	25 Dec	L 0-2	17,410	62	13	8	10	51	40	6	14	11	37	45
12	Gillingham	3	1920-21	22 Jan	D 3-3	7,000	76	15	10	13	59	54	14	6	18	46	55
13	Swansea Town	3	1920-21	5 Feb	L 1-2	7,000	72	21	9	6	54	28	5	10	21	39	72
14	Swindon Town	3	1920-21	19 Feb	L 0-1	10,000	70	17	9	9	58	40	8	8	19	40	61
15	Portsmouth	3	1920-21	5 Mar	L 1-2	8,000	28	7	5	2	29	17	4	2	8	16	27
16	Watford	3	1920-21	19 Mar	W 1-0	6,000	60	14	10	6	53	36	6	12	12	34	48
17	Northampton Town	3	1920-21	26 Mar	D 1-1	7,000	66	22	5	6	66	30	8	9	16	33	61
18	Grimsby Town	3	1920-21	28 Mar	W 5-0	7,000	56	16	0	12	52	31	7	4	17	29	61
19	Southend United	3	1920-21	9 Apr	D 2-2	5,000	90	27	11	7	90	46	7	10	28	45	96
20	Merthyr Town	3	1920-21	25 Apr	D 0-0	7,000	20	4	5	1	19	7	1	1	8	7	26
21	Plymouth Argyle	3	1920-21	2 May	D 0-0	5,000	72	16	14	6	56	29	5	10	21	26	63
22	Charlton Athletic	3(S)	1921-22	24 Sep	L 0-2	13,000	30	9	2	4	23	15	1	4	10	12	26
23	Aberdare Athletic	3(S)	1921-22	26 Dec	W 2-1	15,000	12	2	2	2	7	9	1	1	4	4	11
24	Bristol City	3(S)	1922-23	31 Mar	W 4-0	9,500	58	13	6	10	45	36	9	7	13	29	45
25	Bournemouth	3(S)	1923-24	26 Dec	W 2-0	7,000	90	20	16	9	61	49	12	10	23	46	62
26	Coventry City	3(S)	1926-27	23 Oct	W 7-3	9,099	40	10	4	6	41	34	3	6	11	18	31
27	Walsall	3(S)	1927-28	5 Dec	W 3-2	2,202	58	17	8	4	63	27	10	5	14	39	58
28	Torquay United	3(S)	1927-28	25 Feb	L 1-2	8,355	42	9	6	6	38	27	3	7	11	26	41
29	Fulham	3(S)	1928-29	22 Dec	L 1-2	8,876	40	7	4	9	31	26	4	8	8	21	35
30	Leyton Orient	3(S)	1929-30	4 Sep	W 3-1	9,346	32	11	3	2	36	16	6	5	5	24	23
31	Notts County	3(S)	1930-31	24 Sep	D 2-2	9,999	62	15	11	5	50	27	6	10	15	28	40
32	Thames	3(S)	1930-31	15 Nov	W 6-1	7,211	4	2	0	0	7	1	0	1	1	1	3
33	Mansfield Town	3(S)	1931-32	13 Jan	D 1-1	4,902	38	11	5	3	32	17	5	6	8	20	27
34	Cardiff City	3(S)	1931-32	13 Feb	L 2-3	16,239	34	8	5	4	29	18	1	5	11	14	31
35	Aldershot Town	3(S)	1932-33	24 Dec	W 2-0	11,972	32	8	5	3	29	18	6	5	5	18	20
36	Bradford Park Avenue	2	1933-34	31 Aug	W 2-0	13,667	20	8	2	0	17	4	5	2	3	16	15
37	West Ham United	2	1933-34	2 Sep	W 4-1	19,918	20	3	5	2	15	12	3	2	5	10	17
38	Manchester United	2	1933-34	16 Sep	L 3-4	17,180	10	2	1	2	12	10	2	1	2	7	9
39	Hull City	2	1933-34	30 Sep	D 2-2	14,570	48	11	6	7	41	37	5	3	16	18	45
40	Burnley	2	1933-34	7 Oct	W 5-2	14,797	22	5	4	2	18	11	2	4	5	13	19
41	Bradford City	2	1933-34	11 Nov	W 2-1	12,932	50	14	5	6	55	31	6	5	14	28	45
42	Bury	2	1933-34	23 Dec	L 2-3	12,761	56	12	6	10	51	41	9	9	10	35	41
43	Preston North End	2	1933-34	25 Dec	W 3-2	20,662	40	11	6	3	38	23	3	5	12	31	47
44	Nottingham Forest	2	1933-34	30 Dec	W 2-1	12,795	18	3	5	1	14	12	2	2	5	6	14
45	Bolton Wanderers	2	1933-34	3 Feb	W 3-1	16,037	32	10	4	2	34	17	5	3	8	17	22
46	Oldham Athletic	2	1933-34	24 Feb	W 2-1	15,927	38	9	10	0	32	19	4	5	10	22	38
47	Blackpool	2	1933-34	17 Mar	W 1-0	16,461	51	16	6	3	47	23	9	5	12	34	42
48	Port Vale	2	1933-34	31 Mar	W 2-0	19,758	50	17	3	5	55	21	3	3	19	21	47
49	Lincoln City	2	1933-34	28 Apr	W 5-0	12,184	44	15	4	3	40	20	2	4	16	19	41
50	Barnsley	2	1934-35	15 Dec	W 8-1	11,843	52	14	8	4	53	21	8	11	7	29	30
51	Newcastle United	2	1934-35	5 Jan	W 3-0	26,079	6	2	0	1	5	2	1	0	2	6	8
52	Sheffield United	2	1934-35	4 May	W 3-1	21,017	22	6	2	3	19	15	4	4	3	17	20
53	Blackburn Rovers	1	1935-36	2 Sep	W 3-1	25,047	20	6	1	3	19	14	1	1	8	10	23

		FIRST HOME GAME					COMPLETE RECORD										
	CLUB	Div.	Season	Date	Score	Attend.	Played	Home					Away				
								W	D	L	F	A	W	D	L	F	A
54	Huddersfield Town	1	1935-36	7 Sep	L 1-2	33,481	47	11	6	7	28	21	8	6	9	29	29
55	Aston Villa	1	1935-36	21 Sep	L 1-2	29,781	6	0	0	3	3	8	0	1	2	4	12
56	Sheffield Wednesday	1	1935-36	5 Oct	D 2-2	25,338	20	4	4	2	17	17	3	5	2	14	12
57	Stoke City	1	1935-36	19 Oct	D 0-0	24,960	22	4	4	3	9	12	0	3	8	12	26
58	Arsenal	1	1935-36	2 Nov	W 2-1	26,330	10	4	0	1	8	2	1	3	1	6	6
59	Sunderland	1	1935-36	16 Nov	L 1-5	24,720	14	1	2	4	11	16	2	1	4	9	12
60	Leeds United	1	1935-36	30 Nov	D 2-2	23,914	24	4	5	3	20	16	2	3	7	11	23
61	Liverpool	1	1935-36	14 Dec	L 1-2	18,508	10	2	1	2	10	9	1	2	2	6	7
62	Middlesbrough	1	1935-36	18 Jan	W 1-0	27,779	12	3	2	1	10	6	1	1	4	2	10
63	Wolverhampton W.	1	1935-36	1 Feb	W 5-0	25,123	16	5	1	2	18	10	3	0	5	13	19
64	Birmingham City	1	1935-36	29 Feb	L 0-1	20,523	28	4	2	8	15	19	4	3	7	13	25
65	Manchester City	1	1935-36	14 Mar	D 0-0	28,364	8	2	1	1	6	7	1	0	3	4	8
66	Chelsea	1	1935-36	28 Mar	W 2-1	33,486	10	3	1	1	5	4	1	0	4	8	10
67	Everton	1	1935-36	13 Apr	W 4-1	29,790	17	5	2	1	16	8	2	1	6	7	22
68	West Bromwich Albion	1	1935-36	25 Apr	D 2-2	24,527	12	2	2	2	6	7	0	0	6	5	13
69	Derby County	1	1935-36	2 May	W 6-0	20,521	18	3	3	3	21	16	3	1	5	14	17
70	Leicester City	1	1937-38	5 Feb	D 1-1	21,309	20	2	3	5	13	17	4	5	1	11	13
71	Tottenham Hotspur	2	1947-48	20 Mar	W 2-0	31,297	6	1	1	1	4	5	0	1	2	1	7
72	Chesterfield	2	1947-48	3 Apr	L 0-3	24,164	66	17	12	4	50	31	11	7	15	37	46
73	Doncaster Rovers	2	1947-48	1 May	W 2-0	16,939	48	10	8	6	32	31	7	6	11	24	37
74	Rotherham United	2	1951-52	25 Aug	W 2-0	24,904	50	10	8	7	37	31	6	6	13	29	47
75	Shrewsbury Town	3(S)	1954-55	26 Aug	D 2-2	12,743	42	11	6	4	37	16	4	6	11	19	26
76	Colchester United	3(S)	1954-55	16 Oct	W 3-2	10,218	50	15	7	3	39	23	9	7	9	38	35
77	Ipswich Town	3(S)	1955-56	12 Nov	W 3-2	14,795	4	1	1	0	4	3	0	1	1	1	5
78	Halifax Town	3	1958-59	20 Sep	W 2-0	12,643	22	5	4	2	14	8	0	3	8	5	16
79	Stockport County	3	1958-59	18 Oct	L 1-4	12,488	38	12	3	4	35	18	6	6	7	20	24
80	Rochdale	3	1958-59	13 Dec	W 2-1	9,432	24	10	1	1	28	7	6	5	1	18	12
81	Wrexham	3	1958-59	3 Jan	W 2-1	11,723	40	12	5	3	34	12	9	4	7	32	28
82	Accrington Stanley	3	1958-59	31 Jan	W 2-1	11,260	6	3	0	0	8	2	1	1	1	5	5
83	Tranmere Rovers	3	1958-59	28 Feb	W 5-2	13,138	34	9	3	5	33	18	4	2	11	21	37
84	York City	3	1959-60	21 Nov	L 1-2	13,118	38	10	5	4	40	24	5	6	8	22	25
85	Peterborough United	3	1961-62	17 Feb	W 2-0	10,991	44	12	4	6	34	17	5	7	10	19	45
86	Barrow	4	1962-63	29 Sep	W 2-1	9,541	8	3	0	1	8	5	2	1	1	5	2
87	Hartlepools United	4	1962-63	2 Oct	W 4-0	10,729	34	12	2	3	33	11	5	3	9	14	24
88	Southport	4	1962-63	13 Oct	D 3-3	11,651	16	5	2	1	11	5	2	1	5	5	12
89	Chester	4	1962-63	26 Dec	W 2-1	9,724	44	12	6	4	40	17	9	9	4	31	26
90	Darlington	4	1962-63	23 Feb	L 1-3	9,272	32	10	2	4	33	17	7	4	5	29	27
91	Oxford United	4	1962-63	23 Mar	W 4-0	13,756	26	9	2	2	28	7	5	4	4	16	14
92	Crewe Alexandra	4	1962-63	30 Apr	W 3-1	15,820	38	10	4	5	27	20	4	4	11	27	39
93	Workington	4	1962-63	23 May	W 4-3	13,150	24	8	2	2	27	11	4	4	4	13	15
94	Carlisle United	3	1964-65	19 Dec	W 6-1	8,383	20	2	5	3	13	11	4	1	5	8	11
95	Scunthorpe United	3	1964-65	27 Apr	W 4-0	6,164	34	13	0	4	36	17	2	9	6	19	25
96	Cambridge United	4	1970-71	26 Apr	L 1-2	5,944	28	6	4	4	21	16	2	6	6	12	17
97	Wimbledon	4	1977-78	22 Aug	W 4-1	11,001	8	1	0	3	9	9	1	2	1	4	4
98	Wigan Athletic	3	1982-83	8 Jan	L 1-3	4,939	30	5	2	8	19	21	1	5	9	13	27
99	Barnet	3	1993-94	30 Oct	W 1-0	5,873	6	3	0	0	6	2	2	1	0	5	1
100	Wycombe Wanderers	2	1994-95	21 Mar	D 0-0	9,530	20	3	6	1	6	5	2	2	6	10	19
101	Scarborough	3	1998-99	27 Feb	D 1-1	4,783	2	0	1	0	1	1	0	0	1	1	3
102	Cheltenham Town	2	2002-03	5 Apr	D 2-2	5,011	4	0	1	1	2	4	0	0	2	0	3
103	Rushden and Diamonds	2	2003-04	20 Mar	W 3-2	4,616	2	1	0	0	3	2	1	0	0	1	0
104	Milton Keynes Dons	1	2004-05	5 Feb	W 1-0	5,077	6	2	0	1	2	3	1	2	0	2	1
105	Yeovil Town	1	2005-06	6 Dec	W 3-2	5,131	4	1	0	1	4	4	1	0	1	2	2
106	Dagenham and Redbric	2	2007-08	2 Oct	L 2-3	3,662	2	0	0	1	2	3	1	0	0	2	1
107	Morecambe	2	2007-08	4 Dec	L 0-1	3,155	2	0	0	1	0	1	0	0	1	1	3
108	Macclesfield Town	2	2007-08	8 Mar	W 1-0	3,863	2	1	0	0	1	0	0	0	1	0	1
109	Hereford United	2	2007-08	26 Apr	L 0-3	6,246	2	0	0	1	0	3	0	0	1	0	2

Statistical Notes:

Brentford Who's Who (page 170 - 172): These contain a listing of every player, plus the period in which they were registered with the club - the complete details (including personal and statistical details) are contained in the book *'Timeless Bees'*, which includes every player to the end of the 2005/06 season. Therefore brief summaries are given for the players who joined in the two seasons from 2006/07. Where a single year is given, this refers to a player who was with the club for just one season/year (but may have returned to the club in a later season), or was still with the club to June 2008.

Attendances Summaries (page 179): The figures are given for the total, average, highest and lowest for every Football League season, except from 1920/21 to 1924/25 inclusive, where official numbers were not published. During those seasons, and before, attendances were normally assessed by local reporters and the figures given have been derived on this basis. In the 1932/33 season, Brentford's average was the highest in their division (Third Division South). The 1927/28 season produced the lowest (to date) attendance, and 1938/39 the highest. 1946/47 saw the biggest average and largest total, whilst the lowest average and total was in the 1986/87 season. Until the 1953/54 season, only 21 home games were played (42 teams in the relevant division) and from 1954/55, 23 games have been played. The aggregate total attendance for all League games is 16,867,473, and the overall average is 10,173.

Football League Seasonal Summary (page 179): This is self-explanatory, giving the overall summary of every Football League season, including the division played in, the final position in that division ('Pos') and separate home and away plus overall total records.

Seasonal Statistics (Pages 180 - 317) All details as produced within this book are the copyright of Yore Publications (Dave Twydell), Rob Jex and/or Tony Brown.

The team line-ups for all seasons to 1917/18 are generally known, but due to space and general interest considerations have not been included here.

The information given is generally self-explanatory, the first column providing the (abbreviated) competition name for that match ('F' = a friendly), or where a number is shown this refers to the match number for the league competition that season. Cup matches (first column), various rounds are indicated thus: Q = qualifying round, R = round plus round number, QF = Quarter-final, SF = Semi-final, F= Final. A number following a number refers to a leg, e.g. 2/1, refers to the second round, first leg). The opposition shown in upper case (capitals) was a 'home' match, and in lower case an 'away' match (including a neutral ground where the venue is also given). For all results, Brentford's score is first. All team groups have the line-ups (where known), and the names read from left to right (unless stated otherwise).

Additional information from 1918/19: Goalscorers - names given with number of goals scored (if more than one). (p) = goal scored from a penalty. (og) = an own goal, with the goalscorer's name. Seventh column is the official (or otherwise) attendance, see also above ('Attendance Summaries'). The eighth and subsequent columns give the team members and numbers (although the latter were not required or used until 1939). The generally accepted numbering/positioning convention has been used i.e. 1 = goalkeeper, 2 and 3 = full backs/defenders, 4,5, and 6 = half-backs/defenders/midfielders, 7 and 11 wingers/midfielders, 8,9 and 10 forwards/strikers; for consistency this method has been used throughout despite the new terminology for positions that came about around 1966. The totals at the bottom of the main table refers to the number of appearances, used substitute appearances (where applicable), and goals scored - all in league matches only.

From the 1965/66 season, the use of substitutes was permitted, initially one named substitute (for an injured player) up to the present five named substitutes from which any three can be used. Substitutes that have been used in a match are shown as 12, 13, 14 (regardless of their actual shirt numbers). Substitutes have replaced those players that started the match (numbered 1 to 11), indicated by underlining. In later seasons players actual squad numbers for that season have been ignored, and the 1-11 convention (as above has been used).

Attendances - Summaries

Season	Total	Average	Highest	Lowest
1920/21		8660		
1921/22		8980	1920 - 1925	
1922/23		8240	Unofficial figures	
1923/24		6730		
1924/25		7140		
1925-26	191057	9097	16893	5632
1926/27	201975	9618	17002	4775
1927/28	153942	7331	12513	**2202**
1928/29	171332	8159	20783	3366
1929/30	254645	12126	21966	5041
1930/31	172947	8236	11770	2306
1931/32	238386	11352	26139	4902
1932/33	279305	**13300**	20693	8377
1933/34	343919	16377	26934	12017
1934/35	379302	18062	26079	11843
1935/36	531031	25287	33486	15379
1936/37	515419	**24544**	31745	14103
1937/38	490030	23335	35584	14609
1938/39	485455	23117	**38535**	12761
~ World War Two ~				
1946/47	**541132**	**25768**	35604	17976
1947/48	490168	23341	34483	13723
1948/49	477857	22755	31369	14360
1949/50	474864	22613	33791	16384
1950/51	411451	19593	26393	9808
1951/52	483438	23021	35827	10243
1952/53	366956	17474	27787	8565
1953/54	328137	15626	22845	10652
1954/55	254771	11077	18756	4960
1955/56	236949	10302	17847	5291
1956/57	264097	11482	18760	6088
1957/58	300922	13084	25744	9130
1958/59	320242	13924	28725	9432
1959/60	273968	11912	21634	6328
1960/61	170018	7392	16673	3503
1961/62	195115	8483	18127	3583
1962/63	262604	11418	15820	8340
1963/64	273300	11883	17094	6818
1964/65	247010	10740	16065	6164
1965/66	193568	8416	15209	4457
1966/67	154723	6727	10646	3592
1967/68	142851	6211	9481	3749
1968/69	147640	6419	9806	3361
1969/70	178777	7773	12261	4383
1970/71	155690	6769	10050	4170
1971/72	269850	11733	18520	8710
1972/73	200160	8703	11800	6060
1973/74	116429	5062	8720	3170
1974/75	118940	5171	6485	3983
1975/76	117218	5096	10612	3453
1976/77	117777	5128	8951	3158
1977/78	197302	8578	14496	5492
1978/79	171461	7455	13873	5140
1979/80	179774	7816	13764	4992
1980/81	155297	6752	11610	4883
1981/82	130919	5692	10834	4124
1982/83	141944	6171	12593	4413
1983/84	108851	4733	8042	3391
1984/85	93010	4044	5254	3019
1985/86	90519	3936	6351	2364
1986/87	**90124**	**3918**	7443	3032
1987/88	105536	4589	8712	3122
1988/89	131296	5709	10851	4013
1989/90	130236	5662	7962	4537
1990/91	141319	6144	8021	4812
1991/92	164580	7156	12071	4586
1992/93	194841	8471	11912	6337
1993/94	128073	5568	6841	4305
1994/95	150368	6538	10079	4031
1995/96	110179	4790	7878	3104
1996/97	133961	5824	8679	3675
1997/98	115930	5040	10510	3424
1998/99	125208	5444	9535	3674
1999/00	132257	5750	7125	4055
2000/01	106807	4644	7550	3062
2001/02	154421	6714	11303	4561
2002/03	132466	5759	9168	3990
2003/04	127462	5542	9485	3818
2004/05	140184	6095	9604	4643
2005/06	155814	6775	9903	5131
2006/07	128799	5600	7023	4540
2007/08	103168	4486	6246	3155

Football League - Seasonal Summary

Year	Div	Pos	P	W	D	L	F	A	W	D	L	F	A	W	D	L	F	A	Pts
1920-21	*3*	*21*	42	7	9	5	27	23	2	3	16	15	44	9	12	21	42	67	30
1921-22	*3(S)*	*9*	42	15	2	4	41	17	1	9	11	11	26	16	11	15	52	43	43
1922-23	*3(S)*	*14*	42	9	4	8	27	23	4	8	9	14	28	13	12	17	41	51	38
1923-24	*3(S)*	*17*	42	9	8	4	33	21	5	0	16	21	50	14	8	20	54	71	36
1924-25	*3(S)*	*21*	42	8	7	6	28	26	1	0	20	10	65	9	7	26	38	91	25
1925-26	*3(S)*	*18*	42	12	4	5	44	32	4	2	15	25	62	16	6	20	69	94	38
1926-27	*3(S)*	*11*	42	10	9	2	46	20	3	5	13	24	41	13	14	15	70	61	40
1927-28	*3(S)*	*12*	42	12	4	5	49	30	4	4	13	27	44	16	8	18	76	74	40
1928-29	*3(S)*	*13*	42	11	4	6	34	21	3	6	12	22	39	14	10	18	56	60	38
1929-30	*3(S)*	*2*	42	21	0	0	66	12	7	5	9	28	32	28	5	9	94	44	61
1930-31	*3(S)*	*3*	42	14	3	4	62	30	8	3	10	28	34	22	6	14	90	64	50
1931-32	*3(S)*	*5*	42	11	6	4	40	22	8	4	9	28	30	19	10	13	68	52	48
1932-33	*3(S)*	*1*	42	15	4	2	45	19	11	6	4	45	30	26	10	6	90	49	62
1933-34	*2*	*4*	42	15	2	4	52	24	7	5	9	33	36	22	7	13	85	60	51
1934-35	*2*	*1*	42	19	2	0	59	14	7	7	7	34	34	26	9	7	93	48	61
1935-36	*1*	*5*	42	11	5	5	48	25	6	7	8	33	35	17	12	13	81	60	46
1936-37	*1*	*6*	42	14	5	2	58	32	4	5	12	24	46	18	10	14	82	78	46
1937-38	*1*	*6*	42	10	6	5	44	27	8	3	10	25	32	18	9	15	69	59	45
1938-39	*1*	*18*	42	11	2	8	30	27	3	6	12	23	47	14	8	20	53	74	36
1946-47	*1*	*21*	42	5	5	11	19	35	4	2	15	26	53	9	7	26	45	88	25
1947-48	*2*	*15*	42	10	6	5	31	26	3	8	10	13	35	13	14	15	44	61	40
1948-49	*2*	*18*	42	7	10	4	28	21	4	4	13	14	32	11	14	17	42	53	36
1949-50	*2*	*9*	42	11	5	5	21	12	4	8	9	23	37	15	13	14	44	49	43
1950-51	*2*	*9*	42	13	3	5	44	25	5	5	11	31	49	18	8	16	75	74	44
1951-52	*2*	*10*	42	11	7	3	34	20	4	5	12	20	35	15	12	15	54	55	42
1952-53	*2*	*17*	42	8	8	5	38	29	5	3	13	21	47	13	11	18	59	76	37
1953-54	*2*	*21*	42	9	5	7	25	26	1	6	14	15	52	10	11	21	40	78	31
1954-55	*3(S)*	*11*	46	11	6	6	44	36	5	8	10	38	46	16	14	16	82	82	46
1955-56	*3(S)*	*6*	46	11	8	4	40	30	8	6	9	29	36	19	14	13	69	66	52
1956-57	*3(S)*	*8*	46	12	9	2	55	29	4	7	12	23	47	16	16	14	78	76	48
1957-58	*3(S)*	*2*	46	15	5	3	52	24	9	5	9	30	32	24	10	12	82	56	58
1958-59	*3*	*3*	46	15	5	3	49	22	6	10	7	27	27	21	15	10	76	49	57
1959-60	*3*	*7*	46	13	6	4	46	24	8	3	12	32	37	21	9	16	78	61	51
1960-61	*3*	*17*	46	10	9	4	41	28	3	8	12	15	42	13	17	16	56	70	43
1961-62	*3*	*23*	46	11	3	9	34	29	2	5	16	19	64	13	8	25	53	93	34
1962-63	*4*	*1*	46	18	2	3	59	31	9	6	8	39	33	27	8	11	98	64	62
1963-64	*3*	*16*	46	11	4	8	54	36	4	10	9	33	44	15	14	17	87	80	44
1964-65	*3*	*5*	46	18	4	1	55	18	6	5	12	28	37	24	9	13	83	55	57
1965-66	*3*	*23*	46	9	4	10	34	30	1	8	14	14	39	10	12	24	48	69	32
1966-67	*4*	*9*	46	13	7	3	36	19	5	6	12	22	37	18	13	15	58	56	49
1967-68	*4*	*14*	46	13	4	6	41	24	5	3	15	20	40	18	7	21	61	64	43
1968-69	*4*	*11*	46	12	7	4	40	24	6	5	12	24	41	18	12	16	64	65	48
1969-70	*4*	*5*	46	14	8	1	36	11	6	8	9	22	28	20	16	10	58	39	56
1970-71	*4*	*14*	46	13	3	7	45	27	5	5	13	21	35	18	8	20	66	62	44
1971-72	*4*	*3*	46	16	2	5	52	21	8	9	6	24	23	24	11	11	76	44	59
1972-73	*3*	*22*	46	12	5	6	33	18	3	2	18	18	51	15	7	24	51	69	37
1973-74	*4*	*19*	46	9	7	7	31	20	3	9	11	17	30	12	16	18	48	50	40
1974-75	*4*	*8*	46	15	6	2	38	14	3	7	13	15	31	18	13	15	53	45	49
1975-76	*4*	*18*	46	12	7	4	37	18	2	6	15	19	42	14	13	19	56	60	41
1976-77	*4*	*15*	46	14	3	6	48	27	4	4	15	29	49	18	7	21	77	76	43
1977-78	*4*	*4*	46	15	6	2	50	17	6	8	9	36	37	21	14	11	86	54	56
1978-79	*3*	*10*	46	14	4	5	35	19	5	5	13	18	30	19	9	18	53	49	47
1979-80	*3*	*19*	46	10	6	7	33	26	5	5	13	26	47	15	11	20	59	73	41
1980-81	*3*	*9*	46	7	9	7	30	25	7	10	6	22	24	14	19	13	52	49	47
1981-82	*3*	*8*	46	8	6	9	28	22	11	5	7	28	25	19	11	16	56	47	68
1982-83	*3*	*9*	46	14	4	5	50	28	4	6	13	38	49	18	10	18	88	77	64
1983-84	*3*	*20*	46	8	9	6	41	30	3	7	13	28	49	11	16	19	69	79	49
1984-85	*3*	*13*	46	13	5	5	42	27	3	9	11	20	37	16	14	16	62	64	62
1985-86	*3*	*10*	46	8	8	7	29	29	10	4	9	29	32	18	12	16	58	61	66
1986-87	*3*	*11*	46	9	7	7	39	32	6	8	9	25	34	15	15	16	64	66	60
1987-88	*3*	*12*	46	9	8	6	27	23	7	6	10	26	36	16	14	16	53	59	62
1988-89	*3*	*7*	46	14	5	4	36	21	4	9	10	30	40	18	14	14	66	61	68
1989-90	*3*	*13*	46	11	4	8	41	31	7	3	13	25	35	18	7	21	66	66	61
1990-91	*3*	*6*	46	12	4	7	30	22	9	9	5	29	25	21	13	12	59	47	76
1991-92	*3*	*1*	46	17	2	4	55	29	8	5	10	26	26	25	7	14	81	55	82
1992-93	*1*	*22*	46	7	6	10	28	30	6	4	13	24	41	13	10	23	52	71	49
1993-94	*2*	*16*	46	7	10	6	30	28	6	9	8	27	27	13	19	14	57	55	58
1994-95	*2*	*2*	46	14	4	5	44	15	11	6	6	37	24	25	10	11	81	39	85
1995-96	*2*	*15*	46	12	6	5	24	15	3	7	13	19	34	15	13	18	43	49	58
1996-97	*2*	*4*	46	8	11	4	26	22	12	3	8	30	21	20	14	12	56	43	74
1997-98	*2*	*21*	46	9	7	7	33	29	2	10	11	17	42	11	17	18	50	71	50
1998-99	*3*	*1*	46	16	5	2	45	18	10	2	11	34	38	26	7	13	79	56	85
1999-00	*2*	*17*	46	8	6	9	27	31	5	7	11	20	30	13	13	20	47	61	52
2000-01	*2*	*14*	46	9	10	4	34	30	5	7	11	22	40	14	17	15	56	70	59
2001-02	*2*	*3*	46	17	5	1	48	12	7	6	10	29	31	24	11	11	77	43	83
2002-03	*2*	*16*	46	8	8	7	28	21	6	4	13	19	35	14	12	20	47	56	54
2003-04	*2*	*17*	46	9	5	9	34	38	5	6	12	18	31	14	11	21	52	69	53
2004-05	*1*	*4*	46	15	4	4	34	22	7	5	11	23	38	22	9	15	57	60	75
2005-06	*1*	*3*	46	10	8	5	35	23	10	8	5	37	29	20	16	10	72	52	76
2006-07	*1*	*24*	46	5	8	10	24	41	3	5	15	16	38	8	13	25	40	79	37
2007-08	*2*	*14*	46	7	5	11	25	35	10	3	10	27	35	17	8	21	52	70	59

Seasonal Statistics and Team Groups

1889/90 Season results

Comp.	Date	Opposition	Result
F	23 Nov	KEW	1-1
F	30	HOUNSLOW 2nd XI	2-4
F	14 Dec	BOHEMIANS 2nd XI	2-1
F	21	KEW	_
F	28	HOUNSLOW 2nd XI	0-2
F	4 Jan	SOUTHALL ATHLETIC	1-0
F	11	Bohemians 2nd XI	_
F	18	HOUNSLOW STANDARD	5-2
F	25	PEARS ATHLETIC	1-3
F	1 Feb	BARNES	_
F	8	Grove House	0-0
F	15 Mar	Southall Athletic	0-1
F	22	Hounslow Standard	1-0

1890/91 Season results

Comp.	Date	Opposition	Result
F	11 Oct	PEARS ATHLETIC	1-5
F	18	Bohemians	2-4
F	25	STANLEY	3-1
F	1 Nov	Hanwell	2-1
WMC 1	8	Southall	0-6
F	15	THE FRIARS	3-1

1891/92 Season results

Comp.	Date	Opposition	Result
F	26 Sep	ROYAL FUSILIERS	4-0
F	3 Oct	Borough Road College	0-8
F	10	Southall	2-0
F	17	EALING DEAN	0-3
F	24	HANWELL	2-1
F	31	Uxbridge Caxtonians	0-3
F	12 Nov	Royal Fusiliers	3-1
WMC 1	14	Yiewsley	2-2
WMC 1	21	YIEWSLEY	1-4
F	28	GROVE HOUSE	4-0
WLC	5 Dec	HANWELL	1-5
MJC 1	12	UXBRIDGE CAXTONIANS	3-2
F	19	KEW	_
MJC 2	26	Shortwood Rangers	Won
F	2 Jan	LONDON RIFLE BRIGADE	2-0
MJC 3	9	HILLINGDON	2-2
MJC 3r	16	Hillingdon	3-2
MJC 4	23	Harrow Athletic Res.	2-4
F	30	HOUNSLOW	1-6
F	6 Feb	Knellar Hall	3-2
F	13	THE FRIARS	_
F	20	ST MARY'S COLLEGE	_
F	27	SHORTWOOD RANGERS	_
F	12 Mar	THE LOYOLA (WESTMINSTER)	_
F	26	Hounslow	_

1892/93 Season results
West London Alliance

Comp.	Date	Opposition	Result
F	10 Sep	Royal Fusiliers	2-1
F	17	Salisbury	3-1
F	24	Apsley	6-2
1	1 Oct	Hammersmith Athletic	5-1
F	8	St. Margaret's Athletic	5-1
LJC 1	15	CLARENCE	2-1
2	22	KENSAL	2-1
LJC 2	29	Oxford Athletic	2-0
3	5 Nov	CANTERBURY	6-0
MJC 1	12	Uxbridge Reserves	0-5
LJC 3	19	WESTINGHOUSE	2-5
F	26	ST. THOMAS'	1-3
4	3 Dec	ST. THOMAS'	3-2
F	10	ST. MARGARET'S ATHLETIC	3-1
F	17	Hatherley *	2-0
5	24	Hanwell	2-2
F	14 Jan	UPTON IVANHOE	1-1
6	21	HANWELL	0-0
F	28	BOROUGH ROAD COLLEGE	5-4
7	4 Feb	HAMMERSMITH ATHLETIC	3-0
8	11	Canterbury	3-0
9	18	Q.P.R. RESERVES	5-0
F	4 Mar	Kensal Reserves	0-1
F	8	Southall	4-1
F	11	MILLWALL ATHLETIC RESERVES	1-1
F	18	2nd SCOTS GUARDS RESERVES	2-2
10	25	Q.P.R. Reserves	1-0
F	31	Windsor and Eton	0-0
11	1 Apr	Kensal	1-0
12	8	St. Thomas'	2-0
F	15	Unknown opposition	_
F	29	Rest of West London Alliance	Won

* Initially an Alliance fixture, but Hatherley later withdrew.

Played on a neutral ground.

1893/94 Season results

Comp.	Date	Opposition	Result
F	9 Sep	LONDON CALEDONIANS	3-7
F	16	CALEDONIAN STROLLERS	3-2
F	23	KNELLER HALL	10-1
F	30	KENSAL	3-1
F	7 Oct	Apsley	0-1
F	14	HAMMERSMITH ATHLETIC	6-1
F	21	Borough Road College	2-1
F	28	WEST KILBURN	5-0
LJC 2	4 Nov	Stanley Reserves	1-2
MJC	11	WEST KILBURN	3-0
F	18	ST. MARY'S COLLEGE	0-5
F	25	Paddington	1-0
F	2 Dec	2nd LIFE GUARDS	3-0
F	9	HOUNSLOW	2-0
F	16	BATTERSEA ASSOCIATION	4-0
F	23	QUEENS PARK RANGERS	1-1
F	26	Ipswich Town	0-3
F	30	Hounslow	1-2
MJC 3	13 Jan	Hillingdon #	4-2
F	20	GROVE HOUSE	3-1
F	27	SOUTHALL	4-0
MJC 4	3 Feb	UXBRIDGE RESERVES	6-3
F	10	St. Mary's College	4-1
F	17	2nd COLDSTREAM GUARDS	1-1
MJC 5	24	KENSAL	1-0
F	3 Mar	HANWELL	5-1
F	10	QUEENS PARK RANGERS	3-2
MJC S/F	17	Hornsey United *	0-0
MJC S/Fr	24	Hornsey United **	7-1
F	31	2nd COLDSTREAM GUARDS	0-1
MJC F	7 Apr	Westminster Ponsonby **	2-1
F	14	YIEWSLEY	2-0
F	21	Southall	5-0

A.E.T., Full time 2-2

* Played at Hounslow F.C. ** Played at Crouch End F.C.

1893-94: Back: Bailey, Beckett, Charlton, Ward, Foster, Ray, James, Harriss (Secretary), Strachan (Chairman) Front: Steers, Saunders, Johnson, Pratley, Stevenson.

1894/95 Season results

Comp.	Date	Opposition	Result
F	8 Sep	Chesham Generals	1-4
F	15	PARSONS GREEN	4-6
F	22	LEYTONSTONE	3-1
F	29	ST. JOHN'S COLLEGE	0-1
F	6 Oct	Vampires	1-0
F	13	Queens Park Rangers	0-3
MSC 1	20	STANLEY	1-1
LSC 2	27	Polytechnic	0-5
F	3 Nov	Stanley *	1-1
MSC 1r	10	Stanley	1-1
F	17	8th HUSSARS	3-2
MSC 1 2r	24	STANLEY	2-2
MSC 1 3r	1 Dec	Stanley **	1-2
MSC 1 3r	8	Stanley ***	1-0
MSC 2	15	Darfield	5-0
F	22	8th HUSSARS	0-3
F	26	Ealing	0-2
F	29	LAMBETH	1-2
F	5 Jan	GROVE HOUSE	2-0
WMC 2	18	Hanwell	2-2
MSC 3	26	Olympians	0-0
MSC 3r	16 Feb	OLYMPIANS	3-0
MSC 4	23	Harrow Athletic	2-3
WMC 2r	2 Mar	HANWELL	3-1
WMC 3	16	YIEWSLEY	4-1
F	23	CLARENCE	3-0
WMC s/f	30	Hounslow #	2-0
F	4 Apr	CIVIL SERVICE	1-2
F	6	SOUTHALL	Won
F	11	WEST LONDON LEAGUE XI	1-1
F	12	SOUTHALL	3-1
F	13	1st COLDSTREAM GUARDS	Lost
F	15	MILLWALL ALLIANCE	Lost
WMC f	20	8th Hussars ##	4-2

* Scheduled as a WMC replay match, but no Official could be appointed.

** abandoned after 72 minutes (fog). Played at Barnes Common

*** Played at West Brompton

Played at Hanwell. ## Played at Southall

1895/96 Season results

Comp.	Date	Opposition	Result
F	7 Sep	STANLEY	1-0
F	14	UXBRIDGE	0-5
F	21	1st COLDSTREAM GUARDS	1-2
F	28	LEWISHAM ST. MARY'S	1-0
F	5 Oct	UPTON PARK	2-0
F	12	STANLEY	2-1
LSC 1	19	Marcians	8-0
F	26	WESTMINSTER	4-1
WMC 1	2 Nov	Harrow Athletic	2-1
LSC 2	9	FULHAM	0-1
MSC 2	23	POLYTECHNIC	1-1
F	30	HOUNSLOW	6-0
MSC 2r	7 Dec	Polytechnic	2-2
MSC 2 2R	14	POLYTECHNIC	1-4
F	21	SOUTHALL	1-1
F	25	ROYAL ORDNANCE RESERVES	Won
F	26	PLUMSTEAD	_
F	28	Hanwell	_
F	4 Jan	CHESHAM	4-2
F	11	WEST CROYDON	_
F	18	Hounslow	4-0
WMC 2	25	Uxbridge Reserves	7-1
F	1 Feb	HORNSEY UNITED	_
F	8	FULHAM	5-1
F	15	BOROUGH ROAD COLLEGE	3-1
F	22	Southall	0-0
F	29	2nd Genadier Guards	_
F	7 Mar	READING	1-0
WMC s/f	14	Yiewsley *	4-0
F	21	UPTON PARK	_
F	3 Apr	LIVERPOOL CASUALS	0-2
F	4	1st COLDSTREAM GUARDS	0-1
F	6	MILLWALL ALLIANCE	3-1
WMC	18	Southall **	1-2

* Played at Southall

** Played at Hounslow

1896/97 Season results
London League Second Division

Comp.	Date	Opposition	Result
F	5 Sep	CLAPTON CLIFTON	3-1
F	12	HOUNSLOW	3-1
F	19	BRIGADE OF GUARDS	2-1
F	26	HANWELL	3-0
1	3 Oct	FULHAM	6-1
MSC 1Q	10	BOW	8-0
LSC 1Q	17	NOVOCASTRIANS	3-1
F	24	CRESCENT (HAMPSTEAD)	1-1
F	27	ST.BERNARDS (EDINBURGH)	0-0
F	31	St. Albans	0-3
LSC 2q	7 Nov	Harrow Athletic	3-0
MSC 2q	14	Scots Greys	0-1
2	21	Fulham	2-0
LSC 3Q	28	CRESCENT (HAMPSTEAD)	5-1
3	5 Dec	Bromley	2-2
4	12	WestCroydon	2-2
LSC 4Q	19	OLD ST. MARKS	2-1
F	26	Ealing	0-5
F	28	THAMES IRONWORKS	2-2
F	9 Jan	Stanley	2-3
#	16	Clapton Clifton	4-0
LSC 1Q	6 Feb	OLD FORESTERS	4-2
WMC 1	13	Southall	3-1
5	20	BROMLEY	3-2
LSC 2q	27	BROMLEY	3-1
6	6 Mar	Harrow Athletic	2-2
WMC s/f	13	Harrow Athletic *	5-2
7	18	WEST CROYDON	4-0
8	24	Stanley	2-1
9	27	Forest Swifts	1-1
10	31	Hammersmith Athletic	3-0
11	1 Apr	FOREST SWIFTS	3-2
12	3	HARROW ATHLETIC	5-0
LSC s/f	8	Old Carthusians **	1-5
13	10	QUEENS PARK RANGERS	2-1
14	16	HAMMERSMITH ATHLETIC	4-1
15	17	STANLEY	0-0
F	19	EALING	1-5
16	22	Queens Park Rangers	1-3
WMC f	24	Hanwell **	0-1

* Played at Hanwell

** Played at Essex County Ground, Leyton

*** Played at Southall

Played as League match, but club exelled and record expunged

1892/93 Season: West London Alliance

	P	W	D	L	F	A	Pts
BRENTFORD	12	10	2	0	33	6	22
Kensal	12	7	2	3	20	11	16
Hanwell†	12	5	3	4	27	10	11
St Thomas'	12	5	1	6	18	27	11
Hammersmith Athletic	12	4	2	6	21	28	10
Canterbury	12	3	0	9	11	30	6
QPR Reserves	12	3	0	9	6	24	6

†Two points deducted for fielding an ineligible player

1896/97 Season: London League Second Division

	P	W	D	L	F	A	Pts
Bromley	16	11	3	2	41	17	25
BRENTFORD	16	9	6	1	42	19	24
Queens Park Rangers	16	10	1	5	35	14	21
Stanley	16	7	6	3	22	10	20
Hammersmith Athletic	16	5	3	8	17	23	13
Harrow Athletic	16	4	3	9	19	34	11
Forest Swifts	16	4	2	10	25	37	10
Fulham	16	3	4	9	17	40	10
West Croydon	16	3	4	9	12	33	10

1897-98
(Top) Hargrave, Stevenson, Richardson, Bailey, Dorey (Middle)Swain, Gillett, Lugg, Charlton,Edney
(Bottom) Smith, Dailey, Lloyd, Booth, Field, Knapman

1900-01
Unnamed group of players and officials

1897/98 Season results

London League Second Division

Comp.	Date	Opposition	Result
F	4 Sep	HOUNSLOW	3-0
1	11	Thames Ironworks	0-1
2	18	2nd GRENADIER GUARDS	4-2
FAC 1q	25	1st COLDSTREAM GUARDS	6-1
F	2 Oct	BOSTAL ROVERS	4-0
3	9	Ilford	2-2
FAC 2q	16	3rd GRENADIER GUARDS	1-1
FAC 2qr	20	3rd Genadier Guards	1-4
F	23	QUEENS PARK RANGERS *	3-0
F	30	Ipswich Town	1-1
4	6 Nov	Stanley	1-0
F	13	UPTON PARK	4-0
F	20	2nd COLDSTREAM GUARDS	3-0
F	27	NORTHFLEET	2-3
5	4 Dec	Barking Woodville	2-1
6	11	Bromley	1-0
F	18	3rd GRENADIER GUARDS **	4-3
F	27	Ealing	3-1
F	1 Jan	CIVIL SERVICE	6-3
7	8	LEYTON	8-4
8	15	3rd GENADIER GUARDS	5-1
LSC 1	22	STANLEY	4-2
MSC 1	29	1st SCOTS GUARDS	4-2
LSC 2	5 Feb	CLAPTON ***	2-4
F	12	Hounslow	3-1
F	14	ST. BERNARDS (EDINBURGH)	0-3
LSC 2r	19	CLAPTON	4-1
MSC 2	26	2nd GRENADIER GUARDS	0-0
MSC 2r	5 Mar	2nd GRENADIER GUARDS	3-1
9	10	2nd GRENADIER GUARDS #	2-1
LSC s/f	12	Casuals ^	4-3
MSC s/f	19	3rd Genadier Guards ^^	4-1
LSC 3 f	26	Ilford <> ^	0-0
LSC fr	2 Apr	Ilford + ^	5-1
10	7	BROMLEY	9-1
F	8	HOUNSLOW	1-2
11	9	STANLEY	1-0
MSC f	11	2nd SCOTS GUARDS ##	2-3
12	16	Leyton	1-2
13	16	ILFORD	2-1
14	23	THAMES IRONWORKS	1-0
15	27	3rd GENADIER GUARDS	4-1
MSC f/r	28	2nd Grenadier Guards <	3-2
16	30	BARKING WOODVILLE	0-0

* League match, but QPR later withdrew

** League match but abandoned after 65 mins.

*** Rep. after protest (Clapton - ineligible player)

Away match but played at Brentford

Rep. after protest (Scots G's. - ineligible player) Played at Southall.

< A.E.T. (2-2 at F.T.)

<> Abandoned after 5 mins. (adverse weather)

^Played at County ground, Leyton.

^^ Played at Ealing F.C., Gunnersbury Lane

1898/99 Season results

Southern League Second Division

Comp.	Date	Opposition	Result
1	10 Sep	ST. ALBANS	6-1
2	17	Fulham	4-1
3	24	Thames Ironworks	1-3
4	8 Oct	WATFORD	2-4
5	15	WYCOMBE WANDERERS	9-2
FAC 3q	29	Clapton	1-6
6	5 Nov	Wolverton	2-4
7	12	Southall	3-0
8	24	St. Albans	5-4
9	3 Dec	Uxbridge	0-3
10	17	SHEPHERDS BUSH	1-1
11	24	Watford	1-2
12	31	Chesham	1-2
MSC 1	7 Jan	UXBRIDGE	7-0
LSC 1	14	LONDON CALEDONIANS	1-6
WMC 1	21	CIVIL SERVICE	4-3
MSC 2	4 Feb	BARNET	1-2
13	11	THAMES IRONWORKS	0-2
14	18	Maidenhead	3-0
15	25	FULHAM	2-1
16	4 Mar	WOLVERTON	3-3
17	11	UXBRIDGE	0-1
WMC s/f	18	Harrow Athletic *	1-2
18	18	Shepherds Bush	2-1
19	1 Apr	CHESHAM	5-2
20	8	MAIDENHEAD	6-0
21	15	SOUTHALL	2-1
22	22	Wycombe Wanderers	1-1

* A.E.T. Played at Hanwell

1899/1900 Season results

Southern League Second Division

Comp.	Date	Opposition	Result
1	9 Sep	WYCOMBE WANDERERS	1-0
2	23	Shepherd Bush	2-2
3	7 Oct	Watford	0-4
FAC 3q	28	RICHMOND ASSOCIATION	1-2
4	4 Nov	FULHAM	0-4
5	11	Maidenhead	1-2
6	23 Dec	Chesham	3-3
7	30	Fulham	0-2
8	27 Jan	WATFORD	1-4
9	8 Feb	GRAYS UNITED	0-5
10	17	Wolverton	1-5
11	24	SHEPHERDS BUSH	1-1
12	3 Mar	Southall	0-0
13	17	CHESHAM	1-1
14	24	Grays United	0-7
15	31	DARTFORD	4-0
16	16 Apr	Dartford	1-2
17	21	MAIDENHEAD	3-2
18	26	WOLVERTON	3-1
19	28	SOUTHALL	6-0
20	30	Wycombe Wanderers	2-2

1900/01 Season results

Southern League Second Division

Comp.	Date	Opposition	Result
1	29 Sep	Fulham	2-1
2	13 Oct	Chesham Town	3-0
3	20	SOUTHALL	0-0
FAC 3q	3 Nov	Maidenhead	3-1
4	10	SHEPHERDS BUSH	6-2
FAC 4q	17	Richmond Association	0-1
5	24	Wycombe Wanderers	4-1
6	22 Dec	Maidenhead	1-0
7	29	SHEPPEY UNITED	2-0
8	19 Jan	Southall	9-1
9	9 Feb	Grays United	1-1
10	16	WYCOMBE WANDERERS	11-1
11	2 Mar	FULHAM	5-1
12	9	Sheppey United	5-0
13	18	CHESHAM TOWN	2-1
14	30	Shepherds Bush	2-1
15	5 Apr	MAIDENHEAD	8-0
16	9	GRAYS UNITED	2-1
TM	29	Swindon Town *	0-0

* Played at Elm Park Reading, abandoned after 107 minutes (bad light)

1901/02 Season results

Southern League First Division

Comp.	Date	Opposition	Result
1	7 Sep	Swindon Town	0-0
2	14	West Ham United	0-2
3	21	Kettering	1-3
4	28	LUTON TOWN	0-1
5	5 Oct	Millwall Athletic	1-4
6	12	QUEENS PARK RANGERS	1-1
7	19	Rading	0-2
8	26	Southampton	0-1
FAC	2 Nov	Marlow	3-0
9	9	NEW BROMPTON	3-2
FAC 4q	16	SHEPHERDS BUSH *	2-2
FAC 4q	23	SHEPHERDS BUSH	2-3
10	30	Wellingborough	1-3
11	7 Dec	WELLINGBOROUGH	3-0
12	14	SOUTHAMPTON	1-1
13	21	SWINDON TOWN	2-0
14	4 Jan	KETTERING	1-1
15	11	Luton Town	1-1
16	18	MILLWALL ATHLETIC	0-2
17	25	Queens Park Rangers	2-3
18	1 Feb	READING	0-1
19	15	BRISTOL ROVERS	2-0
20	22	New Brompton	0-2
21	1 Mar	NORTHAMPTON TOWN	4-2
22	3	WEST HAM UNITED	0-2
23	8	Watford	1-2
24	15	TOTTENHAM HOTSPUR	2-1
25	28	Bristol Rovers	0-5
26	29	PORTSMOUTH	1-4
27	1 Apr	Northampton Town	2-2
28	12	WATFORD	4-3
29	19	Portsmouth	1-7
30	26	Tottenham Hotspur	0-3
TM	28	Grays United **	1-1

* Abandoned after 40 minutes (fog)

** Played at Memorial Grounds, Canning Town

Season 1897/98: London League First Division

	P	W	D	L	F	A	Pts
Thames Ironworks	16	12	3	1	47	15	27
BRENTFORD	16	12	2	2	43	17	26
Leyton	16	8	4	4	41	33	20
3rd Grenadier Guards	16	7	3	6	34	33	17
Ilford	16	5	7	4	33	25	17
Stanley	16	5	4	7	22	22	14
Barking Woodville	16	2	6	8	16	37	10
Bromley	16	4	2	10	20	49	10
2nd Grenadier Guards	16	0	3	13	17	42	3

Season 1898/99: Southern League Second Division

	P	W	D	L	F	A	Pts
Thames Ironworks	22	19	1	2	64	16	39
Wolverton	22	13	4	5	88	43	30
Watford	22	14	2	6	62	35	30
BRENTFORD	22	11	3	8	59	39	25
Wycombe Wanderers	22	10	2	10	55	57	22
Southall	22	11	0	11	44	55	22
Chesham	22	9	2	11	45	62	20
St Albans	22	8	3	11	45	59	19
Shepherds Bush	22	7	3	12	37	53	17
Fulham	22	6	4	12	36	44	16
Uxbridge	22	7	2	13	29	48	16
Maidenhead	22	3	2	17	33	86	8

Season 1899/1900: Southern League Second Division

	P	W	D	L	F	A	Pts
Watford	20	14	2	4	57	25	30
Fulham	20	10	4	6	44	23	24
Chesham	20	11	2	7	43	37	24
Wolverton	20	9	6	5	46	36	24
Grays United	20	8	6	6	63	29	22
Shepherds Bush	20	9	4	7	45	37	22
Dartford	20	8	3	9	36	44	19
Wycombe Wanderers	20	8	3	9	35	50	19
BRENTFORD	20	5	7	8	31	48	17
Southall	20	6	3	11	21	44	15
Maidenhead	20	1	2	17	16	64	4

Season 1900/01: Southern League Second Division

	P	W	D	L	F	A	Pts
BRENTFORD	16	14	2	0	63	11	30
Grays United	16	12	2	2	62	12	26
Sheppey United	16	8	1	7	44	26	17
Shepherds Bush	16	8	1	7	30	30	17
Fulham	16	8	0	8	38	26	16
Chesham Town	16	5	1	10	26	39	11
Maidenhead	16	4	1	11	21	49	9
Wycombe Wanderers	16	4	1	11	23	68	9
Southall	16	4	1	11	22	68	9

Season 1901/02: Southern League First Division

	P	W	D	L	F	A	Pts
Portsmouth	30	20	7	3	67	24	47
Tottenham Hotspur	30	18	6	6	61	22	42
Southampton	30	18	6	6	71	28	42
West Ham United	30	17	6	7	45	28	40
Reading	30	16	7	7	57	24	39
Millwall Athletic	30	13	6	11	48	31	32
Luton Town	30	11	10	9	31	35	32
Kettering	30	12	5	13	44	39	29
Bristol Rovers	30	12	5	13	43	39	29
New Brompton	30	10	7	13	39	38	27
Northampton Town	30	11	5	14	53	64	27
Queens Park Rangers	30	8	7	15	34	56	23
Watford	30	9	4	17	36	60	22
Wellingborough	30	9	4	17	34	72	22
BRENTFORD	30	7	6	17	34	61	20
Swindon Town	30	2	3	25	17	93	7

Season 1902/03: Southern League First Division

	P	W	D	L	F	A	Pts
Southampton	30	20	8	2	83	20	48
Reading	30	19	7	4	72	30	45
Portsmouth	30	17	7	6	69	32	41
Tottenham Hotspur	30	14	7	9	47	31	35
Bristol Rovers	30	13	8	9	46	34	34
New Brompton	30	11	11	8	37	35	33
Millwall Athletic	30	14	3	13	52	37	31
Northampton Town	30	12	6	12	39	48	30
Queens Park Rangers	30	11	6	13	34	42	28
West Ham United	30	9	10	11	35	49	28
Luton Town	30	10	7	13	43	44	27
Swindon Town	30	10	7	13	38	46	27
Kettering	30	8	11	11	33	40	27
Wellingborough	30	11	3	16	36	56	25
Watford	30	6	4	20	35	87	16
BRENTFORD	30	2	1	27	16	84	5

1902-03
Back: Lewis (Secretary), Halley, Spice, Nidd, Crone (Trainer)
Middle: Regan, R.Green, Newsome,
Front: Warren, Maher, Turner, Shanks, Pickering

1902/03 Season results

Southern League First Division

Comp.	Date	Opposition	Result
1	6 Sep	Southampton	0-6
2	13	Wellingborough	0-3
3	20	BRISTOL ROVERS	0-2
4	27	Northampton Town	0-2
5	4 Oct	WATFORD	2-3
6	11	Millwall Athletic	1-3
7	18	Tottenham Hotspur	1-3
8	25	WEST HAM UNITED	0-3
FAC 3q	1 Nov	Oxford City	2-2
FAC 3qr	5	Oxford City	5-4
9	8	NEW BROMPTON	1-2
FAC 4q	15	SOUTHALL	5-0
10	22	KETTERING	2-0
FAC 5q	29	SHEPHERDS BUSH *	2-2
FAC 5q	3 Dec	Shepherds Bush **	1-1
11	6	READING	0-3
FAC 5qr	8	Shepherds Bush	1-0
FAC int r	13	WOOLWICH ARSENAL	1-1
FAC int	17	Woolwich Arsenal	0-5
12	20	SOUTHAMPTON	0-4
13	27	WELLINGBOROUGH	1-2
14	3 Jan	Bristol Rovers	0-2
15	10	NORTHAMPTON TOWN	0-2
16	17	Watford	1-3
17	24	MILLWALL ATHLETIC	1-4
18	31	TOTTENHAM HOTSPUR	1-1
19	7 Feb	West Ham United	0-2
20	14	PORTSMOUTH	0-5
21	21	New Brompton	0-4
22	28	SWINDON TOWN	1-0
23	4	Queens Park Rangers	0-3
24	7 Mar	Kettering	2-3
25	14	LUTON TOWN	1-3
26	21	Reading	0-5
27	28	QUEENS PARK RANGERS	0-2
28	11 Apr	Portsmouth	1-4
29	14	Luton Town	0-2
30	18	Swindon Town	0-3
TM	28	Fulham ***	7-2

* Abandoned after 102 mins (Poor light)

** Played at Kensal Rise Athletic Stadium (Q.P.R. F.C.)

*** Played at Womholt Farm (Loftus Road) Shepherds Bush F.C.

1903/04 Season results

Southern League First Division

Comp.	Date	Opposition	Result
1	5 Sep	Queens Park Rangers	0-1
2	7	SWINDON TOWN	2-1
3	12	PLYMOUTH ARGYLE	1-0
4	14	TOTTENHAM HOTSPUR	0-0
5	19	Reading	1-1
6	26	WELLINGBOROUGH	0-1
7	3 Oct	Bristol Rovers	1-5
8	10	BRIGHTON & HOVE ALBION	1-0
9	17	Portsmouth	1-3
10	24	NORTHAMPTON TOWN	4-1
FAC	31	UXBRIDGE	8-0
11	7 Nov	West Ham United	1-0
FAC	14	Oxford City	3-1
12	21	Luton Town	0-1
FAC	28	Wycombe Wanderers	4-1
13	5 Dec	Kettering	4-2
FAC	12	PLYMOUTH ARGYLE	2-2
FAC	16	Plymouth Argyle	1-4
14	26	FULHAM	1-1
15	28	MILLWALL ATHLETIC	1-3
16	2 Jan	QUEENS PARK RANGERS	1-4
17	4	KETTERING	4-2
18	9	Plymouth Argyle	2-2
19	16	READING	0-0
20	23	Wellingborough	0-2
21	30	BRISTOL ROVERS	1-2
22	1 Feb	NEW BROMPTON	1-1
23	8	Brighton & Hove Albion	1-3
24	13	PORTSMOUTH	4-0
25	20	Northampton Town	0-3
26	27	Swindon Town	1-1
27	5 Mar	WEST HAM UNITED	2-0
28	12	Tottenham Hotspur	1-1
29	19	LUTON TOWN	2-1
30	26	New Brompton	0-3
31	2 Apr	SOUTHAMPTON	0-1
32	9	Southampton	0-1
33	16	Fulham	0-0
34	23	Millwall Athletic	0-2

1904/05 Season results

Southern League First Division

Comp.	Date	Opposition	Result
1	3 Sep	WEST HAM UNITED	0-0
2	10	Reading	0-1
3	17	BRISTOL ROVERS	0-1
4	24	Northampton Town	2-3
5	1 Oct	PORTSMOUTH	1-3
6	8	Brighton & Hove Albion	1-0
7	15	Queens Park Rangers	2-3
8	22	MILLWALL ATHLETIC	2-0
9	29	Tottenham Hotspur	1-1
10	5 Nov	LUTON TOWN	3-0
11	12	Swindon Town	3-1
12	19	NEW BROMPTON	0-2
_	26	Fulham *	0-1
13	3 Dec	SOUTHAMPTON	0-1
FAC 6Q	10	Queens Park Rangers	2-1
14	17	WATFORD	1-1
15	24	Plymouth Argyle	0-1
16	31	West Ham United	1-0
17	7 Jan	READING	0-0
FAC int	14	READING	1-1
FAC int r	18	Reading	0-2
18	21	NORTHAMPTON TOWN	3-4
19	28 Feb	POrtsmouth	0-5
20	4	BRIGHTON & HOVE ALBION	1-0
21	11	QUEENS PARK RANGERS	0-0
22	18	Millwall Athletic	1-1
23	25 Mar	TOTTENHAM HOTSPUR	0-0
24	4	Luton Town	0-1
25	11	SWINDON TOWN	1-1
26	18	New Brompton	1-0
27	25	WELLINGBOROUGH	3-0
28	27 Apr	Wellingborough	4-0
29	1	Southampton	0-2
30	8	FULHAM	1-1
31	15	Watford	0-1
32	22	PLYMOUTH ARGYLE	1-0
33	25	Bristol Rovers	0-3
34	29	Fulham	0-1

* Abadoned after 45 mins. (fog)

Season 1903/04: Southern League First Division

	P	W	D	L	F	A	Pts
Southampton	34	22	6	6	75	30	50
Tottenham Hotspur	34	16	11	7	54	37	43
Bristol Rovers	34	17	8	9	66	42	42
Portsmouth	34	17	8	9	41	38	42
Queens Park Rangers	34	15	11	8	53	37	41
Reading	34	14	13	7	48	35	41
Millwall Athletic	34	16	8	10	64	42	40
Luton Town	34	14	12	8	38	33	40
Plymouth Argyle	34	13	10	11	44	34	36
Swindon Town	34	10	11	13	30	42	31
Fulham	34	9	12	13	33	34	30
West Ham United	34	10	7	17	38	43	27
BRENTFORD	34	9	9	16	34	48	27
Wellingborough	34	11	5	18	44	63	27
Northampton Town	34	10	7	17	36	69	27
New Brompton	34	6	13	15	26	43	25
Brighton & Hove Albion	34	6	12	16	45	79	24
Kettering	34	6	7	21	30	78	19

Season 1904/05: Southern League First Division

	P	W	D	L	F	A	Pts
Bristol Rovers	34	20	8	6	74	36	48
Reading	34	18	7	9	57	38	43
Southampton	34	18	7	9	54	40	43
Plymouth Argyle	34	18	5	11	57	39	41
Tottenham Hotspur	34	15	8	11	53	34	38
Fulham	34	14	10	10	46	34	38
Queens Park Rangers	34	14	8	12	51	46	36
Portsmouth	34	16	4	14	61	56	36
New Brompton	34	11	11	12	40	41	33
West Ham United	34	12	8	14	48	42	32
Brighton & Hove Albion	34	13	6	15	44	45	32
Northampton Town	34	12	8	14	43	54	32
Watford	34	14	3	17	41	44	31
BRENTFORD	34	10	9	15	33	38	29
Millwall Athletic	34	11	7	16	38	47	29
Swindon Town	34	12	5	17	41	59	29
Luton Town	34	12	3	19	45	54	27
Wellingborough	34	5	3	26	25	104	13

1903-04
Back: Molyneux (Manager), Leigh, Bellingham, Frail, Watson, Cale, Crone,(Trainer)
Middle: W.Howarth, Turner, Parsonage, Davidson, Underwood, T.C.Howarth, Swarbrick
Front: Jay, Atherton, Brett.

1904-

1905/06 Season results

Southern League First Division

Comp.	Date	Opposition	Result
1	2 Sep	Southampton	1-0
2	9	READING	2-1
3	16	Watford	0-1
4	23	BRIGHTON & HOVE ALBION	2-0
5	30	West Ham United	0-2
6	7 Oct	FULHAM	0-2
7	14	Queens Park Rangers	2-1
8	21	BRISTOL ROVERS	1-0
9	28	New Brompton	1-2
10	4 Nov	PORTSMOUTH	1-1
11	11	Swindon Town	1-1
12	18	MILLWALL ATHLETIC	1-1
13	25	Luton Town	2-0
14	2 Dec	TOTTENHAM HOTSPUR	0-3
FAC 4q	9	WYCOMBE WANDERERS	4-0
15	16	Norwich City	1-1
16	23	PLYMOUTH ARGYLE	1-0
17	30	SOUTHAMPTON	2-1
18	6 Jan	Reading	2-2
FAC 1	13	BRISTOL CITY	2-1
19	20	WATFORD	3-0
20	27	Brighton & Hove Albion	2-3
FAC 2	3 Feb	LINCOLN CITY	3-0
21	10	Fulham	0-2
22	17	QUEENS PARK RANGERS	2-2
FAC 3	24	Liverpool	0-2
23	3 Mar	NEW BROMPTON	3-2
24	10	Portsmouth	0-5
25	12	NORTHAMPTON TOWN	2-1
26	17	SWINDON TOWN	3-1
27	24	Millwall Athletic	1-1
28	31	LUTON TOWN	2-1
29	7 Apr	Tottenham Hotspur	1-4
30	14	Northampton Town	0-4
31	21	NORWICH CITY	0-2
32	23	WEST HAM UNITED	3-1
33	28	Plymouth Argyle	0-2
34	30	Bristol Rovers	1-2

	P	W	D	L	F	A	Pts
Fulham	34	19	12	3	44	15	50
Southampton	34	19	7	8	58	39	45
Portsmouth	34	17	9	8	61	35	43
Luton Town	34	17	7	10	64	40	41
Tottenham Hotspur	34	16	7	11	46	29	39
Plymouth Argyle	34	16	7	11	52	33	39
Norwich City	34	13	10	11	46	38	36
Bristol Rovers	34	15	5	14	56	56	35
BRENTFORD	34	14	7	13	43	52	35
Reading	34	12	9	13	53	46	33
West Ham United	34	14	5	15	42	39	33
Millwall Athletic	34	11	11	12	38	41	33
Queens Park Rangers	34	12	7	15	58	44	31
Watford	34	8	10	16	38	57	26
Swindon Town	34	8	9	17	31	52	25
Brighton & Hove Albion	34	9	7	18	30	55	25
New Brompton	34	7	8	19	20	62	22
Northampton Town	34	8	5	21	32	79	21

1906/07 Season results

Southern League First Division

Comp.	Date	Opposition	Result
1	1 Sep	WATFORD	2-0
2	8	Northampton Town	0-4
3	15	QUEENS PARK RANGERS	4-1
4	22	Fulham	0-1
5	29	SOUTHAMPTON	2-1
6	6 Oct	West ham United	1-3
7	13	TOTTENHAM HOTSPUR	2-2
8	20	Swindon Town	0-2
9	27	NORWICH CITY	2-1
10	3 Nov	Luton Town	0-2
11	10	CRYSTAL PALACE	2-0
12	17	Bristol Rovers	1-3
13	24	Millwall	0-0
14	1 Dec	LEYTON	2-0
15	8	Portsmouth	0-0
16	15	NEW BROMPTON	3-0
17	22	Plymouth Argyle	2-2
18	25	BRIGHTON & HOVE ALBION	3-1
19	27	Reading	0-4
20	29	Watford	4-1
21	5 Jan	NORTHAMPTON TOWN	2-0
FAC 1	12	GLOSSOP	2-1
_	19	Queens Park Rangers *	0-0
22	26	FULHAM	1-0
FAC 2	2 Feb	MIDDLESBROUGH	1-0
23	9	WEST HAM UNITED	0-0
24	16	Tottenham Hotspur	1-2
FAC 3	23	Crystal Palace	1-1
FAC 3r	27	CRYSTAL PALACE	0-1
25	2	Norwich City	1-1
26	9 Mar	LUTON TOWN	0-1
27	11	Queens Park Rangers	1-1
28	16	Crystal Palace	3-0
29	18	Southampton	0-5
30	23	BRISTOL ROVERS	2-1
31	29	Brighton & Hove Albion	1-3
32	30	MILLWALL ATHLETIC	0-2
33	1	READING	4-2
34	6 Apr	Leyton	3-1
35	8	SWINDON TOWN	5-2
36	13	PORTSMOUTH	1-1
37	20	New Brompton	0-5
38	27	PLYMOUTH ARGYLE	2-1

* Abandoned after 85 mins. (fog)

	P	W	D	L	F	A	Pts
Fulham	38	20	13	5	58	32	53
Portsmouth	38	22	7	9	64	36	51
Brighton & Hove Albion	38	18	9	11	53	43	45
Luton Town	38	18	9	11	52	52	45
West Ham United	38	15	14	9	60	41	44
Tottenham Hotspur	38	17	9	12	63	45	43
Millwall Athletic	38	18	6	14	71	50	42
Norwich City	38	15	12	11	57	48	42
Watford	38	13	16	9	46	43	42
BRENTFORD	38	17	8	13	57	56	42
Southampton	38	13	9	16	49	56	35
Reading	38	14	6	18	57	47	34
Leyton	38	11	12	15	38	60	34
Bristol Rovers	38	12	9	17	55	54	33
Plymouth Argyle	38	10	13	15	43	50	33
New Brompton	38	12	9	17	47	59	33
Swindon Town	38	11	11	16	43	54	33
Queens Park Rangers	38	11	10	17	47	55	32
Crystal Palace	38	8	9	21	46	66	25
Northampton Town	38	5	9	24	29	88	19

1907/08 Season results

Southern League First Division

Comp.	Date	Opposition	Result
1	3 Sep	Leyton	0-2
2	7	Bristol Rovers	0-3
3	14	LEYTON	2-0
4	21	Reading	1-5
5	28	WATFORD	4-1
6	5 Oct	Norwich City	2-3
7	12	NORTHAMPTON TOWN	3-1
8	19	Southampton	0-3
9	26	PLYMOUTH ARGYLE	2-1
10	2 Nov	West Ham United	1-4
11	9	QUEENS PARK RANGERS	1-1
12	16	Tottenham Hotspur	0-1
13	23	SWINDON TOWN	2-0
14	30	Crystal Palace	1-2
15	7 Dec	LUTON TOWN	3-1
16	14	Brighton & Hove Albion	0-1
17	21	PORTSMOUTH	1-1
18	25	MILLWALL ATHLETIC	1-2
19	26	New Brompton	1-2
20	28	Bradford (Park Avenue)	0-1
21	4 Jan	BRISTOL ROVERS	0-3
FAC	11	Carlisle United	2-2
FAC	15	CARLISLE UNITED *	1-3
22	18	READING	1-0
23	25	Watford	2-1
24	8 Feb	Northampton Town	0-0
25	15	SOUTHAMPTON	4-0
26	22	Plymouth Argyle	1-2
27	29	WEST HAM UNITED	4-0
28	7 Mar	Queens Park Rangers	0-1
29	9	NORWICH CITY	2-1
30	14	TOTTENHAM HOTSPUR	3-0
3	21	Swindon Town	0-0
32	28	CRYSTAL PALACE	1-1
33	4 Apr	Luton Town	0-1
34	11	BRIGHTON & HOVE ALBION	2-0
35	17	Millwall Athletic	0-2
36	18	Portsmouth	2-3
37	20	NEW BROMPTON	1-0
38	25	BRADFORD PARK AVENUE	1-2

* A.E.T. (1-1 after 90 mins.)

	P	W	D	L	F	A	Pts
Queens Park Rangers	38	21	9	8	82	57	51
Plymouth Argyle	38	19	11	8	50	31	49
Millwall Athletic	38	19	8	11	49	32	46
Crystal Palace	38	17	10	11	54	51	44
Swindon Town	38	16	10	12	55	40	42
Bristol Rovers	38	16	10	12	59	56	42
Tottenham Hotspur	38	17	7	14	59	48	41
Northampton Town	38	15	11	12	50	41	41
Portsmouth	38	17	6	15	63	52	40
West Ham United	38	15	10	13	47	48	40
Southampton	38	16	6	16	51	60	38
Reading	38	15	6	17	55	50	36
Bradford Park Avenue	38	12	12	14	53	54	36
Watford	38	12	10	16	47	59	34
BRENTFORD	38	14	5	19	49	52	33
Norwich City	38	12	9	17	46	49	33
Brighton & Hove Albion	38	12	8	18	46	59	32
Luton Town	38	12	6	20	33	56	30
Leyton	38	8	11	19	51	73	27
New Brompton	38	9	7	22	44	75	25

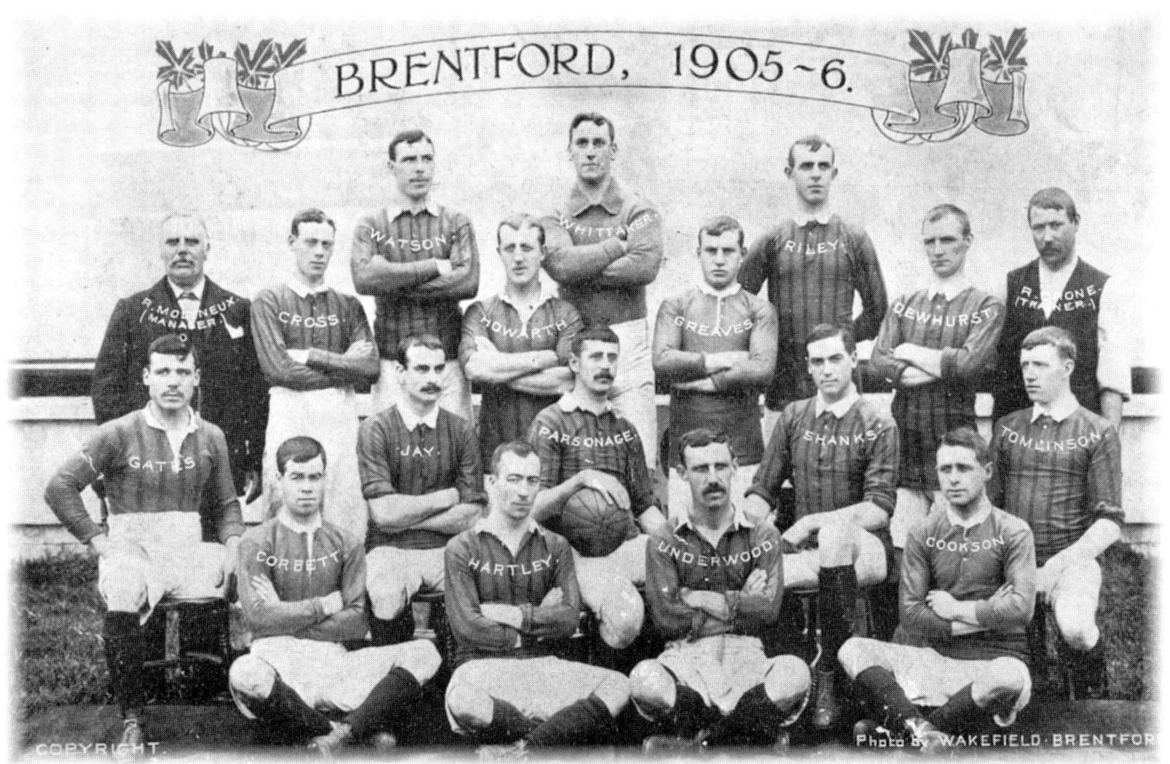

1905-06

1906-07

Back: Campbell, Shanks, Connell, Williams, Brown (Manager), Tomlinson, Crone (Trainer)
Middle: Haworth, Jay, Corbett, Parsonage, Underwood, Watson, Abbott
Front: Taylor, Bull, Hagan, McAllister.

Season 1908/09: Southern League First Division

	P	W	D	L	F	A	Pts
Northampton Town	40	25	5	10	90	45	55
Swindon Town	40	22	5	13	96	55	49
Southampton	40	19	10	11	67	58	48
Portsmouth	40	18	10	12	68	60	46
Bristol Rovers	40	17	9	14	60	63	43
Exeter City	40	18	6	16	56	65	42
New Brompton	40	17	7	16	48	59	41
Reading	40	11	18	11	60	57	40
Luton Town	40	17	6	17	59	60	40
Plymouth Argyle	40	15	10	15	46	47	40
Millwall Athletic	40	16	6	18	59	61	38
Southend United	40	14	10	16	52	54	38
Leyton	40	15	8	17	52	55	38
Watford	40	14	9	17	51	64	37
Queens Park Rangers	40	12	12	16	52	50	36
Crystal Palace	40	12	12	16	62	62	36
West Ham United	40	16	4	20	56	60	36
Brighton & Hove Albion	40	14	7	19	60	61	35
Norwich City	40	12	11	17	59	75	35
Coventry City	40	15	4	21	64	91	34
BRENTFORD	40	13	7	20	59	74	33

Season 1909/10: Southern League First Division

	P	W	D	L	F	A	Pts
Brighton & Hove Albion	42	23	13	6	69	28	59
Swindon Town	42	22	10	10	92	46	54
Queens Park Rangers	42	19	13	10	56	47	51
Northampton Town	42	22	4	16	90	44	48
Southampton	42	16	16	10	64	55	48
Portsmouth	42	20	7	15	70	63	47
Crystal Palace	42	20	6	16	69	50	46
Coventry City	42	19	8	15	71	60	46
West Ham United	42	15	15	12	69	56	45
Leyton	42	16	11	15	60	46	43
Plymouth Argyle	42	16	11	15	61	54	43
New Brompton	42	19	5	18	76	74	43
Bristol Rovers	42	16	10	16	37	48	42
BRENTFORD	42	16	9	17	50	58	41
Luton Town	42	15	11	16	72	92	41
Millwall Athletic	42	15	7	20	45	59	37
Norwich City	42	13	9	20	59	78	35
Exeter City	42	14	6	22	60	69	34
Watford	42	10	13	19	51	76	33
Southend United	42	12	9	21	51	90	33
Croydon Common	42	13	5	24	52	96	31
Reading	42	7	10	25	38	73	24

	P	W	D	L	F	A	Pts
Swindon Town	38	24	5	9	80	31	53
Northampton Town	38	18	12	8	54	27	48
Brighton & Hove Albion	38	20	8	10	58	35	48
Crystal Palace	38	17	13	8	55	48	47
West Ham United	38	17	11	10	63	46	45
Queens Park Rangers	38	13	14	11	52	41	40
Leyton	38	16	8	14	57	52	40
Plymouth Argyle	38	15	9	14	54	55	39
Luton Town	38	15	8	15	67	63	38
Norwich City	38	15	8	15	46	48	38
Coventry City	38	16	6	16	65	68	38
BRENTFORD	38	14	9	15	41	42	37
Exeter City	38	14	9	15	51	53	37
Watford	38	13	9	16	49	65	35
Millwall Athletic	38	11	9	18	42	54	31
Bristol Rovers	38	10	10	18	42	55	30
Southampton	38	11	8	19	42	67	30
New Brompton	38	11	8	19	34	65	30
Southend United	38	10	9	19	47	64	29
Portsmouth	38	8	11	19	34	53	27

Season 1910/11: Southern League First Division

1908/09 Season results

Southern League First Division

Comp.	Date	Opposition	Result
1	2 Sep	Reading	2-2
2	5	SOUTHAMPTON	2-3
3	12	Leyton	0-2
4	19	WEST HAM UNITED	1-0
5	26	Brighton & Hove Albion	0-4
6	28	QUEENS PARK RANGERS	0-0
7	3 Oct	CRYSTAL PALACE	1-3
8	10	Plymouth Argyle	0-2
9	17	Luton Town	1-3
10	24	SWINDON TOWN	1-0
11	31	Portsmouth	3-2
12	7 Nov	Queens Park Rangers	0-3
13	14	Northampton Town	2-4
14	16	EXETER CITY	0-2
15	21	NEW BROMPTON	1-1
16	23	SOUTHEND UNITED	4-1
17	28	Millwall Athletic	1-2
18	12 Dec	Coventry City	2-1
19	19	BRISTOL ROVERS	2-2
20	25	WATFORD	3-1
21	26	Norwich City	1-6
22	28	READING	2-3
23	2 Jan	Southampton	0-1
24	9	LEYTON	0-0
FAC 1	16	GAINSBOROUGH TRINITY	2-0
25	23	West Ham United	0-3
26	30	BRIGHTON & HOVE ALBION	4-0
FAC 2	6 Feb	Nottingham Forest	0-1
27	13	PLYMOUTH ARGYLE	1-0
28	20	LUTON TOWN	2-2
29	27	Swindon Town	1-2
_	6 Mar	PORTSMOUTH *	0-0
30	13	Exeter City	2-1
31	20	NORTHAMPTON TOWN	3-1
32	27	New Brompton	1-1
33	29	PORTSMOUTH	1-2
34	31	Crystal Palace	1-3
35	3 Apr	MILLWALL ATHLETIC	4-2
36	9	NORWICH CITY	3-1
37	10	Southend United	0-1
38	12	Watford	0 2
39	17	COVENTRY CITY	5-2
40	24	Bristol Rovers	2-3

* Abandoned after 41 mins. (Waterlogged pitch)

1909/10 Season results

Southern League First Division

Comp.	Date	Opposition	Result
1	1 Sep	Crystal Palace	0-1
2	4	BRIGHTON & HOVE ALBION	0-0
3	8	Swindon Town	0-4
4	11	West Ham United	2-3
5	13	CRYSTAL PALACE	1-0
6	18	PORTSMOUTH	2-0
7	25	Bristol Rovers	0-3
8	27	SWINDON TOWN	1-1
9	2 Oct	NORWICH CITY	0-1
10	9	Exeter City	1-4
11	11	PLYMOUTH ARGYLE	2-2
12	16	Coventry City	0-3
13	23	WATFORD	2-0
14	30	Reading	0-2
15	6 Nov	SOUTHEND UNITED	4-1
16	13	Leyton	0-0
FAC 4q	20	LUTON TOWN	2-1
17	27	Southampton	0-1
FAC 5q	4 Dec	Accrington Stanley	0-1
18	11	Millwall Athletic	1-1
19	18	NEW BROMPTON	4-1
20	25	NORTHAMPTON TOWN	2-1
21	27	Northampton Town	1-4
22	28	Luton Town	2-4
23	1 Jan	QUEENS PARK RANGERS	0-1
24	8	Brighton & Hove Albion	0-3
25	15	CROYDON COMMON	1-2
26	22	WEST HAM UNITED	0-0
27	29	Portsmouth	2-0
28	5 Feb	Croydon Common	2-1
29	12	Norwich City	1-5
30	14	BRISTOL ROVERS	1-0
31	19	EXETER CITY	3-0
32	26	COVENTRY CITY	3-1
33	5 Mar	Watford	0-0
34	12	READING	1-0
35	19	Southend United	3-0
36	25	Queens Park Rangers	0-0
37	26	LEYTON	1-0
38	28	LUTON TOWN	2-2
39	2 Apr	Plymouth Argyle	0-3
40	9	SOUTHAMPTON	1-0
41	23	MILLWALL ATHLETIC	2-0
42	30	New Brompton	2-3

1910/11 Season results

Southern League First Division

Comp.	Date	Opposition	Result
1	3 Sep	Exeter City	0-0
2	10	SWINDON TOWN	1-1
3	17	Bristol Rovers	1-0
4	24	CRYSTAL PALACE	2-1
5	28	New Brompton	1-2
6	1 Oct	NORWICH CITY	2-0
7	8	Leyton	1-4
8	15	WATFORD	2-0
9	22	Plymouth Argyle	0-2
10	29	SOUTHAMPTON	3-2
11	5 Nov	Southend United	2-0
12	12	COVENTRY CITY	1-0
13	26	MILLWALL ATHLETIC	3-1
14	3 Dec	Queens Park Rangers	0-2
15	10	WEST HAM UNITED	3-0
16	17	Luton Town	1-1
17	24	PORTSMOUTH	2-0
18	26	Northampton Town	0-2
19	27	NORTHAMPTON TOWN	0-0
20	31	EXETER CITY	3-1
21	7 Jan	Swindon Town	0-3
FAC 1	14	PRESTON NORTH END	0-1
22	21	BRISTOL ROVERS	3-0
23	28	Cyrstal Palace	1-1
24	11 Feb	LEYTON	0-0
25	18	Watford	0-1
26	25	PLYMOUTH ARGYLE	1-2
27	4 Mar	Southampton	0-2
28	11	SOUTHEND UNITED	3-1
29	18	Coventry City	0-2
30	25	NEW BROMPTON	0-2
31	1 Apr	Millwall Athletic	1-1
32	8	QUEENS PARK RANGERS	1-1
33	14	Brighton & Hove Albion	0-1
34	15	West Ham United	0-2
35	17	BRIGHTON & HOVE ALBION	1-1
36	18	Norwich City	0-1
37	22	LUTON TOWN	1-0
38	29	Portsmouth	1-2

1908-09

Back: Cowper (Trainer), Sugden, Rarnsden, McCullock, Hisbent, McIvor, Richards, Badger, Blackall, Halliday (Manager)
Middle: Ryalls, Rhodes, Ewing, Nicholson, Beecser, Gordon, Connelly
Front: Hamilton, Jaffray.

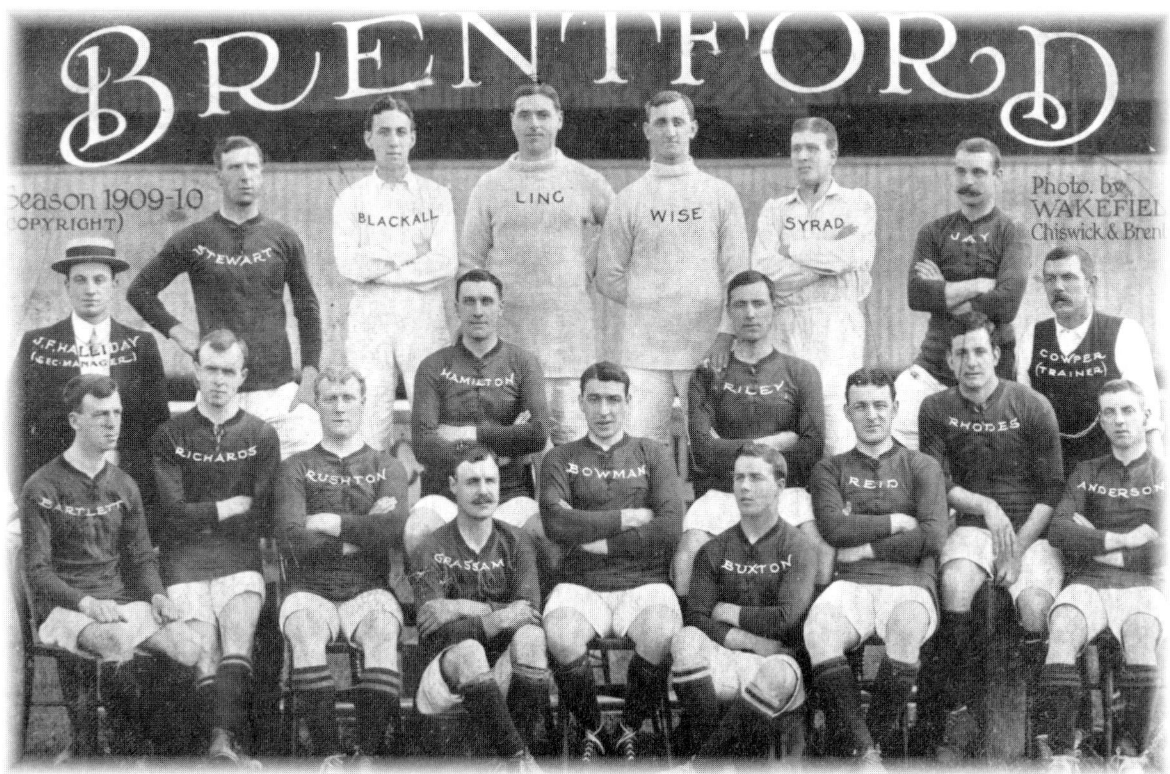

1909-10

1910-11
Back: Stewart, Blackall, Liog, Wise, Syrad, Jay
Middle: Hamilton, Riley, Rhodes,
Front: Bartlett, Richards, Rushton, Grassam, Bowman, Buxton, Reid, Anderson.

1912-13
Back: Kennedy, New, Barclay, Bentley
2nd Row: Halliday (Sec/Manager), Richards, Ling, Price, Wicks, Cowper (Trainer)
3rd Row: Brawn, Fells, Rhodes, McTavish, Spratt
Front: Sibbald, Chapple, Graham, Hickleton, Morrison

1911/12 Season results

Southern League First Division

Comp.	Date	Opposition	Result
1	2 Sep	Reading	0-0
2	6	Brighton & Hove Albion	2-0
3	9	WATFORD	4-2
4	16	New Brompton	1-2
5	23	EXETER CITY	3-1
6	30	LUTON TOWN	0-1
7	7 Oct	Queens Park Rangers	0-4
8	14	MILLWALL ATHLETIC	3-3
9	21	West Ham United	4-7
10	28	BRISTOL ROVERS	2-2
11	4 Nov	Swindon Town	0-2
12	11	NORTHAMPTON TOWN	2-2
FAC 4q	18	1ST BATTALION KING'S ROYAL RIFLES	1-1
FAC 4qr	22	1ST BATTALION KING'S ROYAL RIFLES*	4-1
13	25	STOKE	0-1
FAC 5q	2 Dec	Southend United	1-0
14	9	LEYTON	2-0
15	16	Norwich City	0-2
16	23	CRYSTAL PALACE	1-0
17	25	SOUTHAMPTON	4-0
18	26	Southampton	2-3
19	27	Coventry City	0-9
20	30	READING	0-0
21	6 Jan	Watford	0-3
FAC 1	13	CRYSTAL PALACE	0-0
FAC 1r	17	Crystal Palace	0-4
22	20	NEW BROMPTON	7-1
23	27	Exeter City	0-1
24	3 Feb	Luton Town	0-0
25	10	QUEENS PARK RANGERS	1-2
26	17	Millwall Athletic	0-2
27	2 Mar	Bristol Rovers	3-1
28	16	Northampton Town	3-6
29	23	BRIGHTON & HOVE ALBION	1-1
30	27	WEST HAM UNITED	1-2
31	30	Stoke	1-1
32	5 Apr	PLYMOUTH ARGYLE	4-0
33	6	COVENTRY CITY	3-0
34	8	Plymouth Argyle	0-1
35	13	Leyton	1-1
36	20	NORWICH CITY	3-0
37	24	SWINDON TOWN	2-0
38	27	Crystal Palace	0-2

* Played at Griffin Park (King's R.R. ground unsuitable)

	P	W	D	L	F	A	Pts
Queens Park Rangers	38	21	11	6	59	35	53
Plymouth Argyle	38	23	6	9	63	31	52
Northampton Town	38	22	7	9	82	41	51
Swindon Town	38	21	6	11	82	50	48
Brighton & Hove Albion	38	19	9	10	73	35	47
Coventry City	38	17	8	13	66	54	42
Crystal Palace	38	15	10	13	70	46	40
Millwall Athletic	38	15	10	13	60	57	40
Watford	38	13	10	15	56	68	36
Stoke	38	13	10	15	51	63	36
Reading	38	11	14	13	43	69	36
Norwich City	38	10	14	14	40	60	34
West Ham United	38	13	7	18	64	69	33
BRENTFORD	38	12	9	17	60	65	33
Exeter City	38	11	11	16	48	62	33
Southampton	38	10	11	17	46	63	31
Bristol Rovers	38	9	13	16	41	62	31
New Brompton	38	11	9	18	35	72	31
Luton Town	38	9	10	19	49	61	28
Leyton	38	7	11	20	27	62	25

1912/13 Season results

Southern League First Division

Comp.	Date	Opposition	Result
1	4 Sep	Crystal Palace	1-3
2	7	READING	1-0
3	14	Norwich City	0-2
4	18	CRYSTAL PALACE	2-1
5	21	GILLINGHAM	0-1
6	28	Northampton Town	0-2
7	5 Oct	QUEENS PARK RANGERS	0-2
8	9	Watford	0-1
9	12	Stoke	0-1
10	19	Millwall Athletic	2-3
11	26	BRISTOL ROVERS	0-1
12	2 Nov	Swindon Town	0-2
13	9	PORTSMOUTH	1-0
14	16	Exeter City	0-1
15	23	WEST HAM UNITED	5-1
FAC 4q	30	WATFORD	0-0
FAC 4qr	4 Dec	Watford	1-5
16	7	COVENTRY CITY	2-0
17	21	MERTHYR TOWN	2-0
18	25	PLYMOUTH ARGYLE	2-2
_	26	Plymouth Argyle *	0-2
19	28	Reading	1-4
20	4 Jan	NORWICH CITY	1-0
21	18	Gillingham	4-0
22	25	NORTHAMPTON TOWN	0-0
23	8 Feb	Queens Park Rangers	1-2
24	15	STOKE	4-2
25	22	MILLWALL ATHLETIC	0-0
26	1 Mar	Bristol Rovers	1-1
27	5	Brighton & Hove Albion	2-2
28	8	SWINDON TOWN	0-3
29	12	Plymouth Argyle	0-3
30	15	Portsmouth	0-1
31	21	SOUTHAMPTON	1-2
32	22	EXETER CITY	0-1
33	24	Southampton	1-3
34	29	West Ham United	1-2
35	5 Apr	BRIGHTON & HOVE ALBION	4-1
36	12	Coventry City	0-3
37	19	WATFORD	2-0
38	29	Merthyr Town	1-2

* Abandoned after 49 mins. (waterlogged pitch)

	P	W	D	L	F	A	Pts
Plymouth Argyle	38	22	6	10	77	36	50
Swindon Town	38	20	8	10	66	41	48
West Ham United	38	18	12	8	66	46	48
Queens Park Rangers	38	18	10	10	46	35	46
Crystal Palace	38	17	11	10	55	36	45
Millwall Athletic	38	19	7	12	62	43	45
Exeter City	38	18	8	12	48	44	44
Reading	38	17	8	13	59	55	42
Brighton & Hove Albion	38	13	12	13	48	47	38
Northampton Town	38	12	12	14	61	48	36
Portsmouth	38	14	8	16	41	49	36
Merthyr Town	38	12	12	14	42	60	36
Coventry City	38	13	8	17	53	59	34
Watford	38	12	10	16	43	50	34
Gillingham	38	12	10	16	36	53	34
Bristol Rovers	38	12	9	17	55	64	33
Southampton	38	10	11	17	40	72	31
Norwich City	38	10	9	19	39	50	29
BRENTFORD	38	11	5	22	42	55	27
Stoke	38	10	4	24	39	75	24

1913/14 Season results

Southern League Second Division

Comp.	Date	Opposition	Result
1	13 Sep	Treharris	2-1
2	20	CAERPHILLY	5-0
3	4 Oct	TON PENTRE	7-0
4	11	Abertillery	1-0
5	18	SWANSEA TOWN	3-1
6	25	BARRY	5-0
7	8 Nov	MARDY	4-0
FAC 4q	29	LUTON CLARENCE	1-0
8	6 Dec	Llanelly	3-0
FAC 5q	13	SOUTHEND UNITED	1-1
FAC 5qr	17	Southend United	0-2
9	20	Barry	4-0
10	25	CROYDON COMMON	0-1
11	26	TREHARRIS	7-0
12	27	NEWPORT COUNTY	3-0
13	17 Jan	STOKE	2-0
14	19	Mid-Rhondda	0-0
15	31	PONTYPRIDD	2-0
16	7 Feb	Luton Town	1-3
17	14	LLANELLY	2-0
18	21	PONTYPRIDD	0-0
19	23	Mardy	2-0
20	28	Stoke	1-2
21	14 Mar	MID-RHONDDA	3-1
22	21	Ton Pentre	0-1
23	23	Aberdare	6-3
24	28	ABERTILLERY	5-0
25	4 Apr	Newport County	2-3
26	10	ABERDARE	4-0
27	11	LUTON TOWN	0-0
28	13	Croydon Common	0-1
29	18	Swansea Town	0-0
30	20	Caerphilly	5-1

	P	W	D	L	F	A	Pts
Croydon Common	30	23	5	2	76	14	51
Luton Town	30	24	3	3	92	22	51
BRENTFORD	30	20	4	6	80	18	44
Swansea Town	30	20	4	6	66	23	44
Stoke	30	19	2	9	71	34	40
Newport County	30	14	8	8	49	38	36
Mid Rhondda	30	13	7	10	55	37	33
Pontypridd	30	14	5	11	43	38	33
Llanelly	30	12	4	14	45	39	28
Barry	30	9	8	13	44	70	26
Abertillery	30	8	4	18	44	57	20
Ton Pentre	30	8	4	18	33	61	20
Mardy	30	6	6	18	30	60	18
Caerphilly	30	4	7	19	21	103	15
Aberdare	30	4	5	21	33	87	13
Treharris	30	2	4	24	19	106	8

1914/15 Season results
Southern League Second Division

Comp.	Date	Opposition	Result
1	5 Sep	COVENTRY CITY	3-1
2	12	Barry	1-0
3	14	Mid-Rhondda	0-0
_	19	LEYTON *	5-0
4	26	Ton Pentre	0-0
5	13 Oct	Stalybridge Celtic	1-5
_	17	MARDY **	2-0
6	31	EBBW VALE	3-0
7	7 Nov	Lanelly	0-3
8	14	NEWPORT COUNTY	1-0
FAC 4q	21	Nunhead	1-0
_	28	ABERTILLERY ***	10-0
FAC 5q	5 Dec	Boscombe	0-0
FAC 5qr	9	BOSCOMBE	0-1
9	12	SWANSEA TOWN	2-0
10	25	STOKE	2-2
11	26	Stoke	0-3
12	2 Jan	Coventry City	2-3
13	9	Pontypridd	0-1
14	16	BARRY	0-0
15	30	TON PENTRE	3-3
16	13 Feb	STALYBRIDGE CELTIC	1-3
17	6 Mar	Ebbw Vale	4-1
18	13	LLANELLY	2-2
19	20	Newport County	0-5
20	27	MID-RHONDDA	3-1
21	2 Apr	MERTHYR TOWN	1-1
22	3	Swansea Town	0-8
23	5	Merthyr Town	0-3
24	10	PONTYPRIDD	6-0

	P	W	D	L	F	A	Pts
Stoke	24	17	4	3	62	15	38
Stalybridge Celtic	24	17	3	4	47	22	37
Merthyr Town	24	15	5	4	46	20	35
Swansea Town	24	16	1	7	48	21	33
Coventry City	24	13	2	9	56	33	28
Ton Pentre	24	11	6	7	42	43	28
BRENTFORD	24	8	7	9	35	45	23
Llanelly	24	10	1	13	39	32	21
Barry	24	6	5	13	30	35	17
Newport County	24	7	3	14	27	42	17
Pontypridd	24	5	6	13	31	58	16
Mid Rhondda	24	3	6	15	17	40	12
Ebbw Vale	24	3	1	20	23	88	7

* Leyton resigned in December - Record expunged.
** Mardy resigned in December - Record expunged.
*** Abertillery resigned and disbanded in December. Record expunged

1915
Unnamed Team group.

1915/16 Season results

London Combination

Principal Tournament

Comp.	Date	Opposition	Result
1	4 Sep	WEST HAM UNITED	2-1
2	11	Tottenham Hotspur	1-1
3	18	CRYSTAL PALACE	1-0
4	25	Queens Park Rangers	2-1
5	2 Oct	FULHAM	2-2
6	9	Clapton Orient	3-1
7	16	WATFORD	1-2
8	23	Millwall Athletic	3-3
9	30	CROYDON COMMON	2-1
10	6 Nov	The Arsenal	1-3
11	13	West Ham United	1-4
2	20	TOTTENHAM HOTSPUR	1-1
13	27	Crystal Palace	0-1
14	4 Dec	QUEENS PARK RANGERS	4-0
15	11	Fulham	3-4
16	18	CLAPTON ORIENT	1-1
17	25	CHELSEA	1-2
18	27	Chelsea	1-4
19	1 Jan	Watford	1-3
20	8	MILLWALL ATHLETIC	1-1
21	15	Croydon Common	2-2
22	22	THE ARSENAL	2-2

London Combination

Supplementary Tournament

Comp.	Date	Opposition	Result
23	5 Feb	Luton Town	3-4
24	12	THE ARSENAL	2-1
25	19	Queens Park Rangers	1-1
26	4 Mar	West Ham United	2-4
27	11	CROYDON COMMON	3-1
28	18	The Arsenal	2-5
29	25	QUEENS PARK RANGERS	4-0
30	1 Apr	Crystal Palace	3-6
31	8	WEST HAM UNITED	1-3
32	15	Croydon Common	0-0
33	21	FULHAM	2-1
34	24	Fulham	0-1
35	29	LUTON TOWN	0-3
36	6 May	CRYSTAL PALACE	6-3

Principal Tournament

	P	W	D	L	F	A	Pts
Chelsea	22	17	3	2	71	18	37
Millwall Athletic	22	12	6	4	46	24	30
The Arsenal	22	10	5	7	43	46	25
West Ham United	22	10	4	8	47	35	24
Fulham	22	10	4	8	45	37	24
Tottenham Hotspur	22	8	8	6	38	35	24
BRENTFORD	22	6	8	8	36	40	20
Queens Park Rangers	22	8	3	11	27	41	19
Crystal Palace	22	8	3	11	35	55	19
Watford	22	8	1	13	37	46	17
Clapton Orient	22	4	6	12	22	44	14
Croydon Common	22	3	5	14	24	50	11

Supplementary Tournament

	P	W	D	L	F	A	Pts
Chelsea	14	10	1	3	50	15	21
West Ham United	14	9	2	3	32	16	20
Tottenham Hotspur	14	8	3	3	32	22	19
Fulham	14	9	0	5	38	19	18
Millwall Athletic	14	8	2	4	30	22	18
Crystal Palace	14	8	2	4	41	29	18
Watford	14	5	3	6	22	20	13
BRENTFORD	14	5	2	7	29	33	12
Croydon Common	14	4	3	7	28	27	11
Clapton Orient	14	3	4	7	17	27	10
The Arsenal	14	3	4	7	19	31	10
Luton Town	14	4	1	9	31	44	9
Queens Park Rangers	14	2	5	7	14	37	9
Reading	14	2	2	8	23	64	8

1916/17 Season results

London Combination

Comp.	Date	Opposition	Result
1	2 Sep	Crystal Palace	0-4
2	9	SOUTHAMPTON	1-1
3	16	CHELSEA	0-3
4	23	The Arsenal	0-0
5	30	LUTON TOWN	1-3
6	7 Oct	Reading	2-0
7	14	MILLWALL ATHLETIC	0-3
8	21	Watford	2-4
9	28	CLAPTON ORIENT	3-0
10	4 Nov	Fulham	0-2
11	11	QUEENS PARK RANGERS	1-4
12	18	West Ham United	0-4
13	25	CRYSTAL PALACE	3-1
14	2 Dec	Southampton	1-3
15	9	Chelsea	2-7
16	23	Luton Town	2-5
17	25	TOTTENHAM HORSPUR	1-5
18	26	Tottenham Hotspur	2-5
19	30	PORTSMOUTH	7-0
20	6 Jan	Millwall Athletic	0-3
21	13	WATFORD	4-1
22	20	Clapton Orient	2-5
23	27	FULHAM	1-1
24	3 Feb	Queens Park Rangers	0-2
25	10	WEST HAM UNITED	1-1
26	17	Millwall Athletic	3-2
27	24	FULHAM	1-4
28	3 Mar	CHELSEA	3-0
29	10	Watford	2-5
30	17	LUTON TOWN	1-2
31	24	Queens Park Rangers	2-2
32	31	MILLWALL ATHLETIC	1-3
33	6 Apr	West Ham United	0-2
34	7	Fulham	2-0
35	9	WEST HAM UNITED	1-2
36	14	Chelsea	2-3
37	19	QUEENS PARK RANGERS	0-0
38	21	WATFORD	2-1
39	26	THE ARSENAL	0-0
40	28	Luton Town	0-6

	P	W	D	L	F	A	Pts
West Ham United	40	30	5	5	110	45	65
Millwall Athletic	40	26	6	8	85	48	58
Chelsea	40	24	5	11	93	48	53
Tottenham Hotspur	40	24	5	11	112	64	53
The Arsenal	40	19	10	11	62	47	48
Fulham	40	21	3	16	102	63	45
Luton Town	39	20	3	16	101	82	43
Crystal Palace	38	14	7	17	68	72	35
Southampton	39	13	8	18	57	80	34
Queens Park Rangers	39	10	9	20	48	86	29
Watford	40	8	9	22	69	115	25
BRENTFORD	40	9	7	24	56	99	25
Portsmouth	40	9	4	27	58	117	22
Clapton Orient	40	6	7	27	49	104	19

The following matches were not played:
Crystal Palace v Luton Town
QPR v Watford
Southampton v Crystal Palace

1917/18 Season results

London Combination

Comp.	Date	Opposition	Result
1	1 Sep	CLAPTON ORIENT	1-0
2	8	Millwall Athletic	3-1
3	15	TOTTENHAM HOTSPUR	5-2
4	22	Chelsea	1-3
5	29	Crystal Palace	0-4
6	6 Oct	THE ARSENAL	2-2
7	13	West Ham United	3-8
8	20	FULHAM	1-3
9	27	Clapton Orient	3-1
10	3 Nov	MILLWALL ATHLETIC	0-4
11	10	Tottenham Hotspur	1-6
12	17	CHELSEA	1-0
13	24	CRYSTAL PALACE	3-0
14	1 Dec	The Arsenal	1-4
15	8	WEST HAM UNITED	3-2
16	15	Fulham	0-2
17	22	CLAPTON ORIENT	5-0
18	25	QUEENS PARK RANGERS	1-1
19	26	Queens Park Rangers	4-0
20	29	Millwall Athletic	1-7
21	5 Jan	TOTTENHAM HOTSPUR	2-3
22	12	Chelsea	1-4
23	19	Crystal Palace	4-3
24	26	THE ARSENAL	3-2
25	2 Feb	West Ham United	2-7
26	9	QUEENS PARK RANGERS	6-1
27	16	Clapton Orient	1-1
28	23	MILLWALL ATHLETIC	3-0
29	2 Mar	Tottenham Hotspur	0-3
30	9	CHELSEA	0-1
31	16	CRYSTAL PALACE	0-2
32	23	The Arsenal	3-1
33	29	FULHAM	2-3
34	30	WEST HAM UNITED	3-7
35	1 Apr	Fulham	6-4
36	6	Queens Park Rangers	6-2

	P	W	D	L	F	A	Pts
Chelsea	36	21	8	7	82	39	50
West Ham United	36	20	9	7	103	51	49
Fulham	36	20	7	9	75	60	47
Tottenham Hotspur	36	22	2	12	86	56	46
The Arsenal	36	16	5	15	76	57	37
BRENTFORD	36	16	3	17	81	94	35
Crystal Palace	36	13	4	19	54	83	30
Queens Park Rangers	36	14	2	20	48	73	30
Millwall Athletic	36	12	4	20	52	74	28
Clapton Orient	36	2	4	30	34	104	8

1918/19

1st in London Combination

No.	Month	Day	Opponent	Score	Scorers	Att.	Morris	Rhodes	Amos	McGovern	Stanton	Brandham	Gillies	White	Denyer	Morley	Chalmers	Keenor	James	Chester	Wynn	Perat	Hendren	Pickup	Wright	Alborough	Woodward	Parsons	Wilcox	Lappin	Price	Cock	Baker	Bullock	Green	Hanney	Rosier	Doran	Pick	Hibbert	Carr
1	Sep	7	WEST HAM UNITED	2-0	Stanton, Amos (p)	5000	1	2	3	4	5	6	7	8	9	10	11																								
2		14	Tottenham Hotspur	1-1	Denyer	3000	1	2		4	3			8	9	10		5	6	7	11																				
3		21	CHELSEA	0-0		5996	1	2		4	6			8	9	10		5			7	3	11																	
4		28	The Arsenal	1-1	White	8000			3	4				8	9	10			6			2	11	1	5	7															
5	Oct	5	CRYSTAL PALACE	2-3	Morley, Peart (p)	3000		2		4	8			9		10						3		1			5	6	7	11										
6		12	Queens Park Rangers	1-2	Peart (p)	?	1	2			4		8			10	9		6	7		3			5					11										
7		19	MILLWALL ATHLETIC	4-2	White, Cock 2, Morley	4000		2		4	6			8		10		5				3				7					1	9	11							
8		26	Clapton Orient	2-1	Cock 2	?	1	2		4	5					10	8		6							7						9	11	3						
9	Nov	2	West Ham United	3-1	Wright, Morley 2	6000				6	4					10	8	9				2	7		5						1		11	3						
10		9	TOTTENHAM HOTSPUR	7-1	Chalmers 2, Stanton, Cock 2, Morley 2	6000		2			4	6				10	8					3	7				5				1	9	11							
11		16	Chelsea	2-2	White, Cock	12000		2		6	4			8		10		5	7			3		1								9	11							
12		23	THE ARSENAL	4-1	Hendren 2 1p, White, Cock	5000		2		4	6			8		10		5					7	1			3						9	11							
13		30	Crystal Palace	4-0	Cock 2, White 2	6000		2			5	6		8				10					7				3				1	9	11		4						
14	Dec	7	QUEENS PARK RANGERS	5-1	White 5	8000				4	6			9		10				7		3	8								1		11	2		5					
15		14	Millwall Athletic	1-3	Hendren 2 1p, White, Cock	?				4	6			8		10						2	7								1	9	11	3		5					
16		21	CLAPTON ORIENT	7-0	White 3, Cock 2, Feenor, Chester	5000				6				8		10		4		7		3								1	9	11			5	2				
17		25	FULHAM	2-1	White, Hendren p	10800		2	3	4	6			8		10		5					7								1	9	11							
18		26	Fulham	4-1	Hendren, Cock 2, White	20000		2		4	6			8		10		5				3	7								1	9	11							
19		28	WEST HAM UNITED	3-1	Morley, Keenor, White	10000				4	6			8		10		5				3	7								1	9	11			2					
20	Jan	4	Tottenham Hotspur	1-1	Cock	8000					4			8		10		6					7	1			5						9	11			2	3				
21		11	CHELSEA	1-1	Cock	17000		2	4		6			8		10							7								1	9	11	3		5					
22		18	The Arsenal	3-3	Baker, White, Cock	30000			3		4			8		10		5					7				6				1	9	11			2					
23		25	CRYSTAL PALACE	6-1	Doran 2, Cock 3, Pick	10000			3		4										7							6				1	9		2		5		8	10	11	
24	Feb	1	Queens Park Rangers	0-0		8000				4				8		10		6				3	7								1	9	11	2		5					
25		8	MILLWALL ATHLETIC	2-1	Hendren, Morley	12000								8		10		6				2	7				4				1	9	11	3		5					
26		15	Fulham	2-3	Morley, Cock	20000				4	6			8		10						3	7				2				1	9	11			5					
27		22	West Ham United	1-2	White	16000				4				8				6					7				2				1			3		5		10	9	11	
28	Mar	1	TOTTENHAM HOTSPUR	4-1	White 2, Morley 2	12000				4	8			9		10							7				6				1		11	3		5					
29		8	Chelsea	4-1	Morley, Baker 2, White	30500				6	4			8		10						2	7								1	9	11	3		5					
30		15	THE ARSENAL	2-0	White 2,	15621			4	6	8			9		10						2	7								1		11	3		5					
31		22	Crystal Palace	3-2	Peart p, Baker, Morley	10000			3		4			8		10						2	7								1	9	11			5					
32		29	QUEENS PARK RANGERS	1-1	Baker	12000			3	4	6			8				10				2	7								1	9	11			5					
33	Apr	5	Millwall Athletic	0-3		22000			3	6	4			8		10		7				2	11								1	9				5					
34		12	FULHAM	5-0	Cock 3, McGovern, White	13000			3	4				8		10		6				2	7								1	9	11			5					
35		18	CLAPTON ORIENT	2-0	Morley, Baker	15000			3		6			8		10						2	7								1	9	11			5					4
36		21	Clapton Orient	2-4	White, Cock	7000			3	4				8								2	7				6				1	9				5			10		11
						Apps	5	14	13	26	29	3	2	31	4	31	5	19	5	5	2	25	27	5	3	3	13	1	1	2	26	25	26	12	1	21	2	2	3	2	2
						Goals			1	1	2			26	1	14	2	2		1		3	6		1							25	6						2	1		

Victory Cup

Rd	Month	Day	Opponent	Score	Scorers	Att.	Morris	Rhodes	Amos	McGovern	Stanton	Brandham	Gillies	White	Denyer	Morley	Chalmers	Keenor	James	Chester	Wynn	Perat	Hendren	Pickup	Wright	Alborough	Woodward	Parsons	Wilcox	Lappin	Price	Cock	Baker	Bullock	Green	Hanney	Rosier	Doran	Pick	Hibbert	Carr
R1	Dec	30	CLAPTON ORIENT	3-2	Cock, White	4300			3	4	6			8		10						2	7								1	9	11			5					
R2	Feb	17	CRYSTAL PALACE	0-1		3000				4	6			8		10						3	7				2				1	9	11			5					

1918-19

Back: Peart, Price, McGovern, Cock, Morley, Hendren, Baker, Hanney, Keenor, Amos, White.

1919/20

15th in Southern League Division One

No	Month	Day	Opponent	Score	Scorers	Att	Amos AH	Ashford	Boyne	Cannon	Cartmell JR	Dale	Durston FJ	Embury	Gilboy	Hanks	Hawkins	Hendren	Henery J	Hodson J	Lockwood	Loveday	McGovern	Morley F	Morris S	Parr	Price	Rosier	Searby	Spreadbury BAJ	Taylor F	Thompson AA	Webster
1	Aug	30	BRIGHTON & HOVE ALB.	2-1	Boyne, Morley	12000	6		9		11				7					2			4	10			1				5	8	3
2	Sep	1	MILLWALL	2-2	Boyne, Gilboy	8000	6		9		11				7					2			4	10			1				5	8	3
3		6	Newport County	4-2	Boyne 2, Gilboy, Morley	6500	6		9		11				7					2			4	10			1				5	8	3
4		8	Millwall	2-0	Boyne, Thompson		6		9		11				7		2							10	4		1				5	8	3
5		13	PORTSMOUTH	0-2		10000	6				7				8			11		2				10	4	9	1				5		3
6		20	Northampton Town	1-1	Boyne	6000	5		9						7		3	11					6	10			1				4	8	2
7		24	Exeter City	0-0			5		9						7		3	11					6	10	4		1				8		2
8		27	CRYSTAL PALACE	0-0		8000	5				7						3	11					6	10	4		1				8	9	2
9	Oct	4	Southend United	1-3	Hendren	6000	5		9		7						3	11		2			6	10			1				4	8	
10		11	NORWICH CITY	1-1	Boyne	8000	5		9	8	11				7					2			6	10	4		1	3					
11		18	Watford	0-1		6000	5		9	8	7							11		2			6	10	4		1	3					
12		25	Merthyr Town	1-2	unknown		5		9	8	7					10	3			2			6				1	11			4		
13	Nov	1	PLYMOUTH ARGYLE	0-0		8000	5		9	8	7						3			2			6	10	4		1	11					
14		8	Bristol Rovers	1-3	Cannon	10000	5		9	8	11				7		3			2			6	10	4		1						
15		15	READING	1-0	Amos	6000	5		9	8					7			11		2			6	10	4		1	3					
16		22	Southampton	1-0	Morley	9000	5		8						7			11		2			6	10	4		1	3	9				
17		29	LUTON TOWN	3-1	Searby, Morley, Cartmell	6000	5		8		7							11		2			6	10	4		1	3	9				
18	Dec	6	Gillingham	2-0	Morley, Hendren	7000	5		8						7		3	11		2			6	10	4		1		9				
19		13	SWANSEA TOWN	1-1	Hendren (p)		5		8		7							11		2			6	10	4		1	3	9				
20		25	Queen's Park Rangers	0-2		15000	5		8						7		3	11					6	10	4		1	2	9				
21		26	QUEEN'S PARK RANGERS	2-1	Searby, Boyne	15000	5	6	8		7							11		2				10	4		1	3	9				
22		27	CARDIFF CITY	1-2	Thompson	9000	5	6	8		7	1						11		2					4			3	9			10	
23	Jan	3	Brighton & Hove Albion	0-4		9000	5		8		7		1					11		2					4				9		6	10	3
24		17	NEWPORT COUNTY	2-1	Searby, Embury	7000		6			11		1	10	7					2			5		4			3	9			8	
25		24	Portsmouth	0-3			5				11		1	10	7					2			6		4			3	9			8	
26		31	NORTHAMPTON T	5-0	Boyne 3, Thompson, Hendren (p)		5		9		7		1					11		2			6	10	4			3				8	
27	Feb	7	Crystal Palace	1-1	Thompson	11000	5				7		1	9				11		2			6	10	4			3				8	
28		14	SOUTHEND UNITED	2-0	Cartmell, Lockwood		5				7		1					11		2	9		6	10	4			3				8	
29		21	Norwich City	1-1	Spreadbury	9000	5				7		1				3	11					6	10	4			2		9		8	
30		28	WATFORD	0-3		10000	5				7		1					11		2			6	10	4			3		9		8	
31	Mar	6	MERTHYR TOWN	3-0	Spreadbury 2, Hendren		5				7		1				3	11					6	10	4			2		9		8	
32		13	Plymouth Argyle	2-3	Thompson 2	10000	5				7		1					11				3		10	4					9	6	8	2
33		20	BRISTOL ROVERS	3-0	Hendren, Morley, Spreadbury	8000	5				7		1					11		2				10	4			3		9	6	8	
34		27	Reading	0-1			5				7		1					11		2				10	4			3		9	6	8	
35	Apr	2	SWINDON TOWN	2-0	Morley, Boyne	10000			9		7		1					11		2			6	10	4			3			5	8	
36		3	SOUTHAMPTON	2-3	Taylor, Morley						7		1					11		2			6	10	4			3	9		5	8	
37		5	Swindon Town	1-3	Gilboy	8000		6			7		1		10		2	11		3					4					9	5	8	
38		10	Luton Town	0-0		6000		6			11		1	10	7					2					4			3		9	5	8	
39		17	GILLINGHAM	1-2	Thompson			6	9		7		1		10		3	11		2					4						5	8	
40		24	Swansea Town	0-6		15000		6	9		7		1					11		2					4					10	5	8	3
41		26	EXETER CITY	2-1	Thompson, Boyne	3000		6	9				1					11	7	2				10	4			3			5	8	
42	May	1	Cardiff City	0-2		12000		6	10		11		1		7					2					4			3		9	5	8	
						Apps	33	9	27	6	35	1	20	4	19	1	14	30	1	34	1	1	28	32	36	1	21	26	11	10	22	28	11
						Goals	1		13	1	2			1	3			6			1			8					3	4	1	8	

F.A. Cup

Rd	Month	Day	Opponent	Score	Scorers	Att	Amos AH	Ashford	Boyne	Cannon	Cartmell JR	Dale	Durston FJ	Embury	Gilboy	Hanks	Hawkins	Hendren	Henery J	Hodson J	Lockwood	Loveday	McGovern	Morley F	Morris S	Parr	Price	Rosier	Searby	Spreadbury BAJ	Taylor F	Thompson AA	Webster
R1	Jan	10	Huddersfield Town	1-5	Morris	10000	5		9/		7		1					11		2			6	8	4			3				10	

Season 1919-20: Southern League First Division

	P	W	D	L	F	A	Pts
Portsmouth	42	23	12	7	73	27	58
Watford	42	26	6	10	69	42	58
Crystal Palace	42	22	12	8	69	43	56
Cardiff City	42	18	17	7	70	43	53
Plymouth Argyle	42	20	10	12	57	29	50
Queens Park Rangers	42	18	10	14	62	50	46
Reading	42	16	13	13	51	43	45
Southampton	42	18	8	16	72	63	44
Swansea Town	42	16	11	15	53	45	43
Exeter City	42	17	9	16	57	51	43
Southend United	42	13	17	12	46	48	43
Norwich City	42	15	11	16	64	57	41
Swindon Town	42	17	7	18	65	68	41
Millwall Athletic	42	14	12	16	52	55	40
BRENTFORD	42	15	10	17	52	59	40
Brighton & Hove Albion	42	14	8	20	60	72	36
Bristol Rovers	42	11	13	18	61	78	35
Newport County	42	13	7	22	45	70	33
Northampton Town	42	12	9	21	64	103	33
Luton Town	42	10	10	22	51	76	30
Merthyr Town	42	9	11	22	47	78	29
Gillingham	42	10	7	25	34	74	27

Season 1918-19: London Combination

	P	W	D	L	F	A	Pts
BRENTFORD	36	20	9	7	94	46	49
The Arsenal	36	20	5	11	85	54	45
West Ham United	36	17	7	12	65	51	41
Fulham	36	17	6	13	70	55	40
Queens Park Rangers	36	16	7	13	69	60	39
Chelsea	36	13	11	12	70	53	37
Crystal Palace	36	14	6	16	66	73	34
Tottenham Hotspur	36	13	8	15	52	72	34
Millwall Athletic	36	10	9	17	50	67	29
Clapton Orient	36	3	6	27	35	123	12

1920/21

21st in Division Three

							Amos AH	Anstiss HA	Baker AL	Boyne R	Cartmell JR	Challinor S	Cock H	Durston FJ	Elliott JE	Hendren EH	Henery J	Hodson J	Howe F	Kearney W	King HE	Levitt E	Morley F	Morris S	Rosier HL	Smith GE	Spratt W	Spreadbury BAS	Taylor F	Thompson AA	Young W
1	Aug	28	Exeter City	0-3		6000	6								4		11	2				5	10		3	7		9		8	1
2		30	MILLWALL	1-0	Boyne	11000	6			9		4		1			11	2				5	10		3	7				8	
3	Sep	4	EXETER CITY	0-0		10000	6			8		4		1			11	2			9	5	10		3	7					
4		6	Millwall	0-0		15000	6					4		1			11	2			9	5	10		3	7				8	
5		11	BRIGHTON & HOVE ALB	2-0	Challinor, Amos	8000	6					4		1			11	2			9	5	10		3	7				8	
6		18	Brighton & Hove Albion	0-4		5500	6				7	4		1	5		11	2			9		10		3					8	
7		25	CRYSTAL PALACE	0-4		13000	4			9	7	6		1	5		11	2			8		10		3						
8	Oct	2	Crystal Palace	2-4	King 2	15000	5				11	6		1	4			2			8		10			7	3	9			
9		9	Norwich City	0-0		9000	5	10			7			1	4		11	2			9			6			3			8	
10		16	NORWICH CITY	3-1	King 2, Thompson	8000	5		7		11			1	4			2			8			6			3	9		10	
11		23	Southampton	0-3		10000			7		11			1	4			2		3	8	5		6				9		10	
12		30	SOUTHAMPTON	1-1	Thompson	7000	5		7		11			1	4			2			8			6	3			9		10	
13	Nov	6	Bristol Rovers	1-2	King	8500	5		7		11			1	4			2			8		9	6	3					10	
14		13	BRISTOL ROVERS	0-0		6000	5				11	6		1	4			2			8		9		3				7	10	
15		20	Reading	1-2	Spreadbury	4000	5			9				1	4		11	2			8			6	3			10	7		
16		27	READING	3-2	King, Boyne 2	5000	5			9	11			1	4			2			8			6	3			10	7		
17	Dec	4	Luton Town	0-2		6000	5			9	11			1	4			2						6	3	8		10	7		
18		11	LUTON TOWN	1-0	Boyne	6000	5			9	11			1	4			2			8		10	6	3				7		
19		18	NEWPORT COUNTY	2-2	Griffin (og), King (p)	6000	5			9	11			1	4			2			8		10	6	3				7		
20		25	QUEEN'S PARK RANGERS	0-2		16379	5			9	11	6		1	4						8		10		3		2		7		
21		27	Queen's Park Rangers	0-1		25000	3				11	6			5					2	8			4		7		10	9		1
22	Jan	1	Newport County	1-3	King	4000	3				7	6			5		11			2	8		10	4				9			1
23		15	Gillingham	3-1	Boyne 2, King	7000	5			9	11	6		1	4			2			8		10		3				7		
24		22	GILLINGHAM	3-3	Amos, King (p), Boyne	7000	5			9	11	6		1	4			2			8		10		3				7		
25	Feb	5	SWANSEA TOWN	1-2	Elliott	7000	5	10		9	11	6		1	4					2	8				3				7		
26		12	Swindon Town	0-1		6000		10			7	6			5		11			2	8			4	3				9		1
27		19	SWINDON TOWN	0-1		10000	5	10			7	6			4		11			2	8				3			9			1
28		26	Portsmouth	2-0	Henery, Anstiss	13645	5	10		8		6			9		11	2						4	3				7		1
29	Mar	5	PORTSMOUTH	1-2	Boyne	8000	5	10		8		6			9		11	2						4	3				7		1
30		12	Watford	0-1		5000	3	10		9		6			5		11				8			4	2	7					1
31		19	WATFORD	1-0	Anstiss	6000	3	10		9		6			5		11							4	2				7	8	1
32		25	Grimsby Town	0-2		8000	9	10			11	6			5			2						4	3				7	8	1
33		26	NORTHAMPTON T	1-1	King	7000		10			11	6		1	5			2			9			4	3				7	8	
34		28	GRIMSBY TOWN	5-0	Boyne, King 3, Anstiss	7000	3	10		8		6			5		11	2			9			4					7		1
35	Apr	2	Northampton Town	2-6	King, Elliot	6000	3	10				6			5		11				9			4	2				7	8	1
36		9	SOUTHEND UNITED	2-2	Spreadbury, Boyne	4000		10		8	11	6			5			2						4	3			9	7		1
37		16	Southend United	1-4	Anstiss	6000	9	10		8	11	6		1	5			2						4	3				7		
38		25	MERTHYR TOWN	0-0		7000		10		8	7	6			5	11		2			9			4	3						1
39		28	Swansea Town	1-1	King (p)	5000		10		8	7	6			5		11	2			9			4	3						1
40		30	Merthyr Town	1-3	Challinor	4000	6	10			7	8			5	11		2			9			4	3						1
41	May	2	PLYMOUTH ARGYLE	0-0		5000	5	10				8			4		11	2	6		9				3				7		1
42		7	Plymouth Argyle	0-1		4000		10			11	6	9		5			2	3		8			4					7		1
						Apps	35	19	4	21	29	31	1	24	38	2	20	33	2	6	33	6	16	27	34	9	4	12	23	15	18
						Goals	2	4		10		2			2		1				16							2		2	

One own goal

F.A. Cup

							Amos AH	Anstiss HA	Baker AL	Boyne R	Cartmell JR	Challinor S	Cock H	Durston FJ	Elliott JE	Hendren EH	Henery J	Hodson J	Howe F	Kearney W	King HE	Levitt E	Morley F	Morris S	Rosier HL	Smith GE	Spratt W	Spreadbury BAS	Taylor F	Thompson AA	Young W
R1	Jan	8	HUDDERSFIELD TOWN	1-2	King	14892	5			9	7	6			4		11	2			8		10		3						1

Pl.			Home					Away					F.	A.	Pts
			W	D	L	F	A	W	D	L	F	A	(Total)		
1	Crystal Palace	42	15	4	2	45	17	9	7	5	25	17	70	34	59
2	Southampton	42	14	5	2	46	10	5	11	5	18	18	64	28	54
3	Queen's Park Rgs.	42	14	4	3	38	11	8	5	8	23	21	61	32	53
4	Swindon Town	42	14	5	2	51	17	7	5	9	22	32	73	49	52
5	Swansea Town	42	9	10	2	32	19	9	5	7	24	26	56	45	51
6	Watford	42	14	4	3	40	15	6	4	11	19	29	59	44	48
7	Millwall	42	11	5	5	25	8	7	6	8	17	22	42	30	47
8	Merthyr Town	42	13	5	3	46	20	2	10	9	14	29	60	49	45
9	Luton Town	42	14	6	1	51	15	2	6	13	10	41	61	56	44
10	Bristol Rovers	42	15	3	3	51	22	3	4	14	17	35	68	57	43
11	Plymouth Argyle	42	10	7	4	25	13	1	14	6	10	21	35	34	43
12	Portsmouth	42	10	8	3	28	14	2	7	12	18	34	46	48	39
13	Grimsby Town	42	12	5	4	32	16	3	4	14	17	43	49	59	39
14	Northampton Town	42	11	4	6	32	23	4	4	13	27	52	59	75	38
15	Newport County	42	8	5	8	20	23	6	4	11	23	41	43	64	37
16	Norwich City	42	9	10	2	31	14	1	6	14	13	39	44	53	36
17	Southend United	42	13	2	6	32	20	1	6	14	12	41	44	61	36
18	Brighton & Hove A.	42	11	6	4	28	20	3	2	16	14	41	42	61	36
19	Exeter City	42	9	7	5	27	15	1	8	12	12	39	39	54	35
20	Reading	42	8	4	9	26	22	4	3	14	16	37	42	59	31
21	**BRENTFORD**	**42**	**7**	**9**	**5**	**27**	**23**	**2**	**3**	**16**	**15**	**44**	**42**	**67**	**30**
22	Gillingham	42	6	9	6	19	24	2	3	16	15	50	34	74	28

1920-21

Back: Elliot, Halliday (Sec.), Spratt, Amos, Durston, Morley, Rosier, Witham (Trainer), Challiner
Middle: Thompson, Kearney, Hodson, Spreadbury, Lovett, King
Front: Baker, Cartmell

1921/22

Back: Morris, J.Elliott, Wright, Alton, Young, Bethune, Fisher, Howe, Witham (Trainer)
Middle: Capper, T.Elliott, Shields, Halliday (Secretary), Mitchell (Manager), Norton, Antiss, Amos
Front: Pither, Kerr, Hendren, Bertram, Rosier.

1921/22

9th in Division Three (South)

						Alton C	Amos AH	Anstiss HA	Bertram G	Bethune J	Capper A	Elliott JE	Elliott TW	Fisher C	Hendren EH	Howe F	Hunter C	Kerr J	Mitchell AP	Morris DH	Norton H	Pither GB	Rosier HL	Shields R	Young W
1	Aug 27	MERTHYR TOWN	0-1		11000	2	6		10		7	5	8					4			11		3	9	1
2	29	Southend United	1-1	Morris	6000		6		11	2	7	5	8	4						10			3	9	1
3	Sep 3	Merthyr Town	0-2		6000	2	6		10			5	7	4	11					9			3	8	1
4	5	SOUTHEND UNITED	1-0	Bertram	8000	2	6		10		7	5	8	4						9		11	3		1
5	10	WATFORD	1-1	Morris	10372	2	6		10		7	5	8	4						9		11	3		1
6	14	Bristol Rovers	0-0		7000	2	5		10		7	4	8					6		9		11	3		1
7	17	Watford	0-0		7000		5		10	2	7	4	8					6		9		11	3		1
8	24	CHARLTON ATHLETIC	0-2		13000		5	10		2	7		8		11	4		6					3	9	1
9	Oct 1	Charlton Athletic	1-1	Anstiss	12000		6	10		2	7		8		11			4	5	9			3		1
10	8	NORTHAMPTON T	1-0	Morris	9000		6	10		2	7	4	8		11				5	9			3		1
11	15	Northampton Town	0-2		6000		6	10		2	7	4	8		11				5	9			3		1
12	22	QUEEN'S PARK RANGERS	5-1	T Elliott, Morris 3, Bertram	13836	2	3		10		7	4	8	6	11				5	9					1
13	29	Queen's Park Rangers	1-1	Mitchell (p)	15000	2	3		10		7	4	8	6	11				5	9					1
14	Nov 5	PORTSMOUTH	2-2	Mitchell (p), Morris	11000	2	6		10			4	8		11				5	9	7		3		1
15	12	Portsmouth	0-1		12894	2	6					4	8		11				5	9	7		3	10	1
16	19	Norwich City	0-0		6000	2	6				7		8		11			4	5	9			3	10	1
17	26	NORWICH CITY	2-1	Morris, Shields	5000	2	6				7		8		11			4	5	9			3	10	1
18	Dec 10	Reading	3-0	Anstiss 2, Morris	8000	2	6	10			7	4	8		11				5	9			3		1
19	24	BRISTOL ROVERS	4-2	T Elliott, Anstiss 2, Morris	10000	2	6	10			7	4	8		11				5	9			3		1
20	26	ABERDARE ATHLETIC	2-1	T Elliott, Anstiss	12000	2	6	10		3	7	4	8		11				5	9					1
21	27	Aberdare Athletic	0-2		11000	2	6	10			7	4	8		11		5			9			3		1
22	31	Southampton	0-0		10000	2	6	10			7	4	8		11		5			9			3		1
23	Jan 14	SOUTHAMPTON	1-0	T Elliott (p)	10000	2	6	10			7	4	8		11		5			9			3		1
24	21	PLYMOUTH ARGYLE	3-1	Morris 2, Norton	7000	2	6				7	4	8		11		5			9	10		3		1
25	28	Plymouth Argyle	1-4	Morris	7000	2	6				7	4	8		11		5			9	10		3		1
26	Feb 4	NEWPORT COUNTY	1-0	T Elliott	6000	2	6				7	4	8		11		5			9	10		3		1
27	11	Newport County	1-2	Norton	6500	2	6			3	7	4	8		11		5			9	10				1
28	18	LUTON TOWN	0-2		9000	2				3	7	4	8		11		5	6		9	10				1
29	25	Luton Town	0-3		5000	2				3	7	4	8		11		5	6		9	10				1
30	Mar 4	SWINDON TOWN	3-0	Anstiss, Norton, Amos	5000	2	6	10			7		9		11		5	4			8		3		1
31	11	Swindon Town	1-2	T Elliott	6000	2	6	10			7		9		11		5	4			8		3		1
32	18	Gillingham	0-0		8000	2	6	10					8		11		5	4		9	7		3		1
33	25	GILLINGHAM	0-1		6000	2	6	10					8		11		5	4		9	7		3		1
34	Apr 1	Millwall	1-1	Morris	12000	2	3	10				4			7		5	6		9	8	11			1
35	8	MILLWALL	1-0	Anstiss	6000	2	3	10				4			7		5	6		9	8	11			1
36	14	BRIGHTON & HOVE ALB	4-0	Anstiss 3, Hendren	10000	2	6	10			7		9		11		5	4			8		3		1
37	15	Exeter City	0-1		5000	2	6	10			7		9		11		5	4			8		3		1
38	17	Brighton & Hove Albion	1-2	Anstiss	9008	2	5	10			7		8		11			6		9	4		3		1
39	18	READING	2-0	Anstiss, T Elloitt	5000	2	6	10			7		8		11		5	4		9			3		1
40	22	EXETER CITY	5-2	Anstiss, Kerr, Capper, Morris, Amos	4000	2	6	10			7				11		5	4		9	8		3		1
41	29	Swansea Town	0-1		5000	2	6	10			7		8		11		5	4	1	9			3		
42	May 6	SWANSEA TOWN	3-0	Morris, T Elliott, Anstiss	5000	2	6	10			7		8				5			9		11	3	4	1
					Apps	36	40	23	10	10	35	27	39	6	35	1	21	21	13	36	19	7	34	8	41
					Goals		2	15	2		1		8		1			1	2	16	3			1	

F.A. Cup

						Alton C	Amos AH	Anstiss HA	Bertram G	Bethune J	Capper A	Elliott JE	Elliott TW	Fisher C	Hendren EH	Howe F	Hunter C	Kerr J	Mitchell AP	Morris DH	Norton H	Pither GB	Rosier HL	Shields R	Young W
Q5	Dec 3	DULWICH HAMLET	3-1	Capper, Michell, Morris	9078	2	6				7	4	8		11				5	9			3	10	1
Q6	17	SHILDON	1-0	T Elliott	9250	2	6	10			7	4	8		11				5	9			3		1
R1	Jan 7	TOTTENHAM HOTSPUR	0-2		12964	2	6	10			7	4	8		11				5	9			3		1

	Pl.	Home W	D	L	F	A	Away W	D	L	F	A	F. (Totall)	A.	Pts
1 Southampton	42	14	7	0	50	8	9	8	4	18	13	68	21	61
2 Plymouth Argyle	42	17	4	0	43	4	8	7	6	20	20	63	24	61
3 Portsmouth	42	13	5	3	38	18	5	12	4	24	21	62	39	53
4 Luton Town	42	16	2	3	47	9	6	6	9	17	26	64	35	52
5 Queen's Park Rgs.	42	13	7	1	36	12	5	6	10	17	32	53	44	49
6 Swindon Town	42	10	7	4	40	21	6	6	9	32	39	72	60	45
7 Watford	42	9	9	3	34	21	4	9	8	20	27	54	48	44
8 Aberdare Ath.	42	11	6	4	38	18	6	4	11	19	33	57	51	44
9 BRENTFORD	**42**	**15**	**2**	**4**	**41**	**17**	**1**	**9**	**11**	**11**	**26**	**52**	**43**	**43**
10 Swansea Town	42	11	8	2	40	19	2	7	12	10	28	50	47	41
11 Merthyr Town	42	14	2	5	33	15	3	4	14	12	41	45	56	40
12 Millwall	42	6	13	2	22	10	4	5	12	16	32	38	42	38
13 Reading	42	10	5	6	28	15	4	5	12	12	32	40	47	38
14 Bristol Rovers	42	8	8	5	32	24	6	2	13	20	43	52	67	38
15 Norwich City	42	8	10	3	29	17	4	3	14	21	45	50	62	37
16 Charlton Athletic	42	10	6	5	28	19	3	5	13	15	37	43	56	37
17 Northampton Town	42	13	3	5	30	17	0	8	13	17	54	47	71	37
18 Gillingham	42	11	4	6	36	20	3	4	14	11	40	47	60	36
19 Brighton & Hove A.	42	9	6	6	33	19	4	3	14	12	32	45	51	35
20 Newport County	42	8	7	6	22	18	3	5	13	22	43	44	61	34
21 Exeter City	42	7	5	9	22	29	4	7	10	16	30	38	59	34
22 Southend United	42	7	5	9	23	23	1	6	14	11	51	34	74	27

1922/23

14th in Division 3 (South)

	Date	Opponent	Score	Scorers	Att	Allen PJ	Alton C	Capper A	Clayson WJ	Duncan P	Elliott TW	Haggan J	Hendren EH	Hunter C	Inglis W	James RW	Johnstone GS	Jones H	Kell G	Kerr J	Morris DH	Mulford SR	Parker R	Rosier HL	Stott H	Thain JW	Wright E	Young W
1	Aug 26	Gillingham	0-2		9000		2	7		10	8	6		5						4	9			3	11		1	
2	28	LUTON TOWN	3-2	Morris 3	8000		2	7		10	8	6		5						4	9			3	11		1	
3	Sep 2	GILLINGHAM	2-0	Morris, Haggan	10000		2	7	8	10		6		5						4	9			3	11		1	
4	4	Luton Town	0-4		11000		2	7	8	10		6		5						4	9			3	11		1	
5	9	Norwich City	2-0	Morris, Clayson	8597		2	7	8					5	4	10				6	9			3	11		1	
6	11	QUEEN'S PARK RANGERS	1-3	Clayson	15000		2	7	8			6		5		10				4	9			3	11		1	
7	16	NORWICH CITY	1-4	Alton (p)	7000		2	7	8		10	6		5						4	9			3	11			1
8	23	Northampton Town	1-1	Johnstone	8000		2	7	8					5	4	10	9			6				3	11			1
9	30	NORTHAMPTON T	2-1	Clayson, Morris	7000		2	7	8					5	4		10			6	9			3	11			1
10	Oct 7	Exeter City	2-0	Morris 2	6000		2	7	8					5	4		10			6	9			3	11			1
11	14	EXETER CITY	0-1		7000		2	7	8					5	4		10			6	9			3	11			1
12	21	Brighton & Hove Albion	1-2	Capper	8000		2	7	8				11	5	4					6	9			3	10			1
13	28	BRIGHTON & HOVE ALB	1-2	Morris	7000		2	7	8				11	5				4		6	9	10		3				1
14	Nov 4	MERTHYR TOWN	3-1	Hendren, Morris, Alton (p)	6000		2	7	8	10		6	11	5						4	9			3				1
15	11	Merthyr Town	0-1		5000		2	7	8	10		6	11		5					4	9			3				1
16	18	READING	1-1	Clayson	6000		2	7	10		8	6	11		5					4	9			3				1
17	25	Reading	0-1		5000	3	2	7	9		8	6	11		5					4			10					1
18	Dec 9	Queen's Park Rangers	1-1	Clayson	19000		2	7	10		8	6			5					4		9		3	11			1
19	23	BRISTOL ROVERS	0-1		10000		2	7	8			6	11		5					4	9		10	3				1
20	25	Watford	0-2		8000		2	7		10	8	6	11		5					4	9			3				1
21	26	WATFORD	2-1	Morris, Duncan	10000		2	8		10		6	7		5					4	9			3	11			1
22	Jan 6	PLYMOUTH ARGYLE	2-0	Morris, Duncan	14000		2	8		10		6	7		5					4	9			3	11			1
23	20	Charlton Athletic	1-1	Hendren	6464		2	8		10		6	7		5					4	9			3	11			1
24	27	CHARLTON ATHLETIC	0-3		9000		2	8		10		6	7		5					4	9			3	11			1
25	Feb 3	Swindon Town	0-3		9000		2	8		10		6	7	5						4	9		11	3				1
26	10	SWINDON TOWN	3-0	Thain, Mulford, Morris	4000		3	8					11	5		6			2	4	9	10				7		1
27	17	Aberdare Athletic	0-0		6000		3	8					11	5		6		9	2	4		10				7		1
28	24	ABERDARE ATHLETIC	0-1		5000		3	8					11	5		6		9	2	4		10				7		1
29	Mar 3	Swansea Town	0-0		6000		3	8			9		7	5	4	6			2	10			11					1
30	10	SWANSEA TOWN	0-1		4000		3	8			9		7	5	4	6			2	10					11			1
31	17	NEWPORT COUNTY	0-0		5000		3	7	9	10	8			5		6			2	4					11			1
32	24	Newport County	1-0	James	4000		3	7	8					5	4	9			2	6		10			11			1
33	30	SOUTHEND UNITED	0-0		6000		3	7	8				11		5	6	9		2	4			10					1
34	31	BRISTOL CITY	4-0	Johnstone 2, Parker 2	9500		3	7	8				11		5	6	9		2	4			10					1
35	Apr 2	Southend United	2-1	Clayson, Alton (p)	10000		3	7	8				11		5	6	9		2	4			10					1
36	7	Bristol City	1-1	Johnstone	16000		3	7	8				11		5	6	9		2	4			10					1
37	14	PORTSMOUTH	1-0	Parker	7000		3	7	8				11		5	6	9		2	4			10					1
38	21	Portsmouth	0-3		8106		3	7	8				11		5	6	9		2	4			10					1
39	28	MILLWALL	1-1	Parker	12000		3		8				7	5		6	9		2	4			10		11			1
40	30	Bristol Rovers	1-1	Johnstone	2000		3		8					5		6	9		2	4			10		11	7		1
41	May 2	Plymouth Argyle	0-3		7000		3		8					5		6	9		2	4			10		11	7		1
42	5	Millwall	1-1	Johnstone	12000		3		8					5		6	9		2	4		7	10		11			1
					Apps	1	42	38	29	13	10	18	25	26	25	20	14	3	17	42	23	7	14	24	24	5	6	36
					Goals		3	1	6	2		1	2			1	6				13	1	4			1		

F.A. Cup

	Date	Opponent	Score	Scorers	Att	Allen PJ	Alton C	Capper A	Clayson WJ	Duncan P	Elliott TW	Haggan J	Hendren EH	Hunter C	Inglis W	James RW	Johnstone GS	Jones H	Kell G	Kerr J	Morris DH	Mulford SR	Parker R	Rosier HL	Stott H	Thain JW	Wright E	Young W
Q5	Dec 2	Maidstone United	0-0		10500		2	7	10		8	6	11		5	4					9			3				1
rep	6	MAIDSTONE UNITED	4-0	Clayson 2, Alton (p), Mulford	5408		2	7	10		8	6	11		5					4		9		3				1
Q6	16	MERTHYR TOWN	0-1		12000		2	7	10		8	6	11		5					4		9		3				1

		Pl.	Home					Away					F.	A.	Pts
			W	D	L	F	A	W	D	L	F	A	(Totall)		
1	Bristol City	42	16	4	1	43	13	8	7	6	23	27	66	40	59
2	Plymouth Argyle	42	18	3	0	47	6	5	4	12	14	23	61	29	53
3	Swansea Town	42	13	6	2	46	14	9	3	9	32	31	78	45	53
4	Brighton & Hove A.	42	15	3	3	39	13	5	8	8	13	21	52	34	51
5	Luton Town	42	14	4	3	47	18	7	3	11	21	31	68	49	49
6	Millwall	42	9	10	2	27	13	5	8	8	18	27	45	40	46
7	Portsmouth	42	10	5	6	34	20	9	3	9	24	32	58	52	46
8	Northampton Town	42	13	6	2	40	17	4	5	12	14	27	54	44	45
9	Swindon Town	42	14	4	3	41	17	3	7	11	21	39	62	56	45
10	Watford	42	10	6	5	35	23	7	4	10	22	31	57	54	44
11	Queen's Park Rgs.	42	10	4	7	34	24	6	6	9	20	25	54	49	42
12	Charlton Athletic	42	11	6	4	33	14	3	8	10	22	37	55	51	42
13	Bristol Rovers	42	7	9	5	25	19	6	7	8	10	17	35	36	42
14	**BRENTFORD**	**42**	**9**	**4**	**8**	**27**	**23**	**4**	**8**	**9**	**14**	**28**	**41**	**51**	**38**
15	Southend United	42	10	6	5	35	18	2	7	12	14	36	49	54	37
16	Gillingham	42	13	4	4	38	18	2	3	16	13	41	51	59	37
17	Merthyr Town	42	10	4	7	27	17	1	10	10	12	31	39	48	36
18	Norwich City	42	8	7	6	29	26	5	3	13	22	45	51	71	36
19	Reading	42	9	8	4	24	15	1	6	14	12	40	36	55	34
20	Exeter City	42	10	4	7	27	18	3	3	15	20	66	47	84	33
21	Aberdare Ath.	42	6	8	7	25	23	3	3	15	17	47	42	70	29
22	Newport County	42	8	6	7	28	21	0	5	16	12	49	40	70	27

1923/24

17th in Division Three (South)

						Allen PJ	Alton C	Capper A	Clayson WJ	Garnish TF	Gower HH	Hendren EH	Hughes R	Hunter C	Inglis WJ	James RW	Johnstone GS	Jones H	Kell G	Kerr J	Mulford SR	Parker R	Parkinson H	Pearson JC	Williams H	Young W
1	Aug 25	Queen's Park Rangers	0-1		18000		3	7	8				11	5		6	9		2	4		10				1
2	27	PLYMOUTH ARGYLE	1-1	Hughes	6500		3	7	8				11		5	6	9		2	4		10				1
3	Sep 1	QUEEN'S PARK RANGERS	0-1		12000		3	7	8					5		6	9			4	11	10		2		1
4	3	Plymouth Argyle	1-4	Clayson	10000		3	10	9				7	5	4	6					8	11		2		1
5	8	LUTON TOWN	2-1	Clayson, Parkinson	10000		3	7	8					5		6				4		11	9	2	10	1
6	10	Aberdare Athletic	2-1	Parkinson, Hughes	6000		3	7	8				11	5		6				4			9	2	10	1
7	15	Luton Town	1-2	Hunter	8000		3	7	8				11	5		6	9			4				2	10	1
8	22	BRIGHTON & HOVE ALB	1-2	Hunter	5000		3	7	8				11	5		6				4			9	2	10	1
9	29	Brighton & Hove Albion	0-2		7000	3		8				11	7	5		6				4		10	9	2		1
10	Oct 6	Bristol Rovers	0-2		10000		3	7						5	4	10		6				11	9	2	8	1
11	13	BRISTOL ROVERS	1-2	Mulford	9000		3	7				11		5		6	9	4	2		8	10				1
12	20	Southend United	1-3	Capper	6000	4	3	10				11	7		5	6			2		8	9				1
13	27	SOUTHEND UNITED	3-1	Hughes, Parker 2	5000		3	10				11	7	5	4				2	6	8	9				1
14	Nov 3	Portsmouth	0-3		9867		3	10				11	7	5	4				2	6	8	9				1
15	10	PORTSMOUTH	1-1	Capper	9000			8		7	3	11		4	5				2	6		9			10	1
16	24	EXETER CITY	1-0	Williams	4000					7	3	11			5	6			2	4		9	8		10	1
17	Dec 8	ABERDARE ATHLETIC	1-1	Clayson	6000			8	10	7		11		4	5				2	6		9		3		1
18	22	GILLINGHAM	3-2	Johnstone, Clayson, Parker	5000			7	8			11		4	5		10		2	6		9		3		1
19	25	Bournemouth	4-2	Parker 2, Clayson, Capper	5000			7	8			11		4	5		10		2	6		9		3		1
20	26	BOURNEMOUTH	2-0	Clayson, Parker	7000			7	8			11		4	5		10		2	6		9		3		1
21	29	Millwall	1-4	Parker (p)	9000			7	8			11		4	5		10		2	6		9		3		1
22	Jan 5	MILLWALL	1-3	Amos (og)	7000			11	8	7				4	5		10		2	6		9		3		1
23	26	NEWPORT COUNTY	0-0		5000			7	8			11			5	6	10		2	4		9		3		1
24	Feb 2	Merthyr Town	0-2		6000		2						11	4	5		10			6	7	9	8	3		1
25	9	MERTHYR TOWN	0-0		3000		2	8				11	7				10	4		6		9		3	5	1
26	16	Charlton Athletic	1-3	Parker	3000		2						11		5		9	4		6	7	10		3	8	1
27	23	CHARLTON ATHLETIC	0-0		5000		2		8			11			5		6	4			7	9		3	10	1
28	Mar 1	Norwich City	3-2	Parker 2, Williams	7000		3			7		11			5		6	4			8	9		2	10	1
29	8	NORWICH CITY	3-0	Mulford, Parker, Inglis	7794		3			7		11			5		6	4			8	9		2	10	1
30	15	SWINDON TOWN	2-2	Alton (p), Parker	6000		3			7		11			5		6	4			8	9		2	10	1
31	19	Gillingham	0-6		8000		3			7		11			5		6	4			8	9		2	10	1
32	22	Swindon Town	1-2	Parker	6000		3			7		11		4	5		6		2		8	9			10	1
33	29	WATFORD	4-1	Parker 2, Garnish, Clayson	6500		3			7		11		4	5		6		2		8	9			10	1
34	Apr 2	Exeter City	0-1		3500		3		8	7		11		4	5		6		2			9			10	1
35	5	Watford	1-0	Williams	4500		3		8	7		11		4	5		6		2			9			10	1
36	12	SWANSEA TOWN	2-2	Clayson, Parker	7000		3		8	7		11		4	5		6		2			9			10	1
37	18	Reading	0-1		11782		3		8	7		11		4	5		6		2			9			10	1
38	19	Swansea Town	0-4		6000				8	7			11	4	5		6		2			9		3	10	1
39	21	READING	4-1	Williams 2, Parker, Alton (p)	5000		3		8	7		11		4	5		6		2			9			10	1
40	22	Newport County	2-3	Hughes, Parker	6000		3		8	7			11	5			6	4				9		2	10	1
41	26	NORTHAMPTON T	1-0	Clayson	3000		3		8	7		11		5			6	4				9		2	10	1
42	May 3	Northampton Town	3-2	Hughes 3	4000		3		8	7			11	5		6		4	2			9			10	1
					Apps	2	31	23	25	19	2	27	16	31	30	15	29	12	24	22	15	39	7	26	25	42
					Goals		2	3	9	1			7	2	1		1				2	18	2		5	

One own goal

F.A. Cup

						Allen PJ	Alton C	Capper A	Clayson WJ	Garnish TF	Gower HH	Hendren EH	Hughes R	Hunter C	Inglis WJ	James RW	Johnstone GS	Jones H	Kell G	Kerr J	Mulford SR	Parker R	Parkinson H	Pearson JC	Williams H	Young W
Q5	Dec 1	Botwell Mission	1-1	Parker	7629			8				11	7		5			4	2	6		9		3	10	1
rep	5	BOTWELL MISSION	2-0	Clayson, Parker (p)	6200			8	10	7		11		4	5				2	6		9		3		1
Q6	15	PORTSMOUTH	1-1	Clayson	9059			7	8			11		4	5				2	6		9		3	10	1
rep	19	Portsmouth	0-1	(aet)	11664			7	8			11		4	5				2	6		9		3	10	1

	Pl.	Home					Away					F.	A.	Pts
		W	D	L	F	A	W	D	L	F	A	(Totall)		
1 Portsmouth	42	15	3	3	57	11	9	8	4	30	19	87	30	59
2 Plymouth Argyle	42	13	6	2	46	15	10	3	8	24	19	70	34	55
3 Millwall	42	17	3	1	45	11	5	7	9	19	27	64	38	54
4 Swansea Town	42	18	2	1	39	10	4	6	11	21	38	60	48	52
5 Brighton & Hove A.	42	16	4	1	56	12	5	5	11	12	25	68	37	51
6 Swindon Town	42	14	5	2	38	11	3	8	10	20	33	58	44	47
7 Luton Town	42	11	7	3	35	19	5	7	9	15	25	50	44	46
8 Northampton Town	42	14	3	4	40	15	3	8	10	24	32	64	47	45
9 Bristol Rovers	42	11	7	3	34	15	4	6	11	18	31	52	46	43
10 Newport County	42	15	4	2	39	15	2	5	14	17	49	56	64	43
11 Norwich City	42	13	5	3	45	18	3	3	15	15	41	60	59	40
12 Aberdare Ath.	42	9	9	3	35	18	3	5	13	10	40	45	58	38
13 Merthyr Town	42	11	8	2	33	19	0	8	13	12	46	45	65	38
14 Charlton Athletic	42	8	7	6	26	20	3	8	10	12	25	38	45	37
15 Gillingham	42	11	6	4	27	15	1	7	13	16	43	43	58	37
16 Exeter City	42	14	3	4	33	17	1	4	16	4	35	37	52	37
17 BRENTFORD	**42**	**9**	**8**	**4**	**33**	**21**	**5**	**0**	**16**	**21**	**50**	**54**	**71**	**36**
18 Reading	42	12	2	7	35	20	1	7	13	16	37	51	57	35
19 Southend United	42	11	7	3	35	19	1	3	17	18	65	53	84	34
20 Watford	42	8	8	5	35	18	1	7	13	10	36	45	54	33
21 Bournemouth	42	6	8	7	19	19	5	3	13	21	46	40	65	33
22 Queen's Park Rgs.	42	9	6	6	28	26	2	3	16	9	51	37	77	31

1924/25

21st in Division 3 (South)

No.	Date	Opponent	Score	Scorers	Att.	Allen JWA	Alton C	Broadbent WH	Cain T	Clayson WJ	Cooke ER	Garnish TF	Gilbert AG	Graham JA	Henderson F	Hughes H	Inglis W	Isaac AH	Jones H	Kell G	Lane JW	McCree J	Parker R	Relph W	Rowe R	Rowe V	Shepherd E	Steel JH	Walton J	Williams H	Williams R	Young H	Young W	Johnstone GS	McGuigan C
1	Aug 30	BRIGHTON & HOVE ALB	2-4	Garnish, Parker	8500		3	4		8		7			6		5			2			9	11						10			1		
2	Sep 3	Gillingham	0-1		5000	11	2	4	6	8		7					5						10				3				9		1		
3	6	Plymouth Argyle	1-7	Parker	9000	11	2	4		7						8	5						10				3			6	9		1		
4	8	GILLINGHAM	2-1	Parker, Allen	6000	11	3	4		7					6	8	5			2			9							10			1		
5	13	BRISTOL CITY	1-0	Allen	9000	11	3	4		7					6	8	5			2			9							10			1		
6	15	NEWPORT COUNTY	2-0	Parker 2	7000	11	3	4		7					6	8	5			2			9							10			1		
7	20	Swindon Town	0-2		4000	11	3	4		7					6	8	5			2			9							10			1		
8	27	ABERDARE ATHLETIC	2-2	Parker , H Williams	9000	11	3	4		7					6	8	5			2			9							10			1		
9	Oct 4	Norwich City	0-3		6000	11	3		6						4		5			2			9							10	8		1		7
10	11	QUEEN'S PARK RANGERS	0-1		8000	11	3		6	8			1		4		5			2			9							10					7
11	18	MILLWALL	1-0	R Williams	11000	11	3		6	8	2	7	1				4						10							5	9				
12	22	Bournemouth	0-2		6000	11	3		6	8	2	7	1				4						10							5	9				
13	25	Merthyr Town	0-4		5000	10		3	6		2	7	1			8	4						9	11						5					
14	Nov 1	READING	0-1		2500	11		3	6	7		8	1			4	5			2			9							10					
15	8	Swansea Town	0-7		5000			3	6			7	1			8	4			2			9	11						5	10				
16	15	EXETER CITY	2-5	Garnish, Parker	2500	7	3	4				8	1			6				2			9	11						5	10				
17	22	Bristol Rovers	0-2		5000			4	5		3	7	1			8				2			9	11					6	10					
18	Dec 6	Southend United	1-6	Relph	4000			3		7	2	8	1	5									9	11					4	10				6	
19	13	WATFORD	0-0		4000		3			8		7		5					4	2			9	11						10			1	6	
20	20	Northampton Town	2-0	Allen 2	6000	11	3			8		7					5		4	2			9						6	10			1		
21	25	Charlton Athletic	0-3		7000	11	3			8		7					5		4	2			9						6	10			1		
22	26	CHARLTON ATHLETIC	1-0	Allen	10000	11				8		7		5			3		4	2			9						6	10			1		
23	27	Brighton & Hove Albion	1-4	Parker	2500	11				8	3	7					5		4	2			9		6	10							1		
24	Jan 3	PLYMOUTH ARGYLE	1-0	Graham (p)	8000	11				8		7		5			3		4	2			9						6	10			1		
25	10	SOUTHEND UNITED	2-2	Garnish, V Rowe	7000	11				8		7		5			3		4	2			9			10			6				1		
26	17	Bristol City	0-3		8500	11						8		5			3		4	2		7	9			10			6				1		
27	24	SWINDON TOWN	0-0		7000	11		8				7		5			4			2			9			10		3	6				1		
28	Feb 7	NORWICH CITY	1-1	Allen	7000	11	2			7				5		8			4				9					3	6	10			1		
29	14	Queen's Park Rangers	0-1		10000	11				8				5					4	2		7	9					3	6	10			1		
30	16	Aberdare Athletic	1-2	Hughes	3000	11				8				9		7	5		4	2			10					3	6				1		
31	21	Millwall	0-3		14000	11				8		7		5					4	2			9					3	6	10			1		
32	28	MERTHYR TOWN	2-2	Isaac, H Williams	7000							7		5				8	4	2			9					3	6	10		11	1		
33	Mar 7	Reading	1-3	Allen	6312	7		8						5					4	2			9					3	6	10		11	1		
34	14	SWANSEA TOWN	3-1	Allen 2, Lane	9000	9								5				7	4	2	8		10					3	6			11	1		
35	21	Exeter City	1-5	Lane	3000	9								5		7			4	2	8		10					3	6			11	1		
36	28	BRISTOL ROVERS	1-1	Allen	4000	9								5						2	8	7	10		4			3	6			11	1		
37	Apr 4	Newport County	0-1		5000	9						7		5						2	8		10		4			3	6			11	1		
38	10	LUTON TOWN	3-0	Allen 2, Lane	7000	9						7		5						2	8		10		4			3	6			11	1		
39	13	Luton Town	1-3	Garnish	6000	9						7		5						2	8		10		4			3	6			11	1		
40	18	Watford	1-3	Allen	4000	9						7		5						2	8		10		4			3	6			11	1		
41	25	NORTHAMPTON T	1-3	Lane	5000	9				7				5						2	8		10		4			3	6			11	1		
42	May 2	BOURNEMOUTH	1-2	Allen	4000	9		10		7			1	5			6			2	8				4			3				11			
					Apps	36	17	17	9	26	6	25	10	22	8	14	25	2	16	35	9	3	41	7	8	4	2	16	23	27	7	11	32	2	2
					Goals	14						4		1		1		1			4		8	1		1				2	1				

F.A. Cup

No.	Date	Opponent	Score	Scorers	Att.	Allen JWA	Alton C	Broadbent WH	Cain T	Clayson WJ	Cooke ER	Garnish TF	Gilbert AG	Graham JA	Henderson F	Hughes H	Inglis W	Isaac AH	Jones H	Kell G	Lane JW	McCree J	Parker R	Relph W	Rowe R	Rowe V	Shepherd E	Steel JH	Walton J	Williams H	Williams R	Young H	Young W	Johnstone GS	McGuigan C
5q	Nov 29	St Albans City	3-5	Parker, H Williams, Garnish	8825	7	3	4	5				1	8						2			9	11					6	10					

		Pl.	Home W	D	L	F	A	Away W	D	L	F	A	F. (Total)	A.	Pts
1	Swansea Town	42	17	4	0	51	12	6	7	8	17	23	68	35	57
2	Plymouth Argyle	42	17	3	1	55	12	6	7	8	22	26	77	38	56
3	Bristol City	42	14	5	2	40	10	8	4	9	20	31	60	41	53
4	Swindon Town	42	17	2	2	51	13	3	9	9	15	25	66	38	51
5	Millwall	42	12	5	4	35	14	6	8	7	23	24	58	38	49
6	Newport County	42	13	6	2	35	12	7	3	11	27	30	62	42	49
7	Exeter City	42	13	4	4	37	19	6	5	10	22	29	59	48	47
8	Brighton & Hove A.	42	14	3	4	43	17	5	5	11	16	28	59	45	46
9	Northampton Town	42	12	3	6	34	18	8	3	10	17	26	51	44	46
10	Southend United	42	14	1	6	34	18	5	4	12	17	43	51	61	43
11	Watford	42	12	3	6	22	20	5	6	10	16	27	38	47	43
12	Norwich City	42	10	8	3	39	18	4	5	12	14	33	53	51	41
13	Gillingham	42	11	8	2	25	11	2	6	13	10	33	35	44	40
14	Reading	42	9	6	6	28	15	5	4	12	9	23	37	38	38
15	Charlton Athletic	42	12	6	3	31	13	1	6	14	15	35	46	48	38
16	Luton Town	42	9	10	2	34	15	1	7	13	15	42	49	57	37
17	Bristol Rovers	42	10	5	6	26	13	2	8	11	16	36	42	49	37
18	Aberdare Ath.	42	13	4	4	40	21	1	5	15	14	46	54	67	37
19	Queen's Park Rgs.	42	10	6	5	28	19	4	2	15	14	44	42	63	36
20	Bournemouth	42	8	6	7	20	17	5	2	14	20	41	40	58	34
21	**BRENTFORD**	**42**	**8**	**7**	**6**	**28**	**26**	**1**	**0**	**20**	**10**	**65**	**38**	**91**	**25**
22	Merthyr Town	42	8	3	10	24	27	0	2	19	11	50	35	77	21

1925/26

18th in Division Three (South)

	Month	Day	Opponent	Score	Scorers	Att.	Allen JWA	Beacham AJ	Cain T	Donnelly J	Douglas EAC	Evans ET	Finlayson W	Graham JA	Hendren EH	Lane JW	McClennon JW	Noble AH	Parker R	Price JW	Rae HS	Stanford H	Thomson JY	Walton J	Watkins ET	Watson F	Whitton PA	Young H
1	Aug	29	NORTHAMPTON T	3-4	Allen 2, Graham	12317	9		6	3			10	5		8		7			4		1				2	11
2	Sep	2	Southend United	1-3	Allen	8224	9		6	3			10	5		8		7			4		1				2	11
3		5	Aberdare Athletic	0-3		4140		5		3			10	6		8		7	9		4		1				2	11
4		7	SOUTHEND UNITED	1-3	Douglas	6409				3	11		9	5		10					4		1	6		8	2	7
5		12	BRIGHTON & HOVE ALB	1-6	Parker	8803	7			3				5		8			9		4		1	6		10	2	11
6		19	Watford	2-2	Young, Parker	4771	7	5		3		4				8			9			1		6		10	2	11
7		23	Plymouth Argyle	0-4		8384	7	5				4				8	3		9		10	1		6			2	11
8		26	QUEEN'S PARK RANGERS	1-2	Beacham	9719		5				4				8	3	7	9		10		1	6			2	11
9	Oct	3	Crystal Palace	0-2		15724				2			10	5	7	8	3				4		1	6		9		11
10		10	Bristol City	0-3		11095					11		10	5	7	8	3				4		1	6		9	2	
11		17	Bristol Rovers	2-1	Lane, Whitton	7095				2	11		10	5	7	8	3				4		1	6			9	
12		24	SWINDON TOWN	3-1	Whitton, Finlayson, Graham (p)	8282				2	11		10	5	7	8	3				4		1	6			9	
13		31	Newport County	3-2	Lane 2, Finlayson	4933				2	11	4	10		7	8	3				5		1	6			9	
14	Nov	7	LUTON TOWN	1-0	Lane	7533				2	11		10	5	7	8	3				4		1	6			9	
15		14	Bournemouth	2-3	Whitton 2	4530				2	11	6	10	5	7	8	3	4					1				9	
16		21	CHARLTON ATHLETIC	4-0	Whitton, Allen, Lane, Graham (p)	8017	10			2		6		5	7	8	3	4					1				9	11
17	Dec	5	MERTHYR TOWN	1-1	Graham (p)	6932				2			10	5	7	8	3				4		1	6			9	11
18		19	READING	1-0	Graham	7064				2		6		10	7	8	3	4			5		1				9	11
19		25	Millwall	1-2	Hendren	13333				2				10	7	8	3	4			5		1	6			9	11
20		26	MILLWALL	2-0	Allen 2	16893	9			2			10		7	8	3	4			5		1	6				11
21		28	Exeter City	1-6	Finlayson	5493	9			2			10			8	3	4			5		1	6		7		11
22	Jan	2	Northampton Town	1-6	Allen	4649	9			2			10	5	7	8	3	4					1	6				11
23		9	Gillingham	3-1	Watkins, Douglas 2	6093				2	11			10	7	8		4		3	5		1	6	9			
24		16	ABERDARE ATHLETIC	1-0	Douglas	5632				2	11			10	7	8		4		3	5		1	6	9			
25		23	Brighton & Hove Albion	2-3	Lane, Watkins	6107				2	11			10	7	8		4		3	5		1	6	9			
26		30	WATFORD	4-3	Graham 2, Rae, Hendren	7711				2	11			10	7	8		4		3	5		1	6	9			
27	Feb	6	Queen's Park Rangers	1-1	Plunkett (og)	13085				2	11		10		7	8		4		3	5		1	6	9			
28		13	CRYSTAL PALACE	3-2	Watkins 2, Douglas	10140				2	11		8	10	7			4		3	5		1	6	9			
29		20	BRISTOL CITY	2-1	Watkins, Graham	11956	9			2	11			10	7			4		3	5		1	6	8			
30		27	BRISTOL ROVERS	4-1	Watkins, Douglas, Graham (p), Rae	9902				2	11			10	7	8		4		3	5		1	6	9			
31	Mar	6	Swindon Town	1-2	Hendren	4932				2	11			10	7			4		3	5		1	6	9		8	
32		13	NEWPORT COUNTY	3-3	Watkins 2, Rae	9643				2	11			10	7			4		3	5		1	6	9		8	
33		20	Luton Town	2-4	Lane, Till (og)	6072				2	11		10		7	8	3	4			5		1	6	9			
34		27	BOURNEMOUTH	0-2		7687				2	11				7	8	3	4			5		1	6			9	10
35	Apr	2	NORWICH CITY	5-1	Hendren 2, Watkins 3	11463				2	11				7	8	3	4			5		1	6	9			10
36		3	Charlton Athletic	2-0	Young, Rae	6812				2	11				7	8	3	4			5		1	6	9			10
37		5	Norwich City	0-1		11694				2	11					8	3	4			5		1	6	9	7		10
38		10	GILLINGHAM	0-0		7942				2	11				7	8	3	4			5		1	6	9			10
39		17	Merthyr Town	0-6		2329	7			2	11					8	3	4					1	6	9		5	10
40		24	EXETER CITY	2-0	Finlayson, Douglas	7889				2	11					8	3	4			5		1	6	9		7	10
41		26	PLYMOUTH ARGYLE	2-2	Finlayson, Douglas	10123				2	11					8		4		3	5		1	6	9		7	10
42	May	1	Reading	1-7	Lane	17432				2	11					8		4		3	5		1	6	9		7	10
						Apps	11	4	2	39	27	7	18	25	28	38	24	31	5	12	37	2	40	36	19	7	25	25
						Goals	7	1			8		5	9	5	8			2		4				11		5	2

Two Own Goals

F.A. Cup

	Month	Day	Opponent	Score	Scorers	Att.	Allen JWA	Beacham AJ	Cain T	Donnelly J	Douglas EAC	Evans ET	Finlayson W	Graham JA	Hendren EH	Lane JW	McClennon JW	Noble AH	Parker R	Price JW	Rae HS	Stanford H	Thomson JY	Walton J	Watkins ET	Watson F	Whitton PA	Young H
R1	Nov	28	BARNET	3-1	Lane, Whitton, Graham	9480	10			2		6		5	7	8	3	4					1				9	11
R2	Dec	12	BOURNEMOUTH	1-2	Whitton	8200	11			2			10	5	7	8	3				4		1	6			9	

	Pl.	Home W	D	L	F	A	Away W	D	L	F	A	F. (Total)	A.	Pts
1 Reading	42	16	5	0	49	16	7	6	8	28	36	77	52	57
2 Plymouth Argyle	42	16	2	3	71	33	8	6	7	36	34	107	67	56
3 Millwall	42	14	6	1	52	12	7	5	9	21	27	73	39	53
4 Bristol City	42	14	3	4	42	15	7	6	8	30	36	72	51	51
5 Brighton & Hove A.	42	12	4	5	47	33	7	5	9	37	40	84	73	47
6 Swindon Town	42	16	2	3	48	22	4	4	13	21	42	69	64	46
7 Luton Town	42	16	4	1	60	25	2	3	16	20	50	80	75	43
8 Bournemouth	42	10	5	6	44	30	7	4	10	31	61	75	91	43
9 Aberdare Ath.	42	11	6	4	50	24	6	2	13	24	42	74	66	42
10 Gillingham	42	11	4	6	36	19	6	4	11	17	30	53	49	42
11 Southend United	42	13	2	6	50	20	6	2	13	28	53	78	73	42
12 Northampton Town	42	13	3	5	47	26	4	4	13	35	54	82	80	41
13 Crystal Palace	42	16	1	4	50	21	3	2	16	25	58	75	79	41
14 Merthyr Town	42	13	3	5	51	25	1	8	12	18	50	69	75	39
15 Watford	42	12	5	4	47	26	3	4	14	26	63	73	89	39
16 Norwich City	42	11	5	5	35	26	4	4	13	23	47	58	73	39
17 Newport County	42	11	5	5	39	27	3	5	13	25	47	64	74	38
18 BRENTFORD	**42**	**12**	**4**	**5**	**44**	**32**	**4**	**2**	**15**	**25**	**62**	**69**	**94**	**38**
19 Bristol Rovers	42	9	4	8	44	28	6	2	13	22	41	66	69	36
20 Exeter City	42	13	2	6	54	25	2	3	16	18	45	72	70	35
21 Charlton Athletic	42	9	7	5	32	23	2	6	13	16	45	48	68	35
22 Queen's Park Rgs.	42	5	7	9	23	32	1	2	18	14	52	37	84	21

1925-26

Back: Cain, Steel, Graham, Walton, Donnelly
Middle: Finlayson, Whitton, Thomson, Stanford, Beacham, Rae Front: Noble, Lane, Parker, Allen, Watson, Young.

1926-27

Back: Noble, Dearn, Hodnett, Collins, Ferguson, Craddock, Beacham, Bellamy, Whitton
Middle: Watkins, Winship, Anderson, Rae, Donnelly, Hodgson, Douglas. Front: Berry, Reddock

1926/27

11th in Division Three (South)

							Allen JW	Anderson GR	Beacham AJ	Bellamy H	Berry WG	Butler CJW	Clark AW	Collins AH	Craddock CW	Dearn S	Donnelly J	Douglas EAC	Ferguson JS	Hendren EH	Hodgson JWR	Hodnett JE	Lane JW	Lawson H	Marshall F	Noble AH	Rae HS	Reddock C	Watkins ET	Winship E
1	Aug	28	BRIGHTON & HOVE ALB	4-0	Rae (p), Berry, Watkins 2	12057				6	11				7	10	2		1			4	8				5		9	3
2		30	Luton Town	1-2	Dearn	9090				6	11				7	10	2		1			4	8				5		9	3
3	Sep	4	Northampton Town	3-2	Berry 2, Douglas	10082				6	7					10	2	11	1		3	4	8				5		9	
4		6	SOUTHEND UNITED	3-1	Watkins 2, Dearn	7996				6	7					10	2	11	1		3	5	8			4			9	
5		11	QUEEN'S PARK RANGERS	4-2	Lane, Watkins 2, Douglas	17380				6	7					10	2	11	1		3	5	8			4			9	
6		15	Southend United	1-3	Dearn	6512				6	7					10	2	11	1		3	5	8			4			9	
7		18	MILLWALL	0-0		14125				3	7					10	2	11	1				8			4	5	6	9	
8		25	Bristol Rovers	3-1	Lane, Watkins 2	8311				6	11	3				10	2		1	7			8			4	5		9	
9	Oct	2	SWINDON TOWN	2-2	Watkins 2	15404				6	11	3				10	2		1	7			8			4	5		9	
10		9	Exeter City	1-3	Lane	7152				6	11	3				10	2		1	7			8			4	5		9	
11		16	Crystal Palace	3-4	Berry 2, Lane	14860				6	11	3				10	2		1	7			8			4	5		9	
12		23	COVENTRY CITY	7-3	Hendren 4 (2p), Watkins, Dearn 2	9099				6	11	3				10	2		1	7		4	8				5		9	
13		30	Charlton Athletic	1-1	Rae	8058			4		11					10	2		1	7			8				5	6	9	3
14	Nov	6	BRISTOL CITY	3-0	Anderson 2, Dearn	11457		9	4	6	11					10	2		1	7			8				5			3
15		20	PLYMOUTH ARGYLE	0-0		8481		9	4	6	11	2				10			1	7			8				5			3
16	Dec	4	ABERDARE ATHLETIC	1-4	Baynham (og)	9485				6	11	2				10	3		1	7			8			4	5		9	
17		18	WATFORD	3-0	Watkins, Dearn, Douglas	9631			4	6		2				10		11	1	7			8				5		9	3
18		25	Norwich City	1-2	Hendren	10743			4	6		2				10		11	1	7			8				5		9	3
19		27	NORWICH CITY	3-0	Allen, Watkins, Douglas	17002	10		4	3						6	2	11	1	7			8				5		9	
20	Jan	1	LUTON TOWN	2-2	Dearn, Lane	9116	10		4	3						6	2	11	1	7			8				5		9	
21		15	Brighton & Hove Albion	1-1	Hendren	9517	10					3				6	2	11	1	7			8		4		5		9	
22		22	NORTHAMPTON T	1-1	Allen	4775	10					3				6	2	11	1	7			8		4		5		9	
23	Feb	5	Millwall	0-3		19178	10			6		3					2	11	1	7			8		4		5		9	
24		12	BRISTOL ROVERS	0-2		6630	10	9	4	6	7	3					2	11	1						8		5			
25		26	EXETER CITY	6-1	Watkins 2, Lane 2, Craddock, Douglas	6986				6		3		1	10		2	11		7			8		4		5		9	
26	Mar	5	CRYSTAL PALACE	3-0	Watkins, Allen, Lane	8205	10			6		3		1			2	11		7			8		4		5		9	
27		9	Swindon Town	2-4	Craddock, Hendren	4659				6		3		1	10		2	11		7			8		4		5		9	
28		12	Coventry City	1-3	Watkins	11910				6		3		1	10		2	11		7			8		4		5		9	
29		16	Bournemouth	1-3	Watkins	3195				6		3			10		2	11	1			5	8	7	4				9	
30		19	CHARLTON ATHLETIC	2-0	Donnelly (p), Craddock	6755				6		3			10		2	11	1			5	8	7	4				9	
31		26	Bristol City	0-1		14062			5	6		3			10		2	11	1				8	7		4			9	
32		30	Gillingham	2-1	Watkins, Lawson	2947			5	6		3			10		2	11	1				8	7	4				9	
33	Apr	2	BOURNEMOUTH	0-0		6766		10		6		3	5				2	11	1				8	7	4				9	
34		9	Plymouth Argyle	1-2	Craddock	9556			5	6		3			10		2	11	1				8	7	4				9	
35		15	MERTHYR TOWN	1-1	Lane	9031				6		3				10	2	11	1				8	7	4		5		9	
36		16	NEWPORT COUNTY	1-1	Watkins	7801			5	6		3				10	2	11	1	7			8		4				9	
37		19	Merthyr Town	0-1		3910					11	3			10	6	2		1				8	7	4		5		9	
38		23	Aberdare Athletic	1-3	Craddock	1227		9	5		11	3			10	6	2		1				8	7	4					
39		25	Newport County	0-0		1721		9								10	2	11	1				8	7	4		5	6		3
40		30	GILLINGHAM	0-0		5793					11					10	2		1				8	7	4		5	6	9	3
41	May	5	Queen's Park Rangers	1-1	Lawson	11355		9			11					10	2		1				8	7	4		5	6		3
42		7	Watford	0-0		4999		9	5		11					10	2		1				8	7	4			6		3
						Apps	7	8	14	33	22	27	1	4	12	30	39	26	38	21	4	9	41	13	21	10	30	6	35	11
						Goals	3	2			5				5	8	1	5		7			9	2			2		20	

One own goal

F.A. Cup

							Allen JW	Anderson GR	Beacham AJ	Bellamy H	Berry WG	Butler CJW	Clark AW	Collins AH	Craddock CW	Dearn S	Donnelly J	Douglas EAC	Ferguson JS	Hendren EH	Hodgson JWR	Hodnett JE	Lane JW	Lawson H	Marshall F	Noble AH	Rae HS	Reddock C	Watkins ET	Winship E
R1	Nov	27	Clapton	1-1	Anderson	4412		9	4	6	11	2				10			1	7			8				5			3
rep	Dec	1	CLAPTON	7-3	Watkins 3,.Lane 2, Hendren 2	5936			4	6	11	2				10	3		1	7			8				5		9	
R2		11	Gillingham	1-1	Hendren	10076				6		2				10		11	1	7			8			4	5		9	3
rep		15	GILLINGHAM	1-0	Dearn	6965				6		2				10		11	1	7			8			4	5		9	3
R3	Jan	10	Oldham Athletic	4-2	Allen 3, Watkins	9162	10		4			3				6	2	11	1	7			8				5		9	
R4		29	West Ham United	1-1	Lane	40000	10		4			3				6	2	11	1	7			8				5		9	
rep	Feb	2	WEST HAM UNITED	2-0	Lane, Allen	20799	10		4	6		3					2	11	1	7			8				5		9	
R5		19	Reading	0-1		33042	10		4	6		3					2	11	1	7			8				5		9	

		Pl.	Home W	D	L	F	A	Away W	D	L	F	A	F. (Total)	A. (Total)	Pts
1	Bristol City	42	19	1	1	71	24	8	7	6	33	30	104	54	62
2	Plymouth Argyle	42	17	4	0	52	14	8	6	7	43	47	95	61	60
3	Millwall	42	16	2	3	55	19	7	8	6	34	32	89	51	56
4	Brighton & Hove A.	42	15	4	2	61	24	6	7	8	18	26	79	50	53
5	Swindon Town	42	16	3	2	64	31	5	6	10	36	54	100	85	51
6	Crystal Palace	42	12	6	3	57	33	6	3	12	27	48	84	81	45
7	Bournemouth	42	13	2	6	49	24	5	6	10	29	42	78	66	44
8	Luton Town	42	12	9	0	48	19	3	5	13	20	47	68	66	44
9	Newport County	42	15	4	2	40	20	4	2	15	17	51	57	71	44
10	Bristol Rovers	42	12	4	5	46	28	4	5	12	32	52	78	80	41
11	**BRENTFORD**	**42**	**10**	**9**	**2**	**46**	**20**	**3**	**5**	**13**	**24**	**41**	**70**	**61**	**40**
12	Exeter City	42	14	4	3	46	18	1	6	14	30	55	76	73	40
13	Charlton Athletic	42	13	5	3	44	22	3	3	15	16	39	60	61	40
14	Queen's Park Rgs.	42	9	8	4	41	27	6	1	14	24	44	65	71	39
15	Coventry City	42	11	4	6	44	33	4	3	14	27	53	71	86	37
16	Norwich City	42	10	5	6	41	25	2	6	13	18	46	59	71	35
17	Merthyr Town	42	11	5	5	42	25	2	4	15	21	55	63	80	35
18	Northampton Town	42	13	4	4	36	23	2	1	18	23	64	59	87	35
19	Southend United	42	12	3	6	44	25	2	3	16	20	52	64	77	34
20	Gillingham	42	10	5	6	36	26	1	5	15	18	46	54	72	32
21	Watford	42	9	6	6	36	27	3	2	16	21	60	57	87	32
22	Aberdare Ath.	42	8	2	11	38	48	1	5	15	24	53	62	101	25

1927/28

12th in Division Three (South)

						Bailey H	Beacham AJ	Berry WG	Butler CJW	Cairns J	Craddock CW	Dearn S	Donnelly J	Douglas EAC	Drinnan JMcK	Ferguson JS	Fletcher AW	Hodge W	Lane JW	Lawson H	McCafferty J	Phillips J	Price WJ	Stevenson A	Ward S	Watkins ET	Wiggins JA	Winship E	Hendrie R
1	Aug 27	Brighton & Hove Albion	2-5	Phillips, Drinnan	13164		4					6		11	10	1	5		8	7		9		2				3	
2	29	NORTHAMPTON T	3-0	Phillips 3	8280				2			6		11		1	5	4	8	7		9				10		3	
3	Sep 3	BOURNEMOUTH	2-1	Fletcher, Douglas	11108				2			6		11		1	5	4	8	7		9				10		3	
4	5	Northampton Town	2-3	Lane, Watkins	7220				2			6		11		1	5	4	8	7		9				10		3	
5	10	Queen's Park Rangers	3-2	Watkins, Lane, Phillips	18826		5		2			6		11		1		4	8	7		9				10		3	
6	14	Bristol Rovers	3-1	Phillips, Watkins, Lawson	2578		5		2			6		11		1		4	8	7		9				10		3	
7	17	Luton Town	2-5	Lawson 2	9182		5		2			6		11		1		4	8	7		9				10		3	
8	24	MILLWALL	6-1	Douglas, Watkins (p), Phillips 2, Lawson 2	12513				2			6		11		1	5	4	8	7		9				10		3	
9	Oct 1	Crystal Palace	2-0	Phillips, Lane	11552				2			6		11		1	5	4	8	7		9				10		3	
10	8	EXETER CITY	1-1	Lawson	11326				2			6		11	10	1	5	4	8	7						9		3	
11	15	Torquay United	1-2	Lawson	4185				2			6		11		1	5	4	8	7		9				10		3	
12	22	COVENTRY CITY	4-1	Craddock 2, Hodge, Lane	4666		5		2		9			11		1	6	4	8		7					10		3	
13	29	Newport County	0-3		5790		5		2		9			11		1	6	4	8	7						10		3	
14	Nov 5	SWINDON TOWN	1-4	Lane	9527		5		2			6		11		1		4	8	7		9				10		3	
15	12	Gillingham	1-2	Lawson	3293		4					6		11	10	1	5		8	7				2		9		3	
16	Dec 3	PLYMOUTH ARGYLE	0-2		7537		4		2			6		11	10	1	5		8	7						9		3	
17	5	WALSALL	3-2	Watkins, Dearn (p), Lane	2202				2			6		11		1		4	8	7					5	10	9	3	
18	10	Merthyr Town	1-3	Craddock	2465		4	11	2		8	6				1	5			7						10	9	3	
19	17	CHARLTON ATHLETIC	1-1	Berry	5245	1		11	2		8	10					6	4		7					5	9		3	
20	24	Watford	1-1	Craddock	5226	1		11	2		9	10					6	4	8	7					5			3	
21	26	Southend United	2-3	Craddock 2	3540	1		11	2		9	6						4	8	7					5	10		3	
22	31	BRIGHTON & HOVE ALB	1-3	Lane	6061	1		11	2		9	6						4	8	7					5	10		3	
23	Jan 7	Bournemouth	0-1		4796		5	11	2		10	6				1		4	8	7						9		3	
24	21	QUEEN'S PARK RANGERS	0-3		10430		5	7	2		9	6		11		1	4		8							10		3	
25	28	LUTON TOWN	4-2	Watkins 4	3291		4	7	2		8	6		11	10	1									5	9		3	
26	Feb 4	Millwall	0-3		16885		5	7	2		8	6		11	10	1	4									9		3	
27	11	CRYSTAL PALACE	2-1	Beacham, Drinnan	7580		5	7	2			6		11	10	1	4		8							9		3	
28	18	Exeter City	1-0	Drinnan	7420		5	7	2			6		11	10	1	4		8							9		3	
29	25	TORQUAY UNITED	1-2	Lane	8355		5	7	2			6		11	10	1	4		8			9						3	
30	Mar 3	Coventry City	0-0		8188		5	7	2			6		11	10	1	4		8			9						3	
31	10	NEWPORT COUNTY	3-1	Berry 2, Phillips	5759		5	11	2			6			10	1	4		8	7		9						3	
32	17	Swindon Town	1-1	Phillips	6500	1	5	11	2			6			10		4		8	7		9						3	
33	24	GILLINGHAM	2-0	Lane 2	6107	1	5	11	2			6			10		4		8	7		9						3	
34	31	Walsall	2-4	Drinnan, Phillips	4750	1	5	11	2			6			10		4		8	7		9						3	
35	Apr 6	NORWICH CITY	3-1	Berry, Price, Wiggins	11814	1	5	11	2			6					4		8	7			10				9	3	
36	7	BRISTOL ROVERS	5-1	Wiggins, Cairns, Drinnan 2, Lawson	7894	1	5	11	2	8		6			10		4			7							9	3	
37	9	Norwich City	1-1	Berry (p)	10848	1	5	11	2			6			10		4		8	7		9						3	
38	14	Plymouth Argyle	0-1		5940	1	5	11	2			6			10		4		8	7		9						3	
39	21	MERTHYR TOWN	4-0	Phillips 2, Berry, Lane	4583	1	5	11	2			6			10		4		8	7		9						3	
40	23	SOUTHEND UNITED	2-2	Phillips 2	4889	1		11	2			6	3				4		8	7		9			5	10			
41	28	Charlton Athletic	2-3	Watkins, Phillips	7122	1	5	11	2			6					4		8	7		9				10		3	
42	May 5	WATFORD	1-1	Phillips	4775	1	5	11	2			6					4		8	7		9				10		3	
					Apps	15	29	25	40	1	11	40	1	24	18	27	33	19	37	34	1	23	1	2	7	29	4	41	
					Goals		1	6		1	6	1		2	6		1	1	11	9		18	1			10	2		

F.A. Cup

						Bailey H	Beacham AJ	Berry WG	Butler CJW	Cairns J	Craddock CW	Dearn S	Donnelly J	Douglas EAC	Drinnan JMcK	Ferguson JS	Fletcher AW	Hodge W	Lane JW	Lawson H	McCafferty J	Phillips J	Price WJ	Stevenson A	Ward S	Watkins ET	Wiggins JA	Winship E	Hendrie R
R3	Jan 14	Manchester United	1-7	Jones (og)	18538		5	7			10	6		11		1		4	8							9		2	3

		Pl.	Home W	D	L	F	A	Away W	D	L	F	A	F. (Total)	A.	Pts
1	Millwall	42	19	2	0	87	15	11	3	7	40	35	127	50	65
2	Northampton Town	42	17	3	1	67	23	6	6	9	35	41	102	64	55
3	Plymouth Argyle	42	17	2	2	60	19	6	5	10	25	35	85	54	53
4	Brighton & Hove A.	42	14	4	3	51	24	5	6	10	30	45	81	69	48
5	Crystal Palace	42	15	3	3	46	23	3	9	9	33	49	79	72	48
6	Swindon Town	42	12	6	3	60	26	7	3	11	30	43	90	69	47
7	Southend United	42	14	2	5	48	19	6	4	11	32	45	80	64	46
8	Exeter City	42	11	6	4	49	27	6	6	9	21	33	70	60	46
9	Newport County	42	12	5	4	52	38	6	4	11	29	46	81	84	45
10	Queen's Park Rgs.	42	8	5	8	37	35	9	4	8	35	36	72	71	43
11	Charlton Athletic	42	12	5	4	34	27	3	8	10	26	43	60	70	43
12	**BRENTFORD**	**42**	**12**	**4**	**5**	**49**	**30**	**4**	**4**	**13**	**27**	**44**	**76**	**74**	**40**
13	Luton Town	42	13	5	3	56	27	3	2	16	38	60	94	87	39
14	Bournemouth	42	12	6	3	44	24	1	6	14	28	55	72	79	38
15	Watford	42	10	5	6	42	34	4	5	12	26	44	68	78	38
16	Gillingham	42	10	3	8	33	26	3	8	10	29	55	62	81	37
17	Norwich City	42	9	8	4	41	26	1	8	12	25	44	66	70	36
18	Walsall	42	9	6	6	52	35	3	3	15	23	66	75	101	33
19	Bristol Rovers	42	11	3	7	41	36	3	1	17	26	57	67	93	32
20	Coventry City	42	5	8	8	40	36	6	1	14	27	60	67	96	31
21	Merthyr Town	42	7	6	8	38	40	2	7	12	15	51	53	91	31
22	Torquay United	42	4	10	7	27	36	4	4	13	26	67	53	103	30

1927-28
Back: Rae, Fletcher, Ward, Bailey, Ferguson, Beacham, Donnelly, Butler, Hendrie
Middle: Ratcliffe (Trainer), Watkins, Lawson, Phillips, Lane, Craddock, Drinnant, Dearn, Douglas, Cartmell(Asst.Trainer)
Front: McCafferty, Winship, Reddock, Stevenson, Berry.

1929/30
Unnamed team group (2nd row first player - Bill Lane, second player Jack Lane

1928/29

13th in Division Three (South)

							Bailey H	Bain J	Beacham AJ	Berry WG	Davies R	Dearn S	Douglas EAC	Drinnan JMcK	Dumbrell G	Durnion AJ	Fox FS	Gamble FC	Heeps A	Herod ERB	Hodge W	Lane JW	Lawson H	McKinley CA	Phillips J	Purdy A	Reddock C	Richards AC	Sherlaw DD	Stevenson A	Stone NWB	Ware EAG	Watkins ET	Winship E
1	Aug	25	EXETER CITY	4-2	Phillips 2, Drinnan, Berry	11158	1		5	11	4	6		10						2		8		7	9									3
2	Sep	1	Southend United	1-1	McKinley	8082	1		5	11	4	6		10						2		8		7	9									3
3		3	CHARLTON ATHLETIC	1-0	Lane	6850	1		5	11	4	6		10						2		8		7	9									3
4		8	MERTHYR TOWN	2-1	Lane, Phillips	9153	1		5		4	6	11							2		8		7	9								10	3
5		10	SWINDON TOWN	2-0	Lane, Phillips	7231	1		5		4	6	11							2		8		7	9								10	3
6		15	Bournemouth	1-1	Watkins	7573	1		5	11	4	6		10						2		8		7									9	3
7		22	QUEEN'S PARK RANGERS	1-1	Lane	20783	1		5	11	4	6		10						2		8		7	9									3
8		29	LUTON TOWN	0-1		13758	1		5	11	4	6								3		8		7					9	2			10	
9	Oct	6	Coventry City	0-1		16993	1		5	11	4	6		10						3		8		7						2			9	
10		13	NORTHAMPTON T	2-2	Watkins 2	9260	1		5	11	4	6		10						2		8		7						3			9	
11		20	Bristol Rovers	0-2		9316	1			11	4	6		10						2		8		7		5				3			9	
12		27	WATFORD	0-1		8301	1			11	4									2		8		7			6	9		3			10	
13	Nov	3	Walsall	0-2		7937					4		11				1		5	2		8		7			6			9			10	3
14		10	NEWPORT COUNTY	1-3	Lane	5395				7	4		11	10			1		5	2		8					6						9	3
15		17	Crystal Palace	0-1		11323				7	4		11				1			5	6	8						9	10	2				3
16	Dec	1	Torquay United	1-4	Berry	4614				11	4			10			1			2	6	8	7						9				5	3
17		15	Plymouth Argyle	0-4		10940	1	5			4		11	10						2	6			7					8				9	3
18		22	FULHAM	1-2	Watkins	8876	1	5			4		11	10						2		8							7			6	9	3
19		25	Brighton & Hove Albion	2-3	Douglas, Durnian	8600	1	5			4		11			10				2		8							7			6	9	3
20		26	BRIGHTON & HOVE ALB	5-1	Lane 4, Sherlaw	5117		5			4		11			10	1			2		8							7			6	9	3
21		29	Exeter City	3-2	Drinnan, Watkins, Sherlaw	6124		5			4		11	10			1			2		8							7			6	9	3
22	Jan	5	SOUTHEND UNITED	1-0	Drinnan	4588		5			4		11	10			1			2		8							7			6	9	3
23		12	GILLINGHAM	4-1	Douglas 2, Watkins, Sherlaw	5042	1	5			4		11	10	3					2		8							7			6	9	
24		19	Merthyr Town	2-2	Drinnan, Sherlaw	2500	1	5			4		11	10						2		8							7			6	9	3
25		26	Gillingham	2-1	Watkins, Douglas	3756	1	5			4		11	10						2		8							7			6	9	3
26	Feb	2	Queen's Park Rangers	2-2	Sherlaw 2	10590	1	5			4		11	10						2		8							7			6	9	3
27		9	Luton Town	1-2	Lawson	8148	1	5			4		11	10								8	7							2		6	9	3
28		16	COVENTRY CITY	1-0	Watkins	3950	1	5			4		11	10						2		8	7									6	9	3
29		23	Northampton Town	1-1	Watkins	8555	1	5		11	4			10						2									7			6	9	3
30	Mar	2	BRISTOL ROVERS	2-0	Sherlaw, Drinnan	6991	1	5			4		11	10										7					8	2		6	9	3
31		9	Watford	0-2		10453	1	5		11	4			10									7						8	2		6	9	3
32		13	BOURNEMOUTH	0-0		3366	1	5			4		11	10								8							7	2		6	9	3
33		16	WALSALL	1-0	Douglas	7111	1	5			4		11	10				9					8						7	2		6		3
34		23	Newport County	1-1	Douglas	3090	1	5			4		11					9				8							7	2		6	10	3
35		29	NORWICH CITY	4-0	Stone 2, Watkins 2	10049	1	5			4		11										7						8	2	9	6	10	3
36		30	CRYSTAL PALACE	2-4	Watkins, Berry	13314	1	5	4	7			11																8	2	9	6	10	3
37	Apr	1	Norwich City	4-2	Berry 2, Watkins 2	9713		5	4	7			11		3		1												8	2	9	6	10	
38		6	Swindon Town	1-3	Gamble	3107		5	4	7			11		3		1	9											8	2		6	10	
39		13	TORQUAY UNITED	0-0		4507		5	4	11							1	9				8							7	2		6	10	3
40		22	Charlton Athletic	0-1		8017		5		11		4					1	9				8							7	2		6	10	3
41		27	PLYMOUTH ARGYLE	0-2		6532		5	4	11							1	9					7						8	2		6	10	3
42	May	4	Fulham	0-1		16524		5		11	4						1	8											7	2	9	6	10	3
						Apps	29	26	15	22	36	12	25	25	3	2	13	7	2	28	3	31	7	15	6	1	3	2	27	21	4	25	36	34
						Goals				5			6	5		1		1				9	1	1	4				7		2		14	

Played in one game: A Wood (29, at 8), MH Woosnam (12, at 5)

F.A. Cup

							Bailey H	Bain J	Beacham AJ	Berry WG	Davies R	Dearn S	Douglas EAC	Drinnan JMcK	Dumbrell G	Durnion AJ	Fox FS	Gamble FC	Heeps A	Herod ERB	Hodge W	Lane JW	Lawson H	McKinley CA	Phillips J	Purdy A	Reddock C	Richards AC	Sherlaw DD	Stevenson A	Stone NWB	Ware EAG	Watkins ET	Winship E
R1	Nov	24	BRIGHTON & HOVE ALB.	4-1	Drinnan, Lane 2, Shirlaw	9439				11	4			10			1			2	6	8	7						9				5	3
R2	Dec	8	PLYMOUTH ARGYLE	0-1		10681	1			11	4			10						2	6	8	7						9				5	3

		Pl.	Home W	D	L	F	A	Away W	D	L	F	A	F. (Total)	A.	Pts
1	Charlton Athletic	42	14	5	2	51	22	9	3	9	35	38	86	60	54
2	Crystal Palace	42	14	2	5	40	25	9	6	6	41	42	81	67	54
3	Northampton Town	42	14	6	1	68	23	6	6	9	28	34	96	57	52
4	Plymouth Argyle	42	14	6	1	51	13	6	6	9	32	38	83	51	52
5	Fulham	42	14	3	4	60	31	7	7	7	41	40	101	71	52
6	Queen's Park Rgs.	42	13	7	1	50	22	6	7	8	32	39	82	61	52
7	Luton Town	42	16	3	2	64	28	3	8	10	25	45	89	73	49
8	Watford	42	15	3	3	55	31	4	7	10	24	43	79	74	48
9	Bournemouth	42	14	4	3	54	31	5	5	11	30	46	84	77	47
10	Swindon Town	42	12	5	4	48	27	3	8	10	27	45	75	72	43
11	Coventry City	42	9	6	6	35	23	5	8	8	27	34	62	57	42
12	Southend United	42	10	7	4	44	27	5	4	12	36	48	80	75	41
13	**BRENTFORD**	**42**	**11**	**4**	**6**	**34**	**21**	**3**	**6**	**12**	**22**	**39**	**56**	**60**	**38**
14	Walsall	42	11	7	3	47	25	2	5	14	26	54	73	79	38
15	Brighton & Hove A.	42	14	2	5	39	28	2	4	15	19	48	58	76	38
16	Newport County	42	8	6	7	37	28	5	3	13	32	58	69	86	35
17	Norwich City	42	12	3	6	49	29	2	3	16	20	52	69	81	34
18	Torquay United	42	10	3	8	46	36	4	3	14	20	48	66	84	34
19	Bristol Rovers	42	9	6	6	39	28	4	1	16	21	51	60	79	33
20	Merthyr Town	42	11	6	4	42	28	0	2	19	13	75	55	103	30
21	Exeter City	42	7	6	8	49	40	2	5	14	18	48	67	88	29
22	Gillingham	42	7	8	6	22	24	3	1	17	21	59	43	83	29

1929/30

2nd in Division Three (South)

							Adamson TK	Bain J	Blakemore C	Caesar WC	Davies R	Dumbrell G	Foster JTF	Fox FS	Hodge W	Lane JW	Lane WHC	Payne JF	Salt H	Sherlaw DD	Stevenson A	Ware EAG	Watkins ET	Whipp PL
1	Aug	31	SWINDON TOWN	3-2	Payne 2, Blakemore	11084	3	5	10		4		7	1			9	11	6		2			8
2	Sep	4	CLAPTON ORIENT	3-1	Blakemore, Galbraith (og), W Lane	9346	3	5	10		4		7	1			9	11	6		2			8
3		7	Plymouth Argyle	1-1	W Lane	12161	3	5	10		4		7	1			9	11	6		2			8
4		14	MERTHYR TOWN	6-0	Whipp, W Lane 4, Blakemore	11040	3	5	10		4		7	1			9	11	6		2			8
5		16	Clapton Orient	1-1	Payne	6854	3	5	10		4		7	1			9	11			2	6		8
6		21	Torquay United	1-2	W Lane	5012	3	5	10		4		7	1			9	11	6		2			8
7		25	BRISTOL ROVERS	2-1	Foster, W Lane	6265	3	5	10		4		7	1			9	11	6		2			8
8		28	NEWPORT COUNTY	1-0	Payne	11073	3	5	10		4		7	1			9	11			2	6	8	
9	Oct	5	Watford	2-1	Payne, Bain	10814	3	5	10		4		7	1		8	9	11	6		2			
10		12	COVENTRY CITY	3-1	Blakemore, J Lane, Bain	11957	3	5	10		4		7	1		8	9	11	6		2			
11		19	Fulham	0-2		25891			10	5	4		7	1	3	8	9	11	6		2			
12		26	NORWICH CITY	3-0	W Lane 2, Blakemore	11052		5	10		4		7	1	3	8	9	11	6		2			
13	Nov	2	Crystal Palace	1-2	J Lane	16939	3	5	10		4		7	1		8	9	11	6		2			
14		9	GILLINGHAM	2-1	W Lane 2	9603	3	5	10		4		7	1		8	9	11	6		2			
15		16	Northampton Town	1-1	Foster	6165	3	5	10		4		7	1		8	9	11	6		2			
16		23	EXETER CITY	2-0	Blakemore, J Lane	6502	3	5	10		4		7	1		8	9	11	6		2			
17	Dec	7	LUTON TOWN	2-0	J Lane 2	7167	3	5	10		4		7	1		8	9	11	6		2			
18		21	WALSALL	6-2	W Lane 2, J Lane, Blakemore (p), Payne 2	5041	3	5	10		4		7	1		8	9	11	6		2			
19		25	BRIGHTON & HOVE ALB	5-2	J Lane 2, Payne, Blakemore, W Lane	14612	3	5	10		4		7	1		8	9	11	6		2			
20		26	Brighton & Hove Albion	0-2		19193	3	5	10		4		7	1		8	9	11	6		2			
21		28	Swindon Town	2-0	Blakemore 2	4317	3	5	10		4		7	1		8	9	11	6		2			
22	Jan	4	PLYMOUTH ARGYLE	3-0	Foster, J Lane 2	20511	3	5	10		4		7	1		8	9	11	6		2			
23		11	Southend United	0-2		6456	3	5	10		4		7	1		8	9	11	6		2			
24		18	Merthyr Town	3-2	Blakemore, J Lane 2	2103	3	5	10		4		7	1		8	9	11	6		2			
25		25	TORQUAY UNITED	5-0	J Lane, Foster, W Lane 3	10497	3	5	10		4		7	1		8	9	11	6		2			
26	Feb	1	Newport County	3-1	W Lane 2, Payne	3827	3	5	10		4		7	1		8	9	11	6		2			
27		8	WATFORD	5-0	Blakemore, Payne, J Lane, W Lane 2	11356	3	5	10		4		7	1		8	9	11	6		2			
28		15	Coventry City	1-2	Blakemore	12146	3	5	10		4		7	1		8	9	11	6		2			
29		22	FULHAM	5-1	Blakemore, W Lane, J Lane 3	21966	3	5	10		4		7	1		8	9	11	6		2			
30	Mar	1	Norwich City	2-2	Foster 2	14081	3	5	10		4		7	1		8	9	11	6		2			
31		8	CRYSTAL PALACE	2-0	W Lane, Payne	19555	3	5	10		4		7	1		8	9	11	6		2			
32		15	Gillingham	3-1	Payne 2, W Lane	6749	3	5	10		4		7	1		8	9	11	6		2			
33		22	NORTHAMPTON T	2-0	W Lane 2	16460	3	5	10		4	2	7	1		8	9	11	6					
34		26	Bournemouth	2-1	W Lane, Payne (p)	5494	3	5	10		4		7	1	2	8	9	11	6					
35		29	Exeter City	0-0		7219	3	5	10		4	2	7	1		8	9	11	6					
36	Apr	5	SOUTHEND UNITED	2-1	Payne 2	13255		5	10		4	2	7	1	3	8	9	11	6					
37		12	Luton Town	1-2	W Lane	11150		5	10		4	2	7	1	3	8	9	11	6					
38		18	Queen's Park Rangers	1-2	Blakemore	22179	3	5	10		4	2	7	1		8	9	11	6					
39		19	BOURNEMOUTH	1-0	J Lane	7694		5	10		4	2	7	1	3	8	9	11	6					
40		21	QUEEN'S PARK RANGERS	3-0	W Lane 3	18549		5	10		4	2	7	1	3	8	9	11	6					
41		26	Walsall	2-1	Sherlaw, W Lane	2917		5	10		4	2		1	3	8	9	11	6	7				
42	May	3	Bristol Rovers	1-4	J Lane	6402	3	5	10		4	2	7	1		8	9	11	6					
						Apps	35	41	42	1	42	9	41	42	8	34	42	42	40	1	32	2	1	7
						Goals		2	15				6			18	33	16		1				1

One own goal

F.A. Cup

R1	Nov	30	Southend United	0-1		16890	3	5	10		4		7	1		8	9	11	6		2			

	Pl.	Home W	D	L	F	A	Away W	D	L	F	A	F. (Total)	A.	Pts
1 Plymouth Argyle	42	18	3	0	63	12	12	5	4	35	26	98	38	68
2 BRENTFORD	**42**	**21**	**0**	**0**	**66**	**12**	**7**	**5**	**9**	**28**	**32**	**94**	**44**	**61**
3 Queen's Park Rgs.	42	13	5	3	46	26	8	4	9	34	42	80	68	51
4 Northampton Town	42	14	6	1	53	20	7	2	12	29	38	82	58	50
5 Brighton & Hove A.	42	16	2	3	54	20	5	6	10	33	43	87	63	50
6 Coventry City	42	14	3	4	54	25	5	6	10	34	48	88	73	47
7 Fulham	42	12	6	3	54	33	6	5	10	33	50	87	83	47
8 Norwich City	42	14	4	3	55	28	4	6	11	33	49	88	77	46
9 Crystal Palace	42	14	5	2	56	26	3	7	11	25	48	81	74	46
10 Bournemouth	42	11	6	4	47	24	4	7	10	25	37	72	61	43
11 Southend United	42	11	6	4	41	19	4	7	10	28	40	69	59	43
12 Clapton Orient	42	10	8	3	38	21	4	5	12	17	41	55	62	41
13 Luton Town	42	13	4	4	42	25	1	8	12	22	53	64	78	40
14 Swindon Town	42	10	7	4	42	25	3	5	13	31	58	73	83	38
15 Watford	42	10	4	7	37	30	5	4	12	23	43	60	73	38
16 Exeter City	42	10	6	5	45	29	2	5	14	22	44	67	73	35
17 Walsall	42	10	4	7	45	24	3	4	14	26	54	71	78	34
18 Newport County	42	9	9	3	48	29	3	1	17	26	56	74	85	34
19 Torquay United	42	9	6	6	50	38	1	5	15	14	56	64	94	31
20 Bristol Rovers	42	11	3	7	45	31	0	5	16	22	62	67	93	30
21 Gillingham	42	9	5	7	38	28	2	3	16	13	52	51	80	30
22 Merthyr Town	42	5	6	10	39	49	1	3	17	21	86	60	135	21

1930/31

3rd in Division Three (South)

			Opponent	Score	Scorers	Att	Adamson TK	Allen RSL	Bain J	Bann WE	Berry WG	Blakemore C	Davies R	Foster JTF	Fox FS	Gamble FC	Hodge W	Lane JW	Lane WHC	Lawson H	McDonough FJB	Nash EM	Payne JF	Roberts CL	Robson GC	Salt H	Shaw J	Sherlaw DD	Stevenson A	Thomson NS	Ware EAG	Wilkins L
1	Aug	30	Luton Town	1-1	Foster	11686	3		5				4	7	1	9		8					11	10		6			2			
2	Sep	3	NORTHAMPTON T	0-4		11356	3		5				4	7	1			8	9				11	10		6			2			
3		6	BRISTOL ROVERS	4-0	Blakemore 2, W Lane 2	9919			5	3		10	4	7	1			8	9				11			6			2			
4		8	Fulham	1-1	W Lane	12248	3		5			10	4	7	1			8	9				11			6			2			
5		13	Newport County	2-0	W Lane 2	2758	3		5			10	4	7				8	9		1		11			6			2			
6		17	FULHAM	4-1	W Lane 2, J Lane, Payne	9564	3		5			10	4	7				8	9		1		11			6			2			
7		20	GILLINGHAM	1-1	Payne	9407	3		5			10	4	7				8	9			1	11			6			2			
8		24	NOTTS COUNTY	2-2	Blakemore (p), W Lane	9999	3		5			10	4	7				8	9			1	11			6			2			
9		27	Exeter City	0-4		5352	3		5			10	4	7	1		2	8	9				11			6						
10	Oct	4	BRIGHTON & HOVE ALB	3-2	W Lane, Blakemore, J Lane	9348	3		5		11	10		7	1		2	8	9	4						6						
11		11	Torquay United	3-0	J Lane, Hill (og), W Lane	6944	3		5		11	10	4	7	1			8	9							6			2			
12		18	COVENTRY CITY	1-2	W Lane	10244	3		5		11	10	4	7	1				9					8		6			2			
13		25	Walsall	4-1	W Lane, J Lane 2, Berry	2943	3		5		11	10	4	7	1			8	9							6			2			
14	Nov	1	QUEEN'S PARK RANGERS	5-3	Berry 2, J Lane, Blakemore 2 (1p)	10857	3		5		11	10	4	7	1			8	9							6			2			
15		8	Norwich City	0-3		9172	3		5		11	10	4	7	1			8	9							6			2			
16		15	THAMES	6-1	Berry, J Lane, Blakemore 2, W Lane 2	7211	3		5		11	10	4		1			8	9							6		7	2			
17		22	Clapton Orient	0-3		8319	3		5		11	10	4	7	1			8								6		9	2			
18	Dec	6	Watford	3-1	W Lane, Berry, Blakemore (p)	6775	3		5		11	10	4	7	1			8	9							6			2			
19		18	BOURNEMOUTH	1-2	J Lane	2306			5	3			4	7	1			8	9				11	10		6			2			
20		20	Swindon Town	2-3	Blakemore, J Lane	4728			5	3	11	10	4	7	1			8	9							6			2			
21		25	CRYSTAL PALACE	8-2	J Lane 3, W Lane 3, Berry 2	11770	3		5		11	10	4	7	1			8	9							6			2			
22		26	Crystal Palace	1-5	W Lane	15853	3		5		11	10		7	1			8	9	4						6			2			
23		27	LUTON TOWN	0-1		7353	3		5		11	10		7	1			8	9	4						6			2			
24	Jan	3	Bristol Rovers	5-2	W Lane 3, Berry 2	7449			5		11			7			3	8	9	4		1		10		6			2			
25		17	NEWPORT COUNTY	3-2	W Lane, Berry, J Lane	7170	3		5		11	10	4	7				8	9			1				6			2			
26		28	Gillingham	1-1	J Lane	2547	3		5		11	10	4	7				8	9			1							2		6	
27		31	EXETER CITY	2-1	Gamble, Berry	7575	3		5		11	10	4	7		8	2		9			1									6	
28	Feb	7	Brighton & Hove Albion	0-1		9451	3		5		11		4			9	2					1					10	7		8	6	
29		14	TORQUAY UNITED	0-0		6464	3		5		11	10	4			9	2		8			1						7			6	
30		21	Coventry City	1-0	Blakemore	9651	3		5		11	10	4	7		9	2					1			8						6	
31		28	WALSALL	6-1	Berry 2, Gamble 3, John (og)	7117	3		5		11	10	4	7		9	2					1			8						6	
32	Mar	7	Queen's Park Rangers	1-3	Sherlaw	10331	3		5		11	10	4	7			2					1			8			9			6	
33		14	NORWICH CITY	3-1	Hannah (og), Robson, Wilkins	9013		9	5		11		4	7			3					1			8				2		6	10
34		21	Thames	0-2		3675		9	5		11		4	7			3					1			8				2		6	10
35		28	CLAPTON ORIENT	3-0	W Lane, Robson, Berry	7757	3		5		11	10	4	7			2		9			1			8						6	
36	Apr	3	SOUTHEND UNITED	3-1	W Lane, Blakemore, Robson	6027	3		5		11	10	4	7			2		9			1			8						6	
37		4	Notts County	0-1		14759	3		5		11	10	4	7			2		9			1			8						6	
38		6	Southend United	1-0	Berry	9969	3		5		11	10	4	7			2		9			1			8						6	
39		11	WATFORD	2-1	WLane, Blakemore (p)	8163	3		5		11	10	4	7			2		9			1			8						6	
40		18	Bournemouth	0-1		3662	3		5		11	10	4	7			2		9			1			8						6	
41		25	SWINDON TOWN	5-2	Berry 2, W Lane, Robson 2	4327	3		5		11	10	4	7			2		9			1			8						6	
42	May	2	Northampton Town	2-1	Sherlaw, Berry	3698	3		5		11	10	4	7			2					1			8			9			6	
						Apps	36	2	42	3	32	35	38	39	19	6	19	25	33	4	2	21	10	5	13	25	1	6	26	1	17	2
						Goals					18	13		1		4		14	27				2		5			2				1

Game 17 played at Wembley Stadium

Three own goals

F.A. Cup

			Opponent	Score	Scorers	Att	Adamson TK	Allen RSL	Bain J	Bann WE	Berry WG	Blakemore C	Davies R	Foster JTF	Fox FS	Gamble FC	Hodge W	Lane JW	Lane WHC	Lawson H	McDonough FJB	Nash EM	Payne JF	Roberts CL	Robson GC	Salt H	Shaw J	Sherlaw DD	Stevenson A	Thomson NS	Ware EAG	Wilkins L
R1	Nov	29	Ilford	6-1	W Lane 3, J Lane 3	5718	3		5		11	10	4	7	1			8	9							6			2			
R2	Dec	13	NORWICH CITY	1-0	J Lane	12000	3		5		11	10	4	7	1			8	9							6			2			
R3	Jan	10	CARDIFF CITY	2-2	Berry, W Lane	16500	3		5		11	10		7				8	9	4		1				6			2			
rep		14	Cardiff City	2-1	W Lane, J Lane	25000	3		5		11	10	4	7				8	9			1				6			2			
R4		24	PORTSMOUTH	0-1		23544	3		5		11	10	4	7				8	9			1				6			2			

		Pl.	Home W	D	L	F	A	Away W	D	L	F	A	F. (Total)	A.	Pts
1	Notts County	42	16	4	1	58	13	8	7	6	39	33	97	46	59
2	Crystal Palace	42	17	2	2	71	20	5	5	11	36	51	107	71	51
3	**BRENTFORD**	**42**	**14**	**3**	**4**	**62**	**30**	**8**	**3**	**10**	**28**	**34**	**90**	**64**	**50**
4	Brighton & Hove A.	42	13	5	3	45	20	4	10	7	23	33	68	53	49
5	Southend United	42	16	0	5	53	26	6	5	10	23	34	76	60	49
6	Northampton Town	42	10	6	5	37	20	8	6	7	40	39	77	59	48
7	Luton Town	42	15	3	3	61	17	4	5	12	15	34	76	51	46
8	Queen's Park Rgs.	42	15	0	6	57	23	5	3	13	25	52	82	75	43
9	Fulham	42	15	3	3	49	21	3	4	14	28	54	77	75	43
10	Bournemouth	42	11	7	3	39	22	4	6	11	33	51	72	73	43
11	Torquay United	42	13	5	3	56	26	4	4	13	24	58	80	84	43
12	Swindon Town	42	15	5	1	68	29	3	1	17	21	65	89	94	42
13	Exeter City	42	12	6	3	55	35	5	2	14	29	55	84	90	42
14	Coventry City	42	11	4	6	55	28	5	5	11	20	37	75	65	41
15	Bristol Rovers	42	12	3	6	49	36	4	5	12	26	56	75	92	40
16	Gillingham	42	10	6	5	40	29	4	4	13	21	47	61	76	38
17	Walsall	42	9	5	7	44	38	5	4	12	34	57	78	95	37
18	Watford	42	9	4	8	41	29	5	3	13	31	46	72	75	35
19	Clapton Orient	42	12	3	6	47	33	2	4	15	16	58	63	91	35
20	Thames	42	12	5	4	34	20	1	3	17	20	73	54	93	34
21	Newport County	42	10	5	6	45	31	1	1	19	24	80	69	111	28
22	Norwich City	42	10	7	4	37	20	0	1	20	10	56	47	76	28

1930-31
Back: Shaw, Davies, Stevenson, Fox, Adamson, Kane (Trainer), Salt
Front: Foster, J.Lane, W.Lane, Blakemore, Berry, Bain.

1931-32
Back: Kane (Trainer), Wilkins, Hodge, Nash, Adamson, Ware, Davies
Front: Curtis (Manager), Foster, Allen, W.Lane, Robson, Berry, Bain.

1931/32

5th in Division Three (South)

						Att.	Adamson TK	Allen RSL	Bain J	Bann WE	Berry WG	Burns JC	Cook GW	Crompton A	Foster J	Gibbins WVT	Hodge W	James J	Lane WHC	Lawson H	Nash EM	Robson GC	Salt H	Smith DL	Stephens HJ	Stevenson A	Ware EAG	Weeks GE	Wilkins L
1	Aug	29	QUEEN'S PARK RANGERS	1-0	Robson	20739	3		5		11	4	10		7		2		9		1	8					6		
2	Sep	3	Thames	1-1	Cook	4217	3		5		11	4	10		7		2		9		1	8					6		
3		5	Exeter City	1-4	Lane	7093	3		5		11	4	10		7		2		9		1	8					6		
4		9	Reading	2-1	Lane, Foster	9155	3		5		11	10			7		2		9		1	8	4				6		
5		12	COVENTRY CITY	4-2	Lane 3, Foster	8017	3		5		11	10			7		2		9		1	8	4				6		
6		19	Gillingham	2-0	Lane, Foster	7225	3		5		11	10			7		2		9		1	8	4				6		
7		24	READING	3-0	Lane 2, Foster	8942	3		5		11	10			7		2		9		1	8	4				6		
8		26	LUTON TOWN	1-0	Burns	12540	3		5		11	10			7		2		9		1	8	4				6		
9	Oct	3	Cardiff City	2-3	Burns, Lane	9521	3		5		11	10			7		2		9		1	8	4				6		
10		10	NORTHAMPTON T	2-0	Lane (p), Robson	12694	3		5		11	10			7		2		9		1	8	4				6		
11		17	BRISTOL ROVERS	4-2	Burns, Robson 2 (2p), Berry	11338	3		5		11	10	9		7		2				1	8					6		4
12		24	Torquay United	1-1	Robson (p)	4650	3		5		11	10	9		7		2				1	8					6		4
13		31	CLAPTON ORIENT	3-0	Berry 2, Burns	11295	3		5		11	10			7		2		9		1	8					6		4
14	Nov	7	Swindon Town	3-1	Lane, Foster 2	6415	3		5		11	10			7		2		9		1	8					6		4
15		14	NORWICH CITY	0-1		11484	3		5		11		10		7		2		9		1	8					6		4
16		21	Brighton & Hove Albion	2-1	Lane, Berry	9582	3				11	10			7			5	9		1	8				2	6		4
17	Dec	5	Watford	4-1	Robson, Foster, Lane 2	12086	3		5		11	10			7		2		9		1	8					6		4
18		19	Bournemouth	3-1	Lane, Foster, Burns	5000	3		5		11	10			7		2		9		1	8					6		4
19		25	FULHAM	0-0		26139	3		5		11	10			7		2		9		1	8					6		4
20		26	Fulham	1-2	Robson	29253	3		5		11	10			7		2		9			8		1			6		4
21	Jan	2	Queen's Park Rangers	2-1	Lane 2	33553	3		5		11	10			7		2		9			8		1			6		4
22		13	MANSFIELD TOWN	1-1	Lane	4902	3		5		11	10			7		2		9		1	8					6		4
23		16	EXETER CITY	2-2	Lane, Foster	11981	3		5		11	10			7		2		9		1	8					6		4
24		28	Coventry City	1-0	Berry	6172	3	8	5		11				7		2		9		1	10					6		4
25		30	GILLINGHAM	1-1	Berry	11361	3	9	5		11				7		2		8	4	1	10					6		
26	Feb	6	Luton Town	1-1	Lane	7402	3		5		11	10			7		2		9		1	8					6		4
27		13	CARDIFF CITY	2-3	Crompton, Gibbins	16239	3		5			10		11	7	9	2		8		1						6		4
28		20	Northampton Town	0-3		6533	3		5			6		11	7	10	2		9		1	8	4						
29		27	Bristol Rovers	0-2		6114	3		5		11			10	7		2		9		1	8	4				6		
30	Mar	5	TORQUAY UNITED	3-0	Webster(og), Burns, Gibbins	11293						4		11	7	10		5	9		1	8				2	6	3	
31		12	Clapton Orient	2-2	Crompton, Foster	10700						4		11	7	10		5	9		1	8				2	6	3	
32		19	SWINDON TOWN	2-0	Robson (p), Foster	10179	3				11		10		7			5	9		1	8	4			2	6		
33		25	SOUTHEND UNITED	2-3	Crompton, Lane	15237						4		11	7	10	3	5	9		1	8				2	6		
34		26	Norwich City	0-1		10422			5	3		8	10	11	7	9					1		4			2	6		
35		28	Southend United	0-1		17313			5	3			10	11	7				9		1	8	4			2	6		
36	Apr	2	BRIGHTON & HOVE ALB	2-2	Gibbins 2	9107			5	3		10		11	7	9					1	8	4			2	6		
37		9	Mansfield Town	0-2		4932			5	3	11	10			7	9					1	8				2	6		4
38		13	CRYSTAL PALACE	1-1	Lane	5816	3		5		11	10	8		7				9	4				1		2	6		
39		16	WATFORD	1-2	Burns	6723	2		5		11	10	8						9	4				1	7	3	6		
40		23	Crystal Palace	0-1		12138	3		5			4	10	11					9			8		1	7	2	6		
41		30	BOURNEMOUTH	4-2	Foster, Cook 2, Lane	5906	3		5			4	10	11	7				9			8		1		2	6		
42	May	7	THAMES	1-0	Robson	6364	3		5			4	10	11	7				9			8		1		2	6		
						Apps	35	2	37	4	31	36	14	12	40	8	29	5	37	3	35	38	13	7	2	14	41	2	17
						Goals					6	7	3	3	12	4			23			9							

One own goal

F.A. Cup

						Att.	Adamson TK	Allen RSL	Bain J	Bann WE	Berry WG	Burns JC	Cook GW	Crompton A	Foster J	Gibbins WVT	Hodge W	James J	Lane WHC	Lawson H	Nash EM	Robson GC	Salt H	Smith DL	Stephens HJ	Stevenson A	Ware EAG	Weeks GE	Wilkins L
R1	Nov	28	Tunbridge Wells Rangers	1-1	Burns	5680	3				11	10			7			5	9		1	8				2	6		4
rep	Dec	2	TUNBRIDGE WELLS RGS	2-1	Lane (p), Burns	10000	3				11	10			7			5	9		1	8				2	6		4
R2		12	NORWICH CITY	4-1	Lane 2, Robson, Berry	17000	3		5		11	10			7		2		9		1	8					6		4
R3	Jan	9	BATH CITY	2-0	Lane, Berry	15700	3		5		11	10			7		2		9		1	8					6		4
R4		23	Manchester City	1-6	Lane	56190	3		5		11	4	10		7		2		9		1	8					6		

	Pl.	Home					Away					F.	A.	Pts
		W	D	L	F	A	W	D	L	F	A	(Total)		
1 Fulham	42	15	3	3	72	27	9	6	6	39	35	111	62	57
2 Reading	42	19	1	1	65	21	4	8	9	32	46	97	67	55
3 Southend United	42	12	5	4	41	18	9	6	6	36	35	77	53	53
4 Crystal Palace	42	14	7	0	48	12	6	4	11	26	51	74	63	51
5 BRENTFORD	**42**	**11**	**6**	**4**	**40**	**22**	**8**	**4**	**9**	**28**	**30**	**68**	**52**	**48**
6 Luton Town	42	16	1	4	62	25	4	6	11	33	45	95	70	47
7 Exeter City	42	16	3	2	53	16	4	4	13	24	46	77	62	47
8 Brighton & Hove A.	42	12	4	5	42	21	5	8	8	31	37	73	58	46
9 Cardiff City	42	14	2	5	62	29	5	6	10	25	44	87	73	46
10 Norwich City	42	12	7	2	51	22	5	5	11	25	45	76	67	46
11 Watford	42	14	4	3	49	27	5	4	12	32	52	81	79	46
12 Coventry City	42	17	2	2	74	28	1	6	14	34	69	108	97	44
13 Queen's Park Rgs.	42	11	6	4	50	30	4	6	11	29	43	79	73	42
14 Northampton Town	42	12	3	6	48	26	4	4	13	21	43	69	69	39
15 Bournemouth	42	8	8	5	42	32	5	4	12	28	46	70	78	38
16 Clapton Orient	42	7	8	6	41	35	5	3	13	36	55	77	90	35
17 Swindon Town	42	12	2	7	47	31	2	4	15	23	53	70	84	34
18 Bristol Rovers	42	11	6	4	46	30	2	2	17	19	62	65	92	34
19 Torquay United	42	9	6	6	49	39	3	3	15	23	67	72	106	33
20 Mansfield Town	42	11	5	5	54	45	0	5	16	21	63	75	108	32
21 Gillingham	42	8	6	7	26	26	2	2	17	14	56	40	82	28
22 Thames	42	6	7	8	35	35	1	2	18	18	74	53	109	23

1932/33

Champions of Division Three (South): Promoted

No	Month	Day	Opponent	Score	Scorers	Att	Baker TW	French JP	Addmson TK	Burns JC	Bain J	Watson HL	Foster J	Robson GC	Holliday JW	Scott WR	Crompton A	McKenzie D	Allen RSL	Stevenson A	Berry WG	Muttitt E	Hopkins IJ	Hodge W	James J	Ware EGA	Walsh CH	Stepnens HJ	Wheeler AJ
1	Aug	27	Queen's Park Rangers	3-2	Holliday 2, Crompton	24381	1	2	3	4	5	6	7	8	9	10	11												
2		29	Coventry City	3-2	Foster, Allen 2	18909	1	2	3		5	6	7	8		10	11	4	9										
3	Sep	3	TORQUAY UNITED	3-1	Scott, Holliday, Foster	12567	1	2	3	4	5	6	7	8	9	10	11												
4		8	COVENTRY CITY	2-1	Holliday 2	8377	1		3	4	5	6	7	8	9	10	11			2									
5		10	Exeter City	2-1	Holliday 2	8184	1	2	3	4	5	6	7	8	9	10	11												
6		17	LUTON TOWN	1-0	Robson	15409	1	2	3	4	5	6	7	8	9	10	11												
7		24	Newport County	6-1	Holliday 3, Scott 2, Robson	7343	1		3	6	5	4	7	8	9	10	11			2									
8	Oct	1	BOURNEMOUTH	1-1	Crompton	12963	1		3	6	5	4	7	8	9	10	11			2									
9		8	Swindon Town	0-0		6659	1		3	6	5	4	7	8	9	10	11			2									
10		15	CLAPTON ORIENT	4-2	Holliday 3, Robson	14440	1		3	6	5	4	7	8	9	10				2	11								
11		22	Southend United	1-0	Crompton	9453	1		3	6	5	4	7	8	9	10	11			2									
12		29	CRYSTAL PALACE	2-0	Robson, Holliday	17827	1		3	6	5	4	7	8	9	10				2		11							
13	Nov	5	Gillingham	3-1	Holliday 3	12880	1		3	6	5	4	7	8	9	10				2		11							
14		12	WATFORD	2-1	Robson, Scott	14661	1		3	6	5	4		8	9	10				2		11	7						
15		19	Cardiff City	1-2	Scott	5274	1		3	6	5	4		8	9	10				2		11	7						
16	Dec	3	Norwich City	0-3		14180	1		3	6	5	4	7	8	9	10	11			2									
17		17	Bristol Rovers	4-2	Burns, Scott 2, Allen	15355	1			6	5	4	7		9	10	11		8	2				3					
18		24	ALDERSHOT TOWN	2-0	Crompton 2	11972	1			6	5	4	7	8		10	11		9	2				3					
19		26	Northampton Town	0-1		14210	1			6		4	7	8		10	11		9	2				3	5				
20		27	NORTHAMPTON T	1-0	Scott	18747	1			6		4	7		9	10	11		8	2				3	5				
21		31	QUEEN'S PARK RANGERS	2-0	Hall (og), Crompton	14981	1			6		4	7	8		10	11		9	2				3	5				
22	Jan	7	Torquay United	1-1	Holliday	4882	1					4	7	8	9	10	11			2				3	5	6			
23		21	EXETER CITY	0-2		10769	1						7	8		10	11	4	9	2				3	5	6			
24	Feb	1	Luton Town	5-5	Holliday 5 (1p)	3044	1			6	5				9	10	11			2			7	3		4	8		
25		4	NEWPORT COUNTY	6-0	Hopkins, Holliday 2, Walsh, Scott	10060	1			6	5				9	10	11			2			7	3		4	8		
26		11	Bournemouth	1-1	Crompton	6853	1			6	5				9	10	11			2			7	3		4	8		
27		18	SWINDON TOWN	1-0	Walsh	11559	1				5	6			9	10	11			2			7	3		4	8		
28		25	Clapton Orient	5-1	Scott, Crompton, Holliday 2, Hopkins	7814	1			6	5				9	10	11			2			7	3		4	8		
29	Mar	4	SOUTHEND UNITED	3-1	Holliday 2, Scott	14288	1			6	5				9	10	11			2			7	3		4	8		
30		11	Crystal Palace	1-2	Scott	20261	1			6	5				9	10	11			2			7	3		4	8		
31		18	GILLINGHAM	1-2	Robson	11445	1		3	6	5			8	9	10	11			2			7			4			
32		25	Watford	1-1	Holliday	10057	1		3		5	4			9	10	11						7	2		6	8		
33	Apr	1	CARDIFF CITY	7-3	Muttitt, Holliday 4, Crompton 2	10831	1		3	6	5	4			9	8	11					10	7	2					
34		8	Reading	3-1	Scott, Holliday, Crompton	16089	1		3	6	5	4			9	8	11					10	7	2					
35		14	Bristol City	2-1	Muttitt, Scott	19326	1		3	6	5	4			9	8	11					10	7	2					
36		15	NORWICH CITY	2-2	Stephens, Hopkins	20693	1		3	6	5	4				8						10	7	2			9	11	
37		17	BRISTOL CITY	2-1	Hopkins, Scott	15212	1		3	6	5	4				8			9			10	7	2				11	
38		22	Brighton & Hove Albion	2-1	Holliday, Hopkins	8659	1		3	6	5	4		8	9							10	7	2				11	
39		26	BRIGHTON & HOVE ALB	2-1	Muttitt, Holliday	12638	1		3	6	5	4			9	8						10	7	2				11	
40		29	BRISTOL ROVERS	0-0		10355	1		3	6	5	4			9	8	11					10	7	2					
41	May	3	READING	1-1	Walsh	9511	1			6	5	4		8		10				2		11	7	3			9		
42		6	Aldershot Town	1-1	Wheeler	5145	1		3	6	5	4			9	8						11	7	2					10
						Apps	42	5	27	37	37	34	21	24	34	41	31	2	8	27	1	14	21	25	5	11	10	4	1
						Goals				1			2	6	37	15	11		3			3	6				3	1	1

One own goal

F.A. Cup

Rd	Month	Day	Opponent	Score	Scorers	Att	Baker TW	French JP	Addmson TK	Burns JC	Bain J	Watson HL	Foster J	Robson GC	Holliday JW	Scott WR	Crompton A	McKenzie D	Allen RSL	Stevenson A	Berry WG	Muttitt E	Hopkins IJ	Hodge W	James J	Ware EGA	Walsh CH	Stepnens HJ	Wheeler AJ
R1	Nov	26	Reading	2-3	Scott, Holliday	22809	1		3	6	5		7	8	9	10	11			2						4			

	Pl.	Home W	D	L	F	A	Away W	D	L	F	A	F. (Total)	A. (Total)	Pts
1 BRENTFORD	**42**	**15**	**4**	**2**	**45**	**19**	**11**	**6**	**4**	**45**	**30**	**90**	**49**	**62**
2 Exeter City	42	17	2	2	57	13	7	8	6	31	35	88	48	58
3 Norwich City	42	16	3	2	49	17	6	10	5	39	38	88	55	57
4 Reading	42	14	5	2	68	30	5	8	8	35	41	103	71	51
5 Crystal Palace	42	14	4	3	51	21	5	4	12	27	43	78	64	46
6 Coventry City	42	16	1	4	75	24	3	5	13	31	53	106	77	44
7 Gillingham	42	14	4	3	54	24	4	4	13	18	37	72	61	44
8 Northampton Town	42	16	5	0	54	11	2	3	16	22	55	76	66	44
9 Bristol Rovers	42	13	5	3	38	22	2	9	10	23	34	61	56	44
10 Torquay United	42	12	7	2	51	26	4	5	12	21	41	72	67	44
11 Watford	42	11	8	2	37	22	5	4	12	29	41	66	63	44
12 Brighton & Hove A.	42	13	3	5	42	20	4	5	12	24	45	66	65	42
13 Southend United	42	11	5	5	39	27	4	6	11	26	55	65	82	41
14 Luton Town	42	12	8	1	60	32	1	5	15	18	46	78	78	39
15 Bristol City	42	11	5	5	59	37	1	8	12	24	53	83	90	37
16 Queen's Park Rgs.	42	9	8	4	48	32	4	3	14	24	55	72	87	37
17 Aldershot	42	11	6	4	37	21	2	4	15	24	51	61	72	36
18 Bournemouth	42	10	7	4	44	27	2	5	14	16	54	60	81	36
19 Cardiff City	42	12	4	5	48	30	0	3	18	21	69	69	99	31
20 Clapton Orient	42	7	8	6	39	35	1	5	15	20	58	59	93	29
21 Newport County	42	9	4	8	42	42	2	3	16	19	63	61	105	29
22 Swindon Town	42	7	9	5	36	29	2	2	17	24	76	60	105	29

1932-33

Back: Stevenson, Scott, Wheeler, Robson, Baker, Holliday, Pope, Adamson, Ware
2nd Row: Kane (Trainer), C.Smith, French, Hodge, James, D.L.Smith, McKenzie, Allen, Fulton, Lawson, Cartmell (Asst.Trainer), Curtiss (Sec./Manager)
3rd Row: C.L.Simon (Dir.), Adams (Dir.), F.A.Davis (Vice.Chair.), Bain, L.P.Simon (Chairman), Watson, Barton (Dir.), H.F. Davis, (Dir.), Dodge (Dir.) Front: Foster, Berry, Stephens, Crompton.

1933/34

Back: (Players) James, Bateman, Mathieson, Poyser, Watson, Hopkins
Front: Robson, Holliday, Scott, Fletcher, McKenzie

1933/34

4th in Division Two

							Baker TW	Astley J	Hodge W	Watson HL	Bain J	Smith WS	Hopkins IJ	Scott WR	Holliday JW	Muttitt E	Fletcher CA	Burns JC	McClure JH	Clough JH	Robson GC	McKenzie D	Adamson TK	James J	Stevenson A	Smith C	Bateman A	Allen RSL
1	Aug	26	Nottingham Forest	1-1	Hopkins	12702	1	2	3	4	5	6	7	8	9	10	11											
2		31	BRADFORD PARK AVE.	2-0	Holliday 2	13667	1	2	3	4	5		7	8	9	10	11	6										
3	Sep	2	WEST HAM UNITED	4-1	Holliday 2, Hopkins 2	19918	1	2	3	4	5		7	8	9	10	11	6										
4		6	Bradford Park Avenue	2-5	Hopkins, Muttitt	11982	1	2	3	4	5		7	8	9	10	11		6									
5		9	Plymouth Argyle	1-1	Watson	20945	1	2	3	4	5		7	8	9	10	11	6										
6		16	MANCHESTER UNITED	3-4	Fletcher, Holliday, Muttitt	17180	1	2	3	4	5		7	8	9	10	11	6										
7		23	Bolton Wanderers	2-3	Fletcher, Hopkins	9894		2	3	4	5		7	10	9		11	6		1	8							
8		30	HULL CITY	2-2	Fletcher, Holliday	14570		2	3		5		7	10	9		11	6		1	8	4						
9	Oct	7	BURNLEY	5-2	Hopkins 2, Holliday 2, Muttitt	14797	1	2		4			7	8	9	10	11	6					3	5				
10		14	Oldham Athletic	4-1	James, Hopkins 2, Holliday	9831	1	2		4			7	8	9	10	11	6					3	5				
11		21	Fulham	1-1	Holliday	35421	1	2		4			7	8	9	10	11	6					3	5				
12		28	SOUTHAMPTON	2-0	Hopkins 2	15611	1	2		4			7	8	9	10	11	6					3	5				
13	Nov	4	Blackpool	1-3	Muttitt	14229	1	2		4			7	8	9	10	11	6					3	5				
14		11	BRADFORD CITY	2-1	Holiday, Muttitt	12932	1			4			7	8	9	10	11	6					3	5	2			
15		18	Port Vale	0-1		11349	1	3		4			7	8	9	10	11	6						5	2			
16		25	NOTTS COUNTY	2-2	Holliday, Scott	12110	1	3		4			7	8	9	10	11	6						5	2			
17	Dec	2	Swansea Town	3-2	Fletcher 2, Muttitt	4269	1	2		4			7	8	9	10	11					6	3	5				
18		9	MILLWALL	3-0	Scott 2, Holliday	12017	1	2	3	4			7	8	9	10	11	6						5				
19		16	Lincoln City	2-0	Holliday 2	6080	1	2	3	4			7	8	9	10	11	6						5				
20		23	BURY	2-3	Muttitt, Fletcher	12761	1		2	4			7	8	9	10	11	6					3	5				
21		25	PRESTON NORTH END	3-2	Hopkins 2, Fletcher	20662	1	2	3	4			7	8	9	10	11	6						5				
22		26	Preston North End	2-3	Scott 2	24451	1	2	3	4			7	8	9	10	11	6						5				
23		30	NOTTM. FOREST	2-1	Hopkins, Scott	12795	1	2	3	4			7	8	9	10	11	6						5				
24	Jan	6	West Ham United	2-3	Muttitt, Holliday	24108	1	2	3				7	8	9	10	11					6		5		4		
25		20	PLYMOUTH ARGYLE	3-0	Scott, Fletcher, Holliday	17566		2	3				7	8	9	10	11	6		1		4		5				
26		27	Manchester United	3-1	Muttitt 2, Fletcher	16891		2					7	8	9	10	11	6		1		4		5			3	
27	Feb	3	BOLTON WANDERERS	3-1	Holliday 2, Scott	16037		2		4			7	8	9	10	11			1		6		5			3	
28		10	Hull City	1-0	Hopkins	10566		2		4			7	8	9	10	11	6		1				5			3	
29		17	Burnley	1-3	Holliday	11666		2		4			7	8	9	10	11	6		1				5			3	
30		24	OLDHAM ATHLETIC	2-1	Scott, Muttitt	15927		2		4			7	8	9	10	11			1		6		5			3	
31	Mar	3	FULHAM	1-2	Holliday	25184		2					7	8	9	10	11	6		1		4		5			3	
32		10	Southampton	0-0		10349		2					7	8	9	10	11	6		1		4		5			3	
33		17	BLACKPOOL	1-0	Hopkins	16461		2					7	10	9		11	6		1	8	4		5			3	
34		24	Bradford City	1-2	Hopkins	12394		2					7		9	10	11	6		1	8	4		5			3	
35		30	Grimsby Town	2-2	Hopkins, Holliday	23233		2		4			7	8	9	10	11			1		6		5			3	
36		31	PORT VALE	2-0	Holliday, Scott	19758		2		4			7	8	9	10	11	6		1				5			3	
37	Apr	2	GRIMSBY TOWN	1-2	Holliday	26934		2		4			7	8	9	10	11	6		1				5			3	
38		7	Notts County	2-1	Allen, Hopkins	11657		2		4			7	8		10	11	6		1				5			3	9
39		14	SWANSEA TOWN	2-0	Hopkins, Muttitt	14848		2		4			7	8	9	10	11	6		1				5			3	
40		21	Millwall	0-2		21671		2		4			7	8	9	10	11	6		1				5			3	
41		28	LINCOLN CITY	5-0	Scott, Holliday 3, Hopkins	12184		2		4			7	8	9	10	11	6		1				5			3	
42	May	5	Bury	2-1	Fletcher, Scott	9461		2		4			7	8	9	10	11	6		1				5			3	
						Apps	22	40	16	34	8	1	42	41	41		42	35	1	20	4	12	8	34	3	1	17	1
						Goals				1			21	12	27	12	10							1				1

F.A. Cup

							Baker TW	Astley J	Hodge W	Watson HL	Bain J	Smith WS	Hopkins IJ	Scott WR	Holliday JW	Muttitt E	Fletcher CA	Burns JC	McClure JH	Clough JH	Robson GC	McKenzie D	Adamson TK	James J	Stevenson A	Smith C	Bateman A	Allen RSL
R3	Jan	13	Hull City	0-1		14726		2	3				7	8	9	10	11	6		1		4		5				

	Pl.	Home W	D	L	F	A	Away W	D	L	F	A	F. (Total)	A. (Total)	Pts
1 Grimsby Town	42	15	3	3	62	28	12	2	7	41	31	103	59	59
2 Preston North End	42	15	3	3	47	20	8	3	10	24	32	71	52	52
3 Bolton Wanderers	42	14	2	5	45	22	7	7	7	34	33	79	55	51
4 BRENTFORD	**42**	**15**	**2**	**4**	**52**	**24**	**7**	**5**	**9**	**33**	**36**	**85**	**60**	**51**
5 Bradford Park Ave.	42	16	2	3	63	27	7	1	13	23	40	86	67	49
6 Bradford City	42	14	4	3	46	25	6	2	13	27	42	73	67	46
7 West Ham United	42	13	3	5	51	28	4	8	9	27	42	78	70	45
8 Port Vale	42	14	4	3	39	14	5	3	13	21	41	60	55	45
9 Oldham Athletic	42	12	5	4	48	28	5	5	11	24	32	72	60	44
10 Plymouth Argyle	42	12	7	2	43	20	3	6	12	26	50	69	70	43
11 Blackpool	42	10	8	3	39	27	5	5	11	23	37	62	64	43
12 Bury	42	12	4	5	43	31	5	5	11	27	42	70	73	43
13 Burnley	42	14	2	5	40	29	4	4	13	20	43	60	72	42
14 Southampton	42	15	2	4	40	21	0	6	15	14	37	54	58	38
15 Hull City	42	11	4	6	33	20	2	8	11	19	48	52	68	38
16 Fulham	42	13	3	5	29	17	2	4	15	19	50	48	67	37
17 Nottingham Forest	42	11	4	6	50	27	2	5	14	23	47	73	74	35
18 Notts County	42	9	7	5	32	22	3	4	14	21	40	53	62	35
19 Swansea Town	42	10	9	2	36	19	0	6	15	15	41	51	60	35
20 Manchester United	42	9	3	9	29	33	5	3	13	30	52	59	85	34
21 Millwall	42	8	8	5	21	17	3	3	15	18	51	39	68	33
22 Lincoln City	42	7	7	7	31	23	2	1	18	13	52	44	75	26

1934/35

Champions of Division Two: Promoted

						Mathieson JA	Bateman A	Poyser GH	Watson HL	James J	Burns JC	Hopkins JJ	Scott WR	Holliday JW	Muttitt E	Fletcher CA	Scott AT	Metcalf WF	McKenzie D	Robson GC	Raven J	Astley J
1	Aug 25	NORWICH CITY	2-1	Holliday, Hopkins	21565	1	2	3	4	5	6	7	8	9	10	11						
2	27	Fulham	2-2	Fletcher, Holliday	26656	1	2	3	4	5	6	7	8	9	10	11						
3	Sep 1	Newcastle United	5-2	Muttitt 3, Holliday, Hopkins	23714	1	2	3	4	5	6	7	8	9	10	11						
4	5	FULHAM	1-0	Muttitt	23678	1	2	3	4	5	6	7	8	9	10	11						
5	8	WEST HAM UNITED	4-1	Holliday 3, Burns	20818	1	2	3	4	5	6	7	8	9	10	11						
6	15	Blackpool	2-2	Muttitt, Scott	24223	1	2	3	4	5	6	7	8	9	10	11						
7	22	BURY	2-1	Muttitt 2	13729	1	2	3	4		6	7	8	9	10	11	5					
8	29	Hull City	1-2	Fletcher	7764	1	2		4	5	6	7	8	9	10	11		3				
9	Oct 6	NOTTM. FOREST	1-1	James	16098	1	2	3	4	5	6	7	8	9	10	11						
10	13	Bradford City	0-3		13132	1	2	3	4	5	6	7	8	9	10	11						
11	20	NOTTS COUNTY	4-1	Burns 3, Mills (og)	15313	1	2	3	4	5	10	7	8	9		11			6			
12	27	Southampton	0-1		10268	1	2	3		5	6	7	8	9	10	11			4			
13	Nov 3	BOLTON WANDERERS	1-0	Holliday	22322	1	2	3		5	6	7	10	9		11			4	8		
14	10	Oldham Athletic	3-1	Holliday, Fletcher, Scott	8391	1	2	3		5	6	7	10	9		11			4	8		
15	17	BURNLEY	6-1	Holliday 3, Robson, Hopkins, Scott	15459	1	2	3		5	6	7	10	9		11			4	8		
16	24	Swansea Town	4-2	Scott, Holliday 2, Fletcher	10547	1	2	3		5	6	7	10	9		11			4	8		
17	Dec 1	MANCHESTER UNITED	3-1	Hopkins, Fletcher, Holliday	21744	1	2	3		5	6	7	10	9		11			4	8		
18	8	Port Vale	2-2	Hopkins, Robson	8054	1	2	3		5	6	7	10	9		11			4	8		
19	15	BARNSLEY	8-1	Scott 5, Robson 2, Holliday	11843	1	2	3		5	6	7	10	9		11			4	8		
20	22	Sheffield United	2-1	Fletcher, Hopkins	11115	1	2	3		5	6	7	10	9		11			4	8		
21	25	PLYMOUTH ARGYLE	0-0		23786	1	2	3		5	6	7	10	9		11			4	8		
22	26	Plymouth Argyle	1-1	Scott	32509	1	2	3	6	5		7	10	9		11			4	8		
23	29	Norwich City	1-2	Hopkins	13371	1	2	3		5	6	7	10	9		11			4	8		
24	Jan 5	NEWCASTLE UNITED	3-0	Hopkins, Fletcher 2	26079	1	2	3		5	6	7	10	9		11			4	8		
25	19	West Ham United	0-2		33788	1	2	3	6	5		7	10	9		11			4	8		
26	26	BLACKPOOL	2-1	Cardwell (og), Robson	13087	1	2	3			6	7	10	9		11	5		4	8		
27	Feb 2	Bury	1-4	Hopkins	13687	1	2	3		5	6	7	10	9		11			4	8		
28	9	HULL CITY	2-1	Hopkins, Holliday	14109	1	2	3	4	5	6	7	8	9	10	11						
29	23	BRADFORD CITY	2-0	Fletcher, Hopkins	15824	1	2	3	6	5		7	8	9	10	11			4			
30	28	Nottingham Forest	0-0		8137	1	2	3	6	5		7	8	9	10	11					4	
31	Mar 2	Notts County	1-0	Holliday	10252	1	2	3	6	5		7	10	9		11			4	8		
32	9	SOUTHAMPTON	3-2	Hopkins, Scott 2	13111	1	2	3	6	5		7	10	9		11			4	8		
33	23	OLDHAM ATHLETIC	2-1	Holliday 2	13867	1		3	6	5		7	10	9		11			4	8		2
34	30	Burnley	3-0	Robson, Scott, Hopkins	11206	1	2	3	6	5		7	10	9		11			4	8		
35	Apr 6	SWANSEA TOWN	1-0	Holliday	17212	1	2	3	6	5		7	10	9		11			4	8		
36	13	Manchester United	0-0		32969	1	2	3	6	5		7	10	9		11			4	8		
37	19	BRADFORD PARK AVE.	1-0	Holliday	20447	1	2	3	6	5		7	10	9		11			4	8		
38	20	PORT VALE	8-0	Holiday 3, Robson 3, Burns, Hopkins	18194	1	2	3		5	6	7	10	9		11			4	8		
39	22	Bradford Park Avenue	3-2	Bateman, Hopkins 2	12729	1	2	3	6	5		7	10	9		11			4	8		
40	27	Barnsley	3-3	Scott 3	7021	1	2	3	5		6	7	10	9		11			4	8		
41	May 1	Bolton Wanderers	0-2		46554	1	2	3	6	5		7	10	9		11			4	8		
42	4	SHEFFIELD UNITED	3-1	Fletcher, Holliday, Scott	21017	1	2	3	6	5		7	10	9		11			4	8		
					Apps	42	41	41	27	39	28	42	42	42	14	42	2	1	30	27	1	1
					Goals		1			1	5	16	17	25	7	10				9		

Two own goals

F.A. Cup

						Mathieson JA	Bateman A	Poyser GH	Watson HL	James J	Burns JC	Hopkins JJ	Scott WR	Holliday JW	Muttitt E	Fletcher CA	Scott AT	Metcalf WF	McKenzie D	Robson GC	Raven J	Astley J
R3	Jan 12	PLYMOUTH ARGYLE	0-1		24500	1	2	3		5	6	7	10	9		11			4	8		

	Pl.	Home W	D	L	F	A	Away W	D	L	F	A	F. (Total)	A.	Pts
1 BRENTFORD	**42**	**19**	**2**	**0**	**59**	**14**	**7**	**7**	**7**	**34**	**34**	**93**	**48**	**61**
2 Bolton Wanderers	42	17	1	3	63	15	9	3	9	33	33	96	48	56
3 West Ham United	42	18	1	2	46	17	8	3	10	34	46	80	63	56
4 Blackpool	42	16	4	1	46	18	5	7	9	33	39	79	57	53
5 Manchester United	42	16	2	3	50	21	7	2	12	26	34	76	55	50
6 Newcastle United	42	14	2	5	55	25	8	2	11	34	43	89	68	48
7 Fulham	42	15	3	3	62	26	2	9	10	14	30	76	56	46
8 Plymouth Argyle	42	13	3	5	48	26	6	5	10	27	38	75	64	46
9 Nottingham Forest	42	12	5	4	46	23	5	3	13	30	47	76	70	42
10 Bury	42	14	1	6	38	26	5	3	13	24	47	62	73	42
11 Sheffield United	42	11	4	6	51	30	5	5	11	28	40	79	70	41
12 Burnley	42	11	2	8	43	32	5	7	9	20	41	63	73	41
13 Hull City	42	9	6	6	32	22	7	2	12	31	52	63	74	40
14 Norwich City	42	11	6	4	51	23	3	5	13	20	38	71	61	39
15 Bradford Park Ave.	42	7	8	6	32	28	4	8	9	23	35	55	63	38
16 Barnsley	42	8	10	3	32	22	5	2	14	28	61	60	83	38
17 Swansea Town	42	13	5	3	41	22	1	3	17	15	45	56	67	36
18 Port Vale	42	10	7	4	42	28	1	5	15	13	46	55	74	34
19 Southampton	42	9	8	4	28	19	2	4	15	18	56	46	75	34
20 Bradford City	42	10	7	4	34	20	2	1	18	16	48	50	68	32
21 Oldham Athletic	42	10	3	8	44	40	0	3	18	12	55	56	95	26
22 Notts County	42	8	3	10	29	33	1	4	16	17	64	46	97	25

1934/35
Back: Kane (Trainer), McKenzie, James, Mathieson, Poyser, Burns, Watson
Front: Hopkins, Robson, Holliday, Bateman, Scott, Fletche

1935/36
Back: Dumbrell, James, Holliday, Wilson, Bateman, Poyser
Middle: F A Davis (Vice Chair.), Brown, Briddon, Metcalf, Mathieson, Nichols, Lynch, C Smith, A Scott, Burns, H F Davis (Dir), Kane (Trainer)
Third Row: Cartmell (Asst.Train.), H.Dodge (Dir), Hopkins, Fenton, Dunn, W Scott, Knott, Curtis (Manager), Muttit, McAloon, McCulloch, Richards
Front: L.Smith, MacKenzie, Murray, Gibbons, Reid, Bamford.

1935/36

5th in Division One

							Ashley J	Bateman A	Brown JJ	Burns JC	Dumbrell G	Dunn WM	Fletcher CA	Holliday JW	Hopkins IJ	James J	Mathieson JA	McCulloch D	McKenzie D	Metcalf WF	Muttitt E	Poyser GH	Reid R	Richards DT	Robson GC	Scott AT	Scott WR	Smith CSF	Watson HL	Wilson JW
1	Aug	31	Bolton Wanderers	2-0	Holliday 2	31949		2					11	9	7	5	1		4			3			8		10		6	
2	Sep	5	BLACKBURN ROVERS	3-1	Fletcher 2, Holliday	25047		2					11	9	7	5	1		4			3			8		10		6	
3		7	HUDDERSFIELD T	1-2	Hopkins	33481		2		6			11	9	7	5	1		4			3			8		10			
4		14	Middlesbrough	0-0		38107		2					11	9	7	5	1		4			3			8		10		6	
5		18	Derby County	1-2	Fletcher	21648		2					11	9	7	5	1		4			3			8		10		6	
6		21	ASTON VILLA	1-2	Holliday	29781		2					11	9	7	5	1		4			3			8		10		6	
7		28	Wolverhampton Wan.	2-3	Holliday, W Scott	28431		2		4			11	9	7	5	1			3					8		10		6	
8	Oct	5	SHEFFIELD WEDNESDAY	2-2	Robson, W Scott	25338		2					11	9	7	5	1		4			3			8		10		6	
9		12	Portsmouth	3-1	Hopkins 2, Holliday	22316		2		6			11	9	7	5	1		4			3			8		10			
10		19	STOKE CITY	0-0		24960		2		6			11	9	7	5	1		4			3			8		10			
11		26	Manchester City	1-2	Hopkins	29868		2		6			11	9	7	5	1		4			3			8		10			
12	Nov	2	ARSENAL	2-1	Burns, Hopkins	26330	2			10			11	9	7	5	1		4			3			8				6	
13		9	Birmingham	1-2	Dunn	28673	2			10		9	11		7	5	1		4			3			8				6	
14		16	SUNDERLAND	1-5	Hopkins	24720	2			4			11	9	7	5	1					3			8		10		6	
15		23	Chelsea	1-2	Robson (p)	56624	2		9	10			11		7	5	1					3			8		4		6	
16		30	LEEDS UNITED	2-2	W Scott, McCulloch	23914	2						11		7	5	1	9	4			3		6	8		10			
17	Dec	7	Grimsby Town	1-6	Fletcher	5276					2		11		7	5	1	9	4					6	8		10		3	
18		14	LIVERPOOL	1-2	Robson	18508	2						11	10	7	5	1	9	4			3		6	8					
19		21	West Bromwich Albion	0-1		14272	2							10	7	5	1	9	4		11	3		6			8			
20		25	PRESTON NORTH END	5-2	Holliday, Muttitt, McCulloch 2, W Scott	21474	2							10	7	5	1	9	4		11	3		6			8			
21		26	Preston North End	4-2	Hopkins 3, McCulloch	22937								10	7	5	1	9	4		11	3		6			8			2
22		28	BOLTON WANDERERS	4-0	McCulloch 3, McKenzie	27156								10	7	5	1	9	4		11	3		6			8			2
23	Jan	1	Blackburn Rovers	0-1		24724							10		7	5	1	9	4		11	3		6			8			2
24		4	Huddersfield Town	2-2	McCulloch, Fletcher	17682							11	10	7	5	1	9	4			3		6			8			2
25		18	MIDDLESBROUGH	1-0	W Scott	27779								10	7	5	1	9	4			3	11	6			8			2
26		25	Aston Villa	2-2	Reid, W Scott	40328								10	7	5	1	9	4			3	11	6			8			2
27	Feb	1	WOLVERHAMPTON W.	5-0	Morris (og), McCulloch 2, W Scott, Holliday	25123								10	7	5	1	9	4			3	11	6			8			2
28		8	Sheffield Wednesday	3-3	Holliday, McCulloch, Hopkins	20757								10	7	5	1	9	4			3	11	6			8			2
29		22	Stoke City	2-2	McCulloch, W Scott	18045								10	7		1	9	4			3	11	6		5	8			2
30		29	BIRMINGHAM	0-1		20523								10	7	5	1	9	4			3	11	6			8			2
31	Mar	7	Leeds United	2-1	Reid, Hopkins	10509		3						10	7	5	1	9	4				11	6			8			2
32		14	MANCHESTER CITY	0-0		28364		3						10	7	5	1	9	4				11	6			8			2
33		21	Sunderland	3-1	Holliday, McCulloch 2	26348		3						10	7	5	1	9	4				11	6			8			2
34		25	PORTSMOUTH	3-1	McCulloch 3	15379		3						10	7	5	1	9	4				11	6			8			2
35		28	CHELSEA	2-1	McCulloch, Hopkins	33486		3						10	7	5	1	9	4				11	6			8			2
36	Apr	4	Arsenal	1-1	Holliday	28303		3				9		10	7	5	1		4				11	6			8			2
37		10	Everton	2-1	McCulloch 2	45477		3						10	7	5	1	9	4				11	6			8			2
38		11	GRIMSBY TOWN	3-0	McCulloch 2, Hopkins	24830		3						10	7	5	1	9	4				11	6			8			2
39		13	EVERTON	4-1	Holliday, Hopkins 2, W Scott	29790		3						10	7	5	1	9					11	6			8		4	2
40		18	Liverpool	0-0		28463		3						10	7	5	1	9	4				11				8	6		2
41		25	WEST BROMWICH ALB.	2-2	W Scott, Reid	24527		3						10	7	5	1	9	4				11	6			8			2
42	May	2	DERBY COUNTY	6-0	McCulloch 4, Holliday, W Scott	20521		3						10	7	5	1	9	4				11	6			8			2
						Apps	8	23	1	9	1	2	20	37	42	41	42	26	38	1	5	28	18	26	18	1	39	1	13	22
						Goals				1		1	5	13	15			26	1		1		4		3		11			

F.A. Cup

							Ashley J	Bateman A	Brown JJ	Burns JC	Dumbrell G	Dunn WM	Fletcher CA	Holliday JW	Hopkins IJ	James J	Mathieson JA	McCulloch D	McKenzie D	Metcalf WF	Muttitt E	Poyser GH	Reid R	Richards DT	Robson GC	Scott AT	Scott WR	Smith CSF	Watson HL	Wilson JW
R3	Jan	11	Leicester City	0-1		29750		3						10	7	5	1	9	4		11			6			8			2

	Pl.	Home W	Home D	Home L	Home F	Home A	Away W	Away D	Away L	Away F	Away A	F. (Total)	A. (Total)	Pts
1 Sunderland	42	17	2	2	71	33	8	4	9	38	41	109	74	56
2 Derby County	42	13	5	3	43	23	5	7	9	18	29	61	52	48
3 Huddersfield Town	42	12	7	2	32	15	6	5	10	27	41	59	56	48
4 Stoke City	42	13	3	5	35	24	7	4	10	22	33	57	57	47
5 BRENTFORD	**42**	**11**	**5**	**5**	**48**	**25**	**6**	**7**	**8**	**33**	**35**	**81**	**60**	**46**
6 Arsenal	42	9	9	3	44	22	6	6	9	34	26	78	48	45
7 Preston North End	42	15	3	3	44	18	3	5	13	23	46	67	64	44
8 Chelsea	42	11	7	3	39	27	4	6	11	26	45	65	72	43
9 Manchester City	42	13	2	6	44	17	4	6	11	24	43	68	60	42
10 Portsmouth	42	14	4	3	39	22	3	4	14	15	45	54	67	42
11 Leeds United	42	11	5	5	41	23	4	6	11	25	41	66	64	41
12 Birmingham	42	10	6	5	38	31	5	5	11	23	32	61	63	41
13 Bolton Wanderers	42	11	4	6	41	27	3	9	9	26	49	67	76	41
14 Middlesbrough	42	12	6	3	56	23	3	4	14	28	47	84	70	40
15 Wolverhampton W.	42	13	7	1	59	28	2	3	16	18	48	77	76	40
16 Everton	42	12	5	4	61	31	1	8	12	28	58	89	89	39
17 Grimsby Town	42	13	4	4	44	20	4	1	16	21	53	65	73	39
18 West Bromwich Alb.	42	12	3	6	54	31	4	3	14	35	57	89	88	38
19 Liverpool	42	11	4	6	43	23	2	8	11	17	41	60	64	38
20 Sheffield Wed.	42	9	8	4	35	23	4	4	13	28	54	63	77	38
21 Aston Villa	42	7	6	8	47	56	6	3	12	34	54	81	110	35
22 Blackburn Rovers	42	10	6	5	32	24	2	3	16	23	72	55	96	33

1936/37

6th in Division One

	Date	Opponent	Score	Scorers	Att	Bateman A	Brown W	Dumbrell G	Dunn WM	Holliday JW	Hopkins IJ	James J	Mathieson JA	McCulloch D	McKenzie D	Metcalf WF	Murray J	Muttitt E	Nicholls JH	Poyser GH	Reid R	Richards DT	Scott AT	Scott WR	Smith CSF	Smith LGF	Wilson JW
1	Aug 29	BOLTON WANDERERS	2-2	McCulloch, Wilson (p)	27524	3				10	7	5	1	9	4							6		8		11	2
2	Sep 3	ARSENAL	2-0	Hopkins, McCulloch	31056	3				10	7	5	1	9	4							6		8		11	2
3	5	Everton	0-3		37524	3				10	7	5	1	9	4							6		8		11	2
4	9	Arsenal	1-1	Wilson (p)	44010	3				10	7	5	1	9	4							6		8		11	2
5	12	HUDDERSFIELD T	1-1	McCulloch	25386	3				10	7	5		9	4				1			6		8		11	2
6	17	CHARLTON ATHLETIC	4-2	L Smith, McCulloch, W Scott, McKenzie (p)	21373	2				10	7	5	1	9	4					3		6		8		11	
7	19	Sunderland	1-4	Hopkins	37407	2				10	7	5	1	9	4					3	11	6		8			
8	26	WOLVERHAMPTON W.	3-2	McCulloch 2, McKenzie (p)	23256	2				10	7	5	1	9	4					3	11	6		8			
9	Oct 3	Derby County	3-2	W Scott 2, McCulloch	24545	2				10	7	5	1	9	4					3	11	6		8			
10	10	MANCHESTER UNITED	4-0	Reid, W Scott 2, McCulloch	28019	2				10	7	5	1	9	4					3	11	6		8			
11	17	Grimsby Town	0-2		11858	2				10		5	1	9	4			8		3	11				6	7	
12	24	LIVERPOOL	5-2	McCulloch 3, Holliday, Reid	25934	2				10	7	5	1	9	4					3	11	6		8			
13	31	Leeds United	1-3	Holliday	21498	2			9	10	7	5	1		4					3	11	6		8			
14	Nov 7	BIRMINGHAM	2-1	McCulloch 2	22905	2				10	7	5	1	9	4					3	11	6		8			
15	14	Middlesbrough	0-3		23064	3				10	7	5	1	9	4						11	6		8			2
16	21	WEST BROMWICH ALB.	2-1	Reid, McCulloch	20575	2				10	7	5	1	9	4					3	11	6		8			
17	Dec 5	PORTSMOUTH	4-0	McCulloch 2, Holliday 2	26371	2				10	7	5	1	9	4					3	11	6		8			
18	12	Chelsea	1-2	Reid	51079	2				10	7	5	1	9	4					3	11	6		8			
19	19	STOKE CITY	2-1	Holliday, Tutin (og)	18167	2				10	7	5	1	9	4					3	11	6		8			
20	25	SHEFFIELD WEDNESDAY	2-1	Reid, W Scott	26560	2				10	7	5	1	9	4					3	11	6		8			
21	26	Bolton Wanderers	2-2	McCulloch. W Scott	36962	2				10	7	5	1	9	4					3	11	6		8			
22	28	Sheffield Wednesday	2-0	W Scott, Hopkins	20374	2				10	7	5	1	9	4					3	11	6		8			
23	Jan 2	EVERTON	2-2	Hopkins, McKenzie (p)	20457	2				10	7	5	1	9	4					3	11	6		8			
24	9	Huddersfield Town	1-1	McCulloch	21753	2				10	7	5	1	9	4					3	11		6	8			
25	23	SUNDERLAND	3-3	W Scott 3	29389	2				10	7	5	1	9	4					3	11	6		8			
26	Feb 6	DERBY COUNTY	6-2	Reid 2, Holliday 2, McCulloch 2	31745	2				10	7	5	1	9	4					3	11	6		8			
27	10	Wolverhampton Wan.	0-4		19373			2		10	7	5	1	9	4					3	11	6		8			
28	13	Manchester United	3-1	W Scott, Reid 2	31942			2		10	7	5		9	4				1	3	11	6		8			
29	27	Liverpool	2-2	Reid (p), McCulloch	25005			2		10	7	5		9	4				1	3	11	6		8			
30	Mar 3	GRIMSBY TOWN	2-3	McCulloch 2	14103			2		10	7	5		9	4				1	3	11	6		8			
31	6	LEEDS UNITED	4-1	Holliday, McCulloch 2, Holley (og)	16588					10	7	5		9	4				1	3	11	6		8			2
32	13	Birmingham	0-4		30510					10	7	5		9	4				1	3	11		6	8			2
33	20	MIDDLESBROUGH	4-1	L Smith, McCulloch 3	23872		6			10	7	5		9	4				1	3				8		11	2
34	26	PRESTON NORTH END	1-1	McCulloch	31069		6			10	7	5	1	9	4					3	11			8			2
35	27	West Bromwich Albion	0-1		29858		6			10	7	5	1	9	4					3	11			8			2
36	29	Preston North End	1-1	W Scott	26782		6				7	5	1	9	4		11	10		3				8			2
37	Apr 3	MANCHESTER CITY	2-6	W Scott, Hopkins	29028		6			10	7	5	1	9	4					3				8		11	2
38	7	Manchester City	1-2	McCulloch	24629		2			6	7	5	1	9	4	3		10						8		11	
39	10	Portsmouth	3-1	Hopkins, McCulloch, Muttitt	19208		2			6	7	5	1	9	4	3		10						8		11	
40	17	CHELSEA	1-0	McKenzie (p)	22042		2			6	7	5	1	9	4	3		10						8		11	
41	24	Stoke City	1-5	McKenzie	18451		2			6	7	5	1	9	4	3		10						8		11	
42	May 1	Charlton Athletic	1-2	W Scott	26195		2			6	7	5	1	9	4	3		10						8		11	
					Apps	26	10	4	1	41	41	42						7	7	31	28	29	2	41	1	14	13
					Goals					8	6			31	5			1			10			15		2	2

Two own goals

F.A. Cup

	Date	Opponent	Score	Scorers	Att	Bateman A	Brown W	Dumbrell G	Dunn WM	Holliday JW	Hopkins IJ	James J	Mathieson JA	McCulloch D	McKenzie D	Metcalf WF	Murray J	Muttitt E	Nicholls JH	Poyser GH	Reid R	Richards DT	Scott AT	Scott WR	Smith CSF	Smith LGF	Wilson JW
R3	Jan 16	HUDDERSFIELD TOWN	5-0	Reid 2 (1p), McCulloch 2, Holliday	33000	2				10	7	5	1	9	4					3	11	6		8			
R4	30	Derby County	0-3		27376	2				10	7	5	1	9	4					3	11	6		8			

		Pl.	Home W	D	L	F	A	Away W	D	L	F	A	F. (Total)	A. (Total)	Pts
1	Manchester City	42	15	5	1	56	22	7	8	6	51	39	107	61	57
2	Charlton Athletic	42	15	5	1	37	13	6	7	8	21	36	58	49	54
3	Arsenal	42	10	10	1	43	20	8	6	7	37	29	80	49	52
4	Derby County	42	13	3	5	58	39	8	4	9	38	51	96	90	49
5	Wolverhampton W.	42	16	2	3	63	24	5	3	13	21	43	84	67	47
6	**BRENTFORD**	**42**	**14**	**5**	**2**	**58**	**32**	**4**	**5**	**12**	**24**	**46**	**82**	**78**	**46**
7	Middlesbrough	42	14	6	1	49	22	5	2	14	25	49	74	71	46
8	Sunderland	42	17	2	2	59	24	2	4	15	30	63	89	87	44
9	Portsmouth	42	13	3	5	41	29	4	7	10	21	37	62	66	44
10	Stoke City	42	12	6	3	52	27	3	6	12	20	30	72	57	42
11	Birmingham	42	9	7	5	36	24	4	8	9	28	36	64	60	41
12	Grimsby Town	42	13	3	5	60	32	4	4	13	26	49	86	81	41
13	Chelsea	42	11	6	4	36	21	3	7	11	16	34	52	55	41
14	Preston North End	42	10	6	5	35	28	4	7	10	21	39	56	67	41
15	Huddersfield Town	42	12	5	4	39	21	0	10	11	23	43	62	64	39
16	West Bromwich Alb.	42	13	3	5	45	32	3	3	15	32	66	77	98	38
17	Everton	42	12	7	2	56	23	2	2	17	25	55	81	78	37
18	Liverpool	42	9	8	4	38	26	3	3	15	24	58	62	84	35
19	Leeds United	42	14	3	4	44	20	1	1	19	16	60	60	80	34
20	Bolton Wanderers	42	6	6	9	22	33	4	8	9	21	33	43	66	34
21	Manchester United	42	8	9	4	29	26	2	3	16	26	52	55	78	32
22	Sheffield Wed.	42	8	5	8	32	29	1	7	13	21	40	53	69	30

1936/37
Photograph taken at Grim's Dyke - Unnamed.

Mc Kenzie. James. Mathieson. Poyser. Dumbrell.

Hopkins. Scott. Mc Culloch. Holliday. Reid. Brown.

1937-38

1937/38

6th in Division One

							Bateman A	Brown W	Crozier J	Eastham GR	Edelston M	Holliday JW	Hopkins IJ	James J	Mathieson JA	McAloon GP	McCulloch D	McKenzie D	Poyser GH	Reid R	Scott AT	Scott WR	Smith LGF	Sneddon WC	Wilson JW
1	Aug	28	Bolton Wanderers	0-2		31572		2		10			7	5	1		9	4	3	11		8		6	
2	Sep	1	PRESTON NORTH END	2-1	W Scott, Reid	21228		2		10			7	5	1		9	4	3	11		8		6	
3		4	HUDDERSFIELD T	2-0	McCulloch, McKenzie	26762		2		10			7	5	1		9	4	3	11		8		6	
4		6	Preston North End	1-1	McCulloch	21746		2		10			7	5	1		9	4	3	11		8		6	
5		11	Everton	0-3		36038		2		10			7	5	1		9	4	3	11		8		6	
6		16	BLACKPOOL	2-4	W Scott, McCulloch	14816		2		10			7	5	1		9	4	3	11		8		6	
7		18	WOLVERHAMPTON W.	2-1	McCulloch 2	28945	3	2	1			10	7	5			9	4		11		8		6	
8		20	Blackpool	1-1	McCulloch	20732	3	2	1	8		10	7	5			9	4		11				6	
9		25	Leicester City	1-0	McCulloch	23416		3	1	8			7	5			9	4		11		10		6	2
10	Oct	2	SUNDERLAND	4-0	W Scott, McCulloch 2, Reid	35584		3	1	8			7	5			9	4		11		10		6	2
11		9	Derby County	3-1	McCulloch, Reid 2	19621		3	1	8			7	5			9	4		11		10		6	2
12		16	CHARLTON ATHLETIC	5-2	McCulloch 4, Reid	34861		3	1	8			7	5			9	4		11		10		6	2
13		23	Chelsea	1-2	Smith	56810		3	1	8		10		5			9	4		11			7	6	2
14		30	PORTSMOUTH	2-0	Holliday, W Scott	24138	3	5	1	8		9						4		11		10	7	6	2
15	Nov	6	Liverpool	4-3	Reid 3, McCulloch	30492	3	5	1	8							9	4		11		10	7	6	2
16		13	MIDDLESBROUGH	3-3	W Scott 2, Reid	25682	3	5	1	8							9	4		11		10	7	6	2
17		20	Grimsby Town	1-0	McCulloch	13206	3	5	1	8							9	4		11		10	7	6	2
18		27	WEST BROMWICH ALB.	0-2		16702	3	5	1	8							9	4		11		10	7	6	2
19	Dec	4	Stoke City	0-3		11970	3	2	1	8							9	4		11	5	10	7	6	
20		11	LEEDS UNITED	1-1	McCulloch	18184	3	2	1	8			7	5			9	4				10	11	6	
21		18	Birmingham	0-0		22531	3	2	1	8			7	5			9	4		11		10		6	
22		25	Manchester City	2-0	McKenzie (p), Reid	37478	3	2	1	8			7	5			9	4		11		10		6	
23		27	MANCHESTER CITY	2-1	W Scott, Reid	33887	3	2	1	8			7	5			9	4		11		10		6	
24	Jan	1	BOLTON WANDERERS	1-1	Reid	23210	3	2	1	8			7	5			9	4		11		10		6	
25		15	Huddersfield Town	3-0	Reid, Holliday, McCulloch	11969	3	4	1			10	7	5			9			11		8		6	2
26		26	EVERTON	3-0	McCulloch, W Scott, Hopkins	16917	3	4	1	8			7	5			9			11		10		6	2
27		29	Wolverhampton Wan.	1-2	McCulloch	35989	3	4	1	8			7	5			9			11		10		6	2
28	Feb	5	LEICESTER CITY	1-1	McCulloch	21309	3	4	1	8				5			9			11		10	7	6	2
29		16	Sunderland	0-1		18970	3	6	1	8		10		5			9	4		11			7		2
30		19	DERBY COUNTY	2-3	McKenzie 2 (2p)	20561	3	2	1			10		5			9	4		11		8	7	6	
31		26	Charlton Athletic	0-1		35572	3	2	1	8				5			9	4		11		10	7	6	
32	Mar	9	CHELSEA	1-1	Hopkins	20401	2	4	1	8			7	5			9	6	3	11			10		
33		12	Portsmouth	1-4	Reid	23366	2	5	1	8		6	7				9	4	3	11			10		
34		19	LIVERPOOL	1-3	Hopkins	17754	3	2		8			7	5	1		9	4		11		10		6	
35		26	Middlesbrough	1-0	Hopkins	29339	2	4	1	10			7	5		8	9		3	11				6	
36	Apr	2	GRIMSBY TOWN	6-1	Edelston, McCulloch 2, Reid 2, McAloon	17994	2	4	1		10		7	5		8	9		3	11				6	
37		9	West Bromwich Albion	3-4	McCulloch 2, McAloon	23602	2	4	1	10			7	5		8	9		3				11	6	
38		15	Arsenal	2-0	McAloon, Hopkins	51299	2	4	1	10			7	5		8	9		3	11				6	
39		16	STOKE CITY	0-0		21885	2		1	10	8		7	5			9	4	3	11				6	
40		18	ARSENAL	3-0	McCulloch, McAloon, Reid	34601	2	4	1	10			7	5		8	9		3	11				6	
41		23	Leeds United	0-4		17840	2	4	1	10			7	5		8	9		3	11				6	
42		30	BIRMINGHAM	1-2	McAloon	14609	2	4	1	10			7	5		8	9		3	11				6	
						Apps	31	41	35	38	2	8	31	35	7	7	41	31	16	40	1	29	15	39	15
						Goals	2				1		5				26	4		17		8	1		

F.A. Cup

							Bateman A	Brown W	Crozier J	Eastham GR	Edelston M	Holliday JW	Hopkins IJ	James J	Mathieson JA	McAloon GP	McCulloch D	McKenzie D	Poyser GH	Reid R	Scott AT	Scott WR	Smith LGF	Sneddon WC	Wilson JW
R3	Jan	8	FULHAM	3-1	Hindson (og), McCulloch 2	29867	3	4	1			10	7	5			9			11		8		6	2
R4	Jan	22	PORTSMOUTH	2-1	Wilson (p), McCulloch	36718	3	4	1			10	7	5			9			11		8		6	2
R5	Feb	12	MANCHESTER UNITED	2-0	Holliday, Reid	27747	3	2	1	8		9		5				4		11		10	7	6	
R6	Mar	5	PRESTON NORTH END	0-3		39626	3	2	1			10	7	5			9	4		11		8		6	

		Pl.	Home					Away					F.	A.	Pts
			W	D	L	F	A	W	D	L	F	A	(Total)		
1	Arsenal	42	15	4	2	52	16	6	6	9	25	28	77	44	52
2	Wolverhampton W.	42	11	8	2	47	21	9	3	9	25	28	72	49	51
3	Preston North End	42	9	9	3	34	21	7	8	6	30	23	64	44	49
4	Charlton Athletic	42	14	5	2	43	14	2	9	10	22	37	65	51	46
5	Middlesbrough	42	12	4	5	40	26	7	4	10	32	39	72	65	46
6	**BRENTFORD**	**42**	**10**	**6**	**5**	**44**	**27**	**8**	**3**	**10**	**25**	**32**	**69**	**59**	**45**
7	Bolton Wanderers	42	11	6	4	38	22	4	9	8	26	38	64	60	45
8	Sunderland	42	12	6	3	32	18	2	10	9	23	39	55	57	44
9	Leeds United	42	11	6	4	38	26	3	9	9	26	43	64	69	43
10	Chelsea	42	11	6	4	40	22	3	7	11	25	43	65	65	41
11	Liverpool	42	9	5	7	40	30	6	6	9	25	41	65	71	41
12	Blackpool	42	10	5	6	33	26	6	3	12	28	40	61	66	40
13	Derby County	42	10	5	6	42	36	5	5	11	24	51	66	87	40
14	Everton	42	11	5	5	54	34	5	2	14	25	41	79	75	39
15	Huddersfield Town	42	11	3	7	29	24	6	2	13	26	44	55	68	39
16	Leicester City	42	9	6	6	31	26	5	5	11	23	49	54	75	39
17	Stoke City	42	10	7	4	42	21	3	5	13	16	38	58	59	38
18	Birmingham	42	7	11	3	34	28	3	7	11	24	34	58	62	38
19	Portsmouth	42	11	6	4	41	22	2	6	13	21	46	62	68	38
20	Grimsby Town	42	11	5	5	29	23	2	7	12	22	45	51	68	38
21	Manchester City	42	12	2	7	49	33	2	6	13	31	44	80	77	36
22	West Bromwich Alb.	42	10	5	6	46	36	4	3	14	28	55	74	91	36

1938/39

18th in Division One

					Att	Aiken AV	Anderson DN	Bateman A	Boulter LM	Briddon S	Brown W	Cheetham TM	Crozier J	Eastham GR	Edelston M	Gibbons AH	Gorman WC	Holliday JW	Hopkins IJ	James J	McAloon GP	McCulloch D	Muttitt E	Poyser GH	Reid R	Scott WR	Smith LGF	Sneddon WC	Townsend LF	Wilkins GE	Wilson JW
1	Aug 27	HUDDERSFIELD T	2-1	Brown, McCulloch	26638			2			4		1	10					7	5	8	9		3	11			6			
2	Sep 3	Everton	1-2	Reid	35989			2			4		1	10					7	5	8	9		3	11			6			
3	8	ARSENAL	1-0	McAloon	38535			2			4		1	10		9			7	5	8			3	11			6			
4	10	WOLVERHAMPTON W.	0-1		28027						4		1	10		8			7	5		9		3	11			6			2
5	17	Aston Villa	0-5		49092						4		1	10					7	5	8	9		3	11			6			2
6	19	Blackpool	1-4	Smith	21970						4		1	10					7	5		9		3		8	11	6			2
7	24	SUNDERLAND	2-3	Eastham, McCulloch	26128					4	2		1	10					7	5	8	9		3			11	6			
8	Oct 1	Grimsby Town	0-0		12106						4		1	10	8				7	5		9		3			11	6			2
9	8	DERBY COUNTY	1-3	Scott	23539						3		1		10			6		5		9			11	8	7	4			2
10	15	Stoke City	2-3	Holliday (p), Hopkins	23588						3		1	10				6	7	5		9				8	11	4			2
11	22	CHELSEA	1-0	Reid	31425						4		1	10		9				5				3	11	8	7	6			2
12	29	Charlton Athletic	1-1	Scott	32191						4		1	10				9		5				3	11	8	7	6			2
13	Nov 5	BOLTON WANDERERS	2-2	Atkinson (og), Scott	24594						4		1			10		9		5				3	11	8	7	6			2
14	12	Leeds United	2-3	Edelston, Brown	22555						4		1		10	9				5				3	11	8	7	6			2
15	19	LIVERPOOL	2-1	Holliday 2	20977			2			4		1		10			9	7	5				3		8	11	6			
16	26	Leicester City	1-1	Scott	16634			2			4		1		10			9	7	5				3		8	11	6			
17	Dec 3	MIDDLESBROUGH	2-1	Holliday, Sneddon	21746			2			4		1		10			9	7	5				3		8	11	6			
18	10	Birmingham	1-5	Holliday	23333			2			4		1		10			9	7	5				3	11	8		6			
19	17	MANCHESTER UNITED	2-5	Gibbons, Vose (og)	14919						4		1		10	9	2		7	5				3	11	8		6			
20	24	Huddersfield Town	2-1	Smith, Townsend	11483					4			1		10		2		7	5	8			3			11	6	9		
21	27	Portsmouth	2-2	Townsend, McAloon	31732					4			1		10		2		7	5	8			3			11	6	9		
22	31	EVERTON	2-0	Townsend 2	27861					4	6		1				2		7	5	8			3		10	11		9		
23	Jan 14	Wolverhampton Wan.	2-5	Edelston 2	23944					4	6		1		10		2			5	8			3			11		9	7	
24	28	Sunderland	1-1	Sneddon (p)	19591	4					9		1				2			5	8			3	11	10	7	6			
25	Feb 4	GRIMSBY TOWN	1-2	Scott	17380	4							1		10	9	2			5				3	11	8	7	6			
26	8	ASTON VILLA	2-4	Edelston, Reid (p)	21162				10	4		9	1		8		2			5				3	11		7	6			
27	11	Derby County	2-1	Hopkins, Cheetham	19707				10			9	1		8		2		7	5			6	3	11	4					
28	18	STOKE CITY	1-0	Cheetham	26237				10			9	1				2		7	5			6	3	11	4				8	
29	22	PORTSMOUTH	2-0	McAloon, Scott	14290				10			9	1				2		7	5	8		6	3		4	11				
30	25	Chelsea	3-1	Cheetham 2, Smith	33511				10			9	1				2		7	5	8		6	3		4	11				
31	Mar 4	CHARLTON ATHLETIC	1-0	Hopkins	24440				10		3	9	1				2		7	5	8		6				11	4			
32	11	Bolton Wanderers	1-1	Boutler	15161				10		3	9	1				2		7	5	8		6				11	4			
33	18	LEEDS UNITED	0-1		21480				10		3	9	1		8		2		7	5			6				11	4			
34	25	Liverpool	0-1		18113				10		3	9	1		8		2		7	5			6			4	11				
35	Apr 1	LEICESTER CITY	2-0	Smith, Hopkins	17238				10		3	9	1		8		2		7	5			6			4	11				
36	7	PRESTON NORTH END	3-1	Cheetham 2, Edelston	30780				10		3	9	1		8		2		7	5			6			4	11				
37	8	Middlesbrough	1-3	Cheetham	18191				10			9	1			8	2		7	5			6	3		4	11				
38	10	Preston North End	0-2		22350				10		5	9	1		8		2		7				6	3		4	11				
39	15	BIRMINGHAM	0-1		15298				10		5	9	1			8	2						6	3		4	11			7	
40	22	Manchester United	0-3		15353	6			10		5	9	1			8	2		7					3		4	11				
41	29	BLACKPOOL	1-1	Cheetham	12761		3		8		6	9	1				2	10	7	5						4	11				
42	May 6	Arsenal	0-2		30928						6	9	1			8	2	10	7	5				3		4	11				
					Apps	3	1	7	16	6	33	17	42	11	19							9	13	33	17	28	33	27	4	3	10
					Goals				1		2	8		1	5	1		5	4		3	2			3	7	3	2	4		

F.A. Cup

					Att	Aiken AV	Anderson DN	Bateman A	Boulter LM	Briddon S	Brown W	Cheetham TM	Crozier J	Eastham GR	Edelston M	Gibbons AH	Gorman WC	Holliday JW	Hopkins IJ	James J	McAloon GP	McCulloch D	Muttitt E	Poyser GH	Reid R	Scott WR	Smith LGF	Sneddon WC	Townsend LF	Wilkins GE	Wilson JW
R3	Jan 7	Newcastle United	0-2		27881					4	6		1				2		7	5	8			3		10	11		9		

		Pl.	Home W	D	L	F	A	Away W	D	L	F	A	F. (Total)	A.	Pts
1	Everton	42	17	3	1	60	18	10	2	9	28	34	88	52	59
2	Wolverhampton W.	42	14	6	1	55	12	8	5	8	33	27	88	39	55
3	Charlton Athletic	42	16	3	2	49	24	6	3	12	26	35	75	59	50
4	Middlesbrough	42	13	6	2	64	27	7	3	11	29	47	93	74	49
5	Arsenal	42	14	3	4	34	14	5	6	10	21	27	55	41	47
6	Derby County	42	12	3	6	39	22	7	5	9	27	33	66	55	46
7	Stoke City	42	13	6	2	50	25	4	6	11	21	43	71	68	46
8	Bolton Wanderers	42	10	6	5	39	25	5	9	7	28	33	67	58	45
9	Preston North End	42	13	7	1	44	19	3	5	13	19	40	63	59	44
10	Grimsby Town	42	11	6	4	38	26	5	5	11	23	43	61	69	43
11	Liverpool	42	12	6	3	40	24	2	8	11	22	39	62	63	42
12	Aston Villa	42	11	3	7	44	25	5	6	10	27	35	71	60	41
13	Leeds United	42	11	5	5	40	27	5	4	12	19	40	59	67	41
14	Manchester United	42	7	9	5	30	20	4	7	10	27	45	57	65	38
15	Blackpool	42	9	8	4	37	26	3	6	12	19	42	56	68	38
16	Sunderland	42	7	7	7	30	29	6	5	10	24	38	54	67	38
17	Portsmouth	42	10	7	4	25	15	2	6	13	22	55	47	70	37
18	**BRENTFORD**	**42**	**11**	**2**	**8**	**30**	**27**	**3**	**6**	**12**	**23**	**47**	**53**	**74**	**36**
19	Huddersfield Town	42	11	4	6	38	18	1	7	13	20	46	58	64	35
20	Chelsea	42	10	5	6	43	29	2	4	15	21	51	64	80	33
21	Birmingham	42	10	5	6	40	27	2	3	16	22	57	62	84	32
22	Leicester City	42	7	6	8	35	35	2	5	14	13	47	48	82	29

1938/39
Back: Smith, McKenzie, Brown, Crozier, James, Bateman, Cartmell (Trainer)
Front: Hopkins, Eastham, McCulloch, Scott, Reid, Sneddon.

1945-46
An unnamed team group.

1939/40

Football League Division One

(Suspended Due to the War - 12th on Sept. 2)

No.	Date	Opponent	Score	Scorers	Att.
1	Aug 26	Everton	1-1	Saunders	30466
2	28	Blackpool	1-2	Boulter	21633
3	Sep 2	HUDDERSFIELD TOWN	1-0	Holliday	12079

Regional League (South B) - 5th joint

No.	Date	Opponent	Score	Scorers	Att.
1	Oct 21	CHELSEA	2-2	Holliday; Gorman	6628
2	28	Portsmouth	1-3	Boulter	3396
3	Nov 4	SOUTHAMPTON	3-1	Boulter 2; Manley	4757
4	11	Queens Park Rangers	0-1		8000
5	18	BRIGHTON AND HOVE ALBION	4-1	Holliday 3; Townsend	3533
6	25	Aldershot	0-1		4000
7	Dec 2	READING	3-0	Smith; Holliday 2	4077
8	9	BOURNEMOUTH & BA	5-2	Townsend 2; McKenzie; Hopkins; Boulter	4680
9	16	Fulham	4-2	Holliday 2; Hopkins; Manley	5000
10	25	PORTSMOUTH	4-0	Holliday 3; Manley	4811
11	26	Southampton	3-2	Holliday; Hopkins; Townsend	6000
12	30	QUEENS PARK RANGERS	0-7		3942
13	Jan 6	Brighton and Hove Albion	2-3	Manley 2	2071
14	13	ALDERSHOT	4-3	Townsend 2; Brown; Hopkins	1863
15	20	Reading	1-3	Hopkins	1900
16	24	Chelsea	2-3	Griffith (og); Holliday	2000
17	27	Bournemouth & BA	2-2	James; Holliday	3000
18	Feb 14	FULHAM	2-5	Wilkins; McKenzie	1885

Subsidiary Competition (South C) - 4th

No.	Date	Opponent	Score	Scorers	Att.
1	Feb 10	Arsenal	1-3	Boulter	5000
2	17	WEST HAM UNITED	4-3	Smith; Boulter; McKenzie (p); Wilkins	1885
3	24	Charlton Athletic	2-3	Wilkins; McKenzie (p)	7000
4	Mar 2	CHELSEA	1-1	McCulloch D	7110
5	9	Tottenham Hotspur	1-1	Yorston	9815
6	16	SOUTHAMPTON	5-0	Yorston 2; Hunt 3	3600
7	22	PORTSMOUTH	3-1	Wilkins; McKenzie 2	8000
8	23	Millwall	1-4	Hunt	14490
9	25	Portsmouth	3-1	Holliday; Wilkins; Hunt	6500
10	30	FULHAM	5-0	Hunt 2; Yorston; Wilkins; Brown	6956
11	Apr 6	ARSENAL	2-4	Yorston; Doherty	8000
12	10	Southampton	1-4	Wilkins	4000
13	13	West Ham United	1-1	Hunt	8000
14	17	MILLWALL	1-1	Doherty	5000
15	May 4	TOTTENHAM HOTSPUR	2-3	Wilkins; Hitchins (og)	5521
16	11	CHELSEA	2-0	McKenzie (p); Hopkins	3168
17	18	CHARLTON ATHLETIC	2-1	Hunt; Hopkins	3000
18	Jun 3	Fulham	5-3	Wilkins 2; Burgess 2; Holliday	1000

League Cup

Rd	Date	Opponent	Score	Scorers	Att.
R1/1	Apr 20	Fulham	1-4	Smith	12000
R1/2	27	FULHAM	1-2	Brown J	7865

Competition South 'B' Final Table

	P	W	L	D	F	A	Pts
QPR	18	12	4	2	49	26	26
B'mouth & B A	18	11	5	2	52	37	24
Chelsea	18	9	4	5	43	37	23
Reading	18	10	6	2	47	42	22
Brentford	18	8	8	2	42	41	18
Fulham	18	7	7	4	42	41	18
Portsmouth	18	7	9	2	37	42	16
Aldershot	18	5	9	4	38	49	14
Brighton & HA	18	5	12	1	42	53	11
Southampton	18	4	14	0	41	63	8

Competition South 'C' Final Table

	P	W	L	D	F	A	Pts
Tottenham	18	11	3	4	43	30	26
West Ham	18	10	4	4	53	28	24
Arsenal	18	9	4	5	41	26	23
Brentford	18	8	6	4	42	34	20
Millwall	18	7	6	5	36	30	19
Charlton	18	7	7	4	39	56	18
Fulham	18	8	9	1	38	42	17
Southampton	18	5	10	3	28	55	13
Chelsea	18	4	11	3	33	53	11
Portsmouth	18	3	12	3	26	45	9

1940/41

Football League (South) - 20th

No.	Date	Opponent	Score	Scorers	Att.
1	Aug 31	CLAPTON ORIENT	2-2	Wilkins; McKenzie (p)	1123
2	Sep 7	Chelsea	1-2	Wilkins	3500
3	14	CHARLTON ATHLETIC	1-1	McKenzie (p)	600
4	21	Arsenal	1-3	Hunt	1700
5	Oct 5	Clapton Orient	0-1		500
6	12	Charlton Athletic	4-1	Hunt 2; Townsend 2	800
7	19	FULHAM	8-3	Hunt 3; Hopkins; McKenzie (p); Townsend 2; Muttitt	1300
8	26	ARSENAL	3-3	Townsend 2; Muttitt	1200
9	Nov 2	PORTSMOUTH	3-1	Ferris; Cheetham; Hopkins	500
10	16	WEST HAM UNITED	0-2		400
11	23	Fulham	0-3		600
12	Dec 7	READING	2-3	Hopkins; McKenzie (p)	600
13	14	Millwall	0-3		1250
14	21	Portsmouth	3-2	Holliday 2; Wilkins	1814
15	25	QUEENS PARK RANGERS	2-1	Wilkins; Hunt	3725
16	28	MILLWALL	3-2	Hunt 2; Boulter	1759
17	Mar 15	CRYSTAL PALACE	2-3	Perry; Hopkins	4000
18	22	Crystal Palace	0-5		2638
19	Apr 19	MILLWALL	5-2	Perry 3; Hopkins; Townsend	2500
20	May 3	West Ham United	2-3	Hopkins 2	3000
21	10	FULHAM	2-3	Bamford; Holliday	2670
22	17	Reading	4-1	Perry 3; Holliday	5000
23	24	READING	3-1	Hopkins 3	1520

London War Cup

Rd	Date	Opponent	Score	Scorers	Att.
Grp A	Jan 4	CRYSTAL PALACE	2-2	Muttitt; Boulter	1000
Grp A	11	Crystal Palace	2-2	Muttitt; Smith L	2841
Grp A	25	Chelsea	1-0	Davie	1318
Grp A	Feb 1	Fulham	1-4	Smith L	2500
Grp A	8	FULHAM	7-4	Hunt; Hopkins 3; Perry 2; McKenzie	2428
Grp A	Mar 29	CHELSEA	2-2	Smith L; Townsend	1654
Grp A	Apr 5	ALDERSHOT	4-2	Perry 2; Hopkins	1960
Grp A	12	Aldershot	2-2	Wilkins; Perry	4000
Grp A	14	QUEENS PARK RANGERS	4-2	Hopkins; Perry 2; Smith L	5000
Grp A	26	Queens Park Rangers	0-0		6000
SF	May 31	Tottenham Hotspur	2-0	Perry; Townsend	6495
Final	Jun 7	Reading	2-3	Perry 2	9000

Final played at Stamford Bridge

League Cup

Rd	Date	Opponent	Score	Scorers	Att.
R1/!	Feb 15	Southampton	2-2	Hunt; Wilkins	1815
R1/2	22	SOUTHAMPTON	5-2	James; Smith L; Perry 3	2142
R2/1	Mar 1	CHELSEA	2-2	Hunt; Hopkins	4520
R2/2	8	Chelsea	1-3	Perry	5992

Away to Southampton played at Fratton Park

10 Tottenham	23	9	9	5	53	41	1.292
11 Millwall	31	16	10	5	73	57	1.280
12 Walsall	32	14	11	7	100	80	1.250
13 WBA	28	13	10	5	83	69	1.202
14 Leicester	33	17	11	5	87	73	1.191
15 Northampton	30	14	13	3	84	71	1.183
16 Bristol C	20	10	8	2	55	48	1.145
17 Mansfield	29	12	11	6	77	68	1.132
18 Charlton	19	7	8	4	37	34	1.088
19 Aldershot	24	14	8	2	73	68	1.073
20 Brentford	23	9	11	3	51	51	1.000
21 Chelsea	23	10	9	4	57	58	.981
22 Birmingham	16	7	8	1	38	43	.883
23 Fulham	30	10	13	7	62	73	.849

Only teams local to each played each other, and with a variable number of games played, final positions were based on goal average only. N.B. only teams in final positions 10th to 23rd shown.

1941/42

London War League - 9th

No	Month	Day	Opponent	Score	Scorers	Att
1	Aug	30	ARSENAL	4-1	Hapgood (og); Wilkins; Perry; L Smith	12000
2	Sep	6	Queens Park Rangers	4-3	Hunt; Wilkins; Perry 2	8000
3		13	READING	3-2	Perry 2; Wilkins	6100
4		20	Brighton and Hove Albion	2-2	Perry; Hunt	5000
5		27	Clapton Orient	3-1	Perry; Smith; Hopkins	3500
6	Oct	4	CRYSTAL PALACE	1-2	Perry	4700
7		11	Fulham	3-4	Townsend; Smailes; Perry	6000
8		18	TOTTENHAM HOTSPUR	1-4	Hunt	6000
9		25	Portsmouth	1-2	Hunt	5806
10	Nov	1	CHELSEA	3-1	Perry; James; Hunt	4650
11		8	CHARLTON ATHLETIC	2-1	Smith ; Hunt	6320
12		15	WEST HAM UNITED	0-5		5000
13		22	Watford	6-1	Hopkins 2; Perry 4	4000
14		29	ALDERSHOT	5-1	Hopkins; Hunt 2; Townsend; Duns	4410
15	Dec	6	Millwall	2-4	Muttitt; Townsend	2000
16		13	Arsenal	3-1	L Smith; Duns; Perry	9739
17		20	QUEENS PARK RANGERS	4-3	Townsend 3; Hunt	3500
18		25	Reading	3-4	Townsend; Hopkins; L Smith	5159
19		27	BRIGHTON AND HOVE ALBION	4-2	Townsend 2; Tooze (og); Smith	5000
20	Jan	3	CLAPTON ORIENT	5-2	Barnes (og); Holliday 2; Hopkins; McKenzie	3420
21		10	Crystal Palace	0-2		6000
22		17	FULHAM	2-3	Smith; Hopkins	3000
23		31	PORTSMOUTH	2-5	Wilkins; Holliday	3820
24	Feb	7	Chelsea	1-1	Wilkins	3135
25		14	Charlton Athletic	2-3	Perry; Duncan	3909
26		21	West Ham United	1-2	Hunt	4000
27		28	WATFORD	5-3	Smith; Hunt 2; Hopkins 2	3110
28	Mar	7	Aldershot	3-6	Hopkins; Hunt; McKenzie	3000
29		14	MILLWALL	4-3	Hopkins; Smith; Cardwell (og); Hunt	4500
30	Apr	25	Tottenham Hotspur	1-2	Sneddon	5131

London Cup

Rd	Month	Day	Opponent	Score	Scorers	Att
Grp2	Mar	21	ALDERSHOT	6-2	Hunt 2; Smith; Perry; Wilkins 3	5120
Grp2		28	MILLWALL	3-3	Perry 2; McKenzie (p)	3500
Grp2	Apr	4	Queens Park Rangers	2-1	Cheetham; Hunt	3000
Grp2		6	Millwall	2-2	Cheetham 2	
Grp2		11	QUEENS PARK RANGERS	1-0	Perry	7310
Grp2		18	Aldershot	3-1	Hopkins; Smith L; Smith J	4000
SF	May	2	Arsenal	0-0		41154
replay		16	Arsenal	2-1	Wilkins; Hunt	37600
Final		30	Portsmouth	2-0	Smith 2	69792

SF played at Stamford Bridge; replay at White Hart Lane; Final at Wembley

War Cup Winners' Match

Month	Day	Opponent	Score	Scorers	Att
Jun	6	Wolverhampton Wanderers	1-1	Collett	20174

Match played at Stamford Bridge

1941/42

	P	W	L	D	F	A	Pts
Arsenal	30	23	5	2	108	43	48
Portsmouth	30	20	8	2	105	59	42
West Ham	30	17	8	5	81	44	39
Aldershot	30	17	8	5	85	56	39
Tottenham	30	15	7	8	61	41	38
Crystal Palace	30	14	10	6	70	53	34
Reading	30	13	9	8	76	58	34
Charlton	30	14	11	5	72	64	33
Brentford	30	14	14	2	80	76	30
QPR	30	11	16	3	52	59	25
Fulham	30	10	16	4	79	99	24
Brighton & HA	30	9	17	4	71	108	22
Chelsea	30	8	18	4	56	88	20
Millwall	30	7	18	5	53	82	19
Clapton Orient	30	5	18	7	42	94	17
Watford	30	6	20	4	47	114	16

1942/43

	P	W	L	D	F	A	Pts
Arsenal	28	21	6	1	102	40	43
Tottenham	28	16	6	6	68	28	38
QPR	28	18	8	2	64	49	38
Portsmouth	28	16	9	3	66	52	35
Southampton	28	14	9	5	86	58	33
West Ham	28	14	9	5	80	66	33
Chelsea	28	14	10	4	52	45	32
Aldershot	28	14	12	2	87	77	30
Brentford	28	12	11	5	64	63	29
Charlton	28	13	12	3	68	75	29
Clapton Orient	28	11	12	5	54	72	27
Brighton & HA	28	10	13	5	65	73	25
Reading	28	9	13	6	67	74	24
Fulham	28	10	16	2	69	78	22
Crystal Palace	28	7	16	5	49	75	19
Millwall	28	6	17	5	66	88	17
Watford	28	7	19	2	51	88	16
Luton	28	4	18	6	43	100	14

1942/43

Football League South - 9th

No	Month	Day	Opponent	Score	Scorers	Att
1	Aug	29	CLAPTON ORIENT	2-2	Holliday; Hunt	3210
2	Sep	5	Fulham	1-3	Hunt	4600
3		12	BRIGHTON AND HOVE ALBION	9-4	Townsend 6; Kiernan 2; Hunt	4020
4		19	CHELSEA	0-2		8480
5		26	Queens Park Rangers	1-4	Kiernan	8000
6	Oct	3	WATFORD	3-0	Wilkins; Hopkins; Hunt	3590
7		10	WEST HAM UNITED	6-2	Kiernan 3; Fenton (og); Townsend 2	7000
8		17	Arsenal	2-0	Smith; Kiernan	16700
9		24	ALDERSHOT	4-1	Hunt; Townsend; Aicken; Kiernan	5000
10		31	LUTON TOWN	2-2	Sneddon; Townsend	5000
11	Nov	7	Millwall	2-1	Hunt; Perry	4557
12		14	Charlton Athletic	4-1	Perry 2; Townsend; Hunt	3000
13		21	READING	3-3	Kiernan; Hunt 2	5390
14		28	Clapton Orient	0-2		2500
15	Dec	5	FULHAM	4-2	Townsend 3; McKenzie (p)	5200
16		12	Brighton and Hove Albion	2-7	Townsend; Hunt	4000
17		19	Chelsea	4-2	Holliday; McKenzie 2; Hopkins	8154
18		25	Tottenham Hotspur	1-1	Townsend	14621
19		26	TOTTENHAM HOTSPUR	2-1	Townsend; Hopkins	12542
20	Jan	2	QUEENS PARK RANGERS	2-0	Hunt 2	7500
21		9	Watford	0-2		2177
22		16	West Ham United	1-4	Perry	7500
23		23	ARSENAL	0-1		23180
24		30	Aldershot	1-2	Townsend	4000
25	Feb	6	Luton Town	1-1	Hunt (og)	3000
26		13	MILLWALL	3-1	McCulloch 2; Perry	5150
27		20	CHARLTON ATHLETIC	3-5	James; Armstrong; Smith	4680
28		27	Reading	1-7	Henley	4000

Football League South Cup

Rd	Month	Day	Opponent	Score	Scorers	Att
Grp 2	Mar	6	QUEENS PARK RANGERS	1-2	O'Donnell	10520
Grp 2		13	Clapton Orient	1-1	Hopkins	3707
Grp 2		20	SOUTHAMPTON	1-6	Townsend	6600
Grp 2		27	Queens Park Rangers	0-2		9954
Grp 2	Apr	3	CLAPTON ORIENT	3-2	Hunt 2 (1p); Hopkins	4080
Grp 2		10	Southampton	1-2	Holliday	13000

1943/44

Football League South -7th

No	Month	Day	Opponent	Score	Scorers	Att
1	Aug	28	CLAPTON ORIENT	4-2	Hunt; Smith 2; Stewart	4820
2	Sep	4	Fulham	3-4	Stewart; Hunt 2	7737
3		11	BRIGHTON AND HOVE ALBION	2-3	Hopkins; Hunt	5310
4		18	CHELSEA	3-1	Smith; Hunt; Stewart	6400
5		25	Crystal Palace	1-1	Watson	5131
6	Oct	2	WATFORD	4-1	Durrant; Hunt (p); McKennan 2	6720
7		9	West Ham United	0-0		12000
8		16	Arsenal	3-3	McKennan; Townsend; Hunt	17658
9		23	ALDERSHOT	2-4	McKennan 2	9940
10		30	Luton Town	2-2	Driver; McKennan	5000
11	Nov	6	TOTTENHAM HOTSPUR	0-2		9560
12		13	PORTSMOUTH	2-0	Smith; Hunt (p)	6880
13		27	Clapton Orient	4-1	Smith 2; Little; Mckennan	1000
14	Dec	4	FULHAM	1-1	Smith	7510
15		11	Brighton and Hove Albion	2-0	Thomas; Stewart	2500
16		18	SOUTHAMPTON	7-2	Smith 2; Hunt 2; McKennan 2; Stewart	3000
17		25	QUEENS PARK RANGERS	2-5	Thomas; McKennan	11200
18		27	Queens Park Rangers	2-3	Smith; Stewart	8900
19	Jan	1	Chelsea	3-0	McKennan 2; Hunt	12000
20		8	Tottenham Hotspur	0-1		16917
21		22	Watford	4-4	Hunt 2 (1p); Watson; McKennan	2759
22		29	WEST HAM UNITED	2-1	Townsend; Hunt	11220
23	Feb	5	ARSENAL	4-1	Soo; Westcott; Townsend 2	20270
24		12	Aldershot	2-4	McKennan; Smith	4000
25	Apr	1	LUTON TOWN	2-0	Hopkins; Baynham	2340
26		10	CRYSTAL PALACE	2-0	Stewart; Hollliday	4440
27		15	READING	1-0	Smith	6040
28		22	Southampton	2-2	Townsend; Stewart	9000
29		29	Portsmouth	2-3	Baynham; Townsend	8000
30	May	6	Reading	3-0	Townsend 2; Hunt	3500

Football League South Cup

Rd	Month	Day	Opponent	Score	Scorers	Att
Grp 1	Feb	19	CRYSTAL PALACE	3-4	Townsend 2; Stevens	4110
Grp 1		26	Charlton Athletic	3-5	Townsend; Hunt 2	5023
Grp 1	Mar	4	BRIGHTON AND HOVE ALBION	8-0	Westcott 4; Townsend 3; Hunt	5020
Grp 1		11	Crystal Palace	2-1	Westcott; Shepherd	8659
Grp 1		18	CHARLTON ATHLETIC	2-2	Townsend; Smith	10000
Grp 1		25	Brighton and Hove Albion	0-5		3000

1944/45

Football League South - 3rd

1	Aug	26	BRIGHTON AND HOVE ALBION	6-2	Townsend 2; Hunt 2; Boulter 2	6000
2	Sep	2	Portsmouth	4-2	Hunt; R Thomas 2; Boulter	9500
3		9	CHELSEA	0-5		16100
4		16	Luton Town	3-1	Manley; Boulter; R Thomas	3500
5		23	MILLWALL	4-1	Townsend 2; R Thomas 2	8750
6		30	ALDERSHOT	5-2	Smith 2 (1P); Hunt; R Thomas 2	10270
7	Oct	7	Charlton Athletic	4-0	Boulter 2; Townsend 2	7143
8		14	WATFORD	4-1	Townsend 2; R Thomas; Hopkins	5387
9		21	QUEENS PARK RANGERS	3-1	Rose (og); R Thomas; Townsend	15000
10		28	TOTTENHAM HOTSPUR	2-2	R Thomas; Soo	23207
11	Nov	4	Fulham	2-0		25000
12		11	SOUTHAMPTON	0-1		11080
13		18	CRYSTAL PALACE	1-2	Townsend	11100
14		25	Reading	4-4	Hunt 2; Townsend 2	6000
15	Dec	2	Brighton and Hove Albion	7-2	Townsend 3; Smith; R Thomas 2; Hunt	5000
16		9	PORTSMOUTH	7-1	C Brown 2; Hunt 2 (1p); Townsend 2; Hopkins	9550
17		16	Chelsea	2-0	Hunt; R Thomas	24492
18		23	Arsenal	2-5	R Thomas 2	18527
19		30	LUTON TOWN	6-0	Townsend 4; R Thomas; Smith	6500
20	Jan	6	Millwall	0-0		5438
21		13	Aldershot	1-0	Smith	4000
22		20	CHARLTON ATHLETIC	3-1	Hunt; R Thomas; Baynham	6850
23	Mar	17	Queens Park Rangers	1-1	D Thomas	5900
24		24	TOTTENHAM HOTSPUR	0-2		16750
25		31	FULHAM	2-3	Hopkins; Smith	8780
26	Apr	2	ARSENAL	3-1	R Thomas 2; D Thomas	12700
27		14	Southampton	2-4	Hunt; Townsend	7549
28		21	Crystal Palace	1-6	D Thomas	6492
29		28	READING	7-2	R Thomas 2; D Thomas 2; Smith; Baynham 2	4390
30	May	19	Watford	1-5	Cheetham	2563

Football League South Cup

Grp 2	Feb	3	BRIGHTON AND HOVE ALBION	3-5	Townsend 3	10110
Grp 2		10	Millwall	2-3	R Thomas; Hunt	8553
Grp 2		17	Fulham	0-1		15000
Grp 2		24	Brighton and Hove Albion	4-2	Townsend 3; R Thomas	10000
Grp 2	Mar	3	MILLWALL	2-2	Baynham; R Thomas	11830
Grp 2		10	FULHAM	2-5	Townsend; R Thomas	10380

1944/45 Season

	P	W	L	D	F	A	Pts
Tottenham	30	23	1	6	81	30	52
West Ham	30	22	5	3	96	47	47
Brentford	30	17	9	4	87	57	38
Chelsea	30	16	9	5	100	55	37
Southampton	30	17	10	3	96	69	37
Crystal Palace	30	15	10	5	74	70	35
Reading	30	14	10	6	78	68	34
Arsenal	30	14	13	3	77	67	31
QPR	30	10	10	10	70	61	30
Watford	30	11	13	6	66	84	28
Fulham	30	11	15	4	79	83	26
Portsmouth	30	11	15	4	56	61	26
Charlton	30	12	16	2	72	81	26
Brighton & HA	30	10	18	2	66	95	22
Luton	30	6	17	7	56	104	19
Aldershot	30	7	19	4	44	85	18
Millwall	30	5	18	7	50	84	17
Clapton Orient	30	5	18	7	39	86	17

1943/44 Season

	P	W	L	D	F	A	Pts
Tottenham	30	19	3	8	71	36	46
West Ham	30	17	6	7	74	39	41
QPR	30	14	4	12	69	54	40
Arsenal	30	14	6	10	72	42	38
Crystal Palace	30	16	9	5	75	53	37
Portsmouth	30	16	9	5	68	59	37
Brentford	30	14	9	7	71	51	35
Chelsea	30	16	12	2	79	55	34
Fulham	30	11	10	9	80	73	31
Millwall	30	13	13	4	70	66	30
Aldershot	30	12	12	6	64	73	30
Reading	30	12	15	3	73	62	27
Southampton	30	10	13	7	67	88	27
Charlton	30	9	14	7	57	73	25
Watford	30	6	16	8	58	80	20
Brighton & HA	30	9	19	2	55	82	20
Luton	30	3	22	5	42	104	11
Clapton Orient	30	4	23	3	32	87	11

1945/46

Football League South - 14th

1	Aug	25	NEWPORT COUNTY	2-1	Sloan; Townsend	13980
2	Sep	1	Newport County	5-0	Thomas 2; Sloan; Townsend 2	8862
3		6	LEICESTER CITY	1-2	Sloan	11620
4		8	Wolverhampton Wanderers	0-1		19895
5		12	DERBY COUNTY	0-0		11050
6		15	WOLVERHAMPTON WANDERERS	0-0		20664
7		22	WEST HAM UNITED	1-1	Thomas	18800
8		29	West Ham United	2-0	Sloan; Durrant	23000
9	Oct	6	West Bromwich Albion	4-3	Thomas 2; Tranter (og); Hunt	29821
10		13	WEST BROMWICH ALBION	2-0	Durrant 2	20160
11		20	BIRMINGHAM CITY	2-1	Wilkins 2	20690
12		27	Birmingham City	0-1		34788
13	Nov	3	Tottenham Hotspur	0-1		28603
14		10	TOTTENHAM HOTSPUR	1-3	Thomas	19269
15		17	Swansea Town	1-4	Roberts	16000
16		24	SWANSEA TOWN	2-2	Durrant; Hunt	12090
17	Dec	1	CHELSEA	4-4	Townsend 2; Durrant 2	28170
18		8	Chelsea	2-4	Durrant; Thomas	40000
19		15	MILLWALL	7-0	Thomas; Townsend 4; Watson; Durrant	16190
20		22	Millwall	1-3	Townsend	22000
21		25	SOUTHAMPTON	1-4	McAloon	14350
22		26	Southampton	4-3	Townsend 2; McAloon; Thomas	20000
23		29	Derby County	2-3	McAloon; Durrant	22751
24	Jan	12	Coventry City	0-1		13450
25		19	COVENTRY CITY	1-2	Metcalf (og)	10309
26	Feb	2	Luton Town	4-1	Durrant; Gotts; Scott; Townsend	8348
27		16	ASTON VILLA	0-1		27100
28		23	ARSENAL	6-3	Thomas 3 (1p); Durrant; McAloon; Bamford	22250
29	Mar	16	CHARLTON ATHLETIC	1-1	McAloon	14900
30		23	FULHAM	1-2	McAloon	23400
31		30	Fulham	2-2	Thomas; Townsend	27475
32	Apr	6	Plymouth Argyle	1-1	McAloon	20000
33		10	Charlton Athletic	3-4	Thomas 3	20000
34		13	PLYMOUTH ARGYLE	3-2	G Smith; Thomas; McAloon	13200
35		17	Aston Villa	1-1	McAloon	18000
36		19	PORTSMOUTH	0-2		16184
37		20	Nottingham Forest	0-2		19704
38		22	Portsmouth	0-2		20000
39		24	LUTON TOWN	6-1	McAloon 3; Durrant; Edelston; Jones	7050
40		27	NOTTINGHAM FOREST	5-1	Scott 2; McAloon 3 (1p)	8140
41		29	Arsenal	1-1	Scott	5250
42	May	4	Leicester City	3-1	Durrant; McAloon 2	10000

F.A. Cup played on two-legged basis

3/1	Jan	5	Tottenham Hotspur	2-2	Durrant; Thomas	30202
3/2		10	TOTTENHAM HOTSPUR	2-0	Hopkins 2	21050
4/1		26	Bristol City	1-2	Townsend	35684
4/2		31	BRISTOL CITY	5-0	McAloon 3; Durrant; Guy (og)	18000
5/1	Feb	9	Queens Park Rangers	3-1	Hopkins; McAloon; Durrant	19855
5/2		14	QUEENS PARK RANGERS	0-0		20000
6/1	Mar	2	Charlton Athletic	3-6	McAloon 2; Durrant	44000
6/2		9	CHARLTON ATHLETIC	1-3	Scott	36000

1945/46 Season

	P	W	L	D	F	A	Pts
Birmingham	42	28	9	5	96	45	61
Aston Villa	42	25	6	11	106	58	61
Charlton	42	25	7	10	92	45	60
Derby	42	24	11	7	101	62	55
WBA	42	22	12	8	104	69	52
Wolves	42	20	11	11	75	48	51
West Ham	42	20	11	11	94	76	51
Fulham	42	20	12	10	93	73	50
Tottenham	42	22	17	3	78	81	47
Chelsea	42	19	17	6	92	80	44
Arsenal	42	16	15	11	76	73	43
Millwall	42	17	17	8	79	105	42
Coventry	42	15	17	10	70	69	40
Brentford	42	14	18	10	82	72	38
Nottingham F	42	12	17	13	72	73	37
Southampton	42	14	19	9	97	105	37
Swansea	42	15	20	7	90	112	37
Luton	42	13	22	7	60	92	33
Portsmouth	42	11	25	6	66	87	28
Leicester	42	8	27	7	57	101	23
Newport	42	9	31	2	52	125	20
Plymouth	42	3	31	8	39	120	14

1946/47

21st in Division One (Relegated)

No.	Month	Day	Opponents	Score	Scorers	Att.	Blakeman AG	Brown W	Crozier J	Durrant FH	Gillies JC	Girling HM	Gorman WC	Hopkins IJ	Macaulay AR	Manley TR	McAloon GP	McDonald M	Moore JW	Munro RA	Naylor WH	Oliver HS	Paterson GD	Roberts MES	Scott WR	Shaw A	Smith A	Smith GC	Stewart G	Toulouse CH	Townsend LF	Wilkins GE	Bragg WL	Gallego J	Latimer FJ
1	Aug	31	Everton	2-0	Wilkins (p), McAloon	55338		6	1				2	7			8					3		11	4			5			9	10			
2	Sep	2	Blackpool	2-4	Durrant, Wilkins (p)	24230			1	9			2	7		6	8					3		11	4			5				10			
3		7	HUDDERSFIELD T	2-0	Wilkins, McAloon	31407			1				2	7		6	8					3		11	4			5			9	10			
4		14	Wolverhampton Wan.	2-1	Durrant 2	34446		6	1	9			2	7			8					3		11	4			5				10			
5		18	BLACKPOOL	2-1	McAloon, G Smith	25621		6	1	9			2	7			8					3		11	4			5				10			
6		21	SUNDERLAND	0-3		33766		6	1	9			2	7			8					3		11	4			5				10			
7		28	Aston Villa	2-5	Wilkins (p), McAloon	45350		6	1					7			8			2		3		11	4			5			9	10			
8	Oct	5	DERBY COUNTY	0-3		34746			1				2	7		6				3				11	4			5	8		9	10			
9		12	Arsenal	2-2	Blakeman 2	43367	9		1		11		2	7		6				3					4			5	8			10			
10		19	PRESTON NORTH END	2-3	Blakeman 2	25303	9	4	1				2	7						3				11	8			5	10			6			
11		26	Liverpool	0-1		43892	9		1				2	7						3				11				5	10	4	8	6			
12	Nov	2	BOLTON WANDERERS	1-0	Howe (og)	23782	9		1		11		2	7				10		3						8		5		4		6			
13		9	Chelsea	2-3	Hopkins 2	50242	9		1		11		2	7				10		3						8		5		4		6			
14		16	CHARLTON ATHLETIC	1-4	Townsend	26648			1				2	7	8			10		3			6					5		4	9	11			
15		23	Grimsby Town	2-2	Macaulay, Townsend	16750			1		11		2	7	8			10		3			6					5			9	4			
16		30	LEEDS UNITED	1-1	Townsend	20352			1		11		2	7	8			10		3			6					5			9	4			
17	Dec	7	Manchester United	1-4	Macaulay	31956	11		1				2	7	8			10		3			6					5			9	4			
18		14	STOKE CITY	1-4	MacDonald	30189			1				2	7	8			10		3							11	5		4	9	6			
19		21	Middlesbrough	0-2		28750			1				2	7	4			10		3					8		11	5			9	6			
20		25	Sheffield United	1-6	Townsend	36156			1				2	7	8					3			10				11	5		4	9	6			
21		26	SHEFFIELD UNITED	2-1	A Smith, Wilkins	29535			1				2	7	4			8		3			6				11	5			9	10			
22		28	EVERTON	1-1	Hopkins	29360	9		1				2	7	4			8		3			6				11	5				10			
23	Jan	1	Blackburn Rovers	3-0	Townsend, Wilkins, Stewart	29067			1				2	7	4					3			6				11	5	8		9	10			
24		4	Huddersfield Town	0-3		27759			1				2	7	4			8		3			6				11	5			9	10			
25		18	WOLVERHAMPTON W.	4-1	Wilkins, Stewart, Townsend, A Smith	35604			1				2	7	4					3			6				11	5	8		9	10			
26	Feb	1	ASTON VILLA	0-2		21692			1				2	7	4					3			6		8		11	5			9	10			
27		22	Preston North End	2-5	Townsend, A Smith	25591			1				2	7	4					3	10		6				11	5	8		9				
28	Mar	1	Derby County	1-2	Leuty (og)	18691			1			11	2		4					3	10		6					5	8		9			7	
29		15	CHELSEA	0-2		33498			1			11	2	7	4	5				3	10		6					9	8						
30		22	Charlton Athletic	0-3		29327	9		1			11	2	7	8	5				3	10		6					4							
31		29	GRIMSBY TOWN	0-1		19778			1			11	2		8					3	10		6					5		4	9		7		
32	Apr	4	PORTSMOUTH	1-3	Hopkins	24570			1			11		7	4			10		2		3	6			8		5			9				
33		5	Leeds United	2-1	Naylor, Girling	23962			1			11	2	7	4			8		3	10		6					5			9				
34		7	Portsmouth	0-3		33409		2	1			11		7	4			9		3	10		6			8		5							
35		12	MANCHESTER UNITED	0-0		22035			1			11		7				8		2	10	3	6					5		4	9				
36		19	Stoke City	1-3	Naylor	28966			1			11		7	4					2	10	3	6					5	8		9				
37		26	MIDDLESBROUGH	0-0		19020			1			11		7				10		2		3	6					5	8	4	9				
38	May	3	BLACKBURN ROVERS	0-3		18022			1			11			4					2	10	3	6					5	8	9	7				
39		10	Bolton Wanderers	0-1		19887			1			11	2	7					4		10	3	6					5	8		9				
40		17	LIVERPOOL	1-1	Stewart	18228			1			11	2	7	4	10						3	6					5	8		9				
41		24	Sunderland	1-2	Townsend	20160			1			11	3	7	4	10				2			6					5	8		9				
42		26	ARSENAL	0-1		17976		2	1			11		7	8	9			4	3			6						10						5
						Apps	8	8	42	4	5	15	34	39	26	9	7	16	2	34	11	14	27	10	12	4	10	41	16	10	29	26	1	1	1
						Goals	4			3		1		4	2		4	1			2						3	1	3		8	7			

Two own goals

F.A. Cup

Rd	Month	Day	Opponents	Score	Scorers	Att.	Blakeman AG	Brown W	Crozier J	Durrant FH	Gillies JC	Girling HM	Gorman WC	Hopkins IJ	Macaulay AR	Manley TR	McAloon GP	McDonald M	Moore JW	Munro RA	Naylor WH	Oliver HS	Paterson GD	Roberts MES	Scott WR	Shaw A	Smith A	Smith GC	Stewart G	Toulouse CH	Townsend LF	Wilkins GE	Bragg WL	Gallego J	Latimer FJ
R3	Jan	11	CARDIFF CITY	1-0	Townsend	32894			1				2	7	4					3			6				11	5	8		9	10			
R4		25	LEICESTER CITY	0-0		32112			1				2	7	4					3			6		8		11	5			9	10			
rep		30	Leicester City	0-0	(aet)	20339			1				2	7	4					3			6		8		11	5			9	10			
rep2	Feb	3	Leicester City (Villa Park	1-4	Scott	7500			1				2	7	4					3			6		8		11	5			9	10			

		Pl.	Home W	Home D	Home L	Home F	Home A	Away W	Away D	Away L	Away F	Away A	F. (Total)	A. (Total)	Pts
1	Liverpool	42	13	3	5	42	24	12	4	5	42	28	84	52	57
2	Manchester United	42	17	3	1	61	19	5	9	7	34	35	95	54	56
3	Wolverhampton W.	42	15	1	5	66	31	10	5	6	32	25	98	56	56
4	Stoke City	42	14	5	2	52	21	10	2	9	38	32	90	53	55
5	Blackpool	42	14	1	6	38	32	8	5	8	33	38	71	70	50
6	Sheffield United	42	12	4	5	51	32	9	3	9	38	43	89	75	49
7	Preston North End	42	10	7	4	45	27	8	4	9	31	47	76	74	47
8	Aston Villa	42	9	6	6	39	24	9	3	9	28	29	67	53	45
9	Sunderland	42	11	3	7	33	27	7	5	9	32	39	65	66	44
10	Everton	42	13	5	3	40	24	4	4	13	22	43	62	67	43
11	Middlesbrough	42	11	3	7	46	32	6	5	10	27	36	73	68	42
12	Portsmouth	42	11	3	7	42	27	5	6	10	24	33	66	60	41
13	Arsenal	42	9	5	7	43	33	7	4	10	29	37	72	70	41
14	Derby County	42	13	2	6	44	28	5	3	13	29	51	73	79	41
15	Chelsea	42	9	3	9	33	39	7	4	10	36	45	69	84	39
16	Grimsby Town	42	9	6	6	37	35	4	6	11	24	47	61	82	38
17	Blackburn Rovers	42	6	5	10	23	27	8	3	10	22	26	45	53	36
18	Bolton Wanderers	42	8	5	8	30	28	5	3	13	27	41	57	69	34
19	Charlton Athletic	42	6	6	9	34	32	5	6	10	23	39	57	71	34
20	Huddersfield Town	42	11	4	6	34	24	2	3	16	19	55	53	79	33
21	**BRENTFORD**	**42**	**5**	**5**	**11**	**19**	**35**	**4**	**2**	**15**	**26**	**53**	**45**	**88**	**25**
22	Leeds United	42	6	5	10	30	30	0	1	20	15	60	45	90	18

1946-47
Back: Simon (Dir.), Millard (Dir.), Munroe, Crozier, Manley, Oliver (Dir.), Davis (Dir.) Kane (Trainer)
Front: Hopkins, McAloon, Townsend, Wilkins, Morris, Smith, Brown.

1947-48
Back: Dougall, Dawson, Gorman, Crozier, Oliver, Manley, Munroe, Girling
Front: Gallego, Gibbons, Paterson, Stewart, Moore

1947/48

15th in Division Two

							Blakeman AG	Buchanan PS	Chisholm JR	Crozier J	Dawson T	Dougall T	Gallego J	Gaskell E	Gibbons AH	Girling HM	Gleeson P	Gorman WC	Latimer FJ	Manley TR	McDonald M	Monk FJ	Moore JW	Munro RA	Nelson D	Oliver HS	Paterson GD	Stewart G	Toulouse CH	Ventom EG
1	Aug	23	Fulham	0-5		32823				1	10	7	11		9				5	6			4	2		3		8		
2		27	LUTON TOWN	0-3		17022				1	8	7	11		9			2		5	4			3			6	10		
3		30	COVENTRY CITY	1-4	Gibbons	19107		7		1	8		11		9					5	2			3	4		6	10		
4	Sep	3	Luton Town	0-3		20921		7		1	10		11		9				5		2		4	3	8		6			
5		6	Newcastle United	0-1		56692		7		1	8				9				5	4	2			3	11		6	10		
6		10	NOTTM. FOREST	3-1	Buchanan, Nelson, Blakeman	15005	10	7		1	8				9				5	4	2			3	11		6			
7		13	BIRMINGHAM CITY	1-2	Dawson	25523	10	7		1	8				9				5	4	2			3	11		6			
8		17	Nottingham Forest	0-2		18617	10	7		1	8				9				5	4	2			3	11		6			
9		20	West Bromwich Albion	2-3	Buchanan, Gibbons	29445		7		1	10		11		9		8		5		2			3	4		6			
10		27	BARNSLEY	3-3	Gleeson, Gibbons, Buchanan	22137		7		1	10				9	11	8		5		2			3	4		6			
11	Oct	4	Plymouth Argyle	0-0		23959		7		1	10				9	11	8		5		2			3	4		6			
12		11	BRADFORD PARK AVE.	2-1	Dawson, Girling	24682		7		1	10				9	11	8		5		2			3	4		6			
13		18	CARDIFF CITY	0-0		34483		7		1	10				9	11			5		2			3	4		6	8		
14		25	SHEFFIELD WEDNESDAY	1-0	Gibbons	29112		7		1	10				9	11			5		2			3	4		6	8		
15	Nov	1	Tottenham Hotspur	0-4		42362		7		1	10				9	11			5		2			3	4		6	8		
16		8	MILLWALL	2-1	Buchanan, Girling	26251	9	7		1					10	11	8		5		2			3	4		6			
17		15	Chesterfield	0-4		11320	9	7		1	8				10	11			5		2			3	4		6			
18		22	WEST HAM UNITED	1-1	Dawson	24105		7		1	10				9	11	8			5	2			3	4		6			
19		29	Bury	2-2	Dawson, Gibbons	12856		7		1	10				9	11	8			5	2			3	4		6			
20	Dec	6	SOUTHAMPTON	2-2	Dawson, Nelson	18735		7		1	10				9	11	8				2			3	4		6		5	
21		13	Doncaster Rovers	0-0		16916		7		1	9				10	11	8				2			3	4		6		5	
22		20	FULHAM	0-2		20717		7		1	9				10	11				3	2				4		6	8	5	
23		25	LEICESTER CITY	2-2	Dawson 2	21291	10	7	5	1	9				8	11				6	2				4					3
24		27	Leicester City	2-1	Dawson, Girling	32440	10	7			9			1	8	11		3	5	6	2				4					
25	Jan	3	Coventry City	0-3		20180	10	7	5		9			1	8	11		3		6	2				4					
26		17	NEWCASTLE UNITED	1-0	Gibbons	29684	10	7	5	1	9				8	11		3		6	2				4					
27		31	Birmingham City	0-0		37542	10	7	5	1	9				8	11		3		6	2				4					
28	Feb	7	WEST BROMWICH ALB.	1-0	Nelson	25234	10	7	5	1	9				8	11		3			2				4		6			
29		14	Barnsley	1-1	Gibbons	21399	10	7	5	1	9				8	11		3			2				4		6			
30		21	PLYMOUTH ARGYLE	0-0		13723	10	7	5	1	9					11		3		6	2				8		4			
31		28	Bradford Park Avenue	1-1	Buchanan	11666	10	7	5	1	9				8	11		3		6	2				4					
32	Mar	6	Cardiff City	0-1		41032	10	7	5	1					9	11		3		6	2				8		4			
33		20	TOTTENHAM HOTSPUR	2-0	Buchanan, Monk	31297	10	7	5	1					8	11		3		6	2	9			4					
34		26	LEEDS UNITED	3-0	Girling, Gibbons 2	30538	10	7	5	1					8	11		3		6	2	9			4					
35		27	Millwall	1-0	Monk	27519	10	7	5	1					8	11		3		6	2	9			4					
36		29	Leeds United	1-1	Dawson	26775	10	7	5	1	8				9	11		3		6	2				4					
37	Apr	3	CHESTERFIELD	0-3		24164	10	7	5	1					8	11				6	2	9			4	3				
38		10	West Ham United	1-0	Gibbons	21471	10	7	5	1	8				9	11				6	2				4	3				
39		12	Sheffield Wednesday	1-1	Gibbons	36130	10	7	5	1	8				9	11		3		6	2				4					
40		17	BURY	4-1	Blakeman, Gibbons, Buchanan, Dawson	20419	10	7	5	1	8				9	11		3		6	2				4					
41		24	Southampton	1-2	Gibbons	18511	10	7	5	1	8				9	11		3		6	2				4					
42	May	1	DONCASTER ROVERS	2-0	Buchanan, Girling	16939	10	7	5	1	8				9	11					2				4	3	6			
						Apps	25	40	19	40	36	2	5	2	41	33	9	17	16	27	41	4	2	21	40	4	26	8	3	1
						Goals	2	8			10				13	5	1					2			3					

F.A. Cup

							Blakeman AG	Buchanan PS	Chisholm JR	Crozier J	Dawson T	Dougall T	Gallego J	Gaskell E	Gibbons AH	Girling HM	Gleeson P	Gorman WC	Latimer FJ	Manley TR	McDonald M	Monk FJ	Moore JW	Munro RA	Nelson D	Oliver HS	Paterson GD	Stewart G	Toulouse CH	Ventom EG
R3	Jan	10	Rotherham United	3-0	Dawson, Gibbons, Buchanan	22000	10	7	5	1	9				8	11		3		6	2				4					
R4		24	MIDDLESBROUGH	1-2	Girling	34500	10	7	5	1	9				8	11		3		6	2				4					

		Pl.	Home					Away					F.	A.	Pts
			W	D	L	F	A	W	D	L	F	A	(Total)		
1	Birmingham City	42	12	7	2	34	13	10	8	3	21	11	55	24	59
2	Newcastle United	42	18	1	2	46	13	6	7	8	26	28	72	41	56
3	Southampton	42	15	3	3	53	23	6	7	8	18	30	71	53	52
4	Sheffield Wed.	42	13	6	2	39	21	7	5	9	27	32	66	53	51
5	Cardiff City	42	12	6	3	36	18	6	5	10	25	40	61	58	47
6	West Ham United	42	10	7	4	29	19	6	7	8	26	34	55	53	46
7	West Bromwich Alb.	42	11	4	6	37	29	7	5	9	26	29	63	58	45
8	Tottenham Hotspur	42	10	6	5	36	24	5	8	8	20	19	56	43	44
9	Leicester City	42	10	5	6	36	29	6	6	9	24	28	60	57	43
10	Coventry City	42	10	5	6	33	16	4	8	9	26	36	59	52	41
11	Fulham	42	6	9	6	24	19	9	1	11	23	27	47	46	40
12	Barnsley	42	10	5	6	31	22	5	5	11	31	42	62	64	40
13	Luton Town	42	8	8	5	31	25	6	4	11	25	34	56	59	40
14	Bradford Park Ave.	42	11	3	7	45	30	5	5	11	23	42	68	72	40
15	**BRENTFORD**	**42**	**10**	**6**	**5**	**31**	**26**	**3**	**8**	**10**	**13**	**35**	**44**	**61**	**40**
16	Chesterfield	42	8	4	9	32	26	8	3	10	22	29	54	55	39
17	Plymouth Argyle	42	8	9	4	27	22	1	11	9	13	36	40	58	38
18	Leeds United	42	12	5	4	44	20	2	3	16	18	52	62	72	36
19	Nottingham Forest	42	10	5	6	32	23	2	6	13	22	37	54	60	35
20	Bury	42	6	8	7	27	28	3	8	10	31	40	58	68	34
21	Doncaster Rovers	42	7	8	6	23	20	2	3	16	17	46	40	66	29
22	Millwall	42	7	7	7	27	28	2	4	15	17	46	44	74	29

1948/49

18th in Division Two

							Blakeman AG	Buchanan PS	Chisholm JR	Crozier J	Dare WT	Gaskell E	Gibbons AH	Girling HM	Gorman WC	Greenwood R	Harper AF	Harris K	Keene DC	Manley TR	McDonald M	McKennan PS	Monk FJ	Munro RA	Nelson D	Paterson GD	Quinton W	Smith A	Woodward V
1	Aug	21	COVENTRY CITY	2-2	Nelson, Monk	26090	10	7	5	1				11	3					6	2		9		4				8
2		25	Leeds United	0-0		26625	8	7	5	1				11	3					6	2		9		4				10
3		28	Sheffield Wednesday	0-0		35116	8	7	5	1				11	3					6	2		9		4				10
4	Sep	1	LEEDS UNITED	1-3	Woodward	19212	8	7	5	1				11	3					6	2		9		4				10
5		4	LINCOLN CITY	2-1	Manley, Girling	22414	10	7	5	1				11	3					6	2		9		4				8
6		6	Leicester City	0-0		24151	8	7	5	1				11	3			10		6	2		9		4				
7		11	Chesterfield	1-0	Girling	11057	8	7	5	1				11	3			10		6	2		9		4				
8		15	LEICESTER CITY	1-2	Buchanan	17986		7	5	1			8	11	3		10			6	2		9		4				
9		18	WEST BROMWICH ALB.	0-0		28212		7	5	1				11	3		10			6	2	8	9		4				
10		25	Bury	2-1	Monk 2	22473	10	7	5	1				11	3					6	2	8	9		4				
11	Oct	2	WEST HAM UNITED	0-0		31369		7	5	1			10	11	3					6	2	8	9		4				
12		9	Queen's Park Rangers	0-2		25814		7	5	1			10	11	3					6	2	8	9		4				
13		16	LUTON TOWN	2-0	Gibbons, Buchanan	23211		7	5	1			9	11	3			10		6	2	8			4				
14		23	Bradford Park Avenue	1-3	Blakeman	14906	10	7	5	1			9	11	3					6	2	8			4				
15		30	SOUTHAMPTON	0-0		29887		7	5	1			10	11	3					6		8	9	2	4				
16	Nov	6	Barnsley	2-1	Nelson 2 (1p), Monk	20883		7	5	1			10	11	3					6	2	8	9		4				
17		13	GRIMSBY TOWN	2-0	Keene, Monk	24992		7	5	1			10		3				11	6	2	8	9		4				
18		20	Nottingham Forest	2-1	Gibbons, Monk	19278		7	5	1			10	11	3					6	2	8	9		4				
19	Dec	4	Plymouth Argyle	0-1		25611		7	5	1			10	11	3					6	2	8	9		4				
20		11	BLACKBURN ROVERS	0-1		21421		7	5	1			10	11	3					6	2	8	9		4				
21		18	Coventry City	1-2	Manley	21280		7	5	1					3			10	11	6	2	8	9		4				
22		25	CARDIFF CITY	1-1	Monk	22813		7	5	1					3		10		11	6	2	8	9		4				
23		27	Cardiff City	0-2		49236		7	5	1					3		10		11	6	2	8	9		4				
24	Jan	1	SHEFFIELD WEDNESDAY	2-1	Buchanan, Monk	16753		7	5	1					3		10		11	6	2	8	9		4				
25		15	Lincoln City	1-3	McKennan	13125		7	5	1					3		10		11	6	2	8	9		4				
26		22	CHESTERFIELD	1-1	Monk	25549		7	5	1					3		10		11	6	2	8	9		4				
27	Feb	5	West Bromwich Albion	0-2		39482			5	1			7		3		10		11	6	2	8	9		4				
28		19	BURY	8-2	McKennan 5 (1p), Gibbons, Monk 2	23249		7	5	1			10	11	3					6	2	8	9		4				
29	Mar	5	QUEEN'S PARK RANGERS	0-3		29420		7	5	1			10		3				11	6	2	8	9		4				
30		12	Luton Town	1-2	Chisholm	16682			5	1	7		8	11	3		10			6			9	2	4				
31		19	BRADFORD PARK AVE.	1-0	Manley (p)	18413		11		1	7				2	5	10			6			9	3	8	4			
32		26	Southampton	0-2		25217		11		1	7				2	5				6		8	9	3	4	10			
33	Apr	2	BARNSLEY	0-0		18485				1	7			11	2	5	8			6			9	3	10	4			
34		6	FULHAM	0-0		29160				1	9			11	2	5	8			6			7	3	4				10
35		9	Grimsby Town	0-3		15695				1	9			11	2	5	8			6			7	3	4				10
36		15	Tottenham Hotspur	0-2		39050				1	7				2	5	8			6			9	3	4			11	10
37		16	NOTTM. FOREST	2-1	Gager (og), Dare	15857		7		1	9				2	5	8		11	6	10			3	4				
38		18	TOTTENHAM HOTSPUR	1-1	Dare	19004		7		1	9				2	5	8		11	6	10			3	4				
39		23	Fulham	1-2	Dare	39149		7		1	9				2	5	8		11	6				3	4				10
40		25	West Ham United	1-1	Smith	15553				1	9				2	5	10			6		8	7	3		4		11	
41		30	PLYMOUTH ARGYLE	2-2	Buchanan 2	14360		11		1	9				2	5	10			6		8	7	3		4			
42	May	7	Blackburn Rovers	1-2	Gray (og)	15453					9	1			2	5				6			7		4	8	3	11	10
						Apps	9	34	30	41	13	1	15	24	42	12	19	4	12	42	30	24	37	13	40	6	1	3	10
						Goals	1	5	1		3		3	2					1	3		6	11		2			1	1

Two own goals

F.A. Cup

							Blakeman AG	Buchanan PS	Chisholm JR	Crozier J	Dare WT	Gaskell E	Gibbons AH	Girling HM	Gorman WC	Greenwood R	Harper AF	Harris K	Keene DC	Manley TR	McDonald M	McKennan PS	Monk FJ	Munro RA	Nelson D	Paterson GD	Quinton W	Smith A	Woodward V
R3	Jan	8	MIDDLESBROUGH	3-2	(aet) Harper, Monk, McKennan	30000		7	5	1					3		10		11	6	2	8	9		4				
R4		29	TORQUAY UNITED	1-0	McKennan	24500		7	5	1					3		10		11	6	2	8	9		4				
R5	Feb	12	BURNLEY	4-2	McKennan 2, Gibbons, Monk	34000		7	5	1			10	11	3					6	2	8	9		4				
R6		26	LEICESTER CITY	0-2		38678		7	5	1			10	11	3					6	2	8	9		4				

		Pl.	Home					Away					F.	A.	Pts
			W	D	L	F	A	W	D	L	F	A	(Total)		
1	Fulham	42	16	4	1	52	14	8	5	8	25	23	77	37	57
2	West Bromwich Alb.	42	16	3	2	47	16	8	5	8	22	23	69	39	56
3	Southampton	42	16	4	1	48	10	7	5	9	21	26	69	36	55
4	Cardiff City	42	14	4	3	45	21	5	9	7	17	26	62	47	51
5	Tottenham Hotspur	42	14	4	3	50	18	3	12	6	22	26	72	44	50
6	Chesterfield	42	9	7	5	24	18	6	10	5	27	27	51	45	47
7	West Ham United	42	13	5	3	38	23	5	5	11	18	35	56	58	46
8	Sheffield Wed.	42	12	6	3	36	17	3	7	11	27	39	63	56	43
9	Barnsley	42	10	7	4	40	18	4	5	12	22	43	62	61	40
10	Luton Town	42	11	6	4	32	16	3	6	12	23	41	55	57	40
11	Grimsby Town	42	10	5	6	44	28	5	5	11	28	48	72	76	40
12	Bury	42	12	5	4	41	23	5	1	15	26	53	67	76	40
13	Queen's Park Rgs.	42	11	4	6	31	26	3	7	11	13	36	44	62	39
14	Blackburn Rovers	42	12	5	4	41	23	3	3	15	12	40	53	63	38
15	Leeds United	42	11	6	4	36	21	1	7	13	19	42	55	63	37
16	Coventry City	42	12	3	6	35	20	3	4	14	20	44	55	64	37
17	Bradford Park Ave.	42	8	8	5	37	26	5	3	13	28	52	65	78	37
18	**BRENTFORD**	**42**	**7**	**10**	**4**	**28**	**21**	**4**	**4**	**13**	**14**	**32**	**42**	**53**	**36**
19	Leicester City	42	6	10	5	41	38	4	6	11	21	41	62	79	36
20	Plymouth Argyle	42	11	4	6	33	25	1	8	12	16	39	49	64	36
21	Nottingham Forest	42	9	6	6	22	14	5	1	15	28	40	50	54	35
22	Lincoln City	42	6	7	8	31	35	2	5	14	22	56	53	91	28

1948/49
Back: Nelson, Chisholm, MacDonald, Crozier, Gorman, Manley
Front: Buchanon, McKennan, Monk, Harper, Keene

1950/51
Back: Horne, Harper, Hill, Jeffries, Latimer, Munro
Front: Goodwin, Dare, Monk, Greenwood, Sperrin, Paton.

1949/50

9th in Division Two

No	Month	Day	Opponent	Result	Scorers	Att.	Anders J	Coote KA	Dare WT	Garneys TT	Gaskell E	Girling HM	Goodwin JW	Gorman WC	Greenwood R	Hill JWT	Jefferies AJ	Keene DC	Latimer FJ	Manley TR	Monk FJ	Munro RA	Nelson D	Newton RW	O'Flanagan KP	Paterson GD	Paton JA	Pointon WJ	Quinton W	Rampling DW	Sperrin WT	Woodward V
1	Aug	20	TOTTENHAM HOTSPUR	1-4	Manley (p)	32702		10	9		1	11	8	2	5					6			4						3	7		
2		24	Queen's Park Rangers	3-3	Dare 2, Monk	20931		10	7		1	11	8	2	5					6	9					4			3			
3		27	Bury	2-1	Woodward, Dare	16116		10	7		1	11		2	5					6	9					4			3			8
4		31	QUEEN'S PARK RANGERS	0-2		25741		10	7		1	11		2	5					6	9					4			3			8
5	Sep	3	LEICESTER CITY	0-1		20302	8	10	7		1	11			5	9				6		2	4						3			
6		10	Bradford Park Avenue	2-0	Goodwin, Paton	12754	8	10	9		1		7		5					6		2	4				11		3			
7		14	BLACKBURN ROVERS	2-0	Dare, Paton	19889	8	10	9		1		7		5					6		2	4				11		3			
8		17	CHESTERFIELD	0-0		25270		10	9		1		7		5	8				6		2	4				11		3			
9		19	Blackburn Rovers	1-4	Coote	18613		10	9		1		7		5				6			2	4				11		3			8
10		24	Plymouth Argyle	0-2		17088		10	9		1		7	2	5	8			6				4				11		3			
11	Oct	1	SHEFFIELD WEDNESDAY	1-1	Goodwin	25270		10	9		1		7	2	5				6				4				11		3		8	
12		8	Preston North End	0-2		30178		10	9		1		7	2	5	8				6			4				11		3			
13		15	SWANSEA TOWN	0-0		23871	8	10	9		1			2	5	9				6			4				11		3			
14		22	Leeds United	0-1		27342	8	10	9		1		7		5					6		2	4				11		3			
15		29	SOUTHAMPTON	0-1		21694			8				7		5	10	1			6	9	2	4				11		3			
16	Nov	5	Coventry City	1-1	Woodward	16110			9			11	7		5		1			6		2	4						3		8	10
17		12	LUTON TOWN	1-0	Sperrin	20520			9			11	7		5		1			6		2	4						3		10	8
18		19	Barnsley	1-0	Woodward	14942			9			11	7		5		1			6		2	4						3		10	8
19		26	WEST HAM UNITED	0-2		21887			9			11	7		5		1			6		2	4						3		10	8
20	Dec	3	Sheffield United	1-1	Dare	20649			9			11	7		5		1			6		2	4						3		10	8
21		10	GRIMSBY TOWN	1-0	Girling	16384			9			11	7		5		1			6		2	4						3		10	8
22		17	Tottenham Hotspur	1-1	Sperrin	49297			9				7		5		1			6	2		4		11				3		10	8
23		24	BURY	2-0	Dare 2	17401	8		9				7		5		1		6		2		4		11				3		10	
24		26	HULL CITY	3-1	Dare, Sperrin, Goodwin	33791	8		9				7		5		1		6		2		4		11				3		10	
25		27	Hull City	0-2		48447	8		9				7		5		1		6		2		4		11				3		10	
26		31	Leicester City	1-1	Dare	31919		8	9				7		5		1		6		2		4		11				3		10	
27	Jan	14	BRADFORD PARK AVE.	2-0	Coote, Paton	19781		8	9						5		1		6		2		4		7		11		3		10	
28		21	Chesterfield	1-3	Coote	12075		8	9				7		5		1		6		2		4				11		3		10	
29	Feb	4	PLYMOUTH ARGYLE	0-0		22313	10	8	9				7		5		1			6	2		4				11		3			
30		18	Sheffield Wednesday	3-3	Pointon, Hill, Dare	37923			9			11	7		5	10	1		4	6	2							8	3			
31		25	PRESTON NORTH END	1-0	Goodwin	25387			9			11	7		5	10	1		4	6	2							8	3			
32	Mar	4	Swansea Town	0-3		21239			9			11	7		5	10	1		4	6	2							8	3			
33		11	LEEDS UNITED	0-0		22231			9				7		5	10	1		4	6	2						11	8	3			
34		18	Southampton	3-2	Paton, Dare, Mallett (og)	22429			9				7		5	10	1		4	6	2						11	8	3			
35		25	COVENTRY CITY	2-0	Goodwin, Dare	16921		10	9				7		5		1		4	6	2	3					11	8				
36	Apr	1	West Ham United	2-2	Manley (p), Pointon	18826			9				7		5	10	1		4	6	2						11	8	3			
37		7	CARDIFF CITY	1-0	Goodwin	24584			9				7		5	10	1		4	6	2						11	8	3			
38		8	SHEFFIELD UNITED	1-0	Dare	22411			9				7		5	10	1		4	6	2	3					11	8				
39		10	Cardiff City	0-0		16260			9				7		5	10	1		4	6	2	3					11	8				
40		15	Luton Town	0-1		13991			9				7		5	10	1		4	6	2	3					11	8				
41		22	BARNSLEY	3-0	Paton, Hill, Dare	16514			9				7		5	10			4	6	2	3		1			11	8				
42		29	Grimsby Town	1-4	Garneys	11253		8		9					5	10		7	4	6	2	3		1			11					
						Apps	9	20	41	1	14	14	36	8	42	18	26	1	22	33	25	19	26	2	6	3	23	12	36	1	14	10
						Goals		3	14	1		1	6			2				2	1						5	2			3	3

One own goal

F.A. Cup

Round	Month	Day	Opponent	Result	Scorers	Att.	Anders J	Coote KA	Dare WT	Garneys TT	Gaskell E	Girling HM	Goodwin JW	Gorman WC	Greenwood R	Hill JWT	Jefferies AJ	Keene DC	Latimer FJ	Manley TR	Monk FJ	Munro RA	Nelson D	Newton RW	O'Flanagan KP	Paterson GD	Paton JA	Pointon WJ	Quinton W	Rampling DW	Sperrin WT	Woodward V
R3	Jan	7	CHELSEA	0-1		36000	8		9				7		5		1		6		2		4		11				3		10	

		Pl.	Home W	D	L	F	A	Away W	D	L	F	A	F. (Total)	A. (Total)	Pts
1	Tottenham Hotspur	42	15	3	3	51	15	12	4	5	30	20	81	35	61
2	Sheffield Wed.	42	12	7	2	46	23	6	9	6	21	25	67	48	52
3	Sheffield United	42	9	10	2	36	19	10	4	7	32	30	68	49	52
4	Southampton	42	13	4	4	44	25	6	10	5	20	23	64	48	52
5	Leeds United	42	11	8	2	33	16	6	5	10	21	29	54	45	47
6	Preston North End	42	12	5	4	37	21	6	4	11	23	28	60	49	45
7	Hull City	42	11	8	2	39	25	6	3	12	25	47	64	72	45
8	Swansea Town	42	11	3	7	34	18	6	6	9	19	31	53	49	43
9	**BRENTFORD**	**42**	**11**	**5**	**5**	**21**	**12**	**4**	**8**	**9**	**23**	**37**	**44**	**49**	**43**
10	Cardiff City	42	13	3	5	28	14	3	7	11	13	30	41	44	42
11	Grimsby Town	42	13	5	3	53	25	3	3	15	21	48	74	73	40
12	Coventry City	42	8	6	7	32	24	5	7	9	23	31	55	55	39
13	Barnsley	42	11	6	4	45	28	2	7	12	19	39	64	67	39
14	Chesterfield	42	12	3	6	28	16	3	6	12	15	31	43	47	39
15	Leicester City	42	8	9	4	30	25	4	6	11	25	40	55	65	39
16	Blackburn Rovers	42	10	5	6	30	15	4	5	12	25	45	55	60	38
17	Luton Town	42	8	9	4	28	22	2	9	10	13	29	41	51	38
18	Bury	42	10	8	3	37	19	4	1	16	23	46	60	65	37
19	West Ham United	42	8	7	6	30	25	4	5	12	23	36	53	61	36
20	Queen's Park Rgs.	42	6	5	10	21	30	5	7	9	19	27	40	57	34
21	Plymouth Argyle	42	6	6	9	19	24	2	10	9	25	41	44	65	32
22	Bradford Park Ave.	42	7	6	8	34	34	3	5	13	17	43	51	77	31

1950/51

9th in Division Two

							Anders J	Bristow GA	Broadbent PF	Coote KA	Dare WTC	Garneys TT	Gaskell E	Goodwin JW	Greenwood R	Harper AF	Hill JWT	Horne KW	Jefferies AJ	Kelly BA	Latimer FJ	Manley TR	Monk FJ	Munro RA	Newton RW	Paton JA	Pointon WJ	Quinton W	Sinclair T	Sperrin WT
1	Aug	19	Luton Town	0-2		17721					8			7	5		10		1		4	6	2	3		11	9			
2		21	Blackburn Rovers	2-3	Garneys, Goodwin	30176					8	9		7	5	4	10		1			6	2	3		11				
3		26	LEEDS UNITED	1-2	Manley	20276						9		7	5	4	10		1			6	2	3		11	8			
4		30	BLACKBURN ROVERS	3-2	Hill 2, Manley (p)	12122				8		9		7	5		10		1		4	6	2	3					11	
5	Sep	2	West Ham United	2-1	Dare, Hill	21246					8	9		7	5	4	10		1		6		2	3					11	
6		6	Barnsley	3-2	Hill, Sinclair	15505					8	9		7	5	4	10				6		2	3	1				11	
7		9	SWANSEA TOWN	2-1	Hill, Sinclair	23572	7				8	9			5	4	10				6		2	3	1				11	
8		13	BARNSLEY	0-2		18448					8	9		7	5	4	10				6		2	3	1				11	
9		16	Hull City	0-3		31925				8	7	9			5	4	10				6		2		1			3	11	
10		23	DONCASTER ROVERS	1-1	Dare	21544	11			10	7	9			5	4					6		2		1			3		8
11		30	Preston North End	2-4	Dare 2	29881	11				7		1		5	8	10				4	6	2				9	3		
12	Oct	7	COVENTRY CITY	0-4		19754					8		1	7	5	4	10				6		2				9	3	11	
13		14	Manchester City	0-4		39646		6	7		9				5		10		1		4		2	3					11	8
14		21	BIRMINGHAM CITY	2-1	Sinclair, Goodwin	19273		6	8		9			7	5		10		1		4		2	3					11	
15		28	Cardiff City	1-1	Hill	22885		6	8		9			7	5		10		1		4		2	3		11				
16	Nov	4	NOTTS COUNTY	1-3	Goodwin	26393		6	8					7	5		10		1		4		2	3		11			9	
17		11	Grimsby Town	2-7	Goodwin, Broadbent	14985		6	8		9			7	5		10		1		4			2		11		3		
18		18	LEICESTER CITY	0-0		16277			8		9			7	5		6	2	1		4			3		11				10
19		25	Chesterfield	2-2	Sperrin 2	9719			8		9			7	5		6	2	1		4			3		11				10
20	Dec	2	QUEEN'S PARK RANGERS	2-1	Dare, Goodwin	23121			8		9			7	5		6	2	1		4			3		11				10
21		9	Bury	1-2	Goodwin	10825			8		9			7	5		6	2	1		4			3		11				10
22		16	LUTON TOWN	1-0	Coote	9808				8		9		7	5		6		1		4		2	3		11				10
23		23	Leeds United	0-1		19839			8			9		7	5		6		1		4		2	3		11				10
24		26	SOUTHAMPTON	4-0	Dare 4	22435			8		9				5	6			1		4		2	3		11			7	10
25		30	WEST HAM UNITED	1-1	Paton	19291			8		9				5	6			1		4		2	3		11			7	10
26	Jan	13	Swansea Town	1-2	Sperrin	15422				8	9				5	6			1		4		2	3		7			11	10
27		20	HULL CITY	2-1	Sperrin, Sinclair	20523			8						5	4	6	2	1				9	3		11			7	10
28		27	Queen's Park Rangers	1-1	Dare	26290					8				5	4	6	2	1				9	3		11			7	10
29	Feb	3	Doncaster Rovers	3-0	Sperrin, Monk, Greenwood	20733			8						5	4	6	2	1				9	3		11			7	10
30		10	BURY	4-0	Griffiths (og), Broadbent, Monk 2	14986			8					7	5	4	6	2	1				9	3		11				10
31		17	PRESTON NORTH END	2-4	Goodwin, Monk	23434			8					7	5	4	6	2	1				9	3		11				10
32		24	Coventry City	3-3	Sperrin 2, Monk (p)	22892					8			7	5	4	6	2	1				9	3		11				10
33	Mar	3	MANCHESTER CITY	2-0	Monk (p), Sperrin	24288					8			7	5	4	6	2	1				9	3		11				10
34		17	CARDIFF CITY	4-0	Paton, Monk, Sperrin, Hill	19663					8			7	5	4	6	2	1				9	3		11				10
35		23	SHEFFIELD UNITED	3-1	Harper, Dare, Monk	23188					8			7	5	4	6	2	1				9	3		11				10
36		24	Notts County	3-2	Monk, Sperrin 2	24936					8			7	5	4	6	2	1				9	3		11				10
37		26	Sheffield United	1-5	Monk	20816					8			7	5	4	6	2	1				9	3		11				10
38		31	GRIMSBY TOWN	5-1	Kelly, Monk, Dare, Paton 2	15777					8			10	5	4	6	2	1	7			9	3		11				
39	Apr	7	Leicester City	2-1	Goodwin, Dare	20384					8			7	5	4	6	2	1				9	3		11				10
40		14	CHESTERFIELD	4-0	Goodwin, Dare, Monk	17278					8			7	5	4	6	2	1				9	3		11				10
41		25	Birmingham City	1-1	Dare	13643					8			7	5	4	6	2	1				9	3		11				10
42	May	5	Southampton	1-2	Monk	14441					8			7	5	4	6	2	1				9	3		11				10
						Apps	3	5	16	5	33	11	2	31	42	29	38	20	35	1	24	5	37	38	5	31	4	5	16	26
						Goals			2	1	16	1		9	1	1	7			1		2	13			4			5	11

One own goal

F.A. Cup

							Anders J	Bristow GA	Broadbent PF	Coote KA	Dare WTC	Garneys TT	Gaskell E	Goodwin JW	Greenwood R	Harper AF	Hill JWT	Horne KW	Jefferies AJ	Kelly BA	Latimer FJ	Manley TR	Monk FJ	Munro RA	Newton RW	Paton JA	Pointon WJ	Quinton W	Sinclair T	Sperrin WT
R3	Jan	6	Stockport County	1-2	Paton	16346				8	9				5	6			1		4		2	3		11			7	10

		Pl.	Home W	D	L	F	A	Away W	D	L	F	A	F. (Total)	A. (Total)	Pts
1	Preston North End	42	16	3	2	53	18	10	2	9	38	31	91	49	57
2	Manchester City	42	12	6	3	53	25	7	8	6	36	36	89	61	52
3	Cardiff City	42	13	7	1	36	20	4	9	8	17	25	53	45	50
4	Birmingham City	42	12	6	3	37	20	8	3	10	27	33	64	53	49
5	Leeds United	42	14	4	3	36	17	6	4	11	27	38	63	55	48
6	Blackburn Rovers	42	13	3	5	39	27	6	5	10	26	39	65	66	46
7	Coventry City	42	15	3	3	51	25	4	4	13	24	34	75	59	45
8	Sheffield United	42	11	4	6	44	27	5	8	8	28	35	72	62	44
9	**BRENTFORD**	**42**	**13**	**3**	**5**	**44**	**25**	**5**	**5**	**11**	**31**	**49**	**75**	**74**	**44**
10	Hull City	42	12	5	4	47	28	4	6	11	27	42	74	70	43
11	Doncaster Rovers	42	9	6	6	37	32	6	7	8	27	36	64	68	43
12	Southampton	42	10	9	2	38	27	5	4	12	28	46	66	73	43
13	West Ham United	42	10	5	6	44	33	6	5	10	24	36	68	69	42
14	Leicester City	42	10	4	7	42	28	5	7	9	26	30	68	58	41
15	Barnsley	42	9	5	7	42	22	6	5	10	32	46	74	68	40
16	Queen's Park Rgs.	42	13	5	3	47	25	2	5	14	24	57	71	82	40
17	Notts County	42	7	7	7	37	34	6	6	9	24	26	61	60	39
18	Swansea Town	42	14	1	6	34	25	2	3	16	20	52	54	77	36
19	Luton Town	42	7	9	5	34	23	2	5	14	23	47	57	70	32
20	Bury	42	9	4	8	33	27	3	4	14	27	59	60	86	32
21	Chesterfield	42	7	7	7	30	28	2	5	14	14	41	44	69	30
22	Grimsby Town	42	6	8	7	37	38	2	4	15	24	57	61	95	28

1951/52

10th in Division Two

No.	Month	Date	Opponent	Score	Scorers	Att.	Bowie JD	Bragg WL	Bristow GA	Coote KA	Dare WTC	Dargie IC	Gaskell E	Godwin V	Goodwin JW	Greenwood R	Harper AF	Hill JWT	Horne KW	Jefferies AJ	Jones T	Latimer FJ	Lawton T	Ledgerton T	Monk FJ	Morrad FG	Munro RA	Newton RW	Paton IA	Slater WJ	Sperrin WT
1	Aug	18	Leeds United	1-1	Paton	20268					8				7	5	4	6	2	1					9		3		11		10
2		22	Everton	0-1		32722					8				7	5	4	6	2	1					9		3		11		10
3		25	ROTHERHAM UNITED	2-0	Sperrin, Monk	24904					8				7	5	4	6	2	1					9		3		11		10
4		27	EVERTON	1-0	Sperrin	19525					8				7	5	4	6	2	1					9		3		11		10
5	Sep	1	Cardiff City	0-2		27772					8				7	5	4	6	2	1					9		3		11		10
6		5	Doncaster Rovers	2-1	Goodwin, Monk (p)	21154					10				7	5	4	6	2	1					9		3		11		10
7		8	BIRMINGHAM CITY	1-0	Monk	25029					10				7	5	4	6	2	1					9		3		11		10
8		15	Leicester City	1-1	Monk	23757					10				7	5	4	6	2	1					9		3		11		10
9		22	NOTTM. FOREST	1-1	Hill	26350					10				7	5	4	6	2	1					9		3		11		10
10		29	Queen's Park Rangers	1-3	Monk	25339					8				7	5	4	6	2	1					9		3		11		10
11	Oct	6	NOTTS COUNTY	1-0	Coote	28214				8	7					5	4	6	2	1					9		3		11		10
12		13	Luton Town	2-0	Sperrin, Monk	18521				8	7					5	4	6	2	1					9		3		11		10
13		20	BURY	4-0	Sperrin 2, Coote, Paton	20726				8	7					5	4	6	2	1	3				9				11		10
14		27	Swansea Town	1-1	Sperrin	19235				8	7					5	4	6	2	1					9		3		11		10
15	Nov	3	COVENTRY CITY	1-0	Monk	22899				8	7					5	4	6	2	1					9		3		11		10
16		10	West Ham United	0-1		26288				8	7					5	4	6	2	1					9		3		11		10
17		17	SHEFFIELD UNITED	4-1	Paton, Monk 2, Sperrin	27124				8	7		1			5	4	6	2						9		3		11		10
18		24	Barnsley	0-0		10149				8	7		1			5	4	6	2						9		3		11		10
19	Dec	1	HULL CITY	2-1	Monk 2	26072				8	7		1			5	4	6	2						9		3		11		10
20		8	Blackburn Rovers	0-3		13617				8	7		1			5	4	6	2						9		3		11		10
21		15	LEEDS UNITED	2-1	Dare 2	17957				8	7		1			5	4	6	2						9		3		11		10
22		22	Rotherham United	1-1	Monk	14809				8	7		1			5	4	6	2						9		3		11		10
23		25	SOUTHAMPTON	1-2	Dare	25841				8	7		1			5	4	6	2						9		3		11		10
24		26	Southampton	1-2	Sperrin	21625				8	7		1			5	4	6	2						9		3		11		10
25		29	CARDIFF CITY	1-1	Paton	27547				8	7		1			5	4	6	2						9		3		11		10
26	Jan	5	Birmingham City	2-1	Dare, Badham (og)	28368				8	7		1				4		2			5			9		3		11	6	10
27		19	LEICESTER CITY	1-3	Dare	19923		9		8	7		1				4		2			5					3		11	6	10
28		26	Nottingham Forest	0-2		21649					11		1		7	5	4	8	2						9		3			6	10
29	Feb	9	QUEEN'S PARK RANGERS	0-0		25645			6	10	9		1		8	5	4		3					11	2				7		
30		16	Notts County	2-5	Dare, Sperrin	22503			6	8	9		1			5	4		2					11	7		3				10
31	Mar	1	LUTON TOWN	3-3	Dare 2, Horne	21218				7	8		1			5	4	6	9					11	2		3				10
32		8	Bury	0-1		12140	8			7	9					5	4					6		11	2		3	1			10
33		15	SWANSEA TOWN	3-1	Coote, Dare 2	29753	8			7	10					5	4					6	9	11	2		3	1			
34		22	Coventry City	1-2	Dare	27577	8	6		10	11				7	5	4						9		2		3	1			
35	Apr	5	Sheffield United	4-1	Lawton, Paton, Dare, Harper	23435	8	6			10				7	5	4						9		2		3	1	11		
36		11	SHEFFIELD WEDNESDAY	2-3	Bragg, Dare	35827	8	6			10				7	5	4		2				9				3	1	11		
37		12	BARNSLEY	1-1	Goodwin	19912	8	6			10				7	5							9		2		3	1	11	4	
38		14	Sheffield Wednesday	0-2		43935	8	6			10				7	5							9		2		3	1	11	4	
39		19	Hull City	1-4	Dare	30891	8	4			10	6			7	5							9		2		3	1	11		
40		21	WEST HAM UNITED	1-1	Lawton	12563		6			10			8	7				3				9		2		5	1	11	4	
41		26	BLACKBURN ROVERS	1-1	Slater	16195	8	6			10				7				3				9		2		5	1	11	4	
42		30	DONCASTER ROVERS	1-0	Morrad	10243		6		8	10				7		4			1			9		2	3	5		11		
						Apps	9	10	2	24	42	1	15	1	21	37	37	27	34	17	1	4	10	5	40	1	40	10	36	7	31
						Goals		1		3	14				2		1	1	1				2		12	1			5	1	9

Match 40 originally played March 29, abandoned half-time (snow)

One own goal

F.A. Cup

Round	Month	Date	Opponent	Score	Scorers	Att.	Bowie JD	Bragg WL	Bristow GA	Coote KA	Dare WTC	Dargie IC	Gaskell E	Godwin V	Goodwin JW	Greenwood R	Harper AF	Hill JWT	Horne KW	Jefferies AJ	Jones T	Latimer FJ	Lawton T	Ledgerton T	Monk FJ	Morrad FG	Munro RA	Newton RW	Paton IA	Slater WJ	Sperrin WT
R3	Jan	12	QUEEN'S PARK RANGERS	3-1	Coote, Paton, Sperrin	35000				8	7		1				4		2			5			9		3		11	6	10
R4	Feb	2	Luton Town	2-2	Sperrin 2	25320				8	9		1		7	5	4	6	2								3		11		10
rep		6	LUTON TOWN	0-0	(aet)	31143				8	9		1		7	5	4	6	2								3		11		10
rep2		18	Luton Town	2-3	(aet) Dare 2	37269				8	9		1			5	4	6	2					11	7		3				10

R4 rep 2 at Highbury. R4 - rep and rep 2, both a.e.t.

		Pl.	Home W	D	L	F	A	Away W	D	L	F	A	F. (Total)	A.	Pts
1	Sheffield Wed.	42	14	4	3	54	23	7	7	7	46	43	100	66	53
2	Cardiff City	42	18	2	1	52	15	2	9	10	20	39	72	54	51
3	Birmingham City	42	11	6	4	36	21	10	3	8	31	35	67	56	51
4	Nottingham Forest	42	12	6	3	41	22	6	7	8	36	40	77	62	49
5	Leicester City	42	12	6	3	48	24	7	3	11	30	40	78	64	47
6	Leeds United	42	13	7	1	35	15	5	4	12	24	42	59	57	47
7	Everton	42	12	5	4	42	25	5	5	11	22	33	64	58	44
8	Luton Town	42	9	7	5	46	35	7	5	9	31	43	77	78	44
9	Rotherham United	42	11	4	6	40	25	6	4	11	33	46	73	71	42
10	**BRENTFORD**	**42**	**11**	**7**	**3**	**34**	**20**	**4**	**5**	**12**	**20**	**35**	**54**	**55**	**42**
11	Sheffield United	42	13	2	6	57	28	5	3	13	33	48	90	76	41
12	West Ham United	42	13	5	3	48	29	2	6	13	19	48	67	77	41
13	Southampton	42	11	6	4	40	25	4	5	12	21	48	61	73	41
14	Blackburn Rovers	42	11	3	7	35	30	6	3	12	19	33	54	63	40
15	Notts County	42	11	5	5	45	27	5	2	14	26	41	71	68	39
16	Doncaster Rovers	42	9	4	8	29	28	4	8	9	26	32	55	60	38
17	Bury	42	13	2	6	43	22	2	5	14	24	47	67	69	37
18	Hull City	42	11	5	5	44	23	2	6	13	16	47	60	70	37
19	Swansea Town	42	10	4	7	45	26	2	8	11	27	50	72	76	36
20	Barnsley	42	8	7	6	39	33	3	7	11	20	39	59	72	36
21	Coventry City	42	9	5	7	36	33	5	1	15	23	49	59	82	34
22	Queen's Park Rgs.	42	8	8	5	35	35	3	4	14	17	46	52	81	34

1951-52
Back: Horne, Harper, Hill, Jefferies, Latimer, Munroe
Front: Goodwin, Dare, Monk, Greenwood, Sperrin, Paton.

1952-53
Back: Greenwood, Bragg, Newton, Jeffries, Monk, Munroe
Middle: Latimer, Goodwin, Harper, Lawton, Smith, Coote, Horne
Front: Dare, Sperrin.

1952/53

17th in Division Two

No	Month	Day	Opponent	Score	Scorers	Att	Bloomfield JH	Bragg WL	Bristow GA	Bull MF	Coote KA	D'Arcy SD	Dare WTC	Dargie IC	Godwin V	Goodwin JW	Greenwood R	Harper AF	Horne KW	Jefferies AJ	Jones T	Latimer FJ	Lawton T	Ledgerton T	Monk FJ	Morrad FG	Munro RA	Newton RW	Smith LGF	Sperrin WT
1	Aug	23	LINCOLN CITY	1-0	Goodwin	27787		6					8			7	5	4		1			9		2		3		11	10
2		27	Huddersfield Town	0-0		21358		6					8			7	5	4		1			9		2		3		11	10
3		30	Hull City	2-2	Dare, Monk (p)	35993		6					8			7	5	4		1			9		2		3		11	10
4	Sep	3	HUDDERSFIELD T	1-3	Lawton	21733		6					8			7	5	4		1			9		2		3		11	10
5		6	BLACKBURN ROVERS	3-2	Sperrin, Lawton, Monk (p)	21904		6					8			7	5	4		1			9		2		3		11	10
6		8	Sheffield United	2-3	Goodwin, Ledgerton	17397		6					8			7	5	4		1			9	11	2		3			10
7		13	Nottingham Forest	0-3		26923		6					8	5		7		4		1			9	11	2		3			10
8		17	SHEFFIELD UNITED	0-0		11707		6					10			7	5	8		1		4	9	11	2		3			
9		20	EVERTON	2-4	Lawton, Harper	21042		6					10				5	8		1		4	9	11	2		3		7	
10		27	Bury	0-3		12398							7				5	4	2	1		6	9	11	8		3		10	
11	Oct	4	Doncaster Rovers	2-0	Monk, Goodwin	13465								5		7		4	2	1		6	9	11	8		3		10	
12		11	SOUTHAMPTON	3-0	Lawton, Monk (p), Smith	17225								5		7		4	2	1		6	9	11	8		3		10	
13		18	Notts County	0-4		26033								5		7		4	2	1		6	9	11	8		3		10	
14		25	LEICESTER CITY	4-2	Goodwin, Lawton 2, Dare	21655		6				8	10	5		7		4		1			9	11	2		3			
15	Nov	1	West Ham United	1-3	D'Arcy	23263		6			8	9		5		7		4		1				11	2		3		10	
16		8	FULHAM	2-2	D'Arcy, Monk (p)	29241		6				9	10	5		7			3	1		4		11	2				8	
17		15	Rotherham United	1-4	Monk (p)	15427		6				8	10	5		7			3	1		4	9	11	2					
18		22	PLYMOUTH ARGYLE	1-2	Lawton	17192		6			8		10	5		7			3	1		4	9	11	2					
19		29	Leeds United	2-3	Dare, Ledgerton	16077		6				8	10	5		7			3	1		4	9	11	2					
20	Dec	13	Birmingham City	1-3	Lawton	9963		5				8	10			7		4		1			9	11	2		3		6	
21		20	Lincoln City	0-0		11953		5					8		9	7		4		1		6			2		3		11	10
22		25	BARNSLEY	4-0	Sperrin, Dare, Lawton 2	15976		5					8			7		4		1		6	9	11	2		3			10
23		26	Barnsley	2-0	McNeil (og), Ledgerton	13725		5					8			7		4		1		6	9	11	2		3			10
24	Jan	3	HULL CITY	1-0	D'Arcy	16035		5				8	7					4		1		6	9	11	2		3			10
25		17	Blackburn Rovers	0-3		21487		5				10	8		7			4		1		6	9	11	2		3			
26		24	NOTTM. FOREST	1-1	Ledgerton	15110		5				10	8			7		4		1		6	9	11	2		3			
27	Feb	7	Everton	0-5		36431		5		11	10	8				7		4		1		6	9		2		3			
28		14	BURY	2-2	Sperrin, Bloomfield	9387	7	5		11	10							4		1		6	9		2		3			8
29		21	DONCASTER ROVERS	1-0	Lawton	16716	7	5	6	11	10		8					4		1			9		2		3			
30		28	Southampton	2-0	Ellerington (og), Dare	20327	7	5	6				8					4		1		10	9		2	11	3			
31	Mar	7	NOTTS COUNTY	5-0	Monk (p), Harper 2, Dare, Lawton	16147	7	5			6		8					4		1	3	10	9		2	11				
32		14	Leicester City	3-2	Morrad, Latimer 2	21307	7	5			6		8					4		1	3	10	9		2	11				
33		21	WEST HAM UNITED	1-4	Latimer	18117	7	5			6		8					4		1	3	10	9		2	11				
34		28	Fulham	0-5		25550	7	5			6		8					4		1	3	10	9	11	2					
35	Apr	3	SWANSEA TOWN	0-0		17876	8	5	6		4					7			2			10	9			11	3	1		
36		4	ROTHERHAM UNITED	1-1	Bloomfield	14411	7	5	6		4	8	9						2			10		11			3	1		
37		6	Swansea Town	2-3	Ledgerton, Godwin	21695	7	5	6		4		9		10			8						11	2		3	1		
38		11	Plymouth Argyle	0-1		19955	7	5			6				8			4				10	9	11	2		3	1		
39		18	LEEDS UNITED	3-3	Ledgerton, Coote, Lawton	12783	7	5			6	8						4				10	9	11	2		3	1		
40		22	LUTON TOWN	1-1	Ledgerton	16347	7	5			6	8	9					4				10		11	2		3	1		
41		25	Luton Town	1-0	Dare	15826	7	5			6		9		8			4				10		11	2		3	1		
42	May	1	BIRMINGHAM CITY	1-2	Dare	8565	7	5			6		9		8			4		1		10		11	2		3			
						Apps	15	38	5	3	17	13	33	10	6	24	9	36	10	35	4	30	34	28	40	5	34	7	14	12
						Goals	2				1	3	8		1	4		3				3	13	7	7	1			1	3

Two own goals

F.A. Cup

Rd	Month	Day	Opponent	Score	Scorers	Att	Bloomfield JH	Bragg WL	Bristow GA	Bull MF	Coote KA	D'Arcy SD	Dare WTC	Dargie IC	Godwin V	Goodwin JW	Greenwood R	Harper AF	Horne KW	Jefferies AJ	Jones T	Latimer FJ	Lawton T	Ledgerton T	Monk FJ	Morrad FG	Munro RA	Newton RW	Smith LGF	Sperrin WT
R3	Jan	10	LEEDS UNITED	2-1	Ledgerton, Lawton	22650		5					8			7		4		1		6	9	11	2		3			10
R4		31	Aston Villa	0-0		40627		5					8			7		4		1		6	9	11	2		3			10
rep	Feb	4	ASTON VILLA	1-2	Lawton	21735		5					8			7		4		1		6	9	11	2		3			10

		Pl.	Home					Away					F.	A.	Pts
			W	D	L	F	A	W	D	L	F	A	(Total)		
1	Sheffield United	42	15	3	3	60	27	10	7	4	37	28	97	55	60
2	Huddersfield Town	42	14	4	3	51	14	10	6	5	33	19	84	33	58
3	Luton Town	42	15	1	5	53	17	7	7	7	31	32	84	49	52
4	Plymouth Argyle	42	12	5	4	37	24	8	4	9	28	36	65	60	49
5	Leicester City	42	13	6	2	55	29	5	6	10	34	45	89	74	48
6	Birmingham City	42	11	3	7	44	38	8	7	6	27	28	71	66	48
7	Nottingham Forest	42	11	5	5	46	32	7	3	11	31	35	77	67	44
8	Fulham	42	14	1	6	52	28	3	9	9	29	43	81	71	44
9	Blackburn Rovers	42	12	4	5	40	20	6	4	11	28	45	68	65	44
10	Leeds United	42	13	4	4	42	24	1	11	9	29	39	71	63	43
11	Swansea Town	42	10	9	2	45	26	5	3	13	33	55	78	81	42
12	Rotherham United	42	9	7	5	41	30	7	2	12	34	44	75	74	41
13	Doncaster Rovers	42	9	9	3	26	17	3	7	11	32	47	58	64	40
14	West Ham United	42	9	5	7	38	28	4	8	9	20	32	58	60	39
15	Lincoln City	42	9	9	3	41	26	2	8	11	23	45	64	71	39
16	Everton	42	9	8	4	38	23	3	6	12	33	52	71	75	38
17	**BRENTFORD**	**42**	**8**	**8**	**5**	**38**	**29**	**5**	**3**	**13**	**21**	**47**	**59**	**76**	**37**
18	Hull City	42	11	6	4	36	19	3	2	16	21	50	57	69	36
19	Notts County	42	11	5	5	41	31	3	3	15	19	57	60	88	36
20	Bury	42	10	6	5	33	30	3	3	15	20	51	53	81	35
21	Southampton	42	5	7	9	45	44	5	6	10	23	41	68	85	33
22	Barnsley	42	4	4	13	31	46	1	4	16	16	62	47	108	18

1953/54

21st in Division Two: Relegated

							Avis VCS	Bassham AJ	Bloomfield JH	Bragg WL	Bristow GA	Broome FH	Coote KA	Dare WTC	Dargie IC	Dudley FE	Gazzard G	Goodwin JW	Harper AF	Horne KW	Jefferies AJ	Lattimer FJ	Lawton T	Ledgerton T	Lowden G	McPherson IB	Monk FJ	Newton RW	Rainford JW	Robertson JW	Sperrin WT
1	Aug	19	Stoke City	1-1	Broome	22413		3	7	5		11		10					4		1	6	9			8	2				
2		22	Derby County	1-4	Lawton	18927		3	7	5		11	6	10					4		1		9			8	2				
3		27	BLACKBURN ROVERS	1-4	Ledgerton	16682			7	5		8	6						4		1	3	9	11			2				10
4		29	FULHAM	2-1	Monk (p), Goodwin	21689			8	5	10		6	9				7	4			3		11			2	1			
5		31	Blackburn Rovers	2-2	Dare 2	11793			8	5	10		6	9				7	4			3		11			2	1			
6	Sep	5	BRISTOL ROVERS	0-3		21158				5	10	11	6	9				7	4			3				8	2	1			
7		10	DONCASTER ROVERS	1-4	Lawton	14047				5	6		4	9				7	8				10	11	3		2	1			
8		12	Lincoln City	1-2	Harper	16592			8	5		11	6	10				7	4	3			9				2	1			
9		16	Doncaster Rovers	0-3		19463				5		11	8	10				7	4	3		6	9				2	1			
10		19	NOTTS COUNTY	0-0		12770			8	5			6	9				7	4	3		10					2	1		11	
11		26	Hull City	0-2		19501			8	5			6	9				7	4	3				11			2	1		10	
12	Oct	3	EVERTON	1-0	Dare	17367			8	5			6	9				7	4	3						10	2	1		11	
13		10	West Ham United	1-0	Bloomfield	24934			8	5	10		6	9				7	4			3					2	1		11	
14		17	LEEDS UNITED	2-1	Dare, Bloomfield	18329			10	5			6	9				7	4			3					2	1	8	11	
15		24	Birmingham City	1-5	Dare	23582				5	10		6	9				7	4			3					2	1	8	11	
16		31	NOTTM. FOREST	1-1	Rainford	15384			10	5			6	9				7	4			3					2	1	8	11	
17	Nov	7	Luton Town	1-1	Robertson	15167			10	5			6	9				7	4			3					2	1	8	11	
18		14	PLYMOUTH ARGYLE	1-0	Dare	17327			10	5			6	9				7	4			3					2	1	8	11	
19		21	Swansea Town	0-1		16627			10	5			6	9				7	4			3					2	1	8	11	
20		28	ROTHERHAM UNITED	0-1		16740			10	5			6	9				7	4			3					2	1	8	11	
21	Dec	5	Leicester City	0-6		24036			7	5			6	9					4			3					2	1	10	11	8
22		12	STOKE CITY	0-0		11848	9			5			6	10				7	4	2		3						1	8	11	
23		19	DERBY COUNTY	0-0		10652			7	5			6	10		9			4	2		3						1	8	11	
24		25	OLDHAM ATHLETIC	3-1	Rainford, Dudley, Bloomfield	15309			7	5			6	10		9			4	2		3						1	8	11	
25		26	Oldham Athletic	0-2		14414			8	5	4		6	7		9				2		3						1	10	11	
26	Jan	2	Fulham	1-4	Dudley	24372			8	5	6		2	7		9			4			3		11				1	10		
27		16	Bristol Rovers	0-0		20541			8		4		3	10		9		7				5		11			2	1	6		
28		23	LINCOLN CITY	0-1		11431			7	5	4		6	8		9						3					2	1	10	11	
29		30	Bury	1-1	Robertson	9035			7	2	4		6		5	9	8					3						1	10	11	
30	Feb	6	Notts County	0-2		10507			7	2	4		6		5	9	8					3						1	10	11	
31		13	HULL CITY	2-2	Gazzard 2	11522			7	2	4		6		5	9	8					3						1	10	11	
32		24	Everton	1-6	Gazzard	23145				2	4		6	9	5	11	8					3						1	10	7	
33		27	WEST HAM UNITED	3-1	Gazzard, Dudley (p), Dare	16458				2	4		6	9	5	11	8					3						1	10	7	
34	Mar	6	Leeds United	0-4		16501				2	4		6	9	5	11	8					3						1	10	7	
35		13	BIRMINGHAM CITY	2-0	Dudley 2	12584				2	6			9	5	11	8		4			3						1	10	7	
36		20	Nottingham Forest	1-2	Dudley	15700				2	4		6	9	5	11	8					3						1	10	7	
37		27	SWANSEA TOWN	3-1	Gazzard, Robertson, Dudley	14023				2	4		6	9	5	11	8					3						1	10	7	
38	Apr	3	Rotherham United	1-1	Bragg	9198				2	4		6	9	5	11	8					3						1	10	7	
39		10	LUTON TOWN	0-1		14204				2	4		6	9	5	11	8					3						1	10	7	
40		16	BURY	2-1	Gazzard (p), Dudley	15768				2	4		6	9	5	11	8					3						1	10	7	
41		17	Plymouth Argyle	2-3	Dudley, Robertson	23405				2	4		6	9	5	11	8					3						1	10	7	
42		24	LEICESTER CITY	1-3	Dudley	22845			8	2	4		6	9	5	11				3								1	10	7	
						Apps	1	2	27	41	24	6	40	38	14	20	13	19	26	10	3	36	6	7	1	4	23	39	29	31	2
						Goals			3	1		1		7		10	6	1	1				2	1			1		2	4	

F.A. Cup

							Avis VCS	Bassham AJ	Bloomfield JH	Bragg WL	Bristow GA	Broome FH	Coote KA	Dare WTC	Dargie IC	Dudley FE	Gazzard G	Goodwin JW	Harper AF	Horne KW	Jefferies AJ	Lattimer FJ	Lawton T	Ledgerton T	Lowden G	McPherson IB	Monk FJ	Newton RW	Rainford JW	Robertson JW	Sperrin WT
R3	Jan	9	HULL CITY	0-0		15182			8	5	4		6	7		9						3		11			2	1	10		
rep		14	Hull City	2-2	(aet) Dudley, Rainford	20126				2	4		6	8	5	9		7				3		11				1	10		
rep2		18	Hull City	2-5	Sperrin, Bloomfield	10176			7	5	4		6			9						3		11			2	1	10		8

Replay 2 at Belle Vue, Doncaster

	Pl.	Home W	D	L	F	A	Away W	D	L	F	A	F. (Total)	A. (Total)	Pts
1 Leicester City	42	15	4	2	63	23	8	6	7	34	37	97	60	56
2 Everton	42	13	6	2	55	27	7	10	4	37	31	92	58	56
3 Blackburn Rovers	42	15	4	2	54	16	8	5	8	32	34	86	50	55
4 Nottingham Forest	42	15	5	1	61	27	5	7	9	25	32	86	59	52
5 Rotherham United	42	13	4	4	51	26	8	3	10	29	41	80	67	49
6 Luton Town	42	11	7	3	36	23	7	5	9	28	36	64	59	48
7 Birmingham City	42	12	6	3	49	18	6	5	10	29	40	78	58	47
8 Fulham	42	12	3	6	62	39	5	7	9	36	46	98	85	44
9 Bristol Rovers	42	10	7	4	32	19	4	9	8	32	39	64	58	44
10 Leeds United	42	12	5	4	56	30	3	8	10	33	51	89	81	43
11 Stoke City	42	8	8	5	43	28	4	9	8	28	32	71	60	41
12 Doncaster Rovers	42	9	5	7	32	28	7	4	10	27	35	59	63	41
13 West Ham United	42	11	6	4	44	20	4	3	14	23	49	67	69	39
14 Notts County	42	8	6	7	26	29	5	7	9	28	45	54	74	39
15 Hull City	42	14	1	6	47	22	2	5	14	17	44	64	66	38
16 Lincoln City	42	11	6	4	46	23	3	3	15	19	60	65	83	37
17 Bury	42	9	7	5	39	32	2	7	12	15	40	54	72	36
18 Derby County	42	9	5	7	38	35	3	6	12	26	47	64	82	35
19 Plymouth Argyle	42	6	12	3	38	31	3	4	14	27	51	65	82	34
20 Swansea Town	42	11	5	5	34	25	2	3	16	24	57	58	82	34
21 BRENTFORD	**42**	**9**	**5**	**7**	**25**	**26**	**1**	**6**	**14**	**15**	**52**	**40**	**78**	**31**
22 Oldham Athletic	42	6	7	8	26	31	2	2	17	14	58	40	89	25

1954/55

11th in Division Three (South)

							Bassham AJ	Bragg WL	Bristow GA	Cakebread G	Coote KA	Dare WTC	Dargie IC	Dudley FE	Feehan JI	Francis GE	Geard L	Harper AF	Hart RE	Heath DJ	Horne KW	Latimer FJ	Lowden G	Newton RW	Rainford JW	Robertson JW	Robinson TH	Roe ML	Sperrin WT	Stobbart GC	Taylor JN	Towers EJ
1	Aug	21	Southampton	4-6	Robertson 2, Dudley, Stobbart	21454		2			6		5	9				4		7		3		1	10	11				8		
2		26	SHREWSBURY TOWN	2-2	Dudley, Maloney (og)	12743		2	4		6		5	9						7		3		1	10	11				8		
3		28	COVENTRY CITY	2-3	Stobbart, McDonnell (og)	13057		5			6			9				4		7	2	3		1	10	11				8		
4		30	Shrewsbury Town	2-2	Stobbart, Towers	8352		5						9				4		7	2	3		1	6	11				8		10
5	Sep	4	QUEEN'S PARK RANGERS	1-1	Heath	18756		5						9				4		7	2	3		1	6	11				8		10
6		8	Reading	0-0		9692		5						9	1			4		7	2		3		6	11				8		10
7		11	Brighton & Hove Albion	4-3	Towers, Heath, Robertson, Dudley	17361		5						9	1			4		7	2		3		6	11				8		10
8		16	READING	2-2	Dudley, Stobbart	9639		5						9	1			4		7	2		3		6	11				8		10
9		18	TORQUAY UNITED	4-2	Towers, Heath, Stobbart, Webber (og)	13552							5	9	1			4		7	2		3		6	11				8		10
10		23	GILLINGHAM	3-0	Dudley 2, Heath	9241					6		5	9	1			4		7	2		3			11				8		10
11		25	Bristol City	1-2	Dudley	28980					2		5	9	1			4		7		3			6	11				8		10
12		29	Gillingham	1-2	Towers	8202					2		5	9	1			6		7		3			4	11				8		10
13	Oct	2	WALSALL	0-2		12584			4		2		5	9	1					7			3		6	11				8		10
14		9	Exeter City	2-3	Robertson, Rainford	9700		2	4		6	9	5		1					7			3		10	11				8		
15		16	COLCHESTER UNITED	3-2	Robertson, Stobbart, Rainford	10218			4		2		5		1			6		7			3		10	11			8	9		
16		23	Norwich City	0-1		20148			6	1	2		5							7			3		10	11	4			9		8
17		30	BOURNEMOUTH	1-3	Towers	12037					2		5					6		7			3	1	8	11	4			9		10
18	Nov	6	Aldershot	3-2	Stobbart, Towers, Heath	7178			4		2		5		1					7		3			8	11	6			9		10
19		13	SWINDON TOWN	4-2	Stobbart 2, Heath, Towers	10634			4		2	11	5		1					7		3			8		6			9		10
20		27	NORTHAMPTON T	1-3	Croy (og)	10029					4	11	5		1					7	2	3			8		6			9		10
21	Dec	4	Watford	2-2	Towers 2	10438					3		5		1			6		7	2				8	11	4			9		10
22		18	SOUTHAMPTON	0-3		9318			4		3		5		1			6		7	2				8	11				9		10
23		25	MILLWALL	3-1	Stobbart 2, Towers	13591			6		3	11			1			4		7	2	5			8					9		10
24		27	Millwall	2-2	Anslow (og), Hurley (og)	20034			6		3	7			1			4			2	5			8	11				9		10
25	Jan	1	Coventry City	0-1		14481			6		3	11			1			4		7	2	5			8					9		10
26		15	Queen's Park Rangers	1-1	Dudley	9835			6		3	9	5	10	1			4		7	2					11						8
27		22	BRIGHTON & HOVE ALB	2-3	Stobbart, Bristow	10173			6		3	11		10	1			4		7	2	5			8					9		
28	Feb	5	Torquay United	2-4	Dudley, Sperrin	6117			6		3			11	1			4		7	2	5			8				10	9		
29		12	BRISTOL CITY	2-2	Rainford, Robertson	11563			6		3			11	1			4			2	5			8	7			10	9		
30		19	Walsall	2-2	Robertson, Francis	9028	2		4					10	1	9		6		7	3	5				11				8		
31		26	EXETER CITY	1-0	Stobbart	7454	2		4					11	1	9		6			3	5				7				8		10
32	Mar	5	Colchester United	2-3	Francis, Dudley	8254	2		4		10		5	11	1	9		6			3					7				8		
33		12	NORWICH CITY	1-0	Stobbart	11155	2		4		6			11						7	3	5		1	8					9	10	
34		19	Bournemouth	2-1	Coote, Taylor	8241	2		4		6			11						7	3	5		1	8					9	10	
35		26	ALDERSHOT	1-1	Taylor	8755	2		4		6		5	11							3			1	10					9	8	7
36	Apr	2	Swindon Town	1-1	Taylor	5924	2		4		6			9				11		7	3	5		1						8	10	
37		8	LEYTON ORIENT	2-0	Dudley, Towers (p)	18093	2		4		6			11						7	3	5		1						9	8	10
38		9	CRYSTAL PALACE	3-0	Towers, Dudley 2	12013	2		4		6			9							3	5		1		11				7	8	10
39		11	Leyton Orient	1-0	Dudley	9529	2		4		6			9							3	5		1		11				7	8	10
40		16	Northampton Town	2-1	Taylor, Towers	6980	2		4		6			9					5		3			1		11				7	8	10
41		21	Newport County	1-3	Rainford	7926	2		4		6			9							3	5		1	11					7	8	10
42		23	WATFORD	3-2	Dudley, Towers 2 (1p)	9394	2		4	1	6			7					5		3					11				9	8	10
43		27	Crystal Palace	1-1	Andrews (og)	8170	2							7			4				3	5		1		11	6			9	8	10
44		30	Southend United	2-3	Dudley 2	6464	2			1	6			11						7	3	5					4			9	8	10
45	May	2	NEWPORT COUNTY	1-0	Stobbart	4960	2		4		6			11						7	3	5		1	10					9	8	
46		5	SOUTHEND UNITED	2-2	Heath, Dudley	5812	2		4		6		5	11						7	3			1	8			10		9		
						Apps	17	9	30	3	37	8	20	34	25	3	1	26	2	35	35	28	10	18	33	31	8	1	3	45	13	31
						Goals			1		1			18		2				7					4	7			1	15	4	15

Seven own goals

F.A. Cup

							Bassham AJ	Bragg WL	Bristow GA	Cakebread G	Coote KA	Dare WTC	Dargie IC	Dudley FE	Feehan JI	Francis GE	Geard L	Harper AF	Hart RE	Heath DJ	Horne KW	Latimer FJ	Lowden G	Newton RW	Rainford JW	Robertson JW	Robinson TH	Roe ML	Sperrin WT	Stobbart GC	Taylor JN	Towers EJ
R1	Nov	20	NUNEATON BOROUGH	2-1	Dare, Stobbart	13180					4	11	5		1					7	2	3			8		6			9		10
R2	Dec	11	CROOK TOWN	4-1	Rainford, Stobbart 2, Towers	14300			4		3		5		1			6		7	2				8	11				9		10
R3	Jan	8	BRADFORD CITY	1-1	Dudley	12120			6		3			11	1			4		7	2	5			8					9		10
rep		12	Bradford City	2-2	Dare, Dudley	7963			6		3	7		11	1			4			2	5			8					9		10
rep2		20	Bradford City	1-0	Dare	5961			6		3	7		11	1			4			2	5			8					9		10
R4		29	Newcastle United	2-3	Stobbart, Rainford	46574			6		3			11	1			4		7	2	5			10					9		8

R3 replay a.e.t. R3 replay 2 at Highbury

		Pl.	Home W	D	L	F	A	Away W	D	L	F	A	F. (Total)	A.	Pts
1	Bristol City	46	17	4	2	62	22	13	6	4	39	25	101	47	70
2	Leyton Orient	46	16	2	5	48	20	10	7	6	41	27	89	47	61
3	Southampton	46	16	6	1	49	19	8	5	10	26	32	75	51	59
4	Gillingham	46	12	8	3	41	28	8	7	8	36	38	77	66	55
5	Millwall	46	14	6	3	44	25	6	5	12	28	43	72	68	51
6	Brighton & Hove A.	46	14	4	5	47	27	6	6	11	29	36	76	63	50
7	Watford	46	11	9	3	45	26	7	5	11	26	36	71	62	50
8	Torquay United	46	12	6	5	51	39	6	6	11	31	43	82	82	48
9	Coventry City	46	15	5	3	50	26	3	6	14	17	33	67	59	47
10	Southend United	46	13	5	5	48	28	4	7	12	35	52	83	80	46
11	**BRENTFORD**	**46**	**11**	**6**	**6**	**44**	**36**	**5**	**8**	**10**	**38**	**46**	**82**	**82**	**46**
11	Norwich City	46	13	5	5	40	23	5	5	13	20	37	60	60	46
13	Northampton Town	46	13	5	5	47	27	6	3	14	26	54	73	81	46
14	Aldershot	46	12	6	5	44	23	4	7	12	31	48	75	71	45
15	Queen's Park Rgs.	46	13	7	3	46	25	2	7	14	23	50	69	75	44
16	Shrewsbury Town	46	14	5	4	49	24	2	5	16	21	54	70	78	42
17	Bournemouth	46	7	8	8	32	29	5	10	8	25	36	57	65	42
18	Reading	46	7	10	6	32	26	6	5	12	33	47	65	73	41
19	Newport County	46	8	8	7	32	29	3	8	12	28	44	60	73	38
20	Crystal Palace	46	9	11	3	32	24	2	5	16	20	56	52	80	38
21	Swindon Town	46	10	8	5	30	19	1	7	15	16	45	46	64	37
22	Exeter City	46	9	7	7	30	31	2	8	13	17	42	47	73	37
23	Walsall	46	9	6	8	49	36	1	8	14	26	50	75	86	34
24	Colchester United	46	7	6	10	33	40	2	7	14	20	51	53	91	31

1953-54: Player/Manager Tommy Lawton, pre-season, with the players.

1956-57

Back: Eggleston (Trainer), Parsons, Russell, Morgan, Coote, Cakebread, Dargie, Bragg, Tickridge
Front: Francis, Taylor, Dodgin (Manager), Towers, Newcombe, Rainford.

1955/56

6th in Division Three (South)

No	Month	Date	Opponent	Score	Scorers	Att	Bassham AJ	Bragg WL	Bristow GA	Cakebread G	Coote KA	Dargie IC	Dudley FE	Francis GE	Geard L	Goundry W	Heath DJ	Horne KW	Latimer FJ	Lowden G	Morgan W	Newcombe BJ	Newton RW	Pearson JA	Peplow RR	Rainford JW	Robertson JW	Robinson TH	Roe ML	Sperrin WT	Stobbart GC	Taylor JN	Tickridge S	Towers EJ
1	Aug	20	GILLINGHAM	1-4	Towers (p)	12247		5	4	1	6		11				7	3													9	8	2	10
2		22	Queen's Park Rangers	1-1	Stobbart	11688		5	4	1	6		11					3								10					9	8	2	7
3		27	Bournemouth	0-0		10451		5		1	6		10			7		3								4					9	8	2	11
4		30	QUEEN'S PARK RANGERS	2-0	Towers, Taylor	12947		5		1	6		10			7		3								4					9	8	2	11
5	Sep	3	NORWICH CITY	1-2	Dudley	12565		5		1	6		10			7		3								4					9	8	2	11
6		5	Millwall	0-4		6911		5	4	1	6							3								8	11				7	9	2	10
7		10	Colchester United	3-0	Towers 2, Taylor	7843	2	5		1	6					7								8		4	11					9	3	10
8		12	MILLWALL	2-2	Taylor, Stobbart	7597	2	5		1	6		11				7									4					8	9	3	10
9		17	LEYTON ORIENT	1-0	Taylor	17847	2	5		1	6		11				7									4					8	9	3	10
10		19	WATFORD	0-0		6864	2			1	6	5	11	9			7									4						8	3	10
11		24	Exeter City	3-2	Taylor 3	9454	2	5		1	6		11				7									4				8		9	3	10
12		26	Coventry City	1-2	Taylor	12584				1	6	5	11				7	2								4				8		9	3	10
13	Oct	1	SOUTHEND UNITED	2-1	Taylor, Towers	14329		2		1	6		11				7		5							4					8	9	3	10
14		8	Aldershot	1-4	Towers	7395	2			1	6		11				7		5							4					8	9	3	10
15		15	CRYSTAL PALACE	3-0	Taylor 2, Towers	13636		2		1	6						7		5		8					4	11					9	3	10
16		22	Brighton & Hove Albion	0-3		12771				1	6						7		5	2	8					4	11					9	3	10
17		29	SOUTHAMPTON	2-1	Morgan, Rainford	12300			4	1	6	3				11	7		5		8					10						9	2	
18	Nov	5	Shrewsbury Town	1-1	Morgan	10551				1	6	3	11								8			7		4		5				9	2	10
19		12	IPSWICH TOWN	3-2	Francis, Morgan, Towers	14795				1	3			9							8			7		4		5	6			10	2	11
20		26	TORQUAY UNITED	1-3	Heath	11547				1	3						7				10					4		5	6		8	9	2	11
21	Dec	3	Newport County	2-1	Morgan, Dudley	8035			4	1	3		11						5		8			7		6						9	2	10
22		17	Gillingham	2-1	Francis, Bristow	5867		3	4	1	6			10							7					9	11	5				8	2	
23		24	BOURNEMOUTH	2-1	Coote, Taylor	8592		3	4	1	6			8							7					9	11	5				10	2	
24		26	READING	2-2	Robertson, Rainford	12556		3	4	1	6			8							7					9	11	5				10	2	
25		27	Reading	2-5	Bragg (p), Francis	11910		3	4	1	6			8							7					10	11	5			9		2	
26		31	Norwich City	0-1		18542		3	6	1	4			8							7					9	11	5				10	2	
27	Jan	14	COLCHESTER UNITED	2-2	Rainford, Taylor	8492		3	4	1	6						7				8					9		5				10	2	11
28		21	Leyton Orient	1-2	Morgan	14009		3	4		6					7					8		1			10		5				9	2	11
29	Feb	4	EXETER CITY	2-0	Francis 2	6309			6	1	3			9	4	7											11	5				8	2	10
30		11	Southend United	2-2	Towers, Stirling (og)	5124		5	6	1	3			9	4	7				2							11					8		10
31		18	ALDERSHOT	2-0	Towers 2	7026		5	6	1	3			9	4	7				2							11					8		10
32		25	Crystal Palace	2-0	Towers 2	10054		5	6	1	3			9		7				2						4	11					8		10
33	Mar	3	BRIGHTON & HOVE ALB	4-2	Robertson 2, Goundry, Francis	11061		5	6	1	3			9		7				2						4	11					8		10
34		10	Southampton	1-1	Towers	11678	2		6	1	3			9		7	11		5							4						8		10
35		12	SWINDON TOWN	1-2	Towers	7249			6	1	3			9		7	11		5	2						4						8		10
36		17	SHREWSBURY TOWN	1-1	Towers	9156			4	1	3					7				2						8	11	5	6			9		10
37		24	Ipswich Town	1-1	Towers	13672			4	1	6					7			5	2						8	11					9	3	10
38		31	WALSALL	2-2	Towers, Coote	8933			4	1	6					7			5	2						8	11					9	3	10
39	Apr	2	NORTHAMPTON T	2-1	Towers 2	9527			4	1	6					8	7			2							11	5				9	3	10
40		3	Northampton Town	0-1		8248			4	1	6			9		11	7			2						8		5					3	10
41		7	Torquay United	1-3	Taylor	5574		5	4	1	6					7				2	8						11					9	3	10
42		14	NEWPORT COUNTY	1-1	Towers	5291		5	4	1	6					8				2	7						11					9	3	10
43		21	Swindon Town	1-0	Peplow	5790		5	4	1	6					7				2					10	8						9	3	11
44		23	COVENTRY CITY	1-1	Bragg (p)	6078	2	5		1	6					8						7			10				4			9	3	11
45		28	Watford	2-0	Robinson, Francis	7192	2	5		1	6			9		8						7			10		11	4					3	
46	May	3	Walsall	2-1	Taylor, Newcombe	9033	4	5		1				9						3		7				6	11					8	2	10
						Apps	10	29	27	45	45	4	14	17	3	23	17	7	10	15	16	3	1	4	3	37	22	15	4	2	12	43	39	39
						Goals		2	1		2		2	7		1	1				5	1			1	3	3	1			2	15		21

One own goal

F.A. Cup

Rd	Month	Date	Opponent	Score	Scorers	Att	Bassham AJ	Bragg WL	Bristow GA	Cakebread G	Coote KA	Dargie IC	Dudley FE	Francis GE	Geard L	Goundry W	Heath DJ	Horne KW	Latimer FJ	Lowden G	Morgan W	Newcombe BJ	Newton RW	Pearson JA	Peplow RR	Rainford JW	Robertson JW	Robinson TH	Roe ML	Sperrin WT	Stobbart GC	Taylor JN	Tickridge S	Towers EJ
R1	Nov	19	MARCH TOWN UTD	4-0	Stobbart 2, Towers (p), Francis	13300				1	3			10			7									4		5	6		8	9	2	11
R2	Dec	10	Leyton Orient	1-4	Taylor	17490			4	1	3		11						5		8					10		6				9	2	7

		Pl.	Home W	D	L	F	A	Away W	D	L	F	A	F. (Total)	A. (Total)	Pts
1	Leyton Orient	46	18	3	2	76	20	11	5	7	30	29	106	49	66
2	Brighton & Hove A.	46	20	2	1	73	16	9	5	9	39	34	112	50	65
3	Ipswich Town	46	16	6	1	59	28	9	8	6	47	32	106	60	64
4	Southend United	46	16	4	3	58	25	5	7	11	30	55	88	80	53
5	Torquay United	46	11	10	2	48	21	9	2	12	38	42	86	63	52
6	**BRENTFORD**	**46**	**11**	**8**	**4**	**40**	**30**	**8**	**6**	**9**	**29**	**36**	**69**	**66**	**52**
7	Norwich City	46	15	4	4	56	31	4	9	10	30	51	86	82	51
8	Coventry City	46	16	4	3	54	20	4	5	14	19	40	73	60	49
9	Bournemouth	46	13	6	4	39	14	6	4	13	24	37	63	51	48
10	Gillingham	46	12	3	8	38	28	7	7	9	31	43	69	71	48
11	Northampton Town	46	14	3	6	44	27	6	4	13	23	44	67	71	47
12	Colchester United	46	14	4	5	56	37	4	7	12	20	44	76	81	47
13	Shrewsbury Town	46	12	9	2	47	21	5	3	15	22	45	69	66	46
14	Southampton	46	13	6	4	60	30	5	2	16	31	51	91	81	44
15	Aldershot	46	9	9	5	36	33	3	7	13	34	57	70	90	40
16	Exeter City	46	10	6	7	39	30	5	4	14	19	47	58	77	40
17	Reading	46	10	2	11	40	37	5	7	11	30	42	70	79	39
18	Queen's Park Rgs.	46	10	7	6	44	32	4	4	15	20	54	64	86	39
19	Newport County	46	12	2	9	32	26	3	7	13	26	53	58	79	39
20	Walsall	46	13	5	5	43	28	2	3	18	25	56	68	84	38
21	Watford	46	8	5	10	31	39	5	6	12	21	46	52	85	37
22	Millwall	46	13	4	6	56	31	2	2	19	27	69	83	100	36
23	Crystal Palace	46	7	3	13	27	32	5	7	11	27	51	54	83	34
24	Swindon Town	46	4	10	9	18	22	4	4	15	16	56	34	78	30

1956/57

8th in Division Three (South)

							Bassham AJ	Bragg WL	Bristow GA	Cakebread G	Coote KA	Dargie IC	Dudley FE	Feehan JI	Francis GE	Goundry W	Heath DJ	Horne KW	Lowden G	Morgan W	Newcombe BJ	Newton RW	Parsons EG	Peplow RR	Rainford JW	Robinson TH	Roe ML	Russell SEJ	Taylor JN	Tickridge S	Towers EJ	Avis VC	Bloomfield WG	Pearson JA
1	Aug	18	PLYMOUTH ARGYLE	4-1	Newcombe, Goundry, Taylor, Towers	13710	2	5	4	1	6				9	11					7								8	3	10			
2		21	SWINDON TOWN	4-1	Towers, Taylor 2, Bragg (p)	13510	2	5	4	1					9	11					7				6				8	3	10			
3		25	Aldershot	2-0	Towers, Francis	7043	2	5	4	1	6				9	11					7								8	3	10			
4		29	Swindon Town	3-1	Taylor 2, Francis	11995	2	5	4	1	6				9	11					7								8	3	10			
5	Sep	1	WATFORD	1-5	Towers	18760	2	5	4	1	6				9	11					7								8	3	10			
6		4	BRIGHTON & HOVE ALB	2-5	Goundry, Towers	12191		5	4	1	2		9			11					7				6				8	3	10			
7		8	Shrewsbury Town	2-3	Francis, Taylor	8953		4	2	1	6				9	11				10	7					5			8	3				
8		12	Brighton & Hove Albion	2-1	Goundry, Francis	14317		2	4	1	6				9	10					7					5			8	3	11			
9		15	WALSALL	6-2	Taylor 3, Bristow, Goundry, Francis	11492			4	1	6	5			9	10			2	11	7								8	3				
10		18	GILLINGHAM	3-2	Francis 3	15603			4	1	6	5			9	10			2	11	7								8	3				
11		22	Ipswich Town	0-4		12888			6	1	4	5			9	10			2	11	7								8	3				
12		26	Gillingham	1-2	Morgan	7903			4	1	6	5			9	10		2		11	7								8	3				
13		29	BOURNEMOUTH	2-2	Francis, Newcombe	12604				1	6	5			9	10		2		11	7						4		8	3				
14	Oct	6	NORTHAMPTON T	2-1	Coleman (og), Francis	10733				1	6				9	10		2		11	7					5	4		8	3				
15		13	Southend United	0-1		11463	2			1	6				9					11	7			4	10	5			8	3				
16		20	CRYSTAL PALACE	1-1	Taylor	11345	2	5		1	3				9					11	7			4		6			8		10			
17		27	Exeter City	1-1	Francis	8482	2	5		1	6	3			9	10	7				11			4					8					
18	Nov	3	SOUTHAMPTON	4-0	Francis 4	14198	2			1	6	3			9	10	7				11			4		5			8					
19		10	Coventry City	1-1	Peplow (p)	9884	2			1	6	5			9	10	7				11			4					8	3				
20		24	Colchester United	0-1		7290	2			1	6	5			9	10					11		7	4					8	3				
21	Dec	1	NEWPORT COUNTY	0-0		11130	2			1	6	5			9	10					11		7	4					8	3				
22		15	Plymouth Argyle	0-2		6823		3		1	6	5			9					8	11		7	4						2	10			
23		22	ALDERSHOT	2-2	Parsons, Towers	7284				1	6				9	10					11		7	4		5		3		2	8			
24		25	TORQUAY UNITED	0-0		9024					6				9	10					11	1	7	4		5		3		2	8			
25		26	Torquay United	0-2		9540		5			6				9	10					7	1	11	4				3		2	8			
26		29	Watford	1-1	Dudley	8416		5			6		9			8					7	1	11	4	10			3		2				
27	Jan	12	SHREWSBURY TOWN	3-1	Rainford, Dudley, Goundry	8952		2	4		6		9			8					7	1	11		10	5		3						
28		19	Walsall	0-7		13892		2			6		9			8					7	1	11	4	10	5		3						
29	Feb	2	IPSWICH TOWN	1-1	Rees (og)	10538		2	4		6			1	9	8					7		11			5		3	10					
30		9	Bournemouth	0-3		10898		2	4		6			1	9	8					7		11			5		3	10					
31		16	Northampton Town	1-5	Francis	9306		2			6	5		1	9	11				4			7	8				3	10					
32	Mar	2	Crystal Palace	2-0	Parsons 2	11679		2		1	6	5			9	7				4			11					3	8		10			
33		4	MILLWALL	5-0	Taylor, Towers, Francis, Coote, Goundry	6088		2		1	6	5			9	7				4			11					3	8		10			
34		9	READING	4-0	Francis 2, Taylor, McLaren (og)	10223		2		1	6	5			9					4	11		7					3	8		10			
35		12	SOUTHEND UNITED	3-2	Francis 2, Towers	11941		2		1	6	5			9					4	11		7					3	8		10			
36		16	Southampton	3-3	Parsons, Newcombe, Towers	12166		2		1	6	5			9					4	11		7					3	8		10			
37		18	Millwall	1-1	Towers	8726		2		1	6	5			9	8				4	11		7					3			10			
38		23	COVENTRY CITY	1-1	Taylor	10058		2		1	6	5			9					4	11		7					3	8		10			
39		30	Norwich City	1-1	McNeil (og)	11685		2		1	6	5			9					4	11		7					3	8		10			
40	Apr	6	COLCHESTER UNITED	1-1	Taylor	12846		2		1	6	5			9					4	11		7					3	8		10			
41		13	Newport County	0-3		5415		2	6	1		5			9					4	11		7		10			3	8					
42		19	QUEEN'S PARK RANGERS	2-0	Towers 2	13841		2		1	6	5			9					4	11		7					3	8		10			
43		20	EXETER CITY	3-0	Taylor, Harvey (og), Francis	9262		2		1	6	5			9					4	11		7					3	8		10			
44		22	Queen's Park Rangers	2-2	Dargie, Francis	9661		2		1	6	5			9					4	11		7					3	8				10	
45		27	NORWICH CITY	1-1	Bragg (p)	8764		2		1	6	5			9			3		4	11		7						8		10			
46	May	1	Reading	0-2		4203		2		1	6	5						3		4	11		7						8			9		10
						Apps	12	33	16	38	44	27	4	3	41	31	3	5	3	26	43	5	27	14	7	12	2	22	38	23	24	1	1	1
						Goals		2	1		1	1	2		23	6				1	3		4	1	1				15		12			

Five own goals

F.A. Cup

							Bassham AJ	Bragg WL	Bristow GA	Cakebread G	Coote KA	Dargie IC	Dudley FE	Feehan JI	Francis GE	Goundry W	Heath DJ	Horne KW	Lowden G	Morgan W	Newcombe BJ	Newton RW	Parsons EG	Peplow RR	Rainford JW	Robinson TH	Roe ML	Russell SEJ	Taylor JN	Tickridge S	Towers EJ	Avis VC	Bloomfield WG	Pearson JA
R1	Nov	17	GUILDFORD CITY	3-0	Morton (og), Taylor, Beale (og)	13450	2			1	6	5			9	10	7				11			4					8	3				
R2	Dec	8	CRYSTAL PALACE	1-1	Taylor	16750	2			1	6	5			9	10					11		7	4					8	3				
rep		12	Crystal Palace	2-3	Towers, Francis	23136		5		1	6	3			9					8	11		7	4						2	10			

R2 replay a.e.t.

		Pl.	Home W	Home D	Home L	Home F	Home A	Away W	Away D	Away L	Away F	Away A	F. (Total)	A. (Total)	Pts
1	Ipswich Town	46	18	3	2	72	20	7	6	10	29	34	101	54	59
2	Torquay United	46	19	4	0	71	18	5	7	11	18	46	89	64	59
3	Colchester United	46	15	8	0	49	19	7	6	10	35	37	84	56	58
4	Southampton	46	15	4	4	48	20	7	6	10	28	32	76	52	54
5	Bournemouth	46	15	7	1	57	20	4	7	12	31	42	88	62	52
6	Brighton & Hove A.	46	15	6	2	59	26	4	8	11	27	39	86	65	52
7	Southend United	46	14	3	6	42	20	4	9	10	31	45	73	65	48
8	**BRENTFORD**	**46**	**12**	**9**	**2**	**55**	**29**	**4**	**7**	**12**	**23**	**47**	**78**	**76**	**48**
9	Shrewsbury Town	46	11	9	3	45	24	4	9	10	27	55	72	79	48
10	Queen's Park Rgs.	46	12	7	4	42	21	6	4	13	19	39	61	60	47
11	Watford	46	11	6	6	44	32	7	4	12	28	43	72	75	46
12	Newport County	46	15	6	2	51	18	1	7	15	14	44	65	62	45
13	Reading	46	13	4	6	44	30	5	5	13	36	51	80	81	45
14	Northampton Town	46	15	5	3	49	22	3	4	16	17	51	66	73	45
15	Walsall	46	11	7	5	49	25	5	5	13	31	49	80	74	44
16	Coventry City	46	12	5	6	52	36	4	7	12	22	48	74	84	44
17	Millwall	46	13	7	3	46	29	3	5	15	18	55	64	84	44
18	Plymouth Argyle	46	10	8	5	38	31	6	3	14	30	42	68	73	43
19	Aldershot	46	11	5	7	43	35	4	7	12	36	57	79	92	42
20	Crystal Palace	46	7	10	6	31	28	4	8	11	31	47	62	75	40
21	Exeter City	46	8	8	7	37	29	4	5	14	24	50	61	79	37
22	Gillingham	46	7	8	8	29	29	5	5	13	25	56	54	85	37
23	Swindon Town	46	12	3	8	43	33	3	3	17	23	63	66	96	36
24	Norwich City	46	7	5	11	33	37	1	10	12	28	57	61	94	31

1957/58

2nd in Division Three (South)

			Opponent	Score	Scorers	Att.	Bassham AJ	Bloomfield WG	Bristow GA	Cakebread G	Caven J	Coote KA	Dargie IC	Feehan JI	Fletcher CC	Francis GE	Goundry W	Heath DJ	Horne KW	Morgan W	Newcombe BJ	Parsons EG	Peplow RR	Rainford JW	Russell SEJ	Towers EJ	Wilson TF
1	Aug	24	Queen's Park Rangers	0-1		15734				1		6	5			9				4	11	7		8	3	10	2
2		27	EXETER CITY	1-0	Simpson (og)	12307				1		6	5			9				4	11	7		8	3	10	2
3		31	COLCHESTER UNITED	3-3	Newcombe, Towers 2	12732				1		6	5			9				4	11	7		8	3	10	2
4	Sep	4	Exeter City	5-3	Towers 2, Francis, Parsons 2	8498				1		6	5			9				4	11	7		8	3	10	2
5		7	Norwich City	2-3	Francis 2	19150				1		6	5			9				4	11	7		8	3	10	2
6		10	NORTHAMPTON T	7-1	Parsons, Rainford 2, Towers 2, Francis 2	10697			4	1		6	5			9					11	7		8	3	10	2
7		14	BOURNEMOUTH	4-2	Francis 3, Newcombe	13733			4	1		6	5			9					11	7		8	3	10	2
8		16	Northampton Town	1-3	Francis	4528			4	1		6	5			9					11	7		8	3	10	2
9		21	Walsall	2-0	Towers 2	10775			4	1		6	5			9			3		11	7		8		10	2
10		24	Watford	1-4	Towers	7031	2		4			6	5	1		9			3		11	7		8		10	
11		28	COVENTRY CITY	1-3	Caven	12094	2	10	4	1	11	6	5			9					7			8	3		
12	Oct	1	WATFORD	0-0		10447			4	1	11	2	5			9	10	7	3				6	8			
13		5	Shrewsbury Town	2-0	Francis, Heath	7057			4	1	11	2	5			9	10	7	3				6	8			
14		12	GILLINGHAM	1-0	Towers	12488			4	1	11	2	5			9			3			7	6	8		10	
15		19	Millwall	1-0	Rainford	16293			4	1	9	2	5						3		11	7	6	8		10	
16		26	SWINDON TOWN	0-0		13676			4	1		2	5			9	8		3		11	7	6			10	
17	Nov	2	Aldershot	2-0	Francis 2	7133			4	1			5			9			3		11	7	6	8	2	10	
18		9	PLYMOUTH ARGYLE	2-0	Newcombe, Francis	15594			4	1		2	5			9			3		11	7	6	8		10	
19		23	NEWPORT COUNTY	2-1	Rainford, Towers	13603			4	1		2	5			9			3		11	7	6	8		10	
20		30	Southampton	2-4	Towers, Francis	13690			4	1		2	5			9			3		11	7	6	8		10	
21	Dec	14	Southend United	0-0		7952			4	1		2	5		10	9			3		11	7	6	8			
22		21	QUEEN'S PARK RANGERS	1-1	Rutter (og)	12804			4	1		2	5		10	9			3		11	7	6	8			
23		25	CRYSTAL PALACE	0-3		12394			4	1	11	2	5			9	10	7	3				6	8			
24		26	Crystal Palace	1-2	Coote	16797			4	1		6	5		10	9			3		11	7		8	2		
25		28	Colchester United	1-1	Francis	9548			4	1		6	5			9	10		3		11	7		8	2		
26	Jan	11	NORWICH CITY	7-1	Francis 2, Rainford 2, Parsons, Coote, Newcombe	11850			4	1		6	5			9	10		3		11	7		8	2		
27		18	Bournemouth	0-1		11090			4	1		6	5			9	10		3		11	7		8	2		
28	Feb	1	WALSALL	2-1	Rainford, Parsons (p)	9130			4	1		6	5			9			3		11	7		8	2	10	
29		8	Coventry City	0-0		9391			4	1		6	5			9			3		11	7		8		10	2
30		15	SHREWSBURY TOWN	2-0	Francis, Parsons	12842			4	1		6	5			9			3		11	7		8		10	2
31		22	Gillingham	2-3	Parsons, Towers	6626			4	1		6	5			9			3		11	7		8		10	2
32	Mar	1	MILLWALL	4-1	Towers 3, Francis	12919			4	1		6	5			9			3		11	7		8		10	2
33		8	Swindon Town	1-4	Francis	12755			4	1		6	5			9			3		11	7		8		10	2
34		11	READING	2-1	Towers 2	13230			4	1		6	5			9			3		11	7		8		10	2
35		15	ALDERSHOT	4-2	Heath 2, Towers 2	10482			4	1		6	5			9		7	3		11			8		10	2
36		22	Newport County	2-1	Heath, Rainford	5621			4	1		6	5			9		7	3		11			8		10	2
37		24	Port Vale	1-0	Towers	5149			4	1		6	5			9		7	3		11			8		10	2
38		29	SOUTHEND UNITED	4-2	Towers 2, Francis 2	12890			4	1		6	5			9		7	3		11			8		10	2
39	Apr	4	Torquay United	1-0	Towers	8216			4	1		6	5			9		7	3		11			8		10	2
40		5	Plymouth Argyle	0-0		20021			4	1		6	5			9		7	3		11			8		10	2
41		7	TORQUAY UNITED	0-1		15680			4	1		6	5			9		7	3		11			8		10	2
42		12	SOUTHAMPTON	0-0		11663			4	1		6	5			9	11	7	3					8		10	2
43		19	Brighton & Hove Albion	1-1	Heath	25613			4	1		6	5			9	11	7	3					8		10	2
44		23	Reading	2-1	Towers 2	12852			4	1		6	5			9	11	7	3					8		10	2
45		26	PORT VALE	4-1	Towers 3, Rainford	11923			4	1		6	5			9	11	7	3					8		10	2
46		28	BRIGHTON & HOVE ALB	1-0	Goundry	25744			4	1		6	5			9	11	7	3					8		10	2
						Apps	2	1	41	45	6	45	46	1	3	45	12	15	37	5	37	30	12	45	15	36	27
						Goals					1	2				22	1	5			4	7		9		29	

Two own goals

F.A. Cup

			Opponent	Score	Scorers	Att.	Bassham AJ	Bloomfield WG	Bristow GA	Cakebread G	Caven J	Coote KA	Dargie IC	Feehan JI	Fletcher CC	Francis GE	Goundry W	Heath DJ	Horne KW	Morgan W	Newcombe BJ	Parsons EG	Peplow RR	Rainford JW	Russell SEJ	Towers EJ	Wilson TF
R1	Nov	16	Millwall	0-1		20097			4	1		2	5			9	10		3		11	7	6	8			

		Pl.	Home W	D	L	F	A	Away W	D	L	F	A	F. (Total)	A.	Pts
1	Brighton & Hove A.	46	13	6	4	52	30	11	6	6	36	34	88	64	60
2	**BRENTFORD**	**46**	**15**	**5**	**3**	**52**	**24**	**9**	**5**	**9**	**30**	**32**	**82**	**56**	**58**
3	Plymouth Argyle	46	17	4	2	43	17	8	4	11	24	31	67	48	58
4	Swindon Town	46	14	7	2	47	16	7	8	8	32	34	79	50	57
5	Reading	46	14	5	4	52	23	7	8	8	27	28	79	51	55
6	Southampton	46	16	3	4	78	31	6	7	10	34	41	112	72	54
7	Southend United	46	14	5	4	56	26	7	7	9	34	32	90	58	54
8	Norwich City	46	11	9	3	41	28	8	6	9	34	42	75	70	53
9	Bournemouth	46	16	5	2	54	24	5	4	14	27	50	81	74	51
10	Queen's Park Rgs.	46	15	6	2	40	14	3	8	12	24	51	64	65	50
11	Newport County	46	12	6	5	40	24	5	8	10	33	43	73	67	48
12	Colchester United	46	13	5	5	45	27	4	8	11	32	52	77	79	47
13	Northampton Town	46	13	1	9	60	33	6	5	12	27	46	87	79	44
14	Crystal Palace	46	12	5	6	46	30	3	8	12	24	42	70	72	43
15	Port Vale	46	12	6	5	49	24	4	4	15	18	34	67	58	42
16	Watford	46	9	8	6	34	27	4	8	11	25	50	59	77	42
17	Shrewsbury Town	46	10	6	7	29	25	5	4	14	20	46	49	71	40
18	Aldershot	46	7	9	7	31	34	5	7	11	28	55	59	89	40
19	Coventry City	46	10	9	4	41	24	3	4	16	20	57	61	81	39
20	Walsall	46	10	7	6	37	24	4	2	17	24	51	61	75	37
21	Torquay United	46	9	7	7	33	34	2	6	15	16	40	49	74	35
22	Gillingham	46	12	5	6	33	24	1	4	18	19	57	52	81	35
23	Millwall	46	6	6	11	37	36	5	3	15	26	55	63	91	31
24	Exeter City	46	10	4	9	37	35	1	5	17	20	64	57	99	31

1958/59

3rd in Division Three

							Bristow GA	Cakebread G	Caven J	Coote KA	Dargie IC	Feehan JI	Francis GE	Goundry W	Hales JMcK	Heath DJ	Horn W	Horne KW	McLeod GJ	Newcombe BJ	Parsons EG	Peplow RR	Rainford JW	Russell SEJ	Towers EJ	Wilson TF
1	Aug	23	BRADFORD CITY	4-0	Towers 2, Francis 2	15749	4	1		6	5		9			7		3		11			8		10	2
2		28	Doncaster Rovers	0-1		10654	4	1		6	5		9			7		3		11			8		10	2
3		30	Wrexham	1-2	Towers	16905	4	1		6	5		9			7		3			11		8		10	2
4	Sep	2	DONCASTER ROVERS	0-1		14845	4	1		6	5		9			7		3			11		8		10	2
5		6	SOUTHAMPTON	2-0	Francis, Towers	12997		1		6	5		9	4		7		3			11		8		10	2
6		9	MANSFIELD TOWN	2-0	Towers 2	13625		1		6	5		9	4		7		3			11		8		10	2
7		12	Accrington Stanley	1-1	Rainford	9918		1		6	5		9	4		7		3			11		8		10	2
8		15	Mansfield Town	1-1	Towers	9159		1		6	5		9	4		7		3			11		8		10	2
9		20	HALIFAX TOWN	2-0	Francis, Heath	12643		1		6	5		9	4		7		3			11		8		10	2
10		22	Hull City	1-3	Heath	14172		1		6	5		9	4		7		3			11		8		10	2
11		27	Newport County	1-0	Francis	8220	4	1		6	5		9			7		3			11		8		10	2
12		30	HULL CITY	1-1	Towers	12441	4	1	9	6	5					7		3			11		8		10	2
13	Oct	4	CHESTERFIELD	1-1	Heath	12473	4	1		6	5		9			7		3			11		8		10	2
14		9	Notts County	0-0		4381	4	1		6	5		9			7		3	11				8		10	2
15		11	Tranmere Rovers	2-1	Towers, Rainford	12325	4	1		6	5		9			7		3			11		8		10	2
16		18	STOCKPORT COUNTY	1-4	Towers	12488	4	1		6	5		9			7		3			11		8		10	2
17		25	Reading	1-3	Towers	16186	4			6	5	1	9			7	11	3					8		10	2
18	Nov	1	COLCHESTER UNITED	2-1	Towers, Heath	11945	4	1		6	5		9			7		3	11				8		10	2
19		8	Bournemouth	0-0		11564	4	1		6	5		9			7		3	11				8		10	2
20		22	Queen's Park Rangers	2-1	Drinkwater (og), Towers	13784	4	1		6	5		9			7		3	11				8		10	2
21		29	BURY	0-0		11741	4	1		6	5		9			7		3	11				8		10	2
22	Dec	13	ROCHDALE	2-1	Towers, Dargie	9432	4	1		3	5		9	6		7			11				8		10	2
23		20	Bradford City	0-3		11473	4	1		6	5		9			7		3	11				8		10	2
24		25	SWINDON TOWN	2-2	McLeod, Francis	12504	4	1		6	5		9					3	11		7		8		10	2
25		26	Swindon Town	1-1	Francis	12690	4	1		6	5		9					3	11		7		8		10	2
26	Jan	3	WREXHAM	2-1	Francis 2	11723	4	1		6	5		9					3	11		7		8		10	2
27		31	ACCRINGTON STANLEY	2-1	Francis, Towers	11260	4	1		6	5		9					3	11		7		8		10	2
28	Feb	7	Halifax Town	0-0		4654	4	1		6	5		9					3	11		7		8		10	2
29		14	NEWPORT COUNTY	3-0	McLeod, Bristow, Towers	10392	4	1		6	5		9					3	11		7		8		10	2
30		21	Chesterfield	2-1	Francis, Towers (p)	9649	4	1		6	5		9			7		3	11				8		10	2
31		28	TRANMERE ROVERS	5-2	Towers 2, Francis, Rainford 2	13138	4	1		6	5		9					3	11		7		8		10	2
32	Mar	7	Stockport County	1-1	Towers (p)	7973		1		6	5		9	4				3	11		7		8		10	2
33		9	Southampton	6-0	McLeod, Towers 4, Francis	7756		1		6	5		9	4				3	11		7		8		10	2
34		14	READING	3-1	Francis 2, Rainford	18209		1		6	5		9	4				3	11		7		8		10	2
35		21	Colchester United	4-0	Francis 2, McLeod, Towers	8775	4	1		6	5		9					3	11		7		8		10	2
36		27	PLYMOUTH ARGYLE	3-0	Towers, Rainford, Francis	28725	4	1			5		9	6				3	11		7		8		10	2
37		28	BOURNEMOUTH	1-1	McLeod	15970	4	1			5		9	6		7		3	11				8		10	2
38		30	Plymouth Argyle	1-1	Parsons	27073	4	1		6			9					3	11		7		8	5	10	2
39	Apr	4	Norwich City	1-4	Francis	27870	4	1		6			9					3	11		7		8	5	10	2
40		8	Southend United	0-2		9022	4	1		6			9					3	11		7	5	8		10	2
41		11	QUEEN'S PARK RANGERS	1-0	Rainford	15905	4	1		6			9					3	11		7	5	8		10	2
42		18	Bury	1-1	Towers	7092	4	1		6			9					3	11		7	5	8		10	2
43		21	NOTTS COUNTY	4-0	Francis, Towers 3 (2p)	11738	4	1		6			9					3	11		7	5	8		10	2
44		25	SOUTHEND UNITED	6-1	Rainford, Francis 2, Towers 2, Williamson (og)	11264	4	1		6			9					3	11		7	5	8		10	2
45		27	Rochdale	0-0		2191	4	1		6			9					3	11		7	5	8		10	2
46		30	NORWICH CITY	0-4		19035	4	1		6			9		11			3			7	5	8		10	2
						Apps	37	45	1	44	37	1	45	12	1	25	1	45	29	2	34	7	46	2	46	46
						Goals	1				1		22			4			5		1		8		32	

Two own goals

F.A. Cup

							Bristow GA	Cakebread G	Caven J	Coote KA	Dargie IC	Feehan JI	Francis GE	Goundry W	Hales JMcK	Heath DJ	Horn W	Horne KW	McLeod GJ	Newcombe BJ	Parsons EG	Peplow RR	Rainford JW	Russell SEJ	Towers EJ	Wilson TF
R1	Nov	15	EXETER CITY	3-2	Towers, Francis, Rainford	14600	4	1		6	5		9			7		3	11				8		10	2
R2	Dec	6	KING'S LYNN	3-1	Towers 3	14100	4	1		3	5		9	6		7			11				8		10	2
R3	Jan	10	BARNSLEY	2-0	Towers, Francis	16890	4	1		6	5		9			7		3	11				8		10	2
R4		24	West Bromwich Albion	0-2		41948	4	1		6	5		9			7		3	11				8		10	2

	Pl.	Home					Away					F.	A.	Pts
		W	D	L	F	A	W	D	L	F	A	(Total)		
1 Plymouth Argyle	46	14	7	2	55	27	9	9	5	34	32	89	59	62
2 Hull City	46	19	3	1	65	21	7	6	10	25	34	90	55	61
3 BRENTFORD	**46**	**15**	**5**	**3**	**49**	**22**	**6**	**10**	**7**	**27**	**27**	**76**	**49**	**57**
4 Norwich City	46	13	6	4	51	29	9	7	7	38	33	89	62	57
5 Colchester United	46	15	2	6	46	31	6	8	9	25	36	71	67	52
6 Reading	46	16	4	3	51	21	5	4	14	27	42	78	63	50
7 Tranmere Rovers	46	15	3	5	53	22	6	5	12	29	45	82	67	50
8 Southend United	46	14	6	3	52	26	7	2	14	33	54	85	80	50
9 Halifax Town	46	14	5	4	48	25	7	3	13	32	52	80	77	50
10 Bury	46	12	9	2	51	24	5	5	13	18	34	69	58	48
11 Bradford City	46	13	4	6	47	25	5	7	11	37	51	84	76	47
12 Bournemouth	46	12	9	2	40	18	5	3	15	29	51	69	69	46
13 Queen's Park Rgs.	46	14	6	3	49	28	5	2	16	25	49	74	77	46
14 Southampton	46	12	7	4	57	33	5	4	14	31	47	88	80	45
15 Swindon Town	46	13	4	6	39	25	3	9	11	20	32	59	57	45
16 Chesterfield	46	12	5	6	40	26	5	5	13	27	38	67	64	44
17 Newport County	46	15	2	6	43	24	2	7	14	26	44	69	68	43
18 Wrexham	46	12	6	5	40	30	2	8	13	23	47	63	77	42
19 Accrington Stanley	46	10	8	5	42	31	5	4	14	29	56	71	87	42
20 Mansfield Town	46	11	5	7	38	42	3	8	12	35	56	73	98	41
21 Stockport County	46	9	7	7	33	23	4	3	16	32	55	65	78	36
22 Doncaster Rovers	46	13	2	8	40	32	1	3	19	10	58	50	90	33
23 Notts County	46	5	9	9	33	39	3	4	16	22	57	55	96	29
24 Rochdale	46	8	7	8	21	26	0	5	18	16	53	37	79	28

1958-59

Back: Lowden, Fletcher, Parsons, Curran, Avis, Goundry, Middle: Rainford, Francis, Bristow, Dargie, Bloomfield
Front: With ball - Monk (Trainer). Heath, Towers, Newcombe, Coote, Peplow,

1959-60

Back: Horne, Wilson, Cakebread, Ryecraft, Avis, Gitsham,
3rd Row: Monk (Trainer), Bloomfield, Walsh, Lafferty, Goundry, Bristow, Dargie, Coote, Peplow, McInally, Russell, Holliday (Asst.Trainer)
2nd Row: Docherty, Heath, Curran, Rainford, Francis, Towers, Horn, McLeod, Hales
Front (Sitting): Parsons, Higginson, Summers, Newcombe

1959/60

6th in Division Three

							Avis VCS	Bristow GA	Cakebread G	Coote KA	Dargie IC	Francis GE	Goundry W	Hales J	Heath WDJ	Higginson T	Horne KW	Livingstone WE	McInally C	McLeod GJ	Parsons EG	Peplow RR	Rainford JW	Russell SEJ	Towers EJ	Wilson TF
1	Aug	22	Barnsley	2-1	Francis 2	7553		4	1	6		9			7		3			11			8	5	10	2
2		25	WREXHAM	3-1	Francis, Rainford, Towers (p)	16168		4	1	6		9			7		3			11			8	5	10	2
3		29	SOUTHAMPTON	2-2	Rainford 2	15711		4	1	6		9			7		3			11			8	5	10	2
4	Sep	2	Wrexham	2-3	Towers, McLeod (p)	13283	3	4	1	6		9			7					11			8	5	10	2
5		5	Reading	3-3	Francis 2, Heath	13517	3	4	1	6		9			7			5		11			8		10	2
6		8	BURY	1-1	Rainford	16136	3	4	1	2		9	6		7					11			8	5	10	
7		12	SHREWSBURY TOWN	2-1	Towers, McLeod	12551	3	4	1	6		9			7					11			8	5	10	2
8		15	Bury	0-1		13048		4	1	3		9	6		7			5		11			8		10	2
9		19	Port Vale	1-3	Francis	12817		4	1	3		9	6		7			5		11			8		10	2
10		22	HALIFAX TOWN	1-1	Francis	15744		4	1	3		9	6		7			5		11			8	2	10	
11		26	NORWICH CITY	3-4	Towers 2, Heath	21634		4	1	3		9	6		7			5		11			8	2	10	
12		28	Halifax Town	0-1		8243		4	1	3		9	6		7		2	5		11			8		10	
13	Oct	3	Grimsby Town	3-1	Francis, Rainford 2	11454		4	1	3		9	6	7			2	5		11			8		10	
14		6	COLCHESTER UNITED	2-0	Francis, Towers	14780		4	1	3		9	6	7			2	5		11			8		10	
15		10	TRANMERE ROVERS	2-1	Rainford, Francis	11481		4	1	3		9	6	7			2	5		11			8		10	
16		12	Colchester United	1-2	Francis	7790		4	1	3		9	6	7			2	5		11			8		10	
17		17	Bournemouth	2-1	Towers, Hales	12216		4	1	3		9	6	7			2	5		11			8		10	
18		24	ACCRINGTON STANLEY	3-0	Towers 3	12660		4	1	3		9	6	7			2	5		11			8		10	
19		31	Queen's Park Rangers	4-2	Francis 3, Towers	19532		4	1	3		9	6	7			2	5		11			8		10	
20	Nov	21	YORK CITY	1-2	McLeod (p)	13118			1	3		9	4	7			2	5	6	11			8		10	
21		28	Coventry City	1-2	Towers	14972		4	1	3		9	6	7			2			11			8	5	10	
22	Dec	12	Newport County	2-4	Goundry, Towers	8401		4	1	3		9	6	11			2	5			7		8		10	
23		19	BARNSLEY	3-0	Towers, Francis, Parsons	6527		4	1	3		9	6	11			2	5			7		8		10	
24		26	Southend United	0-2		11771		4	1	3		9	6	11			2	5			7		8		10	
25		28	SOUTHEND UNITED	3-1	Parsons (p), Hales, Rainford	11778		4	1	3		9	6	11			2	5			7		8		10	
26	Jan	2	Southampton	0-2		16793		4	1	3		9	6	11			2	5			7		8		10	
27		9	Swindon Town	0-0		8633			1	6	5	9	4							11	7		8	3	10	2
28		16	READING	2-2	Francis, Parsons	9183			1	6	5	9	4							11	7		8	3	10	2
29		23	Shrewsbury Town	1-1	Wallace (og)	6997		4	1	3	5	9	6							11	7		8	2	10	
30	Feb	6	PORT VALE	2-0	Towers, Francis	10141		4	1	3	5	9	6				2			11	7		8		10	
31		13	Norwich City	1-2	Francis	22387		4	1	3	5	9	6							11	7		8	2	10	
32		20	GRIMSBY TOWN	0-2		10945		4	1	3	5	9	6							11	7		8	2	10	
33		27	Tranmere Rovers	1-2	Parsons	8053		4	1	3	5	9	6			10				11	7		8	2		
34	Mar	5	BOURNEMOUTH	1-0	Francis	9764		4	1	3	5	9	6			10				11	7		8			2
35		8	CHESTERFIELD	3-0	Bristow, McLeod (p), Towers	6328		4	1	3	5	9	6							11	7		8		10	2
36		11	Accrington Stanley	4-3	Parsons, Towers, Francis 2	3464		4	1	3	5	9	6							11	7		8		10	2
37		19	COVENTRY CITY	3-1	Francis 2, Bristow	9938		4	1	3	5	9	6							11	7		8		10	2
38		26	Chesterfield	0-1		4353		4	1	3	5	9	6							11	7		8		10	2
39	Apr	2	SWINDON TOWN	2-1	Towers, Higgins (og)	8595			1	3	5	9	6							11	7	4	8		10	2
40		9	York City	1-0	Towers	4751	3		1		5	9	6							11	7	4	8		10	2
41		15	MANSFIELD TOWN	1-1	Francis	9606	3		1		5	9	6	11							7	4	8		10	2
42		16	QUEEN'S PARK RANGERS	1-1	Towers	16025	3		1		5	9	6							11	7	4	8		10	2
43		18	Mansfield Town	1-0	Parsons	7624	3		1		5	9	6		11		2				7	4	8		10	
44		23	Bradford City	2-0	Francis, Goundry	6509	3		1	2	5	9	6	11							7	4	8		10	
45		30	NEWPORT COUNTY	1-2	Towers	7957	3		1	2	5	9	6	11							7	4	8		10	
46	May	3	BRADFORD CITY	4-0	Hales, Towers 2, Francis	7208	3		1	2	5	9	6	11							7	4	8		10	
						Apps	11	35	46	42	20	46	40	18	13	2	20	19	1	36	25	8	46	15	44	19
						Goals		2				26	2	3	2					4	6		8		23	

Two own goals

F.A. Cup

							Avis VCS	Bristow GA	Cakebread G	Coote KA	Dargie IC	Francis GE	Goundry W	Hales J	Heath WDJ	Higginson T	Horne KW	Livingstone WE	McInally C	McLeod GJ	Parsons EG	Peplow RR	Rainford JW	Russell SEJ	Towers EJ	Wilson TF
R1	Nov	14	ASHFORD TOWN	5-0	Francis 4, Towers	13900		4	1	3		9	6	7			2	5		11			8		10	
R2	Dec	5	Exeter City	1-3	Francis	13047		4	1	3		9	6	11			2	5			7		8		10	

	Pl.	Home W	Home D	Home L	Home F	Home A	Away W	Away D	Away L	Away F	Away A	F. (Total)	A. (Total)	Pts
1 Southampton	46	19	3	1	68	30	7	6	10	38	45	106	75	61
2 Norwich City	46	16	4	3	53	24	8	7	8	29	30	82	54	59
3 Shrewsbury Town	46	12	7	4	58	34	6	9	8	39	41	97	75	52
4 Grimsby Town	46	12	7	4	48	27	6	9	8	39	43	87	70	52
5 Coventry City	46	14	6	3	44	22	7	4	12	34	41	78	63	52
6 BRENTFORD	**46**	**13**	**6**	**4**	**46**	**24**	**8**	**3**	**12**	**32**	**37**	**78**	**61**	**51**
7 Bury	46	13	4	6	36	23	8	5	10	28	28	64	51	51
8 Queen's Park Rgs.	46	14	7	2	45	16	4	6	13	28	38	73	54	49
9 Colchester United	46	15	6	2	51	22	3	5	15	32	52	83	74	47
10 Bournemouth	46	12	8	3	47	27	5	5	13	25	45	72	72	47
11 Reading	46	13	3	7	49	34	5	7	11	35	43	84	77	46
12 Southend United	46	15	3	5	49	28	4	5	14	27	46	76	74	46
13 Newport County	46	15	2	6	59	36	5	4	14	21	43	80	79	46
14 Port Vale	46	16	4	3	51	19	3	4	16	29	60	80	79	46
15 Halifax Town	46	13	3	7	42	27	5	7	11	28	45	70	72	46
16 Swindon Town	46	12	6	5	39	30	7	2	14	30	48	69	78	46
17 Barnsley	46	13	6	4	45	25	2	8	13	20	41	65	66	44
18 Chesterfield	46	13	3	7	41	31	5	4	14	30	53	71	84	43
19 Bradford City	46	10	7	6	39	28	5	5	13	27	46	66	74	42
20 Tranmere Rovers	46	11	8	4	50	29	3	5	15	22	46	72	75	41
21 York City	46	11	5	7	38	26	2	7	14	19	47	57	73	38
22 Mansfield Town	46	11	4	8	55	48	4	2	17	26	64	81	112	36
23 Wrexham	46	12	5	6	39	30	2	3	18	29	71	68	101	36
24 Accrington Stanley	46	4	5	14	31	53	7	0	16	26	70	57	123	27

1960/61

17th in Division Three

	Date		Opponent	Res	Scorers	Att	Avis VCS	Bristow GA	Cakebread G	Coote KA	Curran TW	Dargie IC	Docherty J	Francis GE	Gitsham JW	Goundry W	Hales J	Heath DJ	Higginson T	McLeod GJ	O'Donnell D	Parsons EG	Peplow RR	Rainford JW	Summers G	Towers EJ	Wilson TF
1	Aug	20	TRANMERE ROVERS	4-1	Towers 2, Bristow, Goundry (p)	10267	3	4	1	2		5		9		6		7		11				8		10	
2		23	WATFORD	2-1	Heath, Goundry (p)	16673	3	4	1	2		5		9		6		7		11				8		10	
3		27	Halifax Town	0-1		6379	3	4	1	2		5		9		6		7		11				8		10	
4		30	Watford	1-6	Chung (og)	17883	3	4	1	2		5		9		6		7		11				8		10	
5	Sep	3	SHREWSBURY TOWN	4-0	Francis 3, Towers	8493	3	4	1	2		5		9		6		7		11				8		10	
6		6	TORQUAY UNITED	2-3	Rainford, Bettany (og)	8854	3	4	1	2		5		9		6		7		11				8		10	
7		10	Walsall	0-4		10864		4	1	3	8	5		9		6	11		10			7					2
8		14	Torquay United	1-1	Francis	5936		4	1	3	8	5	7	9		6	11									10	2
9		17	BURY	1-5	Francis	8865		4	1	3	8	5	7	9		6	11		10								2
10		19	Queen's Park Rangers	0-0		12823			1	3		5		9		6		7		11			4	8		10	2
11		24	Chesterfield	1-1	Rainford	5617			1	2		5		9		6		7		11			4	8		10	2
12		27	QUEEN'S PARK RANGERS	2-0	Rainford, Towers	15282			1	3		5		9		6		7		11			4	8		10	2
13	Oct	1	SOUTHEND UNITED	1-1	Rainford	7728			1	3		5		9		6		7		11			4	8		10	2
14		3	Port Vale	2-3	Towers, Peplow	6843			1	3		5		9		6		7		11			4	8		10	2
15		8	Bournemouth	1-0	McLeod	5820			1	3		5		9		6		7		11			4	8		10	2
16		15	BRADFORD CITY	2-2	Towers, Peplow (p)	7305			1	3		5		9		6		7		11			4	8		10	2
17		22	Barnsley	1-1	Peplow (p)	7268			1	3		5		9				7	6	11			4	8		10	2
18		29	NEWPORT COUNTY	2-4	Towers 2	7599			1	3		5						7	6	11			4	8	9	10	2
19	Nov	12	GRIMSBY TOWN	0-1		8120		4	1	3		5		9					6	11		7		8		10	2
20		19	Hull City	0-3		7798		4	1	3		5	7	9					6	11				8		10	2
21	Dec	2	Coventry City	0-2		13613		4	1	3		5	7	9					6	11				8		10	2
22		10	BRISTOL CITY	2-0	Towers, Francis	5205			1	3		5	7	9		4	11		6					8		10	2
23		19	Tranmere Rovers	0-2		5584			1	3	10	5	7	9		4	11		6					8			2
24		23	SWINDON TOWN	2-1	Higginson, Docherty	4410			1	3		5	7	9		4	11		6					8		10	2
25		31	HALIFAX TOWN	2-0	Francis, Towers	6983			1	3		5	7	9		4	11		6					8		10	2
26	Jan	7	Swindon Town	1-1	Docherty	8666			1	3		5	7	9		4	11		6					8		10	2
27		14	Shrewsbury Town	0-3		6397			1	3		5	7	9		4	11		6					8		10	2
28		21	WALSALL	3-1	Francis, Towers 2	6300			1	3		5	7	9		4	11		6					8		10	2
29		28	Colchester United	4-2	Rainford, Bristow, Towers 2	4040		4	1	3		5	7	9					6	11				8		10	2
30	Feb	4	Bury	0-1		5861		4	1	3	10	5	7	9					6	11				8			2
31		11	CHESTERFIELD	2-2	Towers 2	6284		4	1	3		5	7	9					6	11				8		10	2
32		18	Southend United	1-1	Towers	7678		4	1	3		5	7						6	11				8	9	10	2
33		25	COVENTRY CITY	1-1	Summers	5516		4	1	3		5	7						6	11				8	9	10	2
34	Mar	4	Bradford City	1-3	McLeod	7484			1	3		5	7						6	11			4	8	9	10	2
35		11	BARNSLEY	0-0		7041			1	3		5					7		6	11			4	8	9	10	2
36		18	Newport County	1-0	Summers	3756			1	3		5					7		6	11			4	8	9	10	2
37		25	COLCHESTER UNITED	0-0		4617			1	3		5					7		6	11			4	8	9	10	2
38	Apr	1	Grimsby Town	0-0		7734			1	3		5					7		6	11			4	8	9	10	2
39		3	NOTTS COUNTY	3-0	Summers, Towers 2	5416			1	3		5					7		6	11			4	8	9	10	2
40		4	Notts County	0-0		3933		4	1			5					7		6	11	8		3		9	10	2
41		8	HULL CITY	2-2	Towers, McLeod	6390			1			5			3		7		6	11	8		4		9	10	2
42		14	Reading	0-4		8304		4	1			5		9	3		7		6	11				8		10	2
43		22	BOURNEMOUTH	2-2	Summers, Towers	4415		4	1			5			3		7		6	11				8	9	10	2
44		25	PORT VALE	0-0		3503		4	1			5			3		7		6	11				8	9	10	2
45		29	Bristol City	0-3		8656		4	1	3		5					7		6	11				8	9	10	2
46	May	2	READING	2-1	Summers 2	4752		4	1	3		5					7		6	11				8	9	10	2
						Apps	6	23	46	41	5	46	17	31	4	23	22	15	32	36	2	2	17	41	15	42	40
						Goals		2					2	8		2		1	1	3			3	5	6	21	

Two own goals

F.A. Cup

	Date		Opponent	Res	Scorers	Att	Avis VCS	Bristow GA	Cakebread G	Coote KA	Curran TW	Dargie IC	Docherty J	Francis GE	Gitsham JW	Goundry W	Hales J	Heath DJ	Higginson T	McLeod GJ	O'Donnell D	Parsons EG	Peplow RR	Rainford JW	Summers G	Towers EJ	Wilson TF
R1	Nov	5	Watford	2-2	Francis 2	16970		4	1	3		5		9					6	11		7		8		10	2
rep		8	WATFORD	0-2		21000		4	1	3		5		9					6	11		7		8		10	2

F.L. Cup

	Date		Opponent	Res	Scorers	Att	Avis VCS	Bristow GA	Cakebread G	Coote KA	Curran TW	Dargie IC	Docherty J	Francis GE	Gitsham JW	Goundry W	Hales J	Heath DJ	Higginson T	McLeod GJ	O'Donnell D	Parsons EG	Peplow RR	Rainford JW	Summers G	Towers EJ	Wilson TF
R2	Oct	25	SUNDERLAND	4-3	Towers, McLeod, Rainford 2	10400			1	3		5						7	6	11			4	8	9	10	2
R3	Nov	22	BURNLEY	1-1	Rainford	9900		4	1	3		5	7	9					6	11				8		10	2
rep	Dec	6	Burnley	1-2	Docherty	12787			1	3		5	7	9		4			6	11				8		10	2

		Pl.	Home W	D	L	F	A	Away W	D	L	F	A	F. (Total)	A.	Pts
1	Bury	46	18	3	2	62	17	12	5	6	46	28	108	45	68
2	Walsall	46	19	4	0	62	20	9	2	12	36	40	98	60	62
3	Queen's Park Rgs.	46	18	4	1	58	23	7	6	10	35	37	93	60	60
4	Watford	46	12	7	4	52	27	8	5	10	33	45	85	72	52
5	Notts County	46	16	3	4	52	24	5	6	12	30	53	82	77	51
6	Grimsby Town	46	14	4	5	48	32	6	6	11	29	37	77	69	50
7	Port Vale	46	15	3	5	63	30	2	12	9	33	49	96	79	49
8	Barnsley	46	15	5	3	56	30	6	2	15	27	50	83	80	49
9	Halifax Town	46	14	7	2	42	22	2	10	11	29	56	71	78	49
10	Shrewsbury Town	46	13	7	3	54	26	2	9	12	29	49	83	75	46
11	Hull City	46	13	6	4	51	28	4	6	13	22	45	73	73	46
12	Torquay United	46	8	12	3	37	26	6	5	12	38	57	75	83	45
13	Newport County	46	12	7	4	51	30	5	4	14	30	60	81	90	45
14	Bristol City	46	15	4	4	50	19	2	6	15	20	49	70	68	44
15	Coventry City	46	14	6	3	54	25	2	6	15	26	58	80	83	44
16	Swindon Town	46	13	6	4	41	16	1	9	13	21	39	62	55	43
17	**BRENTFORD**	**46**	**10**	**9**	**4**	**41**	**28**	**3**	**8**	**12**	**15**	**42**	**56**	**70**	**43**
18	Reading	46	13	5	5	48	29	1	7	15	24	54	72	83	40
19	Bournemouth	46	8	7	8	34	39	7	3	13	24	37	58	76	40
20	Southend United	46	10	8	5	38	26	4	3	16	22	50	60	76	39
21	Tranmere Rovers	46	11	5	7	53	50	4	3	16	26	65	79	115	38
22	Bradford City	46	8	8	7	37	36	3	6	14	28	51	65	87	36
23	Colchester United	46	8	5	10	40	44	3	6	14	28	57	68	101	33
24	Chesterfield	46	9	6	8	42	29	1	6	16	25	58	67	87	32

1961/62

23rd in Division Three: Relegated

							Belcher JA	Block MJ	Brooks J	Cakebread G	Coote KA	Dargie IC	Edgley BK	Francis GE	Gelson PWJ	Gitsham JW	Hales JMcK	Higginson T	McLeod GJ	O'Donnell D	Rainford JW	Reeves RHE	Summers G	Wilson TF
1	Aug	19	Queen's Park Rangers	0-3		16796	4			1	3	5	8				7	6	11	10			9	2
2		22	HALIFAX TOWN	0-2		7509	4			1	3		8		5		7	6	11	10			9	2
3		26	READING	1-2	Spiers (og)	9630	4			1	3		10		5		7	6	11		8		9	2
4		28	Halifax Town	0-1		7759	4			1	3	5	8					6	11	7	10		9	2
5	Sep	2	Newport County	1-6	Edgley	5757	4			1	2	5	10				7	6	11		8	3	9	
6		5	Grimsby Town	0-1		9115	4			1	2	5	10				7	6	11		8	3	9	
7		9	SOUTHEND UNITED	0-0		7135	4		8	1	2	5	10				7	6	11			3	9	
8		16	Notts County	1-3	Edgley	7979	4		8	1	3	5	9					6	11	10	7			2
9		19	COVENTRY CITY	2-1	Higginson, Belcher	6119	4		8	1	6	5	10			3		9	11		7			2
10		23	SHREWSBURY TOWN	4-0	Edgley, Brooks, Rainford	7008	4		8	1	6	5	10			3		9	11		7			2
11		25	Coventry City	0-2		10276	4		8	1	6	5	10			3		9	11		7			2
12		30	Peterborough United	0-6		12533	4		8	1	6	5	10			3		9	11		7			2
13	Oct	3	Bristol City	0-3		10717	4		8	1	6	5				3		9	11	10	7			2
14		7	SWINDON TOWN	1-0	Rainford	7540			8	1	6	5	10	9		3		4	11		7			2
15		10	BRISTOL CITY	0-2		8579			10	1	6	5		9		3		4	11		8		7	2
16		14	Torquay United	1-3	Brooks	4917			8	1	6	5	10	9		3		4	11				7	2
17		21	PORTSMOUTH	3-2	Brooks, Edgley, Francis	9622	4		8	1	2		10	9	5	3		6	11				7	
18		28	Barnsley	2-2	Summers, Edgley	6561	4		8	1	2		10	9	5	3		6	11				7	
19	Nov	11	Watford	1-2	Francis	8356	4		8	1	2		10	9	5	3		6	11				7	
20		18	BOURNEMOUTH	2-2	Francis, Edgley	9681	4		8	1	2		10	9	5	3		6	11				7	
21	Dec	2	LINCOLN CITY	1-0	Summers	7976	4		8	1	2		10	9	5	3		6	11				7	
22		9	Northampton Town	0-5		10059	4		8	1	2		10	9	5			6	11			3	7	
23		16	QUEEN'S PARK RANGERS	1-4	Francis	11771	4		8	1	2		10	9	5		7	6	11			3		
24		23	Reading	0-4		7285	4		8	1	3		10	9	5			6	11		7			2
25		26	BRADFORD PARK AVE.	2-0	Edgley (p), Francis	5043	4		8	1	3		10	9	5			6	11		7			2
26	Jan	13	NEWPORT COUNTY	3-1	Francis, Higginson, McLeod	7757	4	7	8	1	2	5	10	9		3		6	11					
27		20	Southend United	0-0		6818	4	11	10	1		5				3	7	6	9		8			2
28		27	Crystal Palace	2-2	Brooks, Block	19323	4	7	8	1	2	5	10	9		3		6	11					
29	Feb	2	NOTTS COUNTY	0-1		9227	4	7	8	1	2	5	10	9		3		6	11					
30		10	Shrewsbury Town	3-1	Brooks, Francis, McLeod	6037	4	7	8	1	2	5		9		3		6	11	10				
31		17	PETERBOROUGH UTD.	2-0	Brooks (p), McLeod	10991	4	7	8	1	2	5		9		3		6	11	10				
32		23	Swindon Town	2-5	Summers, Francis	7088	4			1	2	5	10	9		3		6	11	8			7	
33	Mar	3	TORQUAY UNITED	0-2		7464	4	10	8	1	2	5		9		3		6	11				7	
34		10	Portsmouth	0-4		15256		11	8	1	2	5		9	4	3		6	10				7	
35		17	BARNSLEY	1-1	Francis	6096		11	8	1	2	5		9	4	3		6	10				7	
36		24	Hull City	0-3		3849		11	8	1	2	5		9	4	3		6	10				7	
37		30	WATFORD	3-1	Francis 2, Summers	6441		11	8	1	2	5		9	4	3		6	10				7	
38	Apr	4	Bradford Park Avenue	2-1	Francis, Summers	4812		11	8	1	2	5		9	4	3		6	10				7	
39		7	Bournemouth	1-1	Block	10736		11	8	1	2	5		9	4	3		6	10				7	
40		13	CRYSTAL PALACE	4-2	Brooks 2 (1p), Francis, Wood (og)	9926		11	8	1	2	5		9	4	3		6	10				7	
41		20	PORT VALE	1-2	Brooks (p)	11175		11	8	1	2	5		9	4	3		6	10				7	
42		21	Lincoln City	3-3	Summers 2, Gelson	5482		11		1	2	5		9	4	3		6	10	8			7	
43		23	Port Vale	0-3		5928		11	8	1	2	5		9	4	3		6	10				7	
44		27	NORTHAMPTON T	3-0	Francis, Brooks, Summers	6715		11	8	1	2	5		9	4	3		6	10				7	
45	May	1	GRIMSBY TOWN	0-2		18127		11	8	1	2	5		9	4	3		6	10				7	
46		3	HULL CITY	0-2		3583		11	8	1	2	5		9	4	3		6	10				7	
						Apps	30	20	38	46	45	35	27	32	24	34	8	46	46	9	15	5	30	16
						Goals	1	2	10				8	14	1			2	3		2		8	

Two own goals

F.A. Cup

							Belcher JA	Block MJ	Brooks J	Cakebread G	Coote KA	Dargie IC	Edgley BK	Francis GE	Gelson PWJ	Gitsham JW	Hales JMcK	Higginson T	McLeod GJ	O'Donnell D	Rainford JW	Reeves RHE	Summers G	Wilson TF
R1	Nov	4	OXFORD UNITED	3-0	Summers, Edgley 2	13500	4		8	1	2		10	9	5	3		6	11				7	
R2		25	Aldershot	2-2	Edgley, Francis	12846	4		8	1	2		10	9	5	3		6	11				7	
rep		28	ALDERSHOT	2-0	Edgley, Brooks	17800	4		8	1	2		10	9	5	3		6	11				7	
R3	Jan	6	LEYTON ORIENT	1-1	Summers	19700	4		8	1	2		10	9	5	3		6	11				7	
rep		8	Leyton Orient	1-2	Higginson	22690	4		8	1	2	5	10	9		3		6	11		7			

F.L. Cup

							Belcher JA	Block MJ	Brooks J	Cakebread G	Coote KA	Dargie IC	Edgley BK	Francis GE	Gelson PWJ	Gitsham JW	Hales JMcK	Higginson T	McLeod GJ	O'Donnell D	Rainford JW	Reeves RHE	Summers G	Wilson TF
R1	Sep	13	Leeds United	1-4	McLeod	4500	4		7	1	3	5	10					6	11		8		9	2

	Pl.	Home W	D	L	F	A	Away W	D	L	F	A	F. (Total)	A.	Pts
1 Portsmouth	46	15	6	2	48	23	12	5	6	39	24	87	47	65
2 Grimsby Town	46	18	3	2	49	18	10	3	10	31	38	80	56	62
3 Bournemouth	46	14	8	1	42	18	7	9	7	27	27	69	45	59
4 Queen's Park Rgs.	46	15	3	5	65	31	9	8	6	46	42	111	73	59
5 Peterborough Utd.	46	16	0	7	60	38	10	6	7	47	44	107	82	58
6 Bristol City	46	15	3	5	56	27	8	5	10	38	45	94	72	54
7 Reading	46	14	5	4	46	24	8	4	11	31	42	77	66	53
8 Northampton Town	46	12	6	5	52	24	8	5	10	33	33	85	57	51
9 Swindon Town	46	11	8	4	48	26	6	7	10	30	45	78	71	49
10 Hull City	46	15	2	6	43	20	5	6	12	24	34	67	54	48
11 Bradford Park Ave.	46	13	5	5	47	27	7	2	14	33	51	80	78	47
12 Port Vale	46	12	4	7	41	23	5	7	11	24	35	65	58	45
13 Notts County	46	14	5	4	44	23	3	4	16	23	51	67	74	43
14 Coventry City	46	11	6	6	38	26	5	5	13	26	45	64	71	43
15 Crystal Palace	46	8	8	7	50	41	6	6	11	33	39	83	80	42
16 Southend United	46	10	7	6	31	26	3	9	11	26	43	57	69	42
17 Watford	46	10	9	4	37	26	4	4	15	26	48	63	74	41
18 Halifax Town	46	9	5	9	34	35	6	5	12	28	49	62	84	40
19 Shrewsbury Town	46	8	7	8	46	37	5	5	13	27	47	73	84	38
20 Barnsley	46	9	6	8	45	41	4	6	13	26	54	71	95	38
21 Torquay United	46	9	4	10	48	44	6	2	15	28	56	76	100	36
22 Lincoln City	46	4	10	9	31	43	5	7	11	26	44	57	87	35
23 BRENTFORD	**46**	**11**	**3**	**9**	**34**	**29**	**2**	**5**	**16**	**19**	**64**	**53**	**93**	**34**
24 Newport County	46	6	5	12	29	38	1	3	19	17	64	46	102	22

1962/63

Champions of Division Four: Promoted

							Anthony TH	Block MJ	Brooks J	Cakebread G	Coote KA	Crowe MJ	Dargie IC	Dick J	Edgley BK	Fielding JA	Gelson PWJ	Gitsham JW	Hales J	Hawley AJ	Higginson T	McAdams WJ	McLeod GF	Ryecraft F	Scott MD	Summers G
1	Aug	18	Doncaster Rovers	2-0	McAdams 2	8247			8	1	2	4			10		5	3			6	9	11			7
2		21	GILLINGHAM	1-2	Edgley	11914			8		2	4			10		5	3			6	9	11	1		7
3		25	MANSFIELD TOWN	1-3	McAdams	8340			8		2	4			10		5	3			6	9	11	1		7
4		29	Gillingham	4-1	Brooks 3, Block	8822		7	8		2	4			10		5	3			6	9	11	1		
5	Sep	1	Workington	1-3	Summers	3382		7	8		2	4					5	3			6	9	11	1		10
6		8	EXETER CITY	3-1	McAdams, Dick, Hughes (og)	11153		7		1	2	4		10			5	3			6	9	11			8
7		12	Crewe Alexandra	0-3		6302		7		1	2	4	5	10				3			6	9	11			8
8		15	Chesterfield	1-1	McAdams	6114		7		1	2	4	5	10				3			6	9	11			8
9		18	STOCKPORT COUNTY	2-1	Dick, McAdams	10146	2	7	8	1	4	6		10				3			5	9	11			
10		22	ROCHDALE	1-0	McLeod	10753	2	7	8	1	4	6		10				3			5	9	11			
11		29	BARROW	2-1	Dick 2	9541	3	7	8	1	4	6		10						2	5	9	11			
12	Oct	2	HARTLEPOOLS UNITED	4-0	Dick 2, McAdams, Block	10729	3	7	8	1	4	6		10						2	5	9	11			
13		6	Darlington	3-1	Brooks 2 (1p), Block	4692	3	7	8	1	2	6	5	10							4	9	11			
14		13	SOUTHPORT	3-3	McAdams, Brooks 2 (1p)	11651	3	7	8	1	2	6		10			5				4	9	11			
15		20	Aldershot	0-0		8660	3	7	8	1	2	6		10			5				4	9	11			
16		27	NEWPORT COUNTY	3-1	McAdams 2, Block	11312	3	7	8	1	2	6		10			5				4	9	11			
17	Nov	10	BRADFORD CITY	5-2	McAdams 3, McLeod, Brooks (p)	8396		7	8	1	2	6					5	3			4	9	11			10
18		24	Stockport County	1-2	Block	3090	3	7	8	1	2	6					5				4	9	11			10
19	Dec	1	Lincoln City	3-1	Brooks, Summers, McAdams	5620	3		8	1	2	6					5		7		4	9	11			10
20		8	OLDHAM ATHLETIC	2-1	Anthony, Brooks	12144	3	7	8	1	2	6		10			5				4	9	11			
21		15	DONCASTER ROVERS	1-0	Meadows (og)	9589	3	7	8	1	2	6		10			5				4	9	11			
22		22	Mansfield Town	2-1	Brooks 2	9468	3	7	8	1	2	6		10			5				4	9	11			
23		26	CHESTER	2-1	Dick, McAdams	9724	3	7	8	1	2	6		10			5				4	9	11			
24	Feb	16	Barrow	1-1	Summers	4147	3	7	8	1	2	4		10			5				6		11			9
25		23	DARLINGTON	1-3	Dick	9272	3	7	8	1	2	6		10			5				4		11			9
26	Mar	2	Southport	0-1		3136	3	7	8	1	2	6		9			5		11		4		10			
27		4	Tranmere Rovers	2-1	Summers 2	8232	3	7	8	1	2	6		10			5				4		11			9
28		9	ALDERSHOT	4-2	Brooks 2 (1p), Henry (og), McAdams	8390	3	7	8	1	2	6		10			5				4	9	11			
29		12	TORQUAY UNITED	2-2	Block, Brooks	13084	3	7	8	1	2	6		10			5				4	9	11			
30		16	Newport County	4-1	McAdams, Dick 2, Brooks (p)	2891	3	7	8	1	2	6		10							4	9	11		5	
31		20	Rochdale	5-3	Dick 3, McAdams, Brooks	5680	3	7	8	1	2	6		10							4	9	11		5	
32		23	OXFORD UNITED	4-0	Block, Higginson, McAdams 2	13756	3	7	8	1	2	6		10							4	9	11		5	
33		29	Torquay United	1-1	McAdams	5750	3	7	8		2	6		10							4	9	11	1	5	
34	Apr	3	Chester	2-1	Dick 2	5919	3	7	8		2	4		10							6	9	11	1	5	
35		6	TRANMERE ROVERS	4-0	McLeod 2, Dick, Brooks (p)	13383	3	11	8		2	6		10		7					4		9	1	5	
36		12	York City	1-1	Brooks	7904	3	7	8		2	6		10							4		11	1	5	9
37		13	Bradford City	1-2	Dick	3070	3	11	8		2	6		10		7					4		9	1	5	
38		15	YORK CITY	2-1	Dick 2	15070	2	7			4			10		8	5	3			9		11	1	6	
39		20	LINCOLN CITY	3-2	Dick, Block, McAdams	11384		7	8		2	6		10				3			4	9	11	1	5	
40		22	Hartlepools United	1-2	Dick	3465		7	8		2	6		10				3			4	9	11	1	5	
41		27	Oldham Athletic	1-2	Brooks	17774	3	7	8		2			10			5				4	9	11	1	6	
42		30	CREWE ALEXANDRA	3-1	Brooks 2 (1p), Dick	15820	3	7	8		2			10			5				6	9	11	1	4	
43	May	4	CHESTERFIELD	2-1	Dick, Fielding	13903	3	11	8		2			10		7	5				6		9	1	4	
44		11	Oxford United	1-2	Summers	11314	3	7			2			10		8	5				6		11	1	4	9
45		17	Exeter City	2-2	Hales, Scott	4930		7			2			10		8	5	3	11		6		9	1	4	
46		23	WORKINGTON	4-3	Fielding 2, Hales, Brown (og)	13150		7			2			10		8	5	3	11		6		9	1	4	
						Apps	33	42	39	28	46	39	3	38	4	7	29	16	4	2	46	34	46	18	17	15
						Goals	1	8	22					23	1	3			2		1	22	4		1	6

Four own goals

F.A. Cup

							Anthony TH	Block MJ	Brooks J	Cakebread G	Coote KA	Crowe MJ	Dargie IC	Dick J	Edgley BK	Fielding JA	Gelson PWJ	Gitsham JW	Hales J	Hawley AJ	Higginson T	McAdams WJ	McLeod GF	Ryecraft F	Scott MD	Summers G
R1	Nov	3	Aldershot	0-1		12200	3	7	8	1	2	6		10			5				4	9	11			

F.L. Cup

							Anthony TH	Block MJ	Brooks J	Cakebread G	Coote KA	Crowe MJ	Dargie IC	Dick J	Edgley BK	Fielding JA	Gelson PWJ	Gitsham JW	Hales J	Hawley AJ	Higginson T	McAdams WJ	McLeod GF	Ryecraft F	Scott MD	Summers G
R1	Sep	4	WREXHAM	3-0	Summers, McAdams, Edgley	6800		7		1	2	4			10		5	3			6	9	11			8
R2		26	SHEFFIELD UNITED	1-4	Dick	13850	2	7	8	1	4	6		10				3			5	9	11			

	Pl.	Home W	Home D	Home L	Home F	Home A	Away W	Away D	Away L	Away F	Away A	F. (Total)	A. (Total)	Pts
1 BRENTFORD	**46**	**18**	**2**	**3**	**59**	**31**	**9**	**6**	**8**	**39**	**33**	**98**	**64**	**62**
2 Oldham Athletic	46	18	4	1	65	23	6	7	10	30	37	95	60	59
3 Crewe Alexandra	46	15	4	4	50	21	9	7	7	36	37	86	58	59
4 Mansfield Town	46	16	4	3	61	20	8	5	10	47	49	108	69	57
5 Gillingham	46	17	3	3	49	23	5	10	8	22	26	71	49	57
6 Torquay United	46	14	8	1	45	20	6	8	9	30	36	75	56	56
7 Rochdale	46	16	6	1	48	21	4	5	14	19	38	67	59	51
8 Tranmere Rovers	46	15	3	5	57	25	5	7	11	24	42	81	67	50
9 Barrow	46	14	7	2	52	26	5	5	13	30	54	82	80	50
10 Workington	46	13	4	6	42	20	4	9	10	34	48	76	68	47
11 Aldershot	46	9	9	5	42	32	6	8	9	31	37	73	69	47
12 Darlington	46	13	3	7	44	33	6	3	14	28	54	72	87	44
13 Southport	46	11	9	3	47	35	4	5	14	25	71	72	106	44
14 York City	46	12	6	5	42	25	4	5	14	25	37	67	62	43
15 Chesterfield	46	7	10	6	43	29	6	6	11	27	35	70	64	42
16 Doncaster Rovers	46	9	10	4	36	26	5	4	14	28	51	64	77	42
17 Exeter City	46	9	6	8	27	32	7	4	12	30	45	57	77	42
18 Oxford United	46	10	10	3	44	27	3	5	15	26	44	70	71	41
19 Stockport County	46	9	7	7	34	29	6	4	13	22	41	56	70	41
20 Newport County	46	11	6	6	44	29	3	5	15	32	61	76	90	39
21 Chester	46	11	5	7	31	23	4	4	15	20	43	51	66	39
22 Lincoln City	46	11	1	11	48	46	2	8	13	20	43	68	89	35
23 Bradford City	46	8	5	10	37	40	3	5	15	27	53	64	93	32
24 Hartlepools United	46	5	7	11	33	39	2	4	17	23	65	56	104	25

1962-63
Back: Crowe, Gelson, Gitsham, Ryecraft, Coote, Higginson,
Front: Summers, Brooks, McAdams, Edgley, McLeod.

1963-64
Back: Jones, Scott, Brodie, Hawley, McLaughlin, Higginson
Front: Lazarus, Ward, Fielding, McAdams, Thomson

1963/64

16th in Division Three

No	Month	Day	Opponent	Res	Scorers	Att	Block MJ	Brodie CTG	Brooks J	Cakebread G	Coote KA	Crowe MJ	Dick J	Fielding JA	Gelson PWJ	Hales J	Hawley AJ	Higginson T	Jones AP	Lazarus M	McAdams WJ	McLaughlin H	McLeod GJ	Ryecraft F	Scott MD	Slater WJ	Smith W	Soutar TJ	Summers G	Thomson GM	Ward D	Phillips GD	Anthony TH
1	Aug	24	NOTTS COUNTY	4-1	Block, McAdams, Brooks, Loxley (og)	13320	7		8		2	6	10					4	3		9		11	1	5								
2		27	BRISTOL CITY	1-2	Dick	16843	7		8		2	6	10					4	3		9		11	1	5								
3		31	Crewe Alexandra	1-1	McLeod	6729	7				2		10	8				4	3		9	6	11	1	5								
4	Sep	7	CRYSTAL PALACE	2-1	Block, McAdams	15883	7		8		2	6	10					4	3		9		11	1	5								
5		10	Bristol City	3-3	Dick 2, Kurila (og)	12689	7				2	6	10	8				4	3		9		11	1	5								
6		14	Walsall	2-2	McAdams, Block	6448	7				2	6	10	8				4	3		9		11	1	5								
7		16	Port Vale	0-3		11539	7				2	6	10	8				4	3		9		11	1	5								
8		21	READING	4-2	Dick 3, Block	12394	7				2	6	10	8					3		9		11	1	5		4						
9		28	Luton Town	2-0	Dick, McAdams	7379	7				2	6	10	8					3		9		11	1	5		4						
10	Oct	1	PORT VALE	1-2	McAdams	11914	7				2	6	10	8					3		9		11	1	5		4						
11		5	COVENTRY CITY	2-3	Dick, McAdams	15829	7		8		2	6	10			11			3		9			1	5		4						
12		9	Wrexham	4-2	Slater 2, McAdams, Dick	8047						6	10	7		11	2		3		9			1	5	4			8				
13		12	BRISTOL ROVERS	2-5		13371						6	10	7		11	2		3		9			1	5	4			8				
14		15	WREXHAM	9-0	McAdams 2,Ward 2,Brooks 2,Fox (og),Hales,Summers	10569			8	1	2					11		6	3		9				5	4			7		10		
15		19	Barnsley	1-1	Brooks	6775			7	1	2		10			11		6	3		9				5	4					8		
16		21	Mansfield Town	2-2	Dick, Ward	12118					2		10			11		6	3		9			1	5	4			7		8		
17		26	MILLWALL	3-1	McAdams, Block 2	15234	11			1	2		10					6	3		9				5		4		7		8		
18		29	MANSFIELD TOWN	4-0	Ward 3, Dick	14910	11			1	2		10	7				6	3		9				5		4				8		
19	Nov	2	Colchester United	2-1	Block, Dick	7117	11			1	2		10	7				6	3		9				5		4				8		
20		9	WATFORD	1-2	Dick	17094	7				2	6	10					4	3		9		11	1	5						8		
21		23	PETERBOROUGH UTD.	2-0	Dick 2	15990	7	1				6	10					4	3		9		11		5					2	8		
22		30	Oldham Athletic	1-4	Block (p)	14395	7	1					10					6	3				11		5		4		9	2	8		
23	Dec	14	Notts County	0-2		3744	7	1			2	6	10					4			9		11		5					3	8		
24		21	CREWE ALEXANDRA	2-2	Fielding, Dick	7580	7	1				6	10	8		11		4	2						5					3	9		
25		28	Bournemouth	0-2		7507	7	1				6	10	8		11		4	2						5					3	9		
26	Jan	11	Crystal Palace	0-1		16630	11	1				6	10					4	2	7	9				5					3	8		
27		18	WALSALL	1-1	Ward	10663	11	1				6	10					4	2	7	9				5					3	8		
28	Feb	1	Reading	3-4	Block, Lazarus, Ward	10887	11	1						8	5			6	2	7	9						4			3	10		
29		8	LUTON TOWN	2-6	McAdams, Lazarus	9003	11	1						8	5			6	2	7	9						4			3	10		
30		15	Coventry City	2-2	Dick, Ward	22775	11	1				6	10					4	2	7	9				5					3	8		
31		22	Bristol Rovers	1-3	Block	8701	11	1				6	10					4	2	7	9				5					3	8		
32		29	QUEEN'S PARK RANGERS	2-2	Block, Lazarus	12226	11	1				6		8				4	2	7	9				5					3	10		
33	Mar	7	Millwall	3-1	McAdams, Ward 2	9140	11	1				6		8				4	2	7	9				5					3	10		
34		14	COLCHESTER UNITED	3-1	Ward 2, Lazarus	7057	11	1				6		8				4	2	7	9				5					3	10		
35		16	Southend United	1-2	Ward	6814	11	1				6		8				4	2	7	9				5					3	10		
36		20	Queen's Park Rangers	2-2	Ward 2	9351	11			1		6		8				4	2	7	9				5					3	10		
37		28	SOUTHEND UNITED	3-0	Higginson, Fielding, McAdams	9250	11	1				6		8			2	4	3	7	9				5						10		
38		30	SHREWSBURY TOWN	0-1		10047	11	1				6		8			3	4	2	7					5				9		10		
39		31	Shrewsbury Town	1-1	Summers	5493	11	1				6	10	7			3	4	2						5				9		8		
40	Apr	4	Peterborough United	0-3		5550	11	1				6	10				2	4	3	7					5					9	8		
41		11	OLDHAM ATHLETIC	2-0	Ward 2	8925		1							7			2	4	3	11	9	6			5					10	8		
42		13	BOURNEMOUTH	2-0	Jones, Ward	10029		1				6		11			2		3	7	9				5		4			10	8		
43		18	Hull City	0-0		6798		1				6		7			2		3	11	10				5		4			9	8		
44		21	Watford	2-2	Fielding, McAdams	19381		1				6		11			2	4	3	7	9				5					10	8		
45		25	BARNSLEY	1-1	Thomson	8351		1				6		11			2	4	3	7	9				5					10	8		
46		28	HULL CITY	1-3	Hales	6818		1								11	2		3	7				5		4	10	9	6	8		
						Apps	35	25	6	6	19	34	30	28	2	9	12	37	45	20	39	2	14	15	44	5	13	1	9	23	33		
						Goals	11		4				18	4		2		1	1	4	14		1			2			2	1	19		

Three own goals

F.A. Cup

Rd	Month	Day	Opponent	Res	Scorers	Att	Block MJ	Brodie CTG	Brooks J	Cakebread G	Coote KA	Crowe MJ	Dick J	Fielding JA	Gelson PWJ	Hales J	Hawley AJ	Higginson T	Jones AP	Lazarus M	McAdams WJ	McLaughlin H	McLeod GJ	Ryecraft F	Scott MD	Slater WJ	Smith W	Soutar TJ	Summers G	Thomson GM	Ward D	Phillips GD	Anthony TH
R1	Nov	16	MARGATE	2-2	Block, Dick	12150	7				2	6	10						3		9		11		5		4				8	1	
rep		20	Margate	2-0	Ward 2	6212	7					6	10					4	3		9		11	1	5						8		
R2	Dec	7	GRAVESEND & N'FLEET	1-0	Block	11850	7	1				6	10					4	2		9		11		5					3	8		2
R3	Jan	4	MIDDLESBROUGH	2-1	Dick, McAdams	16100	7	1				6	10			11		4	2		9				5					3	8		
R4		25	Oxford United	2-2	Block, Ward	15517	7	1				6	10			11		4	2		9				5					3	8		
rep		28	OXFORD UNITED	1-2	McAdams	25000	7	1				6	10			11		4	2		9				5					3	8		

F.L. Cup

Rd	Month	Day	Opponent	Res	Scorers	Att	Block MJ	Brodie CTG	Brooks J	Cakebread G	Coote KA	Crowe MJ	Dick J	Fielding JA	Gelson PWJ	Hales J	Hawley AJ	Higginson T	Jones AP	Lazarus M	McAdams WJ	McLaughlin H	McLeod GJ	Ryecraft F	Scott MD	Slater WJ	Smith W	Soutar TJ	Summers G	Thomson GM	Ward D	Phillips GD	Anthony TH
R1	Sep	4	Reading	1-1	Block	7582	7		8		2		10						3		9	6	11	1	5		4						
rep		23	READING	2-0	Spiers (og), McLoughlin	10360	7				2		10	8		9			3			6	11	1	5		4						
R2		25	BOURNEMOUTH	0-0		10830	7				2	6	10	8					3		9		11	1	5		4						
rep	Nov	4	Bournemouth	0-2		8047	11		8		2		10	7				6	3		9			1	5		4						

		Pl.	Home W	D	L	F	A	Away W	D	L	F	A	F. (Total)	A.	Pts
1	Coventry City	46	14	7	2	62	32	8	9	6	36	29	98	61	60
2	Crystal Palace	46	17	4	2	38	14	6	10	7	35	37	73	51	60
3	Watford	46	16	6	1	57	28	7	6	10	22	31	79	59	58
4	Bournemouth	46	17	4	2	47	15	7	4	12	32	43	79	58	56
5	Bristol City	46	13	7	3	52	24	7	8	8	32	40	84	64	55
6	Reading	46	15	5	3	49	26	6	5	12	30	36	79	62	52
7	Mansfield Town	46	15	8	0	51	20	5	3	15	25	42	76	62	51
8	Hull City	46	11	9	3	45	27	5	8	10	28	41	73	68	49
9	Oldham Athletic	46	13	3	7	44	35	7	5	11	29	35	73	70	48
10	Peterborough Utd.	46	13	6	4	52	27	5	5	13	23	43	75	70	47
11	Shrewsbury Town	46	13	6	4	43	19	5	5	13	30	61	73	80	47
12	Bristol Rovers	46	9	6	8	52	34	10	2	11	39	45	91	79	46
13	Port Vale	46	13	6	4	35	13	3	8	12	18	36	53	49	46
14	Southend United	46	9	10	4	42	26	6	5	12	35	52	77	78	45
15	Queen's Park Rgs.	46	13	4	6	47	34	5	5	13	29	44	76	78	45
16	**BRENTFORD**	**46**	**11**	**4**	**8**	**54**	**36**	**4**	**10**	**9**	**33**	**44**	**87**	**80**	**44**
17	Colchester United	46	10	8	5	45	26	2	11	10	25	42	70	68	43
18	Luton Town	46	12	2	9	42	41	4	8	11	22	39	64	80	42
19	Walsall	46	7	9	7	34	35	6	5	12	25	41	59	76	40
20	Barnsley	46	9	9	5	34	29	3	6	14	34	65	68	94	39
21	Millwall	46	9	4	10	33	29	5	6	12	20	38	53	67	38
22	Crewe Alexandra	46	10	5	8	29	26	1	7	15	21	51	50	77	34
23	Wrexham	46	9	4	10	50	42	4	2	17	25	65	75	107	32
24	Notts County	46	7	8	8	29	26	2	1	20	16	66	45	92	27

1964/65

5th in Division Three

							Block MJ	Bloomfield JH	Bonson J	Brodie CTG	Cobb WW	Dick JH	Fielding JA	Gelson PWJ	Hawley AJ	Higginson T	Jones AP	Lawther WI	Lazarus M	McAdams WJ	McLaughlin H	Phillips GD	Scott MD	Smith W	Summers G	Thomson GM	Ward D	McKenzie JT
1	Aug	22	LUTON TOWN	2-2	Bonson 2	10883			9	1			11	5		6	2		7	8			4			3	10	
2		24	Mansfield Town	1-4	Fielding	11426		8	9	1			11	5		6	2		7				4			3	10	
3		28	Carlisle United	1-0	Bonson	11023		8	9	1			11	5		6	2		7				4			3	10	
4		31	MANSFIELD TOWN	1-0	Lazarus	10592		8	9	1			11	5		6	2		7				4			3	10	
5	Sep	5	PORT VALE	4-0	Summers, Dick 2 (1p), Bonson	8397		8	9	1		10	11	5		6	2						4		7	3		
6		9	Grimsby Town	1-2	Ward	9629		8	9	1			11	5		6	2		7				4			3	10	
7		12	Colchester United	3-0	Fielding 2, Lazarus	3977		8	9	1			11	5		6	2		7				4			3	10	
8		15	GRIMSBY TOWN	2-0	Ward, Lazarus	12759		8	9	1			11	5		6	2		7				4			3	10	
9		19	GILLINGHAM	2-0	Fielding, Bonson	13075	7	8	9	1			11	5		6	2			10			4			3		
10		26	BRISTOL ROVERS	1-1	Summers	14208	7	8	9	1			11	5			2				6		4		10	3		
11		28	Peterborough United	1-3	Dick	13311	7	8	9	1		10	11	5			2				6		4			3		
12	Oct	3	Oldham Athletic	1-1	Fielding	11896	7	8	9	1	10		11	5		6	2						4			3		
13		6	PETERBOROUGH UTD.	3-1	Fielding 2, Cobb	12448	7	8	9	1	10		11	5		6	2						4			3		
14		9	Queen's Park Rangers	3-1	Bonson 2, Lazarus	11063		8	9	1	10		11	5		6	2		7				4			3		
15		14	Exeter City	0-0		6865		8	9	1	10		11	5	2	6			7				4			3		
16		17	SHREWSBURY TOWN	2-0	Fielding, Bonson	11372		8	9	1	10		11	5	2	6			7				4			3		
17		20	EXETER CITY	2-1	Lazarus, Bloomfield	12137		8	9	1	10		11	5	2	6			7				4			3		
18		24	Reading	1-1	Lazarus	12296		8	9	1	10		11	5		6	2		7				4			3		
19		27	HULL CITY	1-3	Higginson	12745		8	9	1	10		11	5		6	2		7				4			3		
20		31	SOUTHEND UNITED	2-1	Dick, Lazarus	11215		8	9	1	6	10	11	5			2		7				4			3		
21	Nov	7	Barnsley	1-3	Bonson	4252		8	9	1	6	10	11	5			2		7				4			3		
22		21	Walsall	3-4	Cobb 2, Bonson	8227		8	9	1	10		11	5	3		2		7				4			6		
23		28	WATFORD	5-1	Cobb 2, Bloomfield, Lazarus 2 (1p)	12955		8		1	10		11	5		6	2	9	7				4			3		
24	Dec	12	Luton Town	2-4	Lazarus, Lawther	6104		8		1	10		11	5		6	2	9	7				4			3		
25		19	CARLISLE UNITED	6-1	Cobb 3, Lawther, Lazarus 2	8383		8		1	10		11	5	2	6		9	7				4			3		
26		26	BRISTOL CITY	2-1	Lawther, Bloomfield	16065		8		1	10		11	5		6	2	9	7				4			3		
27	Jan	2	Port Vale	1-2	Lawther	4533		8		1	10		11	5		6	2	9	7				4			3		
28		16	COLCHESTER UNITED	1-0	Gelson	9049		8		1	6		11	5			2	9	7				4			3	10	
29		23	Gillingham	0-1		14475		8		1	6		11	5	2			9	7				4			3	10	
30	Feb	6	Bristol Rovers	2-1	Lawther, Lazarus	14575		8		1	10			5	2	6		9	7				4			3	11	
31		13	OLDHAM ATHLETIC	2-2	Lazarus, Lawther	10306		8		1	6		11	5	2			9	7				4			3	10	
32		20	QUEEN'S PARK RANGERS	5-2	Higginson, Cobb 3, Bedford (og)	12398	11			1	8			5	2	6		9	7				4			3	10	
33		27	Shrewsbury Town	0-1		5564	11	8		1	10			5	2	6		9	7				4			3		
34	Mar	2	Bristol City	2-3	Cobb, Block (p)	11150	11			1	10			5	2	6	3	9	7				4				8	
35		13	Southend United	1-0	Lawther	7888	7	8		1	10		11		2	4	3	9					5			6		
36		17	Workington	1-1	Cobb	3747	11	8		1	10			5		4	3	9	7				2			6		
37		20	BARNSLEY	1-0	Cobb	7954	11	8		1	10			5		4	3	9	7				2			6		
38		26	Scunthorpe United	0-2		5081	11	8		1	10			5		4	3	9	7				2			6		
39	Apr	3	WALSALL	0-0		7511	11	8			4			5			3	9	7			1	2			6	10	
40		7	WORKINGTON	3-0	Lawther 2, Cobb	6946	7	8		1	10		11	5	2		3	9					6	4				
41		10	Watford	1-1	Lawther	7373	7	8		1	10		11	5	2		3	9					6	4				
42		16	BOURNEMOUTH	2-1	Fielding 2	10519	7	8		1	10		11	5	2		3	9					6	4				
43		17	READING	2-1	Evans (og), Block	8929	7			1	10		11		2	6	3	9	8				5	4				
44		19	Bournemouth	1-0	Gater (og)	6196	7	8		1	10		11	5			3	9					2	4		6		
45		24	Hull City	1-2	Lawther	14924	7	8		1	10		11		2		3	9					5	4		6		
46		27	SCUNTHORPE UNITED	4-0	Bonson 2, Block, Bloomfield	6164	7	8	9	1	10		11		2		3						5	4		6		
						Apps	20	42	23	45	35	4	38	42	18	31	37	23	33	2	2	1	46	7	2	41	14	
						Goals	3	4	12		15	4	10	1		2		11	14						2		2	

Three own goals

F.A. Cup

							Block MJ	Bloomfield JH	Bonson J	Brodie CTG	Cobb WW	Dick JH	Fielding JA	Gelson PWJ	Hawley AJ	Higginson T	Jones AP	Lawther WI	Lazarus M	McAdams WJ	McLaughlin H	Phillips GD	Scott MD	Smith W	Summers G	Thomson GM	Ward D	McKenzie JT
R1	Nov	14	Wisbech Town	2-0	Bonson, Cobb	3473		8	9	1	10		11	5	3		2		7				4			6		
R2	Dec	5	NOTTS COUNTY	4-0	Bonson, Fielding, Cobb, 2	9400		8	9	1	10		11	5		6	2		7				4			3		
R3	Jan	9	Burnley	1-1	Lazarus	15100		8	9	1	10		11	5		6	2		7				4			3		
rep		12	BURNLEY	0-2		30448		8	9	1	10		11	5		6	2		7				4			3		

F.L. Cup

							Block MJ	Bloomfield JH	Bonson J	Brodie CTG	Cobb WW	Dick JH	Fielding JA	Gelson PWJ	Hawley AJ	Higginson T	Jones AP	Lawther WI	Lazarus M	McAdams WJ	McLaughlin H	Phillips GD	Scott MD	Smith W	Summers G	Thomson GM	Ward D	McKenzie JT
R1	Sep	2	SOUTHEND UNITED	0-2		5380	11	8	9	1						6	2		7				4			3	10	5

		Pl.	Home					Away					F.	A.	Pts
			W	D	L	F	A	W	D	L	F	A	(Total)		
1	Carlisle United	46	14	5	4	46	24	11	5	7	30	29	76	53	60
2	Bristol City	46	14	6	3	53	18	10	5	8	39	37	92	55	59
3	Mansfield Town	46	17	4	2	61	23	7	7	9	34	38	95	61	59
4	Hull City	46	14	6	3	51	25	9	6	8	40	32	91	57	58
5	**BRENTFORD**	**46**	**18**	**4**	**1**	**55**	**18**	**6**	**5**	**12**	**28**	**37**	**83**	**55**	**57**
6	Bristol Rovers	46	14	7	2	52	21	6	8	9	30	37	82	58	55
7	Gillingham	46	16	5	2	45	13	7	4	12	25	37	70	50	55
8	Peterborough Utd.	46	16	3	4	61	33	6	4	13	24	41	85	74	51
9	Watford	46	13	8	2	45	21	4	8	11	26	43	71	64	50
10	Grimsby Town	46	11	10	2	37	21	5	7	11	31	46	68	67	49
11	Bournemouth	46	12	4	7	40	24	6	7	10	32	39	72	63	47
12	Southend United	46	14	4	5	48	24	5	4	14	30	47	78	71	46
13	Reading	46	12	8	3	45	26	4	6	13	25	44	70	70	46
14	Queen's Park Rgs.	46	15	5	3	48	23	2	7	14	24	57	72	80	46
15	Workington	46	11	7	5	30	22	6	5	12	28	47	58	69	46
16	Shrewsbury Town	46	10	6	7	42	38	5	6	12	34	46	76	84	42
17	Exeter City	46	8	7	8	33	27	4	10	9	18	25	51	52	41
18	Scunthorpe United	46	9	8	6	42	27	5	4	14	23	45	65	72	40
19	Walsall	46	9	4	10	34	36	6	3	14	21	44	55	80	37
20	Oldham Athletic	46	10	3	10	40	39	3	7	13	21	44	61	83	36
21	Luton Town	46	6	8	9	32	36	5	3	15	19	58	51	94	33
22	Port Vale	46	7	6	10	27	33	2	8	13	14	43	41	76	32
23	Colchester United	46	7	6	10	30	34	3	4	16	20	55	50	89	30
24	Barnsley	46	8	5	10	33	31	1	6	16	21	59	54	90	29

1964-65
Back: Jones, Gelson, Brodie, Higginson, Bonson, Thomson
Front: Lazarus, Ward, Scott, Bloomfield, Fielding

1965-66
Back: Jones, Higginson, Brodie, Gelson, Thomson, Crisp,
Front: Lawther, Block, Bonson, Scott, Cobb, Fielding

1965/66

23rd in Division Three: Relegated

	Date	Opponent	Res	Scorers	Att	Block MJ	Bloomfield JH	Bonson J	Brodie CTG	Cobb WW	Crisp RJ	Curley T	Docherty J	Etheridge BG	Fielding JA	Gelson PWJ	Hawley AJ	Higginson T	Jones AP	Lawther WI	Lazarus M	McKenzie JT	McLaughlin H	Phillips GD	Reeve EG	Regan MJ	Ross RH	Scott MD	Smith W	Thomson GM	Thornley BE
1	Aug 21	QUEEN'S PARK RANGERS	6-1	Fielding, Block 3 (1p), Bonson, Lawther	15209	7		8	1	10					11	5		4	2	9								6		3	
2	24	Grimsby Town	2-3	Block, Gelson	5238	7		8	1	10	4				11	5			2	9								6		3	
3	28	Bristol Rovers	1-1	Cobb	12156	7		8	1	10					11	5		4	2	9								6		3	
4	Sep 4	YORK CITY	0-1		10457	7		8	1	10					11	5		4	2	9								6		3	
5	11	Oxford United	0-2		10113		8		1	10					11	5		4	2	9	7							6		3	
6	14	SHREWSBURY TOWN	4-0	Lazarus 2, Lawther, Cobb	10997	7		8	1	10							2	4	3	9	11							5		6	
7	18	SWANSEA TOWN	2-0	Lawther, Block	10329	7	8	10	1								2	4	3	9	11							5		6	
8	25	Walsall	1-1	Cobb	8386	7		8	1	10							2	4	3	9	11							5		6	
9	Oct 2	WORKINGTON	0-1		8712	7			1	10	8						2	4	3	9	11							5		6	
10	6	Shrewsbury Town	0-0		4982	7			1	10	8						2		3	9	11							5	4	6	
11	9	SCUNTHORPE UNITED	0-1		7729	7			1	10	8						2		3	9	11							5	4	6	
12	16	Watford	1-1	Lawther	12339	7			1	8						5		4	3	9	11							2		6	10
13	23	OLDHAM ATHLETIC	0-0		8114	7			1	8						5		4	3	9	11		12					2		6	10
14	30	Gillingham	0-1		8235	11		9	1		8	7				5	2	6	3	10								4			
15	Nov 6	MILLWALL	1-2	Higginson	14805	7		8	1	10					11	5	2	12	3	9								4		6	
16	20	EXETER CITY	1-2	Cobb	5942	7		8		10					11	5	2	6	3	9				1				4			
17	23	GRIMSBY TOWN	3-2	Cobb, Thomson, Lawther	5181	11			1	10					7	5	2	6	3	9								4		8	
18	27	Reading	0-2		6272	11			1	10	12				7	5	2	6	3	9								4		8	
19	Dec 11	Mansfield Town	0-2		3617	11		9	1				7			5		4	2	8					6					3	10
20	Jan 1	Scunthorpe United	2-3	Block, Docherty	5738	11		9	1	10			7			5	3		2	8								4		6	
21	8	PETERBOROUGH UTD.	1-0	Lawther	7388	11			1	8			7			5	3		2	9								4		6	10
22	15	Oldham Athletic	1-1	Cobb	12010	11			1	8			7			5	3		2	9								4		6	10
23	29	Queen's Park Rangers	0-1		14506	11			1	10			7			5	3	8	2	9								4		6	
24	Feb 5	BRISTOL ROVERS	0-5		6242	11			1	8			7			5	3		2	9								4		6	10
25	12	Swindon Town	1-2	Docherty	12551				1			7	11	10		5	3	8	2	9								4		6	
26	26	OXFORD UNITED	5-1	Lawther 2, Docherty, Cobb, Etheridge	7121				1	12	4	7	11	10			3	8	2	9								5		6	
27	Mar 1	SOUTHEND UNITED	2-0	Lawther, Curley	9007					8	5	7	11	10			3		2	9				1				4		6	
28	5	SWINDON TOWN	0-1		9913					8	5	7	11	10			3	6	2	9				1				4		12	
29	7	Southend United	0-1		7088					8		7	11	10			3	4	2	9				1				5		6	
30	12	Swansea Town	1-1	Regan	7925							7	11	10			3	4	2					1		9	8	5		6	
31	19	WALSALL	2-2	Regan, Docherty (p)	7897							7	11	10			3	4	2					1		9	8	5		6	
32	26	Workington	1-1	Docherty	2207							7	11	10		5	3	4	2					1		9	8			6	
33	28	York City	1-1	Etheridge	2702	11							7	10		5	3		2					1		9	8		4	6	
34	Apr 2	Millwall	0-1		13385	11			1				7	10		5	3	4	2							9	8			6	
35	8	Brighton & Hove Albion	0-2		17177				1			7	11	10		5	3	4	2	9							8			6	
36	9	HULL CITY	2-4	Lawther, Docherty	9919							7	11	10		5	3		2	9				1			8	4		6	
37	11	BRIGHTON & HOVE ALB	2-0	Regan, Curley	7671					12		7	11	10		5			3			2		1		9	8		4	6	
38	16	Exeter City	0-5		4975							7	11	10		5			2			3		1		9	8		6	4	
39	23	READING	1-1	Gelson	7813				1				7	8		5	2		3	10						9	11	4		6	
40	26	Bournemouth	1-0	Regan	5408				1				7			5	2	6	3	10						9	11	4		8	
41	30	Hull City	1-4	Regan	25039				1		8		7			5	2	6		10						9	11	4		3	
42	May 7	MANSFIELD TOWN	0-3		7970	7			1	8						5	2		3	10						9	11	4		6	
43	10	WATFORD	1-1	Thomson	5563	11			1	8			7			5	2		3	9							10	4		6	
44	17	BOURNEMOUTH	1-0	Docherty	5132				1				7			5	2	6	3							9	10	4		8	11
45	21	Peterborough United	0-3		3935	11			1	9			7			5	2	6	3								10	4		8	
46	28	GILLINGHAM	0-2		4457	11			1		4	7		8		5	2			9					6		10			3	
					Apps	29	2	12	35	27	10	14	26	16	9	34	36	29	44	37	9	2	0	11	2	12	17	38	5	43	7
					Subs					2	1							1					1							1	
					Goals	6		1		7		2	7	2	1	2		1		10	2					5				2	

F.A. Cup

	Date	Opponent	Res	Scorers	Att	Block MJ	Bloomfield JH	Bonson J	Brodie CTG	Cobb WW	Crisp RJ	Curley T	Docherty J	Etheridge BG	Fielding JA	Gelson PWJ	Hawley AJ	Higginson T	Jones AP	Lawther WI	Lazarus M	McKenzie JT	McLaughlin H	Phillips GD	Reeve EG	Regan MJ	Ross RH	Scott MD	Smith W	Thomson GM	Thornley BE
R1	Nov 13	YEOVIL TOWN	2-1	Fielding 2	9320	7		8		10					11	5	2	6	3	9				1				4			
R2	Dec 4	Reading	0-5		10582	11			1	10	4				7	5	2	6	3	9										8	

F.L. Cup

	Date	Opponent	Res	Scorers	Att	Block MJ	Bloomfield JH	Bonson J	Brodie CTG	Cobb WW	Crisp RJ	Curley T	Docherty J	Etheridge BG	Fielding JA	Gelson PWJ	Hawley AJ	Higginson T	Jones AP	Lawther WI	Lazarus M	McKenzie JT	McLaughlin H	Phillips GD	Reeve EG	Regan MJ	Ross RH	Scott MD	Smith W	Thomson GM	Thornley BE
R2	Sep 22	Workington	0-0		3374	7		8	1	10							2	4	3	9	11							5		6	
rep	30	WORKINGTON	1-2	Lawther	4720	7		8	1	10							2	4	3	9	11							5		6	

		Pl.	Home W	D	L	F	A	Away W	D	L	F	A	F. (Total)	A.	Pts
1	Hull City	46	19	2	2	64	24	12	5	6	45	38	109	62	69
2	Millwall	46	19	4	0	47	13	8	7	8	29	30	76	43	65
3	Queen's Park Rgs	46	16	3	4	62	29	8	6	9	33	36	95	65	57
4	Scunthorpe United	46	9	8	6	44	34	12	3	8	36	33	80	67	53
5	Workington	46	13	6	4	38	18	6	8	9	29	39	67	57	52
6	Gillingham	46	14	4	5	33	19	8	4	11	29	35	62	54	52
7	Swindon Town	46	11	8	4	43	18	8	5	10	31	30	74	48	51
8	Reading	46	13	5	5	36	19	6	8	9	34	44	70	63	51
9	Walsall	46	13	7	3	48	21	7	3	13	29	43	77	64	50
10	Shrewsbury Town	46	13	7	3	48	22	6	4	13	25	42	73	64	49
11	Grimsby Town	46	15	6	2	47	25	2	7	14	21	37	68	62	47
12	Watford	46	12	4	7	33	19	5	9	9	22	32	55	51	47
13	Peterborough Utd.	46	13	6	4	50	26	4	6	13	30	40	80	66	46
14	Oxford United	46	11	3	9	38	33	8	5	10	32	41	70	74	46
15	Brighton & Hove A.	46	13	4	6	48	28	3	7	13	19	37	67	65	43
16	Bristol Rovers	46	11	10	2	38	15	3	4	16	26	49	64	64	42
17	Swansea Town	46	14	4	5	61	37	1	7	15	20	59	81	96	41
18	Bournemouth	46	9	8	6	24	19	4	4	15	14	37	38	56	38
19	Mansfield Town	46	10	5	8	31	36	5	3	15	28	53	59	89	38
20	Oldham Athletic	46	8	7	8	34	33	4	6	13	21	48	55	81	37
21	Southend United	46	15	1	7	43	28	1	3	19	11	55	54	83	36
22	Exeter City	46	9	6	8	36	28	3	5	15	17	51	53	79	35
23	**BRENTFORD**	**46**	**9**	**4**	**10**	**34**	**30**	**1**	**8**	**14**	**14**	**39**	**48**	**69**	**32**
24	York City	46	5	7	11	30	44	4	2	17	23	62	53	106	27

1966/67

9th in Division Four

							Basey PJ	Bedford NB	Brodie CTG	Cobb WW	Crisp RJ	Curley T	Dobson GR	Docherty J	Etheridge BG	Gelson PWJ	Hawley AJ	Higginson T	Hooker KW	Jones AP	Lawther WI	MacKenzie JT	Ogburn MG	Phillips GD	Reeve EG	Regan MJ	Richardson JP	Ross RH	Scott MD	South JE	Thomson GM	Wilson R
1	Aug	20	Barnsley	1-0	Ross	2564			1	7	4			9		5	2				10	3				8		11	6			
2		27	LUTON TOWN	1-0	Cobb	6769			1	7	4			9		5	2	8			10	3						11	6			
3	Sep	3	Aldershot	1-3	Docherty	5583			1		4			9	7	5	2				10	3				8		11	6			
4		7	Lincoln City	1-3	Richardson	4505			1	7	4			9		5	2	8				3					10	11	6			
5		10	WREXHAM	1-1	Docherty	5517			1	8	4			7		5	2				9				6		10	11	3			
6		17	Southend United	0-3		8184					4			7		5	2	8			9	3		1	6		10	11				
7		24	TRANMERE ROVERS	1-1	Bedford	5625	11	8	1	9				7		5	2	4		3	12				6			10				
8		27	LINCOLN CITY	2-2	Grummett (og), Ross	6231	11	10	1					7		5	2	8		3					6		4	9				
9	Oct	1	Bradford City	0-2		4005		9		10		7				5	2	8		3				1	6		4	11				
10		8	Chesterfield	0-3		4968			1		4	7		9		5	2	8			10	3			12			11	6			
11		11	ALDERSHOT	1-0	Lawther	6116		10				7				5	3	4			9		2	1	6		8	11				
12		15	STOCKPORT COUNTY	2-1	Curley, Docherty	5714		10				7		8		5	3	4			9		2	1	6			11				
13		18	HALIFAX TOWN	1-0	Docherty (p)	6093		10				7		8		5	3	4			9		2	1	6			11				
14		22	Rochdale	3-1	Lawther 2, Ross	2632		10				7		11		5	3	4			9		2	1	6			8				
15		29	SOUTHPORT	2-1	Ross, Higginson	6764		10				7		11		5	3	4			9		2	1	6			8				
16	Nov	5	Notts County	2-3	Bedford 2	3883		10		3		7		11		5		4			9		2	1			6	8				
17		12	CHESTER	4-0	Docherty, Bedford, Lawther 2	6606		10				7		11		5		4		3	9		2	1				8	6			
18		15	Halifax Town	2-3	Jones, Curley	2671		10				7		11		5		4		3	9		2	1				8	6			
19		19	Bradford Park Avenue	2-2	Docherty, Curley	4182		10				7		11		5		4		3	9		2	1	6			8				
20	Dec	10	BARROW	0-3		5412						7		11		5		4		3	10		2	1			9	8	6			
21		17	BARNSLEY	3-1	Lawther, Docherty, Bradford	4255		10						11	7	5		4		3	9		2	1			8	6				
22		26	Hartlepools United	2-2	Scott, Docherty	8420		10						11		5		4		3	9		2	1				8	7		6	
23		27	HARTLEPOOLS UNITED	1-2	Docherty	5775		10						11		5		4		3	9	2		1				8	7		6	
24		31	Luton Town	0-3		8531						7		11	10	12		4		2	9			1			8	6	5		3	
25	Jan	14	Wrexham	0-0		11272								7		5	2	4	10	3	9			1	12		8	11			6	
26		21	SOUTHEND UNITED	1-1	Lawther	10646								7		5	2	4		3	10			1	12		8	11		9	6	
27	Feb	3	Tranmere Rovers	0-0		9836						11		7	9		2	4		3	8			1			5	10			6	
28		11	BRADFORD CITY	2-0	Docherty, Ross	7462						11		7		5	2	4		3	8			1			10	9			6	
29		18	YORK CITY	1-1	Lawther	7629						11		7		5	2	4		3	8			1			10	9			6	
30		25	CHESTERFIELD	1-0	Docherty	7013							11	7		5	2	4		3	8			1			10	9			6	
31	Mar	3	Stockport County	2-1	Bedford, Docherty	8288		9						11		5	2	4	8	3				1			10	7			6	
32		11	York City	0-0		1933		9						11		5	2	4	12	3	8			1			10	7			6	
33		18	ROCHDALE	4-0	Docherty, Ross 2, Lawther	6610						7		11		5	2	4			9	3		1			10	8			6	
34		25	Port Vale	3-1	Richardson, Lawther, Curley	3434						7		11		5	2	4	12		9	3		1			10	8			6	
35		27	NEWPORT COUNTY	1-1	Ross	9600						7		11		5	2	4	10	3	9			1				8			6	
36		28	Newport County	1-1	Lawther	2541						7			8	5	2	4	10		9	3		1				11			6	
37	Apr	1	NOTTS COUNTY	1-0	Hooker	6283						7		11	8	5	2	4	10			3		1				9			6	
38		8	Chester	2-1	Bedford, Higginson	2683		9				7		11		5	2	4				3		1	10			8			6	
39		11	EXETER CITY	3-1	Bedford 3	7794		9				7		11		5	2	4				3		1	10			8			6	
40		15	BRADFORD PARK AVE.	1-1	Ross	10021						7		11		5	2	4			9	3		1	10			8			6	
41		22	Southport	0-2		5314		8						7		5	2	4			9	3		1	10			11			6	
42		25	Exeter City	0-1		2934						7		11		5	2	4			9	3		1	10			8			6	
43		29	CREWE ALEXANDRA	0-2		5715		9				7		11		5	2	4			8	3		1				10			6	
44	May	6	Barrow	0-1		8769							7	11		5	2	4	10	3	9			1				8			6	
45		10	Crewe Alexandra	0-1		3403								11		5	2	4	10	3	9			1	7			8			6	
46		13	PORT VALE	2-0	James (og), Wilson	3592								7		5	2	4	10	3	9			1				11			6	8
						Apps	2	21	8	7	7	26	2	43	6	44	37	43	8	23	38	17	12	38	17	2	20	46	12	1	25	1
						Subs										1			2		1				3							
						Goals		10		1		4		13				2	1	1	11						2	9	1			1

Two own goals

F.A. Cup

							Basey PJ	Bedford NB	Brodie CTG	Cobb WW	Crisp RJ	Curley T	Dobson GR	Docherty J	Etheridge BG	Gelson PWJ	Hawley AJ	Higginson T	Hooker KW	Jones AP	Lawther WI	MacKenzie JT	Ogburn MG	Phillips GD	Reeve EG	Regan MJ	Richardson JP	Ross RH	Scott MD	South JE	Thomson GM	Wilson R
R1	Nov	26	CHELMSFORD CITY	1-0	Docherty (p)	8530		10				7		11		5		4		3	9		2	1	6			8				
R2	Jan	7	Orient	0-0		8094								7	9	5	2	4		3	8			1			10	11			6	
rep		10	ORIENT	3-1	Docherty 2, Richardson	10078								11		5	2	4		3	8			1			9	10		7	6	
R3		28	Sunderland	2-5	Docherty 2	36908								7	9	5	2	4		3	10			1			8	11			6	

F.L. Cup

							Basey PJ	Bedford NB	Brodie CTG	Cobb WW	Crisp RJ	Curley T	Dobson GR	Docherty J	Etheridge BG	Gelson PWJ	Hawley AJ	Higginson T	Hooker KW	Jones AP	Lawther WI	MacKenzie JT	Ogburn MG	Phillips GD	Reeve EG	Regan MJ	Richardson JP	Ross RH	Scott MD	South JE	Thomson GM	Wilson R
R1	Aug	24	MILLWALL	0-0		7350			1	7	4			9		5	2	8			10	3						11	6			
rep		29	Millwall	1-0	Docherty	5222			1	7	4			9		5	2	8			10	3						11	6			
R2	Sep	13	IPSWICH TOWN	2-4	Crisp, Ross	5860			1		8			7		5	2	4			9	3			6		10	11				

		Pl.	Home					Away					F.	A.	Pts
			W	D	L	F	A	W	D	L	F	A	(Total)		
1	Stockport County	46	16	5	2	41	18	10	7	6	28	24	69	42	64
2	Southport	46	19	2	2	47	15	4	11	8	22	27	69	42	59
3	Barrow	46	12	8	3	35	18	12	3	8	41	36	76	54	59
4	Tranmere Rovers	46	14	6	3	42	20	8	8	7	24	23	66	43	58
5	Crewe Alexandra	46	14	5	4	42	26	7	7	9	28	29	70	55	54
6	Southend United	46	15	5	3	44	12	7	4	12	26	37	70	49	53
7	Wrexham	46	11	12	0	46	20	5	8	10	30	42	76	62	52
8	Hartlepools United	46	15	3	5	44	29	7	4	12	22	35	66	64	51
9	**BRENTFORD**	**46**	**13**	**7**	**3**	**36**	**19**	**5**	**6**	**12**	**22**	**37**	**58**	**56**	**49**
10	Aldershot	46	14	4	5	48	19	4	8	11	24	38	72	57	48
11	Bradford City	46	13	4	6	48	31	6	6	11	26	31	74	62	48
12	Halifax Town	46	10	11	2	37	27	5	3	15	22	41	59	68	44
13	Port Vale	46	9	7	7	33	27	5	8	10	22	31	55	58	43
14	Exeter City	46	11	6	6	30	24	3	9	11	20	36	50	60	43
15	Chesterfield	46	13	6	4	33	16	4	2	17	27	47	60	63	42
16	Barnsley	46	8	7	8	30	28	5	8	10	30	36	60	64	41
17	Luton Town	46	15	5	3	47	23	1	4	18	12	50	59	73	41
18	Newport County	46	9	9	5	35	23	3	7	13	21	40	56	63	40
19	Chester	46	8	5	10	24	32	7	5	11	30	46	54	78	40
20	Notts County	46	10	7	6	31	25	3	4	16	22	47	53	72	37
21	Rochdale	46	10	4	9	30	27	3	7	13	23	48	53	75	37
22	York City	46	11	5	7	45	31	1	6	16	20	48	65	79	35
23	Bradford Park Ave.	46	7	6	10	30	34	4	7	12	22	45	52	79	35
24	Lincoln City	46	7	8	8	39	39	2	5	16	19	43	58	82	31

1966-67

Back: Gelson, McKenzie, Reeve, Hooker, McLaughlin, Smith, Curley, Crisp.
Middle: Lawther, Block, Ogburn, Phillips, Thornley, Brodie, Hawley, Gadston, Soutar.
Front: Regan, Docherty, Jones, Scott, Etheridge, Higginson, Thomson, Cobb.

1967/68

(Left-Right): Dobson, Ross, Fenton, Mansley, Lawther, Terry, Richardson, Gelson, Hawley, Jones, Higginson, Brodie, Phillips, Hooker, Hunt, Nelmes, Burke.

1967/68

14th in Division Four

							Brodie CTG	Dobson GR	Docherty J	Edwards D	Fenton R	Gelson PWJ	Hawley AJ	Higginson T	Hooker KW	Jones AP	Lawther WI	Mansley A	Myers CW	Nelmes AV	Phillips GD	Reeve EG	Richardson JP	Ross RH	Still RG	Thomson GM
1	Aug	19	Hartlepools United	0-2		5372			11			5	2	4	6	3	8		10		1			7	9	
2		26	NEWPORT COUNTY	3-1	Docherty, Lawther, Dobson	4511		7	11			5	2	4	10	3	9				1	12		8		6
3	Sep	2	York City	1-0	Docherty	4682		7	11			5	2	4	10	3	9				1			8		6
4		5	Swansea Town	1-2	Docherty (p)	6559		7	11			5	2	4	10	3	9				1			8		6
5		9	ROCHDALE	4-0	Ross, Docherty, Lawther, Melledew (og)	5646		7	11			5	2	4	10	3	9		12		1			8		6
6		16	HALIFAX TOWN	0-0		6892		7	11	9		5	2	4	12	3	10				1			8		6
7		23	Bradford Park Avenue	0-1		3403		7	11	10		5	2	4		3	9				1			8		6
8		26	SWANSEA TOWN	2-1	Lawther, Docherty	7596		7	11	8		5	2	4		3	9		10		1					6
9		30	DONCASTER ROVERS	4-2	Lawther, Edwards, Jones, Thomson	7308		7	11	8		5	2	4		3	9		10		1					6
10	Oct	2	Wrexham	2-1	Smith (og), Docherty	8670		7	11	8		5	2	4		3	9				1			10		6
11		7	Crewe Alexandra	0-2		6246		7	11	8		5	2	6		3	9				1			10		4
12		14	NOTTS COUNTY	2-1	Edwards, Lawther	7443		7	11	10		5	2	4	12	3	9				1			8		6
13		21	Port Vale	1-4	Higginson	5944		7	11				2	4	8	3	9			5	1	10				6
14		24	WREXHAM	0-0		7962		7	11				2	4	6		9		8	5	1			10		3
15		28	CHESTER	3-1	Hooker, Thomson, Hawley	6285		7	11				2	4	8	3	9		12	5	1			10		6
16	Nov	4	Chesterfield	1-2	Higginson	9644		7	11			5	2	10		3	9			4	1			8		6
17		11	EXETER CITY	5-1	Lawther 2, Ross, Wilkinson (og), Docherty	7218		7	11	9		5	2	6		3	8				1			10		4
18		14	YORK CITY	3-1	Lawther, Gelson, Dobson	7968		7	11	9		5	2	4		3	8				1			10		6
19		18	Darlington	3-2	Gelson, Docherty, Albeson (og)	4789		7	11			5	2	8	12	3	9			4	1			10		6
20		25	ALDERSHOT	1-1	Docherty	9481		7	11	10		5	2	8		3	9				1			4		6
21	Dec	2	Workington	0-2		1809			11	9		5	2	8		3	10			4	1			7		6
22		16	HARTLEPOOLS UNITED	0-1		6210			11			5	2	10		3			7	4	1		8	9		6
23		23	Newport County	2-2	Docherty 2	2426			11			5	2	8		3	9		10	4	1			7		6
24		26	SOUTHEND UNITED	1-2	Richardson	8363			11			5	2	10		3	9		7	4	1		12	8		6
25		30	Southend United	0-1		9181			11			5	2	8		3	9			4	1		10	7		6
26	Jan	6	BARNSLEY	0-1		5176			11			5	3	4	6		9			2	1		8	7		10
27		20	Halifax Town	0-3		4610			11			5	3	8	4	12	9			2	1		6	7		10
28		27	BRADFORD CITY	0-1		5594			7		8	5	3	12	4		9	11		2	1			10		6
29	Feb	3	BRADFORD PARK AVE.	2-1	Dobson, Fenton	4313		7			10	5	2		4	3	9	11		6	1			8		
30		10	Doncaster Rovers	0-2		7183		7			10	5	2		4	3	9	11		6	1			8		12
31		17	LUTON TOWN	0-2		7726		7			8	5	2		4	3		11			1		6	9		10
32		24	DARLINGTON	2-0	Lawther 2	4163	1	7			10	5	2	4		3	9	11					6	8		
33	Mar	2	Notts County	1-2	Nelmes	4486					10	5	2	4	8	3		11		9	1		6	7		
34		9	Bradford City	3-2	Fenton 2, Gelson (p)	7118		7			8	5	4	10		3	9	11		2	1		6	12		
35		16	PORT VALE	3-1	Fenton, Hawley, Mansley	5111		7			8	5	2	4		3	9	11		10	1		6			
36		18	Rochdale	1-1	Cockcroft (og)	1725		7			8	5	4	10		3	9	11		2	1		6	12		
37		23	Chester	0-3		2861		7			8	5	2	10		3	9	11		4	1		6			
38		30	CHESTERFIELD	1-1	Lawther	3844		7			8	5	4			3	9	11		2	1		6	10		
39	Apr	6	Exeter City	3-0	Higginson, Fenton 2	3900		7			10	5	4	9		3		11		2	1		6	8		
40		13	CREWE ALEXANDRA	2-1	Mansley 2	5389		7			8	5	4	10		3		11		2	1		6	9		
41		15	Barnsley	0-3		12405		7			8	5	4	10		3		11		2	1		6	9		
42		20	Aldershot	0-0		5183		7			8	5	2	4		3	10	11			1		6	9		
43		23	LINCOLN CITY	1-3	Gelson (p)	4903		7			8	5	2	4		3	10	11			1		6	9		
44		27	WORKINGTON	2-1	Mansley, Gelson	3749		7			8	5	2	4	12	3	10	11			1		6	9		
45	May	4	Lincoln City	0-1		8071		7			8	5	2	4	12	3	10	11			1		6	9		
46		11	Luton Town	1-2	Moore (og)	14643		7			8	5	2	4	12	3	10	11			1		6	9		
						Apps	1	36	28	11	19	43	46	41	15	42	40	19	7	24	45	1	20	39	1	28
						Subs								1	6	1			2			1	1	2		1
						Goals		3	11	2	6	5	2	3	1	1	11	4		1			1	2		2

Six own goals

F.A. Cup

							Brodie CTG	Dobson GR	Docherty J	Edwards D	Fenton R	Gelson PWJ	Hawley AJ	Higginson T	Hooker KW	Jones AP	Lawther WI	Mansley A	Myers CW	Nelmes AV	Phillips GD	Reeve EG	Richardson JP	Ross RH	Still RG	Thomson GM
R1	Dec	14	GUILDFORD CITY	2-2	Docherty, Myers	10050			11			5	2	10	8	3	9		12	4	1			7		6
rep		18	Guildford City	1-2	Myers	7200			11			5	2	10		3			7	4	1		9	8		6

R1 - December 9 abandoned 53 minutes (snow)

F.L. Cup

							Brodie CTG	Dobson GR	Docherty J	Edwards D	Fenton R	Gelson PWJ	Hawley AJ	Higginson T	Hooker KW	Jones AP	Lawther WI	Mansley A	Myers CW	Nelmes AV	Phillips GD	Reeve EG	Richardson JP	Ross RH	Still RG	Thomson GM
R1	Aug	23	Southend United	0-1		7905		7	11			5	2	4	6	3	9		10	12	1			8		

		Pl.	Home					Away					F.	A.	Pts
			W	D	L	F	A	W	D	L	F	A	(Total)		
1	Luton Town	46	19	3	1	55	16	8	9	6	32	28	87	44	66
2	Barnsley	46	17	6	0	43	14	7	7	9	25	32	68	46	61
3	Hartlepools United	46	15	7	1	34	12	10	3	10	26	34	60	46	60
4	Crewe Alexandra	46	13	10	0	44	18	7	8	8	30	31	74	49	58
5	Bradford City	46	14	5	4	41	22	9	6	8	31	29	72	51	57
6	Southend United	46	12	8	3	45	21	8	6	9	32	37	77	58	54
7	Chesterfield	46	15	4	4	47	20	6	7	10	24	30	71	50	53
8	Wrexham	46	17	3	3	47	12	3	10	10	25	41	72	53	53
9	Aldershot	46	10	11	2	36	19	8	6	9	34	36	70	55	53
10	Doncaster Rovers	46	12	8	3	36	16	6	7	10	30	40	66	56	51
11	Halifax Town	46	10	6	7	34	24	5	10	8	18	25	52	49	46
12	Newport County	46	11	7	5	32	22	5	6	12	26	41	58	63	45
13	Lincoln City	46	11	3	9	41	31	6	6	11	30	37	71	68	43
14	**BRENTFORD**	**46**	**13**	**4**	**6**	**41**	**24**	**5**	**3**	**15**	**20**	**40**	**61**	**64**	**43**
15	Swansea Town	46	11	8	4	38	25	5	2	16	25	52	63	77	42
16	Darlington	46	6	11	6	31	27	6	6	11	16	26	47	53	41
17	Notts County	46	10	7	6	27	27	5	4	14	26	52	53	79	41
18	Port Vale	46	10	5	8	41	31	2	10	11	20	41	61	72	39
19	Rochdale	46	9	8	6	35	32	3	6	14	16	40	51	72	38
20	Exeter City	46	9	7	7	30	30	2	9	12	15	35	45	65	38
21	York City	46	9	6	8	44	30	2	8	13	21	38	65	68	36
22	Chester	46	6	6	11	35	38	3	8	12	22	40	57	78	32
23	Workington	46	8	8	7	35	29	2	3	18	19	58	54	87	31
24	Bradford Park Ave.	46	3	7	13	18	35	1	8	14	12	47	30	82	23

1968/69

11th in Division Four

	Date	Opponent	Score	Scorers	Att.	Brodie CTG	Caterer B	Deakin P	Dobson GR	Fenton R	Foster RE	Gelson PWJ	Hawley AJ	Higginscn T	Hooker KW	Hunt DP	Jones AF	Kirby G	Mansley A	Neilson G	Nelmes AV	Phillips GD	Renwick R	Richardson JP	Ross RH	Terry PA	Willis RI
1	Aug 10	COLCHESTER UNITED	4-0	Deakin, Moughton (og), Terry, Ross	7586			8	7			5		4		3	2		11		6	1			10	9	
2	17	Scunthorpe United	1-1	Terry	3685			8	7	12		5		4		3			11		2	1		6	10	9	
3	24	PORT VALE	3-1	Mansley, Fenton 2	7443			8	7	12		5		4		3	2		11		6	1			10	9	
4	26	ROCHDALE	1-1	Deakin	9149			7		8		5		4		3	2		11		6	1			10	9	
5	31	Exeter City	2-2	Terry, Richardson	8835				12	10		5		8		3	2		11		6	1		4	7	9	
6	Sep 7	CHESTERFIELD	1-0	Fenton	9703			12	7	10		5		4			2		11		3	1		6	8	9	
7	14	Peterborough United	1-2	Dobson	6435			11	7	10		5		4			2				3	1		6	8	9	
8	18	Chester	2-2	Terry, Ross	8638				7	8		5		4		3	2				6	1		10	11	9	
9	21	YORK CITY	5-1	Terry 3, Ross, Carr (og)	8360	1			7	8		5	12	4		3	2				6			10	11	9	
10	28	Bradford City	0-3		6491			8		10			4	6			2		11		3			5	7	9	1
11	Oct 5	NEWPORT COUNTY	1-1	Mansley	7825	1		10		4				6			2		11	7	3			5	8	9	
12	7	Rochdale	0-0		5181	1	6			10				4	8		3		11	7	2			5		9	
13	12	Swansea Town	3-2	Neilson, Terry, Fenton	6912	1				8		5		4		3	2		11	7	6			10		9	
14	19	WREXHAM	1-1	Mansley	7791	1				8		5		4		3	2		11	7	10			6	9		
15	26	Notts County	2-0	Mansley 2	4173	1				10		5		4			3	9	11	7	2			6	8		
16	Nov 2	ALDERSHOT	2-4	Mansley, Higginson	9806					10		5		4			3	8	11	7	2	1		6	12	9	
17	4	DARLINGTON	0-1		8550							5		4			3	8	11	7	2	1		6	10	9	
18	9	Lincoln City	0-1		6121					10		5	8	6			3			7	4	1		2	11	9	
19	23	Bradford Park Avenue	2-0	Kirby, Fenton	2391	1				10			4	6			3	9	11	7	2			5	8		
20	30	HALIFAX TOWN	1-1	Mansley	6002	1				10		5	4				3	9	11	7	2			6	8		
21	Dec 14	SWANSEA TOWN	2-1	Hawley, Terry	4321	1			11	10		5	4				3			7	2			6	8	9	
22	21	Wrexham	0-2		4867	1			7	10		5	4				3		11	12	2			6	8	9	
23	26	Newport County	1-1	Gelson	3750	1			12			5	10	4			3		11	7	2			6	8	9	
24	Jan 4	WORKINGTON	0-3		6081	1				10		5	4	12			3		11	7	2			6	8	9	
25	11	Aldershot	2-1	Mansley 2	9280				7	10		5		4		2	3		11	12		1		6	8	9	
26	18	LINCOLN CITY	2-2	Ross, Terry	6572				7	8		5		4		2	3		11			1		6	10	9	
27	25	Darlington	1-3	Dobson	5184				7	10		5		4			3		11	9	2	1		6	8		
28	31	Southend United	0-4		11154					8		5				3	2		11	7	4	1		6	10	9	
29	Feb 22	GRIMSBY TOWN	4-2	Richardson, Neilson 2, Terry	5697	1				10		5					2		11	7	4		3	6	8	9	
30	28	Colchester United	1-2	Neilsen	7268	1				10		5					2		11	7	6		3	4	8	9	
31	Mar 5	Workington	0-1		2318	1			12	10		5		4			2		11	7	8		3	6	9		
32	8	SCUNTHORPE UNITED	2-1	Neilson, Nelmes	5456	1				10		5		9			2		11	7	4		3	6	8		
33	10	SOUTHEND UNITED	1-1	Terry	6030	1			12			5		4			2		11	7	6		3	8	10	9	
34	15	Port Vale	1-4	Ross (p)	4478	1			12			5		10			2		11	7	4		3	6	8	9	
35	22	EXETER CITY	0-1		5242				7	10		5					2		11		4	1	3	6	8	9	
36	26	NOTTS COUNTY	0-0		3361				7	8	10	5					2		11		6	1	3	4	9		
37	29	Chesterfield	2-1	Mansley, Neilson	3261				12	8	10	5		4			3		11	7	2	1		6	9		
38	Apr 8	Doncaster Rovers	0-5		11561					8	10	5		6			2		11	7	4	1	3	12	9		
39	12	York City	1-2	Mansley	3767	1			7	8		5		6			2		11	12	4		3	9	10		
40	14	DONCASTER ROVERS	1-0	Richardson	4222	1			7	10		5		6			2		11		4		3	8	9		
41	19	PETERBOROUGH UTD.	2-0	Fenton, Mansley	4492				7	10		5		9			2		11		4	1	3	8	8		
42	21	BRADFORD PARK AVE.	3-0	Fenton 2, Ross (p)	4137				7	10		5	12	6			2		11		4	1	3	8	9		
43	28	Halifax Town	0-2		6488				7	10		5		6			2		11	12	4	1	3	8	9		
44	30	CHESTER	2-1	Mansley, Fenton	4090				7	10		5		6			2		11		4	1	3		8	9	
45	May 3	Grimsby Town	2-0	Gelson, Dobson	1833	1			7	10	12	5		4			2		11		6		3	9	8		
46	5	BRADFORD CITY	2-1	Richardson, Mansley	5724	1			7	10		5		6			2		11		4		3	8	9		
					Apps	22	1	7	22	39	3	42	8	37	1	12	45	5	41	23	44	23	17	41	43	29	1
					Subs			1	6	2	1		2	1						4				1	1		
					Goals			2	3	9		2	1	1				1	14	6	1			4	6	12	

Two own goals

F.A. Cup

	Date	Opponent	Score	Scorers	Att.	Brodie CTG	Caterer B	Deakin P	Dobson GR	Fenton R	Foster RE	Gelson PWJ	Hawley AJ	Higginscn T	Hooker KW	Hunt DP	Jones AF	Kirby G	Mansley A	Neilson G	Nelmes AV	Phillips GD	Renwick R	Richardson JP	Ross RH	Terry PA	Willis RI
R1	Nov 16	WOKING	2-0	Fenton, Ross	5990	1				10		5	4				3	9	11	7	2			6	8		
R2	Dec 7	Watford	0-1		12883	1				10		5	8	4			3	12	11	7	2			6	9		

F.L. Cup

	Date	Opponent	Score	Scorers	Att.	Brodie CTG	Caterer B	Deakin P	Dobson GR	Fenton R	Foster RE	Gelson PWJ	Hawley AJ	Higginscn T	Hooker KW	Hunt DP	Jones AF	Kirby G	Mansley A	Neilson G	Nelmes AV	Phillips GD	Renwick R	Richardson JP	Ross RH	Terry PA	Willis RI
R1	Aug 14	Aldershot	4-2	Rafferty (og), Deakin, Mansley, Terry	5977			8	7			5		4		3	2		11		6	1			10	9	
R2	Sep 4	HULL CITY	3-0	Mansley 2, Fenton	11485			8	7	10		5		4			2		11		3	1		6	9		
R3	24	NORWICH CITY	0-2		17425	1			7	10		5		4		3	2		11		12			6	8	9	

		Pl.	Home W	Home D	Home L	Home F	Home A	Away W	Away D	Away L	Away F	Away A	F. (Total)	A. (Total)	Pts
1	Doncaster Rovers	46	13	8	2	42	16	8	9	6	23	22	65	38	59
2	Halifax Town	46	15	5	3	36	18	5	12	6	17	19	53	37	57
3	Rochdale	46	14	7	2	47	11	4	13	6	21	24	68	35	56
4	Bradford City	46	11	10	2	36	18	7	10	6	29	28	65	46	56
5	Darlington	46	11	6	6	40	26	6	12	5	22	19	62	45	52
6	Colchester United	46	12	8	3	31	17	8	4	11	26	36	57	53	52
7	Southend United	46	15	3	5	51	21	4	10	9	27	40	78	61	51
8	Lincoln City	46	13	6	4	38	19	4	11	8	16	33	54	52	51
9	Wrexham	46	13	7	3	41	22	5	7	11	20	30	61	52	50
10	Swansea Town	46	11	8	4	35	20	8	3	12	23	34	58	54	49
11	**BRENTFORD**	**46**	**12**	**7**	**4**	**40**	**24**	**6**	**5**	**12**	**24**	**41**	**64**	**65**	**48**
12	Workington	46	8	11	4	24	17	7	6	10	16	26	40	43	47
13	Port Vale	46	12	8	3	33	15	4	6	13	13	31	46	46	46
14	Chester	46	12	4	7	43	24	4	9	10	33	42	76	66	45
15	Aldershot	46	13	3	7	42	23	6	4	13	24	43	66	66	45
16	Scunthorpe United	46	10	5	8	28	22	8	3	12	33	38	61	60	44
17	Exeter City	46	11	8	4	45	24	5	3	15	21	41	66	65	43
18	Peterborough Utd.	46	8	9	6	32	23	5	7	11	28	34	60	57	42
19	Notts County	46	10	8	5	33	22	2	10	11	15	35	48	57	42
20	Chesterfield	46	7	7	9	24	22	6	8	9	19	28	43	50	41
21	York City	46	12	8	3	36	25	2	3	18	17	50	53	75	39
22	Newport County	46	9	9	5	31	26	2	5	16	18	48	49	74	36
23	Grimsby Town	46	5	7	11	25	31	4	8	11	22	38	47	69	33
24	Bradford Park Ave.	46	5	8	10	19	34	0	2	21	13	72	32	106	20

1968-69
Back: Jones, Richardson, Gelson, Nelmes, Phillips, Hawley, Ross
Front: Dobson, Neilson, Higginson, Fenton, Mansley.

1969-70
Back:Jones, Higginson, Richardson, Brodie,Ross, Phillips, Renwick, Gelson, Hawley
Front: Dobson, Brown, Neilson, Fenton, Mansley, Frude, Nelmes.

1969/70

5th in Division Four

			Opponent	Score	Scorers	Att.	Baker GA	Brodie CTG	Brown WFT	Cocks AW	Cook MJ	Cross RG	Dobson GR	Docherty J	Fenton R	Frude RG	Gelson PWJ	Harney D	Hawley AJ	Higginson T	Jones AP	Mansley A	Neilson G	Nelmes AV	Renwick R	Richardson JP	Ross RH	Tawse B	Turner BA
1	Aug	9	Hartlepool	0-0		3020		1			8		12			9	5		2	6			7	4	3	10	11		
2		16	NOTTS COUNTY	1-0	Ross	6364		1			8				12		5		2	6		11	7	4	3	9	10		
3		23	Crewe Alexandra	2-1	Renwick, Cook	3051		1			9		7			12	5		2	6		11	8	4	3		10		
4		27	Chester	2-1	Dobson, Ross	4426		1			9		7				5		2	6		11	8	4	3		10		
5		30	DARLINGTON	1-1	Dobson	7442		1			9		7				5		2	6		11	8	4	3		10		
6	Sep	6	Newport County	0-1		3193		1			9				8		5		2	6		11	7	4	3		10		
7		13	SWANSEA TOWN	2-2	Mansley, Ross (p)	7139		1	9		12		7		8		5		2	6		11		4	3		10		
8		15	SOUTHEND UNITED	3-1	Mansley, Neilson, Fenton	7446		1	9						8		5		2	6		11	7	4	3		10		
9		20	Bradford Park Avenue	1-0	Ross	2887		1	9						8		5		2	6		11	7	4	3		10		
10		27	WREXHAM	0-0		8610		1	9		12				8		5		2	6		11	7	4	3		10		
11		29	LINCOLN CITY	2-1	Gelson, Cook	8210		1			9				8		5		2	6		11	7	4	3		10		
12	Oct	4	Workington	2-1	Mansley, Ross	1882		1			9		12		8		5		2	6		11	7	4	3		10		
13		8	Notts County	0-1		4664		1			9		7		8		5	12	2	6		11		4	3		10		
14		11	SCUNTHORPE UNITED	3-0	Cook, Mansley 2	7493		1			9				8		5		2	6		11	7	4	3		10		
15		18	OLDHAM ATHLETIC	1-1	Cook	8674		1			9		12		8		5		2	6		11	7	4	3		10		
16		25	Chesterfield	0-1		11212	9	1							8		5		2	6		11	7	4	3		10		
17	Nov	1	PETERBOROUGH UTD.	5-2	Baker, Wile (og), Ross, Higginson, Fenton	8650	9	1			12				8		5		2	6		11	7	4	3		10		
18		8	Exeter City	2-2	Renwick 2	4897	9	1							8		5		2	6		11	7	4	3		10		
19		22	Northampton Town	1-1	Dobson	5315	9	1					7		8		5		2	6	3	11		4			10		
20		24	GRIMSBY TOWN	3-0	Baker, Ross, Mansley	7647	9	1					7		8		5		2	6		11		4	3		10		
21	Dec	13	Swansea Town	0-1		7423		1			9		7		10		5		2	6		11		4	3		8		
22		20	NEWPORT COUNTY	1-0	Ross	4383		1					9		8		5		2	6	12	11	7	4	3		10		
23		26	CREWE ALEXANDRA	1-1	Ross	9307		1					8		9		5		2	6	12	11	7	4	3		10		
24		27	Darlington	2-1	Fenton, Ross	2507	9	1					12		8		5		2	6	3	11	7	4			10		
25	Jan	3	Lincoln City	0-1		4991	9	1							8		5		2	6	3	11	7	4			10		
26		10	BRADFORD PARK AVE.	1-1	Fenton	5847	11	1			9		12		10		5		2		3		7	6			8		4
27		17	Wrexham	0-1		8451		1			9				10		5		2	12	3	11	7	6			8		4
28		24	PORT VALE	1-0	Boulton (og)	8661		1			10		7		8		5		2	9				6	3		11		4
29		31	WORKINGTON	1-0	Dobson	7756		1		8	9		7		12		5		2	10				6	3		11		4
30	Feb	10	Scunthorpe United	1-1	Gelson	5316		1		9			11		8		5		2	10			7	6	3		4		
31		21	CHESTERFIELD	0-1		10540		1		9			11		8		5		2	10			7	6	3		4		
32		23	HARTLEPOOL	3-0	Gelson, Turner, Hawley	7352		1		9			11		8		5		2	10			7	6	3		4		12
33		28	Peterborough United	0-0		7512		1		9					8				2	10			7	6	3		4	11	5
34	Mar	7	NORTHAMPTON T	1-0	Cocks	7292		1		9					8				2	10	12		7	6	3		4	11	5
35		9	YORK CITY	0-0		8124		1		9	12								4	10	2	8	7		3		6	11	5
36		14	Colchester United	1-1	Ross	4878		1				10		11			5		2	6				4	3		8	7	9
37		16	Port Vale	0-0		7947		1		8		9		11			5		2	10				6	3		4	7	
38		21	ALDERSHOT	0-0		12261		1				9		11	8		5		2	10				6	3		4	7	12
39		27	EXETER CITY	2-0	Cross, Ross (p)	10111		1		9		10		11			5		2		3			6			8	7	4
40		28	York City	2-4	Docherty, Neilson	2833		1		8		9		11			5		2	10	3		12	6			4	7	
41		31	Oldham Athletic	1-4	Cross	5078		1		8		9		11			5		2	10				6	3		4	7	
42	Apr	4	CHESTER	2-0	Gelson, Docherty	4748		1				9		8			5		2				7	6	3		10	11	4
43		7	Grimsby Town	1-2	Cross	3973		1				9		8			5		2				7	6	3		10	11	4
44		13	Southend United	2-2	Neilson, Ross	6805		1				9		8			5		2				7	6	3		10	11	4
45		18	COLCHESTER UNITED	2-0	Renwick, Docherty	4720		1				9		8			5		2	10	12		7	6	3		11		4
46		24	Aldershot	2-1	Cross 2	7497		1				9		8			5		2				7	6	3		10	11	4
						Apps	8	46	4	11	16	11	15	11	29	1	43	0	46	39	8	26	33	45	39	2	46	13	14
						Subs					4		5		2	1		1		1	4		1						2
						Goals	2			1	4	5	4	3	4		4		1	1		6	3		4		13		1

Two own goals

F.A. Cup

			Opponent	Score	Scorers	Att.	Baker GA	Brodie CTG	Brown WFT	Cocks AW	Cook MJ	Cross RG	Dobson GR	Docherty J	Fenton R	Frude RG	Gelson PWJ	Harney D	Hawley AJ	Higginson T	Jones AP	Mansley A	Neilson G	Nelmes AV	Renwick R	Richardson JP	Ross RH	Tawse B	Turner BA
R1	Nov	15	PLYMOUTH ARGYLE	0-0		9963		1			9				8		5		2	6		11	7	4	3		10		
rep		19	Plymouth Argyle	0-2		11554		1			9		12		8		5			6	2	11	7	4	3		10		

F.L. Cup

			Opponent	Score	Scorers	Att.	Baker GA	Brodie CTG	Brown WFT	Cocks AW	Cook MJ	Cross RG	Dobson GR	Docherty J	Fenton R	Frude RG	Gelson PWJ	Harney D	Hawley AJ	Higginson T	Jones AP	Mansley A	Neilson G	Nelmes AV	Renwick R	Richardson JP	Ross RH	Tawse B	Turner BA
R1	Aug	12	Southend United	2-2	Mansley 2	9256		1			8						5		2	6		11	7	4	3	9	10		
rep		18	SOUTHEND UNITED	0-0		7941		1			8					12	5		2	6		11	7	4	3	9	10		
rep2		21	SOUTHEND UNITED	2-3	Mansley, Gelson	2068		1			8		12			9	5		2	6		11	7	4	3		10		

Replay and replay 2 a.e.t. (replay 2 at Millwall)

		Pl.	Home W	Home D	Home L	Home F	Home A	Away W	Away D	Away L	Away F	Away A	F. (Total)	A. (Total)	Pts
1	Chesterfield	46	19	1	3	55	12	8	9	6	22	20	77	32	64
2	Wrexham	46	17	6	0	56	16	9	3	11	28	33	84	49	61
3	Swansea Town	46	14	8	1	43	14	7	10	6	23	31	66	45	60
4	Port Vale	46	13	9	1	39	10	7	10	6	22	23	61	33	59
5	**BRENTFORD**	**46**	**14**	**8**	**1**	**36**	**11**	**6**	**8**	**9**	**22**	**28**	**58**	**39**	**56**
6	Aldershot	46	16	5	2	52	22	4	8	11	26	43	78	65	53
7	Notts County	46	14	4	5	44	21	8	4	11	29	41	73	62	52
8	Lincoln City	46	11	8	4	38	20	6	8	9	28	32	66	52	50
9	Peterborough Utd.	46	13	8	2	51	21	4	6	13	26	48	77	69	48
10	Colchester United	46	14	5	4	38	22	3	9	11	26	41	64	63	48
11	Chester	46	14	3	6	39	23	7	3	13	19	43	58	66	48
12	Scunthorpe United	46	11	6	6	34	23	7	4	12	33	42	67	65	46
13	York City	46	14	7	2	38	16	2	7	14	17	46	55	62	46
14	Northampton Town	46	11	7	5	41	19	5	5	13	23	36	64	55	44
15	Crewe Alexandra	46	12	6	5	37	18	4	6	13	14	33	51	51	44
16	Grimsby Town	46	9	9	5	33	24	5	6	12	21	34	54	58	43
17	Southend United	46	12	8	3	40	28	3	2	18	19	57	59	85	40
18	Exeter City	46	13	5	5	48	20	1	6	16	9	39	57	59	39
19	Oldham Athletic	46	11	4	8	45	28	2	9	12	15	37	60	65	39
20	Workington	46	9	9	5	31	21	3	5	15	15	43	46	64	38
21	Newport County	46	12	3	8	39	24	1	8	14	14	50	53	74	37
22	Darlington	46	8	7	8	31	27	5	3	15	22	46	53	73	36
23	Hartlepool	46	7	7	9	31	30	3	3	17	11	52	42	82	30
24	Bradford Park Ave.	46	6	5	12	23	32	0	6	17	18	64	41	96	23

1970/71

14th in Division Four

							Bence PJ	Brodie CTG	Cross RG	Dawson AD	Docherty J	Gelson PWJ	Graham JJ	Hawley AJ	Heath MF	Mansley A	Maskell MR	Neilson G	Nelmes AV	O'Mara J	Phillips GD	Renwick R	Ross RH	Tawse B	Turner BA
1	Aug	15	CHESTER	1-2	Docherty	6477		1	9		8	5	10	2		11		7	6				4		3
2		22	Lincoln City	0-2		6813	6	1	9		8	5	10	2				7	3				4	11	12
3		29	SOUTHPORT	0-1		5324	3	1	9		7	5	10	2		11			6				8	12	4
4		31	Cambridge United	0-1		6654	3	1	9		8	5	10			11			6				4	7	2
5	Sep	5	Oldham Athletic	1-5	Tawse	4866	5	1	9		8		10			11	3	12	6				4	7	2
6		12	PETERBOROUGH UTD.	1-1	Ross	4176	10	1	9		12	5		2		11			6			3	8	7	4
7		19	Notts County	0-0		10281	10	1	9		7	5		2		11			6			3	8		4
8		23	Crewe Alexandra	3-5	Cross, Gater (og), Turner	1909	4	1	9		10	5				11			6			3	8	7	2
9		26	DARLINGTON	1-0	Docherty	4841	2	1	9		7	5	10						6			3	8	11	4
10		28	Stockport County	0-1		4387	2	1	10	9	7	5	11						6			3	8		4
11	Oct	3	Northampton Town	0-1		6282	2	1	10	9	7	5	11						6			3	8		4
12		10	BOURNEMOUTH	1-2	Graham	5965	2		10	9	7	5	11						6		1	3	8	12	4
13		17	Chester	2-1	Dawson, Cross	5834	2		10	9	7	5	11						6		1	3	8		4
14		19	ALDERSHOT	2-3	Dawson, Ross	7648	2		10	9	7	5	11						6		1	3	8		4
15		24	Southend United	3-4	Docherty, Dawson, Ross	6052	2		10	9	7	5	11						6		1	3	8		4
16		31	EXETER CITY	5-0	Docherty 2, Cross, Graham, Ross	5267	2		10	9	7	5	11						6		1	3	8		4
17	Nov	7	Newport County	1-0	Dawson	2407	2		10	9	7	5	11						6		1	3	8		4
18		9	YORK CITY	6-4	Docherty 3, Cross 2, Dawson	5955	2		10	9	7	5	11						6		1	3	8		4
19		14	GRIMSBY TOWN	2-0	Dawson, Ross (p)	5497	2		10	9	7	5						11	6		1	3	8		4
20		28	Colchester United	0-4		4673		1	9		7	5	10	2				11	6			3	8		4
21	Dec	5	BARROW	2-1	Cross, Ross	5632	2		9		7	5	10					11	6		1	3	8		4
22		19	LINCOLN CITY	2-1	Graham, Bence	5966	11		9		7	5	10	2					6		1	3	8		4
23		26	Scunthorpe United	1-1	Cross	4960	11		9		7	5	10	2					6		1	3	8		4
24	Jan	9	STOCKPORT COUNTY	3-0	Docherty, Ross, Cross	7340	11		9		7	5	10	2					6		1	3	8		4
25		16	Aldershot	0-1		7533	3		9		7	5	10	2		12		11	6		1		8		4
26	Feb	6	Barrow	1-0	Bence	2338	11		9		7	5	10	2					6		1	3	8		4
27		20	York City	0-0		3366	11	1	9		7	5	10	2					6			3	8		4
28		24	HARTLEPOOL	1-0	Graham	9246	11	1	9		7	5	10	2					6			3	8		4
29		27	Exeter City	0-1		3892	11		9		7	5	10	2					6		1	3	8		4
30	Mar	6	SOUTHEND UNITED	4-2	Cross 2, Ross 2 (2p)	6348	11	1	9		7	5	10	2				12	6			3	8		4
31		8	CREWE ALEXANDRA	3-1	Bence, Neilson, Ross	7631	4		9		7	5	10	2				11	6		1	3	8		
32		13	Grimsby Town	5-1	Ross 2, Cross 2, Bence	3336	11	1	9		7	5	10	2		12			6			3	8		4
33		15	Hartlepool	0-0		2936	11		9		7	5	10	2					6		1	3	8		4
34		20	NEWPORT COUNTY	0-3		8421	11	1	9		7	5	10	2				12	6			3	8		4
35		24	Workington	1-1	Docherty	1731	4		9		7	5	10	2				11	6		1	3	8		
36		27	OLDHAM ATHLETIC	1-1	Renwick	7207	4		9		7	5	10	2				11	6		1	3	8		12
37		29	COLCHESTER UNITED	1-0	Neilson	9209	11		9			5	10	2				7	6		1	3	8		4
38	Apr	3	Southport	0-2		2026	11		9			5	10	2					6	8	1	3	7		4
39		9	NORTHAMPTON T	3-0	Ross 2, Turner	10058	2		10			5	11					7	6	9	1	3	8		4
40		10	SCUNTHORPE UNITED	0-1		7561	2		9			5	11						4	10	1	3	8	7	6
41		12	Peterborough United	2-1	Neilson, Ross	3841	2		10			5	11					7	6	9	1	3	8		4
42		17	Bournemouth	0-1		11206	2		10			5	11					7	6	9	1	3	8		4
43		24	NOTTS COUNTY	2-2	Cross, Graham	9299	2		10			5	11					7	6	9	1	3	8		4
44		26	CAMBRIDGE UNITED	1-2	O'Mara	5994	7		10			5	11	2					6	9	1	3	8		4
45	May	1	Darlington	1-2	Cross	1629	4		10			5	11	2				7	6	9	1	3	8		
46		7	WORKINGTON	3-0	Neilson, Graham, O'Mara	4781	2		10			5	11	12	8			7	6	9	1	3	4		
						Apps	44	17	46	10	35	45	42	25	1	7	1	16	46	9	29	40	46	7	40
						Subs					1			1		2		3						2	2
						Goals	4		14	6	10		6					4		2		1	15	1	2

One own goal

F.A. Cup

							Bence PJ	Brodie CTG	Cross RG	Dawson AD	Docherty J	Gelson PWJ	Graham JJ	Hawley AJ	Heath MF	Mansley A	Maskell MR	Neilson G	Nelmes AV	O'Mara J	Phillips GD	Renwick R	Ross RH	Tawse B	Turner BA
R1	Nov	21	GILLINGHAM	2-1	Docherty, Dawson	8000	2	1	10	9	7	5	11					12	6			3	8		4
R2	Dec	12	WALSALL	1-0	Cross	8500	2		9		7	5	10					11	6		1	3	8		4
R3	Jan	2	Workington	1-0	Docherty	5953	10		11		7	5	4	2					6		1	3	9		8
R4		23	Cardiff City	2-0	Graham, Docherty	23335	4		9		7	5	10	2				11	6		1	3	8		
R5	Feb	13	Hull City	1-2	Ross	29709	11		9		7	5	10	2					6		1	3	8		4

F.L. Cup

							Bence PJ	Brodie CTG	Cross RG	Dawson AD	Docherty J	Gelson PWJ	Graham JJ	Hawley AJ	Heath MF	Mansley A	Maskell MR	Neilson G	Nelmes AV	O'Mara J	Phillips GD	Renwick R	Ross RH	Tawse B	Turner BA
R1	Aug	18	Aldershot	0-1		6899	6	1	9		8	5	10	2				7	3				4	11	12

		Pl.	Home					Away					F.	A.	Pts
			W	D	L	F	A	W	D	L	F	A	(Total)		
1	Notts County	46	19	4	0	59	12	11	5	7	30	24	89	36	69
2	Bournemouth	46	16	5	2	51	15	8	7	8	30	31	81	46	60
3	Oldham Athletic	46	14	6	3	57	29	10	5	8	31	34	88	63	59
4	York City	46	16	6	1	45	14	7	4	12	33	40	78	54	56
5	Chester	46	17	2	4	42	18	7	5	11	27	37	69	55	55
6	Colchester United	46	14	6	3	44	19	7	6	10	26	35	70	54	54
7	Northampton Town	46	15	4	4	39	24	4	9	10	24	35	63	59	51
8	Southport	46	15	2	6	42	24	6	4	13	21	33	63	57	48
9	Exeter City	46	12	7	4	40	23	5	7	11	27	45	67	68	48
10	Workington	46	13	7	3	28	13	5	5	13	20	36	48	49	48
11	Stockport County	46	12	8	3	28	17	4	6	13	21	48	49	65	46
12	Darlington	46	15	3	5	42	22	2	8	13	16	35	58	57	45
13	Aldershot	46	8	10	5	32	23	6	7	10	34	48	66	71	45
14	**BRENTFORD**	**46**	**13**	**3**	**7**	**45**	**27**	**5**	**5**	**13**	**21**	**35**	**66**	**62**	**44**
15	Crewe Alexandra	46	13	1	9	49	35	5	7	11	26	41	75	76	44
16	Peterborough Utd.	46	14	3	6	46	23	4	4	15	24	48	70	71	43
17	Scunthorpe United	46	9	7	7	36	23	6	6	11	20	38	56	61	43
18	Southend United	46	8	11	4	32	24	6	4	13	21	42	53	66	43
19	Grimsby Town	46	13	4	6	37	26	5	3	15	20	45	57	71	43
20	Cambridge United	46	9	9	5	31	27	6	4	13	20	39	51	66	43
21	Lincoln City	46	11	4	8	45	33	2	9	12	25	38	70	71	39
22	Newport County	46	8	3	12	32	36	2	5	16	23	49	55	85	28
23	Hartlepool	46	6	10	7	28	27	2	2	19	6	47	34	74	28
24	Barrow	46	5	5	13	25	38	2	3	18	26	52	51	90	22

1970-71
Back: Lyons (Trainer), Turner, Renwick, Brodie, Gelson, Nelmes, Cross, Phillips, Bence Hawley, Blunstone (Manager)
Front: Tawse, Docherty, Ross, Neilson, Graham, Mansley.

1971-72
Back: Bence, Gelson, Turner, Nelmes, Phillips, O'Mara, Allen, Hawley
Front: Neilson, Docherty, Tom, Ross, Scales, Graham.

1971/72

3rd in Division Four: Promoted

No.	Month	Day	Opponents	Result	Scorers	Att.	Allen M	Bence PI	Cross RG	Dawkins TA	Docherty J	Gelson PWJ	Graham JJ	Hawley AJ	Houston SM	Neilson G	Nelmes AV	O'Mara J	Phillips GD	Ross RH	Scales TA	Tom SE	Turner BA	Wallace KR
1	Aug	14	Bury	2-0	Gelson, Tom	2957		2	10			4	8				3	9	1	11	5	7	6	
2		21	ALDERSHOT	1-1	Turner	8920		2	10		11	4	8				3	9	1	7	5		6	
3		28	Darlington	0-0		2514		2	10		11	4	8				3	9	1	6	5	7		
4		30	BARROW	4-0	O'Mara, Cross, Tuner, Ross	8866		2	10		11	4	8				3	9	1	7	5		6	
5	Sep	4	HARTLEPOOL	6-0	Turner 2, O'Mara 3, Cross	8712		2	10		11	4	8				3	9	1	7	5		6	
6		11	Grimsby Town	1-3	O'Mara	11683		2			11	4	8				3	9	1	10	5	7	6	
7		18	PETERBOROUGH UTD.	5-1	Neilson, Graham, Docherty, O'Mara, Ross	8770		2			11	4	8			7	3	9	1	10	5		6	
8		25	Chester	0-0		4088		2			11	4	8			7	3	9	1	10	5		6	
9		27	STOCKPORT COUNTY	2-0	Ross 2	10445		2		7	11	4	8				3	9	1	10	5		6	
10	Oct	2	NORTHAMPTON T	6-1	O'Mara 3, Gelson, Docherty, Neilson	11004		2			7	4	10			11	3	9	1	8	5	12	6	
11		8	Southport	0-0		5371		7		12	11		8	2			3	9	1	10	5	4	6	
12		16	BURY	2-0	O'Mara, Graham	9851		2		8	7		11	5			3	9	1	10		4	6	
13		20	Reading	1-2	O'Mara	10473		2		7	11		8	5		12	3	9	1	10		4	6	
14		23	SOUTHEND UNITED	1-2	O'Mara	14001		8			7	4	10	2			3	9	1	11	5		6	
15		30	Scunthorpe United	0-0		6121	6	2			11		7				3	9	1	10	5	4	8	
16	Nov	6	NEWPORT COUNTY	3-1	Docherty, Ross 2 (1p)	10484	4	2			11		10				3	9	1	7	5	6	8	
17		13	Colchester United	1-1	O'Mara	6898	7	2			11		8				3	9	1	10	5	4	6	
18		27	GILLINGHAM	1-3	Ross	10945	7	2			11		8			12	3	9	1	10	5	4	6	
19	Dec	4	Exeter City	1-0	O'Mara	3809	7	2			11	6	8				3	9	1	10	5		4	
20		11	SOUTHPORT	1-0	Peat (og)	9624	4	2			11	5	10			7	3	9	1	8		12	6	
21		18	Hartlepool	2-1	Allen 2	2199	7	2			9	4	8			11	3		1	10	5		6	
22		27	CREWE ALEXANDRA	1-0	O'Mara	18237	7	2			11	4	8			12	3	9	1	10	5		6	
23	Jan	1	Peterborough United	2-2	O'Mara 2	7027	7	2			11	5	8				3	9	1	10	4		6	
24		8	DARLINGTON	6-2	Ross (p), O'Mara 2, Docherty 3	10582	7	2			11	4	8				3	9	1	10	5		6	
25		15	Lincoln City	1-4	O'Mara	7552	7	2			11	4	8				3	9	1	10	5		6	
26		21	Stockport County	1-0	Ross	3247	7	2			11	4	8				3	9	1	10	5		6	
27		29	READING	1-2	Docherty	12144	7	2			11	4	8				3	9	1	10	5		6	
28	Feb	5	Cambridge United	1-1	Graham	6861	7	2			11	4	8				3		1	10	5		6	9
29		12	Southend United	1-3	Ross (p)	9841	7	2			11	4	8				3		1	10	5		6	9
30		19	SCUNTHORPE UNITED	0-3		11912	8	6			10	4		2		11	3		1	12	5	7		9
31		26	Newport County	0-0		3271	7				10	4	8	2		11	3		1	9	5		6	
32	Mar	4	COLCHESTER UNITED	0-2		9210	7	2			11	12	8		5	9	3		1	10	4		6	
33		13	LINCOLN CITY	2-0	O'Mara, Scales	12065					11	4	8	2	10	12	3	9	1	7	5		6	
34		18	Aldershot	2-1	O'Mara, Ross	6989	12				11	4	8	2	10		3	9	1	7	5		6	
35		21	Doncaster Rovers	3-0	Graham 2, Ross	5256	7					4	8	2	10		3	9	1	11	5	12	6	
36		25	GRIMSBY TOWN	2-0	Docherty, O'Mara	14635	7				11	4	8	2	10		3	9	1	6	5		12	
37		27	WORKINGTON	2-0	Docherty, Houston	13972	7				11	4	8	2	10		3	9	1	6	5			
38		31	CHESTER	1-1	Docherty	18521	7				11	4	8	2	10		3	9	1		5		6	
39	Apr	1	Crewe Alexandra	1-2	Docherty	2072		7			11	4	8	2	10		3	9	1	6	5	12		
40		3	Northampton Town	0-0		5314	7				11	4	8	2	10		3	9	1	6	5			
41		8	CAMBRIDGE UNITED	2-1	Docherty, Graham	9061	7	12			11		8	2	10		3	9	1	6	5	4		
42		15	Gillingham	1-0	Docherty	5819	7				11		8	2	10		3	9	1	6	5	4		
43		17	DONCASTER ROVERS	2-1	O'Mara 2	13484	7				11	4	8	2	10		3	9	1	6	5	12		
44		22	EXETER CITY	1-0	Ross (p)	14540	6				11	4	8	2	10		3	9	1	7	5			
45		24	Barrow	3-0	Houston, Allen, Graham	2646	7				11	4	8	2	10		3	9	1	6	5			
46		29	Workington	0-3		1751	7	12			11	4	8	2	10		3	9	1	6	5			
						Apps	29	32	5	3	44	36	45	20	15	8	46	40	46	44	43	13	34	3
						Subs	1	2		1		1				4				1		5	1	
						Goals	3		2		13	2	7		2	2		25		13	1	1	4	

F.A. Cup

Rd	Month	Day	Opponents	Result	Scorers	Att.	Allen M	Bence PI	Cross RG	Dawkins TA	Docherty J	Gelson PWJ	Graham JJ	Hawley AJ	Houston SM	Neilson G	Nelmes AV	O'Mara J	Phillips GD	Ross RH	Scales TA	Tom SE	Turner BA	Wallace KR
R1	Nov	20	Swansea City	1-1	O'Mara	7915	7	2	9			5				11		10	1	8	3	4	6	
rep		22	SWANSEA CITY	2-3	Ross, O'Mara	15000	7	2	9			5				11		10	1	8	3	4	6	

F.L. Cup

Rd	Month	Day	Opponents	Result	Scorers	Att.	Allen M	Bence PI	Cross RG	Dawkins TA	Docherty J	Gelson PWJ	Graham JJ	Hawley AJ	Houston SM	Neilson G	Nelmes AV	O'Mara J	Phillips GD	Ross RH	Scales TA	Tom SE	Turner BA	Wallace KR
R1	Aug	18	Colchester United	1-3	Ross	6125		2	9		12	5	10				4	7	1	8	3	11	6	

		Pl.	Home					Away					F.	A.	Pts
			W	D	L	F	A	W	D	L	F	A	(Total)		
1	Grimsby Town	46	18	3	2	61	26	10	4	9	27	30	88	56	63
2	Southend United	46	18	2	3	56	26	6	10	7	25	29	81	55	60
3	**BRENTFORD**	**46**	**16**	**2**	**5**	**52**	**21**	**8**	**9**	**6**	**24**	**23**	**76**	**44**	**59**
4	Scunthorpe United	46	13	8	2	34	15	9	5	9	22	22	56	37	57
5	Lincoln City	46	17	5	1	46	15	4	9	10	31	44	77	59	56
6	Workington	46	12	9	2	34	7	4	10	9	16	27	50	34	51
7	Southport	46	15	5	3	48	21	3	9	11	18	25	66	46	50
8	Peterborough Utd.	46	14	6	3	51	24	3	10	10	31	40	82	64	50
9	Bury	46	16	4	3	55	22	3	8	12	18	37	73	59	50
10	Cambridge United	46	11	8	4	38	22	6	6	11	24	38	62	60	48
11	Colchester United	46	13	6	4	38	23	6	4	13	32	46	70	69	48
12	Doncaster Rovers	46	11	8	4	35	24	5	6	12	21	39	56	63	46
13	Gillingham	46	11	5	7	33	24	5	8	10	28	43	61	67	45
14	Newport County	46	13	5	5	34	20	5	3	15	26	52	60	72	44
15	Exeter City	46	11	5	7	40	30	5	6	12	21	38	61	68	43
16	Reading	46	14	3	6	37	26	3	5	15	19	50	56	76	42
17	Aldershot	46	5	13	5	27	20	4	9	10	21	34	48	54	40
18	Hartlepool	46	14	2	7	39	25	3	4	16	19	44	58	69	40
19	Darlington	46	9	9	5	37	24	5	2	16	27	58	64	82	39
20	Chester	46	10	11	2	34	16	0	7	16	13	40	47	56	38
21	Northampton Town	46	8	9	6	43	27	4	4	15	23	52	66	79	37
22	Barrow	46	8	8	7	23	26	5	3	15	17	45	40	71	37
23	Stockport County	46	7	10	6	33	32	2	4	17	22	55	55	87	32
24	Crewe Alexandra	46	9	4	10	27	25	1	5	17	16	44	43	69	29

1972/73

22nd in Division Three: Relegated

	Date	Opponent	Score	Scorers	Att.	Allen M	Baker KR	Bence PJ	Court DJ	Cross RG	Docherty J	Gelson PWJ	Graham JJ	Hawley AJ	Houston SM	Jenkins DJ	Murray A	Nelmes AV	O'Mara J	Phillips GD	Priddy PJ	Ross RH	Salvage BJ	Scales TA	Webb SJ	Woon AG
1	Aug 12	HALIFAX TOWN	0-1		10164	7					11	4	8	2	10		6	3			1	9		5		
2	19	Oldham Athletic	1-1	Houston	6106	7		12			11	4	8	2	10		6	3			1	9		5		
3	26	BLACKBURN ROVERS	4-0	Arentoft (og), Houston, O'Mara, Graham	9427	7						4	8	2	10	11	6	3	9		1			5		
4	28	BOLTON WANDERERS	2-1	Allen, Murray	11803	7						4	8	2	10	11	6	3	9		1			5		
5	Sep 2	Plymouth Argyle	1-0	Murray	7833	7			12			4	8	2	10	11	6	3	9		1			5		
6	9	SWANSEA CITY	0-2		9986	7			8			4		2	10	11	6	3	9		1			5		
7	16	Port Vale	0-1		4663	7		9				4		2	10	11	6	3			1	8		5		
8	20	Chesterfield	0-3		6507	8		7	12			4		2	10	11	6	3		1		9		5		
9	23	BOURNEMOUTH	1-1	Docherty	11100	8		7			11	4		2		9	6	3			1	10		5		
10	25	BRISTOL ROVERS	2-1	Docherty, Jenkins	9720	8		7	12		10	4		2		11	6	3			1	9		5		
11	30	Notts County	0-1		8152	8		7	12		11	4		2		9	6	3			1	10		5		
12	Oct 7	Scunthorpe United	0-1		3378	7		9			11	4	8	2	10		6	3			1			5		
13	9	TRANMERE ROVERS	2-0	Docherty, D'Arcy (og)	8154	7		9			11	4	8	2	10	12	6	3			1			5		
14	14	WALSALL	2-0	Houston, Docherty	9493	8		7			11	4		2	10	9	6	3			1			5		
15	21	Southend United	0-4		7205	8		7			11	4		2	10	9	6	3			1			5		
16	28	ROCHDALE	1-0	Docherty	9201	8		7			11	4		2	10	12	6	3		1				5	9	
17	Nov 4	Bristol Rovers	1-3	Houston	7916	8		7			11	4		2	10	9	6	3		1				5		
18	11	CHESTERFIELD	3-1	Murray (p), Webb, Houston	8078	8					11	4	7	2	10		6	3		1				5	9	
19	25	YORK CITY	2-0	Webb, Graham	7111			6			11	4	8	2	10		7	3		1				5	9	
20	28	Charlton Athletic	1-2	Docherty	6192			7			11	4	8	2	10		6	3			1			5	9	
21	Dec 2	Shrewsbury Town	0-2		2079			6			11	4	8	2	10		7	3			1			5	9	
22	16	Grimsby Town	0-4		9110			2	7		11	4	8		10		6	3			1			5	9	
23	23	WREXHAM	1-0	Docherty	6067			2	7		11	4	8		10	12	6	3			1			5	9	
24	26	Bournemouth	2-3	Houston, Graham	14372			8	7		11	4	10	2	5	12	6	3			1				9	
25	30	OLDHAM ATHLETIC	1-1	Webb	7719	5		7			11	4	8	2	10	12	6	3			1				9	
26	Jan 6	Blackburn Rovers	1-2	Graham	6534	6		7	8		11	12	10	2	5	9	4	3			1					
27	13	ROTHERHAM UNITED	1-1	Cross	7446			8	7	10	11	4	5	2			6	3		1					9	12
28	20	PLYMOUTH ARGYLE	0-2		7075			12	7	10	11	4	8	2			6	3		1				5	9	
29	26	Swansea City	1-2	Murray	2119			7		10	11		8	2	4		6	3		1				5	9	
30	Feb 2	Tranmere Rovers	2-6	Court, Murray	6650			8	7		11		10	2	4		6	3		1				5	9	
31	10	PORT VALE	5-0	Woon 3, Graham, Salvage	6694			2		10	7	4	8	3	6					1			11	5		9
32	24	GRIMSBY TOWN	0-1		9302			2		10	7	4	8	3	6		12			1			11	5		9
33	26	CHARLTON ATHLETIC	1-0	Salvage	9929		1	7		10		3	8	2	4		6						11	5	9	
34	Mar 3	SCUNTHORPE UNITED	1-0	Murray	7896		1	7		10	12	3	8	2	4		6						11	5	9	
35	6	Rotherham United	1-2	Webb	3758		1	7		10	12		8	2	4		6	3					11	5	9	
36	10	Walsall	0-3		4192		1	7		10	9		8	2	4		6	3					11	5		
37	17	SOUTHEND UNITED	1-2	Cross	8051	7		6		10	8	3		2	4		12			1			11	5		9
38	19	WATFORD	1-1	Cross	8232	5	1	6		10	8	3	7	2	4		12						11			9
39	24	Rochdale	1-0	Allen	1747	7	1			10	8	3		2	4		6						11	5	9	
40	31	York City	1-0	Allen	2307	8				9	7	3		2	4		6			1			11	5	10	
41	Apr 4	Halifax Town	2-3	Webb, Allen	970	7				10	8	3		2	4		6	12		1			11	5	9	
42	7	SHREWSBURY TOWN	1-2	Salvage	6758	7				10	8	3		2			6	4		1			11	5	9	
43	14	Watford	2-2	Cross, Murray	7813			12		10	8	4	7	2			6	3			1		11	5	9	
44	20	NOTTS COUNTY	1-1	Graham	11658			8		10		3	7	2	4		6				1		11	5	9	
45	23	Wrexham	1-4	Webb	2611			8		10		3	7	2	4		6				1		11	5	9	
46	28	Bolton Wanderers	0-2		21917			2		10		4	12		8		6	3			1		11	5	7	9
					Apps	26	6	33	8	19	34	41	30	43	39	13	42	35	4	15	25	7	16	41	24	5
					Subs			3	4		2	1	1			5	3	1								1
					Goals	4			1	4	7		6		6	1	7		1				3		6	3

Two own goals

F.A. Cup

	Date	Opponent	Score	Scorers	Att.	Allen M	Baker KR	Bence PJ	Court DJ	Cross RG	Docherty J	Gelson PWJ	Graham JJ	Hawley AJ	Houston SM	Jenkins DJ	Murray A	Nelmes AV	O'Mara J	Phillips GD	Priddy PJ	Ross RH	Salvage BJ	Scales TA	Webb SJ	Woon AG
R1	Nov 18	Yeovil Town	1-2	Allen	9447	8		2			11	4	7		10		6	3		1				5	9	

F.L. Cup

	Date	Opponent	Score	Scorers	Att.	Allen M	Baker KR	Bence PJ	Court DJ	Cross RG	Docherty J	Gelson PWJ	Graham JJ	Hawley AJ	Houston SM	Jenkins DJ	Murray A	Nelmes AV	O'Mara J	Phillips GD	Priddy PJ	Ross RH	Salvage BJ	Scales TA	Webb SJ	Woon AG
R1	Aug 16	CAMBRIDGE UNITED	1-0	Docherty	7750	7					11	4	8	2	10		6	3			1	9		5		
R2	Sep 5	Rotherham United	0-2		4996				7			4	8	2	10	11	6	3	9		1	12		5		

		Pl.	Home W	D	L	F	A	Away W	D	L	F	A	F. (Total)	A.	Pts
1	Bolton Wanderers	46	18	4	1	44	9	7	7	9	29	30	73	39	61
2	Notts County	46	17	4	2	40	12	6	7	10	27	35	67	47	57
3	Blackburn Rovers	46	12	8	3	34	16	8	7	8	23	31	57	47	55
4	Oldham Athletic	46	12	7	4	40	18	7	9	7	32	36	72	54	54
5	Bristol Rovers	46	17	4	2	55	20	3	9	11	22	36	77	56	53
6	Port Vale	46	15	6	2	41	21	6	5	12	15	48	56	69	53
7	Bournemouth	46	14	6	3	44	16	3	10	10	22	28	66	44	50
8	Plymouth Argyle	46	14	3	6	43	26	6	7	10	31	40	74	66	50
9	Grimsby Town	46	16	2	5	45	18	4	6	13	22	43	67	61	48
10	Tranmere Rovers	46	12	8	3	38	17	3	8	12	18	35	56	52	46
11	Charlton Athletic	46	12	7	4	46	24	5	4	14	23	43	69	67	45
12	Wrexham	46	11	9	3	39	23	3	8	12	16	31	55	54	45
13	Rochdale	46	8	8	7	22	26	6	9	8	26	28	48	54	45
14	Southend United	46	13	6	4	40	14	4	4	15	21	40	61	54	44
15	Shrewsbury Town	46	10	10	3	31	21	5	4	14	15	33	46	54	44
16	Chesterfield	46	13	4	6	37	22	4	5	14	20	39	57	61	43
17	Walsall	46	14	3	6	37	26	4	4	15	19	40	56	66	43
18	York City	46	8	10	5	24	14	5	5	13	18	32	42	46	41
19	Watford	46	11	8	4	32	23	1	9	13	11	25	43	48	41
20	Halifax Town	46	9	8	6	29	23	4	7	12	14	30	43	53	41
21	Rotherham United	46	12	4	7	34	27	5	3	15	17	38	51	65	41
22	**BRENTFORD**	**46**	**12**	**5**	**6**	**33**	**18**	**3**	**2**	**18**	**18**	**51**	**51**	**69**	**37**
23	Swansea City	46	11	5	7	37	29	3	4	16	14	44	51	73	37
24	Scunthorpe United	46	8	7	8	18	25	2	3	18	15	47	33	72	30

1972-73
Back: Hawley, Nelmes, Bence, Priddy, Phillips, Scales, Allen, Court, Gelson
Front: Docherty, Jenkins, Houston, Ross, Graham, Murray, O'Mara.

1973-74
Back: Bence, Nelmes, Webb, Priddy, Towse, Cross, Houston, Scales
Middle: Woon, Docherty, Gelson, Hawley, Graham, Salvage, Allen. Front: Harding, Oliver, Poole

1973/74

19th in Divison Four

	Date		Opponent	Score	Scorers	Att	Allen M	Bence PI	Brown MJL	Cotton RWL	Cross RG	Docherty J	Gabriel J	Gelson PWJ	Graham JJ	Harding KRC	Hawley AJ	Houston SM	Metchick DJ	Nelmes AV	Poole RJ	Priddy PJ	Reed HD	Riddick GG	Salvage BJ	Scales TA	Sherwood S	Simmons DJ	Towse GT	Webb SJ	Woon AG
1	Aug	25	Hartlepool	0-1		3447	10	4			8	7		5				6		2		1			11	3				9	
2	Sep	1	EXETER CITY	0-1		4814	10	7			8			5			4	6		2		1			11	3				9	12
3		8	Darlington	2-1	Cross, Woon	2287		4			9	10		5			2	6				1			11	3				7	8
4		10	TORQUAY UNITED	0-0		5581		4			9	10					2	6		5					11	3			1	7	8
5		15	DONCASTER ROVERS	2-0	Cross 2	4957	12	4			9	10					2	6		5					11	3			1	7	8
6		17	READING	0-1		8717	12	4			9	10					2	6		5					11	3			1	7	8
7		22	Bury	0-3		4329	10	4			9	12					2	6		5		1			11	3				7	8
8		29	BARNSLEY	5-1	Scales, Docherty, Woon 2, Metchick	5010		4	5		9	7					2	6	10			1			11	3					8
9	Oct	3	Reading	0-1		11267		4	5		9						2	6	10			1	7		11	3					8
10		6	Lincoln City	2-3	Cross, Woon	4056			6		9			5			2	10	11			1	7	4		3					8
11		13	PETERBOROUGH UTD.	0-1		6141	12				9			5			2	6	10			1	7	4	11	3					8
12		20	ROTHERHAM UNITED	1-1	Webb	4419	12				9			5	7		2	6	10			1		4	11	3				8	
13		24	Torquay United	0-3		4445		10			9			5	7		2	6					12	4	11	3			1	8	
14		27	Scunthorpe United	1-4	Cross	2523		4			9			5	7		2	6	10						11	3			1	8	12
15	Nov	3	MANSFIELD TOWN	4-1	Houston, Cross 3 (1p)	4331					8			5	10		2	6	7			1		4	11	3					9
16		10	Workington	2-0	Woon, Riddick	970					8			5	7			6	10	2		1		4	11	3					9
17		12	Stockport County	1-1	Riddick	1948					8			5	7			6	10	2		1		4	11	3				12	9
18		17	CHESTER	3-0	Cross 3	5166					8			5	7			6	10	2		1		4	11	3					9
19	Dec	1	GILLINGHAM	0-3		5748	12				8	7		5	10			6	11	2		1		4		3					9
20		8	Bradford City	1-1	Webb	3243	11				8	7		5	10		4	6		2		1				3				9	
21		15	DARLINGTON	0-0		3166	11				8	7		5	10		4	6		2		1		12		3				9	
22		22	Barnsley	1-2	Cross	2458	11			12	8			5	10		4	6		2		1		7		3					9
23		26	NEWPORT COUNTY	1-1	Graham	5445					8			5	10		4	6	9	2		1		7	11	3					
24	Jan	1	Exeter City	1-2	Salvage	5754					8			5	7		4		10	2		1		6	11	3					9
25		5	SWANSEA CITY	0-2		3501					8			5	7		2		10	6		1		4	11	3					9
26		12	Doncaster Rovers	2-1	Woon 2	3009	8				12			5	7		2		10	6				4	11	3	1				9
27		19	HARTLEPOOL	1-2	Allen	4646	8				12			5	7		2		10	6				4	11	3	1				9
28		26	Crewe Alexandra	0-0		1380	12	2			8			5	7				10	6		1		4	11	3					9
29	Feb	2	Northampton Town	0-0		4130	11	2		10	8			5	7					6		1		4		3				12	9
30		9	BURY	1-2	Cross	4015	12	2			8			5	7				10	6		1		4		3				11	9
31		16	Peterborough United	0-1		7645	3	2			8	7		5					10	6		1		4	11						9
32		23	LINCOLN CITY	2-1	Cross, Salvage	4171	3	2			8	7		5					10	6	9	1		4	11						12
33	Mar	2	Newport County	1-1	Salvage	2167	3	2			9	7		5		8			10	6				4	11		1				
34		9	SCUNTHORPE UNITED	2-1	Allen, Salvage	4053	3	2			9	7		5		8			10	6				4	11		1				
35		16	Rotherham United	1-1	Metchick	2536	3	2			9		4	5	7				10	6					11		1	8			
36		18	NORTHAMPTON T	3-1	Cross, Salvage, Simmons	3686	3	2			9		4	5	7				10	6					11		1	8			
37		23	WORKINGTON	1-1	Cross	5008	3	2			9		4	5	7				10	6					11		1	8			
38		26	Swansea City	0-0		2220	3	2			9		4	5	7				10	6					11		1	8			
39		30	Mansfield Town	1-1	Graham	1909	3	2			9		4	5	7				10	6					11		1	8			
40	Apr	1	CREWE ALEXANDRA	3-0	Cross, Metchick, Simmons	5552	3	2			9		4	5	7				10	6					11		1	8			
41		6	STOCKPORT COUNTY	0-0		5625	3	2			9		4	5	7				10	6					11		1	8			
42		12	Colchester United	1-2	Simmons	8154	3	2					4	5	7				10	6	9				11		1	8			
43		13	Chester	0-0		2775	3	2					4	5	7	10			11		12			6			1	8			9
44		16	COLCHESTER UNITED	0-0		7478	3	2						5	7	4			10		9			6		11	1	8			
45		20	BRADFORD CITY	2-0	Poole, Simmons	5224	3	2						5	7	4			12		9			6	11	10	1	8			
46		27	Gillingham	0-1		9319	3	2						5	7				4		9			6	11	10	1	8			
						Apps	25	30	3	1	39	13	9	40	31	5	22	23	33	33	5	25	3	26	37	33	16	12	5	13	24
						Subs	7			1	2	1							1		1		1	1						2	3
						Goals	2				17	1			2			1	3		1			2	5	1		4		2	7

F.A. Cup

	Date		Opponent	Score	Scorers	Att	Allen M	Bence PI	Brown MJL	Cotton RWL	Cross RG	Docherty J	Gabriel J	Gelson PWJ	Graham JJ	Harding KRC	Hawley AJ	Houston SM	Metchick DJ	Nelmes AV	Poole RJ	Priddy PJ	Reed HD	Riddick GG	Salvage BJ	Scales TA	Sherwood S	Simmons DJ	Towse GT	Webb SJ	Woon AG
R1	Nov	24	Plymouth Argyle	1-2	Allen	11050	12				8	7		5	10			6	11	2		1		4		3					9

F.L. Cup

	Date		Opponent	Score	Scorers	Att	Allen M	Bence PI	Brown MJL	Cotton RWL	Cross RG	Docherty J	Gabriel J	Gelson PWJ	Graham JJ	Harding KRC	Hawley AJ	Houston SM	Metchick DJ	Nelmes AV	Poole RJ	Priddy PJ	Reed HD	Riddick GG	Salvage BJ	Scales TA	Sherwood S	Simmons DJ	Towse GT	Webb SJ	Woon AG
R1	Aug	28	ORIENT	1-2	Webb	6620	10	7			8			5			4	6		2		1			11	3				9	12

	Pl.	Home W	Home D	Home L	Home F	Home A	Away W	Away D	Away L	Away F	Away A	F. (Total)	A. (Total)	Pts
1 Peterborough Utd.	46	19	4	0	49	10	8	7	8	26	28	75	38	65
2 Gillingham	46	16	5	2	51	16	9	7	7	39	33	90	49	62
3 Colchester United	46	16	5	2	46	14	8	7	8	27	22	73	36	60
4 Bury	46	18	3	2	51	14	6	8	9	30	35	81	49	59
5 Northampton Town	46	14	7	2	39	14	6	6	11	24	34	63	48	53
6 Reading	46	11	9	3	37	13	5	10	8	21	24	58	37	51
7 Chester	46	13	6	4	31	19	4	9	10	23	36	54	55	49
8 Bradford City	46	14	7	2	45	20	3	7	13	13	32	58	52	48
9 Newport County	46	13	6	4	39	23	3	8	12	17	42	56	65	45
10 Exeter City *	45	12	5	6	37	20	6	3	13	21	35	58	55	44
11 Hartlepool	46	11	4	8	29	16	5	8	10	19	31	48	47	44
12 Lincoln City	46	10	8	5	40	30	6	4	13	23	37	63	67	44
13 Barnsley	46	15	5	3	42	16	2	5	16	16	48	58	64	44
14 Swansea City	46	11	6	6	28	15	5	5	13	17	31	45	46	43
15 Rotherham United	46	10	9	4	33	22	5	4	14	23	36	56	58	43
16 Torquay United	46	11	7	5	37	23	2	10	11	15	34	52	57	43
17 Mansfield Town	46	13	8	2	47	24	0	9	14	15	45	62	69	43
18 Scunthorpe United	*45	12	7	3	33	17	2	5	16	14	47	47	64	42
19 BRENTFORD	**46**	**9**	**7**	**7**	**31**	**20**	**3**	**9**	**11**	**17**	**30**	**48**	**50**	**40**
20 Darlington	46	9	8	6	29	24	4	5	14	11	38	40	62	39
21 Crewe Alexandra	46	11	5	7	28	30	3	5	15	15	41	43	71	38
22 Doncaster Rovers	46	10	7	6	32	22	2	4	17	15	58	47	80	35
23 Workington	46	10	8	5	33	26	1	5	17	10	48	43	74	35
24 Stockport County	46	4	12	7	22	25	3	8	12	22	44	44	69	34

* (Scunthorpe United versus Exeter City match not played)

1974/75

8th in Division Four

							Allen M	Bence PI	Brown W	Cross RG	Filby IF	French MJ	Gelson PWJ	Graham JJ	Harding KRC	Johnson T	Lawrence KD	Metchick DJ	Nelmes AV	Poole RJ	Riddick GG	Salvage BJ	Scales TA	Sherwood S	Simmons DJ	Smith G (Graham)	Smith GM (Gary)	Smith NP	Stagg W	Woon AG
1	Aug	17	NORTHAMPTON T	1-0	Woon	5147	3	2		9				7			5	10			6	11	4	1						8
2		24	Southport	0-3		1285	3	2		9				7			5	10			6	11	4	1	12					8
3		31	SWANSEA CITY	1-0	Cross	4908	3	2		9				7			5	10			6	11	4	1	12					8
4	Sep	7	Chester	0-2		2625	3	2		9			7				5	10			6	11	4	1	8					
5		14	CAMBRIDGE UNITED	1-0	Simmons	5313	3	2		9	12		7				5	10			6	11	4	1	8					
6		16	ROTHERHAM UNITED	3-4	Bence, Metchick, Simmons	5979	3	2		9			7				5	10			6	11	4	1	8					
7		21	Newport County	0-1		3022	3	2		9	11			7			5	10			6		4	1	8					12
8		23	Rochdale	0-0		1587	3	2		9				7			5	10			6		4	1	8				11	12
9		28	CREWE ALEXANDRA	1-0	Simmons	5442		2						7			5	10			6	11	3	1	9				8	4
10		30	Stockport County	1-1	Woon	1982		2						7			5	10			6	11	3	1	8				9	4
11	Oct	5	Doncaster Rovers	1-2	Simmons	1692					12			7	2		5	10			6	11	3	1	8				9	4
12		12	LINCOLN CITY	1-1	Lawrence	4973								7	2		5	10		9	6	11	3	1	8	4				
13		19	Shrewsbury Town	0-1		4099								7	2		5	10		9	6	11	3	1	8	4				12
14		23	Bradford City	0-1		2932		2						4			5	10		9	6	11	3	1	8	7				
15		26	TORQUAY UNITED	3-1	Graham, Simmons 2	4496		2		10				7			5				6	11	3	1	9	4				8
16	Nov	2	Barnsley	1-1	Simmons	4158		2		10				7			5				6	11	3	1	9	4				8
17		4	BRADFORD CITY	0-0		5131		2		10				7			5	12			6	11	3	1	9	4				8
18		9	MANSFIELD TOWN	2-3	C Foster (og), Simmons	5553		2		10				7			5	8	12		6	11	3	1	9	4				
19		16	Hartlepool	2-3	Simmons, Johnson	2864		2	8					7		4	5	10			6	11	3	1	9					
20		30	Workington	1-0	Brown	1325	3	2	9					7		4	5				6	11	10	1						8
21	Dec	7	DARLINGTON	3-0	Johnson, Brown 2	4925	3	2	9					7		4	5				6	11	10	1						8
22		21	SCUNTHORPE UNITED	2-0	Brown 2	4364	3	2	9					7		4	5				6	11	10	1	12					8
23		26	Cambridge United	0-2		3959	3	2	9					7		4	5				6	11	10	1	8					
24		28	EXETER CITY	2-0	Simmons, Johnson	5608	3	4	9	12				10		7		11	2		6			1	8		5			
25	Jan	4	Northampton Town	0-0		4735	3	4	9					10		7		11	2		6			1	8		5			
26		11	Darlington	1-2	Johnson	2095	3	4	9					10		7		11	2		6			1	8		5			
27		18	WORKINGTON	2-2	Simmons, Brown	3983	3	2	9					7		4	5	10			6	11		1	8					
28		25	READING	1-0	Brown	6485	3	2	9					7		4	5	10			6	11		1						8
29	Feb	1	Mansfield Town	1-1	Graham	11362		2	9					7		4	5	10			6	11	3	1	8					
30		4	Rotherham United	0-3		4541	3	2	9					7		4	5	10		8	6	11		1						12
31		8	BARNSLEY	3-0	Simmons, Brown, French	5080	3	2	9			12		7		4	5				6	11	10	1	8					
32		15	Reading	0-1		6013	3	2	9			8		7		4	5			12	6	11	10	1						
33		22	HARTLEPOOL	1-0	Johnson	5516	3	2	9	12		8		7		4	5				6	11	10	1						
34		28	Swansea City	1-0	Brown	1706	3	2	9	6		8		7		4	5					11	10	1						
35	Mar	8	ROCHDALE	3-0	Graham, Cross, Johnson	4460	3	2		9		8		7		4	5	12			6	11	10	1						
36		15	Crewe Alexandra	1-1	Johnson	2356	3	2		9		10		7		4	5				6	11	8	1	12					
37		22	CHESTER	1-1	Cross	5827		2		9		10		7		4	5		3		6	11	8	1	12					
38		31	Exeter City	0-1		3301		2		9		10		7		4	5		3		6		8	1	11					
39	Apr	1	NEWPORT COUNTY	0-0		5569	3	2		9		10		7		4	5				6	11	8	1						
40		5	Torquay United	2-3	Scales, Cross	2555	3	2		9		10		7		4	5		12		6	11	8	1						
41		7	STOCKPORT COUNTY	3-0	Riddick, French 2	4434	11	2		9		10		7		4	5	12	3		6		8	1						
42		12	DONCASTER ROVERS	1-1	French	5147	11	2		9		10		7		4	5		3		6		8	1						
43		15	Scunthorpe United	2-1	Cross, Johnson	1556	11	2		9		10		7		4	5		3	12	6		8	1						
44		19	Lincoln City	1-1	Cross	6956	11	2		9		10		7		4	5	6	3	12			8	1						
45		21	SOUTHPORT	1-0	French	4796	3	2		9		10		7		4	5		12	11			8	1				6		
46		26	SHREWSBURY TOWN	2-1	Graham, Cross	5810	3	4		8				7		11	5		2				10	1	9			6		
						Apps	32	43	16	25	1	14	3	43	3	28	43	24	10	5	42	34	40	46	25	7	3	2	4	13
						Subs				2	2	1						3	3	3					5					4
						Goals		1	9	8		4		4		8	1	1			1		1		12					2

One own goal

F.A. Cup

							Allen M	Bence PI	Brown W	Cross RG	Filby IF	French MJ	Gelson PWJ	Graham JJ	Harding KRC	Johnson T	Lawrence KD	Metchick DJ	Nelmes AV	Poole RJ	Riddick GG	Salvage BJ	Scales TA	Sherwood S	Simmons DJ	Smith G (Graham)	Smith GM (Gary)	Smith NP	Stagg W	Woon AG
R1	Nov	23	Slough Town	4-1	Graham, Woon 2, Simmons	3394		2						7		4	5	10			6	11	3	1	9					8
R2	Dec	14	Brighton & Hove Albion	0-1		13287	3	2	9					7		4	5				6	11	10	1	12					8

F.L. Cup

							Allen M	Bence PI	Brown W	Cross RG	Filby IF	French MJ	Gelson PWJ	Graham JJ	Harding KRC	Johnson T	Lawrence KD	Metchick DJ	Nelmes AV	Poole RJ	Riddick GG	Salvage BJ	Scales TA	Sherwood S	Simmons DJ	Smith G (Graham)	Smith GM (Gary)	Smith NP	Stagg W	Woon AG
R1	Aug	21	ALDERSHOT	3-0	Scales, Woon, Cross (p)	5702	3	2		9				7			5	10			6	11	4	1						8
R2	Sep	10	Liverpool	1-2	Cross	21413	3	2		9			7				5	10			6	11	4	1	8					12

		Pl.	Home W	Home D	Home L	Home F	Home A	Away W	Away D	Away L	Away F	Away A	F. (Total)	A. (Total)	Pts
1	Mansfield Town	46	17	6	0	55	15	11	6	6	35	25	90	40	68
2	Shrewsbury Town	46	16	3	4	46	18	10	7	6	34	25	80	43	62
3	Rotherham United	46	13	7	3	40	19	9	8	6	31	22	71	41	59
4	Chester	46	17	5	1	48	9	6	6	11	16	29	64	38	57
5	Lincoln City	46	14	8	1	47	14	7	7	9	32	34	79	48	57
6	Cambridge United	46	15	5	3	43	16	5	9	9	19	28	62	44	54
7	Reading	46	13	6	4	38	20	8	4	11	25	27	63	47	52
8	**BRENTFORD**	**46**	**15**	**6**	**2**	**38**	**14**	**3**	**7**	**13**	**15**	**31**	**53**	**45**	**49**
9	Exeter City	46	14	3	6	33	24	5	8	10	27	39	60	63	49
10	Bradford City	46	10	5	8	32	21	7	8	8	24	30	56	51	47
11	Southport	46	13	7	3	36	19	2	10	11	20	37	56	56	47
12	Newport County	46	13	5	5	43	30	6	4	13	25	45	68	75	47
13	Hartlepool	46	13	6	4	40	24	3	5	15	12	38	52	62	43
14	Torquay United	46	10	7	6	30	25	4	7	12	16	36	46	61	42
15	Barnsley	46	10	7	6	34	24	5	4	14	28	41	62	65	41
16	Northampton Town	46	12	6	5	43	22	3	5	15	24	51	67	73	41
17	Doncaster Rovers	46	10	9	4	41	29	4	3	16	24	50	65	79	40
18	Crewe Alexandra	46	9	9	5	22	16	2	9	12	12	31	34	47	40
19	Rochdale	46	9	9	5	35	22	4	4	15	24	53	59	75	39
20	Stockport County	46	10	8	5	26	27	2	6	15	17	43	43	70	38
21	Darlington	46	11	4	8	38	27	2	6	15	16	40	54	67	36
22	Swansea City	46	9	4	10	25	31	6	2	15	21	42	46	73	36
23	Workington	46	7	5	11	23	29	3	6	14	13	37	36	66	31
24	Scunthorpe United	46	7	8	8	27	29	0	7	16	14	49	41	78	29

1974-75
Back: Everitt (Manager), Simmons, Riddick, Woon, Cross, Priddy, Lawrence, Nelmes, Smith
Middle: Bence, Scales, Metchick, Salvage, Graham, Allen, Gelson
Front: Tripp, Stagg, Poole, Johnson, Harding.

1975-76
Back: Tripp, Cross, Scales, Cox, Riddick, Sharp, Priddy, Oxley, Graham, Bence, French, Lawrence
Front: Salman, Smith, Sweetzer, Johnson, Poole, Nelmes, Allen.

1975/76

18th in Division Four

						Allen M	Bence PI	Cross RG	French MJ	Glazier WJ	Graham JJ	Horn GR	Johnson T	Lawrence KD	McCulloch A	Nelmes AV	Poole RJ	Priddy PJ	Riddick GG	Salman DMM	Scales TA	Sharp TA	Simmons DJ	Smith NP	Sweetzer GEP
1	Aug 16	Bradford City	1-1	Johnson	2385	3	7		10	1	8		11	5		2					4		9	6	
2	23	HARTLEPOOL	1-1	Cross	4948	3	7	10		1	8		11	5		2			12		4		9	6	
3	30	Torquay United	3-2	Allen, Graham, Cross	3179	3	4	10		1	7		11	5		2					8		9	6	
4	Sep 6	BARNSLEY	1-0	Cross	5605	3	4	10	12	1	7		11	5		2					8		9	6	
5	15	Doncaster Rovers	1-1	Johnson	6353	3	4		10	1	7		11	5		2					8		9	6	
6	20	STOCKPORT COUNTY	2-1	Simmons, Riddick	6282	3	4		10	1	7		11	5		2			12		8		9	6	
7	24	Bournemouth	0-3		4113	3	4		10	1	7		11	5		2			12		8		9	6	
8	27	Huddersfield Town	1-2	Sweetzer	4160	3	4	10			7		11			2		1	5		8		9	6	12
9	Oct 4	NEWPORT COUNTY	1-3	Graham	5678	3	4	10	12	1	7		11	5		2					8		9	6	
10	11	Lincoln City	1-3	Graham	6312	3	4	9		1	7		11	5			12		2		8			6	10
11	18	SOUTHPORT	1-0	Johnson	4515	3	2	10			7		11	5			12	1	4		8		9	6	
12	21	Northampton Town	1-3	Scales	6225	3	4	9	12		7		11	5		2	10	1	6		8				
13	25	Cambridge United	1-2	French	2596	3	2	9	4		7		11	5				1			8			6	10
14	Nov 1	SCUNTHORPE UNITED	5-2	Graham, French, Johnson, Cross 2	4227	3	2	9	4		7		11	5				1			8			6	10
15	3	WORKINGTON	4-0	French, Johnson (p), Cross, Sweetzer	5379	3	2	9	4		7		11	5				1			8			6	10
16	7	Tranmere Rovers	1-5	Cross	4326	3	2	9	4		7	1	11	5			12				8			6	10
17	15	WATFORD	1-0	Scales	6934	3	2	9	4		7	1	11						5	12	8			6	10
18	29	Crewe Alexandra	0-1		2248	3	4	9			7	1	11	5		2					8			6	10
19	Dec 6	ROCHDALE	3-0	Johnson (p), Cross, Riddick	4853	3	8	9			7		11	5		2		1	4					6	10
20	20	DARLINGTON	3-0	Cross, Sweetzer 2	4193	3	4	9			7		11	5		2		1			8			6	10
21	26	Exeter City	0-0		4912	3	4	9			7		11	5		2		1			8			6	10
22	27	READING	2-2	Scales, Johnson	10612	3	4	9			7		11	5		2		1			8			6	10
23	Jan 10	TORQUAY UNITED	1-1	Johnson	5687	3	4	9			7		11	5		2	12	1	10		8			6	
24	16	Stockport County	0-2		2267	3	4	9			7		11	5		2	12	1	10		8			6	
25	24	DONCASTER ROVERS	0-1		4885	3	2	9	11		7		4					1	5		8	12		6	10
26	31	NORTHAMPTON T	2-1	Johnson (p), Cross	4114	3	2	9	11		7		4					1	5		8			6	10
27	Feb 7	Workington	1-1	French	1231	3	2	9	11		7		4					1	5		8	12		6	10
28	14	TRANMERE ROVERS	0-1		4725	3	2	9	11		7		4					1	5		8			6	10
29	21	Watford	2-3	Bristow (og), Sweetzer	6223	3	2	9	11		7		4			12		1	5		8	6			10
30	23	BOURNEMOUTH	1-2	Graham	4585	3	2	9	11		7		4	5				1		6	8	12			10
31	28	CAMBRIDGE UNITED	0-0		4095	3	2	9	11		7		4	5				1			8	12		6	10
32	Mar 6	Scunthorpe United	1-2	Sharp	3377	3	2		11		7		4	5			9	1			8	12		6	10
33	8	Newport County	0-1		1150	3	2		11		7		4	5	9			1			8			6	10
34	13	LINCOLN CITY	1-0	Cross	5386	3	2	11			7		4		9			1	5		8	12		6	10
35	16	Southport	0-2		1506	3	2	11			7		4	5	9			1	8			12		6	10
36	20	CREWE ALEXANDRA	0-0		3851	3	2	11			7		4	5	9	8		1	6			12			10
37	27	Rochdale	2-1	French, McCulloch	894	3	4		11		7		10	5	9	2		1	6		8				
38	29	Darlington	0-2		1758	3	4		10		7		11	5	9	2		1	6		8				12
39	Apr 3	BRADFORD CITY	2-2	Cross, McCulloch	3453	3	7	10	12				11	5	9	2		1	4		8			6	
40	5	HUDDERSFIELD T	0-0		4413	3	4	11	10				7		9	2		1	6		8	12		5	
41	10	Barnsley	1-1	Cross	3877	3	4	10	11				7	5	9	2		1		12	8			6	
42	16	SWANSEA CITY	1-0	Johnson	4623	3	4	11	10				7		9	2		1	6		8			5	
43	17	EXETER CITY	5-1	Bence, French 2, Cross, McCulloch	4175	3	4	10	11				7		9	2		1	5		8			6	
44	19	Reading	0-1		12972	3	4	11	10				7	6	9	2		1	5	12	8				
45	24	Hartlepool	0-1		1276	6	4		11				7	5	9	2		1		3	8	12			10
46	26	Swansea City	2-2	French, Johnson	1480		4	11	10				7	6		2		1		3	8	5			9
					Apps	45	46	37	27	9	38	3	46	35	13	28	2	34	23	3	43	2	10	37	25
					Subs				4							1	5		3	3		10			2
					Goals	1	1	14	8		5		11		3				2		3	1	1		5

One own goal

F.A. Cup

						Allen M	Bence PI	Cross RG	French MJ	Glazier WJ	Graham JJ	Horn GR	Johnson T	Lawrence KD	McCulloch A	Nelmes AV	Poole RJ	Priddy PJ	Riddick GG	Salman DMM	Scales TA	Sharp TA	Simmons DJ	Smith NP	Sweetzer GEP
R1	Nov 22	NORTHAMPTON T	2-0	Sweetzer 2	6645	3	2	9	4		7		11	5		12		1			8			6	10
R2	Dec 13	Wimbledon	2-0	Johnson 2 (1p)	8375	3	4	9			7		11	5		2		1			8			6	10
R3	Jan 3	BOLTON WANDERERS	0-0		12452	3	4		12		7		11	5		2		1	9		8			6	10
rep	6	Bolton Wanderers	0-2		18538	3	4	9			7		11	5		2		1	12		8			6	10

F.L. Cup

						Allen M	Bence PI	Cross RG	French MJ	Glazier WJ	Graham JJ	Horn GR	Johnson T	Lawrence KD	McCulloch A	Nelmes AV	Poole RJ	Priddy PJ	Riddick GG	Salman DMM	Scales TA	Sharp TA	Simmons DJ	Smith NP	Sweetzer GEP
R1/1	Aug 19	BRIGHTON & HOVE ALB.	2-1	Johnson (p), Cross	5360	3	4	12	10	1	7		11	5		2					8		9	6	
R1/2	27	Brighton & Hove Albion	1-1	Cross	11016	3	4	10		1	7		11	5		2			12		8		9	6	
R2	Sep 10	Manchester United	1-2	Lawrence	25286	3	4	10	9	1	7		11	5		2					8		12	6	

		Pl.	Home					Away					F.	A.	Pts
			W	D	L	F	A	W	D	L	F	A	(Total)		
1	Lincoln City	46	21	2	0	71	15	11	8	4	40	24	111	39	74
2	Northampton Town	46	18	5	0	62	20	11	5	7	25	20	87	40	68
3	Reading	46	19	3	1	42	9	5	9	9	28	42	70	51	60
4	Tranmere Rovers	46	18	3	2	61	16	6	7	10	28	39	89	55	58
5	Huddersfield Town	46	11	6	6	28	17	10	8	5	28	24	56	41	56
6	Bournemouth	46	15	5	3	39	16	5	7	11	18	32	57	48	52
7	Exeter City	46	13	7	3	37	17	5	7	11	19	30	56	47	50
8	Watford	46	16	4	3	38	18	6	2	15	24	44	62	62	50
9	Torquay United	46	12	6	5	31	24	6	8	9	24	39	55	63	50
10	Doncaster Rovers	46	10	6	7	42	31	9	5	9	33	38	75	69	49
11	Swansea City	46	14	8	1	51	21	2	7	14	15	36	66	57	47
12	Barnsley	46	12	8	3	34	16	2	8	13	18	32	52	48	44
13	Cambridge United	46	7	10	6	36	28	7	5	11	22	34	58	62	43
14	Hartlepool	46	10	6	7	37	29	6	4	13	25	49	62	78	42
15	Rochdale	46	7	11	5	27	23	5	7	11	13	31	40	54	42
16	Crewe Alexandra	46	10	7	6	36	21	3	8	12	22	36	58	57	41
17	Bradford City	46	9	7	7	35	26	3	10	10	28	39	63	65	41
18	**BRENTFORD**	**46**	**12**	**7**	**4**	**37**	**18**	**2**	**6**	**15**	**19**	**42**	**56**	**60**	**41**
19	Scunthorpe United	46	11	3	9	31	24	3	7	13	19	35	50	59	38
20	Darlington	46	11	7	5	30	14	3	3	17	18	43	48	57	38
21	Stockport County	46	8	7	8	23	23	5	5	13	20	53	43	76	38
22	Newport County	46	8	7	8	35	33	5	2	16	22	57	57	90	35
23	Southport	46	6	6	11	27	31	2	4	17	14	46	41	77	26
24	Workington	46	5	4	14	19	43	2	3	18	11	44	30	87	21

1976/77

15th in Division Four

						Allen M	Aylott SJ	Bain J	Bence PI	Burns AJ	Carlton DG	Cox GP	Cross RG	Fraser J	French MJ	Glover AR	Goldthorpe RJ	Graham JJ	Johnson T	Kruse PK	McCulloch A	Phillips SE	Priddy PJ	Pritchett KB	Redknapp HJ	Riddick GG	Rolph GL	Salman DMM	Scales TA	Scrivens SJ	Sharp TA	Shrubb PJ	Smillie N	Smith NP	Sweetzer GEP	Walker PJ
1	Aug 21	BARNSLEY	0-1		3903	8			4				9	2	12		5	11			10		1	3					7					6		
2	23	Stockport County	0-2		3191	8			4				10		9		5	11	12				1	3				2	7					6		
3	28	Huddersfield Town	0-1		4559				4				10		9		5	11	7				1	3				2	8					6		
4	Sep 4	DONCASTER ROVERS	2-2	French, Johnson	3804		2		4				10		9		5	7	11				1	3					8		12			6		
5	10	Aldershot	1-1	French	5129				2				10		9		5	8	11				1	3	7				4					6		12
6	18	SOUTHPORT	3-0	Cross, Graham, Johnson	4185				2				10	3	9		5	7	11				1	4					8					6		
7	25	Torquay United	1-1	Cross	2456				2				10	3	9		5	7	11				1	4					8					6		
8	Oct 2	Bradford City	2-3	Cross 2	4809				4				10	2	9		5	7	11				1	3					8					6		
9	9	NEWPORT COUNTY	1-1	Goldthorpe	5894	3			2				10		12	4	5	7	9				1	11					8					6		
10	15	Swansea City	3-5	Pritchett, Goldthorpe, Allen	3656	6							10			4	5	7	9				1	11				2	8		3					
11	23	DARLINGTON	0-3		4303	6							10			4		7	9		12		1	11		5		2	8		3					
12	25	WORKINGTON	5-0	Cross, Fraser, McCulloch 2, Sweetzer	3158	3							10	2		8	5	9	7		6		1			4									11	
13	30	Colchester United	1-2	Cross	3607	3					12		9	2		8	5	10	7		6		1			4									11	
14	Nov 3	Exeter City	2-3	Graham, McCulloch	2779	3					6		9	2	12	8	5	7	11		10		1			4										
15	6	BOURNEMOUTH	3-2	French, Cross, McCulloch	4254	3					6		9	2	11		5	7	8		10		1			4										
16	13	Hartlepool	0-2		1888	3					6		9	2	11		5	7	8		10		1			4		12								
17	27	CAMBRIDGE UNITED	0-2		5040	3					6		9	7	11		5	8	12		10		1			4		2								
18	Dec 27	Southend United	1-2	Cross (p)	9239	5					6		9	7				8					1			4	10	2		11				3		
19	Jan 1	Bournemouth	1-3	Cross	4268	5					6	1	9	7				8			12					4	10	2		11				3		
20	3	COLCHESTER UNITED	1-4	McCulloch	4629	5						1		7				8			9					4	10	2		11				3	12	6
21	8	Crewe Alexandra	2-3	McCulloch, Sweetzer	2198	5					6	1	10	7				8			9					4		2		11				3	12	
22	15	STOCKPORT COUNTY	4-0	Fraser, Sweetzer 3	3981	3				1	4		9	7				8								5		2		11				6	10	
23	22	Barnsley	0-2		4095	3				1	4			7	9			8								5	11	2						6	10	
24	25	Scunthorpe United	1-2	Sweetzer	2867	3			11	1	6			7	10			8									12	2	5					4	9	
25	29	HALIFAX TOWN	2-1	French, Sweetzer	4517	3	8			1	6			7	10											4		2					11	5	9	
26	Feb 5	HUDDERSFIELD T	1-3	Salman	4833	3	11		12	1	4			7	9											5	10	2						6	8	
27	12	Doncaster Rovers	0-5		4095	3	5			1	4			7	9			8									10	2			12		11	6		
28	19	ALDERSHOT	0-1		4542	5	3	6			10			2	12			8				11	1										7	4	9	
29	22	ROCHDALE	3-2	Johnson, Sweetzer, Phillips	3307	3		6			10			2			5	8	7			11	1											4	9	
30	Mar 5	TORQUAY UNITED	3-2	Sweetzer 3 (1p)	4172	3		6			10			2			5	8	7			11	1											4	9	
31	8	Southport	2-1	Johnson (p), Sweetzer	969	3		6			10			2			5	8	7			11	1									12		4	9	
32	12	BRADFORD CITY	4-0	Johnson, Bain, Phillips, Shrubb	5742	3		6						2				8	7	5		11	1									10		4	9	
33	18	Newport County	1-3	Sweetzer	1747	3		6			10			2				8	7	5		11	1											4	9	
34	23	WATFORD	3-0	Graham, Sweetzer 2	7602	3		6			10			2				8	7	5		11	1									12		4	9	
35	26	SWANSEA CITY	4-0	Johnson 2 (1p), Sweetzer, Phillips	6201	3		6			10			2				8	7	5		11	1											4	9	
36	Apr 2	Darlington	2-2	Johnson, Sweetzer	1681	3		6			10			2				8	7	5		11	1									12		4	9	
37	8	SOUTHEND UNITED	1-0	Phillips	8951	3		6			10			2				8	7	5		11	1											4	9	
38	9	Watford	1-0	McCulloch	9382	3					10			2				8		5	7	11	1					4				6			9	
39	12	EXETER CITY	1-0	Sweetzer	7641	3		12			10			2				6	7	5	8	11	1									4			9	
40	16	Workington	3-1	McCulloch, Sweetzer, Phillips	1032	3		6			10			2						5	7	11	1									8		4	9	
41	19	Halifax Town	0-0		1464	3		7			10			2				9		5	8	11	1									6		4		
42	23	HARTLEPOOL	3-1	McCulloch, Sweetzer (p), Kruse	5978	3		4			10			2				7		5	8	11	1									6		12	9	
43	30	Cambridge United	2-3	Graham, Sweetzer	5617	3		4			10			2				7		5	8	11	1									6			9	
44	May 2	CREWE ALEXANDRA	0-0		5842	3		4			10			2				7	12	5	8	11	1									6			9	
45	7	SCUNTHORPE UNITED	4-2	Sweetzer 2, Phillips, Kruse	5298	3		4			10			2				7		5	8	11	1									6		12	9	
46	14	Rochdale	3-2	McCulloch, Phillips, Shrubb	977	3		4			10			2						5	8	11	1					12				7		6	9	
					Apps	40	5	17	10	6	31	3	21	39	15	6	19	42	24	15	18	19	37	11	1	15	6	16	12	5	2	10	3	32	25	1
					Subs			1	1		1				4				3		2						1	2			2	3		2	2	1
					Goals	1		1					9	2	4		2	4	8	2	10	7		1				1				2			23	

F.A. Cup

						Allen M	Aylott SJ	Bain J	Bence PI	Burns AJ	Carlton DG	Cox GP	Cross RG	Fraser J	French MJ	Glover AR	Goldthorpe RJ	Graham JJ	Johnson T	Kruse PK	McCulloch A	Phillips SE	Priddy PJ	Pritchett KB	Redknapp HJ	Riddick GG	Rolph GL	Salman DMM	Scales TA	Scrivens SJ	Sharp TA	Shrubb PJ	Smillie N	Smith NP	Sweetzer GEP	Walker PJ
R1	Nov 20	CHESHAM UNITED	2-0	French, Cross	5633	3					6		9	2	11		5	8	7				1			4		12							10	
R2	Dec 20	Colchester United	2-3	Rolph, Fraser	4730	5					6		9	7	11		12	8					1			4	10	2	3							

R2 - on Dec 11 abandoned after 62 minutes

F.L. Cup

						Allen M	Aylott SJ	Bain J	Bence PI	Burns AJ	Carlton DG	Cox GP	Cross RG	Fraser J	French MJ	Glover AR	Goldthorpe RJ	Graham JJ	Johnson T	Kruse PK	McCulloch A	Phillips SE	Priddy PJ	Pritchett KB	Redknapp HJ	Riddick GG	Rolph GL	Salman DMM	Scales TA	Scrivens SJ	Sharp TA	Shrubb PJ	Smillie N	Smith NP	Sweetzer GEP	Walker PJ
R1/1	Aug 14	Watford	1-1	Cross	4827				4				10		9		5	11					1	3				2	7		12			6		8
R1/2	17	WATFORD	0-2		5542				4				10		9		5	11					1	3				2	7					6		8

		Pl.	Home W	D	L	F	A	Away W	D	L	F	A	F. (Total)	A.	Pts
1	Cambridge United	46	16	5	2	57	18	10	8	5	30	22	87	40	65
2	Exeter City	46	17	5	1	40	13	8	7	8	30	33	70	46	62
3	Colchester United	46	19	2	2	51	14	6	7	10	26	29	77	43	59
4	Bradford City	46	16	7	0	51	18	7	6	10	27	33	78	51	59
5	Swansea City	46	18	3	2	60	30	7	5	11	32	38	92	68	58
6	Barnsley	46	16	5	2	45	18	7	4	12	17	21	62	39	55
7	Watford	46	15	7	1	46	13	3	8	12	21	37	67	50	51
8	Doncaster Rovers	46	16	2	5	47	25	5	7	11	24	40	71	65	51
9	Huddersfield Town	46	15	5	3	36	15	4	7	12	24	34	60	49	50
10	Southend United	46	11	9	3	35	19	4	10	9	17	26	52	45	49
11	Darlington	46	13	5	5	37	25	5	8	10	22	39	59	64	49
12	Crewe Alexandra	46	16	6	1	36	15	3	5	15	11	45	47	60	49
13	Bournemouth	46	13	8	2	39	13	2	10	11	15	31	54	44	48
14	Stockport County	46	10	10	3	29	19	3	9	11	24	38	53	57	45
15	**BRENTFORD**	**46**	**14**	**3**	**6**	**48**	**27**	**4**	**4**	**15**	**29**	**49**	**77**	**76**	**43**
16	Torquay United	46	12	5	6	33	22	5	4	14	26	45	59	67	43
17	Aldershot	46	10	8	5	29	19	6	3	14	20	40	49	59	43
18	Rochdale	46	8	7	8	32	25	5	5	13	18	34	50	59	38
19	Newport County	46	11	6	6	33	21	3	4	16	9	37	42	58	38
20	Scunthorpe United	46	11	6	6	32	24	2	5	16	17	49	49	73	37
21	Halifax Town	46	11	6	6	36	18	0	8	15	11	40	47	58	36
22	Hartlepool	46	8	9	6	30	20	2	3	18	17	53	47	73	32
23	Southport	46	3	12	8	17	28	0	7	16	16	49	33	77	25
24	Workington	46	3	7	13	23	42	1	4	18	18	60	41	102	19

1976-77
Back: Graham, Salman, Russell, Fraser, Aylott, Scales
Middle: Docherty (Manager), Smith, Sharp, Priddy, Goldthorpe, Riddick, Cox, Pritchett, Allen, Lyons (Trainer)
Front: Sweetzer, French, Johnson, Bence, Cross, McCulloch, Rolph.

1977-78
Back: Fraser, Allen, McCulloch, Aylott, Sweetzer
Middle: Rolfe, Carlton, Cox, Kruse, Smith
Front: Shrubb, Walker, Graham, Lloyd, Phillips.

1977/78

4th in Division Four: Promoted

No	Date		Opponents	Score	Scorers	Att	Allder DS	Allen M	Aylott SJ	Baldwin T	Bond LA	Carlton DG	Cox GP	Fraser J	Graham JJ	Graham WV	Kruse PK	Lloyd BD	McCulloch A	Murray J	Phillips SE	Rolph GL	Salman DMM	Shrubb PJ	Smith NP	Sweetzer GEP	Tucker WB	Walker PJ	Glynn TR
1	Aug	20	NORTHAMPTON T	3-0	Lloyd, McCulloch, Phillips	5492		3			1			2	8		5	4	10		11			6		9		7	
2		22	WIMBLEDON	4-1	Lloyd, Sweetzer, McCulloch, Phillips	11001		3			1			2	8		5	4	10		11			6	12	9		7	
3		27	READING	1-1	Sweetzer (p)	8176					1			2	8		5	4	10		11			3	6	9		7	
4	Sep	3	Crewe Alexandra	6-4	Collier (og), Sweetzer 3, Carlton 2	1837					1	7		2	8		5	4	10		11		12	3	6	9			
5		10	BOURNEMOUTH	1-1	Phillips	7702					1	7		2	8			4	10		11		3	6	5	9			
6		13	Rochdale	2-1	Kruse, McCulloch	1164					1	7		2	8		5	4	10		11		3	6		9			
7		17	Doncaster Rovers	1-3	Phillips	3044					1	7		2	8		5	4	10		11	12	3	6		9			
8		24	SCUNTHORPE UNITED	2-0	McCulloch, Phillips	6115		3			1	7		2	8	9		4	10		11		5	6					
9		26	Stockport County	1-1	Sweetzer	4121		3				7	1	2	8			4	10		11		5	6		9			
10	Oct	1	HALIFAX TOWN	4-1	Lloyd, Graham J, Phillips 2 (1p)	6239		3			1	7		2	8			4	10		11		5	6		9			
11		3	WATFORD	0-3		14496		3			1	7		2	8		5	4	10		11			6		9		12	
12		8	Torquay United	1-2	McCulloch	2538		3			1	7		2	8		5	4	10		11			6		9			
13		15	SOUTHPORT	0-0		6141				9	1	7		2	8			4	10		11		5	6	3			12	
14		22	Hartlepool United	1-3	Phillips	2470				9	1	7		2	8			4	10		11		5	6	3				
15		29	SOUTHEND UNITED	1-0	McCulloch	7435	9				1	7		2	8		5	4	10		11		3	6					
16	Nov	5	YORK CITY	1-0	Phillips	5985	9				1	7		2	8	12	5	4	10		11		3	6					
17		12	Barnsley	0-0		4209	9				1	7		2		8	5	4	10		11	12	3	6					
18		19	SWANSEA CITY	0-2		6337	9				1			2		8	5	4	10		11	7	3	6					
19	Dec	2	Darlington	3-1	McCulloch, Phillips, Rolph	2058		3			1	7		2	8	9	5	6	10		11	12	4						
20		10	GRIMSBY TOWN	3-1	McCulloch 2, Phillips	5762	9	3			1				8	7	5	6	10		11		4	2					
21		26	Aldershot	0-1		8175	9	3	12		1	8				7	5	6	10		11		4	2					
22		27	NEWPORT COUNTY	3-3	Phillips (p), Baldwin, Allder	8972	9	3		8	1					7	5	6			11		4	2		10			
23		31	York City	2-3	McCulloch, Phillips	2329	8	3			1					7	5	6	10		11		4	2		9			
24	Jan	2	HUDDERSFIELD T	1-1	Shrubb	9475	9	3		8	1					7	5	6	10		11		4	2					
25		7	Wimbledon	1-1	Sweetzer	5411	9	3	6		1					7	5		10		11		4	2		8			
26		14	Northampton Town	2-2	McCulloch 2	4050	9	3			1				7	8	5		10		11		4	2	6				
27		28	CREWE ALEXANDRA	5-1	Sweetzer, McCulloch, Phillips 2 (1p), Graham W	6871	9	3			1				7	12	5		10		11		2	6	4	8			
28	Feb	4	Bournemouth	2-3	Sweetzer, McCulloch	3417	9	3			1				7	12	5		10		11		2	6	4	8			
29		25	Halifax Town	1-1	Carlton	1764	9				1	6				8	5	12	10	7	11		2	4			3		
30	Mar	4	TORQUAY UNITED	3-0	Darke (og), Sweetzer 2 (1p)	6551	9				1	6				7	5		10		11		2	4		8	3		
31		6	ROCHDALE	4-0	Lloyd, Sweetzer, McCulloch, Phillips	7215	9				1	7				6	5	12	10		11		2	4		8	3		
32		11	Southport	3-1	McCulloch, Phillips 2	1691	9				1	7			8	6	5		10	12	11		2	4			3		
33		14	Scunthorpe United	1-1	Murray	3053	9				1	7			8	6	5		10	12	11		2	4			3		
34		18	HARTLEPOOL UNITED	2-0	McCulloch, Phillips	7499	9				1	7			8	6	5		10		11		2	4			3		
35		24	Southend United	1-2	Phillips	11810	9				1	7			8	6	5		10	12	11		2	4			3		
36		25	Newport County	2-1	Graham J, McCulloch	4953	9	2			1	7			12		5	6	10	8	11			4			3		
37		27	ALDERSHOT	2-0	Phillips 2 (1p)	12579	9	2			1	7			8	6	5		10		11			4			3		
38	Apr	1	Huddersfield Town	3-1	Phillips 3	6345	9	2			1				8	6	5	7	10		11			4			3		
39		3	STOCKPORT COUNTY	4-0	McCulloch 2, Phillips 2	11674	9	2			1	7			8	6	5		10		11			4			3		
40		8	BARNSLEY	2-0	Phillips (p), Allder	12139	9				1	7			8	6	5		10		11		2	4			3		
41		12	Reading	0-0		7384	9				1	7			8	6	5		10		11		2	4			3		
42		15	Swansea City	1-2	Graham W	16152	9				1	7			8	6	5	12	10		11		2	4			3		
43		18	DONCASTER ROVERS	2-2	Phillips 2	11512	9				1	7			8	6	5		10		11		2	4			3		
44		22	DARLINGTON	2-0	McCulloch, Phillips (p)	11934	9				1	7			8	6	5	12	10		11		2	4			3		
45		25	Watford	1-1	McCulloch	16544	9				1	7			8	6	5		10		11		2	4			3		
46		29	Grimsby Town	1-2	Phillips	4712	9				1	7			8	6	5	12	10		11		2	4			3		
						Apps	31	21	1	4	45	33	1	19	35	28	40	26	45	2	46	1	36	45	8	18	18	3	
						Subs			1						1	3		5		3		3	1		1			2	
						Goals	2			1		3			2	2	1	4	22	1	32	1		1		12			

Two own goals

F.A. Cup

Rd	Date		Opponents	Score	Scorers	Att	Allder DS	Allen M	Aylott SJ	Baldwin T	Bond LA	Carlton DG	Cox GP	Fraser J	Graham JJ	Graham WV	Kruse PK	Lloyd BD	McCulloch A	Murray J	Phillips SE	Rolph GL	Salman DMM	Shrubb PJ	Smith NP	Sweetzer GEP	Tucker WB	Walker PJ	Glynn TR
R1	Nov	26	FOLKSTONE & SHEPWA'	2-0	Phillips 2	5981	9	3			1			2	8		5	6	10		11		4	7					
R2	Dec	17	Swindon Town	1-2	Phillips (p)	8447	9	3			1				8	7	5	6	10		11	12	4	2					

F.L. Cup

Rd	Date		Opponents	Score	Scorers	Att	Allder DS	Allen M	Aylott SJ	Baldwin T	Bond LA	Carlton DG	Cox GP	Fraser J	Graham JJ	Graham WV	Kruse PK	Lloyd BD	McCulloch A	Murray J	Phillips SE	Rolph GL	Salman DMM	Shrubb PJ	Smith NP	Sweetzer GEP	Tucker WB	Walker PJ	Glynn TR
R1/1	Aug	13	CRYSTAL PALACE	2-1	Sweetzer 2	8929		3			1			2	8		5	4	10		11		7	6		9			
R1/2		16	Crystal Palace	1-5	Phillips	11586		3			1			2	8		5	4	10		11		7	6		9			12

		Pl.	Home W	Home D	Home L	Home F	Home A	Away W	Away D	Away L	Away F	Away A	F. (Total)	A. (Total)	Pts
1	Watford	46	18	4	1	44	14	12	7	4	41	24	85	38	71
2	Southend United	46	15	5	3	46	18	10	5	8	20	21	66	39	60
3	Swansea City	46	16	5	2	54	17	7	5	11	33	30	87	47	56
4	**BRENTFORD**	**46**	**15**	**6**	**2**	**50**	**17**	**6**	**8**	**9**	**36**	**37**	**86**	**54**	**56**
5	Aldershot	46	15	8	0	45	16	4	8	11	22	31	67	47	54
6	Grimsby Town	46	14	6	3	30	15	7	5	11	27	36	57	51	53
7	Barnsley	46	15	4	4	44	20	3	10	10	17	29	61	49	50
8	Reading	46	12	7	4	33	23	6	7	10	22	29	55	52	50
9	Torquay United	46	12	6	5	43	25	4	9	10	14	31	57	56	47
10	Northampton Town	46	9	8	6	32	30	8	5	10	31	38	63	68	47
11	Huddersfield Town	46	13	5	5	41	21	2	10	11	22	34	63	55	45
12	Doncaster Rovers	46	11	8	4	37	26	3	9	11	15	39	52	65	45
13	Wimbledon	46	8	11	4	39	26	6	5	12	27	41	66	67	44
14	Scunthorpe United	46	12	6	5	31	14	2	10	11	19	41	50	55	44
15	Crewe Alexandra	46	11	8	4	34	25	4	6	13	16	44	50	69	44
16	Newport County	46	14	6	3	43	22	2	5	16	22	51	65	73	43
17	Bournemouth	46	12	6	5	28	20	2	9	12	13	31	41	51	43
18	Stockport County	46	14	4	5	41	19	2	6	15	15	37	56	56	42
19	Darlington	46	10	8	5	31	22	4	5	14	21	37	52	59	41
20	Halifax Town	46	7	10	6	28	23	3	11	9	24	39	52	62	41
21	Hartlepool United	46	12	4	7	34	29	3	3	17	17	55	51	84	37
22	York City	46	8	7	8	27	31	4	5	14	23	38	50	69	36
23	Southport	46	5	13	5	30	32	1	6	16	22	44	52	76	31
24	Rochdale	46	8	6	9	29	28	0	2	21	14	57	43	85	24

1978/79

10th in Division Three

	Date		Opponent	Score	Scorers	Att.	Allder DS	Allen M	Bond LA	Booker R	Carlton DG	Eames WA	Fraser J	Frost LA	Glover AR	Graham JJ	Graham WV	Kruse PK	McCulloch A	McNichol JA	Phillips SE	Porter TJ	Rolph GL	Salman DMM	Shrubb PJ	Silman DA	Smith D	Smith NP	Tucker WB	Walker PJ	Baldwin T	Wilkins SM
1	Aug	19	Shrewsbury Town	0-1		2346	9	12			7		2			6	8	5	10		11	1			4				3			
2		21	COLCHESTER UNITED	1-0	Kruse	6802	9	3			7					8	6	5	10		11	1			4			12	2			
3		26	CHESTERFIELD	0-3		6162	9	12			7					8	6	5	10		11	1		2	4				3			
4	Sep	2	Exeter City	2-2	McCulloch 2	3645	9	3			7					8	6	5	10		11	1		4					2	12		
5		9	HULL CITY	1-0	Phillips	6528	9	3			7					8	6	5	10		11	1		4					2	12		
6		12	Swindon Town	0-2		6902	9	3			7					8	6	5	10		11	1						4	2	12		
7		16	Peterborough United	1-3	Kruse	5884	9	3			7		10			8	6	5			11	1						4	2	12		
8		23	GILLINGHAM	0-2		6977					7		2			8		5	10		11	1	9	6	4				3	12		
9		25	LINCOLN CITY	2-1	Graham J, Eames	6107						9	6			8	12	5	10		11	1		2	4				3	7		
10		30	Swansea City	1-2	McCulloch	11370					8	9	6					5	10		11	1		2	4				3	7		
11	Oct	7	BURY	0-1		5855	12				7		6	9		8		5	10		11	1		2	4				3			
12		14	Watford	0-2		15180			1	6	7		12	9		8		5	10		11			2	4				3			
13		17	Rotherham United	0-1		3881	5		1	6	7			9		8			10		11			2	4				3			
14		21	TRANMERE ROVERS	2-0	McCulloch 2	5883			1		6		4	9		8			10	5	11			3	2		7					
15		28	Chester	1-3	McCulloch	4495			1		7			4		8		5	10	6	11			12	2		9		3			
16	Nov	4	OXFORD UNITED	3-0	McCulloch, Smith D 2	6863			1		8			12		6		5	10	4	11			2	7		9		3			
17		11	EXETER CITY	0-0		6387	9		1	12	8					6		5	10	4	11			2	7				3			
18		18	Chesterfield	0-0		4584			1		8				9	6		5	10	4	11			2	7				3			
19	Dec	2	WALSALL	1-0	McCulloch	5140			1				7		9	8	12	5	10	6	11			2	4				3			
20		9	Mansfield Town	1-2	McCulloch	4003			1						8	6		5	10	4	11			2	7		9		3			
21		23	Southend United	1-1	Phillips	13703			1		8				9	6		5	10	4	11			2	7				3			
22		26	PLYMOUTH ARGYLE	2-1	Smith D 2	7367	10		1				12		8	6	7	5		4	11			2			9		3			
23		30	CARLISLE UNITED	0-0		6477	10		1		7				8	6		5		4	11			2			9		3			
24	Jan	20	PETERBOROUGH UTD.	0-0		5760	12		1		7		3		8	6		5	10	4	11			2			9					
25		27	Gillingham	0-0		6899	10		1		7		3			6		5		4	11			2	8		9					
26	Feb	10	SWANSEA CITY	1-0	Carlton	7264			1		8					6		5	10	4	11			2	7		9		3			
27		24	WATFORD	3-3	Phillips 2 (1p), Smith D	13873			1		7					6		5	10	4	11			2	8		9		3			
28	Mar	3	Tranmere Rovers	1-0	Phillips	1882			1		7				12	6		5	10	4	11			2	8		9		3			
29		6	Hull City	0-1		3418	12		1						7	6		5	10	4	11			2	8		9		3			
30		10	CHESTER	6-0	Phillips 3, McCulloch, Glover 2	6421	12		1						7	6		5	10	4	11			2	8		9		3			
31		13	Sheffield Wednesday	0-1		10383	12		1		7				10	6		5			11			2	8	4	9		3			
32		21	Lincoln City	0-1		2060			1		7				9	6		5	10	4	11			2	8		12		3			
33		24	Colchester United	1-1	Shrubb	3528	12		1		7				9	6		5		4	11			2	8		10		3			
34		26	SHREWSBURY TOWN	2-3	McCulloch, Smith D	7756	12		1		7					6		5	10	4	11			2	8		9		3			
35		31	BLACKPOOL	3-2	Phillips, McNichol 2	6364	12		1		7					6		5	10	4	11			2	8		9		3			
36	Apr	4	Oxford United	1-0	Shrubb	5242	12		1		7		2		6			5	10	4	11				8		9		3			
37		7	Walsall	3-2	Kruse, Phillips 2	3840	9		1				6		7		12	5	10	4	11			2	8				3			
38		13	SOUTHEND UNITED	3-0	Salman, Kruse, McCulloch	11509	9		1				6		8			5	10	4	11			7	2				3			
39		14	Plymouth Argyle	1-2	Carlton	6344	9		1		7		8			10		5		6	11			4	2		12		3			
40		17	SHEFFIELD WEDNESDAY	2-1	McNichol 2	9050	9		1				6		8			5	10	4	11			7	2		12		3			
41		21	Carlisle United	0-1		3967	9		1		12		6		8			5	10	4	11			7	2				3			
42		23	ROTHERHAM UNITED	1-0	Smith D	6758			1		7		6					5	10	4	11			8	2		9		3			
43		28	MANSFIELD TOWN	1-0	Phillips	6838	12		1		7		6					5	10	4	11			8	2		9		3			
44	May	5	Blackpool	1-0	McCulloch	3464	9		1		7		8					5	10	6	11			4	2				3			
45		8	SWINDON TOWN	1-2	Smith D	13317	12		1		7		6					5	10	4	11			8	2		9		3			
46		15	Bury	3-2	Phillips 2, McCulloch	2512	12		1		7		6		8			5	10	4	11				2		9		3			
						Apps	18	5	35	2	36	2	21	5	18	35	8	44	39	32	46	11	1	39	39	1	22	2	43	2		
						Subs	12	2		1	1		2	1	1		3							1			3	1		5		
						Goals					2	1			2	1		4	14	4	14			1	2		8					

F.A. Cup

	Date		Opponent	Score	Scorers	Att.	Allder DS	Allen M	Bond LA	Booker R	Carlton DG	Eames WA	Fraser J	Frost LA	Glover AR	Graham JJ	Graham WV	Kruse PK	McCulloch A	McNichol JA	Phillips SE	Porter TJ	Rolph GL	Salman DMM	Shrubb PJ	Silman DA	Smith D	Smith NP	Tucker WB	Walker PJ	Baldwin T	Wilkins SM
R1	Nov	25	Exeter City	0-1		3810			1		7				9	8		5	10	6	11			2	4		12		3			

F.L. Cup

	Date		Opponent	Score	Scorers	Att.	Allder DS	Allen M	Bond LA	Booker R	Carlton DG	Eames WA	Fraser J	Frost LA	Glover AR	Graham JJ	Graham WV	Kruse PK	McCulloch A	McNichol JA	Phillips SE	Porter TJ	Rolph GL	Salman DMM	Shrubb PJ	Silman DA	Smith D	Smith NP	Tucker WB	Walker PJ	Baldwin T	Wilkins SM
R1/1	Aug	12	Watford	0-4		9292	9				8		12			6	7	5			11	1		2	4				3		10	
R1/2		15	WATFORD	1-3	Rolph	7414	9				8					6	7	5			11	1	10	2	4				3			12

	Pl.	Home W	D	L	F	A	Away W	D	L	F	A	F. (Total)	A.	Pts
1 Shrewsbury Town	46	14	9	0	36	11	7	10	6	25	30	61	41	61
2 Watford	46	15	5	3	47	22	9	7	7	36	30	83	52	60
3 Swansea City	46	16	6	1	57	32	8	6	9	26	29	83	61	60
4 Gillingham	46	15	7	1	39	15	6	10	7	26	27	65	42	59
5 Swindon Town	46	17	2	4	44	14	8	5	10	30	38	74	52	57
6 Carlisle United	46	11	10	2	31	13	4	12	7	22	29	53	42	52
7 Colchester United	46	13	9	1	35	19	4	8	11	25	36	60	55	51
8 Hull City	46	12	9	2	36	14	7	2	14	30	47	66	61	49
9 Exeter City	46	14	6	3	38	18	3	9	11	23	38	61	56	49
10 BRENTFORD	**46**	**14**	**4**	**5**	**35**	**19**	**5**	**5**	**13**	**18**	**30**	**53**	**49**	**47**
11 Oxford United	46	10	8	5	27	20	4	10	9	17	30	44	50	46
12 Blackpool	46	12	5	6	38	19	6	4	13	23	40	61	59	45
13 Southend United	46	11	6	6	30	17	4	9	10	21	32	51	49	45
14 Sheffield Wed.	46	9	8	6	30	22	4	11	8	23	31	53	53	45
15 Plymouth Argyle	46	11	9	3	40	27	4	5	14	27	41	67	68	44
16 Chester	46	11	9	3	42	21	3	7	13	15	40	57	61	44
17 Rotherham United	46	13	3	7	30	23	4	7	12	19	32	49	55	44
18 Mansfield Town	46	7	11	5	30	24	5	8	10	21	28	51	52	43
19 Bury	46	6	11	6	35	32	5	9	9	24	33	59	65	42
20 Chesterfield	46	10	5	8	35	34	3	9	11	16	31	51	65	40
21 Peterborough Utd.	46	8	7	8	26	24	3	7	13	18	39	44	63	36
22 Walsall	46	7	6	10	34	32	3	6	14	22	39	56	71	32
23 Tranmere Rovers	46	4	12	7	26	31	2	4	17	19	47	45	78	28
24 Lincoln City	46	5	7	11	26	38	2	4	17	15	50	41	88	25

1978-79
Back: Walker, Smith, Rolph, Fraser, Shrubb,
Middle: Salman, Alder, Cox, Silkman, Bond, Kruse, Allen
Front: Lyons (Physio), Carlton, Murray, Tucker, Dodgin (Manager), J.Graham, Phillips, W.Graham, Baldwin (Player/Coach).

1979-80
Back: Carlton, Holmes, Benning, Booker, Porter, Kruse, Bond, McNichol, Smith, Fraser, Glover
Front: Walker, Johns, Shrubb, Phillips, J.Graham, Tucker, Allder, O'Mahoney, , W.Graham, Walsh.

1979/80

19th in Division Three

	Date	Opponents	Score	Scorers	Att	Allder DS	Bond LA	Booker R	Carlton DG	Fear KW	Fraser J	Funnell A	Glover AR	Graham JJ	Graham WV	Harding SJ	Holmes LJ	Holmes WG	Jenkins IC	Kruse PK	McNichol JA	Parkinson ND	Phillips SE	Porter TJ	Salman DMM	Shrubb PJ	Smith D	Tucker WB	Walker PJ
1	Aug 18	Reading	2-2	Henderson (og), Fraser	8140	12	1		7		6		8				9			5	4		11		3	2	10		
2	25	Swindon Town	0-4		7204		1		7		6		12	8			9			5	4		11		3	2	10		
3	Sep 1	CHESTERFIELD	3-1	Fraser, Carlton, Holmes W	5762	10	1		7		6			8			9	12		5	4		11			2		3	
4	8	Sheffield Wednesday	2-0	Holmes L, Phillips	11778	10	1		7		6			8			9	12		5	4		11		3	2			
5	15	GRIMSBY TOWN	1-0	Salman	7121	10	1		7					8			9	6		5	4		11		3	2		12	
6	17	EXETER CITY	0-2		7809	10	1		7					8			9	6		5	4		11		2	12		3	
7	22	Wimbledon	0-0		5524	12	1		7					8				10		5	4		11		2	6	9	3	
8	29	SOUTHEND UNITED	2-0	McNichol, Phillips	6928		1		7		6			8			9	10			5		11		4	2		3	
9	Oct 3	Exeter City	0-0		3297		1		7		6			8			9	10		5	4		11		2	12		3	
10	6	BARNSLEY	3-1	Kruse, Holmes L, Smith	7292		1				6			8			9	10		5	4		11		2		7	3	
11	10	Oxford United	2-0	McNichol, Phillips	6362		1				6			8			9	10		5	4		11		2	12	7	3	
12	13	Blackpool	4-5	McNichol, Carlton, Phillips, Holmes W	5386	12	1		7		6			8				10		5	4		11		2		9	3	
13	20	BLACKBURN ROVERS	2-0	McNichol, Phillips	7970	10	1		7		6			8				12		5	4		11		2		9	3	
14	22	SHEFFIELD UNITED	1-2	Smith	13764	10	1		7		6						12			5	4		11		2	8	9	3	
15	27	Plymouth Argyle	1-0	Graham J	5203		1		7		6			8			9			5	4		11		2		10	3	
16	Nov 3	READING	2-2	Smith 2	10011	12	1		7		6			8			10			5	4		11		2		9	3	
17	6	Sheffield United	2-0	Tibbott (og), Smith	14808	8	1		7		6						10	12		5	4		11			2	9	3	
18	10	COLCHESTER UNITED	1-0	McNichol	9070	10	1		7		6			8						5	4		11		2	12	9	3	
19	17	Rotherham United	2-4	McNichol 2 (1p)	4709	7	1			12	6			8			9			5	4		11		2		10	3	
20	Dec 1	Carlisle United	1-3	Holmes L	4275		1		7	8	6						10	12		5	4		11			2	9	3	
21	8	HULL CITY	7-2	Kruse, Phillips 2, Fear, Booker 3	6793			9	7	10	6		8							5	4		11	1		2		3	
22	15	OXFORD UNITED	1-1	Salman	7592			9	7	8	6		10							5	4		11	1	12	2		3	
23	21	Bury	2-4	Fraser, Booker	2443		1	9	7	8	6			12						5	4		11		10	2		3	
24	26	CHESTER	2-2	McNichol, Fear	10139		1		7	8				10						5	4		11		6	2	9	3	
25	29	SWINDON TOWN	1-3	Fraser	12122		1	9	7	10	6			8			12		4	5			11		3	2			
26	Jan 5	GILLINGHAM	0-2		7849		1	9		8	6			10						5	4		11		2	7		3	12
27	12	Chesterfield	0-1		5529	10	1		7		6			8			9			5			11		4	2	12	3	
28	19	SHEFFIELD WEDNESDAY	2-2	Holmes L, Phillips	8389	10	1	12	7		6			8		5	9						11		4	2		3	
29	Feb 2	Grimsby Town	1-5	Phillips	9817	9	1		7		6			8		12	10			5			11		4	2		3	
30	9	WIMBLEDON	0-1		7383	9	1		7		6					4	10			5			11		2	8	12	3	
31	16	Southend United	2-3	Shrubb, Phillips	4198	12	1				6			8	7	4				5			11		2	10	9	3	
32	23	BLACKPOOL	2-1	Salman, Booker	6403	7	1	12			6			10						5	4	8	11		2	9		3	
33	Mar 1	Blackburn Rovers	0-3		10227	12	1	9	7		6			10						5	4	8	11		2			3	
34	8	PLYMOUTH ARGYLE	0-0		6462		1	12	7		6	9								5	4	8	11		2	10		3	
35	10	Mansfield Town	0-0		3461		1		7		2	10		6						5	4	8	11			9		3	
36	15	Barnsley	0-1		9368		1		7		2	10		6						5	4	8	11		12	9		3	
37	18	Millwall	1-3	Kruse	6107	12			7		2	10					9			5		8	11	1	4	6		3	
38	22	Colchester United	1-6	Funnell	3821				7		2	10					9			5	4	8	11	1	6	12		3	
39	29	ROTHERHAM UNITED	0-1		4992	12	1	9	7		2	10		8						5			11		4	6		3	
40	Apr 5	Chester	1-1	Phillips	2930	9	1		7		2			8						5		12	11		4	6	10	3	
41	7	MANSFIELD TOWN	2-0	Holmes L, Phillips	6057	10	1				2						7			5		8	11		4	6	9	3	
42	8	BURY	0-0		6751	10	1				2	7						12		5		8	11		4	6	9	3	
43	12	Gillingham	1-0	Booker	5889	10	1	9	7		2						8			5			11		4	6		3	
44	19	CARLISLE UNITED	0-3		6130	10	1	9	8		2						7	12		5			11		4	6		3	
45	26	Hull City	1-2	Holmes L	5382		1		7		2	12		8			9			5			11		4	6		3	10
46	May 3	MILLWALL	1-0	Funnell	7033		1		8		2	11					9			5			12		4	6	10	3	7
					Apps	19	42	9	38	7	42	8	3	30	1	3	26	8	1	44	31	9	45	4	39	34	20	41	2
					Subs	8		3		1		1	1	1		1	2	7				1	1		2	5	2	1	1
					Goals			6	2	2	4	2		1			6	2		3	8		12		3	1	5		

Two own goals

F.A. Cup

	Date	Opponents	Score	Scorers	Att	Allder DS	Bond LA	Booker R	Carlton DG	Fear KW	Fraser J	Funnell A	Glover AR	Graham JJ	Graham WV	Harding SJ	Holmes LJ	Holmes WG	Jenkins IC	Kruse PK	McNichol JA	Parkinson ND	Phillips SE	Porter TJ	Salman DMM	Shrubb PJ	Smith D	Tucker WB	Walker PJ
R1	Nov 24	Swindon Town	1-4	Smith	9472	10	1		7		6			8						5	4		11		2	12	9	3	

F.L. Cup

	Date	Opponents	Score	Scorers	Att	Allder DS	Bond LA	Booker R	Carlton DG	Fear KW	Fraser J	Funnell A	Glover AR	Graham JJ	Graham WV	Harding SJ	Holmes LJ	Holmes WG	Jenkins IC	Kruse PK	McNichol JA	Parkinson ND	Phillips SE	Porter TJ	Salman DMM	Shrubb PJ	Smith D	Tucker WB	Walker PJ
R1/1	Aug 15	Southend United	1-2	Holmes L	4780	12	1		7		6		8				9			5	4		11		3	2	10		
R1/2	21	SOUTHEND UNITED	1-4	Allder	7818	3	1		7		6		8				9			5	4		11			2	10		

		Pl.	Home W	Home D	Home L	Home F	Home A	Away W	Away D	Away L	Away F	Away A	F. (Total)	A. (Total)	Pts
1	Grimsby Town	46	18	2	3	46	16	8	8	7	27	26	73	42	62
2	Blackburn Rovers	46	13	5	5	34	17	12	4	7	24	19	58	36	59
3	Sheffield Wed.	46	12	6	5	44	20	9	10	4	37	27	81	47	58
4	Chesterfield	46	16	5	2	46	16	7	6	10	25	30	71	46	57
5	Colchester United	46	10	10	3	39	20	10	2	11	25	36	64	56	52
6	Carlisle United	46	13	6	4	45	26	5	6	12	21	30	66	56	48
7	Reading	46	14	6	3	43	19	2	10	11	23	46	66	65	48
8	Exeter City	46	14	5	4	38	22	5	5	13	22	46	60	68	48
9	Chester	46	14	6	3	29	18	3	7	13	20	39	49	57	47
10	Swindon Town	46	15	4	4	50	20	4	4	15	21	43	71	63	46
11	Barnsley	46	10	7	6	29	20	6	7	10	24	36	53	56	46
12	Sheffield United	46	13	5	5	35	21	5	5	13	25	45	60	66	46
13	Rotherham United	46	13	4	6	38	24	5	6	12	20	42	58	66	46
14	Millwall	46	14	6	3	49	23	2	7	14	16	36	65	59	45
15	Plymouth Argyle	46	13	7	3	39	17	3	5	15	20	38	59	55	44
16	Gillingham	46	8	9	6	26	18	6	5	12	23	33	49	51	42
17	Oxford United	46	10	4	9	34	24	4	9	10	23	38	57	62	41
18	Blackpool	46	10	7	6	39	34	5	4	14	23	40	62	74	41
19	**BRENTFORD**	**46**	**10**	**6**	**7**	**33**	**26**	**5**	**5**	**13**	**26**	**47**	**59**	**73**	**41**
20	Hull City	46	11	7	5	29	21	1	9	13	22	48	51	69	40
21	Bury	46	10	4	9	30	23	6	3	14	15	36	45	59	39
22	Southend United	46	11	6	6	33	23	3	4	16	14	35	47	58	38
23	Mansfield Town	46	9	9	5	31	24	1	7	15	16	34	47	58	36
24	Wimbledon	46	6	8	9	34	38	4	6	13	18	43	52	81	34

1980/81

9th in Division Three

						Bocker R	Crown DI	Frost LA	Funnell A	Graham WV	Harris RE	Hill MS	Hurlock TA	Jenkins IC	Johnson GJ	Johnson RN	Kruse PK	McCullough PJ	McKellar DN	McNichol JA	Roberts GPM	Salman DMM	Shrubb PJ	Silkman B	Smith D	Teer KP	Tucker WB	Walker PJ
1	Aug 16	Charlton Athletic	1-3	Hill	5125	9	11		12		6	3		4			5	1				7	2	8				10
2	18	MILLWALL	1-0	Funnell	6524	9	11		7		6	3					5	1				4	2	8				10
3	23	READING	1-2	Funnell	6717	9	11		7		6	3					5	1				4	2	8				10
4	30	Walsall	3-2	Hill, Walker, Funnell	4586	9	11		7		2	3	6				5	1				4		8				10
5	Sep 6	Portsmouth	2-0	Booker, Funnell	16971	9	11		7			3	6				5	1				4	2	8				10
6	13	FULHAM	1-3	Booker	11610	9	11		7			3	6				5	1				4	2	8				10
7	15	BARNSLEY	1-1	Funnell	6935	9	11		7			3	6	12			5	1				4	2	8				10
8	20	Blackpool	3-0	Walker, Crown 2	3738	9	11		7				6	2			5		1	12		4	3	8				10
9	27	HULL CITY	2-2	Jenkins, Funnell	6305	9	11		7				6	2			5		1			4	3	8				10
10	30	Barnsley	1-0	Walker	11227	9	11		7				6	2			5		1			4	3	8				10
11	Oct 4	NEWPORT COUNTY	0-1		7309	9	11		7				6	2			5		1			4	3	8	12			10
12	8	Exeter City	0-0		4665	9	11		7				6	2			5		1			4	3	8				10
13	11	Carlisle United	2-1	Silkman (p), Walker	3030	9	11					12	6	2			5		1		7	4	3	8				10
14	18	CHESTER	0-1		6604	9	11				2		6	12			5		1		7	4	3	8				10
15	20	GILLINGHAM	3-3	Crown, Smith, Hurlock	6786		11		7	8	2	3	6				5		1			4			9			10
16	25	Burnley	0-2		7324		11		7		8	3	6				5		1	12		4	2		9			10
17	28	Plymouth Argyle	1-0	Smith	7249	9	11				8	3	6				5		1			4	2		7			10
18	Nov 1	OXFORD UNITED	3-0	Hill, Crown 2	6549		11		7		8	3	6				5		1			4	2		9			10
19	3	EXETER CITY	0-1		6593		11		7		8	3	6	12			5		1			4	2		9			10
20	8	Chesterfield	1-2	Graham	7127	9	11		7	8		3	6	2					1	5		4	12					10
21	11	Millwall	2-2	Booker, Hurlock	4279	9	11		7	8		3	6	2					1	5		4	12					10
22	15	CHARLTON ATHLETIC	0-1		8181	9	11		7	8		3	6	2					1	5		4	12					10
23	29	Huddersfield Town	0-3		8871	9	11		7	8		3	6				5		1	12		4	2					10
24	Dec 6	SWINDON TOWN	1-1	Kruse	5727		11		7		8		6				5		1		12	4	2		9		3	10
25	20	Rotherham United	1-4	Johnson G	5913		11	8				3	6	5	9				1		7	4	12				2	10
26	26	COLCHESTER UNITED	2-1	Kruse, Hurlock	6241		11	8				3	6		9		5		1		7	4					2	10
27	27	Sheffield United	0-0		13130		11	8			7	3	6		9		5		1			4	10				2	
28	Jan 3	BURNLEY	0-0		6379		11	8	12		10	3	6		9		5		1			4	7				2	
29	10	Chester	0-0		2237		11	8			10	3	6		9		5		1			4	7				2	
30	17	HUDDERSFIELD TOWN	0-0		5831		11	8			10	3	6		9		5		1			4	7				2	
31	24	WALSALL	4-0	Shrubb, Frost, Johnson G 2	5503		11	8			10	3	6		9		5		1		12	4	7				2	
32	31	Reading	0-0		6374		11	8			10	3	6		9		5		1			4	7				2	
33	Feb 7	Fulham	1-1	Roberts	8627		11	8			10	3	6		9		5		1		12	4	7				2	
34	14	PORTSMOUTH	2-2	Roberts, Tucker (p)	10162			8			10	3	6		9		5		1	4	11		7				2	
35	21	Hull City	0-0		4535			8			10	3	6		9		5		1	4	11		7				2	
36	28	BLACKPOOL	2-0	Frost, Johnson G	5850			8			10	3	6		9		5		1	4	11		7				2	
37	Mar 7	Newport County	1-1	Crown	5270		11	8			10	3	6		9		5		1	4	12		7				2	
38	14	CARLISLE UNITED	1-1	Frost	6209		11	8			10	3	6		9		5		1	4			7				2	
39	21	Gillingham	0-2		3916		11	8			10	3	6		9		5		1		12	4	7				2	
40	28	PLYMOUTH ARGYLE	0-1		5868	12	11		7			3	6		9		5		1		8	4					2	10
41	Apr 4	Oxford United	1-1	Booker	4085	8					6	3			9		5		1		11	4	7				2	10
42	11	CHESTERFIELD	3-2	Roberts, Johnson G, Ridley (og)	4883	8	12				10	3	6		9		5		1		11	4	7				2	
43	18	SHEFFIELD UNITED	1-1	Booker	5622	8					10	3	6		9		5		1	4	11		7				2	
44	20	Colchester United	2-0	Shrubb, Booker	2609	8					10		6		9	3	5		1	4	11		7				2	
45	25	ROTHERHAM UNITED	2-1	Booker, Hurlock	6909	8					10	3	6		9		5		1	4	11		7				2	
46	May 2	Swindon Town	0-0		8968	8						3	6		9		5		1		11	4	7			12	2	10
					Apps	25	37	15	21	5	29	37	42	11	22	1	42	7	39	11	14	38	38	14	6	0	23	29
					Subs	1	1		2			1		3						3	5		4		1	1		
					Goals	7	6	3	6	1		3	4	1	5		2				3		2	1	2		1	4

One own goal

F.A. Cup

						Bocker R	Crown DI	Frost LA	Funnell A	Graham WV	Harris RE	Hill MS	Hurlock TA	Jenkins IC	Johnson GJ	Johnson RN	Kruse PK	McCullough PJ	McKellar DN	McNichol JA	Roberts GPM	Salman DMM	Shrubb PJ	Silkman B	Smith D	Teer KP	Tucker WB	Walker PJ
R1	Nov 22	ADDLESTONE & WEYBRIDGE TOWN	2-2	Booker, Funnell (p)	6536	9	11		7	8		3	6	2					1	5		4	12					10
rep	25	ADDLESTONE & WEYBRIDGE TOWN	2-0	Crown, Funnell	7678	9	11		7		8	3	6				5		1	4			2					10
R2	Dec 13	Fulham	0-1		11261	9	11		12		8		6				5		1			4	2		7		3	10

R1 was an Addlestone home game but played at Griffin Park.

F.L. Cup

						Bocker R	Crown DI	Frost LA	Funnell A	Graham WV	Harris RE	Hill MS	Hurlock TA	Jenkins IC	Johnson GJ	Johnson RN	Kruse PK	McCullough PJ	McKellar DN	McNichol JA	Roberts GPM	Salman DMM	Shrubb PJ	Silkman B	Smith D	Teer KP	Tucker WB	Walker PJ
R1/1	Aug 9	CHARLTON ATHLETIC	3-1	Walker, Crown, Smith	5847	9	11				6	3		4			5	1					2	8	7			10
R1/2	12	Charlton Athletic	0-5		3764	9	11				6	3		4			5	1				12	2	8	7			10

		Pl.	Home					Away					F.	A.	Pts
			W	D	L	F	A	W	D	L	F	A	(Total)		
1	Rotherham United	46	17	6	0	43	8	7	7	9	19	24	62	32	61
2	Barnsley	46	15	5	3	46	19	6	12	5	26	26	72	45	59
3	Charlton Athletic	46	14	6	3	36	17	11	3	9	27	27	63	44	59
4	Huddersfield Town	46	14	6	3	40	11	7	8	8	31	29	71	40	56
5	Chesterfield	46	17	4	2	42	16	6	6	11	30	32	72	48	56
6	Portsmouth	46	14	5	4	35	19	8	4	11	20	28	55	47	53
7	Plymouth Argyle	46	14	5	4	35	18	5	9	9	21	26	56	44	52
8	Burnley	46	13	5	5	37	21	5	9	9	23	27	60	48	50
9	**BRENTFORD**	**46**	**7**	**9**	**7**	**30**	**25**	**7**	**10**	**6**	**22**	**24**	**52**	**49**	**47**
10	Reading	46	13	5	5	39	22	5	5	13	23	40	62	62	46
11	Exeter City	46	9	9	5	36	30	7	4	12	26	36	62	66	45
12	Newport County	46	11	6	6	38	22	4	7	12	26	39	64	61	43
13	Fulham	46	8	7	8	28	29	7	6	10	29	35	57	64	43
14	Oxford United	46	7	8	8	20	24	6	9	8	19	23	39	47	43
15	Gillingham	46	9	8	6	23	19	3	10	10	25	39	48	58	42
16	Millwall	46	10	9	4	30	21	4	5	14	13	39	43	60	42
17	Swindon Town	46	10	6	7	35	27	3	9	11	16	29	51	56	41
18	Chester	46	11	5	7	25	17	4	6	13	13	31	38	48	41
19	Carlisle United	46	8	9	6	32	29	6	4	13	24	41	56	70	41
20	Walsall	46	8	9	6	43	43	5	6	12	16	31	59	74	41
21	Sheffield United	46	12	6	5	38	20	2	6	15	27	43	65	63	40
22	Colchester United	46	12	7	4	35	22	2	4	17	10	43	45	65	39
23	Blackpool	46	5	9	9	19	28	4	5	14	26	47	45	75	32
24	Hull City	46	7	8	8	23	22	1	8	14	17	49	40	71	32

1980-81
Back: Lyons (Physio), Bowen, Salman, Bateman, McCullough, Booker, Kruse, Hill, Jenkins, Callaghan (Manager)
Middle: Crown, Walker, Funnell, Shrubb, Harris, Smith, McNichol, Silkman
Front: Eden, Tear, Mahoney, Graham, Rowe, Pullen.

1981-82
Back: Kamara, Bowen, McNichol, Booker, McKellar, Whitehead, Johnson, Roberts, Sweetzer
Front: Harris, Bowles, Rowe, Hurlock, Salman, Tucker.

1981/82

8th in Division Three

							Booker R	Bowen KB	Bowles S	Crown DI	Harris RE	Hill MS	Hurlock TA	Johnson GJ	Johnson RN	Kamara C	Kemp DM	Kruse PK	McKellar DN	McNichol JA	Priddy PJ	Roberts GPM	Rowe NTS	Salman DMM	Shrubb PJ	Spencer AR	Sweetzer GEP	Tonge KA	Tucker WB	Walker PJ	Whitehead A
1	Aug	29	Fulham	2-1	Brown (og), Tucker (p)	7632	9			11	10	3	6						1			8		4	7				2	12	5
2	Sep	5	WALSALL	0-0		5353	9			11	10	3	6						1			8		4	7				2		5
3		12	Portsmouth	2-2	Booker, Crown	10364	9			11	10	3	6						1			8		4					2	7	5
4		19	PLYMOUTH ARGYLE	0-0		4943	9				10	3	6						1			8		4	7				2	11	5
5		21	GILLINGHAM	0-1		5425	9	8			10		6		3				1			11		4	2					7	5
6		26	Doncaster Rovers	0-1		5494		8		11	10	3	6	9					1					4					2	7	5
7		29	Newport County	1-0	Tucker	4040	12	8		11	10	3	6	9					1					4					2	7	5
8	Oct	3	CARLISLE UNITED	1-2	Johnson G	4587	7	8		11	10	3	6	9					1			12		4					2		5
9		10	Exeter City	1-3	Crown	3589	7	8		11		3	6	9					1			10		4					2		5
10		17	LINCOLN CITY	3-1	Tucker, Whitehead, Booker	4187	7	8				3	6	9					1	10		11		4					2		5
11		19	SOUTHEND UNITED	0-1		5403	7	8		12		3	6	9					1	10		11		4					2		5
12		24	Chesterfield	2-0	Roberts, Bowen	5525	7	8			10		6	9					1	4		11		2					3		5
13		31	BURNLEY	0-0		6929		8	10				6	9		7			1	4		11		2					3		5
14	Nov	3	Swindon Town	3-0	Bowen, Johnson G, Kamara	6649	12	8	10				6	9		7			1	4		11		2					3		5
15		7	BRISTOL CITY	0-1		6758	12	8	10				6	9		7			1	4		11		2					3		5
16		14	Oxford United	2-1	Johnson G 2	5693	10	8			2		6	9		7			1	4		11							3		5
17		28	CHESTER	1-0	McNichol	5201	10	8			2		6	9		7				4	1	11							3		5
18	Dec	5	Preston North End	3-1	Bowen 2, Johnson G	4171		8	10				6	9		7			1	4		11		2					3		5
19		28	Millwall	1-0	Roberts	7474		8	10				6	9		7			1	4		11		2					3		5
20	Jan	2	HUDDERSFIELD T	0-1		5438	12	8	10				6	9		7			1	4		11		2					3		5
21		19	Walsall	0-3		3853		8	10		6			9		7			1	4		11		2					3	12	5
22		23	FULHAM	0-1		10834	12	8	10		2			9		7			1	4		11							3	6	5
23		27	Reading	1-4	Sweetzer	3710	8		10		2		6			7		5	1	4							9	12	3	11	
24		30	Plymouth Argyle	0-1		5008	8	12	10				6			7			1	4		11		2			9		3		5
25	Feb	6	PORTSMOUTH	2-2	Tucker (p), Bowles	5947	12	8	10				6			7			1	4		11		2			9		3		5
26		9	Gillingham	1-1	Bowles	3931		8	10			11	6			7			1	4				2			9		3		5
27		13	Carlisle United	0-1		4942		9	10				6			7			1	4		11		2			8		3		5
28		20	NEWPORT COUNTY	2-0	Roberts, Kamara	4297	6	9	10							7			1			11	2	4			8		3		5
29		27	EXETER CITY	2-0	Whitehead, Bowen	4934	6	9	10		7			12					1			11	2	4			8		3		5
30	Mar	6	Lincoln City	0-1		2880	11	9	10		7	12	6				8		1				2	4					3		5
31		8	Southend United	1-1	Kemp	4058	12		10			11	6			7	8		1				2	4			9		3		5
32		13	CHESTERFIELD	2-0	Roberts, Kamara	5374	12		10			3	6	9		7	8		1			11	2	4							5
33		20	Burnley	0-0		7906	10	9				3	6	8		7			1			11	2	4							5
34		22	BRISTOL ROVERS	1-0	Bowles (p)	5840	12	9	10			3	6	8		7			1			11	2	4							5
35		27	Bristol City	1-0	Bowen	6243		9	10			3	6	8		7			1	2		11		4							5
36	Apr	3	OXFORD UNITED	1-2	Booker	5786	6	9	10					8		7			1	2		11		4			12		3		5
37		9	MILLWALL	4-1	Roberts, Booker, Johnson G, McNichol	7460	6	9	10					8		7			1	2		11		4					3		5
38		12	Wimbledon	2-1	Hurlock, Roberts	4513	7	9	10		12		6	8					1	2		11		4					3		5
39		17	PRESTON NORTH END	0-0		5627	5	9	10				6	8		7			1	2		11		4					3		
40		19	SWINDON TOWN	4-2	Hurlock, Bowen, McNichol, Bowles	5374	5	9	10				6	8		7			1	2		11		4					3		
41		24	Chester	2-1	Johnson G, Kamara	1484	5	9	10				6	8		7			1	2		11		4					3		12
42		26	WIMBLEDON	2-3	Johnson G, Bowles	6612	12	9	10				6	8		7			1	2		11		4					3		5
43	May	1	DONCASTER ROVERS	2-2	Whitehead, Bowen	4124	12	9	10			3	6	8		7			1			11		4					2		5
44		3	Bristol Rovers	2-1	Roberts, Kamara	4314	4	9	10		8		6			7			1			11	2			3					5
45		8	Huddersfield Town	1-1	Bowles (p)	4542	4	9	10		8		6			7			1			11	2			3					5
46		15	READING	1-2	Roberts	4502	9		10		8		6			7			1			11	2	4		3					5
						Apps	27	37	31	7	19	17	40	29	1	31	3	1	45	26	1	39	10	40	4	3	8	0	38	7	42
						Subs	11	1		1	1	1		1								1					1	1		2	1
						Goals	4	8	6	2			2	8		5	1			3		8					1		4		3

One own goal

F.A. Cup

							Booker R	Bowen KB	Bowles S	Crown DI	Harris RE	Hill MS	Hurlock TA	Johnson GJ	Johnson RN	Kamara C	Kemp DM	Kruse PK	McKellar DN	McNichol JA	Priddy PJ	Roberts GPM	Rowe NTS	Salman DMM	Shrubb PJ	Spencer AR	Sweetzer GEP	Tonge KA	Tucker WB	Walker PJ	Whitehead A
R1	Nov	21	EXETER CITY	2-0	Bowen 2	6416	10	8			2		6	9		7			1	4		11							3		5
R2	Dec	16	COLCHESTER UNITED	1-1	Roberts	5448		8	10				6	9		7			1	4		11		2					3		5
rep		30	Colchester United	0-1		5532	11	8	10				6	9		7			1	4				2					3		5

F.L. Cup (Milk Cup)

							Booker R	Bowen KB	Bowles S	Crown DI	Harris RE	Hill MS	Hurlock TA	Johnson GJ	Johnson RN	Kamara C	Kemp DM	Kruse PK	McKellar DN	McNichol JA	Priddy PJ	Roberts GPM	Rowe NTS	Salman DMM	Shrubb PJ	Spencer AR	Sweetzer GEP	Tonge KA	Tucker WB	Walker PJ	Whitehead A
R1/1	Sep	2	Oxford United	0-1		3621	9			11	10	3	6						1			8		4	7				2		5
R1/2		15	OXFORD UNITED	0-2		5490	9			11	10	3	6						1			8		4					2	7	5

		Pl.	Home					Away					F.	A.	Pts
			W	D	L	F	A	W	D	L	F	A	(Total)		
1	Burnley	46	13	7	3	37	20	8	10	5	29	25	66	45	80
2	Carlisle United	46	17	4	2	44	21	6	7	10	21	29	65	50	80
3	Fulham	46	12	9	2	44	22	9	6	8	33	29	77	51	78
4	Lincoln City	46	13	7	3	40	16	8	7	8	26	24	66	40	77
5	Oxford United	46	10	8	5	28	18	9	6	8	35	31	63	49	71
6	Gillingham	46	14	5	4	44	26	6	6	11	20	30	64	56	71
7	Southend United	46	11	7	5	35	23	7	8	8	28	28	63	51	69
8	**BRENTFORD**	**46**	**8**	**6**	**9**	**28**	**22**	**11**	**5**	**7**	**28**	**25**	**56**	**47**	**68**
9	Millwall	46	12	4	7	36	28	6	9	8	26	34	62	62	67
10	Plymouth Argyle	46	12	5	6	37	24	6	6	11	27	32	64	56	65
11	Chesterfield	46	12	4	7	33	27	6	6	11	24	31	57	58	64
12	Reading	46	11	6	6	43	35	6	5	12	24	40	67	75	62
13	Portsmouth	46	11	10	2	33	14	3	9	11	23	37	56	51	61
14	Preston North End	46	10	7	6	25	22	6	6	11	25	34	50	56	61
15	Bristol Rovers	46	12	4	7	35	28	6	5	12	23	37	58	65	61
16	Newport County	46	9	10	4	28	21	5	6	12	26	33	54	54	58
17	Huddersfield Town	46	10	5	8	38	25	5	7	11	26	34	64	59	57
18	Exeter City	46	14	4	5	46	33	2	5	16	25	51	71	84	57
19	Doncaster Rovers	46	9	9	5	31	24	4	8	11	24	44	55	68	56
20	Walsall	46	10	7	6	32	23	3	7	13	19	32	51	55	53
21	Wimbledon	46	10	6	7	33	27	4	5	14	28	48	61	75	53
22	Swindon Town	46	9	5	9	37	36	4	8	11	18	35	55	71	52
23	Bristol City	46	7	6	10	24	29	4	7	12	16	36	40	65	46
24	Chester	46	2	10	11	16	30	5	1	17	20	48	36	78	32

1982/83

9th in Division Three

							Booker R	Bowen KB	Bowles S	Cassells KB	Harris RE	Holmes JP	Hurlock TA	Johnson GJ	Joseph F	Kamara C	Mahoney AJ	McNichol JA	Roberts GPM	Roche PJC	Rowe NTS	Salman DMM	Spencer AR	Strong L	Tucker WB	Walker PJ	Whitehead A	Wilkins GG
1	Aug	28	BRISTOL ROVERS	5-1	Joseph 2, Mahoney, Roberts 2	5542			10				6		8	7	9	4	11	1					2		5	3
2	Sep	4	Wigan Athletic	2-3	Joseph, Mahoney	5019	4		10				6	12	8	7	9		11	1					2		5	3
3		8	Reading	1-1	Joseph	3790	4		10				6		8	7	9		11	1					2		5	3
4		11	SOUTHEND UNITED	4-2	Joseph, Mahoney 2, Roberts	5604	4		10				6	12	8	7	9		11	1					2		5	3
5		18	Orient	3-3	Mahoney, Roberts, Booker	3458	5	12	10				6		8	7	9	4	11	1	2				3			
6		25	MILLWALL	1-1	McNichol	6455	5		10				6		8	7	9	4	11	1	2							3
7		28	NEWPORT COUNTY	2-0	Joseph, Mahoney	5706	12		10				6		8	7	9	4	11	1	2						5	3
8	Oct	2	Walsall	1-2	Kamara	2723	12		10				6		8	7	9	4	11	1	2						5	3
9		9	CHESTERFIELD	4-2	Hurlock, Joseph 2, Bowles (p)	5706	12		10				6		8	7	9	4	11	1			3				5	2
10		16	Doncaster Rovers	4-4	McNichol, Mahoney, Roberts, Booker	3266	5	12	10				6		8	7	9	4	11	1		2						3
11		20	Oxford United	2-2	Joseph, Mahoney	6324	5		10				6		8	7	9	4	11	1	2							3
12		23	LINCOLN CITY	2-0	Joseph, Bowen	8017		12	10				6		8	7	9	4	11	1	2						5	3
13		30	Plymouth Argyle	0-2		4036	8	12	10		3		6			7	9	4	11	1	2						5	
14	Nov	2	PRESTON NORTH END	3-1	McNichol, Kamara, Roberts	6142		8	10				6			7	9	4	11	1	2		3				5	
15		6	BRADFORD CITY	0-2		6669			10				6		8	7	9	4	11	1	2		3				5	
16		13	Huddersfield Town	0-2		10034	12				10		6		8	7	9	4	11	1	2						5	3
17		27	Sheffield United	2-1	Joseph, Booker	10202	6		10					12	8	7	9	4	11	1	2						5	3
18	Dec	4	WREXHAM	4-1	Kamara, Joseph 2, Mahoney	5606	4		10						8	7	9		11	1	2					6	5	3
19		18	EXETER CITY	4-0	Whitehead, Bowles, Booker, Walker	5580	4		10				6	9	8	7				1	2					11	5	3
20		27	Portsmouth	1-2	Joseph	14476	4		10				6	9	8	7			11	1				2		12	5	3
21		28	GILLINGHAM	1-1	Joseph	7796	4	12	10					9	8	7			11	1				2		6	5	3
22	Jan	1	Bournemouth	3-4	Joseph 2, Roberts	5593	4	9	10		6			12	8				11	1	3			2		7	5	
23		3	CARDIFF CITY	1-3	Bowles (p)	7602	4		10				6	9	8				11	1	2			3		7	5	
24		8	WIGAN ATHLETIC	1-3	Roberts	4939		9					6		8	7			11	1	2		4	3		10	5	
25		15	Bristol Rovers	0-2		5450	4	12	10				6		8	7			11	1	2					9	5	3
26		22	ORIENT	5-2	Hurlock, Bowles (p), Roberts, Booker 2	5209	4		10		3		6		8	7			11	1	2					9	5	
27		29	Southend United	2-4	Kamara, Roberts	3310	4	12	10		3		6		8	7			11	1	2					9	5	
28	Feb	6	Newport County	0-0		3401		9	10			3	6		8	7		4	11	1	2						5	
29		12	READING	1-2	Bowles (p)	6273	12		10	9		3	6		8	7		4	11	1							5	2
30		19	Chesterfield	1-2	Cassells	2291	2	12	10	9			6		8	7		4	11	1			3				5	
31		26	DONCASTER ROVERS	1-0	Bowles (p)	4413	12		10	9		3	6		8	7		4	11	1	2						5	
32	Mar	1	Preston North End	0-3		3663	12	9	10			3	6		8	7		4	11	1	2						5	
33		5	Lincoln City	1-2	Cassells	3698	12		10	9			6		8	7		4	11	1	2						5	3
34		11	PLYMOUTH ARGYLE	2-0	Kamara, Joseph	4967			10	9			6		8	7		4	11	1	2						5	3
35		19	Bradford City	1-0	Cassells	3828	4		10	9	6				8	7			11	1	2						5	3
36		22	OXFORD UNITED	1-1	Bowles	5086	6		10	9					8	7		4	11	1	2					12	5	3
37		26	HUDDERSFIELD T	1-0	Bowles (p)	6277	3		10	9			6		8	7		4	11	1	2						5	
38	Apr	1	PORTSMOUTH	1-1	Joseph	12593	3		10	9			6		8	7		4	11	1	2						5	
39		2	Gillingham	2-2	Kamara 2	4168	3			9	10		6		8	7		4	11	1	2						5	
40		8	Wrexham	4-3	Kamara, Joseph 2, Cassells	2104	3		10	9			6		8	7		4	11	1	2						5	12
41		16	WALSALL	2-3	Bowles (p), Cassells	4868	8		10	9	6					7		4	11	1	2					12	5	3
42		23	Exeter City	7-1	Kamara 2, Joseph 2, Roberts, Cassells 2	2759	5		10	9			6		8	7		4	11	1	2		3					
43		30	SHEFFIELD UNITED	2-1	Hurlock, Roberts	4987	2		10	9			6		8	7		4	11	1			3			12	5	
44	May	2	Cardiff City	1-3	Kamara	9112	2		10	9			6		8	7		4	11	1			3			12	5	
45		8	Millwall	0-1		9097	2			9	10		6		8	7		4	11	1	3					12	5	
46		14	BOURNEMOUTH	2-1	Joseph, Bowles (p)	6191	9		10				6		8	7		4	11	1	2		3			12	5	
						Apps	31	5	42	16	9	4	39	4	43	44	18	32	45	46	34	1	9	5	5	9	41	24
						Subs	8	8						4												7		1
						Goals	6	1	10	7			3		24	11	9	3	12							1	1	

F.A. Cup

							Booker R	Bowen KB	Bowles S	Cassells KB	Harris RE	Holmes JP	Hurlock TA	Johnson GJ	Joseph F	Kamara C	Mahoney AJ	McNichol JA	Roberts GPM	Roche PJC	Rowe NTS	Salman DMM	Spencer AR	Strong L	Tucker WB	Walker PJ	Whitehead A	Wilkins GG
R1	Nov	20	WINDSOR & ETON	7-0	McNichol, Hurlock 2, Joseph, Mahoney 3	6309	12		10		3		6		8	7	9	4	11	1	2						5	
R2	Dec	11	Swindon Town	2-2	Roberts, Bowen	7176	4	12	10				6		8	7	9		11	1	2						5	3
rep		14	SWINDON TOWN	1-3	Roberts	7883	4	12	10				6		8	7	9		11	1	2						5	3

R1 played at Griffin Park by arrangement. R2 replay a.e.t.

F.L. Cup (Milk Cup)

							Booker R	Bowen KB	Bowles S	Cassells KB	Harris RE	Holmes JP	Hurlock TA	Johnson GJ	Joseph F	Kamara C	Mahoney AJ	McNichol JA	Roberts GPM	Roche PJC	Rowe NTS	Salman DMM	Spencer AR	Strong L	Tucker WB	Walker PJ	Whitehead A	Wilkins GG
R1/1	Aug	30	Wimbledon	1-1	Roberts	2907	4		10				6		8	7	9		11	1			3		2		5	
R1/2	Sep	14	WIMBLEDON	2-0	Mahoney 2	5747			10				6		8	7	9	4	11	1	2				3		5	
R2/1	Oct	5	BLACKBURN ROVERS	3-2	Hurlock, Joseph, Bowles (p)	6201			10				6		8	7	9	4	11	1	2						5	3
R2/2		27	Blackburn Rovers	0-0		4137	6		10		3				8	7	9	4	11	1	2						5	
R3	Nov	9	SWANSEA CITY	1-1	Roberts	15262	12		10		3		6		8	7	9	4	11	1	2						5	
rep		17	Swansea City	2-1	Mahoney, Roberts	6676			10		3		6		8	7	9	4	11	1	2						5	
R4	Dec	1	Notingham Forest	0-2		16479	4	12	10		6				8	7	9		11	1	2						5	3

		Pl.	Home					Away					F.	A.	Pts
			W	D	L	F	A	W	D	L	F	A	(Total)		
1	Portsmouth	46	16	4	3	43	19	11	6	6	31	22	74	41	91
2	Cardiff City	46	17	5	1	45	14	8	6	9	31	36	76	50	86
3	Huddersfield Town	46	15	8	0	56	18	8	5	10	28	31	84	49	82
4	Newport County	46	13	7	3	40	20	10	2	11	36	34	76	54	78
5	Oxford United	46	12	9	2	41	23	10	3	10	30	30	71	53	78
6	Lincoln City	46	17	1	5	55	22	6	6	11	22	29	77	51	76
7	Bristol Rovers	46	16	4	3	55	21	6	5	12	29	37	84	58	75
8	Plymouth Argyle	46	15	2	6	37	23	4	6	13	24	43	61	66	65
9	**BRENTFORD**	**46**	**14**	**4**	**5**	**50**	**28**	**4**	**6**	**13**	**38**	**49**	**88**	**77**	**64**
10	Walsall	46	14	5	4	38	19	3	8	12	26	44	64	63	64
11	Sheffield United	46	16	3	4	44	20	3	4	16	18	44	62	64	64
12	Bradford City	46	11	7	5	41	27	5	6	12	27	42	68	69	61
13	Gillingham	46	12	4	7	37	29	4	9	10	21	30	58	59	61
14	Bournemouth	46	11	7	5	35	20	5	6	12	24	48	59	68	61
15	Southend United	46	10	8	5	41	28	5	6	12	25	37	66	65	59
16	Preston North End	46	11	10	2	35	17	4	3	16	25	52	60	69	58
17	Millwall	46	12	7	4	41	24	2	6	15	23	53	64	77	55
18	Wigan Athletic	46	10	4	9	35	33	5	5	13	25	39	60	72	54
19	Exeter City	46	12	4	7	49	43	2	8	13	32	61	81	104	54
20	Orient	46	10	6	7	44	38	5	3	15	20	50	64	88	54
21	Reading	46	10	8	5	37	28	2	9	12	27	51	64	79	53
22	Wrexham	46	11	6	6	40	26	1	9	13	16	50	56	76	51
23	Doncaster Rovers	46	6	8	9	38	44	3	3	17	19	53	57	97	38
24	Chesterfield	46	6	6	11	28	28	2	7	14	15	40	43	68	37

1982-83
Back: Callaghan (Manager), Bowles, McNichol, Whitehead, Borota, Booker, Bowen, Johnson, Lyons (Physio), Harris (Player/Coach)
Front: Roberts, Hurlock, Mahoney, Joseph, Kamara, Rowe, Tucker, Wilkins, Walker.

1983-84
Back: Roberts, McNichol, Garner, Swinburne, Booker, Roche, Whitehead, Mahoney, Salman
Front: Spencer, Cassells, Hurlock, Kamara, Bullivant, Joseph, Wilkins, Rowe.

1983/84

20th in Division Three

No	Month	Day	Opponent	Res	Scorers	Att	Bolton IR	Booker R	Bowles S	Bullivant TP	Cassells KB	Davies IC	Finney T	Fisher RP	Garner WD	Gray NR	Harris RE	Hurlock TA	Joseph F	Kamara C	Lynch AJ	Mahoney AJ	McNichol JA	Roberts GPM	Roberts P	Roche PJC	Roffey WR	Rollings AN	Rowe NTS	Salman DMM	Spencer AR	Swinburne T	Whitehead A	Wilkins GG
1	Aug	27	MILLWALL	2-2	Kamara, Joseph	6224				10	9							6	8	7			4	11					2		3	1	5	
2	Sep	3	Preston North End	3-3	Joseph, Cassells, Roberts G	3957		2		10	9				12			6	8	7				11						4	3	1	5	
3		6	Bristol Rovers	1-3	Joseph	5148		2		10	9							6	8	7				11					12	4	3	1	5	
4		10	LINCOLN CITY	3-0	Kamara, Joseph 2	4777		11		10	9							6	8	7			12		3				2	4		1	5	
5		17	Wigan Athletic	1-2	Garner	3034		9		10					11			6	8	7			4		3				2		12	1	5	
6		24	BURNLEY	0-0		8042		11		10	9				8		6			7			4		3				2			1	5	12
7	Oct	1	Gillingham	2-4	McNichol, Kamara	3268		6		10										7			9	11	8				2	4	3	1	5	
8		8	Oxford United	1-2	Kamara	7326		12		10							6		8	7	9		2	11						4		1	5	3
9		15	HULL CITY	1-1	Joseph	4258		10			9						6		8	7			2	11						4		1	5	3
10		18	PORT VALE	3-1	McNichol, Bullivant, Roberts G	3903		6		10									8	7	9		2	11						4		1	5	3
11		22	Sheffield United	0-0		9848		6		10									8	7			9	11					2	4		1	5	3
12		29	BOURNEMOUTH	1-1	Joseph	4630		6		10	9								8	7		12	2	11						4		1	5	3
13		31	Southend United	0-6		3182		6		10	9								8	7		12		11					2	4	3	1	5	
14	Nov	5	PLYMOUTH ARGYLE	2-2	Cassells, Mahoney	4183		6		10	9								8			7		11	3				2	4		1	5	
15		12	Orient	0-2		3650				10		3							8	7		9		11	2					4		1	5	6
16		26	BRADFORD CITY	1-4	Roberts G	3738				10		6							8	7		9	2	11	3	1		5	12	4				
17	Dec	3	Bolton Wanderers	0-1		5416			10										8	7		9	4	11	6				2			1	5	3
18		17	Walsall	0-1		3965	4	12	10									6	8	7		9	2	11	3	1							5	
19		24	WIMBLEDON	3-4	McNichol, Hurlock, Kamara	6689	4		10		12							6	8	7		9	2	11	3							1	5	
20		27	Exeter City	2-1	Cassells, Roberts G	4303	4		10	7	12							6	8			9	5	11	3	1			2					
21		31	NEWPORT COUNTY	2-0	Hurlock, Roberts G	4631	4		10	7	12							6	8			9	5	11	3	1			2					
22	Jan	2	Scunthorpe United	4-4	McNichol, Joseph, Cassells (p), Mahoney	2239	4	12		7	10							6	8			9	5	11	3	1			2					
23		15	Millwall	2-1	Joseph 2	5370	4			7	10							6	8			9		11	3	1			2	5				
24		21	WIGAN ATHLETIC	0-1		3972	4		12	7	10							6	8			9		11	3	1			2	5				
25	Feb	1	Lincoln City	0-2		2266	4	2	10	7	9							6	8			12	5	11		1								3
26		4	GILLINGHAM	2-3	Joseph, Bolton	4317	4	3	10	7	9								8	6		12	5	11		1								2
27		11	Burnley	2-2	Kamara, Cassells	7027	5			8	10								9	7			2	11	6	1				4				3
28		14	SOUTHEND UNITED	0-0		3961	5				10		8					6	9	7				11	2	1				4				3
29		18	Bournemouth	3-0	Cassells 3	4308	5				10		8	2				6	9	7				11	3	1				4				
30		25	SHEFFIELD UNITED	1-3	Roberts G	5100	5				10		8	2				6	9	7		12		11	3	1				4				
31	Mar	3	Port Vale	3-4	Joseph, Roberts G, Gray	3704	5				9		8	2		4		6	10	7				11	3							1		
32		6	Plymouth Argyle	1-1	Hurlock	4322					10		8	3		5		6	9	7		12		11	4	1								2
33		10	ORIENT	1-1	Joseph	4358				7			8	3		5		6	9	12		10		11	4	1				2				
34		17	OXFORD UNITED	1-2	Roberts G	5936							8	2		5		6	9	7		10		11	4	1	3							
35		20	ROTHERHAM UNITED	2-1	Booker, Mahoney (p)	3391		11					8	2		5		6	9	7		10				1	3			4				
36		24	Hull City	0-2		5572		11			10		8	2		5		6	9	7					4	1	3		12					
37		31	BRISTOL ROVERS	2-2	Hurlock, Booker	4067		11					8	2		5		6	12	7				9	4	1	3		10					
38	Apr	3	PRESTON NORTH END	4-1	Kamara, Roberts G, Booker, Finney	3446		10					8			5		6	9	7				11	4	1	3		2					
39		7	Rotherham United	0-4		3705		10					8	2		5		6	9	7				11	4	1	3							
40		14	BOLTON WANDERERS	3-0	Joseph 2, Deakin (og)	3831		10			12		8	2		5		6	9	7				11	4	1	3							
41		20	EXETER CITY	3-0	Joseph, Booker, Finney	5620		10					8	2		5		6	9	7				11	4	1	3							
42		21	Wimbledon	1-2	Joseph	5487		10			11			2		5		6	9	7				12	4	1	3		8					
43		28	Bradford City	1-1	Cassells	3755		10			8			2		5		6	9	7		12		11	4	1	3							
44	May	5	SCUNTHORPE UNITED	3-0	Rowe, Joseph, Roffey	4561		10			8			2		5		6	9			12		11	4		3		7			1		
45		7	Newport County	1-1	Roberts G	2154		10			8			2		5		6		7		9		11	4		3					1		
46		12	WALSALL	1-1	Caswell (og)	5281		10			8		12	2		5		6	9	7				11	4		3					1		
						Apps	14	26	7	24	26	2	14	17	2	16	3	32	42	37	2	15	19	40	34	25	13	1	18	21	5	21	18	12
						Subs		3	1		4		1		1				1	1		8	1	1					3		1			1
						Goals	1	4		1	9		2		1	1		4	18	7		3	4	10			1		1					

Two own goals

F.A. Cup

Rd	Month	Day	Opponent	Res	Scorers	Att	Bolton IR	Booker R	Bowles S	Bullivant TP	Cassells KB	Davies IC	Finney T	Fisher RP	Garner WD	Gray NR	Harris RE	Hurlock TA	Joseph F	Kamara C	Lynch AJ	Mahoney AJ	McNichol JA	Roberts GPM	Roberts P	Roche PJC	Roffey WR	Rollings AN	Rowe NTS	Salman DMM	Spencer AR	Swinburne T	Whitehead A	Wilkins GG
R1	Nov	19	Dagenham	2-2	Joseph, Roberts P	2146				10								6	8	7		9	2	11	3	1				4			5	
rep		22	DAGENHAM	2-1	Roberts G, Mahoney	3936				10								6	8	7		9	2	11	3	1				4			5	12
R2	Dec	10	WIMBLEDON	3-2	Kamara, Joseph, Roberts G	5666			10									6	8	7		9	4	11	3				2			1	5	
R3	Jan	7	Gillingham	3-5	Hurlock, Cassells, Roberts G	6509	4	12		7	10							6	8			9	5	11	3	1			2					

F.L. Cup (Milk Cup)

Rd	Month	Day	Opponent	Res	Scorers	Att	Bolton IR	Booker R	Bowles S	Bullivant TP	Cassells KB	Davies IC	Finney T	Fisher RP	Garner WD	Gray NR	Harris RE	Hurlock TA	Joseph F	Kamara C	Lynch AJ	Mahoney AJ	McNichol JA	Roberts GPM	Roberts P	Roche PJC	Roffey WR	Rollings AN	Rowe NTS	Salman DMM	Spencer AR	Swinburne T	Whitehead A	Wilkins GG
1/1	Aug	30	CHARLTON ATHLETIC	3-0	Joseph, Roberts G, Berry (og)	4858		2		10	9							6	8	7				11						4	3	1	5	
1/2	Sep	13	Charlton Athletic	1-2	Joseph	3622		9		10							11	6	8	7			4						2		3	1	5	
2/1	Oct	5	LIVERPOOL	1-4	Roberts G	17859		12		10							6		8	7		9	2	11					3	4		1	5	
2/2		25	Liverpool	0-4		9092		6		10	9								8	7			2	11					12	4		1	5	3

A.M. Cup

Rd	Month	Day	Opponent	Res	Scorers	Att	Bolton IR	Booker R	Bowles S	Bullivant TP	Cassells KB	Davies IC	Finney T	Fisher RP	Garner WD	Gray NR	Harris RE	Hurlock TA	Joseph F	Kamara C	Lynch AJ	Mahoney AJ	McNichol JA	Roberts GPM	Roberts P	Roche PJC	Roffey WR	Rollings AN	Rowe NTS	Salman DMM	Spencer AR	Swinburne T	Whitehead A	Wilkins GG
R1	Feb	21	LEYTON ORIENT	3-2	Finney, Joseph 2	2301	5	3			12		8	2				6	9		7	10		11						4		1		
R2	Mar	26	Plymouth Argyle	0-2		2308	5	10			12			2		4		6	9	7	11			14	3				8			1		

R2 a.e.t.

		Pl.	Home W	Home D	Home L	Home F	Home A	Away W	Away D	Away L	Away F	Away A	F. (Total)	A. (Total)	Pts
1	Oxford United	46	17	5	1	58	22	11	6	6	33	28	91	50	95
2	Wimbledon	46	15	5	3	58	35	11	4	8	39	41	97	76	87
3	Sheffield United	46	14	7	2	56	18	10	4	9	30	35	86	53	83
4	Hull City	46	16	5	2	42	11	7	9	7	29	27	71	38	83
5	Bristol Rovers	46	16	5	2	47	21	6	8	9	21	33	68	54	79
6	Walsall	46	14	4	5	44	22	8	5	10	24	39	68	61	75
7	Bradford City	46	11	9	3	46	30	9	2	12	27	35	73	65	71
8	Gillingham	46	13	4	6	50	29	7	6	10	24	40	74	69	70
9	Millwall	46	16	4	3	42	18	2	9	12	29	47	71	65	67
10	Bolton Wanderers	46	13	4	6	36	17	5	6	12	20	43	56	60	64
11	Orient	46	13	5	5	40	27	5	4	14	31	54	71	81	63
12	Burnley	46	12	5	6	52	25	4	9	10	24	36	76	61	62
13	Newport County	46	11	9	3	35	27	5	5	13	23	48	58	75	62
14	Lincoln City	46	11	4	8	42	29	6	6	11	17	33	59	62	61
15	Wigan Athletic	46	11	5	7	26	18	5	8	10	20	38	46	56	61
16	Preston North End	46	12	5	6	42	27	3	6	14	24	39	66	66	56
17	Bournemouth	46	11	5	7	38	27	5	2	16	25	46	63	73	55
18	Rotherham United	46	10	5	8	29	17	5	4	14	28	47	57	64	54
19	Plymouth Argyle	46	11	8	4	38	17	2	4	17	18	45	56	62	51
20	**BRENTFORD**	**46**	**8**	**9**	**6**	**41**	**30**	**3**	**7**	**13**	**28**	**49**	**69**	**79**	**49**
21	Scunthorpe United	46	9	9	5	40	31	0	10	13	14	42	54	73	46
22	Southend United	46	8	9	6	34	24	2	5	16	21	52	55	76	44
23	Port Vale	46	10	4	9	33	29	1	6	16	18	54	51	83	43
24	Exeter City	46	4	8	11	27	39	2	7	14	23	45	50	84	33

1984/85

13th in Division Three

							Alexander RS	Booker R	Bullivant TP	Butler S	Cassells KB	Cooke RL	Finney T	Fisher RP	Hurlock TA	Joseph F	Joseph RA	Kamara C	Key RM	Lynch AJ	Millen KD	Murray JG	Phillips GC	Roberts GPM	Roberts P	Rowe NTS	Salman DMM	Swinburne T	Torrance GC	Wignall SL
1	Aug	25	ORIENT	0-1		4171					10		8	2	6	9		7				3		11	4		5	1		
2	Sep	1	Walsall	1-0	Booker	4747		10			12		8	2	6	9		7				3		11	4		5	1		
3		8	WIGAN ATHLETIC	2-0	Salman, Cassells	3724		10			12			2	6	9		7				3		11	4		5	1		8
4		18	Rotherham United	1-1	Hurlock	3644		10			9			2	6				1	8		3		11	4	7				5
5		22	SWANSEA CITY	3-0	Hurlock, Cassells 2	4298		10			9			2	6			7		12		3		11	4		8	1		5
6		29	Cambridge United	2-1	Kamara, Cassells	2580	10				9			2	6			7				3		11	4		8	1		5
7	Oct	2	DONCASTER ROVERS	1-1	Harle (og)	4901	10	7			9			2	6							3		11	4		8	1		5
8		6	BRADFORD CITY	0-1		4196		7			9			2	6			10		12		3		11	4		8	1		5
9		13	Millwall	0-2		5385	10				9			2	6			7		12		3		11	4		8	1		5
10		20	GILLINGHAM	5-2	Cassells, Roberts G 3, Alexander	4053	10	8			9			2	6			7				3		11	4			1		5
11		23	Burnley	1-3	Malley (og)	2916	10				9			2	6			7				3		11	4		8	1		5
12		27	YORK CITY	2-1	Salman, Roberts G	4261	10	12			9			2	6			7				3		11	4		8	1		5
13	Nov	3	Bristol City	1-1	Kamara	7674	10	8			9			2	6			7				3		11	4		5	1		
14		7	Derby County	0-1		10530	10				9		8		6			7				3		11	4		2	1		5
15		10	LINCOLN CITY	2-2	Cassells, Booker	4115	10	8			9		6					7				3		11	4		2	1		5
16		24	Bournemouth	0-1		4113	10				9		6	2	8			7				3		11	4		5	1		
17		27	Newport County	0-2		1589	10	6			9			2	8			7				3		11	4		5	1		
18	Dec	1	BOLTON WANDERERS	2-1	Kamara, Cassells	3668	10	12			9			2	8			7				3		11	4		5	1		6
19		15	Preston North End	1-1	Roberts G	2818	10	9						2	8			7				3		11	4		5	1		6
20		22	Hull City	0-4		6354	10	12		9				2	8							3		11	4		5	1	7	6
21		26	BRISTOL ROVERS	0-3		5254	10	7			9			2	8							3	1	11	4		6			5
22		29	READING	2-1	Booker, Richardson (og)	5161	12	9			10			2	8			7				3	1	11	4				6	5
23	Jan	1	Plymouth Argyle	1-1	Alexander	6926	12	4			9	8						7				3	1	11	2		5		10	6
24		19	Wigan Athletic	1-1	Cooke	3358	10	5			9	8			6			7				3			2		11	1	4	
25		26	NEWPORT COUNTY	2-5	Kamara (p), Cooke	3962		2		9		8		12	6			7		10		3			5		4	1	11	
26	Feb	2	CAMBRIDGE UNITED	2-0	Torrance, Cooke	3254		2			9	11			6			7		10		3			12		4	1	8	5
27		9	Swansea City	2-3	Kamara, Cooke	4440		2			9	8			6			7		10		3					4	1	11	5
28		16	Doncaster Rovers	2-2	Salman, Cooke	3129		9				11		2	6			7				3			4		10	1	8	5
29		23	BRISTOL CITY	1-2	Booker	4526		9				11		2	6			7		12		3	1		4		10		8	5
30	Mar	2	York City	0-1		4288	9	5				10		2	6			7		8	12	3	1	11			4			
31		5	BURNLEY	2-1	Butler, Cooke	3267				9	8	11		2	6			7			5	3	1	10			4			
32		9	Gillingham	0-2		5799					9	10		2	6			7			8	3	1	11			4			5
33		23	Bradford City	4-5	Booker, Cooke 3	6038		9			10	8		2	6						7	3	1				4		11	5
34		27	WALSALL	3-1	Hurlock, Roberts G, Cooke	3021		10			9	8			6			7			4	3	1	11			2			5
35		30	DERBY COUNTY	1-1	Roberts G	4423		10			9	8			6			7			4	3	1	11			2			5
36	Apr	6	Bristol Rovers	0-3		4419		10			9	8			6			7			4	3	1	11			2			5
37		8	PLYMOUTH ARGYLE	3-1	Cassells 2 (1p), Roberts G	4043		10			9	8		5	6			7			4	3	1	11			2			
38		13	Lincoln City	1-1	Cooke	1980		10	6		9	8						7			4	3	1	11			2			5
39		16	Orient	1-0	Booker	3164		10			9	8			6			7			4	3	1	11			2			5
40		20	BOURNEMOUTH	0-0		3559		10	7		9	8			6						4	3	1	11			2			5
41		23	ROTHERHAM UNITED	3-0	Cassells, Roberts G 2	3019		9	7		10	8			6						4	3	1	11			2			5
42		27	Bolton Wanderers	1-1	Kamara	4230		9	7		10	8			6			12			4	3	1	11			2			5
43	May	4	PRESTON NORTH END	3-1	Roberts G, Booker, Cooke	3476		9	6		10	8						7		12	4	3	1	11			2			5
44		6	Reading	0-0		3898		9			10	8						7			4	3	1	11			2		6	5
45		11	HULL CITY	2-1	Skipper (og), Cassells (p)	4309		9			10	8			6			7			4	3	1	11			2		12	5
46		19	MILLWALL	1-1	Cassells	5050		10			9	8					2	7			4	3	1	11			6		12	5
						Apps	17	35	5	3	38	24	5	27	40	3	1	38	1	5	16	46	21	39	27	1	43	24	11	36
						Subs	2	3			2			1				1		5	1				1				2	
						Goals	2	7		1	12	12			3			6						11			3		1	

Four own goals

F.A. Cup

							Alexander RS	Booker R	Bullivant TP	Butler S	Cassells KB	Cooke RL	Finney T	Fisher RP	Hurlock TA	Joseph F	Joseph RA	Kamara C	Key RM	Lynch AJ	Millen KD	Murray JG	Phillips GC	Roberts GPM	Roberts P	Rowe NTS	Salman DMM	Swinburne T	Torrance GC	Wignall SL
R1	Nov	17	BISHOP'S STORTFORD	4-0	Cassells 2, Alexander 2	3948	10	12			9		6	2	8			7				3		11	4		5	1		
R2	Dec	8	NORTHAMPTON T	2-2	Cassells (p), Alexander	4449	10				9			2	8			7				3		11	4		5	1		6
rep		17	Northampton Town	2-0	Hurlock, Cassells	3610		10			9			2	8			7				3		11	4		5	1		6
R3	Jan	5	Oldham Athletic	1-2	Kamara	4163	10	2			9				8			7				3		11			5	1	4	6

F.L. Cup (Milk Cup)

							Alexander RS	Booker R	Bullivant TP	Butler S	Cassells KB	Cooke RL	Finney T	Fisher RP	Hurlock TA	Joseph F	Joseph RA	Kamara C	Key RM	Lynch AJ	Millen KD	Murray JG	Phillips GC	Roberts GPM	Roberts P	Rowe NTS	Salman DMM	Swinburne T	Torrance GC	Wignall SL
R1/1	Aug	28	CAMBRIDGE UNITED	2-0	Roberts G 2	3037		10					8	2	6	9		7				3		11	4		5	1		
R1/2	Sep	4	Cambridge United	0-1		2347		10					8	2	6	9		7				3		11	4		5	1		
R2/1		26	Leicester City	2-4	Kamara, Alexander	7638	10				9			2	6			7				3		11	4		8	1		5
R2/2	Oct	9	LEICESTER CITY	0-2		6291	10				9			2	6			7		12		3		11	4		8	1		5

A.M. Cup (Freight Rover Trophy)

							Alexander RS	Booker R	Bullivant TP	Butler S	Cassells KB	Cooke RL	Finney T	Fisher RP	Hurlock TA	Joseph F	Joseph RA	Kamara C	Key RM	Lynch AJ	Millen KD	Murray JG	Phillips GC	Roberts GPM	Roberts P	Rowe NTS	Salman DMM	Swinburne T	Torrance GC	Wignall SL
R1/1	Feb	6	Reading	3-1	Torrance 2, Roberts P	2500		5			9	8			6			7		10		3	1	12	2		4		11	
R1/2		26	READING	2-0	Wignall, Roberts D	2011		9				11		2	6			7		8		3	1	10	12		4		14	5
R2	Mar	19	CAMBRIDGE UNITED	1-0	Cooke	2003	12		11	8	9	10		2	6						7	3	1				4		14	5
QF	Apr	11	Swansea City	2-0	Booker 2	1653		10	6		9	8						7			4	3	1	11			2			5
SFS		30	Bournemouth	3-2	Cooke 2, Kamara	4657		9	7			8			6			10			4	3	1	11			2			5
FS	May	17	NEWPORT COUNTY	6-0	Cassells 2 (1p), Roberts G 4	8214		9	12		10	8			6			7			4	3	1	11			2			5
F	Jun	1	Wigan Athletic	1-3	Cooke	39897		9	12		10	8			6			7			4	3	1	11			2			5

Final at Wembley Stadium

		Pl.	Home W	D	L	F	A	Away W	D	L	F	A	F. (Total)	A.	Pts
1	Bradford City	46	15	6	2	44	23	13	4	6	33	22	77	45	94
2	Millwall	46	18	5	0	44	12	8	7	8	29	30	73	42	90
3	Hull City	46	16	4	3	46	20	9	8	6	32	29	78	49	87
4	Gillingham	46	15	5	3	54	29	10	3	10	26	33	80	62	83
5	Bristol City	46	17	2	4	46	19	7	7	9	28	28	74	47	81
6	Bristol Rovers	46	15	6	2	37	13	6	6	11	29	35	66	48	75
7	Derby County	46	14	7	2	40	20	5	6	12	25	34	65	54	70
8	York City	46	13	5	5	42	22	7	4	12	28	35	70	57	69
9	Reading	46	8	7	8	31	29	11	5	7	37	33	68	62	69
10	Bournemouth	46	16	3	4	42	16	3	8	12	15	30	57	46	68
11	Walsall	46	9	7	7	33	22	9	6	8	25	30	58	52	67
12	Rotherham United	46	11	6	6	36	24	7	5	11	19	31	55	55	65
13	**BRENTFORD**	**46**	**13**	**5**	**5**	**42**	**27**	**3**	**9**	**11**	**20**	**37**	**62**	**64**	**62**
14	Doncaster Rovers	46	11	5	7	42	33	6	3	14	30	41	72	74	59
15	Plymouth Argyle	46	11	7	5	33	23	4	7	12	29	42	62	65	59
16	Wigan Athletic	46	12	6	5	36	22	3	8	12	24	42	60	64	59
17	Bolton Wanderers	46	12	5	6	38	22	4	1	18	31	53	69	75	54
18	Newport County	46	9	6	8	30	30	4	7	12	25	37	55	67	52
19	Lincoln City	46	8	11	4	32	20	3	7	13	18	31	50	51	51
20	Swansea City	46	7	5	11	31	39	5	6	12	22	41	53	80	47
21	Burnley	46	6	8	9	30	24	5	5	13	30	49	60	73	46
22	Orient	46	7	7	9	30	36	4	6	13	21	40	51	76	46
23	Preston North End	46	9	5	9	33	41	4	2	17	18	59	51	100	46
24	Cambridge United	46	2	3	18	17	48	2	6	15	20	47	37	95	21

1984-85

Back: Lyons (Physio), Finney, Kamara, Roberts, Swinburne, Key, Booker, Wignall, Salman
Middle: McLintock (Manager), Bullivant, Cassells, Fisher, Hurlock, Murray, Joseph, Roberts, Docherty (Asst.Manager)
Front: Myers, Brophy, Lynch, Millen, Spencer, Rowe

1985-86

Back: Salman, Millen, Butler, Evans, Booker, Bates. Wignall
Middles: Alexander, Torrance, F.Joseph, Phillips, R.Joseph, Cooke, Murray
Front: McLintock (Manager), Lyons (Physio), Lynch, Hurlock, Bullivant, Fisher, Docherty (Asst. Manager), Hills (Youth Team Coach).

1985/86

10th in Division Three

						Alexander RS	Booker R	Bullivant TP	Burke SJ	Butler S	Cooke RL	Cooper GJ	Evans TW	Holloway IS	Hurlock TA	Joseph F	Joseph RA	Key RM	Lynch AJ	Millen KD	Murray JG	Phillips GC	Roberts GPM	Salman DMM	Sinton A	Torrance GC	Wignall SL
1	Aug 17	WOLVERHAMPTON W.	2-1	Murray, Bullivant	5576		9	11		10	8		12		6				7	4	3	1		2			5
2	24	Bristol Rovers	1-0	Lynch	4140		9	10			8		5		6				7		3	1		2		11	4
3	26	BOURNEMOUTH	1-0	Cooke	4283		9	10			8		5		6				7		3	1		2		11	4
4	31	Wigan Athletic	0-4		2871		9				8		5		6		7		12	10	3	1		2		11	4
5	Sep 7	PLYMOUTH ARGYLE	1-1	Lynch	3927	10	9				8	11			6				7	4	3	1		2		12	5
6	13	Doncaster Rovers	0-1		2831		9				8	11			6	10			7	4	3	1		2			5
7	17	READING	1-2	Booker	6351	12	9				8	11			6	10			7	4	3	1		2			5
8	21	Lincoln City	0-3		1856	12	9				8	11			6				7	4	3	1		2		10	5
9	28	ROTHERHAM UNITED	1-1	Alexander	3257	8	9				10	11			6				7	4	3	1		2		12	5
10	Oct 1	Darlington	5-3	Lynch, Booker, Alexander 3	2447	11	9				12	10			6		8		7	4	3	1		2			5
11	5	SWANSEA CITY	1-0	Alexander	3508	10	9				6	11					8		7	4	3	1		2		12	5
12	12	Bolton Wanderers	2-1	Wignall, Cooke	4106	10	9				8	11			6		2		7	4	3	1					5
13	19	NEWPORT COUNTY	0-0		3646	10	9				8	11			6		2		12	4	3	1		7			5
14	22	Walsall	2-1	Wignall, Hurlock	4318	10	9				8				6		2		7		3	1		4		11	5
15	26	Blackpool	0-4		5448	10	9				8	12			6		2		7		3	1		4		11	5
16	Nov 2	CARDIFF CITY	3-0	Hurlock, Lynch, Cooke	3934	10	9			12	8		4		6				7		3	1		2		11	5
17	6	DERBY COUNTY	3-3	Murray, Cooke, Butler	4707		9			10	8		4		6				7		3	1		2		11	5
18	9	Bristol City	0-0		6598		9			10	8		4		6				7		3	1		2		11	5
19	23	CHESTERFIELD	1-0	Roberts	3502	10	9	6		8			4								3	1	7	2		11	5
20	30	York City	0-1		3674	10	9			8			4		6				12		3	1	7	2		11	5
21	Dec 14	BURY	1-0	Sinton (p)	4038		11			9	10		5		6					4	3	1	7	2	8		
22	22	BRISTOL ROVERS	1-0	Cooke	5724	9	11				10		5		6		2				3	1		4	8	7	
23	28	Bournemouth	0-0		4006	9	11				10		5		6		2				3	1		4	8	7	
24	Jan 4	Cardiff City	0-1		3398	9	11				10		5		6		2			12	3	1		4	8	7	
25	11	WIGAN ATHLETIC	1-3	Booker	4048	6	11			9	10		5				2			12	3	1		4	8	7	
26	18	Wolverhampton Wan.	4-1	Cooke 2, Sinton 2	3420	9					10		5		6		2	1	11		3			4	8	7	
27	21	NOTTS COUNTY	1-1	Evans	4002	9					10		5		6		2	1	7		3			4	8	11	
28	24	DONCASTER ROVERS	1-3	Cooke	3568	12	11			9	10		5		6		2	1	7		3			4	8		
29	Feb 1	Plymouth Argyle	0-2		4873	12	11				10		5		6		2		7	9	3	1		4	8		
30	4	WALSALL	1-3	Alexander	3015	9	11				10		5		6		2		7	3		1		4	8		
31	Mar 1	Rotherham United	2-1	Cooke, Booker	3260	9	11	6			10								7	4	3	1		2	8		5
32	8	Swansea City	0-2		3683	9	11	6			10						12		7	4	3	1		2	8		5
33	11	Newport County	2-1	Lynch, Cooke	1508	9	11	6			10						5		7	4	3	1		2	8		
34	14	BOLTON WANDERERS	1-1	Booker	3284	9	6				10			11			2		7	4	3	1		5	8		
35	18	Gillingham	2-1	Cooke, Booker	3558	9	11	12			10			7			2			4	3	1		5	8	6	
36	22	BLACKPOOL	1-1	Cooke	3528	9	6			12	10			11			2		7	4	3	1		5	8		
37	29	Notts County	4-0	Cooke 2, Holloway, Burke	3857		6		7	9	10			11			2			4	3	1		5	8		
38	31	GILLINGHAM	1-2	Cooke	4702		6		11	9	10			7						4	3	1		2	8		5
39	Apr 5	Derby County	1-1	Holloway	11026		6		11	9	10			7					12	4	3	1		2	8		5
40	13	BRISTOL CITY	1-2	Millen	3701		6		11	9	10			7					12	4	3	1		2	8		5
41	16	Reading	1-3	Murray	6855		6		7	9	10			11		12	2			4	3	1			8		5
42	19	Chesterfield	3-1	Cooke, Booker, Butler	2344		6		11	9	10			7		12	2			4	3	1			8		5
43	22	LINCOLN CITY	0-1		3011		6		7	9	10			11		12	2			4	3	1		5	8		
44	26	YORK CITY	3-3	Hood (og), Joseph R, Joseph F	2864		6		7		10			11		9	2			4	3	1			8		5
45	May 3	Bury	0-0		2953		6		7	12	10			11		9	2		5	4	3	1			8		
46	5	DARLINGTON	2-1	Millen, Cooke	2824		6		7		10			11		9	2		5	4	3	1			8		
					Apps	24	44	7	10	15	43	9	18	13	27	5	27	3	28	30	45	43	3	40	26	18	28
					Subs	4		1		3	1	1	1			3	1		5	2						3	
					Goals	6	7	1	1	2	17		1	2	2	1	1		5	2	3		1		3		2

One own goal

F.A. Cup

						Alexander RS	Booker R	Bullivant TP	Burke SJ	Butler S	Cooke RL	Cooper GJ	Evans TW	Holloway IS	Hurlock TA	Joseph F	Joseph RA	Key RM	Lynch AJ	Millen KD	Murray JG	Phillips GC	Roberts GPM	Salman DMM	Sinton A	Torrance GC	Wignall SL
R1	Nov 16	BRISTOL ROVERSS	1-3	Evans	4716	10	9	6			8		4						7		3	1		2		11	5

F.L. Cup (Milk Cup)

						Alexander RS	Booker R	Bullivant TP	Burke SJ	Butler S	Cooke RL	Cooper GJ	Evans TW	Holloway IS	Hurlock TA	Joseph F	Joseph RA	Key RM	Lynch AJ	Millen KD	Murray JG	Phillips GC	Roberts GPM	Salman DMM	Sinton A	Torrance GC	Wignall SL
R1/1	Aug 20	Cambridge United	1-1	Booker	1794		9	10			8		5		6		2		7	4	3	1				11	
R1/2	Sep 3	CAMBRIDGE UNITED	2-0	Hurlock, Cooke (p)	2512	12	9				8				6		2		7	4	3	1		10		11	5
R2/1	25	SHEFFIELD WEDNESDA	2-2	Alexander 2	5352	10	9				8				6				7	4	3	1		2		11	5
R2/2	Oct 15	Sheffield Wednesday	0-2		11132	10	9				8				6		2		7	4	3	1				11	5

A.M. Cup (Freight Rover Trophy)

						Alexander RS	Booker R	Bullivant TP	Burke SJ	Butler S	Cooke RL	Cooper GJ	Evans TW	Holloway IS	Hurlock TA	Joseph F	Joseph RA	Key RM	Lynch AJ	Millen KD	Murray JG	Phillips GC	Roberts GPM	Salman DMM	Sinton A	Torrance GC	Wignall SL
R1	Jan 15	DERBY COUNTY	0-0		2531	12				9	10		5				2		11	6	3	1		4	8	7	
R1	29	Gillingham	1-1	Murray	1464	9	11				10		5		6		2		7		3	1		4	8		

		Pl.	Home					Away					F.	A.	Pts
			W	D	L	F	A	W	D	L	F	A	(Total)		
1	Reading	46	16	3	4	39	22	13	4	6	28	29	67	51	94
2	Plymouth Argyle	46	17	3	3	56	20	9	6	8	32	33	88	53	87
3	Derby County	46	13	7	3	45	20	10	8	5	35	21	80	41	84
4	Wigan Athletic	46	17	4	2	54	17	6	10	7	28	31	82	48	83
5	Gillingham	46	14	5	4	48	17	8	8	7	33	37	81	54	79
6	Walsall	46	15	7	1	59	23	7	2	14	31	41	90	64	75
7	York City	46	16	4	3	49	17	4	7	12	28	41	77	58	71
8	Notts County	46	12	6	5	42	26	7	8	8	29	34	71	60	71
9	Bristol City	46	14	5	4	43	19	4	9	10	26	41	69	60	68
10	**BRENTFORD**	**46**	**8**	**8**	**7**	**29**	**29**	**10**	**4**	**9**	**29**	**32**	**58**	**61**	**66**
11	Doncaster Rovers	46	7	10	6	20	21	9	6	8	25	31	45	52	64
12	Blackpool	46	11	6	6	38	19	6	6	11	28	36	66	55	63
13	Darlington	46	10	7	6	39	33	5	6	12	22	45	61	78	58
14	Rotherham United	46	13	5	5	44	18	2	7	14	17	41	61	59	57
15	Bournemouth	46	9	6	8	41	31	6	3	14	24	41	65	72	54
16	Bristol Rovers	46	9	8	6	27	21	5	4	14	24	54	51	75	54
17	Chesterfield	46	10	6	7	41	30	3	8	12	20	34	61	64	53
18	Bolton Wanderers	46	10	4	9	35	30	5	4	14	19	38	54	68	53
19	Newport County	46	7	8	8	35	33	4	10	9	17	32	52	65	51
20	Bury	46	11	7	5	46	26	1	6	16	17	41	63	67	49
21	Lincoln City	46	7	9	7	33	34	3	7	13	22	43	55	77	46
22	Cardiff City	46	7	5	11	22	29	5	4	14	31	54	53	83	45
23	Wolverhampton W.	46	6	6	11	29	47	5	4	14	28	51	57	98	43
24	Swansea City	46	9	6	8	27	27	2	4	17	16	60	43	87	43

1986/87

11th in Division Three

No	Month	Day	Opponent	Score	Scorers	Att	Bater PT	Bates JA	Blissett GP	Booker R	Carroll R	Cooke RL	Droy MR	Evans TW	Geddis D	Holloway IS	Hughton HT	Joseph F	Joseph RA	Maddy PM	Merson PC	Millen KD	Murray IG	Nogan LM	Obi AL	Perryman SJ	Phillips GC	Power J	Priest P	Sinton A	Stevens GM	Turner WL	Wignall SL	Key RM
1	Aug	23	BOURNEMOUTH	1-1	Cooke (p)	3856				6		9				7		10	2	11		4	3				1			8			5	
2		30	Doncaster Rovers	0-2		1675	3			6		9				11		12	2			4			7		1			8	10		5	
3	Sep	6	PORT VALE	0-2		3150	3					9						10	2	11		4			7		1			8	12	6	5	
4		13	Fulham	3-1	Joseph R, Cooke, Stevens	4820	3					10				11			2			4	5		7		1			8	9	6		
5		16	Carlisle United	0-0		2904	3	5				10				11			2			4			7		1			8	9	6		
6		20	DARLINGTON	5-3	Cooke 2 (1p), Bater, Stevens 2	3265	3					10				11			2			4	5		7		1			8	9	6		
7		27	Gillingham	0-2		4710		12				10		5		11	3		2			4			7		1			8	9	6		
8		30	BURY	0-2		3238										11	5	10	2	12		4	3		7		1			8	9	6		
9	Oct	4	NEWPORT COUNTY	2-0	Sinton, Maddy	3231		5				10					6		2	11		4	3		7		1			8	9			
10		11	Mansfield Town	0-1		3456		5				10						12	2	11		4	3		7		1			8	9	6		
11		18	YORK CITY	3-1	Cooke, Stevens 2	3457		5				10							2	11		4	3		7		1			8	9	6		
12		25	Walsall	2-5	Millen, Cooke	4495	8	5				10							2	11		4	3				1			7	9	6		
13	Nov	1	BOLTON WANDERERS	1-2	Maddy	3522	3	5			7	10							2	11		4					1			8	9	6		
14		4	NOTTS COUNTY	1-0	Carroll	3057	3	5			7	10					12		2	11		4					1			8	9	6		
15		8	Chester City	1-1	Cooke	2055						10	5				2			11		4	3			8	1			7	9	6		
16		22	BLACKPOOL	1-1	Stevens	4471	2					10	5			11							4	3			7	1			8	9	6		
17		30	Rotherham United	3-2	Sinton, Cooke 2	3148	2					10	5		9	11	12			6		4	3			7	1			8				
18	Dec	13	Wigan Athletic	1-1	Cooke	2411	6				7	9	5		10	12	4						3			2	1			8	11			
19		21	MIDDLESBROUGH	0-1		5504	6				7	9	5		10		12					4	3			2	1			8	11			
20		26	Swindon Town	0-2		8086	11				7	9	5		10							4	3			2	1			8	12	6		
21		28	BRISTOL ROVERS	1-2	Cooke	4500	11					10	5			7		12				4	3			2	1			8	9	6		
22	Jan	1	CHESTERFIELD	2-2	Cooke, Bater	3622	7					10	5						11	2	12		4	3				1			8	9	6		
23		3	Blackpool	0-2		4384	11	5			7	9						10	2			4	3			6	1			8				
24		10	Bournemouth	1-1	Millen	4682	11					10	5						9	2	7		4	3			6	1			8	12			
25		24	Port Vale	1-4	Cooke	3062	4				7	9						10	2	6	12		3				1			8	5	11		
26	Feb	1	FULHAM	3-3	Sinton, Stevens, Bates	5340	4	5			12							10	2	6	7					3	1			8	9	11		
27		7	CARLISLE UNITED	3-1	Joseph F, Maddy, Wright (og)	3032		5			12							10	2	6	7		3			4	1			8	9	11		
28		15	Darlington	1-1	Droy	2303		4			12	11	5					10		6	7		3			2	1			8	9			
29		21	GILLINGHAM	3-2	Cooke, Maddy, Stevens	4015		4				10	5							6	7		3			2	1			8	9	11		
30		28	Bury	1-1	Stevens	2317		4				10	5							6	7		3			2	1			8	9	11		
31	Mar	3	Bolton Wanderers	2-0	Cooke (p), Stevens	3465		5			12	10								6	7	4	3			2	1			8	9	11		
32		7	WALSALL	0-1		3442		5			7	10				12				6		4	3			2	1			8	9	11		
33		14	York City	1-2	Cooke	2426					7	10	5			11				6		4	3			2	1			8	9			
34		17	BRISTOL CITY	1-1	Maddy	4051					7	9	5							6		4	3			2	1			8	10	11		
35		21	MANSFIELD TOWN	3-1	Cooke, Carroll 2	3336		12			7	9	5						2	6		4	3			11	1			8	10			
36	Apr	4	CHESTER CITY	3-1	Droy 2, Blissett (p)	3496			10		7		5						2	6		4	3	9		11	1		12	8				
37		7	Newport County	2-2	Nogan, Blissett	1596		5	10			9							2	6		4	3	7			1		12	8		11		
38		11	Notts County	1-1	Priest	4358		12	10			9							2	6		4	3	7		5	1		11	8				
39		14	DONCASTER ROVERS	1-1	Blissett	3426			10		12	9							2	6		4	3	7		5	1		11	8				
40		18	Chesterfield	2-1	Cooke, Williamson (og)	2116		5	10		12	9							2	6		4	3	7			1			8		11		
41		20	SWINDON TOWN	1-1	Cooke	7443			10			9	5						2	6		4	3	7			1			8		11		
42		25	Middlesbrough	0-2		9942		12				9	5						2	6		4	3	7			1		10	8		11		
43		28	Bristol City	2-0	Carroll, Blissett	9050			10		7	9	5						2			4	3	12		6	1			8		11		
44	May	2	ROTHERHAM UNITED	2-0	Cooke, Nogan	3425		5	10		7	9				12			2			4	3	6			1			8		11		
45		4	Bristol Rovers	1-0	Sinton	3513		5	10		7					9			2			4	3	6		12		1		8		11		
46		9	WIGAN ATHLETIC	2-3	Sinton, Blissett (p)	4235		5	10		7					9			2			4	3	6				1		8		11		
						Apps	19	20	10	2	16	40	19	1	4	13	5	10	32	29	6	39	39	10	10	23	44	2	3	46	29	32	3	
						Subs		4			6				3	3	3		2	1					1			2		3			
						Goals	2	1	5		4	20	3					1	1	5		2		2					1	5	10			

Two own goals

F.A. Cup

Rd	Month	Day	Opponent	Score	Scorers	Att	Bater PT	Bates JA	Blissett GP	Booker R	Carroll R	Cooke RL	Droy MR	Evans TW	Geddis D	Holloway IS	Hughton HT	Joseph F	Joseph RA	Maddy PM	Merson PC	Millen KD	Murray IG	Nogan LM	Obi AL	Perryman SJ	Phillips GC	Power J	Priest P	Sinton A	Stevens GM	Turner WL	Wignall SL	Key RM
R1	Dec	3	Bristol Rovers	0-0		3035	7					10	5			11				6		4	3			2	1			8	9			
rep		6	BRISTOL ROVERS	2-0	Stevens 2	3848	11					10	5			7	12			6		4	3			2	1			8	9			
R2		9	Cardiff City	0-2		2531	6				11	10	5			7	14	12				4	3			2	1			8	9			

F.L. Cup (Littlewoods Cup)

Rd	Month	Day	Opponent	Score	Scorers	Att	Bater PT	Bates JA	Blissett GP	Booker R	Carroll R	Cooke RL	Droy MR	Evans TW	Geddis D	Holloway IS	Hughton HT	Joseph F	Joseph RA	Maddy PM	Merson PC	Millen KD	Murray IG	Nogan LM	Obi AL	Perryman SJ	Phillips GC	Power J	Priest P	Sinton A	Stevens GM	Turner WL	Wignall SL	Key RM
R1/1	Aug	26	Southend United	0-1		1539	12			6		9				7		10	2	11		4	3				1			8	13		5	
R1/2	Sep	2	SOUTHEND UNITED	2-3	Cooke, Joseph F	2632	3			6		12				7		10	2	11		4					1			8	9		5	

A.M. Cup (Freight Rover Trophy)

Rd	Month	Day	Opponent	Score	Scorers	Att	Bater PT	Bates JA	Blissett GP	Booker R	Carroll R	Cooke RL	Droy MR	Evans TW	Geddis D	Holloway IS	Hughton HT	Joseph F	Joseph RA	Maddy PM	Merson PC	Millen KD	Murray IG	Nogan LM	Obi AL	Perryman SJ	Phillips GC	Power J	Priest P	Sinton A	Stevens GM	Turner WL	Wignall SL	Key RM
PR	Dec	15	Leyton Orient	5-1	Cooke 4, Geddis	749					7	9	5		10	12	2					4	3				1			8	11	6		
PR	Jan	6	SWINDON TOWN	4-2	Stevens, Sinton 2, Carroll	1110		5			7			4				10	2	6		12	3								8	9	11		1
R1		26	WALSALL	4-2	Joseph F 2, Stevens, Maddy	1774	4	5				9						10	2	6	12		3				1			8	7	11		
QF	Feb	10	Bristol City	0-3		7425		4			14	12	5						10	2	6	7		3				1			8	9	11		

		Pl.	Home W	Home D	Home L	Home F	Home A	Away W	Away D	Away L	Away F	Away A	F. (Total)	A. (Total)	Pts
1	Bournemouth	46	19	3	1	44	14	10	7	6	32	26	76	40	97
2	Middlesbrough	46	16	5	2	38	11	12	5	6	29	19	67	30	94
3	Swindon Town	46	14	5	4	37	19	11	7	5	40	28	77	47	87
4	Wigan Athletic	46	15	5	3	47	26	10	5	8	36	34	83	60	85
5	Gillingham	46	16	5	2	42	14	7	4	12	23	34	65	48	78
6	Bristol City	46	14	6	3	42	15	7	8	8	21	21	63	36	77
7	Notts County	46	14	6	3	52	24	7	7	9	25	32	77	56	76
8	Walsall	46	16	4	3	50	27	6	5	12	30	40	80	67	75
9	Blackpool	46	11	7	5	35	20	5	9	9	39	39	74	59	64
10	Mansfield Town	46	9	9	5	30	23	6	7	10	22	32	52	55	61
11	**BRENTFORD**	**46**	**9**	**7**	**7**	**39**	**32**	**6**	**8**	**9**	**25**	**34**	**64**	**66**	**60**
12	Port Vale	46	8	6	9	43	36	7	6	10	33	34	76	70	57
13	Doncaster Rovers	46	11	8	4	32	19	3	7	13	24	43	56	62	57
14	Rotherham United	46	10	6	7	29	23	5	6	12	19	34	48	57	57
15	Chester City	46	7	9	7	32	28	6	8	9	29	31	61	59	56
16	Bury	46	9	7	7	30	26	5	6	12	24	34	54	60	55
17	Chesterfield	46	11	5	7	36	33	2	10	11	20	36	56	69	54
18	Fulham	46	8	8	7	35	41	4	9	10	24	36	59	77	53
19	Bristol Rovers	46	7	8	8	26	29	6	4	13	23	46	49	75	51
20	York City	46	11	8	4	34	29	1	5	17	21	50	55	79	49
21	Bolton Wanderers	46	8	5	10	29	26	2	10	11	17	32	46	58	45
22	Carlisle United	46	7	5	11	26	35	3	3	17	13	43	39	78	38
23	Darlington	46	6	10	7	25	28	1	6	16	20	49	45	77	37
24	Newport County	46	4	9	10	26	34	4	4	15	23	52	49	86	37

1986-87
Back: Hills (Youth Team Man.), Rudgeley (Youth Coach), Stevens, Millen, Evans, Booker, Bates, Maddy, Woolnough (Physio),
Middle: Cooke, Key, Phillips, Murray,
Front: Mancini (Coach), Bater, Sinton, R.Joseph, Lange (Chairman), Wignall, Evans (KLM), F.Joseph, Holloway, Allen, McLintock (Manager).

1987-88
Back: Blissett, Millen, Lee, Phillips, Booker, Evans, Bates
Middle: Carroll, Joseph, Priddie, Gravette, Cooke
Front: Clare (Physio), Murray, Turner, Perryman (Manager), Sinton, Holloway, Holder (Asst.Manager)

1987/88

12th in Division Three

No	Month	Day	Opponent	Result	Scorers	Att	Bates JA	Birch PA	Blissett GP	Booker R	Buckle PJ	Carroll R	Cockram AC	Cooke RL	Evans TW	Feeley AJ	Ferdinand L	Gravette W	Holloway IS	Howard MJ	Jones KA	Joseph RA	Lee C	Millen KD	Murray JG	Oliver AJ	Perryman SJ	Phillips GC	Priddle SP	Rix G	Sinton A	Smith PS	Stanislaus REP	Stewart IE	Thorne ST	Turner WL	Williams PA
1	Aug	15	SUNDERLAND	0-1		7509			10			12		9		7			11			2	5	4	3			1	6		8						
2		29	BRISTOL CITY	0-2		4328			10			11		9		6						2	5	4	3		12	1			8	7					
3		31	Grimsby Town	1-0	Blissett	3361	2		10					9		6		12					5	4	3		11	1			8	7					
4	Sep	5	ROTHERHAM UNITED	1-1	Jones	3604	2		10					9		6					5			4	3		11	1			8	7					
5		9	Northampton Town	1-2	Cooke (p)	5748	10		12					9		3					11	2	5	4			6	1			8	7					
6		12	Southend United	3-2	Sinton, Cooke, Blissett	2418	5		10	12				9		3					6	2		4				1	11		8	7					
7		15	CHESTERFIELD	2-0	Benjamin (og), Cooke (p)	3183	10			12				9		3		14			6	2	5	4				1	11		8	7					
8		19	BLACKPOOL	2-1	Sinton, Smith	3886	5			10				9		3		12			6	2		4				1	11		8	7					
9		26	Aldershot	1-4	Sinton	3651	5		10			14		9		3					6	2		4			12	1	11		8	7					
10		29	Preston North End	2-1	Sinton, Carroll	4241	5		10			7		9							6	2		4			11	1	12		8		3				
11	Oct	3	PORT VALE	1-0	Sinton	4007	5		10					9		12					6	2	14	4			11	1			8	7	3				
12		10	Bury	2-2	Sinton, Bates	2300	5		10					9							6	2	7	4			11	1			8		3				
13		17	WALSALL	0-0		5056	5		10			7		9							6	2		4			11	1			8	12	3				
14		20	CHESTER CITY	1-1	Cooke	4027	5		10					9		12					6	2		4			11	1			8		3				7
15		24	Brighton & Hove Albion	1-2	Stanislaus	7600	5		10					9		12					6	2		4			11	1			8	14	3				7
16		31	BRISTOL ROVERS	1-1	Williams	4487	5		10					12							6	2		4			11	1			8	7	3				9
17	Nov	3	Gillingham	1-0	Thorne	4513			10						5	12					6	2		4			11	1			8		3		7		9
18		7	Notts County	0-3		5634			10	12					5	7					6	2		4			11	1			8		3				9
19		21	WIGAN ATHLETIC	2-1	Sinton (p), Williams	3625	4			12					5	6						2	9				11	1			8		3			7	10
20		28	Doncaster Rovers	1-0	Williams	1360	4		10						5	6						2	12				11	1			8		3			7	9
21	Dec	12	MANSFIELD TOWN	2-2	Blissett, Carroll	3729	4		10			9				6						2	5				11	1			8		3			7	
22		18	York City	1-1	Turner	1801	4	12	10			9			5	6						2	11					1			8		3			7	
23		26	ALDERSHOT	3-0	Millen, Sinton, Birch	5578		9	10						5	6					14	2		4			12	1		11	8		3			7	
24		28	Fulham	2-2	Evans, Birch	9369		9	10						5	6					12	2		4				1		11	8		3			7	
25	Jan	1	Bristol City	3-2	Sinton, Blissett 2	12877	14	9	10						5						6	2		4			12	1		11	8		3			7	
26		2	SOUTHEND UNITED	1-0	Stanislaus	5752		9	10			12			5							2		4			6	1		11	8		3			7	
27		9	NORTHAMPTON T	0-1		6025			10			14			5	6						2	9	4			12	1		11	8		3			7	
28		16	Blackpool	1-0	Millen	3911		10		12					5	6						2	9	4				1		11	8		3			7	
29	Feb	14	FULHAM	3-1	Millen, Blissett, Elkins (og)	8712	12	9	10						5						6	2		4				1			8	14	3	11		7	
30		17	Rotherham United	0-2		2572		9	10						5						6	2		4				1			8		3	11		7	
31		20	Sunderland	0-2		15458		9	10						5	12					6	2		4				1			8	14	3	11		7	
32		23	GRIMSBY TOWN	0-2		3534		10		12					5	9					6	2		4				1			8	14	3	11		7	
33		27	Port Vale	0-1		3876	12	9	10						5	11					6	2		4		1					8		3	14		7	
34	Mar	1	PRESTON NORTH END	2-0	Blissett, Evans	3505		9	10						5	11					6	2		4		1					8	12	3			7	
35		5	Walsall	2-4	Blissett, Evans	4548		9	10						5	11		14			6	2		4		1					8		3	12		7	
36		12	BURY	0-3		3920		9	10						5	11					6	2		4		1					8		3	12		7	
37		19	Bristol Rovers	0-0		3380			10	12					5	11		9			6		2	4		1					8		3			7	
38		26	BRIGHTON & HOVE ALB	1-1	Lee	5331			10						5	11	9				6	2	14	4		1					8	12	3			7	
39	Apr	2	NOTTS COUNTY	1-0	Blissett	4388			10	12			7		5		9				6	2	11	4		1					8		3				
40		4	Wigan Athletic	1-1	Evans	3597			10	12			7		5		9				6	2	11	4		1					8		3				
41		9	GILLINGHAM	2-2	Sinton 2	3875		12	10			9	7		5						6	2	11	4		1					8		3				
42		19	Chesterfield	1-2	Turner	2010			10	12			9		5						6	2	11	4		1					8		3			7	
43		23	Chester City	1-1	Cockram	1793			10				9		5	3					6	2	11	4		1					8		12			7	
44		30	DONCASTER ROVERS	1-1	Cockram	3122			10	14			9		5	12					6	2	11	4				1			8		3			7	
45	May	2	Mansfield Town	1-2	Carroll	2664	4	12	10			9			5	14					6	2	11					1			8		3			7	
46		7	YORK CITY	1-2	Carroll	4180	4		10		14	9	11		5	7				12	6	2						1			8		3				
						Apps	20	13	40	1	0	8	7	15	29	27	3	1	1	0	34	43	19	40	4	11	16	35	5	6	46	10	36	4	1	24	7
						Subs	3	3	1	11	1	4		1		7		4		1	2		3				5		1			7	1	3			
						Goals	1	2	9			4	2	4	4						1		1	3							11	1	2		1	2	3

Two own goals

F.A. Cup

Rd	Month	Day	Opponent	Result	Scorers	Att	Bates JA	Birch PA	Blissett GP	Booker R	Buckle PJ	Carroll R	Cockram AC	Cooke RL	Evans TW	Feeley AJ	Ferdinand L	Gravette W	Holloway IS	Howard MJ	Jones KA	Joseph RA	Lee C	Millen KD	Murray JG	Oliver AJ	Perryman SJ	Phillips GC	Priddle SP	Rix G	Sinton A	Smith PS	Stanislaus REP	Stewart IE	Thorne ST	Turner WL	Williams PA
R1	Nov	14	BRIGHTON & HOVE ALB.	0-2		6358				14		12		9	5	4					6	2	10				11	1			8		3		7		

F.L. Cup (Littlewoods Cup)

Rd	Month	Day	Opponent	Result	Scorers	Att	Bates JA	Birch PA	Blissett GP	Booker R	Buckle PJ	Carroll R	Cockram AC	Cooke RL	Evans TW	Feeley AJ	Ferdinand L	Gravette W	Holloway IS	Howard MJ	Jones KA	Joseph RA	Lee C	Millen KD	Murray JG	Oliver AJ	Perryman SJ	Phillips GC	Priddle SP	Rix G	Sinton A	Smith PS	Stanislaus REP	Stewart IE	Thorne ST	Turner WL	Williams PA
R1/1	Aug	18	SOUTHEND UNITED	2-1	Sinton, Blissett	2837			10			11		9		7						2	5	4	3		6	1			8						
R1/2		25	Southend United	2-4	Cooke, Carroll	2111	6		10			11		9		7						2	5	4	3		12	1			8						

A.M. Cup (Sherpa Van Trophy)

Rd	Month	Day	Opponent	Result	Scorers	Att	Bates JA	Birch PA	Blissett GP	Booker R	Buckle PJ	Carroll R	Cockram AC	Cooke RL	Evans TW	Feeley AJ	Ferdinand L	Gravette W	Holloway IS	Howard MJ	Jones KA	Joseph RA	Lee C	Millen KD	Murray JG	Oliver AJ	Perryman SJ	Phillips GC	Priddle SP	Rix G	Sinton A	Smith PS	Stanislaus REP	Stewart IE	Thorne ST	Turner WL	Williams PA
PR	Oct	28	Northampton Town	0-1		3076	5		10	12				9							6	2		4			11	1			8	7	3				
PR	Nov	24	NOTTS COUNTY	3-2	Williams 3	2005	4		10						5	6						2					11	1			8	12	3			7	9
R1	Jan	19	Wolverhampton Wan.	0-4		6298		10		14		12			5	6						2	9	4			11	1			8		3			7	

	Team	Pl.	Home W	Home D	Home L	Home F	Home A	Away W	Away D	Away L	Away F	Away A	F. (Total)	A. (Total)	Pts
1	Sunderland	46	14	7	2	51	22	13	5	5	41	26	92	48	93
2	Brighton & Hove A.	46	15	7	1	37	16	8	8	7	32	31	69	47	84
3	Walsall	46	15	6	2	39	22	8	7	8	29	28	68	50	82
4	Notts County	46	14	4	5	53	24	9	8	6	29	25	82	49	81
5	Bristol City	46	14	6	3	51	30	7	6	10	26	32	77	62	75
6	Northampton Town	46	12	8	3	36	18	6	11	6	34	33	70	51	73
7	Wigan Athletic	46	11	8	4	36	23	9	4	10	34	38	70	61	72
8	Bristol Rovers	46	14	5	4	43	19	4	7	12	25	37	68	56	66
9	Fulham	46	10	5	8	36	24	9	4	10	33	36	69	60	66
10	Blackpool	46	13	4	6	45	27	4	10	9	26	35	71	62	65
11	Port Vale	46	12	8	3	36	19	6	3	14	22	37	58	56	65
12	**BRENTFORD**	**46**	**9**	**8**	**6**	**27**	**23**	**7**	**6**	**10**	**26**	**36**	**53**	**59**	**62**
13	Gillingham	46	8	9	6	45	21	6	8	9	32	40	77	61	59
14	Bury	46	9	7	7	33	26	6	7	10	25	31	58	57	59
15	Chester City	46	9	8	6	29	30	5	8	10	22	32	51	62	58
16	Preston North End	46	10	6	7	30	23	5	7	11	18	36	48	59	58
17	Southend United	46	10	6	7	42	33	4	7	12	23	50	65	83	55
18	Chesterfield	46	10	5	8	25	28	5	5	13	16	42	41	70	55
19	Mansfield Town	46	10	6	7	25	21	4	6	13	23	38	48	59	54
20	Aldershot	46	12	3	8	45	32	3	5	15	19	42	64	74	53
21	Rotherham United	46	8	8	7	28	25	4	8	11	22	41	50	66	52
22	Grimsby Town	46	6	7	10	25	29	6	7	10	23	29	48	58	50
23	York City	46	4	7	12	27	45	4	2	17	21	46	48	91	33
24	Doncaster Rovers	46	6	5	12	25	36	2	4	17	15	48	40	84	33

1988/89

7th in Division Three

	Date	Opponents	Score	Scorers	Att	Ansah A	Bates JA	Birch PA	Blissett GP	Booker R	Buttigieg J	Cadette RR	Cockram AC	Driscoll A	Evans TW	Feeley AJ	Gayle MA	Godfrey KA	Holdsworth DC	Jones KA	Lee C	Millen KD	Parks A	Pearce GC	Perryman SJ	Purdie J	Ratcliffe S	Roberts J	Sealy AJ	Sinton A	Smeulders J	Smillie N	Stanislaus REP
1	Aug 27	HUDDERSFIELD T	1-0	Cockram	5016			12	10			9	6		5	2				7		4	1							8		11	3
2	Sep 3	Northampton Town	0-1		4488		2	14	10	12		9	6		5					7		4	1							8		11	3
3	10	WIGAN ATHLETIC	1-1	Blissett	4081		12		10			9	6		5	2				7		4	1							8		11	3
4	17	Swansea City	1-1	Millen	5015		2		10	6		9			5					7		4	1		12					8		11	3
5	21	Bristol Rovers	2-1	Cadette 2	3836		2		10	6		9			5					7		4	1							8		11	3
6	24	SHEFFIELD UNITED	1-4	Sinton (p)	6577		2		10	6		9			5					7		4	1		12					8		11	3
7	Oct 1	GILLINGHAM	1-0	Sinton (p)	4839		2		10	6		9	12		5	3				7		4	1							8		11	
8	5	Chester City	2-3	Cadette, Blissett	1999		2		10	6		9	14		5	3				7		4	1							8		11	12
9	9	SOUTHEND UNITED	4-0	Evans, Cockram, Sinton 2	5016		2		10			9	6		5	12				7		4								8	1	11	3
10	15	Bury	1-3	Cockram	2359		2		10	14		9	6		5	11			12	7		4								8	1		3
11	22	PRESTON NORTH END	0-2		5584		5			14		9				2	12		10	7		4		11	6					8	1		3
12	25	Chesterfield	2-2	Cadette 2	1876		3		10			9			5	12			11	7	14	4		2	6					8	1		
13	29	PORT VALE	2-1	Jones, Holdsworth	5212		2		10			9			5	6		11	14	7		4			12					8	1		3
14	Nov 5	Reading	2-2	Sinton 2 (1p)	7974		2		10			9			5	6			12	7		4		11						8	1		3
15	8	NOTTS COUNTY	2-1	Cadette 2	4013		2		10		4	9			5	6			12	7				11						8	1		3
16	12	Mansfield Town	0-1		3196		2		10		4	9			5	6			12	7				11						8	1		3
17	25	Cardiff City	0-1		3405		2		10		11	9	12		5	6				7		4						1		8			3
18	Dec 3	BOLTON WANDERERS	3-0	Evans, Cadette 2	4628				10		6	9	2		5			11		7		4		3				1		8		12	
19	18	Aldershot	0-0		4012						2	9	6		5		12	10		7		4	1							8		11	3
20	26	BLACKPOOL	1-0	Sinton	6021							9	6		5	2		10		7		4	1							8		11	3
21	31	WOLVERHAMPTON W.	2-2	Jones, Godfrey	8020							9	6		5	2		10		7		4	1							8		11	3
22	Jan 2	Fulham	3-3	Sinton, Cadette, Godfrey	8120						12	9	6		5	2		10		7		4	1							8		11	3
23	14	NORTHAMPTON T	2-0	Stanislaus, Cadette	6043							9	6		5	2		10		7		4	1				12			8		11	3
24	21	Wigan Athletic	1-1	Sinton	2514				14			9	6		5	2		10		7		4	1				12			8		11	3
25	Feb 4	Gillingham	0-0		4002				10			9	6		5	2						4	1	12			7			8		11	3
26	11	CHESTER CITY	0-1		5748				10			9	6		5	2	12					4	1				7			8		11	3
27	25	BURY	2-2	Blissett, Godfrey	6077		12		10			9	14		5	2		11		7		4					6	1		8			3
28	28	CHESTERFIELD	1-0	Cadette	4192		12					9	11		5	2		10		7		4					6	1		8			3
29	Mar 4	Preston North End	3-5	Bates, Godfrey, Ratcliffe	8191		2				9		10		5			11		7		4		14			6	1		8		12	3
30	11	READING	3-2	Millen, Evans, Sinton (p)	6866		2		10			9	12		5			11		7		4	1				6			8			3
31	13	Port Vale	2-3	Millen, Godfrey	5577		12		10			9	14		5	2		11		7		4	1				6			8			3
32	24	FULHAM	0-1		10851	12	2		10				6		5	7		11			4		1	9					8				3
33	27	Blackpool	3-0	Cockram 2 (1p), Godfrey	3053		4		10		12		6		5	2		11		7			1	8		14			9				3
34	Apr 1	ALDERSHOT	2-1	Jones, Sealy	5200		4		10		12		6		5	2		11		7			1			9			8			14	3
35	4	BRISTOL CITY	3-0	Cockram (p), Sealy 2	4627		4		10		2		6		5			14		7			1	12		9			8			11	3
36	8	Wolverhampton Wan.	0-2		14356		4		10		2		6		5	12		14		7			1			9			8			11	3
37	11	Bristol City	1-0	Evans	4339		4		10				6		5	2		14		7			1	12		9			8			11	3
38	15	BRISTOL ROVERS	2-1	Blissett, Smillie	7558		4		10		2		6		5			14		7			1	12		9			8			11	3
39	18	Southend United	1-1	Smillie	4194	12	4		10		2		6		5			9		7			1						8			11	3
40	22	Sheffield United	2-2	Godfrey, Sealy	12613		2		10				6		5			9		7		4	1						8			11	3
41	25	Huddersfield Town	2-1	Blissett, Godfrey	3538	12	2		10				6		5			9		7		4	1						8			11	3
42	29	MANSFIELD TOWN	1-0	Cockram	5231		2		10		12		6		5	8		9		7		4	1	14								11	3
43	May 1	Notts County	0-3		4989	14	2				12	9	6		5	8		10		7		4	1	11									3
44	6	Bolton Wanderers	2-4	Ansah 2	4627	10	2				7		6	12	5	8		11				4	1	3									9
45	9	SWANSEA CITY	1-1	Blissett	4415	7	2		10		12		6		5	8		11				4	1	3					14				9
46	13	CARDIFF CITY	1-1	Evans	4865	9	12		10		2	14	6		5	7		11				4	1						8				3
					Apps	3	31	0	35	5	12	31	31	0	45	30	0	24	2	40	1	36	33	11	2	5	7	5	11	31	8	25	42
					Subs	4	5	2	1	3	6	1	6	1		3	3	4	5		1			6	3	1	2		1			3	1
					Goals	2	1		6			12	7		5			8	1	3		3					1		4	10		2	1

F.A. Cup

	Date	Opponents	Score	Scorers	Att	Ansah A	Bates JA	Birch PA	Blissett GP	Booker R	Buttigieg J	Cadette RR	Cockram AC	Driscoll A	Evans TW	Feeley AJ	Gayle MA	Godfrey KA	Holdsworth DC	Jones KA	Lee C	Millen KD	Parks A	Pearce GC	Perryman SJ	Purdie J	Ratcliffe S	Roberts J	Sealy AJ	Sinton A	Smeulders J	Smillie N	Stanislaus REP
R1	Nov 19	HALESOWEN TOWN	2-0	Evans, Sinton	4514		2		10		14	9	12		5	6		11		7		4		3				1		8			
R2	Dec 10	Peterborough United	0-0		5609				10			9	6		5	2		14		7		4	1	3	12					8		11	
rep	14	PETERBOROUGH UTD	3-2	Cockram, Cadette, Smillie	5605				10			9	6		5	2		8		7		4	1		12							11	3
R3	Jan 7	Walsall	1-1	Jones	5375							9	6		5	2		10		7		4	1	12						8		11	3
rep	10	WALSALL	1-0	Cockram	8163							9	6		5	2		10		7		4	1							8		11	3
R4	28	MANCHESTER CITY	3-1	Jones, Blissett 2	12100				10			9	6		5	2				7		4	1				12			8		11	3
R5	Feb 18	Blackburn Rovers	2-0	Blissett 2	15280				10			9			5	2		12		7		4	1				6			8		11	3
R6	Mar 18	Liverpool	0-4		42376				10			9	6		5	2		11		7		4	1						12	8			3

F.L. Cup (Littlewoods Cup)

	Date	Opponents	Score	Scorers	Att	Ansah A	Bates JA	Birch PA	Blissett GP	Booker R	Buttigieg J	Cadette RR	Cockram AC	Driscoll A	Evans TW	Feeley AJ	Gayle MA	Godfrey KA	Holdsworth DC	Jones KA	Lee C	Millen KD	Parks A	Pearce GC	Perryman SJ	Purdie J	Ratcliffe S	Roberts J	Sealy AJ	Sinton A	Smeulders J	Smillie N	Stanislaus REP
R1/1	Aug 30	Fulham	2-2	Stanislaus, Sinton	5489				10			9	6		5	2				7		4	1							8		11	3
R1/2	Sep 6	FULHAM	1-0	Blissett	7707		12	14	10			9	6		5	2				7		4	1							8		11	3
R2/1	27	Blackburn Rovers	1-3	Blissett	4606		2		10	6		9			5					7		4	1		12					8		11	3
R2/2	Oct 12	BLACKBURN ROVERS	4-3	Jones, Sinton, Cadette 2	3844		2		10	14		9	6		5	12				7		4								8	1	11	3

R1/2 a.e.t.

A.M. Cup (Sherpa Van Trophy)

	Date	Opponents	Score	Scorers	Att	Ansah A	Bates JA	Birch PA	Blissett GP	Booker R	Buttigieg J	Cadette RR	Cockram AC	Driscoll A	Evans TW	Feeley AJ	Gayle MA	Godfrey KA	Holdsworth DC	Jones KA	Lee C	Millen KD	Parks A	Pearce GC	Perryman SJ	Purdie J	Ratcliffe S	Roberts J	Sealy AJ	Sinton A	Smeulders J	Smillie N	Stanislaus REP
PR	Nov 22	Fulham	2-0	Blissett, Cadete	2376					2	1	10	7		12		14		3	8	11	5	6							9			4
PR	29	GILLINGHAM	2-0	Blissett, Cockram	3713				10			9	6		5	2		11		7		4			3			1		8			
R1	Jan 17	NOTTS COUNTY	2-0	Godfrey, Cadete	3194							9	6		5	2		10		7		4					12	1		8		11	3
QF	Feb 21	Chesterfield	1-0	Blissett	4207				10			9			5	2		12		7		4	1				6			8		11	3
SFS	Mar 21	TORQUAY UNITED	0-1		5802		7		10			9	6		5	2		11				4	1						12	8			3

		Pl.	Home W	Home D	Home L	Home F	Home A	Away W	Away D	Away L	Away F	Away A	F. (Total)	A. (Total)	Pts
1	Wolverhampton W.	46	18	4	1	61	19	8	10	5	35	30	96	49	92
2	Sheffield United	46	16	3	4	57	21	9	6	8	36	33	93	54	84
3	Port Vale	46	15	3	5	46	21	9	9	5	32	27	78	48	84
4	Fulham	46	12	7	4	42	28	10	2	11	27	39	69	67	75
5	Bristol Rovers	46	9	11	3	34	21	10	6	7	33	30	67	51	74
6	Preston North End	46	14	7	2	56	31	5	8	10	23	29	79	60	72
7	**BRENTFORD**	**46**	**14**	**5**	**4**	**36**	**21**	**4**	**9**	**10**	**30**	**40**	**66**	**61**	**68**
8	Chester City	46	12	6	5	38	18	7	5	11	26	43	64	61	68
9	Notts County	46	11	7	5	37	22	7	6	10	27	32	64	54	67
10	Bolton Wanderers	46	12	8	3	42	23	4	8	11	16	31	58	54	64
11	Bristol City	46	10	3	10	32	25	8	6	9	21	30	53	55	63
12	Swansea City	46	11	8	4	33	22	4	8	11	18	31	51	53	61
13	Bury	46	11	7	5	27	22	5	6	12	28	45	55	67	61
14	Huddersfield Town	46	10	8	5	35	25	7	1	15	28	48	63	73	60
15	Mansfield Town	46	10	8	5	32	22	4	9	10	16	30	48	52	59
16	Cardiff City	46	10	9	4	30	16	4	6	13	14	40	44	56	57
17	Wigan Athletic	46	9	5	9	28	22	5	9	9	27	31	55	53	56
18	Reading	46	10	6	7	37	29	5	5	13	31	43	68	72	56
19	Blackpool	46	10	6	7	36	29	4	7	12	20	30	56	59	55
20	Northampton Town	46	11	2	10	41	34	5	4	14	25	42	66	76	54
21	Southend United	46	10	9	4	33	26	3	6	14	23	49	56	75	54
22	Chesterfield	46	9	5	9	35	35	5	2	16	16	51	51	86	49
23	Gillingham	46	7	3	13	25	32	5	1	17	22	49	47	81	40
24	Aldershot	46	7	6	10	29	29	1	7	15	19	49	48	78	37

1988-89
Back: Stanislaus, Feeley, Phillips, Blissett, Joesph,
Middle: Holder (Asst.Manager), Lee (Youth Devt.), Bates, Booker, Evans, Millen, Birch, Clare (Physio.)
Front: Cockram, Jones, Turner, Perryman (Player/Manager), Sinton, Cadetts, Smillie

1989-90
Back: Courvish (Coach), Millen, Larkin, Ratcliffe, Buttigieg, Evans, Thomas, Blissett, Haag, Bates, Clare (Physio)
2nd Row: Warde, Tuckerman, Stanislaus, Howard, Bayes, Gayle, Parks, Jones, Godrey, Cousins, Moore
3rd Row: Buckle, May, Cockram, Ansah, Perryman (Manager), Jones, Holder (Asst. Manager),
Cadette, Smillie, Peters, Fleming
Front: Turner, Moabi, Ryder, Brand, Driscoll, Dale, Ivers, Jagroop, Webb, Moyse

1989/90

13th in Division Three

						Ansah A	Bates JA	Bayes AJ	Blissett GP	Branagan KG	Buckle PJ	Buttigieg J	Cadette RR	Cockram AC	Cousins JM	Driscoll A	Evans TW	Fleming MJ	Gayle MA	Godfrey KA	Haag KJ	Holdsworth DC	Jones KA	May ES	Millen KD	Miller PR	Moncur JF	Parks A	Perryman SJ	Peters RAA	Ratcliffe S	Scott CG	Smillie N	Sparham SR	Stanislaus REP
1	Aug 19	Bristol Rovers	0-1		5851				10			2					5			9	12		7	8	4			1			6		11		3
2	26	CHESTER CITY	1-1	Evans	5153	14	12		10			2					5			9			7	8	4			1			6		11		3
3	Sep 2	Cardiff City	2-2	May 2	3499				10			2					5			9	12		7	8	4			1			6		11		3
4	9	BURY	0-1		5010				10			2	9				5			12			7	8	4			1			6		11		3
5	16	Huddersfield Town	0-1		5578		12		10			2		14			5			11	9		7	8	4			1			6				3
6	23	BIRMINGHAM CITY	0-1		5386				10			2	9	14			5				12		7	8	4			1			6		11		3
7	26	Crewe Alexandra	3-2	Smillie, Jones, Godfrey	3496							2	9				5			10	12		7	8	4			1			6		11		3
8	30	WIGAN ATHLETIC	3-1	Blissett, Holdsworth, May	4647		12		10			2	14				5	3				9	7	8	4			1			6		11		
9	Oct 7	BRISTOL CITY	0-2		7421		2		10				12	14			5	3		11		9	7	8	4			1			6				
10	14	Preston North End	2-4	May, Holdsworth	5956		12		10					14				3		5		9	7	8	4			1	2		6		11		
11	17	BOLTON WANDERERS	1-2	Holdsworth	4537				10					12			5	3				9	7	8	4			1	2		6		11		
12	21	Shrewsbury Town	0-1		3073				10				12				5	3				9	7	8	4		6	1			2		11		
13	28	FULHAM	2-0	Evans, Smillie	7962				10			12					5	3				9	7	8	4		6	1			2		11		
14	31	Notts County	1-3	Moncur	4586				10			12					5	3		14		9	7	8	4		6	1			2		11		
15	Nov 4	TRANMERE ROVERS	2-4	May, Ratcliffe	5720		4		14			12	10				5	3				9		8			6	1	2		7		11		
16	11	Blackpool	0-4		2512		3						10				5			12		9	7	8	4		6	1			2		11		
17	25	Northampton Town	2-0	May, Holdsworth	3165				10	1		12		2			5	3		14		9	7	8		4					6		11		
18	Dec 3	LEYTON ORIENT	4-3	Smillie, May, Holdsworth (p), Blissett	6434				10	1				6			5	3				9		8		4					2		11		7
19	17	MANSFIELD TOWN	2-1	Holdsworth 2	5022				10					6			5	2		12		9	7	8		4		1					11		3
20	26	Reading	0-1		5590		4		10					6			5	2		12		9	7	8				1					11		3
21	30	Swansea City	1-2	Blissett	4537		4		10				12	6			5					9	7	8				1			2		11		3
22	Jan 1	WALSALL	4-0	Blissett, Smillie, Holdsworth, Jones	5259		4		10				12	6			5	14				9	7	8				1			2		11		3
23	6	ROTHERHAM UNITED	4-2	Holdsworth 3, Stanislaus	5624		4		10					6			5	12				9	7	8				1			2		11		3
24	12	Chester City	1-1	Cockram	2302		4		10					6			5			12		9	7	8				1			2		11		3
25	20	BRISTOL ROVERS	2-1	Ratcliffe, Cadette	7414		4						10	6			5					9	7	8				1			2		11		3
26	27	Bury	2-0	May, Holdsworth	2963		4					14	10	6	5					12		9	7	8				1			2		11		3
27	Feb 10	HUDDERSFIELD T	2-1	Holdsworth 2	6774				10				12	6	4		5					9	7	8				1			2		11		3
28	18	Leyton Orient	1-0	Holdsworth	6572				10				12	6			5			8		9	7		4			1			2		11		3
29	21	CARDIFF CITY	0-1		5174				10				12	6			5					9	7	8	4			1			2		11		3
30	25	NORTHAMPTON T	3-2	Blissett 2, Holdsworth	6391				10					6			5					9	7	8	4			1			2		11		3
31	Mar 3	Rotherham United	1-2	Blissett	5603				10					6			5			12		9	7	8	4			1		14	2		11		3
32	6	Wigan Athletic	1-2	Blissett	1938				10					6	14		5		12	8		9	7		4			1			2		11		3
33	10	CREWE ALEXANDRA	0-2		5815				10		14				6		5		12	8		9	7		4			1			2		11		3
34	13	Birmingham City	1-0	Holdsworth	8169				10		6	14			2		5		12	8		9	7		4			1					11		3
35	17	Bristol City	0-2		10813				10		6	4	12		2	14	5		7	8		9						1		3			11		
36	20	PRESTON NORTH END	2-2	Holdsworth, Blissett	4673			1	10		6	14				8	5	3	12			9	7		4						2		11		
37	24	Bolton Wanderers	1-0	Holdsworth	6156				10			6			11	8	5	3	12			9	7		4						2	1			
38	31	SHREWSBURY TOWN	1-1	Smillie	5387				10		7	14			2	8	5	3	12			9			4						6	1	11		
39	Apr 7	NOTTS COUNTY	0-1		5105				10		6	2				8	5		12			9	7		4							1	11	3	
40	10	Fulham	0-1		6729							10				8	5		12			9	7		4						6	1	11	2	3
41	14	Walsall	1-2	Sparham	2903						6	14			2	8	5			12		9	7		4							1	11	10	3
42	16	READING	1-1	Driscoll	5594						12			6		8	5			10		9	7		4							1	11	2	3
43	21	Mansfield Town	3-2	Holdsworth2 (1p), Blissett	2347				10			12		6	4	14	5			8		9	7					1					11	2	3
44	28	BLACKPOOL	5-0	Evans,Cockram,Holdsworth,Driscoll,Blissett	4784		12		10					6	2	8	5			14		9	7		4			1					11		3
45	May 2	SWANSEA CITY	2-1	Holdsworth 2	4950						12			6	2	8	5			10		9	7		4			1					11		3
46	5	Tranmere Rovers	2-2	Godfrey, Steel (og)	5379						12			6	2	8	5			10		9	7		4			1					11		3
					Apps	0	10	1	36	2	6	12	7	21	12	10	44	15	1	16	1	39	42	30	32	3	5	37	3	1	35	6	43	5	31
					Subs	1	5		1		4	10	9	5	1	2		2	8	11	4									1					
					Goals				11				1	2		2	3			2		24	2	8			1				2		5	1	1

One own goal

F.A. Cup

						Ansah A	Bates JA	Bayes AJ	Blissett GP	Branagan KG	Buckle PJ	Buttigieg J	Cadette RR	Cockram AC	Cousins JM	Driscoll A	Evans TW	Fleming MJ	Gayle MA	Godfrey KA	Haag KJ	Holdsworth DC	Jones KA	May ES	Millen KD	Miller PR	Moncur JF	Parks A	Perryman SJ	Peters RAA	Ratcliffe S	Scott CG	Smillie N	Sparham SR	Stanislaus REP
R1	Nov 18	COLCHESTER UNITED	0-1		4171				10								5			14	12	9	7	8	4			1	2	3	6		11		

F.L. Cup (Littlewoods Cup)

						Ansah A	Bates JA	Bayes AJ	Blissett GP	Branagan KG	Buckle PJ	Buttigieg J	Cadette RR	Cockram AC	Cousins JM	Driscoll A	Evans TW	Fleming MJ	Gayle MA	Godfrey KA	Haag KJ	Holdsworth DC	Jones KA	May ES	Millen KD	Miller PR	Moncur JF	Parks A	Perryman SJ	Peters RAA	Ratcliffe S	Scott CG	Smillie N	Sparham SR	Stanislaus REP
R1/1	Aug 23	Brighton & Hove Albior	3-0	Millen, Godfrey, May	6405	14	12		10			2					5			9			7	8	4			1			6		11		3
R1/2	29	BRIGHTON & HOVE ALE	1-1	Blissett	4306		12		10			2		14			5			9			7	8	4			1			6		11		3
R2/1	Sep 19	MANCHESTER CITY	2-1	Evans, Blissett	6065				10			2	9	14			5				12		7	8	4			1			6		11		3
R2/2	Oct 4	Manchester City	1-4	May	17864		2		10			12	14				5					9	7	8	4			1			6		11		3

A.M. Cup (Leyland Daf Cup)

						Ansah A	Bates JA	Bayes AJ	Blissett GP	Branagan KG	Buckle PJ	Buttigieg J	Cadette RR	Cockram AC	Cousins JM	Driscoll A	Evans TW	Fleming MJ	Gayle MA	Godfrey KA	Haag KJ	Holdsworth DC	Jones KA	May ES	Millen KD	Miller PR	Moncur JF	Parks A	Perryman SJ	Peters RAA	Ratcliffe S	Scott CG	Smillie N	Sparham SR	Stanislaus REP
PR	Nov 7	LEYTON ORIENT	3-0	Holdsworth 2, May	2544		4					12	10				5			14		9	7	8			6	1	3		2		11		
PR	Dec 9	Mansfield Town	1-2	Holdsworth	1445				10	1				6	12		5	3		14		9		8		4					2		11		7
R1	Jan 23	READING	2-1	May, Cadette	3928		4						10	6			5			12		9	7	8				1			2		11		3
QF	Feb 6	BRISTOL ROVERS	2-2	Smillie, Holdsworth	4409		5		14			12	10	6	4							9	7	8				1			2		11		3

QF lost 2-4 on penalties a.e.t.

		Pl.	Home W	D	L	F	A	Away W	D	L	F	A	F. (Total)	A.	Pts
1	Bristol Rovers	46	15	8	0	43	14	11	7	5	28	21	71	35	93
2	Bristol City	46	15	5	3	40	16	12	5	6	36	24	76	40	91
3	Notts County	46	17	4	2	40	18	8	8	7	33	35	73	53	87
4	Tranmere Rovers	46	15	5	3	54	22	8	6	9	32	27	86	49	80
5	Bury	46	11	7	5	35	19	10	4	9	35	30	70	49	74
6	Bolton Wanderers	46	12	7	4	32	19	6	8	9	27	29	59	48	69
7	Birmingham City	46	10	7	6	33	19	8	5	10	27	40	60	59	66
8	Huddersfield Town	46	11	5	7	30	23	6	9	8	31	39	61	62	65
9	Rotherham United	46	12	6	5	48	28	5	7	11	23	34	71	62	64
10	Reading	46	10	9	4	33	21	5	10	8	24	32	57	53	64
11	Shrewsbury Town	46	10	9	4	38	24	6	6	11	21	30	59	54	63
12	Crewe Alexandra	46	10	8	5	32	24	5	9	9	24	29	56	53	62
13	**BRENTFORD**	**46**	**11**	**4**	**8**	**41**	**31**	**7**	**3**	**13**	**25**	**35**	**66**	**66**	**61**
14	Leyton Orient	46	9	6	8	28	24	7	4	12	24	32	52	56	58
15	Mansfield Town	46	13	2	8	34	25	3	5	15	16	40	50	65	55
16	Chester City	46	11	7	5	30	23	2	8	13	13	32	43	55	54
17	Swansea City	46	10	6	7	25	27	4	6	13	20	36	45	63	54
18	Wigan Athletic	46	10	6	7	29	22	3	8	12	19	42	48	64	53
19	Preston North End	46	10	7	6	42	30	4	3	16	23	49	65	79	52
20	Fulham	46	8	8	7	33	27	4	7	12	22	39	55	66	51
21	Cardiff City	46	6	9	8	30	35	6	5	12	21	35	51	70	50
22	Northampton Town	46	7	7	9	27	31	4	7	12	24	37	51	68	47
23	Blackpool	46	8	6	9	29	33	2	10	11	20	40	49	73	46
24	Walsall	46	6	8	9	23	30	3	6	14	17	42	40	72	41

1990/91

6th in Division Three

							Bates JA	Benstead GM	Blissett GP	Brooke GJ	Buckle PJ	Cadette RR	Carstairs JW	Cash SP	Cockram AC	Cousins JM	Evans TW	Fleming MJ	Gayle MA	Godfrey KA	Goodyear C	Holdsworth DC	Jones KA	May ES	Millen KD	Parks A	Peters RAA	Ratcliffe S	Rostron JW	Smillie N
1	Aug	25	BOURNEMOUTH	0-0		5669	5	1			6	12				2		3		10		9	7	8	4					11
2	Sep	1	Mansfield Town	2-0	Smillie, Godfrey	2513	5	1		12	6	9				2		3		10			7	8	4					11
3		8	CHESTER CITY	0-1		4812	2	1		9	6				12		5	3		10			7	8	4			14		11
4		15	Swansea City	2-2	Bates, Jones (p)	4127	2	1		12	6	14		3			5			10		9	7	8	4					11
5		18	Rotherham United	2-2	Holdsworth, Smillie	4298	2	1		12	6	14		3			5			10		9	7	8	4					11
6		22	BOLTON WANDERERS	4-2	May, Brooke, Jones, Holdsworth	5077	2	1		6		14		3			5			10		9	7	8	4			12		11
7		29	GRIMSBY TOWN	1-0	Jones	5951	2	1		6		9		3		5				10			7	8	4					11
8	Oct	2	Preston North End	1-1	Godfrey	5025	2	1		6		9		3		5				10			7	8	4					11
9		6	Bradford City	1-0	Godfrey	6402	2	1		6	14	9		3		5				10			7	8	4			12		11
10		14	CAMBRIDGE UNITED	0-3		6833	5	1		6		9		3		2			14	10			7	8	4			12		11
11		20	HUDDERSFIELD T	1-0	May	5509	5	1		6				3	12	2			9	10			7	8				4		11
12		23	Reading	2-1	Gayle, Holdsworth	6562	2	1						3			5		6	10		9	7	8				4		11
13		26	Tranmere Rovers	1-2	Holdsworth (p)	7173	2							3			5		6	10		9	7	8	12	1		4		11
14	Nov	4	SOUTHEND UNITED	0-1		8021	4	1	12	6				3			5		9	10			7	8				2		11
15		10	BURY	2-2	Blissett, Cockram	5303		1	12						14		5	3	6	10		9	7	8	4			2		11
16		24	Exeter City	1-1	Blissett	3826		1	10						6		5	3		12		9	7	8	4			2		11
17	Dec	2	LEYTON ORIENT	1-0	Godfrey	7383	12	1	10		6						5	3	14	8		9	7		4			2		11
18		16	Stoke City	2-2	Cadette, Smillie	10847		1	10		6	9				5		3	12	8			7		4			2		11
19		23	WIGAN ATHLETIC	1-0	Blissett (p)	6495		1	10		6	9					5	3	12	8			7		4			2		11
20		26	Birmingham City	2-0	Blissett 2	6612		1	10		6	9			14		5	3	12	8			7		4			2		11
21		29	Crewe Alexandra	3-3	Blissett, Cadette, Cockram	3636		1	10		6	9			14		5	3	12	8			7		4			2		11
22	Jan	1	SHREWSBURY TOWN	3-0	Blissett (p), Gayle, Cockram	7064		1	10		6				8		5	3	11			9	7	12	4			2		
23		12	MANSFIELD TOWN	0-0		6064		1	10		6				12		5		8			9	7		4			2	3	11
24		19	Bournemouth	0-2		7167		1	10		6	9			12		5		8				7		4			2	3	11
25		26	SWANSEA CITY	2-0	Blissett, Jones	5373	12	1	10		6	9			14		5		8				7		4			2	3	11
26	Feb	2	ROTHERHAM UNITED	1-2	Jones	5540		1	10		6	9					5	3	8	12		14	7		4			2		11
27		5	Bolton Wanderers	0-1		6731		1	10		6	9					5	3	12	8		14	7		4			2		11
28		16	EXETER CITY	1-0	Millen	5118		1	10		6	12	3		14		5					9	7		4			2	8	11
29		23	Bury	1-1	Cadette	2956	4	1			6	9	3		8		5		12	10			7					2	14	11
30	Mar	3	Leyton Orient	2-1	Cadette, Holdsworth	5313		1			6	10	3		8		5			12		9	7		4			2	14	11
31		9	STOKE CITY	0-4		7249		1			6	10	3		8		5	4	12			9	7					2	14	11
32		12	PRESTON NORTH END	2-0	Bates, Blissett	4856	4	1	10		6	12	3		14		5					9	7					2	8	11
33		16	Grimsby Town	0-2		6685	4	1	10		6	9	3				5		12	11		14	7					2	8	
34		19	Cambridge United	0-0		4931	4	1	12			10	3				5		8	11		9	7					2	6	
35		23	BRADFORD CITY	6-1	Oliver (og),Evans,Jones,Cadette2,Gayle	5601	4	1	12		14	9	3				5		6	11		10	7					2	8	
36		30	BIRMINGHAM CITY	2-2	Ratcliffe, Blissett	6757	4	1	10			12					5		6	11	3	9	7					2	8	
37	Apr	1	Wigan Athletic	0-1		2160	4	1	10			12			14		5	11	6		3	9	7					2	8	
38		6	CREWE ALEXANDRA	1-0	Fleming	5066	4	1	10		11	12			14			3	6		5	9	7					2	8	
39		13	Shrewsbury Town	1-1	Ratcliffe	2841	4	1	10		11				7			3	6		5	9						2	8	12
40		16	FULHAM	1-2	Rostron	7839	4	1							12		5	3	10		6	9	7					2	8	11
41		20	Huddersfield Town	2-1	Peters, Gayle	6489	4	1									5		10		6	9	7		3		11	2	8	
42		23	Fulham	1-0	Rostron	6765	4	1									5		10	12	6	9	7		3		11	2	8	
43		27	READING	1-0	Millen	6398	3	1							6		5		10	12	2	9	7		4		11		8	14
44		30	Chester City	2-1	Gayle, Evans	1275	3	1	10								5		11		2	9	7		4		8		6	
45	May	4	TRANMERE ROVERS	0-2		7341	3	1	10								5		11		6	9	7		4		8	2	14	12
46		11	Southend United	1-0	Gayle	9666	3	1	10								5		9	12			7		4		6	2	8	11
						Apps	30	45	22	8	24	19	8	11	7	8	36	18	23	26	10	27	45	16	31	1	6	34	18	33
						Subs	2		4	3	2	9			13				10	6		3		1	1			4	4	3
						Goals	2		10	1		6			3		2	1	6	4		5	6	2	2		1	2	2	3

One own goal

Play Offs

							Bates JA	Benstead GM	Blissett GP	Brooke GJ	Buckle PJ	Cadette RR	Carstairs JW	Cash SP	Cockram AC	Cousins JM	Evans TW	Fleming MJ	Gayle MA	Godfrey KA	Goodyear C	Holdsworth DC	Jones KA	May ES	Millen KD	Parks A	Peters RAA	Ratcliffe S	Rostron JW	Smillie N
SF1	May	19	TRANMERE ROVERS	2-2	Evans, Godfrey	9330	3	1	10								5		8	12		9	7		4		14	2	6	11
SF"		22	Tranmere Rovers	0-1		11438	3	1	10								5		12	8		9	7		4			2	6	11

F.A. Cup

							Bates JA	Benstead GM	Blissett GP	Brooke GJ	Buckle PJ	Cadette RR	Carstairs JW	Cash SP	Cockram AC	Cousins JM	Evans TW	Fleming MJ	Gayle MA	Godfrey KA	Goodyear C	Holdsworth DC	Jones KA	May ES	Millen KD	Parks A	Peters RAA	Ratcliffe S	Rostron JW	Smillie N
R1	Nov	17	YEOVIL TOWN	5-0	Blissett, Holdsworth 2, May, Jones	4893		1	12	14					11		5	3	6	10		9	7	8	4			2		
R2	Dec	12	Birmingham City	3-1	Blissett, Millen, Jones	5072		1	10		6	9			14		5	3	12	8			7		4			2		11
R3	Jan	5	Oldham Athletic	1-3	Holdsworth	12588		1	10		6				12		5	3	11	8		9	7		4			2		

F.L. Cup (Rumbelows Cup)

							Bates JA	Benstead GM	Blissett GP	Brooke GJ	Buckle PJ	Cadette RR	Carstairs JW	Cash SP	Cockram AC	Cousins JM	Evans TW	Fleming MJ	Gayle MA	Godfrey KA	Goodyear C	Holdsworth DC	Jones KA	May ES	Millen KD	Parks A	Peters RAA	Ratcliffe S	Rostron JW	Smillie N
R1/1	Aug	28	HEREFORD UNITED	2-0	Bates, Godfrey	2993	5	1			6	12				2		3		10		9	7	8	4					11
R1/2	Sep	5	Hereford United	0-1		2445	5	1			6	9				2	12	3		10			7	8	4			14		11
R2/1		26	Sheffield Wednesday	1-2	Evans	11022	2	1	10	6		12		3			5					9	7	8	4			14		11
R2/2	Oct	9	SHEFFIELD WEDNESDAY	1-2	Jones (p)	8227	5	1	12	6		9		3		2				10			7	8	4					11

A.M. Cup (Leyland Daf Cup)

							Bates JA	Benstead GM	Blissett GP	Brooke GJ	Buckle PJ	Cadette RR	Carstairs JW	Cash SP	Cockram AC	Cousins JM	Evans TW	Fleming MJ	Gayle MA	Godfrey KA	Goodyear C	Holdsworth DC	Jones KA	May ES	Millen KD	Parks A	Peters RAA	Ratcliffe S	Rostron JW	Smillie N
PR	Nov	27	Fulham	1-1	Blissett	2761		1	10					14	6		5	3	12	9			7	8	4			2		11
PR	Jan	29	LEYTON ORIENT	2-0	Blissett 2	2576		1	10		6	9			12		5	3	8	14			7		4			2		11
R1	Feb	21	WREXHAM	0-0	*	2247	4	1			14	10	3		6	2	5		8	12		9	7							11
QF		28	Hereford United	2-0	Smillie, Holdsworth	2207	4	1			6	9	3		8		5			10		12	7					2	14	11
SFS	Mar	5	Southend United	3-0	Smillie, Jones, Cadette	3937		1			6	10	3		8		5		12			9	7		4			2	14	11
FS1		26	Birmingham City	1-2	Gayle	16219	4	1	12			10					5	3	8	11		9	7					2	6	
FS2	Apr	9	BIRMINGHAM CITY	0-1		8745	4	1	10		7	9			14	12		3	6		5	11						2	8	

* a.e.t. - won 3-0 on penalties

		Pl.	Home W	D	L	F	A	Away W	D	L	F	A	F. (Total)	A.	Pts
1	Cambridge United	46	14	5	4	42	22	11	6	6	33	23	75	45	86
2	Southend United	46	13	6	4	34	23	13	1	9	33	28	67	51	85
3	Grimsby Town	46	16	3	4	42	13	8	8	7	24	21	66	34	83
4	Bolton Wanderers	46	14	5	4	33	18	10	6	7	31	32	64	50	83
5	Tranmere Rovers	46	13	5	5	38	21	10	4	9	26	25	64	46	78
6	**BRENTFORD**	**46**	**12**	**4**	**7**	**30**	**22**	**9**	**9**	**5**	**29**	**25**	**59**	**47**	**76**
7	Bury	46	13	6	4	39	26	7	7	9	28	30	67	56	73
8	Bradford City	46	13	3	7	36	22	7	7	9	26	32	62	54	70
9	Bournemouth	46	14	6	3	37	20	5	7	11	21	38	58	58	70
10	Wigan Athletic	46	14	3	6	40	20	6	6	11	31	34	71	54	69
11	Huddersfield Town	46	13	3	7	37	23	5	10	8	20	28	57	51	67
12	Birmingham City	46	8	9	6	21	21	8	8	7	24	28	45	49	65
13	Leyton Orient	46	15	2	6	35	19	3	8	12	20	39	55	58	64
14	Stoke City	46	9	7	7	36	29	7	5	11	19	30	55	59	60
15	Reading	46	11	5	7	34	28	6	3	14	19	38	53	66	59
16	Exeter City	46	12	6	5	35	16	4	3	16	23	36	58	52	57
17	Preston North End	46	11	5	7	33	29	4	6	13	21	38	54	67	56
18	Shrewsbury Town	46	8	7	8	29	22	6	3	14	32	46	61	68	52
19	Chester City	46	10	3	10	27	27	4	6	13	19	31	46	58	51
20	Swansea City	46	8	6	9	31	33	5	3	15	18	39	49	72	48
21	Fulham	46	8	8	7	27	22	2	8	13	14	34	41	56	46
22	Crewe Alexandra	46	6	9	8	35	35	5	2	16	27	45	62	80	44
23	Rotherham United	46	5	10	8	31	38	5	2	16	19	49	50	87	42
24	Mansfield Town	46	5	8	10	23	27	3	6	14	19	36	42	63	38

1990-91
Back: Godfrey, Ratcliffe, Millen, Evans, Benstead, Bates, Blissett, Holdsworth, Gayle.
Middle: Gadston (Youth Manager), Peters, Cockram, Cousins, Bayes, Cash, Moore, Moabi, Clare (Physio).
Front: Fleming, Buckle, Brooke, Jones, Holder (Manager), Cadette, Smillie, Driscoll, May.

1991-92
Back: Holdsworth, Bates, Millen, Bayes, Benstead, Evans, Blissett, Godfrey.
Middle: Gadston (Youth Team Manager), Buckle, Peters, Line, Ratcliffe, Gayle, Driscoll, Clare (Physio).
Front: Manuel, Cadette, Rostron (Asst. Manager), Holder (Manager), Smillie, Jones, Turner.

1991/92

Champions of Division Three: Promoted

			Opponent	Score	Scorers	Att.	Bates JA	Bayes AJ	Benstead GM	Blissett GP	Booker R	Buckle PJ	Cadette RR	Driscoll A	Evans TW	Finnigan A	Gayle MA	Godfrey KA	Holdsworth DC	Hughton CWG	Jones KA	Kruszynski Z	Luscombe LJ	Manuel WAJ	Millen KD	Peters RAA	Ratcliffe S	Rostron JW	Sealy AJ	Smillie N	Statham B	Suckling PJ	Line S
1	Aug	17	LEYTON ORIENT	4-3	Holdsworth 3, Evans	6156	4	1		12		6	10		5		14	8	9		7						2	3		11			
2		24	Exeter City	2-1	Gayle, Blissett	3518	4		1	10		6			5		2	8	9		7			3		12		14		11			
3		31	HUDDERSFIELD T	2-3	Jones, Godfrey	5459	4		1	10		6	9		5		12	8			7			3		2		14		11			
4	Sep	3	Hartlepool United	0-1		3660	4		1	12		6	10		5		7	8	9					3		14		2		11			
5		7	Shrewsbury Town	0-1		3193	4		1	11		12	10		5			8	9		7			3		14		6		2			
6		14	READING	1-0	Cadette	5775	4		1	10			12		5		8	7	9					3	6	14		2		11			
7		17	HULL CITY	4-1	Evans, Smillie, Buckley (og), Holdsworth	4586	4		1	12			10		5		8	7	9					3	6			2		11			
8		21	Darlington	2-1	Smillie, Holdsworth	3418	4		1	12			10		5		8	7	9					3	6	14		2		11			
9		28	BOLTON WANDERERS	3-2	Holdsworth 2, Gayle	5658	2		1	12			10		5		8	7	9					3	4			6		11			
10	Oct	5	Fulham	1-0	Evans	7710	2		1				10		5		9	8			7			3	4	12		6		11			
11		12	PETERBOROUGH UTD.	2-1	Evans, Smillie	7705	2						10		5		7	8	9		3				4		12	6		11		1	
12		19	WEST BROMWICH ALB.	1-2	Gayle	8575	2			14			10		5		8	7						3	4		12	6	9	11		1	
13		26	Bury	3-0	Holdsworth 2, Gayle	2280	2			10					5		8	7	9					3	4		6		12	11		1	
14	Nov	2	Bradford City	1-0	Smillie	5359	2			10					5			7	9					3	4		6	8		11		1	
15		6	BIRMINGHAM CITY	2-2	Smillie, Blissett	8798	2			10					5		8	7	9					3	4		6	12		11		1	
16		9	WIGAN ATHLETIC	4-0	Blissett 2, Holdsworth 2	6675	2			10					5		8	7	9					3	4		6		12	11		1	
17		22	Bournemouth	0-0		6035	2				10				5		8	12	9					3	4		6		7	11		1	
18		30	SWANSEA CITY	3-2	Holdsworth, Ratcliffe, Blissett	6669	2			10		14			5		12	8	9					3	4		6	11	7			1	
19	Dec	14	Torquay United	1-1	Godfrey	2475	2		1	10		8			5		6	3	9						4	12			7	11			
20		22	EXETER CITY	3-0	Blissett 2, Gayle	7226	2		1	10		12			5		14	8					9		4		6	3	7	11			
21		26	Huddersfield Town	1-2	Blissett (p)	10605	2		1	10		8			5		9	3					12		4		6	11	7				
22		28	Leyton Orient	2-4	Luscombe 2	7347	2		1			11			5			8	12				9	14	4		6	3	7	10			
23	Jan	1	HARTLEPOOL UNITED	1-0	Holdsworth	7102	2		1		5	12						8	9				10	3	4	14	6		7	11			
24		4	Stockport County	1-2	Francis (og)	4421	2		1		10				5			8	9				7	3	4		6		12	11			
25		11	STOKE CITY	2-0	Luscombe, Holdsworth	9004	2		1	10	8				5		14	12	9				7	3	4		6			11			
26		18	Chester City	1-1	Booker	1447			1	10	8				5				9				7	3	4		6			11	2		
27		25	PRESTON NORTH END	1-0	Evans	7559	3		1		8	12			5		10		9				7		4		6			11	2		
28	Feb	1	West Bromwich Albion	0-2		15984	3		1		8				5		10		9				7	14	4		6		12	11	2		
29		8	BURY	0-3		6789	3		1	10	8			12	5		7		9					14	4		6			11	2		
30		11	Swansea City	1-1	Millen	3582	6		1	10	8	14			5	7	12		9					3	4					11	2		
31		15	TORQUAY UNITED	3-2	Booker, Blissett, Bates	6079	3		1	10	8				5	7	12		9					6	4		14			11	2		
32		22	Stoke City	1-2	Blissett	16396	2		1	10	8				5	7	12		9					3	4		6		14	11			
33		29	STOCKPORT COUNTY	2-1	Smillie, Holdsworth	7484	2		1	10	12				5		7		9					3	4		6		14	11	8		
34	Mar	3	CHESTER CITY	2-0	Blissett, Holdsworth (p)	6869			1	10	8				5		7		9	3					4		6		12	11	2		
35		7	Preston North End	2-3	Smillie, Buckle	3548	4		1	10		8			5		7		9	3							6			11	2		
36		10	Birmingham City	0-1		13290	5		1		8	14					12	7	9	3			10				6		4	11	2		
37		14	BRADFORD CITY	3-4	Evans, Blissett, Holdsworth	6791	4		1	10	8				5			12	9	3			7	6					14	11	2		
38		20	Wigan Athletic	1-2	Holdsworth	2371	4		1	10	12				5			7	9	3				6			8		14	11	2		
39		29	BOURNEMOUTH	2-2	Godfrey, Blissett	7605	3		1	10					5		12	7	9			4		8			6			11	2		
40	Apr	1	Reading	0-0		5660			1	10					5		7		9	3		8			4		6			11	2		
41		4	SHREWSBURY TOWN	2-0	Holdsworth, Evans	5561	2		1	10					5		7		9	3		8	12	14	4		6			11			
42		11	Hull City	3-0	Holdsworth 2, Blissett	3770	2		1	10					5		7		9	3		8	12	14	4		6			11			
43		17	DARLINGTON	4-1	Holdsworth 2, Toman (og), Blissett	8383	4		1	10					5		7	12	9	3		8		14			6			11	2		
44		20	Bolton Wanderers	2-1	Evans, Spooner (og)	4382	4		1	10					5		7	12	9	3		8		14			6			11	2		
45		26	FULHAM	4-0	Holdsworth, Gayle, Blissett, Ratcliffe	12071			1	10					5		7		9	3		8			4		6			11	2		
46	May	2	Peterborough United	1-0	Blissett	14539	12		1	10					5		7		9	3		8		14	4		6			11	2		
						Apps	41	1	37	31	14	8	10	0	44	3	28	26	40	12	6	8	10	27	34	1	31	15	9	44	18	8	
						Subs	1			6	2	7	1	1			10	5	1				3	8		8	3	3	9				
						Goals	1			17	2	1	1		8		6	3	24		1		3		1		2			7			

Four own goals

F.A. Cup

			Opponent	Score	Scorers	Att.	Bates JA	Bayes AJ	Benstead GM	Blissett GP	Booker R	Buckle PJ	Cadette RR	Driscoll A	Evans TW	Finnigan A	Gayle MA	Godfrey KA	Holdsworth DC	Hughton CWG	Jones KA	Kruszynski Z	Luscombe LJ	Manuel WAJ	Millen KD	Peters RAA	Ratcliffe S	Rostron JW	Sealy AJ	Smillie N	Statham B	Suckling PJ	Line S
R1	Nov	18	GILLINGHAM	3-3	Holdsworth 2, Blissett	5830	2	1		10					5		8	7	9					3	4		6		12	11			
rep		26	Gillingham	3-1	Holdsworth 2, Sealy	7328	2	1		10		12			5			7	9					3	4		6		8	11			
R2	Dec	7	Bournemouth	1-2	Bates	6538	2		1	10		8			5		14	12	9					3	4		6		7	11			

F.L. Cup (Rumbelows Cup)

			Opponent	Score	Scorers	Att.	Bates JA	Bayes AJ	Benstead GM	Blissett GP	Booker R	Buckle PJ	Cadette RR	Driscoll A	Evans TW	Finnigan A	Gayle MA	Godfrey KA	Holdsworth DC	Hughton CWG	Jones KA	Kruszynski Z	Luscombe LJ	Manuel WAJ	Millen KD	Peters RAA	Ratcliffe S	Rostron JW	Sealy AJ	Smillie N	Statham B	Suckling PJ	Line S
R1/1	Aug	20	Barnet	5-5	Cadette 2, Godfrey, Holdsworth 2	2927	4	1		12		6	10		5		14	8	9		7			3			2			11			
R1/2		27	BARNET	3-1	Holdsworth, Godfrey, Evans	5563	4		1	10		6			5			8	9		7			3		2				11			12
R2/1	Sep	24	BRIGHTON & HOVE ALE	4-1	Godfrey, Cadette, Holdsworth 2	4927	2		1	12			10		5		7	8	9					3	4	14		6		11			
R2/2	Oct	9	Brighton & Hove Albion	2-4	Cadette, Holdsworth	4502	2	1					10		5		9	8	12		7			3		14	4	6		11			
R3	Nov	30	Norwich City	1-4	Manuel	7394	2	1		10		14			5		8	7	9					3	4		6	12		11			

A.M. Cup (Autoglass Trophy)

			Opponent	Score	Scorers	Att.	Bates JA	Bayes AJ	Benstead GM	Blissett GP	Booker R	Buckle PJ	Cadette RR	Driscoll A	Evans TW	Finnigan A	Gayle MA	Godfrey KA	Holdsworth DC	Hughton CWG	Jones KA	Kruszynski Z	Luscombe LJ	Manuel WAJ	Millen KD	Peters RAA	Ratcliffe S	Rostron JW	Sealy AJ	Smillie N	Statham B	Suckling PJ	Line S
PR	Oct	22	Aldershot	2-0	Sealy 2	1348	2			10		7					8		12					3	4	14	5	6	9	11		1	
PR	Dec	17	BARNET	3-6	Luscombe, Holdsworth 2	1871	2		1	10		6			5		4	8	9				7			3	12			11			
R1	Jan	21	Leyton Orient	2-3	Holdsworth 2	1856			1	10		12			5	8	14	2	9				7	3	4		6			11			

	Pl.	Home W	D	L	F	A	Away W	D	L	F	A	F. (Total)	A. (Total)	Pts
1 BRENTFORD	**46**	**17**	**2**	**4**	**55**	**29**	**8**	**5**	**10**	**26**	**26**	**81**	**55**	**82**
2 Birmingham City	46	15	6	2	42	22	8	6	9	27	30	69	52	81
3 Huddersfield Town	46	15	4	4	36	15	7	8	8	23	23	59	38	78
4 Stoke City	46	14	5	4	45	24	7	9	7	24	25	69	49	77
5 Stockport County	46	15	5	3	47	19	7	5	11	28	32	75	51	76
6 Peterborough Utd.	46	13	7	3	38	20	7	7	9	27	38	65	58	74
7 West Bromwich Alb.	46	12	6	5	45	25	7	8	8	19	24	64	49	71
8 Bournemouth	46	13	4	6	33	18	7	7	9	19	30	52	48	71
9 Fulham	46	11	7	5	29	16	8	6	9	28	37	57	53	70
10 Leyton Orient	46	12	7	4	36	18	6	4	13	26	34	62	52	65
11 Hartlepool United	46	12	5	6	30	21	6	6	11	27	36	57	57	65
12 Reading	46	9	8	6	33	27	7	5	11	26	35	59	62	61
13 Bolton Wanderers	46	10	9	4	26	19	4	8	11	31	37	57	56	59
14 Hull City	46	9	4	10	28	23	7	7	9	26	31	54	54	59
15 Wigan Athletic	46	11	6	6	33	21	4	8	11	25	43	58	64	59
16 Bradford City	46	8	10	5	36	30	5	9	9	26	31	62	61	58
17 Preston North End	46	12	7	4	42	32	3	5	15	19	40	61	72	57
18 Chester City	46	10	6	7	34	29	4	8	11	22	30	56	59	56
19 Swansea City	46	10	9	4	35	24	4	5	14	20	41	55	65	56
20 Exeter City	46	11	7	5	34	25	3	4	16	23	55	57	80	53
21 Bury	46	8	7	8	31	31	5	5	13	24	43	55	74	51
22 Shrewsbury Town	46	7	7	9	30	31	5	4	14	23	37	53	68	47
23 Torquay United	46	13	3	7	29	19	0	5	18	13	49	42	68	47
24 Darlington	46	5	5	13	31	39	5	2	16	25	51	56	90	37

1992/93

22nd in Division One (formerly Division Two): Relegated

#	Date	Opponent	Score	Scorers	Att	Allon JB	Bates JA	Bayes AJ	Bennett MR	Benstead GM	Blissett GP	Booker R	Buckle PJ	Chalmers G	Dickens AW	Evans TW	Gayle MA	Godfrey KA	Hughton CWG	Jones ML	Kruszynski Z	Luscombe LJ	Manuel WAJ	Millen KD	Mortimer PH	Peters RAA	Peyton GJ	Ratcliffe S	Rostron IW	Sansom KG	Smillie N	Statham B	Stephenson P	Westley SLM
1	Aug 15	WOLVERHAMPTON W.	0-2		9069				7	1	10					5	12	9	3	14				4				6	8		11	2		
2	22	Bristol Rovers	1-2	Blissett (p)	5831		5		7	1	10	8					12	9	3		14			4				6			11	2		
3	29	SOUTHEND UNITED	2-1	Bennett, Millen	6431		5		7	1*	10						12	14	3	9			8	4				6			11	2		
4	Sep 1	PORTSMOUTH	4-1	Bennett, Smillie, Gayle, Blissett	8471		5	1	7		10						9		3				8	4				6			11	2		
5	4	Cambridge United	0-1		5082		5		7	1	10						9	14	3				8	4				6	12		11	2		
6	13	LUTON TOWN	1-2	Blissett	7413		5	1	7		10						9		3	11		12	8	4				6				2		
7	19	Leicester City	0-0		12972		5		7		10	12					9		3		8	11		4			1	6			14	2		
8	26	MILLWALL	1-1	Ratcliffe	8823		5				10						9	14	3		8	11	12	4			1	6			7	2		
9	Oct 4	NEWCASTLE UNITED	1-2	Blissett	10131		5		7		10						14	9	3		8		12	4			1	6			11	2		
10	10	Peterborough United	0-0		5818		5		7		10			6			9	14	3			12	8	4			1				11	2		
11	17	WATFORD	1-1	Putney (og)	8490		5		7		10			6			9		3			12	8	4			1				11	2		
12	24	Barnsley	2-3	Blissett 2	4928		5				10		7	6			9		3	14		12	8	4			1				11	2		
13	31	BRISTOL CITY	5-1	Millen 2, Chalmers, Blissett 2	8726						10			6			9		3	14		7	8	4			1	12			11	2		5
14	Nov 3	Swindon Town	2-0	Blissett, Luscombe	7988						10		12	11			9		3	14		7	8	4			1	6				2		5
15	7	CHARLTON ATHLETIC	2-0	Luscombe 2	9354						10			6			9		3			7	8	4			1	12			11	2		5
16	14	Tranmere Rovers	2-3	Blissett, Gayle	7852				7		10						9	12	3			11	8	4			1	6				2		5
17	21	GRIMSBY TOWN	1-3	Allon (p)	7439	7					10			6			9		3			12	8	4			1	14			11	2		5
18	28	OXFORD UNITED	1-0	Allon (p)	8017	7			11		10						9	14	3			12	8	4			1	8				2		5
19	Dec 5	Birmingham City	3-1	Blissett, Ratcliffe, Manuel	8583	7			11		10						9	12	3				8	4			1	6				2		5
20	12	Sunderland	3-1	Blissett 2, Bennett	16954	7			11		10						9	14	3			12	8	4			1	6				2		5
21	20	WEST HAM UNITED	0-0		11912	7			7	1	10						11	14				8	3	4				6			12	2		5
22	26	DERBY COUNTY	2-1	Allon, Goulooze (og)	10226	7			3	1	10			12						14		9	8	4				6			11	2		5
23	28	Notts County	1-1	Westley	6892	7			3	1	10						6			12		9	8	4							11	2		5
24	Jan 9	LEICESTER CITY	1-3	Blissett	8698	7	4		9	1	10						3				8	11	6									2		5
25	17	Millwall	1-6	Blissett	7574	7	5		9	1	10		4	6			3	12			8	11										2		
26	23	Portsmouth	0-1		10267	7	5		9	1	10		2	6			3	8		14		12		4	11									
27	30	BRISTOL ROVERS	0-3		7527	7			8	1	10			14			12	9				11	6	4	3							2		5
28	Feb 6	Wolverhampton Wan.	2-1	Allon 2 (1p)	12361	7	5		8	1	10						11	9				12	6	4	3							2		14
29	9	Luton Town	0-0		7248	7	5		8	1	10		9					12				11	6	4	3							2		
30	14	CAMBRIDGE UNITED	0-1		7318	7	5		8	1	10							9		12		11	6	4	3							2		
31	21	Southend United	0-3		4173		5		8	1	10							9		7		11	6	4	3	12						2		
32	27	PETERBOROUGH UTD.	0-1		6334	12	5		8	1	10				14			7		9		11	6	4				3				2		
33	Mar 6	Newcastle United	1-5	Scott (og)	29819	7	5		8	1	10				12								6	4				3				2	11	9
34	9	TRANMERE ROVERS	0-1		7526	12	5		3	1	10				6					9		7	6	4								2	11	
35	13	Charlton Athletic	0-1		7115	12	5		3	1	10				8					9		11	6	4				14				2	7	
36	20	BIRMINGHAM CITY	0-2		7532	9	5		3	1	10				8		12			14			11	4				6				2	7	
37	23	Grimsby Town	1-0	Blissett	4384	9	3			1	10	14			8	5	12						11	4				6				2	7	
38	27	SWINDON TOWN	0-0		10197					1	10				8	5	9			12			11	4				6		3		2	7	
39	Apr 3	Oxford United	2-0	Blissett, Bennett	5465	12			14	1	10				8	5	9						11	4				6		3		2	7	
40	6	SUNDERLAND	1-1	Gayle	9302				12	1	10				8	5	9						11	4				6		3		2	7	
41	10	Derby County	2-3	Gayle, Millen	12366				3	1	10				8	5	9	12					11	4				6				2	7	14
42	12	NOTTS COUNTY	2-2	Dickens, Blissett	8045	12			14		10				8	5	9						11	4			1	6		3		2	7	
43	17	West Ham United	0-4		16522				11		10				8	5	9						6				1			3	12	2	7	4
44	24	Watford	0-1		9045				12		10				8	5	9					7	6	4			1			3	11	2		
45	May 1	BARNSLEY	3-1	Blissett 2 (1p), Allon	7958	12			7		10				8	5	9					14	6	4			1			3	11	2		
46	8	Bristol City	1-4	Blissett	12695	12			7		10				8	5	9						6	4			1	14		3	11	2		
					Apps	17	24	2	34	24	46	1	4	9	13	11	31	9	20	6	5	19	39	43	6	0	19	25	1	8	18	45	11	15
					Subs	7			4			2	1	2	2		7	12		10	1	10	2			1		5	1		3			2
					Goals	6			4		21			1	1		4					3	1	4				2			1			1

* Game 3: Gayle substituted Benstead (injured), and Blissett took over in goal

Three own goals

F.A. Cup

Rd	Date	Opponent	Score	Scorers	Att	Allon JB	Bates JA	Bayes AJ	Bennett MR	Benstead GM	Blissett GP	Booker R	Buckle PJ	Chalmers G	Dickens AW	Evans TW	Gayle MA	Godfrey KA	Hughton CWG	Jones ML	Kruszynski Z	Luscombe LJ	Manuel WAJ	Millen KD	Mortimer PH	Peters RAA	Peyton GJ	Ratcliffe S	Rostron IW	Sansom KG	Smillie N	Statham B	Stephenson P	Westley SLM
R3	Jan 2	GRIMSBY TOWN	0-2		6880	7			3	1	10			4			6					9	8								11	2		5

F.L. Cup (Coca Cola Cup)

Rd	Date	Opponent	Score	Scorers	Att	Allon JB	Bates JA	Bayes AJ	Bennett MR	Benstead GM	Blissett GP	Booker R	Buckle PJ	Chalmers G	Dickens AW	Evans TW	Gayle MA	Godfrey KA	Hughton CWG	Jones ML	Kruszynski Z	Luscombe LJ	Manuel WAJ	Millen KD	Mortimer PH	Peters RAA	Peyton GJ	Ratcliffe S	Rostron IW	Sansom KG	Smillie N	Statham B	Stephenson P	Westley SLM
R1/1	Aug 18	Fulham	2-0	Booker, Blissett	5067		5		7	1	10	8					12	9	3	14				4				6			11	2		
R1/2	25	FULHAM	2-0	Bates, Blissett	4806		5		7	1	10	8					14	12	3	9				4				6			11	2		
R2/1	Sep 21	Tottenham Hotspur	1-3	Blissett	19365		5	1			10	12					9	14	3		8	7		4				6			11	2		
R2/2	Oct 7	TOTTENHAM HOTSPUI	2-4	Blissett, Millen	11445		5	1	12		10			8			9		3			7	14	4				6			11	2		

Anglo-Italian Cup

Rd	Date	Opponent	Score	Scorers	Att	Allon JB	Bates JA	Bayes AJ	Bennett MR	Benstead GM	Blissett GP	Booker R	Buckle PJ	Chalmers G	Dickens AW	Evans TW	Gayle MA	Godfrey KA	Hughton CWG	Jones ML	Kruszynski Z	Luscombe LJ	Manuel WAJ	Millen KD	Mortimer PH	Peters RAA	Peyton GJ	Ratcliffe S	Rostron IW	Sansom KG	Smillie N	Statham B	Stephenson P	Westley SLM
PR	Sep 16	Swindon Town	2-1	Gayle, Godfrey	3189		5	1	7		10						9	12	3		8	11		4				6				2		
PR	29	OXFORD UNITED	2-0	Retcliffe, Blissett	2607		5				10		14				12	9	3			7	8	4			1	6			11	2		
IS	Nov 11	Ascoli	3-1	Bates, Gayle, Blissett	880		5		7		10			6			9	12	3	14		11	8	4			1					2		
IS	24	LUCCHESE	1-0	Allon	4339	9	5		12		10			8			14		3			11		4			1	6			7	2		
IS	Dec 8	Cesena	1-0	Allon	450	7	5		11	1	10						9	12	3			14	8	4				6				2		
IS	16	BARI	2-1	Godfrey, Luscombe	4554	9	5		7	1	10			6			11	3		14		4	8								12	2		
SF1	Jan 27	DERBY COUNTY	3-4	Allon 3	5227	7			2	1	10		14	8			12	9				11	6	4	3							5		
SF2	Feb 3	Derby County	2-1	Blissett 2	14494	7	5		8	1	10		14				11	9				12	6	4	3							2		

		Pl.	Home W	D	L	F	A	Away W	D	L	F	A	F. (Total)	A.	Pts
1	Newcastle United	46	16	6	1	58	15	13	3	7	34	23	92	38	96
2	West Ham United	46	16	5	2	50	17	10	5	8	31	24	81	41	88
3	Portsmouth	46	19	2	2	48	9	7	8	8	32	37	80	46	88
4	Tranmere Rovers	46	15	4	4	48	24	8	6	9	24	32	72	56	79
5	Swindon Town	46	15	5	3	41	23	6	8	9	33	36	74	59	76
6	Leicester City	46	14	5	4	43	24	8	5	10	28	40	71	64	76
7	Millwall	46	14	6	3	46	21	4	10	9	19	32	65	53	70
8	Derby County	46	11	2	10	40	33	8	7	8	28	24	68	57	66
9	Grimsby Town	46	12	6	5	33	25	7	1	15	25	32	58	57	64
10	Peterborough Utd.	46	7	11	5	30	26	9	3	11	25	37	55	63	62
11	Wolverhampton W.	46	11	6	6	37	26	5	7	11	20	30	57	56	61
12	Charlton Athletic	46	10	8	5	28	19	6	5	12	21	27	49	46	61
13	Barnsley	46	12	4	7	29	19	5	5	13	27	41	56	60	60
14	Oxford United	46	8	7	8	29	21	6	7	10	24	35	53	56	56
15	Bristol City	46	10	7	6	29	25	4	7	12	20	42	49	67	56
16	Watford	46	8	7	8	27	30	6	6	11	30	41	57	71	55
17	Notts County	46	10	7	6	33	21	2	9	12	22	49	55	70	52
18	Southend United	46	9	8	6	33	22	4	5	14	21	42	54	64	52
19	Birmingham City	46	10	4	9	30	32	3	8	12	20	40	50	72	51
20	Luton Town	46	6	13	4	26	26	4	8	11	22	36	48	62	51
21	Sunderland	46	9	6	8	34	28	4	5	14	16	36	50	64	50
22	**BRENTFORD**	**46**	**7**	**6**	**10**	**28**	**30**	**6**	**4**	**13**	**24**	**41**	**52**	**71**	**49**
23	Cambridge United	46	8	6	9	29	32	3	10	10	19	37	48	69	49
24	Bristol Rovers	46	6	6	11	30	42	4	5	14	25	45	55	87	41

1992-93

Back: Gayle, Tripp, Jones, Millen, Bayes, Evans, Benstead, Booker, Sparks, Bates
Middle: Gadston, Bennett, Kruszynski, Luscombe, Blissett, Ratcliffe, Chalmers, Godfrey, Peters, Clare (Physio)
Front: Rostron (Asst. Manager), Statham, Manuel, Hughton, Holder (Manager), Smillie, Buckle, Bircham, Pearce (Coach)

1993-94

Back: Millen, Gayle, Benstead, Evans, Fernandez (ex-Aouf), Bates, Westley, Williams
Middle: Webb (Manager), Lock (Asst. Man.), Allon, Sains, Hutchings, Ratcliffe, Scott Morgan, Stuart Morgan (Youth Manager), Clarke (Physio)
Front: Bennett, Stephenson, Statham, Chalmers, Manuel, Buckle, Peters, Smith, Ravenscroft.

1993/94

16th in Division Two

	Date	Opponent	Score	Scorers	Att	Allon JB	Annon DC	Ashby BJ	Bates JA	Benjamin IT	Bennett MR	Benstead GM	Cornwell JA	Dearden KC	Fernandes TH	Gayle MA	Grainger MR	Harvey LD	Hutchings CE	Manuel WAJ	Metcalf MA	Morgan S	Mundee DWJ	Peters RAA	Ratcliffe S	Ravenscroft CA	Smith PW	Statham B	Stephenson P	Taylor RA	Thompson DG	Tilson SB	Watson KE	Westley SLM	Williams DA	Williams DP	Buckle PJ	Millen KD
1	Aug 14	EXETER CITY	2-1	Allon, Gayle	5537	10			4		9	1				11			8	3					6			2	7					5				
2	21	Blackpool	1-1	Allon	4024	10			4		9	1							8	3				11	6			2	7					5				
3	28	READING	1-0	Allon	6848	10			4		9	1				8				3			12	11	6			2	7					5				
4	31	Hull City	0-1		4517	10			4		9	1				2				3			8	11	6				7					5	12			
5	Sep 4	Rotherham United	0-2		4333	10			4			1				2			12	3			8	11	6				7					5	9	14		
6	11	SWANSEA CITY	1-1	Ratcliffe	5042	10			4		9					2				3			8	11	6	12			7					5		1		
7	14	LEYTON ORIENT	0-1		5149	10			4		9					2			14	3			8	11	6	12			7					5		1		
8	18	Brighton & Hove Albion	1-2	DAWilliams	5734				4				11			2				3			8	12	6				7			10		5	9	1		
9	25	PORT VALE	1-2	Gayle	5107				4	9			11			2				3	14		8	12	6				7			10		5		1		
10	Oct 2	Cambridge United	1-1	Benjamin	3612				4	9	14		11			2			3		10		8	12	6				7					5		1		
11	9	Hartlepool United	1-0	Benjamin	1802					9			11			2			3		10	4	8		6				7					5		1		
12	16	WREXHAM	2-1	Ratcliffe, Allon	5801	10			4	9				1		2			3		12		8		6		11		7					5				
13	23	York City	2-0	Smith, Allon	3513	10			4	9				1		8	2		3				12		6		11		7					5				
14	30	BARNET	1-0	Allon	5873	10			4					1		9	2		3		8			12	6		11		7					5				
15	Nov 2	CARDIFF CITY	1-1	Allon	4756	10			4					1		8	2		3					9	6		11		7					5				
16	6	Plymouth Argyle	1-1	Allon	6407	10			4		12			1		11	2		3					9	6		8		7					5				
17	20	BURNLEY	0-0		6085				4					1		9	2	11	3				10		6	12	8		7					5				
18	27	Huddersfield Town	3-1	Mundee 2 (2p), Ravenscroft	4544				4					1		8	3	11					10		6	9	7	2						5				
19	Dec 11	BLACKPOOL	3-0	Gayle, Mundee 2	4769				4	9				1		8	3	12					11		6		10	2	7					5				
20	18	Exeter City	2-2	Gayle, Mundee (p)	4250				4	9				1		8	3	7					11		6		10	2						5				
21	27	Bournemouth	3-0	Mundee (p), Harvey, Bartram (og)	6422				4	9				1		8	3	7					11		6		10	2						5				
22	29	BRADFORD CITY	2-0	Ratcliffe, Smith	6059				4	9				1		8	3	7					11		6		10	2						5				
23	Jan 1	Fulham	0-0		9797				4	9				1		8	3	7					11		6		10	2						5				
24	3	STOCKPORT COUNTY	1-1	Miller (og)	6410				4	9				1		8	3	7	12				11		6		10	2						5				
25	8	BRISTOL ROVERS	3-4	Mundee 3	6841				4	9				1		8	3	7			12		11		6		10	2						5				
26	15	Wrexham	2-1	Gayle, Bates	3701				4	12				1		8	3		7	11			9		6	10		2						5				
27	22	HARTLEPOOL UNITED	1-0	Bates	6334				4	12				1		8	3		7	11	14		9		6	10		2						5				
28	29	Barnet	0-0		2544	10			4					1		8	3		12	11			9		6			2	7					5				
29	Feb 5	YORK CITY	1-1	Mundee	5712				4					1		8	3	11					9		6		10	2	7					5				
30	12	Bristol Rovers	4-1	Gayle, Allon 3	5684	10			4					1		8	3						9		6		11	2	7		5							
31	19	Reading	1-2	Thompson	9056	10			4					1		8	3	12					9		6		11	2	7		5							
32	22	HULL CITY	0-3		4361	10			4					1		8	3	14	12				9		6		11	2	7					5				
33	26	ROTHERHAM UNITED	2-2	Mundee, Allon	4980	10			4					1			3	11	12				9		6		8	2	7					5				
34	Mar 5	Swansea City	1-1	Harvey	3187	10			4					1		8	3	11					9		6		7	2			5							
35	12	BRIGHTON & HOVE ALB	1-1	Ratcliffe	6728	10	12		4					1		8		11	3				9		6		7	2			5							
36	15	Leyton Orient	1-1	Allon	3185	10	12		4					1		8	3	11					9		6		7	2			5							
37	19	Port Vale	0-1		8269	10	12		4					1		8		11	3				9		6		7	2			5							
38	26	CAMBRIDGE UNITED	3-3	Taylor, Statham, Granger	5052		8		4					1			3	11	12				9		6		7	2		10	5		14					
39	29	Stockport County	1-3	Annon	4361		8	5	4					1			3	11	2				9				7			10			6					
40	Apr 2	BOURNEMOUTH	1-1	Grainger	4305		8	5	4					1			3	11	12				9		6		7	2		10								
41	4	Bradford City	0-1		6703			5	4					1			9	11	8	3					6		7	2		10								
42	9	FULHAM	1-2	Taylor	6638			5	4					1			3	11	12	14			9		6		8	2	7	10								
43	16	Cardiff City	1-1	Harvey	5268			6	4					1				11	8	3			9		12		7	2			5		10					
44	23	PLYMOUTH ARGYLE	1-1	Smith	6173		9	6	4					1			3	11	8	10					12		7	2			5							
45	30	Burnley	1-4	Ashby	11559		10	5	4					1	12		6	11	8	3			9				7	2										
46	May 7	HUDDERSFIELD T	1-2	Harvey	4483		14	5	4					1			6	11	8	3			9			10	7	2			12							
					Apps	21	5	8	45	12	6	5	4	35	0	35	31	23	20	17	3	1	37	8	41	4	32	31	25	5	9	2	2	31	2	6		
					Subs		4			2	2				1			3	9	1	4		2	4	2	3					1		1		1	1		
					Goals	13	1	1	2	2						6	2	4					11		4	1	3	1		2	1				1			

Two own goals

F.A. Cup

Rd	Date	Opponent	Score	Scorers	Att	Allon JB	Annon DC	Ashby BJ	Bates JA	Benjamin IT	Bennett MR	Benstead GM	Cornwell JA	Dearden KC	Fernandes TH	Gayle MA	Grainger MR	Harvey LD	Hutchings CE	Manuel WAJ	Metcalf MA	Morgan S	Mundee DWJ	Peters RAA	Ratcliffe S	Ravenscroft CA	Smith PW	Statham B	Stephenson P	Taylor RA	Thompson DG	Tilson SB	Watson KE	Westley SLM	Williams DA	Williams DP	Buckle PJ	Millen KD
R1	Nov 13	VS Rugby	3-0	Allon 2 (1p), Gayle	3006	10			4					1		8	2		3				9		6		11		7					5				
R2	Dec 4	CARDIFF CITY	1-3	Gayle	4845				4	9				1		8	7	6	3				10				11	2	12					5				

F.L. Cup (Coca Cola Cup)

Rd	Date	Opponent	Score	Scorers	Att	Allon JB	Annon DC	Ashby BJ	Bates JA	Benjamin IT	Bennett MR	Benstead GM	Cornwell JA	Dearden KC	Fernandes TH	Gayle MA	Grainger MR	Harvey LD	Hutchings CE	Manuel WAJ	Metcalf MA	Morgan S	Mundee DWJ	Peters RAA	Ratcliffe S	Ravenscroft CA	Smith PW	Statham B	Stephenson P	Taylor RA	Thompson DG	Tilson SB	Watson KE	Westley SLM	Williams DA	Williams DP	Buckle PJ	Millen KD
1/1	Aug 17	WATFORD	2-2	Peters, Westley	4297	10			4		9	1				11			8	3			14	12	6			2	7					5			8	
1/2	24	Watford	1-3	Westley	4937	10			4		9	1							14	3			12	11	6			2	7					5				

Autoglass Trophy

Rd	Date	Opponent	Score	Scorers	Att	Allon JB	Annon DC	Ashby BJ	Bates JA	Benjamin IT	Bennett MR	Benstead GM	Cornwell JA	Dearden KC	Fernandes TH	Gayle MA	Grainger MR	Harvey LD	Hutchings CE	Manuel WAJ	Metcalf MA	Morgan S	Mundee DWJ	Peters RAA	Ratcliffe S	Ravenscroft CA	Smith PW	Statham B	Stephenson P	Taylor RA	Thompson DG	Tilson SB	Watson KE	Westley SLM	Williams DA	Williams DP	Buckle PJ	Millen KD
R1	Oct 19	Barnet	2-2	Allon 2	1269	10			4	9				1					3			2	12	8	6		11		7					5				
R1	Nov 9	WYCOMBE WANDERERS	2-3	Ratcliffe, Smith	3165	10								1					3		9	2	12	8	6		11		7					5				4
R2	30	Hereford	2-1	Mundee 2	1049				4		9			1		8			3				10	12	6	7	11	2						5				
QF	Jan 11	Leyton Orient	0-1		3683				4	7				1		8		9	3	14	12		10		6		11	2						5				

		Pl.	Home W	D	L	F	A	Away W	D	L	F	A	F. (Total)	A.	Pts
1	Reading	46	15	6	2	40	16	11	5	7	41	28	81	44	89
2	Port Vale	46	16	6	1	46	18	10	4	9	33	28	79	46	88
3	Plymouth Argyle	46	16	4	3	46	26	9	6	8	42	30	88	56	85
4	Stockport County	46	15	3	5	50	22	9	10	4	24	22	74	44	85
5	York City	46	12	7	4	33	13	9	5	9	31	27	64	40	75
6	Burnley	46	17	4	2	55	18	4	6	13	24	40	79	58	73
7	Bradford City	46	13	5	5	34	20	6	8	9	27	33	61	53	70
8	Bristol Rovers	46	10	8	5	33	26	10	2	11	27	33	60	59	70
9	Hull City	46	9	9	5	33	20	9	5	9	29	34	62	54	68
10	Cambridge United	46	11	5	7	38	29	8	4	11	41	44	79	73	66
11	Huddersfield Town	46	9	8	6	27	26	8	6	9	31	35	58	61	65
12	Wrexham	46	13	4	6	45	33	4	7	12	21	44	66	77	62
13	Swansea City	46	12	7	4	37	20	4	5	14	19	38	56	58	60
14	Brighton & Hove A.	46	10	7	6	38	29	5	7	11	22	38	60	67	59
15	Rotherham United	46	11	4	8	42	30	4	9	10	21	30	63	60	58
16	**BRENTFORD**	**46**	**7**	**10**	**6**	**30**	**28**	**6**	**9**	**8**	**27**	**27**	**57**	**55**	**58**
17	Bournemouth	46	8	7	8	26	27	6	8	9	25	32	51	59	57
18	Leyton Orient	46	11	9	3	38	26	3	5	15	19	45	57	71	56
19	Cardiff City	46	10	7	6	39	33	3	8	12	27	46	66	79	54
20	Blackpool	46	12	2	9	41	37	4	3	16	22	38	63	75	53
21	Fulham	46	7	6	10	20	23	7	4	12	30	40	50	63	52
22	Exeter City	46	8	7	8	38	37	3	5	15	14	46	52	83	45
23	Hartlepool United	46	8	3	12	28	40	1	6	16	13	47	41	87	36
24	Barnet	46	4	6	13	22	32	1	7	15	19	54	41	86	28

1994/95

Second in Division Two

No	Date		Opponent	Score	Scorers	Att	Abrahams P	Annon DC	Ansah A	Ashby BJ	Bailey DL	Bates JA	Benjamin IT	Dearden KC	Fernandes TH	Forster NM	Grainger MR	Harvey LD	Hooker JW	Hurdle AAJ	Hutchings CE	McGhee DC	Mundee DWJ	Parris GMR	Ratcliffe S	Ravenscroft CA	Smith PW	Statham B	Stephenson P	Taylor RA	Westley SLM	Asaba C
1	Aug	13	Plymouth Argyle	5-1	Smith, Forster 2, Stephenson, Taylor	7976						5			1	10		8		2	3			7			6		11	9	4	
2		20	PETERBOROUGH UTD.	0-1		5516		12				5		1		10		8		2	3			7			6		11	9	4	
3		27	Stockport County	1-0	Taylor	4399				5		4		1		10		8		2	3		12	7			6		11	9		
4		30	ROTHERHAM UNITED	2-0	Taylor, Forster	4031				5		4		1		10				2	3		8	7			6		11	9		
5	Sep	3	WREXHAM	0-2		5820				5		4		1		10	14	12		2	3		8	7			6		11	9		
6		10	Wycombe Wanderers	3-4	Taylor, Stephenson, Cousins (og)	6847				5		4		1		10	3	8		2	7		12				6		11	9		
7		13	York City	1-2	Taylor	2836				5		4		1		10	3	8			7				12		6	2	11	9		
8		17	BLACKPOOL	3-2	Forster, Smith, Grainger (p)	4157				5		4	9	1		10	3	8			7		12				6	2	11		14	
9		24	Crewe Alexandra	2-0	Forster, Taylor	3839				5				1		10	3	8			7		12				6	2	11	9	4	
10	Oct	1	SHREWSBURY TOWN	1-0	Taylor	4556				5				1		10	3	8			7		12			11	6	2		9	4	
11		8	BRISTOL ROVERS	3-0	Forster 2, Taylor	5330				5		4		1		10	3	8		12	7		14				6	2	11	9		
12		15	Bournemouth	1-0	Forster	4411				5				1	14	10	3	8			7		12				6	2	11	9	4	
13		22	BIRMINGHAM CITY	1-2	Ward (og)	7779				5				1		10	3	8			7		12				6	2	11	9	4	
14		29	Cambridge United	0-0		3108				5					1	10	3	8							7		6	2	11	9	4	
15	Nov	2	Bradford City	0-1		4105				5				1		10	3	8					12		7		6	2	11	9	4	
16		5	HULL CITY	0-1		5455			11	5				1		10	3	8					12		7		6	2		9	4	
17		19	Huddersfield Town	0-1		10889			11	5				1		10	3	8		12	7						6	2		9	4	
18		26	BRIGHTON & HOVE ALB	2-1	Ashby, Ansah	4728		11	14	5		7		1		10	3	8					12				6	2		9	4	
19	Dec	10	Peterborough United	2-2	Taylor, Forster	4102		7		5		4			1	10		8	12	3			11				6	2		9		
20		17	PLYMOUTH ARGYLE	7-0	Annon, Smith, Taylor 2, Forster, Mundee, Harvey	4492		11		5		4		1		10	3	8			2		12		7		6			9		
21		26	LEYTON ORIENT	3-0	Mundee, Ratcliffe, Forster	6125		7		5		4		1		10	3	8			2		11		6					9		
22		27	Chester City	4-1	Forster 3, Grainger	2266		7		5		4		1		10	3	8			2		11		6					9		
23		31	OXFORD UNITED	2-0	Forster, Taylor	7125		7				5		1		10	3	8			2		11		6			12		9	4	
24	Jan	2	Cardiff City	3-2	Harvey, Forster, Taylor	5253		7				5		1		10	3	8			2		11		6			12		9	4	
25		14	SWANSEA CITY	0-0		7211		7		5		4		1		10	3	8			2		11		6			12		9		
26		21	Hull City	2-1	Mundee, Grainer	3823		7		5		4		1		10	3	8			2	14	11		6			12		9		
27		28	CAMBRIDGE UNITED	6-0	Taylor 2, Forster, Grainger (p), Bailey 2	6390				5	8	4		1		10	3				2		11		6			12	7	9		
28	Feb	4	Brighton & Hove Albion	1-1	Bailey	9499				5	8	4		1		10	3				2	14	11		6			12	7	9		
29		11	BRADFORD CITY	4-3	Mundee, Taylor, Grainge (p), Forster	6019				5	8	4		1		10	3				2		11		6			12	7	9		
30		17	Swansea City	2-0	Forster 2	3935				5	8	4		1		10	3				2		11		6				7	9		
31		21	HUDDERSFIELD T	0-0		9562				5	8	4		1		10	3				2	7	9		6			12	11			
32		25	Shrewsbury Town	1-2	Forster	4570				5	8	4		1		10	3				2	14	9		7		6	12	11			
33	Mar	4	CREWE ALEXANDRA	2-0	Mundee, Taylor	7143				5		4		1		10	3				2		8		7		6	12	11	9		
34		7	Wrexham	0-0		2834						5		1		10					2		8		7		6	3	11	9	4	
35		11	STOCKPORT COUNTY	1-0	Taylor	6513						5		1		10					2		8		7		6	3	11	9	4	
36		18	Rotherham United	2-0	Forster, Abrahams	2964	11			5		4		1		10	3				2						6	8	7	9		
37		21	WYCOMBE WANDERERS	0-0		9530	12			5		4		1		10	3				2		11				6	8	7	9		
38		25	Blackpool	2-1	Bates, Taylor	4663	11			5		4		1		10	3				2		12				6	8	7	9		
39	Apr	1	YORK CITY	3-0	Grainger, Forster, Taylor	6474	11			5		4		1		10	3				2						6	8	7	9		
40		8	Oxford United	1-1	Taylor	7845	11			5		4		1		10	3				2		12				6	8	7	9		
41		15	CHESTER CITY	1-1	Abrahams	8020	11			5		4		1		10	3				2	14	12				6	8	7	9		
42		17	Leyton Orient	2-0	Bates, Forster	4459				5		4		1		10	3						8		7		6	2	11	9		
43		22	CARDIFF CITY	2-0	and Blissett took over in goal	8268	14			5		4		1		10	3				12		8		7		6	2	11	9		
44		26	Birmingham City	0-2		25581	12			5		4		1		10	3						8		7		6	2	11	9		
45		29	BOURNEMOUTH	1-2	Abrahams	10079	11			5		4		1		10					3	14	12		8		6	2	7	9		
46	May	6	Bristol Rovers	2-2	McGhee, Taylor	8256	11			5		4		1		10					3	14	12		8		6	2	7	9		
						Apps	7	9	2	40	6	38	1	43	3	46	36	24	0	7	38	1	22	5	24	1	35	26	34	43	15	
						Subs	3	1	1						1		1	1	1	2	1	6	17		1			10			1	
						Goals	3	1	1	1	3	2				24	7	2				1	5		1		3		2	23		

Play Offs

Rd	Date		Opponent	Score	Scorers	Att	Abrahams P	Annon DC	Ansah A	Ashby BJ	Bailey DL	Bates JA	Benjamin IT	Dearden KC	Fernandes TH	Forster NM	Grainger MR	Harvey LD	Hooker JW	Hurdle AAJ	Hutchings CE	McGhee DC	Mundee DWJ	Parris GMR	Ratcliffe S	Ravenscroft CA	Smith PW	Statham B	Stephenson P	Taylor RA	Westley SLM	Asaba C
S/F1	May	14	Huddersfield Town	1-1	Forster	14160				5		4		1		10	3				12		8		7		6	2	11	9		
S/F2		17	HUDDERSFIELD T *	1-1	Grainger (p)	11161	11			5		4		1		10	3						12		8		6	2	7	9		

* A.E.T. Lost on penalties

F.A. Cup

Rd	Date		Opponent	Score	Scorers	Att	Abrahams P	Annon DC	Ansah A	Ashby BJ	Bailey DL	Bates JA	Benjamin IT	Dearden KC	Fernandes TH	Forster NM	Grainger MR	Harvey LD	Hooker JW	Hurdle AAJ	Hutchings CE	McGhee DC	Mundee DWJ	Parris GMR	Ratcliffe S	Ravenscroft CA	Smith PW	Statham B	Stephenson P	Taylor RA	Westley SLM	Asaba C
R1	Nov	12	Cambridge United	2-2	Annon, Taylor	3353		11		5				1		10	3	8		12	7						6	2		9	4	
rep		22	CAMBRIDGE UNITED	1-2	Grainger	4096				5		7		1		10	3	8			12		11				6	2		9	4	

F.L. Cup (Coca Cola Cup)

Rd	Date		Opponent	Score	Scorers	Att	Abrahams P	Annon DC	Ansah A	Ashby BJ	Bailey DL	Bates JA	Benjamin IT	Dearden KC	Fernandes TH	Forster NM	Grainger MR	Harvey LD	Hooker JW	Hurdle AAJ	Hutchings CE	McGhee DC	Mundee DWJ	Parris GMR	Ratcliffe S	Ravenscroft CA	Smith PW	Statham B	Stephenson P	Taylor RA	Westley SLM	Asaba C
R1/1	Aug	16	Colchester United	2-0	Stephenson, Taylor	2521						5	12	1		10		8		2	3			7			6		11	9	4	
R1/2		23	COLCHESTER UNITED	2-0	Parris, Smith	2315				5		4		1		10		8		2	3		14	7	12		6		11	9		
R2/1	Sep	20	Tranmere Rovers	0-1		3754				5				1		10	3	8			7						6	2	11	9	4	
R2/2		27	TRANMERE ROVERS	0-0		4076				5				1		10	3	8			7						6	2	11	9	4	

Auto Windscreens Shield

Rd	Date		Opponent	Score	Scorers	Att	Abrahams P	Annon DC	Ansah A	Ashby BJ	Bailey DL	Bates JA	Benjamin IT	Dearden KC	Fernandes TH	Forster NM	Grainger MR	Harvey LD	Hooker JW	Hurdle AAJ	Hutchings CE	McGhee DC	Mundee DWJ	Parris GMR	Ratcliffe S	Ravenscroft CA	Smith PW	Statham B	Stephenson P	Taylor RA	Westley SLM	Asaba C
R1	Oct	19	Brighton & Hove Alb.	1-0	Foster	1104				5				1		10	3	8			6		9		7			2	11		4	
R1	Nov	8	GILLINGHAM	3-1	Annon. Asaba. Ansah	1795		7	11	10		4		1	12	14	3			2	5					13	6			9		8
R2	Dec	3	Oxford United	1-2	Grainger (p)	2410		14	11	5		6		1		10	3	8			12		7					2		9	4	

		Pl.	Home W	D	L	F	A	Away W	D	L	F	A	F. (Total)	A.	Pts
1	Birmingham City	46	15	6	2	53	18	10	8	5	31	19	84	37	89
2	**BRENTFORD**	**46**	**14**	**4**	**5**	**44**	**15**	**11**	**6**	**6**	**37**	**24**	**81**	**39**	**85**
3	Crewe Alexandra	46	14	3	6	46	33	11	5	7	34	35	80	68	83
4	Bristol Rovers	46	15	7	1	48	20	7	9	7	22	20	70	40	82
5	Huddersfield Town	46	14	5	4	45	21	8	10	5	34	28	79	49	81
6	Wycombe Wands.	46	13	7	3	36	19	8	8	7	24	27	60	46	78
7	Oxford United	46	13	6	4	30	18	8	6	9	36	34	66	52	75
8	Hull City	46	13	6	4	40	18	8	5	10	30	39	70	57	74
9	York City	46	13	4	6	37	21	8	5	10	30	30	67	51	72
10	Swansea City	46	10	8	5	23	13	9	6	8	34	32	57	45	71
11	Stockport County	46	12	3	8	40	29	7	5	11	23	31	63	60	65
12	Blackpool	46	11	4	8	40	36	7	6	10	24	34	64	70	64
13	Wrexham	46	10	7	6	38	27	6	8	9	27	37	65	64	63
14	Bradford City	46	8	6	9	29	32	8	6	9	28	32	57	64	60
15	Peterborough Utd.	46	7	11	5	26	29	7	7	9	28	40	54	69	60
16	Brighton & Hove A.	46	9	10	4	25	15	5	7	11	29	38	54	53	59
17	Rotherham United	46	12	6	5	36	26	2	8	13	21	35	57	61	56
18	Shrewsbury Town	46	9	9	5	34	27	4	5	14	20	35	54	62	53
19	Bournemouth	46	9	4	10	30	34	4	7	12	19	35	49	69	50
20	Cambridge United	46	8	9	6	33	28	3	6	14	19	41	52	69	48
21	Plymouth Argyle	46	7	6	10	22	36	5	4	14	23	47	45	83	46
22	Cardiff City	46	5	6	12	25	31	4	5	14	21	43	46	74	38
23	Chester City	46	5	6	12	23	42	1	5	17	14	42	37	84	29
24	Leyton Orient	46	6	6	11	21	29	0	2	21	9	46	30	75	26

1994-95

Back: Taylor, Ratcliffe, Thompson, Judge, Fernandes, Dearden, Westley, Ashby, Bates
Middle: Booker (Youth Coach), Lock (Asst. Manager), McGhee, Peters, Smith, Benjamin, Campbell, Hurdle, Manuel, Hutchings, Johnson (Physio), Mason (Asst. Physio)
Front: Grainger, Statham, Annon, Mundee, Webb (Manager), Forster, Ravenscroft, Stephenson, Harvey

1995-96

Back: Omigie, Hurdle, Bates, Ashby, Taylor, Asaba, Hutchings, Campbell, Burke (Asst. Physio)
Middle: Booker (Youth Coach), Grainger, McGhee, Smith, Fernandes, Dearden, Mundee, Abrahams, Anderson, Johnson (Physio)
Front: Hooker, Annon, Harvey, Webb (Manager), Lock (Coach), Forster, Statham, Ravenscroft

1995/96

15th in Division Two

							Abrahams P	Anderson IM	Annon DC	Ansah A	Asaba CE	Ashby BJ	Bates JA	Bent MN	Canham SW	Davis PV	Dearden KC	Fernandes TH	Forster NM	Grainger MR	Greene DM	Harvey LD	Hooker JW	Hurdle AAJ	Hutchings CE	Martin DE	McGhee DC	Mundee DWJ	Omigie JE	Ravenscroft CA	Smith PW	Statham B	Sussex AR	Taylor RA
1	Aug	12	York City	2-2	Smith, Forster	3239		10				4	5				1		9	3		7		6							8	2		11
2		19	OXFORD UNITED	1-0	Taylor	5614		10				4	5				1		9	3		7		6							8	2		11
3		26	Burnley	0-1		9586		10					5				1		9	3		7		6			4	12			8	2		11
4		29	HULL CITY	1-0	Taylor	4535		10					5				1		9	3		7					4	6			8	2		11
5	Sep	2	SWINDON TOWN	0-2		7878		10	14			12	5				1		9	3		7					4	6			8	2		11
6		9	Rotherham United	0-1		2963		10			12	6	5				1		9	3		7					4				8	2		11
7		12	Bristol City	0-0		5054					12	6	5				1		9	3			10				4	7			8	2		11
8		16	WALSALL	1-0	Taylor	4717						6	5			4	1		9	3			10					7			8	2		11
9		23	Bristol Rovers	0-2		5120					14	6	5			4	1		9	3			10				12	7			8	2		11
10		30	CHESTERFIELD	1-2	McGhee	4734					10	6	5			4	1		9	3				12			7				8	2		11
11	Oct	7	BLACKPOOL	1-2	McGhee	5313	12	3				6				4	1		9			10			5		7				8	2		11
12		14	Stockport County	1-1	Smith	6228						6	5				1		9	3		4				10	7				8	2		11
13		21	PETERBOROUGH UTD.	3-0	Bates 2, Grainger (p)	4201					14	6	5				1		9	3		4		12		10	7			11	8	2		
14		28	Crewe Alexandra	1-3	Forster	3835		11			12	6					1		9	3		4		5		10	7				8	2		
15	Nov	1	Notts County	0-4		3958	11				7	6					1		9	3		4				10	5				8	2		
16		4	SHREWSBURY TOWN	0-2		4104					7			9		4		1		3		12	11		5	10	6				8	2		
17		18	Bournemouth	0-1		3894				3			5	7				1		3		2			4	10	6				8			11
18		25	BRADFORD CITY	2-1	Taylor 2	4237				7		6	5	14				1		3		12			4	10	9				8	2		11
19	Dec	9	BRISTOL ROVERS	0-0		5679				7		6	5	12			1			3		2			4	10	9				8			11
20		16	Chesterfield	2-2	Smith, Ansah	4016				7			5				1			3		2			4	10	6				8		9	11
21		22	Wrexham	2-2	Taylor, Martin	3670				7			5	12			1			3		2			4	10	6				8		9	11
22		26	BRIGHTON & HOVE ALB	0-1		5794				7			5				1			3		2			4	10	6		12		8		9	11
23	Jan	13	Oxford United	1-2	Ashby	5566						6	5	10			1		9	3		2			4	12	7				8			11
24		20	YORK CITY	2-0	Bates, Taylor	3915						6	5	10	7		1		9	3		2			4				12		8			11
25		30	WYCOMBE WANDERERS	1-0	Taylor	4668						6	5	10	7		1		9	3		2			4	12					8			11
26	Feb	3	BURNLEY	1-0	Forster	5195						6	5		7		1		9	3		2			4	10					8			11
27		10	Carlisle United	1-2	Bates	5143						6	5		7		1		9	3		2			4	10	12				8			11
28		17	BRISTOL CITY	2-2	McGhee, Taylor	5213		3					5	10	7		1		9			2			4	12	6		14		8			11
29		21	Swindon Town	2-2	Abrahams 2	9733	7	3					5				1		9			2			4	10	6				8			11
30		24	Walsall	1-0	Abrahams	3506	7	10				6	5				1		9	3		2				12	4		14		8			11
31		27	ROTHERHAM UNITED	1-1	Grainger	3446	7	10				6	5				1		9	3		2				12	4				8			11
32	Mar	2	Brighton & Hove Albion	0-0		5914	7	10					5				1		9	3	6	2		4							8			11
33		5	Hull City	1-0	Anderson	2284	7	10					5				1		9	3	6	2		4	12						8			11
34		9	WREXHAM	1-0	Anderson	4579	7	10					5				1		9		6	2		4	3		12				8			11
35		12	Swansea City	1-2	Forster	3538	7	10					5				1		9		6	2		4	3		12				8			11
36		16	Wycombe Wanderers	1-2	Forster	4912		10				4	5		7		1		9	3	6	2							12		8			11
37		19	CARLISLE UNITED	1-1	Grainger	3102		10				12	5		7		1		9	3	6	2			4						8			11
38		23	SWANSEA CITY	0-0		4378	14	6				4	5		7		1		9	3		2					12		10		8			11
39		30	Blackpool	0-1		5899	10	3				4			7		1		9		6	2					5		12		8			11
40	Apr	2	STOCKPORT COUNTY	1-0	Smith	3274	10	3				4			7		1		9		6	2					5				8			11
41		6	CREWE ALEXANDRA	2-1	Taylor 2	4408	10	3				4			7		1		9		6	2					5		12		8			11
42		8	Peterborough United	1-0	McGhee	4343	10	3				4			7		1				6	2			12		5		8		8			11
43		13	NOTTS COUNTY	0-0		4588	10					4			7		1		14		6	2		12	3		5		9		8			11
44		20	Shrewsbury Town	1-2	McGhee	2711	10	3				4		12	7		1		9			2		6			5				8			11
45		26	Bradford City	1-2	Bent	7730		3			10	4	5	7				1	9					2	12		6				8			11
46	May	4	BOURNEMOUTH	2-0	Asaba 2	6091	12				10	4	5	7				1	9					2	3		6				8			11
						Apps	14	25	0	6	5	31	36	8	14	5	41	5	37	33	11	38	4	11	20	14	31	5	3	1	46	17	3	42
						Subs	3		1		5	2		4					1			2		3	3	5	5	1	7					
						Goals	3	2		1	2	1	4	1					5	3						1	5				4			11

F.A. Cup

							Abrahams P	Anderson IM	Annon DC	Ansah A	Asaba CE	Ashby BJ	Bates JA	Bent MN	Canham SW	Davis PV	Dearden KC	Fernandes TH	Forster NM	Grainger MR	Greene DM	Harvey LD	Hooker JW	Hurdle AAJ	Hutchings CE	Martin DE	McGhee DC	Mundee DWJ	Omigie JE	Ravenscroft CA	Smith PW	Statham B	Sussex AR	Taylor RA
R1	Nov	11	FARNBOROUGH TOWN	1-1	Bent	4711					7		5	11				1	9	3		2	12		4	10	6				8			
rep		22	Farnborough Town#	4-0	Smith, Taylor 2, Bent	3581						6	5	7				1		3		2	12		4	10	9				8			11
R2	Dec	2	Bournemouth	1-0	Taylor	4451		12				6	5	7			1			3		14			4	10	9				8	2		11
R3	Jan	6	Norwich City	2-1	OG, Bent	10082		14				6	5	10			1		9	3		2			4	12	7				8			11
R4	Feb	7	Charlton Athletic	2-3	Ashby, Smith	15000		7				6	5				1		9	3		2			4	10					8			11

F.L. Cup (Coca Cola Cup)

							Abrahams P	Anderson IM	Annon DC	Ansah A	Asaba CE	Ashby BJ	Bates JA	Bent MN	Canham SW	Davis PV	Dearden KC	Fernandes TH	Forster NM	Grainger MR	Greene DM	Harvey LD	Hooker JW	Hurdle AAJ	Hutchings CE	Martin DE	McGhee DC	Mundee DWJ	Omigie JE	Ravenscroft CA	Smith PW	Statham B	Sussex AR	Taylor RA
R1/1	Aug	15	Walsall	2-2	Harvey, Foster	2405		10				4	5				1		9	3		7		6							8	2		11
R1/2		22	WALSALL	3-2	Taylor, Anderson, McGhee	3549		10				4	5				1		9	3		7		6			12	14			8	2		11
R2/1	Sep	19	Bolton Wanderers	0-1		5243						6	5			4	1		9	3			10					7			8	2		11
R2/2	Oct	3	BOLTON WANDERERS	2-3	Foster, Grainger (p)	4861					10	6	5			4	1		9	3		12					7				8	2		11

Auto Windscreens Shield

							Abrahams P	Anderson IM	Annon DC	Ansah A	Asaba CE	Ashby BJ	Bates JA	Bent MN	Canham SW	Davis PV	Dearden KC	Fernandes TH	Forster NM	Grainger MR	Greene DM	Harvey LD	Hooker JW	Hurdle AAJ	Hutchings CE	Martin DE	McGhee DC	Mundee DWJ	Omigie JE	Ravenscroft CA	Smith PW	Statham B	Sussex AR	Taylor RA
R1	Sep	27	Bournemouth	1-0	Taylor	1092					10	6	5			4	1		9	3							7				8	2		11
R1	Oct	17	EXETER CITY	1-1	Foster	1431		12				6	5				1		9	3		4			14	10	7				8	2		11
R2	Nov	28	FULHAM	0-1		3760				7		6	5	9				1		3					4	10	12				8	2		11

		Pl.	Home W	Home D	Home L	Home F	Home A	Away W	Away D	Away L	Away F	Away A	F. (Total)	A. (Total)	Pts
1	Swindon Town	46	12	10	1	37	16	13	7	3	34	18	71	34	92
2	Oxford United	46	17	4	2	52	14	7	7	9	24	25	76	39	83
3	Blackpool	46	14	5	4	41	20	9	8	6	26	20	67	40	82
4	Notts County	46	14	6	3	42	21	7	9	7	21	18	63	39	78
5	Crewe Alexandra	46	13	3	7	40	24	9	4	10	37	36	77	60	73
6	Bradford City	46	15	4	4	41	25	7	3	13	30	44	71	69	73
7	Chesterfield	46	14	6	3	39	21	6	6	11	17	30	56	51	72
8	Wrexham	46	12	6	5	51	27	6	10	7	25	28	76	55	70
9	Stockport County	46	8	9	6	30	20	11	4	8	31	27	61	47	70
10	Bristol Rovers	46	12	4	7	29	28	8	6	9	28	32	57	60	70
11	Walsall	46	12	7	4	38	20	7	5	11	22	25	60	45	69
12	Wycombe Wands.	46	9	8	6	36	26	6	7	10	27	33	63	59	60
13	Bristol City	46	10	6	7	28	22	5	9	9	27	38	55	60	60
14	Bournemouth	46	12	5	6	33	25	4	5	14	18	45	51	70	58
15	**BRENTFORD**	**46**	**12**	**6**	**5**	**24**	**15**	**3**	**7**	**13**	**19**	**34**	**43**	**49**	**58**
16	Rotherham United	46	11	7	5	31	20	3	7	13	23	42	54	62	56
17	Burnley	46	9	8	6	35	28	5	5	13	21	40	56	68	55
18	Shrewsbury Town	46	7	8	8	32	29	6	6	11	26	41	58	70	53
19	Peterborough Utd.	46	9	6	8	40	27	4	7	12	19	39	59	66	52
20	York City	46	8	6	9	28	29	5	7	11	30	44	58	73	52
21	Carlisle United	46	11	6	6	35	20	1	7	15	22	52	57	72	49
22	Swansea City	46	8	8	7	27	29	3	6	14	16	50	43	79	47
23	Brighton & Hove A.	46	6	7	10	25	31	4	3	16	21	38	46	69	40
24	Hull City	46	4	8	11	26	37	1	8	14	10	41	36	78	31

1996/97

4th in Division Two

No	Date	Opponent	Res	Scorers	Att	Abrahams P	Anderson IM	Asaba CE	Ashby BJ	Bates JA	Bent MN	Canham SW	Dearden KC	Dennis KJ	Fernandes TH	Forster NM	Goddard-Crawley RL	Harvey LD	Hurdle AAJ	Hutchings CE	Janney M	McGhee DC	McPherson M	Omigie JE	Rapley KJ	Slade SA	Smith PW	Statham B	Taylor RA
1	Aug 17	Bury	1-1	Taylor	3373		3	7	4	5	10		1			9			2			6					8		11
2	24	LUTON TOWN	3-2	Asaba, Bates, Taylor	5409	9	3	7	4	5	10		1					12	2	14		6					8		11
3	27	GILLINGHAM	2-0	Abrahams	5384	9	3	7	4	5	10		1						2			6					8		11
4	31	Shrewsbury Town	3-0	Asaba 3	3530	9	3	7	4	5	10		1					12	2	14		6					8		11
5	Sep 7	Chesterfield	2-0	Bates, Forster	3643		3	7	4	5	10		1			9			2	12		6					8		11
6	10	PLYMOUTH ARGYLE	3-2	Smith, Asaba, Bent	5377		3	7	4	5	10		1			9			2	12		6					8		11
7	14	BLACKPOOL	1-1	Asaba	5908	12	3	7	4	5	10	6	1			9			2								8		11
8	21	Wycombe Wanderers	1-0	Bent	5330	14	3	7	4	5	10	6	1			9			2			12					8		11
9	28	YORK CITY	3-3	Taylor, Asaba	5243	14	3	7	4		10	6	1			9		12	2			5					8		11
10	Oct 1	Bristol City	2-1	Asaba, Forster	9520	10	3	7	4		14		1			9		12	2	6		5					8		11
11	5	ROTHERHAM UNITED	4-2	Asaba 2, Taylor, Forster	6137	10	3	7	4		14		1			9		12	2	6		5					8		11
12	12	Crewe Alexandra	0-2		4313		3	7	4		10		1	14		9		12	2	6		5					8		11
13	15	Peterborough United	1-0	Taylor	5037		3	7	4		10		1			9			2	6		5					8		11
14	19	WALSALL	1-1	Hutchings	5419		3	7	4		10		1			9		12	2	6		5					8		11
15	26	MILLWALL	0-0		7691		3	7	4			10	1			9			2	6		5					8		11
16	29	Bristol Rovers	1-2	Hutchings	5163		3	7	4		12	10	1			9			2	6		5					8		11
17	Nov 2	Watford	0-2		11448		3	7	4		10		1			9			2	6		5		12			8		11
18	9	STOCKPORT COUNTY	2-2	Canham, Forster	5076		3			5	10	6	1			9		12	2			4		7			8		11
19	19	Bournemouth	1-2	Anderson	2747		3	7	4	5		10	1			9		12	2			6					8		11
20	23	WREXHAM	2-0	Forster, Asaba	4885		3	7	4	5		10	1			9		12	2			6					8		11
21	29	Millwall	0-0		7845		3	7	4	5		10	1			9		12	2			6					8		11
22	Dec 3	NOTTS COUNTY	2-0	Bent, Asaba	3675		3	7	4	5	10		1			9		12	2			6					8		11
23	14	Burnley	2-1	Asaba, Forster	10575		3	7	4	5			1			9		11	2	12		6		10			8		
24	21	PRESTON NORTH END	0-0		5365		3	7	4	5	12		1			9		11	2			6		10			8		
25	26	Plymouth Argyle	4-1	Forster 2, Asbab, Omigie	9525		3	7	4	5	11		1			9			2			6		10			8	12	
26	Jan 11	York City	4-2	Asaba 2, Forster 2	3085		3	7	4	5	10		1			9			2			6					8	12	11
27	18	BRISTOL CITY	0-0		7606		3	7	4	5			1			9			2			6					8	10	11
28	21	BRISTOL ROVERS	0-0		4191		3	7	4	5			1			9			2			6	10	14			8	12	11
29	Feb 1	Stockport County	2-1	McGhee, Taylor	8650		3	7	4	5	9	10	1							2		6					8		11
30	8	WATFORD	1-1	Asaba	8679		3	7	4	5	9	10	1							2		6		14			8	12	11
31	22	BOURNEMOUTH	1-0	Asaba	6071		3	7	4	5	9		1							2		6				10	8	12	11
32	Mar 1	Notts County	1-1	Ashby	4323		3	7	4	5	9				1					2		6				10	8	12	11
33	4	WYCOMBE WANDERERS	0-0		5375		3	7	4	5	9				1							6				10	8	2	11
34	8	Preston North End	0-1		9489		3		4	5	9		1						14	2		6	7			10	8	12	11
35	15	BURNLEY	0-3		6624		3	7	4	5	9	10	1							2		6		12			8		11
36	21	Luton Town	0-1		8680		3	7	4	5	9		1	12						2		6		10			8		11
37	25	Wrexham	2-0	Asaba 2 (1p)	4216		3	7		5	9		1	10						2		6					8	4	11
38	29	BURY	0-2		7823		3	7		5	9		1	10						2		6		12			8	4	11
39	31	Gillingham	2-1	Janney, Asaba	7359		3	7	4	5			1	10						2	12	6					8	9	11
40	Apr 5	SHREWSBURY TOWN	0-0		5521		3	7	4	5			1	10						2	9	6					8	12	11
41	11	Rotherham United	1-0	Taylor	1797		3	7	4	5	12		1	10						2		9					8	6	11
42	15	CHESTERFIELD	1-0	Asaba	5216		3	7	4	5	9		1	10					12			6		14			8	2	11
43	19	CREWE ALEXANDRA	0-2		6183		3	7	4	5	9		1	10					12			6					8	2	11
44	22	Blackpool	0-1		4030		3	7		5			1	10						4		6		9			8	2	11
45	26	Walsall	0-1		5359		3	7		5			1	10						4		6		9	12		8	2	11
46	May 3	PETERBOROUGH UTD.	0-1		5274		3	7		5		10	1	12			14			4		6			9		8	2	11
					Apps	5	46	44	40	37	29	13	44	9	2	25	0	2	28	23	1	44	2	7	1	4	46	11	43
					Subs	3					5			3			1	12	3	5	1	1		6	1			8	
					Goals	2	1	23	1	2	3	1				10				2	1	1		1			1		7

Play Offs

No	Date	Opponent	Res	Scorers	Att	Abrahams P	Anderson IM	Asaba CE	Ashby BJ	Bates JA	Bent MN	Canham SW	Dearden KC	Dennis KJ	Fernandes TH	Forster NM	Goddard-Crawley RL	Harvey LD	Hurdle AAJ	Hutchings CE	Janney M	McGhee DC	McPherson M	Omigie JE	Rapley KJ	Slade SA	Smith PW	Statham B	Taylor RA
SF1	May 11	Bristol City	2-1	Smith, Taylor	15581		3	7		5	9		1						2	4		6					8	10	11
SF2	14	BRISTOL CITY	2-1	Taylor, Bent	9496		3			5	9	12	1	7					2	4		6					8	10	11
F	25	Crewe Alexandra	0-1		34149		3	7	12	5	9	14	1						2	4		6					8	10	11

Final at Wembley Stadium

F.A. Cup

No	Date	Opponent	Res	Scorers	Att	Abrahams P	Anderson IM	Asaba CE	Ashby BJ	Bates JA	Bent MN	Canham SW	Dearden KC	Dennis KJ	Fernandes TH	Forster NM	Goddard-Crawley RL	Harvey LD	Hurdle AAJ	Hutchings CE	Janney M	McGhee DC	McPherson M	Omigie JE	Rapley KJ	Slade SA	Smith PW	Statham B	Taylor RA
R1	Nov 16	BOURNEMOUTH	2-0	Smith, Foster	4509		3	7	4	5		10	1			9			2			6		12			8		11
R2	Dec 7	Sudbury Town	3-1	McGhee, Taylor 2	3973		3	7	4	5	10		1			9		12	2			6		14			8		11
R3	Jan 25	MANCHESTER CITY	0-1		12019			7	4	5	10		1			9				3		6		12			8	2	11

F.L. Cup (Coca Cola Cup)

No	Date	Opponent	Res	Scorers	Att	Abrahams P	Anderson IM	Asaba CE	Ashby BJ	Bates JA	Bent MN	Canham SW	Dearden KC	Dennis KJ	Fernandes TH	Forster NM	Goddard-Crawley RL	Harvey LD	Hurdle AAJ	Hutchings CE	Janney M	McGhee DC	McPherson M	Omigie JE	Rapley KJ	Slade SA	Smith PW	Statham B	Taylor RA
R1/1	Aug 21	PLYMOUTH ARGYLE	1-0	Taylor	3043		3	7	4	5	10		1			9		12	2			6					8		11
R1/2	Sep 3	Plymouth Argyle	0-0		5180	9	3	7	4	5	10		1					12	2	14		6					8		11
R2/1	17	BLACKBURN ROVERS	1-2	Foster	8938	12	3	7	4	5	10	6	1			9			2								8		11
R2/2	25	Blackburn Rovers	0-2		9599	14	3	7	4	5	10	6	1			9			2			12					8		11

Auto Windscreens Shield

No	Date	Opponent	Res	Scorers	Att	Abrahams P	Anderson IM	Asaba CE	Ashby BJ	Bates JA	Bent MN	Canham SW	Dearden KC	Dennis KJ	Fernandes TH	Forster NM	Goddard-Crawley RL	Harvey LD	Hurdle AAJ	Hutchings CE	Janney M	McGhee DC	McPherson M	Omigie JE	Rapley KJ	Slade SA	Smith PW	Statham B	Taylor RA
R1	Dec 10	Bristol Rovers	2-0	Omigie, Asaba	2752			7	4	5				10	1			2				6	8	9				3	11
R2	Jan 7	BARNET	2-1	Foster, Taylor	1455		3	7	4	5	12		1			9			2			6		10			8		11
R3	28	COLCHESTER UNITED	0-1		2253			7	4	5	10		1	9						2		6	12	14			8	3	11

R2 won in sudden death extra time

		Pl.	Home W	Home D	Home L	Home F	Home A	Away W	Away D	Away L	Away F	Away A	F. (Total)	A. (Total)	Pts
1	Bury	46	18	5	0	39	7	6	7	10	23	31	62	38	84
2	Stockport County	46	15	5	3	31	14	8	8	7	28	27	59	41	82
3	Luton Town	46	13	7	3	38	14	8	8	7	33	31	71	45	78
4	**BRENTFORD**	**46**	**8**	**11**	**4**	**26**	**22**	**12**	**3**	**8**	**30**	**21**	**56**	**43**	**74**
5	Bristol City	46	14	4	5	43	18	7	6	10	26	33	69	51	73
6	Crewe Alexandra	46	15	4	4	38	15	7	3	13	18	32	56	47	73
7	Blackpool	46	13	7	3	41	21	5	8	10	19	26	60	47	69
8	Wrexham	46	11	9	3	37	28	6	9	8	17	22	54	50	69
9	Burnley	46	14	3	6	48	27	5	8	10	23	28	71	55	68
10	Chesterfield	46	10	9	4	25	18	8	5	10	17	21	42	39	68
11	Gillingham	46	13	3	7	37	25	6	7	10	23	34	60	59	67
12	Walsall	46	12	8	3	35	21	7	2	14	19	32	54	53	67
13	Watford	46	10	8	5	24	14	6	11	6	21	24	45	38	67
14	Millwall	46	12	4	7	27	22	4	9	10	23	33	50	55	61
15	Preston North End	46	14	5	4	33	19	4	2	17	16	36	49	55	61
16	Bournemouth	46	8	9	6	24	20	7	6	10	19	25	43	45	60
17	Bristol Rovers	46	13	4	6	34	22	2	7	14	13	28	47	50	56
18	Wycombe Wands.	46	13	4	6	31	14	2	6	15	20	42	51	56	55
19	Plymouth Argyle	46	7	11	5	19	18	5	7	11	28	40	47	58	54
20	York City	46	8	6	9	27	31	5	7	11	20	37	47	68	52
21	Peterborough Utd.	46	7	7	9	38	34	4	7	12	17	39	55	73	47
22	Shrewsbury Town	46	8	6	9	27	32	3	7	13	22	42	49	74	46
23	Rotherham United	46	4	7	12	17	29	3	7	13	22	41	39	70	35
24	Notts County	46	4	9	10	20	25	3	5	15	13	34	33	59	35

1996-97
Back: Omigie, Bent, Taylor, Ashby, Goddard, Bates, MacPherson, Asaba
Middle: Booker (Youth Coach), Hurdle, McGhee, Smith, Fernandes, Dearden, Myall, Hutchings, Johnson (Physio)
Front: Abrahams, Anderson, Harvey, Webb (Manager), Lock (Coach), Forster, Dennis, Rapley

1997-98
Back: Bent, McGhee, Goddard, Taylor, Bates,.Hutchings, Hurdle
Middle: Omigie, Duffy, Harvey, Fernandes, Dearden, Benstead, Myall, Dennis
Front: Denys, Spencer,.Anderson, Oatway, Canham, Wormull, Rapley, Barrowcliff

1997/98

21st in Division Two: Relegated

No	Date		Opponent	Score	Scorers	Att	Anderson IM	Aspinall WG	Barrowcliff PJ	Bates JA	Benstead GM	Bent MN	Blaney SD	Bryan DK	Canham SW	Clark DW	Cockerill G	Colgan NV	Cullip D	Dearden KC	Dennis KJ	Denys RH	Gleghorn NW	Hall GD	Hogg GJ	Hurdle AAJ	Hutchings CE	McGhee DC	McPherson M	Myall ST	Oatway APDTF	Omigie JE	Pollitt MF	Rapley KJ	Reina EI	Scott A	Spencer SD	Taylor RA	Thompson NJ	Townley L	Watson PD	Wormull SJ	Adams MR	Goddard-Crawley RL
1	Aug	9	Millwall	0-3		8951	3		10	5		9								1		12				2	4	6									7	11				8		
2		16	CHESTERFIELD	0-0		4000	3		6	5		10			8					1		9				2	4					13		12				11				7		
3		23	Watford	1-3	Taylor (p)	10125	3		6	5		10			8					1		9				2	4				7			12				11						
4		30	GRIMSBY TOWN	3-1	Rapley, Taylor 2	3875	3			5		9			8					1		7				2	4				6			10				11						
5	Sep	2	GILLINGHAM	2-0	Bent, Taylor (p)	4903	3			5		9			8					1		7				2	4				6			10				11						
6		5	Southend United	1-3	Rapley	3387	3			5		9			8					1		7				2	4				6			10				11				12		
7		13	Plymouth Argyle	0-0		4394	3			5		9		12	8					1		7				2	4				6			10				11						
8		19	WYCOMBE WANDERERS	1-1	Taylor	3755	3			5		9								1		7				2	4	12			8			10				11		6				
9		27	BURNLEY	2-1	Hutchings, Rapley	4317	3			5		9			13					1		7				2	4	12			8			10				11		6				
10	Oct	4	Preston North End	1-2	Bent	8954	3			5		9								1				7		2	4	12			8			10	13			11		6				
11		11	York City	1-3	Taylor	2831	3			5	1	9										12		7		2	4	6			8			10	13			11						
12		18	WALSALL	3-0	Taylor, Denys, Bent	4874	3			5		9		13				1				7		6			4	12			8			10				11		2				
13		21	BRISTOL ROVERS	2-3	Bent, Rapley	3967	3			5		9		13				1				7		6			4	12			8			10				11		2				
14		25	Luton Town	0-2		6494	3			5		9			12			1				7		6			4	2			8			10				11						
15	Nov	1	Bournemouth	0-0		4772	3			5		9						1						2			4	6		7	8			10				11						
16		4	CARLISLE UNITED	0-1		3424	3			5		9			12			1				13				2	4	6		7	8			10				11						
17		8	BRISTOL CITY	1-4	Reina	6162	3			5		9					8			1		12				2	4	7			6				10			11						
18		18	Northampton Town	0-4		5227			12	5		9					8			1		13	3			2	4	7			6			14	10			11						
19		22	Oldham Athletic	1-1	Scott	5012		10	14	5							8			1			3			2	4		12		6				13	9		11		7				
20		29	WREXHAM	1-1	Aspinall	3748		10	13	5		11					8			1			3				4	12	2		6			14		9				7				
21	Dec	2	Fulham	1-1	Gleghorn	10783		10	11			12		13			8			1			3				4	5	2		6					9				7				
22		13	BLACKPOOL	3-1	Taylor, Townley	3725		10	13			12		14						1			8				4	5	2		6					9		11		7	3			
23		20	Wigan Athletic	0-4		3301		9	13			12					8			1			11				4	5	2		6				14			10		7	3			
24		26	SOUTHEND UNITED	1-1	Taylor	5341		10	13	5		12								1		14	8				4		2		6					9		11		7	3			
25		29	Gillingham	1-3	Taylor	5786		10	2	5		12			14					1	13		8				4				6					9		11		7	3			
26	Jan	3	Chesterfield	0-0		4049		10		5							8			1			2			4					6					9		11		7	3			
27		10	MILLWALL	2-1	Taylor, Aspinall	5529		10		5					6					1		8	2			4								13		9		11		7	3	12		
28		17	Grimsby Town	0-4		4886		10		5					4					1		13	2					12			6			14		9		11		7	3	8		
29		24	WATFORD	1-2	Rapley	6969		10		5							8								6		2				4		1	7		9		11			3			
30		31	PLYMOUTH ARGYLE	3-1	Bates, Scott, Hogg	4783				5					10	14	8				13				6		2	12			4		1	7		9		11			3			
31	Feb	7	Wycombe Wanderers	0-0		6328				5					12		8								6		2	10	7		4		1	13		9		11			3			
32		14	PRESTON NORTH END	0-0		4952		10		5						13	8								6		2	4	7				1	12		9		11			3			
33		21	Burnley	1-1	Taylor	10097		10		5									4						6		2	8	12				1	7		9		11			3			
34		24	Walsall	0-0		3166		10		5									4	1					6		2	8			12			7		9		11			3			
35		28	YORK CITY	1-2	McGhee	4490		10						13	12		8		4	1					6		2	5						7		9		11	14		3			
36	Mar	3	Bristol City	2-2	Bryan, Rapley	10398		10						9	12		5		4	1					6		2	8			7			13				11	14		3			
37		7	BOURNEMOUTH	3-2	Hutchings, Bryan, Rapley	4973		10		5				7	12		8		4	1							2	6						13		14		11	9		3			
38		14	Carlisle United	2-1	Hogg, Scott	6021		10							12		8		5	1					6		2	7			4			13		14		11	9		3			
39		21	NORTHAMPTON T	0-0		5746		10		5					13	14	8		4	1					6		2							11		9		12	7		3			
40		28	OLDHAM ATHLETIC	2-1	Scott, Taylor	4547				5					7		8		4	1					6		2	12						10		9		11			3			
41	Apr	4	Wrexham	2-2	Rapley, Hutchings	3654				5			14		7	13	8		4	1					6		2	10						11		9				12	3			
42		11	FULHAM	0-2		10510		10		5				14	13		8		4	1					6		2	12						7		9		11			3			
43		13	Blackpool	2-1	Hutchings, Aspinall (p)	3926		10		5			7	12			8		4	1					6		2							13		9			11		3			
44		18	WIGAN ATHLETIC	0-2		4480		10		5			4	12			8			1	13				6		2							7		9			11		3			
45		25	LUTON TOWN	2-2	Scott, Hutchings	6598		10		5			7				8		4	1	14				6		2				13			12		9			11		3			
46	May	2	Bristol Rovers	1-2	Rapley	9043		10		5			7				8		4	1	14				6		2				12			13		9		11			3			
						Apps	17	24	5	40	1	19	4	2	11	0	23	5	13	35	0	12	11	6	17	17	43	19	7	2	30	0	5	23	2	24	1	39	6	15	25	3		
						Subs			6			5	1	9	11	4					5	7						10	2		3	1		14	4	2		1	2	1		2		
						Goals		3		1		4		2								1	1		2		5	1						9	1	5		13		2				

F.A. Cup

Rd	Date		Opponent	Score	Scorers	Att	Anderson IM	Aspinall WG	Barrowcliff PJ	Bates JA	Benstead GM	Bent MN	Blaney SD	Bryan DK	Canham SW	Clark DW	Cockerill G	Colgan NV	Cullip D	Dearden KC	Dennis KJ	Denys RH	Gleghorn NW	Hall GD	Hogg GJ	Hurdle AAJ	Hutchings CE	McGhee DC	McPherson M	Myall ST	Oatway APDTF	Omigie JE	Pollitt MF	Rapley KJ	Reina EI	Scott A	Spencer SD	Taylor RA	Thompson NJ	Townley L	Watson PD	Wormull SJ	Adams MR	Goddard-Crawley RL
R1	Nov	15	COLCHESTER UNITED	2-2	Taylor 2	2899			3	5		9					8			1						2	4	7			6			12	10			11						
rep		25	Colchester United	0-0		3612			11	5		9					8			1						12	4	7	2		6				10					3				

F.L. Cup (Coca Cola Cup)

Rd	Date		Opponent	Score	Scorers	Att	Anderson IM	Aspinall WG	Barrowcliff PJ	Bates JA	Benstead GM	Bent MN	Blaney SD	Bryan DK	Canham SW	Clark DW	Cockerill G	Colgan NV	Cullip D	Dearden KC	Dennis KJ	Denys RH	Gleghorn NW	Hall GD	Hogg GJ	Hurdle AAJ	Hutchings CE	McGhee DC	McPherson M	Myall ST	Oatway APDTF	Omigie JE	Pollitt MF	Rapley KJ	Reina EI	Scott A	Spencer SD	Taylor RA	Thompson NJ	Townley L	Watson PD	Wormull SJ	Adams MR	Goddard-Crawley RL
R1/1	Aug	12	SHREWSBURY TOWN	1-1	Denys	2040	3		10	5					12					1		7				2	4	6						13			9	11				8		13
R1/2		26	Shrewsbury Town	5-3	Rapley 2, Taylor 2, Bent	2136	3		6	5		9			8					1		7				2	4							10				11				12		
R2/1	Sep	17	Southampton	1-3	Taylor	8004	3		6	5		9			8					1		7				2	4							10				11						12
R2/2		30	SOUTHAMPTON	0-2		3952	3			5		9			12					1		7				2	4	8						10	13			11		6				

Auto Windscreens Shield

Rd	Date		Opponent	Score	Scorers	Att	Anderson IM	Aspinall WG	Barrowcliff PJ	Bates JA	Benstead GM	Bent MN	Blaney SD	Bryan DK	Canham SW	Clark DW	Cockerill G	Colgan NV	Cullip D	Dearden KC	Dennis KJ	Denys RH	Gleghorn NW	Hall GD	Hogg GJ	Hurdle AAJ	Hutchings CE	McGhee DC	McPherson M	Myall ST	Oatway APDTF	Omigie JE	Pollitt MF	Rapley KJ	Reina EI	Scott A	Spencer SD	Taylor RA	Thompson NJ	Townley L	Watson PD	Wormull SJ	Adams MR	Goddard-Crawley RL
R2	Jan	13	Luton Town	1-2	Townley	3106		10		5					4	14				1	13	6	2											8		9		11		7		3	12	

		Pl.	Home W	D	L	F	A	Away W	D	L	F	A	F. (Total)	A.	Pts
1	Watford	46	13	7	3	36	22	11	9	3	31	19	67	41	88
2	Bristol City	46	16	5	2	41	17	9	5	9	28	22	69	39	85
3	Grimsby Town	46	11	7	5	30	14	8	8	7	25	23	55	37	72
4	Northampton Town	46	14	5	4	33	17	4	12	7	19	20	52	37	71
5	Bristol Rovers	46	13	2	8	43	33	7	8	8	27	31	70	64	70
6	Fulham	46	12	7	4	31	14	8	3	12	29	29	60	43	70
7	Wrexham	46	10	10	3	31	23	8	6	9	24	28	55	51	70
8	Gillingham	46	13	7	3	30	18	6	6	11	22	29	52	47	70
9	Bournemouth	46	11	8	4	28	15	7	4	12	29	37	57	52	66
10	Chesterfield	46	13	7	3	31	19	3	10	10	15	25	46	44	65
11	Wigan Athletic	46	12	5	6	41	31	5	6	12	23	35	64	66	62
12	Blackpool	46	13	6	4	35	24	4	5	14	24	43	59	67	62
13	Oldham Athletic	46	13	7	3	43	23	2	9	12	19	31	62	54	61
14	Wycombe Wands.	46	10	10	3	32	20	4	8	11	19	33	51	53	60
15	Preston North End	46	10	6	7	29	26	5	8	10	27	30	56	56	59
16	York City	46	9	7	7	26	21	5	10	8	26	37	52	58	59
17	Luton Town	46	7	7	9	35	38	7	8	8	25	26	60	64	57
18	Millwall	46	7	8	8	23	23	7	5	11	20	31	43	54	55
19	Walsall	46	10	8	5	26	16	4	4	15	17	36	43	52	54
20	Burnley	46	10	9	4	34	23	3	4	16	21	42	55	65	52
21	**BRENTFORD**	**46**	**9**	**7**	**7**	**33**	**29**	**2**	**10**	**11**	**17**	**42**	**50**	**71**	**50**
22	Plymouth Argyle	46	10	5	8	36	30	2	8	13	19	40	55	70	49
23	Carlisle United	46	8	5	10	27	28	4	3	16	30	45	57	73	44
24	Southend United	46	8	7	8	29	30	3	3	17	18	49	47	79	43

1998/99

Champions of Division Three: Promoted

	Date	Opponents	Score	Scorers	Att	Anderson IM	Aspinall WG	Bates JA	Boxall DJ	Broughton DO	Bryan DK	Coyne CJ	Cullip D	Dearden KC	Evans PS	Folan AS	Fortune-West LF	Freeman DBA	Hebel DJ	Hreidarsson H	Jenkins SM	Mahon GA	Oatway APDTF	Owusu LM	Partridge SM	Pearcey JK	Powell DD	Quinn RJ	Rapley KJ	Rowlands MC	Scott A	Watson PD	Woodman AJ
1	Aug 8	MANSFIELD TOWN	3-0	Rapley 2, Freeman	4846		8	6	2				4					13					12	9		1	5		10	7	11	3	
2	15	Halifax Town	0-1		3876		8	6	2				4	1				13						12			5	9	10	7	11	3	
3	22	BRIGHTON & HOVE ALB	2-0	Thomas (og), Scott	6355	13	8	6	2			4						7						12		1	5	9	14	10	11	3	
4	29	Barnet	3-0	Quinn, Rowlands, Owusu	2710	13	8	6	2			4											12	7		1	5	9	14	10	11	3	
5	31	ROCHDALE	2-1	Powell, Rapley	4873	2	8	6				4							13				12	7		1	5	9	14	10	11	3	
6	Sep 5	Hull City	3-2	Owusu, Aspinall, Scott	4058	2	8	6				4							13				12	7		1	5	9	14	10	11	3	
7	8	Torquay United	1-3	Bates	2340		12	6	2			4							10				8	7		1	5	9	13		11	3	
8	12	ROTHERHAM UNITED	0-3		4803		8	6	2			4						12	13					7		1	5	9	14	10	11	3	
9	19	Scarborough	1-3	Owusu	2028	3	12	6	2			4						7	8					13		1	5	9	14	10	11		
10	26	DARLINGTON	3-0	Powell, Rowlands, Owusu	4486	3	8	6	2							13		7		4				9		1	5	12	14	10	11		
11	Oct 3	Peterborough United	4-2	Freeman, Scott 2, Folan	6056	3	8	6	2							13		7	14	4				9		1	5	12		10	11		
12	17	HARTLEPOOL UNITED	3-1	Freeman, Aspinall (p), Rowlands	4883	3	8	6	2							13		7	12	4				9		1	5	14		10	11		
13	20	SCUNTHORPE UNITED	2-1	Scott, Owusu	4700	3	8	6	2							13		7		4				9		1	5	12		10	11		
14	Nov 3	Plymouth Argyle	0-3		4650	3	8	6	2							7			12	4				9		1	5	14	13	10	11		
15	7	Shrewsbury Town	0-2		2799		8	6	2	11	13					7			12	3				9		1	5	14	4	10			
16	10	SOUTHEND UNITED	4-1	Owusu 3, Freeman	4285		8	6	2		13					11		7	12	4				9		1		5		10		3	
17	21	Leyton Orient	1-2	Folan	6340	2	8				13					11	10		12	4		6	7	9		1		5				3	
18	28	CHESTER CITY	2-1	Owusu, Rowlands	5173	2		6								11		7	8			4		9		1		5		10		3	
19	Dec 12	Exeter City	1-0	Owusu	2793			6	2		13			1		11		7	4	3		8	12	9				5		10			
20	18	CAMBRIDGE UNITED	1-0	Folan	5069	3		6						1		11	12	7	8	4		2	13	9				5		10			
21	26	Brighton & Hove Albion	1-3	Freeman	4838	3		6			13			1		2	12	7	8	4		11	14	9				5		10			
22	28	CARDIFF CITY	1-0	Hreidarsson	9535	3		6	2		13			1		8	12	7		4		11		9				5		10			
23	Jan 2	BARNET	3-1	Freeman, Bryan, Mahon	6011	3			2		6			1		8	12	7		4		11	14	9				5		10	13		
24	9	Mansfield Town	1-3	Owusu	4095	3	8				6			1			12			4		7	13	9			2	5		10	11		
25	23	Rochdale	0-2		2113	3		6	2							7	12	13		4		8	14	9				5		10	11		1
26	30	Cardiff City	1-4	Boxall	11509	3	8	6	2							12		7		4		9	13	14				5		10	11		1
27	Feb 2	CARLISLE UNITED	1-1	Barr (og)	3674	12		6	2							11		7		4		8	13	9				5		10	3		1
28	6	HULL CITY	0-2		5086	3		6	2							11	10	7		4		8		9			5	13			12		1
29	13	TORQUAY UNITED	3-2	Owusu, Bryan, Hreidarsson	4299	3		6	2		7					11	12			4		8		9			5	13		10			1
30	16	Swansea City	1-2	Hreidarsson	5109	3			2		7					11	12	13		4		8		9			5	6		10			1
31	20	Rotherham United	4-2	Mahon, Owusu 3	3894				2		7					11	12			4		8	14	9	13		5	6		10		3	1
32	27	SCARBOROUGH	1-1	Bryan	4783	3			2		7					11				4		8	12	9	13		5	6		10			1
33	Mar 9	PETERBOROUGH UTD.	3-0	Partridge, Mahon, Owusu	4195	3		5	2		11				7							6		9	8					10	4		1
34	13	SHREWSBURY TOWN	0-0		5082	3			2		12				11	7				4		6		9	8		5			13	10		1
35	16	HALIFAX TOWN	1-1	Partridge	3713	3			2						11	7				4		6	12	9	8		5	14		10	13		1
36	20	Carlisle United	1-0	Partridge	2564	3			2		12				11							6	7	9	8		5	4			10		1
37	Apr 3	Hartlepool United	1-0	Owusu	2719	3									11	12				4	13		6	9	8		5	2		10	7		1
38	5	PLYMOUTH ARGYLE	3-1	Evans, Mahon, Folan	6979	3			14		13				11	12				4		10	6	9	8		5	2			7		1
39	10	Scunthorpe United	0-0		5604	3			2						11	12				4		10		9	8		5	6			7		1
40	13	Chester City	3-1	Anderson, Evans, Bryan	1766	3			2		10				11	12				4		6		9			5	8			7		1
41	17	LEYTON ORIENT	0-0		8245	3			2		10				11	12				4		6		9			5	8			7		1
42	24	Southend United	4-1	Owusu 3, Partridge	5273	3			2						11			12		4		6	5	9	10			8		13	7		1
43	27	Darlington	2-2	Scott, Partridge	2288	3			2						11							6	5	9	10		4	8		12	7		1
44	May 1	EXETER CITY	3-0	Quinn, Scott, Partridge	6977	3			2		13				11					4		6	12	9	10		5	8		14	7		1
45	4	SWANSEA CITY	4-1	Owusu,Evans,Hreidarsson,Partridge	7156	3			2		12				11					4		6		9	10		5	8			7		1
46	8	Cambridge United	1-0	Owusu	8936	3			2						11					4		6	12	9	10		5	8			7		1
					Apps	35	17	27	37	1	9	7	2	7	14	19	2	16	6	33	0	29	7	42	12	17	33	34	3	32	31	12	22
					Subs	3	2		1		11					10	9	6	9		1		17	4	2			9	9	4	3		
					Goals	1	2	1	1		4				3	4		6		4		4		22	7		2	2	3	4	7		

Two own goals

F.A. Cup

	Date	Opponents	Score	Scorers	Att	Anderson IM	Aspinall WG	Bates JA	Boxall DJ	Broughton DO	Bryan DK	Coyne CJ	Cullip D	Dearden KC	Evans PS	Folan AS	Fortune-West LF	Freeman DBA	Hebel DJ	Hreidarsson H	Jenkins SM	Mahon GA	Oatway APDTF	Owusu LM	Partridge SM	Pearcey JK	Powell DD	Quinn RJ	Rapley KJ	Rowlands MC	Scott A	Watson PD	Woodman AJ
R1	Nov 14	CAMBERLEY	5-0	Bates,Quinn,Folan 2,Hreidarsson	4783		8	6	2		14					11		7	12	4				9		1		5	13	10		3	
R2	Dec 5	Oldham Athletic	1-1	Freeman (p)	4217	2		6			12					11		7	4				8	9		1		5		10		3	
rep	15	OLDHAM ATHLETIC	2-2	Owusu, Freeman	4375	14	12	6	2					1		3	13	7	11	4			8	9				5		10			

R2 replay lost 2-4 on penalties a.e.t.

F.L. Cup (Worthington Cup)

	Date	Opponents	Score	Scorers	Att	Anderson IM	Aspinall WG	Bates JA	Boxall DJ	Broughton DO	Bryan DK	Coyne CJ	Cullip D	Dearden KC	Evans PS	Folan AS	Fortune-West LF	Freeman DBA	Hebel DJ	Hreidarsson H	Jenkins SM	Mahon GA	Oatway APDTF	Owusu LM	Partridge SM	Pearcey JK	Powell DD	Quinn RJ	Rapley KJ	Rowlands MC	Scott A	Watson PD	Woodman AJ
R1/1	Aug 11	West Bromwich Albion	1-2	Rapley	8460	3	8	6	2				4	1				7					14	13				10	12	9	11	5	
R1/2	18	WEST BROMWICH ALB.	3-0	Bates, Oatway, Owusu	4664		8	6	2				4					7					14	13		1	3	10	12	9	11	5	
R2/1	Sep 15	TOTTENHAM HOTSPUR	2-3	Scott, Freeman	11831	3	8	6	2			4						7						13		1	5	9	12	10	11		
R2/2	23	Tottenham Hotspur	2-3	Scott, Owusu	22980	3	8	6	2							14		7					4	13		1	5	9	12	10	11		

Auto Windscreens Shield

	Date	Opponents	Score	Scorers	Att	Anderson IM	Aspinall WG	Bates JA	Boxall DJ	Broughton DO	Bryan DK	Coyne CJ	Cullip D	Dearden KC	Evans PS	Folan AS	Fortune-West LF	Freeman DBA	Hebel DJ	Hreidarsson H	Jenkins SM	Mahon GA	Oatway APDTF	Owusu LM	Partridge SM	Pearcey JK	Powell DD	Quinn RJ	Rapley KJ	Rowlands MC	Scott A	Watson PD	Woodman AJ
R1	Dec 8	PLYMOUTH ARGYLE	2-0	Hreidarsson, Rowlands	1580			6			2					3	11		7	4		8		9		1		5		10			
R2	Jan 5	Wycombe Wanderers	4-1	Fortune-West, Scott 2, Quinn	2010	3	8		2		12			1			9		7	4		6		14				5		10	11	13	
R3	19	WALSALL	0-0		2048	3		6	2					1		8	14			4		7	12	9			13	5		10	11		

R3 lost 3-4 on penalties a.e.t.

		Pl.	Home W	Home D	Home L	Home F	Home A	Away W	Away D	Away L	Away F	Away A	F. (Total)	A. (Total)	Pts
1	**BRENTFORD**	**46**	**16**	**5**	**2**	**45**	**18**	**10**	**2**	**11**	**34**	**38**	**79**	**56**	**85**
2	Cambridge United	46	13	6	4	41	21	10	6	7	37	27	78	48	81
3	Cardiff City	46	13	7	3	35	17	9	7	7	25	22	60	39	80
4	Scunthorpe United	46	14	3	6	42	28	8	5	10	27	30	69	58	74
5	Rotherham United	46	11	8	4	41	26	9	5	9	38	35	79	61	73
6	Leyton Orient	46	12	6	5	40	30	7	9	7	28	29	68	59	72
7	Swansea City	46	11	9	3	33	19	8	5	10	23	29	56	48	71
8	Mansfield Town	46	15	2	6	38	18	4	8	11	22	40	60	58	67
9	Peterborough Utd.	46	11	4	8	41	29	7	8	8	31	27	72	56	66
10	Halifax Town	46	10	8	5	33	25	7	7	9	25	31	58	56	66
11	Darlington	46	10	6	7	41	24	8	5	10	28	34	69	58	65
12	Exeter City	46	13	5	5	32	18	4	7	12	15	32	47	50	63
13	Plymouth Argyle	46	11	6	6	32	19	6	4	13	26	35	58	54	61
14	Chester City	46	6	12	5	28	30	7	6	10	29	36	57	66	57
15	Shrewsbury Town	46	11	6	6	36	29	3	8	12	16	34	52	63	56
16	Barnet	46	10	5	8	30	31	4	8	11	24	40	54	71	55
17	Brighton & Hove A.	46	8	3	12	25	35	8	4	11	24	31	49	66	55
18	Southend United	46	8	6	9	24	21	6	6	11	28	37	52	58	54
19	Rochdale	46	9	8	6	22	21	4	7	12	20	34	42	55	54
20	Torquay United	46	9	9	5	29	20	3	8	12	18	38	47	58	53
21	Hull City	46	8	5	10	25	28	6	6	11	19	34	44	62	53
22	Hartlepool United	46	8	7	8	33	27	5	5	13	19	38	52	65	51
23	Carlisle United	46	8	8	7	25	21	3	8	12	18	32	43	53	49
24	Scarborough	46	8	3	12	30	39	6	3	14	20	38	50	77	48

1998-99

Back: Powell, Bates, Owusu, Pearcey, Taylor, Townley, Scott,
Middle: Sparrow (Coach), Bullivant (Coach), Freeman, McGhee, Cullip, Oatway, Bryan, Quinn, Thompson, Delahunt (Physio), Lewington (Coach)
Front: Watson, Boxall, Anderson, Rapley, Griffin (Scout), Noades (Manager), Clark, Aspinall, Denys, Dennis.

1999-2000

Back: McEwan, Hreidarsson, Theobald, Pearcey, Owusu, Woodman, Powell, Townley, Scott
Middle: Kennedy, Bryan, Clark, Saroya, Jenkins, Quinn, Cullip, Mahon
Front: Anderson, Boxall, Partridge, Rowlands, Evans, Folan, James, Dobson, Warner.

1999/2000

17th in Division Two

	Date	Opponent	Score	Scorers	Att	Agyemang P	Anderson IM	Boxall DJ	Bryan DK	Charles J	Clement N	Einarsson G	Evans PS	Folan AS	Glass JR	Graham GL	Hreidarsson H	Hutchings CE	Ingimarsson I	James CJ	Jenkins SM	Jones SG	Kennedy RJM	Mahon GA	Marshall SR	O'Connor KP	Owusu LM	Partridge SM	Pearcey JK	Pinamonte CL	Powell DD	Quinn RJ	Rowlands MC	Saroya N	Scott A	Theobald DJ	Warner P	Woodman AJ
1	Aug 7	Bristol Rovers	0-0		8514		3	2	13				11				4				14			6			9	10			5	8	12		7			1
2	14	OLDHAM ATHLETIC	2-0	Hreidarsson, Bryan	5074		3	2	13				11				4							6			9	10			5	8	12		7			1
3	21	Bury	2-2	Partridge, Rowlands	3491		3	2	9				11								12			6				10			5	4	8		7			1
4	28	BLACKPOOL	2-0	Hreidarsson, Evans	5353		3	2	9				11	13			4							6				10			5		8		7		12	1
5	Sep 11	Cambridge United	2-2	Scott, Evans	4234		3		9				11				4							6				10			5	2	8		7		12	1
6	18	LUTON TOWN	2-0	Powell, Partridge	7039		3		13				11	12			4							6			9	10			5	2	8		7			1
7	25	PRESTON NORTH END	2-2	Partridge, Evans	7100		3		12				11				4							6			9	10			5	2	8		7			1
8	28	CARDIFF CITY	2-1	Scott, Owusu	5247		3		14				11				4						12	6			9	10			5	2	8		7	13		1
9	Oct 2	Burnley	2-2	Partridge, Evans	10907		3		12				11				4						14	6			9	10			5	2	8		7	13		1
10	16	OXFORD UNITED	2-0	Powell, Owusu	6237			2	12				11	3										6	4		9	10			5	14	8		7		13	1
11	19	GILLINGHAM	1-2	Owusu	6264	12		2					11											6	4		9	10			5	3	8		7		13	1
12	23	Preston North End	1-2	Mahon	10382	13		2					11	12										6	4		9	10			5	3	8		7			1
13	26	Notts County	1-0	Evans	5075			2					11								3			6	4		9	10			5	8			7		12	1
14	Nov 2	READING	1-1	Folan	6774	13		2					11	12										6	4		9	10			5	3	8		7			1
15	6	Wrexham	1-0	Marshall	2473			2	12				11											6	4		9	10			5	3	8		7		13	1
16	12	SCUNTHORPE UNITED	4-3	Mahon, Owusu 2, Partridge	4657	11	3	2																6	4		9	10				5	8		7		12	1
17	19	Colchester United	3-0	Owusu, Partridge, Rowlands	3382	13	3	2											11		12			6	4		9	10				5	8		7		14	1
18	23	Bournemouth	1-4	Owusu	4202	12		2			3								11				13	6	4		9	10				5	8				7	1
19	27	Wycombe Wanderers	0-2		5879			2			3								11				/	6	4		9	10				5	8				12	1
20	Dec 4	BRISTOL ROVERS	0-3		6843			2	12				11						7		3			6	4		9	10				5	8					1
21	10	CHESTERFIELD	1-1	Owusu	4286			2	7		3		11						12					6	4		9	10				5	8				13	1
22	18	Wigan Athletic	0-1		5498	12		2	7		3					13			11					6	4		9	10				5	8					1
23	26	BRISTOL CITY	2-1	Owusu, Rowlands	7125	12				13	3		11						7					6	4		9	10				5	8			2		1
24	28	Millwall	2-3	Mahon, Rowlands	12077	13		2			3		11			14			7					6	4		9	10				5	8			12		1
25	Jan 3	STOKE CITY	0-1		5274	11	12		14		3								7				13	6	4		9	10			5	8				2		1
26	8	Chesterfield	0-1		2746	14	3		13		12								11				7	6			9	10			5	4	8			2		1
27	15	Oldham Athletic	0-3		4957	10		2	14			13							11				7	6			9				5	4	8		12	3		1
28	22	BURY	2-1	Scott, Rowlands	5605		3	2	13			12	11						10			9		6							5	4	8		7		14	1
29	29	Blackpool	1-0	Ingimarsson	5270		3	2					11						10			9					12	6	1		5	4	8		7		13	
30	Feb 5	NOTTS COUNTY	0-2		5106		3	2		12			11						6			9								10	5	4	8		7		13	1
31	12	Cardiff City	1-1	Rowlands	5478		3	2					11					4	10			9		6			13			12	5		8		7			1
32	19	WYCOMBE WANDERERS	0-0		5961		3	2								12			7			13		6		11	9			10	5	4	8					1
33	26	Luton Town	2-1	Owusu, Evans	6029		3	2					11						7			10		6			9	13			5	4	8		12			1
34	Mar 4	CAMBRIDGE UNITED	1-1	Evans (p)	4987		3					2	11					12	7			10		6			9	8		13	5	4			14			1
35	7	WREXHAM	0-2		4055		3						11			12		4	7					6			9	10		13	5	2	8		14			1
36	11	Reading	0-1		11427		3						11					2	4			14		6		10	9	13	1	12		5	8		7			
37	18	BOURNEMOUTH	0-2		4578		3									12		2	4					6		11	9	10	1	14	5	13	8		7			
38	21	Scunthorpe United	0-0		2686		3									11		2	13					6			9	10	1	12	5	4	8		7			
39	25	Bristol City	0-1		8804		3									11		2	12				14	6			9	10	1	13	5	4	8		7			
40	Apr 1	WIGAN ATHLETIC	0-2		4479		3						11		12			2					6			10	9	14	1	13	5	4	8		7			
41	8	Stoke City	0-1		9955		3						11			12				14					4		9	10		13	5	6	8		7	2		1
42	15	MILLWALL	1-3	Pinamonte	6779		3									11									4		9	6		10	5	2	8		7			1
43	22	Oxford United	1-1	Owusu	5342								11	14		8			12						4		9	6		10	5	2		13	7	3		1
44	24	BURNLEY	2-3	Owusu, Marshall	6595		3						11	13		12			8						4		9	6		10	5	2			7			1
45	29	Gillingham	0-2		9001		3						11	13		8									4	10	9	6			5	2			7	12		1
46	May 6	COLCHESTER UNITED	0-0		5297		3						11	14	1	13									4	10	9	6		12	5	2	8		7			
					Apps	3	30	25	5	0	7	1	33	1	1	5	8	7	21	0	2	6	4	37	22	6	39	38	6	5	36	42	38	0	32	6	1	39
					Subs	9	1		13	2	1	2		8	1	8		1	4	1	3	2	5				2	3		10		2	2	1	4	4	13	
					Goals				1				7	1			2		1					3	2		12	6		1	2		6		3			

F.A. Cup

	Date	Opponent	Score	Scorers	Att	Agyemang P	Anderson IM	Boxall DJ	Bryan DK	Charles J	Clement N	Einarsson G	Evans PS	Folan AS	Glass JR	Graham GL	Hreidarsson H	Hutchings CE	Ingimarsson I	James CJ	Jenkins SM	Jones SG	Kennedy RJM	Mahon GA	Marshall SR	O'Connor KP	Owusu LM	Partridge SM	Pearcey JK	Pinamonte CL	Powell DD	Quinn RJ	Rowlands MC	Saroya N	Scott A	Theobald DJ	Warner P	Woodman AJ
R1	Oct 30	PLYMOUTH ARGYLE	2-2	Owusu, Marshall	4287			2					11								3			6	4		9	10			5	8	12		7			1
rep	Nov 9	Plymouth Argyle	1-2	Quinn	5409	10		2	12					13										6	4		9	14			5	11	8		7		3	1

Replay a.e.t.

F.L. Cup (Worthington Cup)

	Date	Opponent	Score	Scorers	Att	Agyemang P	Anderson IM	Boxall DJ	Bryan DK	Charles J	Clement N	Einarsson G	Evans PS	Folan AS	Glass JR	Graham GL	Hreidarsson H	Hutchings CE	Ingimarsson I	James CJ	Jenkins SM	Jones SG	Kennedy RJM	Mahon GA	Marshall SR	O'Connor KP	Owusu LM	Partridge SM	Pearcey JK	Pinamonte CL	Powell DD	Quinn RJ	Rowlands MC	Saroya N	Scott A	Theobald DJ	Warner P	Woodman AJ
R1/1	Aug 11	IPSWICH TOWN	0-2		4825		3	2	12				11	14			4							6			9	10			5	8	13		7			1
R1/2	24	Ipswich T	0-2		9748		3	2	9				11	7			4							6				10	1		5	12	8		13		14	

Auto Windscreens Shield

	Date	Opponent	Score	Scorers	Att	Agyemang P	Anderson IM	Boxall DJ	Bryan DK	Charles J	Clement N	Einarsson G	Evans PS	Folan AS	Glass JR	Graham GL	Hreidarsson H	Hutchings CE	Ingimarsson I	James CJ	Jenkins SM	Jones SG	Kennedy RJM	Mahon GA	Marshall SR	O'Connor KP	Owusu LM	Partridge SM	Pearcey JK	Pinamonte CL	Powell DD	Quinn RJ	Rowlands MC	Saroya N	Scott A	Theobald DJ	Warner P	Woodman AJ
R2	Jan 11	Peterborough United	1-0	Owusu	2430			2											11				7	6			9	10			5	4	8			3		1
R3	25	OXFORD UNITED	1-0	Bryan, Scott	2942		3	2	13			14	11						10			9		6				12			5	4	8		7			1
SFS	Feb 15	Exeter City	2-3	Powell, Evans (p)	2392		3	2					11						10			9		6		14	13			12	5	4	8		7			1

		Pl.	Home W	D	L	F	A	Away W	D	L	F	A	F. (Total)	A.	Pts
1	Preston North End	46	15	4	4	37	23	13	7	3	37	14	74	37	95
2	Burnley	46	16	3	4	42	23	9	10	4	27	24	69	47	88
3	Gillingham	46	16	3	4	46	21	9	7	7	33	27	79	48	85
4	Wigan Athletic	46	15	3	5	37	14	7	14	2	35	24	72	38	83
5	Millwall	46	14	7	2	41	18	9	6	8	35	32	76	50	82
6	Stoke City	46	13	7	3	37	18	10	6	7	31	24	68	42	82
7	Bristol Rovers	46	13	7	3	34	19	10	4	9	35	26	69	45	80
8	Notts County	46	9	6	8	32	27	9	5	9	29	28	61	55	65
9	Bristol City	46	7	14	2	31	18	8	5	10	28	39	59	57	64
10	Reading	46	10	9	4	28	18	6	5	12	29	45	57	63	62
11	Wrexham	46	9	6	8	23	24	8	5	10	29	37	52	61	62
12	Wycombe Wands.	46	11	4	8	32	24	5	9	9	24	29	56	53	61
13	Luton Town	46	10	7	6	41	35	7	3	13	20	30	61	65	61
14	Oldham Athletic	46	8	5	10	27	28	8	7	8	23	27	50	55	60
15	Bury	46	8	10	5	38	33	5	8	10	23	31	61	64	57
16	Bournemouth	46	11	6	6	37	19	5	3	15	22	43	59	62	57
17	**BRENTFORD**	**46**	**8**	**6**	**9**	**27**	**31**	**5**	**7**	**11**	**20**	**30**	**47**	**61**	**52**
18	Colchester United	46	9	4	10	36	40	5	6	12	23	42	59	82	52
19	Cambridge United	46	8	6	9	38	33	4	6	13	26	32	64	65	48
20	Oxford United	46	6	5	12	24	38	6	4	13	19	35	43	73	45
21	Cardiff City	46	5	10	8	23	34	4	7	12	22	33	45	67	44
22	Blackpool	46	4	10	9	26	37	4	7	12	23	40	49	77	41
23	Scunthorpe United	46	4	6	13	16	34	5	6	12	24	40	40	74	39
24	Chesterfield	46	5	7	11	17	25	2	8	13	17	38	34	63	36

2000/01

14th in Division Two

No			Opponent	Score	Scorers	Att	Anderson IM	Austin KL	Charles J	Crowe JWR	Dobson MW	Evans PS	Folan AS	Gibbs PD	Gottskalksson O	Graham GL	Hutchinson ES	Ingimarsson I	Javary J-P	Kennedy RJM	Lovett J	Mahon GA	Marsh STP	Marshall SR	McCammon MJ	O'Connor KP	Owusu LM	Partridge SM	Pinamonte CL	Powell DD	Quinn RJ	Rowlands MC	Scott A	Smith JM	Smith PD	Somner MJ	Tabb JA	Theobald DJ	Williams MR
1	Aug	12	Northampton Town	1-1	Ingimarsson	6379	3					11	12	2	1			8				6		4	10		9		13		5		7						
2		19	SWANSEA CITY	0-0		5036					13	11		3	1			2	12			6		4	10		9		14		5	8	7						
3		26	Oxford United	1-0	Folan	4752						11	3		1			2	8			6		4	9			12			5	10	7						
4		28	BRISTOL ROVERS	2-6	Scott, Evans (p)	5434					13	11	3		1			2	8			6		4	9				12		5	10	7						
5	Sep	2	WYCOMBE WANDERERS	0-0		4699						11	13		1			2	8			6	3	4	9			12	10		5		7						
6		9	Reading	0-4		10222						11	14		1			2	8			6	13	4	9			3	12		5	10	7						
7		16	MILLWALL	1-1	Scott	5495				2		11			1			8				6	3	4	9						5	10	7						12
8		23	Notts County	2-2	McCammon, Partridge	4164				2		11	12		1			8		3		6		4	9			13			5	10	7						14
9		30	BOURNEMOUTH	3-2	Scott 2, Pinamonte	4210				2		11	13		1			8				6	3	4				12	9		5	10	7						
10	Oct	14	PETERBOROUGH UTD.	1-0	Scott	4479				2		11		3	1			8				6		4				13	9		5	10	7						12
11		17	COLCHESTER UNITED	1-0	Scott	3595				2		11	13		1			8				6		4				9			5	10	7					3	12
12		21	Luton Town	1-3	Scott	5382				2		11	12	3	1			8				6		4				9	13		5	10	7						14
13		24	Port Vale	1-1	Owusu	3338						11	14	3	1			8			2	6		4			13	12			5	10	7						9
14		28	WALSALL	2-1	Scott, Evans	4007		4		2		11		3	1			8				6					12				5	10	7						9
15	Nov	4	Cambridge United	1-1	Scott	4083		4		2		11	12	3	1			8	13			6					14				5	10	7						9
16		11	ROTHERHAM UNITED	0-3		4544		5		2		11		3	1			8				6		4	13		9					10	7						12
17	Dec	2	WIGAN ATHLETIC	2-2	Scott, Evans (p)	4144					12	11		3	1			8			2	6		4		9	13	10			5		7						14
18		12	Bristol City	2-1	Mahon, Partridge	8096					3	11			1			8			2	6		4			12	9			5	10	7						
19		16	Wrexham	1-2	Rowlands	2287						11		3	1			8			2	6		4		13	14	9			5	10	7						12
20		23	OLDHAM ATHLETIC	1-1	Rowlands	5317					2	11		3	1			8				6		4	9	13		7			5	10							12
21		26	Swindon Town	3-2	Scott, Owusu, Evans (p)	7252					2	11		3	1			8			13	6		4		9	12	10			5		7						
22	Jan	1	OXFORD UNITED	3-0	Scott 2, Partridge	5020					2	11		3	1			8				6		4		12		9			5	10	7						
23		6	NORTHAMPTON T	1-1	Owusu	5361					2	11		3	1			8				6		4		12	13	9			5	10	7						14
24		13	Bristol Rovers	0-0		6933					2	11		3	1			8			12	6		4	13		9	7		5		10							
25		17	Stoke City	0-1		9350					3	11			1			8			2	6		4	14	13	9	7		5		10							12
26		23	Bury	1-0	Owusu	2274					3	11		13	1			8			2	6		4	14		9	7		5		10			12				
27		27	Oldham Athletic	0-3		4964					2	11		3	1			8			5	6		4	12		9	7				10							13
28	Feb	3	Wycombe Wanderers	0-0		6604					3	11			1			8			2	6		4	13		9	7		5		10							12
29		10	READING	1-2	McCammon	7550					3			11	1			8			2			4	13		9	7		5		10						6	12
30		16	Millwall	0-1		10233					2	11		3	1			8				6		4	10		9	7		5									12
31		20	BRISTOL CITY	2-1	Partridge, O'Connor	4823					2	11		3	1			8			13	6		4	12	10	9	7		5									
32		24	NOTTS COUNTY	3-1	Owusu, Evans, Partridge	4366					2	11		3	1			8			13	6			12	10	9	7		5								4	
33	Mar	3	Bournemouth	0-2		4438					2	11		3	1			8				6			12		9	7		5		10						4	13
34		6	Peterborough United	1-1	Ingimarsson	4479			12		4	11		3	1			2				6			8		9	7		5		10							
35		10	STOKE CITY	2-2	Owusu, Williams	5518			7			11		3	1			8			2	6			9		13			5		10						4	12
36		16	Colchester United	1-3	Owusu	3415					3	11	13		1			8			2	6				10	9	7		5								4	12
37		31	WREXHAM	1-0	Powell	4449			13		4	11	3		1			8			2	6				12	9	7		5		10							
38	Apr	7	Wigan Athletic	3-1	Gibbs, Owusu, Partridge	6502			12			11	3	2	1						5	6					9	7				10						4	8
39		10	SWINDON TOWN	0-1		4180			12			11	3	2	1		13				5	6					9	7				10						4	8
40		14	PORT VALE	1-1	Evans	3871			7			11		3	1		12				2	6			8		9			5		10						4	13
41		17	Walsall	2-3	McCammon, Roper (og)	4540			10		3	11	7		1		8				2	6			9					5				13				4	12
42		25	CAMBRIDGE UNITED	2-2	Owusu, Evans	3062			12		3	11	6		1			8			2						9	10		5								4	7
43		28	Rotherham United	1-2	Owusu	9670					3	11	6		1		7	8			2						9	10		5								4	12
44	May	1	Swansea City	0-6		2002			10		3	11	6				7	8			2						9	14		5					1	12		4	13
45		3	LUTON TOWN	2-2	Partridge, Williams	3287							3		1	13	7	8			5						9	10						11		2	6	4	12
46		5	BURY	3-1	Ingimarsson, Folan, Partridge	4596			13		3		6		1		7	8			5						9	10						11		2	12	4	14
						Apps	1	3	4	9	23	43	11	26	45	0	5	42	4	1	21	40	3	29	14	5	24	29	3	18	22	32	22	2	1	2	1	15	6
						Subs			6		3		10	1		1	2		2		4		1		10	6	9	7	5					1	1	1	1		24
						Goals						7	2	1				3				1			3	1	10	8	1	1		2	13						2

F.A. Cup

Rd			Opponent	Score	Scorers	Att	Anderson IM	Austin KL	Charles J	Crowe JWR	Dobson MW	Evans PS	Folan AS	Gibbs PD	Gottskalksson O	Graham GL	Hutchinson ES	Ingimarsson I	Javary J-P	Kennedy RJM	Lovett J	Mahon GA	Marsh STP	Marshall SR	McCammon MJ	O'Connor KP	Owusu LM	Partridge SM	Pinamonte CL	Powell DD	Quinn RJ	Rowlands MC	Scott A	Smith JM	Smith PD	Somner MJ	Tabb JA	Theobald DJ	Williams MR
R1	Nov	18	KINGSTONIAN	1-3	Pinamonte	3809						11		3	1			8				6		4			9	2	13		5	10	7						12

F.L. Cup (Worthington Cup)

Rd			Opponent	Score	Scorers	Att	Anderson IM	Austin KL	Charles J	Crowe JWR	Dobson MW	Evans PS	Folan AS	Gibbs PD	Gottskalksson O	Graham GL	Hutchinson ES	Ingimarsson I	Javary J-P	Kennedy RJM	Lovett J	Mahon GA	Marsh STP	Marshall SR	McCammon MJ	O'Connor KP	Owusu LM	Partridge SM	Pinamonte CL	Powell DD	Quinn RJ	Rowlands MC	Scott A	Smith JM	Smith PD	Somner MJ	Tabb JA	Theobald DJ	Williams MR
R1/1	Aug	22	Bristol City	2-2	McCammon, Rowlands	3471						11		3	1			2	8			6		4	10		9	12			5	13	7						
R1/2	Sep	5	BRISTOL CITY	2-1	Scott 2	2310						11	13		1			2	8			6	3	4	9			12			5	10	7						
R2/1		19	TOTTENHAM HOTSPUR	0-0		8580				2		11			1			8				6	3	4	9						5	10	7						
R2/2		26	Tottenham Hotspur	0-2		26909				2	12	11	3		1			8				6		4				7	9		5	10							13

LDV Vans Trophy

Rd			Opponent	Score	Scorers	Att	Anderson IM	Austin KL	Charles J	Crowe JWR	Dobson MW	Evans PS	Folan AS	Gibbs PD	Gottskalksson O	Graham GL	Hutchinson ES	Ingimarsson I	Javary J-P	Kennedy RJM	Lovett J	Mahon GA	Marsh STP	Marshall SR	McCammon MJ	O'Connor KP	Owusu LM	Partridge SM	Pinamonte CL	Powell DD	Quinn RJ	Rowlands MC	Scott A	Smith JM	Smith PD	Somner MJ	Tabb JA	Theobald DJ	Williams MR
R1	Dec	5	OXFORD UNITED	4-1	Lovett, Partridge 2, Marshall	1517					2	11			1					14	8	6		4		13	12	9			5	10	7					3	
R2	Jan	9	Brighton & Hove Albion	2-2	Marshall, McCammon	2482					2	11		3	1			8	6		5			4	7		9					10							12
R3		30	Barnet	2-1	Rowlands, Evans	1438					2	11		3	1			8			5	6		4	12		9	7				10							
SFS	Feb	14	Swansea City	3-2	Evans (p), McCammon, Owusu	2222					2	11		3	1			8				6		4	10		9	7		5									
FS1	Mar	13	Southend United	2-1	Dobson 2	5055					2	11		3	1			8			12	6			13		9	7		5		10						4	
FS2		20	SOUTHEND UNITED	2-1	Ingimarsson, Owusu	6579					2	11		3	1			8			13	6			14		9	7		5		10			12			4	
F	Apr	22	Port Vale	1-2	Dobson	25654					2	11		3	1			8				6			13		9	7		5		10						4	12

R2 won 4-2 on penalties a.e.t. Final at the Millennium Stadium, Cardiff

		Pl.	Home W	Home D	Home L	Home F	Home A	Away W	Away D	Away L	Away F	Away A	F. (Total)	A. (Total)	Pts
1	Millwall	46	17	2	4	49	11	11	7	5	40	27	89	38	93
2	Rotherham United	46	16	4	3	50	26	11	6	6	29	29	79	55	91
3	Reading	46	15	5	3	58	26	10	6	7	28	26	86	52	86
4	Walsall	46	15	5	3	51	23	8	7	8	28	27	79	50	81
5	Stoke City	46	12	6	5	39	21	9	8	6	35	28	74	49	77
6	Wigan Athletic	46	12	9	2	29	18	7	9	7	24	24	53	42	75
7	Bournemouth	46	11	6	6	37	23	9	7	7	42	32	79	55	73
8	Notts County	46	10	6	7	37	33	9	6	8	25	33	62	66	69
9	Bristol City	46	11	6	6	47	29	7	8	8	23	27	70	56	68
10	Wrexham	46	10	6	7	33	28	7	6	10	32	43	65	71	63
11	Port Vale	46	9	8	6	35	22	7	6	10	20	27	55	49	62
12	Peterborough Utd.	46	12	6	5	38	27	3	8	12	23	39	61	66	59
13	Wycombe Wands.	46	8	7	8	24	23	7	7	9	22	30	46	53	59
14	**BRENTFORD**	**46**	**9**	**10**	**4**	**34**	**30**	**5**	**7**	**11**	**22**	**40**	**56**	**70**	**59**
15	Oldham Athletic	46	11	5	7	35	26	4	8	11	18	39	53	65	58
16	Bury	46	10	6	7	25	22	6	4	13	20	37	45	59	58
17	Colchester United	46	10	5	8	32	23	5	7	11	23	36	55	59	57
18	Northampton Town	46	9	6	8	26	28	6	6	11	20	31	46	59	57
19	Cambridge United	46	8	6	9	32	31	6	5	12	29	46	61	77	53
20	Swindon Town	46	6	8	9	30	35	7	5	11	17	30	47	65	52
21	Bristol Rovers	46	6	10	7	28	26	6	5	12	25	31	53	57	51
22	Luton Town	46	5	6	12	24	35	4	7	12	28	45	52	80	40
23	Swansea City	46	5	9	9	26	24	3	4	16	21	49	47	73	37
24	Oxford United	46	5	4	14	23	34	2	2	19	30	66	53	100	27

2000-01

Back: House, Hutchinson, Theobald, Owusu, Powell, P.Smith, Marshall, McCannon, Pinamonte, Ingimarsson, Saroya.
Middle: McLoughlin, Bullivant, Griffin, Downes, Charles, Graham, O'Connor, Bryan, Pearcey, Woodman, Gottskalksson, Quinn, Mahon, Folan, Booker, Taylor, Quinn, Levitt
Front: Dobson, Kennedy, Anderson, Partridge, Boxall, Lewington, Noades, Evans, Rowlands, Gibbs, J.Smith, Williams

2001-02

Back: Marshall, Price, Lovett, Powell, Gottskalksson, P.Smith, Owusu, Ingimarsson, Theobald, McCammon
Middle: Dobson, Charles, Hutchinson, O.Connor, Julian, Fieldwick, Somner, J.Smith, Mahon
Front: Williams, Folan, Partridge, Bryan, Boxall, Evans, Gibbs, Rowlands, Anderson, Hunt.

2001/02

3rd in Division Two

	Month	Day	Opponent	Score	Scorers	Att	Anderson IM	Boxall DJ	Bryan DK	Burgess BK	Caceres AC	Dobson MW	Evans PS	Gibbs PD	Gottskalksson O	Hunt S	Hutchinson ES	Ingimarsson I	Lovett J	Mahon GA	McCammon MJ	O'Connor KP	Owusu LM	Partridge SM	Powell DD	Price JJ	Rowlands MC	Sidwell SJ	Smith PD	Tabb JA	Theobald DJ	Williams MR	Smith JM
1	Aug	11	Wigan Athletic	1-1	Ingimarsson	5952	3					2	11	8	1			4		6		10	9	12	5	7							
2		18	PORT VALE	2-0	Evans, Burgess	4561	3			9		2	11	8	1	13		4		6		10			5	7						12	
3		25	Chesterfield	1-0	Evans	3571				9		2	11	3	1	8		4		6		10			5	7							
4		27	CAMBRIDGE UNITED	2-1	Evans 2 (1p)	4674				10		2	11	3	1	8		4		6		13	9		5	7						12	
5	Sep	8	TRANMERE ROVERS	4-0	Owusu, Evans, Burgess, Williams	5211				10	8	2	11	3	1			4		6		14	9		5	7	13					12	
6		15	Notts County	0-0		5043				10	8	2	11	3	1			4		6		13	9		5	7	12						
7		18	BRISTOL CITY	2-2	Powell, Burgess	6342				10	8		11	3	1			4	2	6		14	9		5	7	13					12	
8		22	OLDHAM ATHLETIC	2-2	Owusu, Evans (p)	5525	14			10	8	2	11	3	1			4		6			9		5	7	13					12	
9		25	Swindon Town	0-2		5519	13			10	8		11	3	1			4	2	6			9		5	7	14					12	
10		29	COLCHESTER UNITED	4-1	Owusu, Evans 2 (1p), Burgess	5179	3			10		2	11	8	1			4		6			9		5	7	12					13	
11	Oct	5	Brighton & Hove Albion	2-1	Ingimarsson, Rowlands	6823	3						11	2	1			4		6		10	9		5	7	8					12	
12		13	PETERBOROUGH UTD.	2-1	Owusu, Evans	11097			12	7		13	11	3	1	8		4		6		10	9		5	2							
13		20	Bournemouth	2-0	Hunt 2	3934	3			7				11	1	8	13	4		6	12	10	9		5	2						14	
14		23	BURY	5-1	Gibbs 2 (2p), Owusu 2, Burgess	5389	3			10				11	1	8	14	4		6	13		9		5	2		7				12	
15		27	Reading	2-1	Ingimarsson, Price	14680	3			10				11	1	8	12	4		6			9		5	2		7					
16	Nov	3	BLACKPOOL	2-0	Owusu, Sidwell	7605	3			10		2		11	1			4		6		8	9		5			7					
17		10	Stoke City	2-3	Owusu, Burgess	17953	3			10		2			1		11	4		6	12	8	9		5		13	7				14	
18		20	Huddersfield Town	1-1	Burgess	8518				10		2	11	3	1	7	14	4		6	13	8	9		5		12						
19		24	QUEEN'S PARK RANGERS	0-0		10849				10		2	11	3	1	7		4		6		13	9		5		8	12					
20	Dec	1	Wycombe Wanderers	3-5	Owusu, Evans (p), Burgess	8013				10		2	11	3	1	8		4		6	12		9		5			7					
21		4	Cardiff City	1-3	Evans	10184				10		2	11	3	1	8	12	4		6	13	14	9		5			7					
22		15	WREXHAM	3-0	Ingimarsson, Burgess, Hunt	5326	3			10		2	11		1	8		4		6	13	14	9		5			7				12	
23		21	NORTHAMPTON T	3-0	Owusu, Evans (p), Burgess	5142	3			10		2	11		1	8		4		6			9		5			7				12	
24		26	Cambridge United	1-2	Burgess	3989	3			10		2	11		1	8		4		6	13		9					7			5	12	
25		29	Tranmere Rovers	0-1		9389	3			10		2	11		1	8		4		6	13		9		5			7				12	
26	Jan	12	Port Vale	1-2	Owusu	4588	3			10		2	11		1	7		4		6	13	8	9		5							12	
27		19	WIGAN ATHLETIC	0-1		5549	3			10		2	11		1	7		4		6		8	9		5								
28		22	Northampton Town	0-1		4184	3			10		2			1	7	6	4		12	9	8	13		5			11					
29		24	BRIGHTON & HOVE ALB	4-0	Ingimarsson, Burgess 2, Sidwell	7475	3			10		2	11			8		4		6			9		5			7	1	12			
30	Feb	2	Colchester United	1-1	Owusu	3657				10		2	11	3		8		4		6		12	9		5			7	1				
31		9	BOURNEMOUTH	1-0	Owusu	6698	3			10		2	11	12		8		4		6	13		9		5			7	1				
32		12	CARDIFF CITY	2-1	Burgess, Hunt	6718	3			10		2	11			8		4		6			9		5			7	1				
33		16	Peterborough United	1-1	Owusu	5100	3			10		2	11	12		8		4		6			9		5			7	1				
34		23	NOTTS COUNTY	2-1	Evans (p), Burgess	5367	3			10		2	11			8		4		6			9		5		12	7	1				
35		26	Oldham Athletic	2-3	Burgess 2	4935	3			10			11	2		8		4		6			9		5		12	7	1				
36	Mar	2	Bristol City	2-0	Owusu, Rowlands	11421	3			10		2	11			8		4					9		5		6	7	1				
37		5	SWINDON TOWN	2-0	Owusu 2	5644	3			10		2	11	13		8		4					9		5		6	7	1			12	
38		9	Wrexham	3-0	Evans, Rowlands 2	3343	3	12		10		2	11	13		8		4				14	9		5		6	7	1				
39		12	CHESTERFIELD	0-0		5372	3			10		2	11	8				4				12	9		5		6	7	1			13	
40		16	WYCOMBE WANDERERS	1-0	Ingimarsson	7165	3			10		2	11			8		4					9				6	7	1	12	5		
41		19	Blackpool	3-1	Owusu 2, Rowlands	4865	3	12		10		2	11			8		4				14	9				6	7	1	13	5		
42		30	STOKE CITY	1-0	Sidwell	8837	3	13		10		2	11			8	12	4				14	9				6	7	1		5		
43	Apr	1	Bury	0-2		4332	3					2	11			8	13	4				10	9				6	7	1		5	12	
44		6	HUDDERSFIELD T	3-0	Owusu, Rowlands, Sidwell	7393	3	13		10		2	11			8		4			14		9		5		6	7	1		12		
45		13	Queen's Park Rangers	0-0		18346	3	12		10		2	11			8		4			13		9		5		6	7	1				
46		20	READING	1-1	Rowlands	11303	3			10		2	11			8		4					9		5		6	7	1			12	
						Apps	33	0	0	43	5	38	40	23	28	34	2	46	2	34	1	13	43	0	41	15	13	29	18	0	5	0	
						Subs	2	5	1			1		4		1	7			1	13	12	1	1			10	1		3	1	20	
						Goals				17			14	2		4		6					20		1	1	7	4				1	

Play Offs

	Month	Day	Opponent	Score	Scorers	Att	Anderson IM	Boxall DJ	Bryan DK	Burgess BK	Caceres AC	Dobson MW	Evans PS	Gibbs PD	Gottskalksson O	Hunt S	Hutchinson ES	Ingimarsson I	Lovett J	Mahon GA	McCammon MJ	O'Connor KP	Owusu LM	Partridge SM	Powell DD	Price JJ	Rowlands MC	Sidwell SJ	Smith PD	Tabb JA	Theobald DJ	Williams MR	Smith JM
SF1	Apr	28	Huddersfield Town	0-0		16523	3			10		2	11			8		4					9		5		6	7	1				
SF2	May	1	HUDDERSFIELD TOWN	2-1	Powell, Owusu	11191	3	13		10		2	11			8		4				12	9		5		6	7	1				
F		11	Stoke City	0-2		42523	2				8		12					3	6	5		9		11	4			13		1	7	10	

Final at the Millennium Stadium, Cardiff

F.A. Cup

	Month	Day	Opponent	Score	Scorers	Att	Anderson IM	Boxall DJ	Bryan DK	Burgess BK	Caceres AC	Dobson MW	Evans PS	Gibbs PD	Gottskalksson O	Hunt S	Hutchinson ES	Ingimarsson I	Lovett J	Mahon GA	McCammon MJ	O'Connor KP	Owusu LM	Partridge SM	Powell DD	Price JJ	Rowlands MC	Sidwell SJ	Smith PD	Tabb JA	Theobald DJ	Williams MR	Smith JM
R1	Nov	17	MORECAMBE	1-0	Gibbs	4026	3			10		2		11	1		12	4		6	14	8	9		5		13	7					
R2	Dec	8	Scunthorpe United	2-3	Dobson, Burgess	3457				10		2	11	3	1	8		4		6		12	9		5			7				13	

F.L. Cup (Worthington Cup)

	Month	Day	Opponent	Score	Scorers	Att	Anderson IM	Boxall DJ	Bryan DK	Burgess BK	Caceres AC	Dobson MW	Evans PS	Gibbs PD	Gottskalksson O	Hunt S	Hutchinson ES	Ingimarsson I	Lovett J	Mahon GA	McCammon MJ	O'Connor KP	Owusu LM	Partridge SM	Powell DD	Price JJ	Rowlands MC	Sidwell SJ	Smith PD	Tabb JA	Theobald DJ	Williams MR	Smith JM
R1	Aug	21	NORWICH CITY	1-0	O'Connor	4111	3			9		2	11	8	1	12		4		6		10		13	5	7							
R2	Sep	12	Newcastle U	1-4	Owusu	25366	3			10		2	11	8	1			4		6		13	9		5	7	14					12	

R2 a.e.t.

LDV Vans Trophy

	Month	Day	Opponent	Score	Scorers	Att	Anderson IM	Boxall DJ	Bryan DK	Burgess BK	Caceres AC	Dobson MW	Evans PS	Gibbs PD	Gottskalksson O	Hunt S	Hutchinson ES	Ingimarsson I	Lovett J	Mahon GA	McCammon MJ	O'Connor KP	Owusu LM	Partridge SM	Powell DD	Price JJ	Rowlands MC	Sidwell SJ	Smith PD	Tabb JA	Theobald DJ	Williams MR	Smith JM
R1	Oct	17	Wycombe Wanderers	0-1		2051	3			10			11	13		7	6	4				8	9			2			1		5	12	14

		Pl.	Home W	Home D	Home L	Home F	Home A	Away W	Away D	Away L	Away F	Away A	F. (Total)	A. (Total)	Pts
1	Brighton & Hove A.	46	17	5	1	42	16	8	10	5	24	26	66	42	90
2	Reading	46	12	7	4	36	20	11	8	4	34	23	70	43	84
3	**BRENTFORD**	**46**	**17**	**5**	**1**	**48**	**12**	**7**	**6**	**10**	**29**	**31**	**77**	**43**	**83**
4	Cardiff City	46	12	8	3	39	25	11	6	6	36	25	75	50	83
5	Stoke City	46	16	4	3	43	12	7	7	9	24	28	67	40	80
6	Huddersfield Town	46	13	7	3	35	19	8	8	7	30	28	65	47	78
7	Bristol City	46	13	6	4	38	21	8	4	11	30	32	68	53	73
8	Queen's Park Rgrs.	46	11	10	2	35	18	8	4	11	25	31	60	49	71
9	Oldham Athletic	46	14	6	3	47	27	4	10	9	30	38	77	65	70
10	Wigan Athletic	46	9	6	8	36	23	7	10	6	30	28	66	51	64
11	Wycombe Wands.	46	13	5	5	38	26	4	8	11	20	38	58	64	64
12	Tranmere Rovers	46	10	9	4	39	19	6	6	11	24	41	63	60	63
13	Swindon Town	46	10	7	6	26	21	5	7	11	20	35	46	56	59
14	Port Vale	46	11	6	6	35	24	5	4	14	16	38	51	62	58
15	Colchester United	46	9	6	8	35	33	6	6	11	30	43	65	76	57
16	Blackpool	46	8	9	6	39	31	6	5	12	27	38	66	69	56
17	Peterborough Utd.	46	11	5	7	46	26	4	5	14	18	33	64	59	55
18	Chesterfield	46	9	3	11	35	36	4	10	9	18	29	53	65	52
19	Notts County	46	8	7	8	28	29	5	4	14	31	42	59	71	50
20	Northampton Town	46	9	4	10	30	33	5	3	15	24	46	54	79	49
21	Bournemouth	46	9	4	10	36	33	1	10	12	20	38	56	71	44
22	Bury	46	6	9	8	26	32	5	2	16	17	43	43	75	44
23	Wrexham	46	7	7	9	29	32	4	3	16	27	57	56	89	43
24	Cambridge United	46	7	7	9	29	34	0	6	17	18	59	47	93	34

2002/03

16th in Division Two

No.	Date	Opponent	Result	Scorers	Att.	Anderson IM	Antoine-Curier M	Blackman LJ	Chorley BF	Constantine L	Dobson MW	Evans SJ	Fieldwick LP	Frampton AJK	Fullarton J	Hughes ST	Hunt S	Hutchinson ES	Julian AJ	Lovett J	Marshall SR	McCammon MJ	O'Connor KP	Peters MW	Roget LTE	Rowlands MC	Smith JM	Smith PD	Somner MJ	Sonko I	Tabb JA	Traynor RT	Vine RL	Williams MR
1	Aug 10	Huddersfield Town	2-0	Vine, Fullarton	9635					12	2				11		8	6				9	7		5		13	1	3	4			10	
2	13	BRISTOL CITY	1-0	Hunt (p)	7130						2						8	6				9	7		5		11	1	3	4			10	
3	17	OLDHAM ATHLETIC	0-0		5356					13	2						8	6				9	7		5		11	1	3	4			10	12
4	24	Colchester United	1-0	Hunt (p)	3135					12	2						8	6				9	7		5		11	1	3	4			10	
5	26	SWINDON TOWN	3-1	McCammon, Vine 2	6299					12	2						8	6				9	7		5		11	1	3	4			10	
6	31	Notts County	2-2	McCammon, Williams	5551						2				13		8	6				9	7		5		11	1	3	4			10	12
7	Sep 7	LUTON TOWN	0-0		7145	3					2				14	13	8	6				9	7				11	1	5	4			10	12
8	14	Tranmere Rovers	1-3	O'Connor	6626	3				13	2				14		8	6				9	7				11	1	5	4			10	12
9	17	Cardiff City	0-2		12032	3				10	2	13			11		8	6				9	7					1	5	4			14	12
10	21	WYCOMBE WANDERERS	1-0	Hunt (p)	6172	3			4	12	2				11		8	6				9	7		5			1					10	
11	28	Peterborough United	1-5	Vine	5066	3		9	4	14	2						8	6					7		5		11	1	12				10	13
12	Oct 5	BARNSLEY	1-2	McCammon	5394	3				13	2	12			11		8	6				9	7		5			1		4			10	
13	12	Northampton Town	2-1	Sonko, Vine	5739	3				12	2				11		8	6				9	7		5			1		4			10	
14	19	PORT VALE	1-1	Hunt (p)	5177	3					2				11		8	6			12	9	7	14	5			1		4			10	13
15	26	Stockport County	3-2	McCammon 2, Marshall	4601						2	3			11		8	6			4	9	7					1	5				10	12
16	29	PLYMOUTH ARGYLE	0-0		6431						2	3		13	11		8	6			4	9	7					1	5				10	12
17	Nov 2	BLACKPOOL	5-0	Sonko 2, Vine, Evans 2	5888					13	2	6		12	11		8				5	9	7					1	3	4			10	14
18	9	Crewe Alexandra	1-2	Sonko	5663					13	2	6		12	11		8				5	9	7			14		1	3	4				10
19	23	WIGAN ATHLETIC	0-1		5454	3					2	6					8					9	7			12	11	1	5	4	14		10	13
20	30	Cheltenham Town	0-1		5013						2	6					8				5	9	7			10	11	1	3	4	12		13	
21	Dec 14	CHESTERFIELD	2-1	Hunt, Vine	5151						2	6			13		8				5	12	7			10	11	1	3	4			9	
22	21	Queen's Park Rangers	1-1	O'Connor	15559						2	6			11		8				5	12	7			10		1	3	4			9	
23	26	Swindon Town	1-2	Vine	6045						2	6			11		8		1		5	13	7			10			3	4			9	12
24	28	MANSFIELD TOWN	1-0	O'Connor	5844						2	6			11		8		1		5	9	7						3	4			10	12
25	Jan 14	Oldham Athletic	1-2	O'Connor	5039						13	6		3			8			2	5	9	7			12	11	1		4		14		10
26	18	NOTTS COUNTY	1-1	Vine	5112						2			3			8				5	9	7	13			11	1		4		12	10	6
27	Feb 4	Mansfield Town	0-0		3735					13	2	6			11		8				5		7			12	10	1	3	4			9	
28	8	CREWE ALEXANDRA	1-2	Hunt	5424						2	6			11		8				5	13	7			10	12	1	3	4			9	
29	11	Bristol City	0-0		9084						2	6			11		8				5	12	7				10	1	3	4			9	
30	15	Blackpool	0-1		6203						2				11	6	8				5	12	7				10	1	3	4			9	13
31	22	Luton Town	1-0	Vine	6940						2		4	3	11		8	12				9	7				6	1	5				10	
32	25	HUDDERSFIELD T	1-0	McCammon	4366						2		5				8	6				9	7				11	1	3	4			10	
33	Mar 1	TRANMERE ROVERS	1-2	Sonko	5396					10	2		5			8		6			12	9	7	14			11	1	3	4			13	
34	4	CARDIFF CITY	0-2		5727					13	2			3				6				9	7	12		8	11	1	5	4			10	
35	8	Wycombe Wanderers	0-4		5930					12	2			3				6			4	9	7	13		8	11	1	5				10	
36	11	COLCHESTER UNITED	1-1	McCammon	3990		11				2		5	3							4	9	7	12		8	13	1	6				10	
37	15	STOCKPORT COUNTY	1-2	Antoine-Curier	4790		11				2		5	3			13	12			4	9	7			8		1	6				10	
38	18	Port Vale	0-1		3241		11				2		12	3			8	6				9	7	14		13		1	5	4			10	
39	22	Plymouth Argyle	0-3		6835		11				2			3			8					9	7			6		1	5	4			10	12
40	29	NORTHAMPTON T	3-0	Somner, Hunt, Rowlands	5354		11				2	6	4	12			8								5	10	7	1	3				9	13
41	Apr 5	CHELTENHAM TOWN	2-2	Dobson, O'Connor	5011		11				2	6		13	14		8						12		5	10	7	1	3	4			9	
42	12	Wigan Athletic	0-2		7204		9			13	2	6			11		8						7		5	10		1	3	4			12	
43	19	QUEEN'S PARK RANGERS	1-2	Peters	9168		9				2	12			11		8				5		7	10				1	3	4	6			
44	21	Chesterfield	2-0	Antoine-Curier 2	3296		9				2	6		12	11		8				5		7	10				1	3	4	13			14
45	26	Barnsley	0-1		9065		9				2	6			11		8		1		5		7	10					3	4			13	12
46	May 3	PETERBOROUGH UTD.	1-1	Evans	6687		11				2	6					8				5		7	13				1	3	4	12		9	10
					Apps	9	11	1	2	2	45	20	6	9	22	2	41	21	3	1	22	31	44	3	14	13	23	43	39	37	1	0	37	4
					Subs					15	1	3	1	6	5	1	1	2			2	6	1	8		5	3		1		4	2	5	18
					Goals		3				1	3			1		7				1	7	5	1		1			1	5			10	1

F.A. Cup

Rd	Date	Opponent	Result	Scorers	Att.	Anderson IM	Antoine-Curier M	Blackman LJ	Chorley BF	Constantine L	Dobson MW	Evans SJ	Fieldwick LP	Frampton AJK	Fullarton J	Hughes ST	Hunt S	Hutchinson ES	Julian AJ	Lovett J	Marshall SR	McCammon MJ	O'Connor KP	Peters MW	Roget LTE	Rowlands MC	Smith JM	Smith PD	Somner MJ	Sonko I	Tabb JA	Traynor RT	Vine RL	Williams MR
R1	Nov 16	Wycombe Wanderers	4-2	Somner, O'Connor, Vine 2	5673						2	6			11		8				5	9	7					1	3	4	12		10	
R2	Dec 7	York City	2-1	Hunt, McCammon	3517						2	6		3			8				5	9	7			10	11	1	12	4				
R3	Jan 4	DERBY COUNTY	1-0	Hunt	8709						2	6		3		12	8				5	9	7			11		1		4			10	
R4	25	BURNLEY	0-3		9563						2			3		9	8				6		7	14	5		11	1	13	4			10	12

F.L. Cup (Worthington Cup)

Rd	Date	Opponent	Result	Scorers	Att.	Anderson IM	Antoine-Curier M	Blackman LJ	Chorley BF	Constantine L	Dobson MW	Evans SJ	Fieldwick LP	Frampton AJK	Fullarton J	Hughes ST	Hunt S	Hutchinson ES	Julian AJ	Lovett J	Marshall SR	McCammon MJ	O'Connor KP	Peters MW	Roget LTE	Rowlands MC	Smith JM	Smith PD	Somner MJ	Sonko I	Tabb JA	Traynor RT	Vine RL	Williams MR
R1	Sep 10	Bournemouth	3-3	O'Connor 2, Vine	3302	3			5	9	2	10			11		14	8			6		7					1	13	4			12	
R2	Oct 1	MIDDLESBROUGH	1-4	Sonko	7558	3				14	2	13			11		8	6				9	7		5			1		4			10	12

R1 won 4-2 on penalties a.e.t.

LDV Vans Trophy

Rd	Date	Opponent	Result	Scorers	Att.	Anderson IM	Antoine-Curier M	Blackman LJ	Chorley BF	Constantine L	Dobson MW	Evans SJ	Fieldwick LP	Frampton AJK	Fullarton J	Hughes ST	Hunt S	Hutchinson ES	Julian AJ	Lovett J	Marshall SR	McCammon MJ	O'Connor KP	Peters MW	Roget LTE	Rowlands MC	Smith JM	Smith PD	Somner MJ	Sonko I	Tabb JA	Traynor RT	Vine RL	Williams MR
R2	Nov 12	Plymouth Argyle	1-0	Hunt	3565						2	6		3	11		8	13	1		5					10	12			4	7		9	
R3	Dec 10	KIDDERMINSTER HARR.	2-1	O'Connor, Marshall	1541							6		3	11						5		7			10	8	1	2	4	12		9	
SFS	Jan 21	CAMBRIDGE UNITED	1-2	McCammon	2878						2			3		12	8				4	9	7		5		6	1				13	10	11

SFS lost in sudden death extra time

		Pl.	Home W	D	L	F	A	Away W	D	L	F	A	F. (Total)	A.	Pts
1	Wigan Athletic	46	14	7	2	37	16	15	6	2	31	9	68	25	100
2	Crewe Alexandra	46	11	5	7	29	19	14	6	3	47	21	76	40	86
3	Bristol City	46	15	5	3	43	15	9	6	8	36	33	79	48	83
4	Queen's Park Rgrs.	46	14	4	5	38	19	10	7	6	31	26	69	45	83
5	Oldham Athletic	46	11	6	6	39	18	11	10	2	29	20	68	38	82
6	Cardiff City	46	12	6	5	33	20	11	6	6	35	23	68	43	81
7	Tranmere Rovers	46	14	5	4	38	23	9	6	8	28	34	66	57	80
8	Plymouth Argyle	46	11	6	6	39	24	6	8	9	24	28	63	52	65
9	Luton Town	46	8	8	7	32	28	9	6	8	35	34	67	62	65
10	Swindon Town	46	10	5	8	34	27	6	7	10	25	36	59	63	60
11	Peterborough Utd.	46	8	7	8	25	20	6	9	8	26	34	51	54	58
12	Colchester United	46	8	7	8	24	24	6	9	8	28	32	52	56	58
13	Blackpool	46	10	8	5	35	25	5	5	13	21	39	56	64	58
14	Stockport County	46	8	8	7	39	38	7	2	14	26	32	65	70	55
15	Notts County	46	10	7	6	37	32	3	9	11	25	38	62	70	55
16	**BRENTFORD**	**46**	**8**	**8**	**7**	**28**	**21**	**6**	**4**	**13**	**19**	**35**	**47**	**56**	**54**
17	Port Vale	46	9	5	9	34	31	5	6	12	20	39	54	70	53
18	Wycombe Wands.	46	8	7	8	39	38	5	6	12	20	28	59	66	52
19	Barnsley	46	7	8	8	27	31	6	5	12	24	33	51	64	52
20	Chesterfield	46	11	4	8	29	28	3	4	16	14	45	43	73	50
21	Cheltenham Town	46	6	9	8	26	31	4	9	10	27	37	53	68	48
22	Huddersfield Town	46	7	9	7	27	24	4	3	16	12	37	39	61	45
23	Mansfield Town	46	9	2	12	38	45	3	6	14	28	52	66	97	44
24	Northampton Town	46	7	4	12	23	31	3	5	15	17	48	40	79	39

2002-03

Back: Somner, Hutchinson, Evans, Marshall, Powell, Smith, McCannon, Constantine, Lovett, Hughes, Dobson
Middle: Taylor (Coaching staff), Hiron (Physio), Traynor, Fieldwick, O'Connor, Gottskalksson, Griffin (Scout), Julian, Smith, Blackman, Rowlands, Forzoni (Coach), McLoughlin (Coach)
Front: Tabb, Hunt, Anderson, Downes (Manager), Allen-Page, Williams, Peters.

2003-04

Back: Frampton, Harrold, Roget, P.Smith, Julian, Sonko, Thomas, Hutchinson
Middle: Allen-Page, Fieldwick, O'Connor, Hughes, Somner, J.Smith, Peters
Front: Hunt, Blackman, Dobson, Traynor, Tabb,

2003/04

17th in Division Two

	Date	Opponent	Score	Scorers	Att.	Beadle PCWJ	Blackman LJ	Bull RR	Dobson MW	Evans SJ	Fieldwick LP	Fitzgerald SB	Frampton AJK	Harrold MJ	Hughes ST	Hunt S	Hutchinson ES	Julian AJ	Kitamirike JD	May BS	Nelson SJ	O'Connor KP	Olugbodi JM	Peters MW	Rhodes AG	Roget LTE	Rougier AL	Smith JM	Smith PD	Somner MJ	Sonko I	Tabb JA	Talbot SD	Wells DT	Wright TA	Allen-Page D
1	Aug 9	Tranmere Rovers	1-4	Hunt (p)	7307	9			2		12		11			8	6					7		13		5		10	1	3	4	14				
2	16	PETERBOROUGH UTD.	0-3		4463		13		2	12							6					7		9		5	10	8	1	3	4	11				
3	23	Wrexham	0-1		4048		12		2	11					10		6					7		13		5	9	8	1	3	4					
4	25	OLDHAM ATHLETIC	2-1	Hutchinson, Rougier	4073				2	11	5					12	6			10		7					9	8	1	3	4					
5	30	Port Vale	0-1		5257				2	11						12	6	1		10		7				5	9	8		3	4	13				
6	Sep 6	PLYMOUTH ARGYLE	1-3	May	5688				2	13	3					8	6	1		10				9		5	7	11			4	12				
7	13	Rushden & Diamonds	1-0	Hunt	4396						3				12	8	6	1		10		7				5	9	11		2	4				13	
8	16	BLACKPOOL	0-0		3818				2		3					8	6			10		7				5	9	11	1	12	4	14			13	
9	20	HARTLEPOOL UNITED	2-1	Sonko, Wright	4501				2	12						8	6		5	10		7					11		1	3	4	13			9	
10	27	Chesterfield	2-1	Hunt, Wright	3257				2							8	6		5	10		7					11	12	1	3	4				9	
11	30	Colchester United	1-1	Rougier	3343				2					12		8	6		5	10		7					11	13	1	3	4				9	
12	Oct 4	SHEFFIELD WEDNESDAY	0-3		8631				2							8	6		5	10		7	14			4	11		1	3		12		13	9	
13	18	LUTON TOWN	4-2	Hunt, Tabb 2, May	5579				2	6						8			5	10		7				4	11	13	1	3	12	14			9	
14	21	BRIGHTON & HOVE ALB	4-0	Hunt 2 (2p), Tabb, May	6532				2				12			8	6		5	10		7		13			9		1	3	4	11				
15	25	Notts County	0-2		4145				2	13			3			8	6		5	10		7	12				9		1	4		11				
16	Nov 1	BARNSLEY	2-1	Hutchinson, Rougier	4789				2					10	12	8	6		5			7		13			9		1	3	4	11				
17	11	Queen's Park Rangers	0-1		15865				2	12				13		8	6		5	10		7					9		1	3	4	11			14	
18	15	Wycombe Wanderers	2-1	Hutchinson, Tabb	6445				2				12		14	8	6		5	10		7					11		1	3	4	13			9	
19	22	GRIMSBY TOWN	1-3	Hunt (p)	4685				2					13	14	8	6		5	10		7					9	12	1	3	4	11				
20	29	Bournemouth	0-1		6674				2	12					13	8			5	10		7		14			9	6	1	3	4	11				
21	Dec 13	Stockport County	1-1	Jackman (og)	4081				2	10						8			5	12		7				6			1	3	4	11			9	
22	20	SWINDON TOWN	0-2		5077				2	10						8			5	13		7				4	12	6	1	3		11			9	
23	26	BRISTOL CITY	1-2	May	5912				2	11						8			5	10		7			12	6			1	3	4				9	
24	28	Plymouth Argyle	0-2		17882				2	11					12	8			5	10		7				6			1	3	4				9	
25	Jan 3	Oldham Athletic	1-1	May	4990				2	11			12			8			5	10		7				6		13	1	3	4				9	
26	10	TRANMERE ROVERS	2-2	Hunt, May	4105			3	2	6			11		12	8				10		13				5	7		1		4				9	
27	17	Peterborough United	0-0		4658			3		6			2			8				10		12					7	11	1	5	4	13			9	
28	24	WREXHAM	0-1		4567			3					2		12	8		1		10		7					9	6		5	4	11			13	
29	31	PORT VALE	3-2	Hunt, Tabb, Rougier	4306		12	3	2							8	6	1	5	10		7		13			9				4	11				
30	Feb 7	Bristol City	1-3	Hutchinson	13029			3	2							8	6	1	5			7		12			9				4	11			10	
31	14	QUEEN'S PARK RANGERS	1-1	O'Connor	8418				2							8	6	1	5	10		7					9			3	4	11				
32	21	Luton Town	1-4	Wright	6273			3	2	13							6	1	5	10		7					11			12	4	14	8		9	
33	28	NOTTS COUNTY	2-3	Hutchinson, Evans	4478			3	2	11			5				6	1		10							7				4	12	8		9	
34	Mar 2	Brighton & Hove Albion	0-1		6007			3	2	7			6				11		12	10	1	14								5	4	13	8		9	
35	6	Swindon Town	1-2	May	7649			3	2	11							6			10	1	/					13			5	4	9	8		12	
36	13	STOCKPORT COUNTY	0-2		6615			3	2							8	11			10	1	7					9			5	4	13	6		12	
37	16	Blackpool	1-1	Hunt (p)	4617			3	2	14		6		13		8	11	1		10		12					9			5	4		7			
38	20	RUSHDEN & DIAMONDS	3-2	Hunt, Tabb, Talbot	4616			3	2	12		5	14	9		8	6	1		10		13									4	11	7			
39	27	Hartlepool United	2-1	Dobson, Tabb	5206			3	2			5	14	12		8	6	1		10		9								13	4	11	7			
40	Apr 3	CHESTERFIELD	1-1	Evans	4962			3	2	14		5		13		8	6	1		10		9								12	4	11	7			
41	10	Sheffield Wednesday	1-1	Sonko	20004			3	2			5	11			8	6			10	1	9								14	4	13	7		12	
42	12	COLCHESTER UNITED	3-2	Sonko, Tabb, Harrold	5017			3	2				5	10		8	6			13	1	14								12	4	11	7		9	
43	17	Barnsley	2-0	Tabb, Talbot	9824			3	2	14		5		13		8	6			10	1	9								12	4	11	7			
44	24	WYCOMBE WANDERERS	1-1	Harrold	7145			3	2			5		12		8	6			10	1	9								13	4	11	7			
45	May 1	Grimsby Town	0-1		6856			3				5	2	9		8	6			10	1	14			12					13	4	11	7			
46	8	BOURNEMOUTH	1-0	Rhodes	9485			3	2			5	12	9		8	6			10	1				13						4	11	7			
					Apps	1	0	20	42	14	4	9	10	5	1	38	36	13	21	38	9	36	0	2	0	15	29	12	24	30	42	22	15	0	18	
					Subs		3			11	1		6	8	8	2			1	3		7	2	7	3		2	5		9	1	14		1	7	
					Goals				1	2				2		11	5			7		1			1		4				3	9	2		3	

One own goal

F.A. Cup

	Date	Opponent	Score	Scorers	Att.	Beadle PCWJ	Blackman LJ	Bull RR	Dobson MW	Evans SJ	Fieldwick LP	Fitzgerald SB	Frampton AJK	Harrold MJ	Hughes ST	Hunt S	Hutchinson ES	Julian AJ	Kitamirike JD	May BS	Nelson SJ	O'Connor KP	Olugbodi JM	Peters MW	Rhodes AG	Roget LTE	Rougier AL	Smith JM	Smith PD	Somner MJ	Sonko I	Tabb JA	Talbot SD	Wells DT	Wright TA	Allen-Page D
R1	Nov 8	GAINSBOROUGH TRINITY	7-1	Harrold 3, Rougier, Purkiss (og), Frampton, O'Connor	3041					12			3	10	13	8	6					7	14				9	2	1	5	4	11				
R2	Dec 6	Telford United	0-3		2996				2	12					13	8			5	10		7		14			9	6	1	3	4	11				

F.L. Cup (Carling Cup)

	Date	Opponent	Score	Scorers	Att.	Beadle PCWJ	Blackman LJ	Bull RR	Dobson MW	Evans SJ	Fieldwick LP	Fitzgerald SB	Frampton AJK	Harrold MJ	Hughes ST	Hunt S	Hutchinson ES	Julian AJ	Kitamirike JD	May BS	Nelson SJ	O'Connor KP	Olugbodi JM	Peters MW	Rhodes AG	Roget LTE	Rougier AL	Smith JM	Smith PD	Somner MJ	Sonko I	Tabb JA	Talbot SD	Wells DT	Wright TA	Allen-Page D
R1	Aug 12	West Bromwich Albion	0-4		10440		12		2				3		13	8	6	14				7		9				10	1	5	4	11				

LDV Vans Trophy

	Date	Opponent	Score	Scorers	Att.	Beadle PCWJ	Blackman LJ	Bull RR	Dobson MW	Evans SJ	Fieldwick LP	Fitzgerald SB	Frampton AJK	Harrold MJ	Hughes ST	Hunt S	Hutchinson ES	Julian AJ	Kitamirike JD	May BS	Nelson SJ	O'Connor KP	Olugbodi JM	Peters MW	Rhodes AG	Roget LTE	Rougier AL	Smith JM	Smith PD	Somner MJ	Sonko I	Tabb JA	Talbot SD	Wells DT	Wright TA	Allen-Page D
R1	Oct 14	Barnet	3-3	Hunt, Tabb 2	1248				2	11			3			8	13		5	10		14	9			4	7	12	1			6				
R2	Nov 4	Peterborough United	2-3	Dobson, Hunt	1821				2	6			3	10	14	8			5			7	13	9				11	1	4						12

R1 won 3-1 on penalties a.e.t.

		Pl.	Home W	D	L	F	A	Away W	D	L	F	A	F. (Total)	A.	Pts
1	Plymouth Argyle	46	17	5	1	52	13	9	7	7	33	28	85	41	90
2	Queen's Park Rgs.	46	16	7	0	47	12	6	10	7	33	33	80	45	83
3	Bristol City	46	15	6	2	34	12	8	7	8	24	25	58	37	82
4	Brighton & H. A.	46	17	4	2	39	11	5	7	11	25	32	64	43	77
5	Swindon Town	46	12	7	4	41	23	8	6	9	35	35	76	58	73
6	Hartlepool United	46	10	8	5	39	24	10	5	8	37	37	76	61	73
7	Port Vale	46	15	6	2	45	28	6	4	13	28	35	73	63	73
8	Tranmere Rovers	46	13	7	3	36	18	4	9	10	23	38	59	56	67
9	Bournemouth	46	11	8	4	35	25	6	7	10	21	26	56	51	66
10	Luton Town	46	14	6	3	44	27	3	9	11	25	39	69	66	66
11	Colchester United	46	11	8	4	33	23	6	5	12	19	33	52	56	64
12	Barnsley	46	7	12	4	25	19	8	5	10	29	39	54	58	62
13	Wrexham	46	9	6	8	27	21	8	3	12	23	39	50	60	60
14	Blackpool	46	9	5	9	31	28	7	6	10	27	37	58	65	59
15	Oldham Athletic	46	9	8	6	37	25	3	13	7	29	35	66	60	57
16	Sheffield Wed.	46	7	9	7	25	26	6	5	12	23	38	48	64	53
17	**BRENTFORD**	**46**	**9**	**5**	**9**	**34**	**38**	**5**	**6**	**12**	**18**	**31**	**52**	**69**	**53**
18	Peterborough Utd.	46	5	8	10	36	33	7	8	8	22	25	58	58	52
19	Stockport County	46	6	8	9	31	36	5	11	7	31	34	62	70	52
20	Chesterfield	46	9	7	7	34	31	3	8	12	15	40	49	71	51
21	Grimsby Town	46	10	5	8	36	26	3	6	14	19	55	55	81	50
22	Rushden & Diam.	46	9	5	9	37	34	4	4	15	23	40	60	74	48
23	Notts County	46	6	9	8	32	27	4	3	16	18	51	50	78	42
24	Wycombe Wands.	46	5	7	11	31	39	1	12	10	19	36	50	75	37

2004/05

4th in League One (Formerly Duivsion 2)

No	Date	Opponent	Score	Scorers	Att	Bankole A	Burton DJ	Charles WDD	Claridge SE	Dobson MW	Fitzgerald SB	Fitzgerald SP	Frampton AJK	Gayle MA	Hargreaves C	Harrold MJ	Hunt S	Hutchinson ES	Ide CJ	Lawrence JH	May BS	Moleski GK	Myers AJ	Nelson SJ	O'Connor KP	Osborne KAJ	Pacquette RF	Peters RV	Pratley DA	Rankin I	Rhodes AG	Salako JA	Smith JM	Sobers JR	Sodje SO	Somner MJ	Tabb JA	Talbot SD	Turner MT	Watts RD
1	Aug 7	Chesterfield	1-3	Rhodes	4651		9			2	5		13		11								3	1	12					10	14	7					6	8	4	
2	10	DONCASTER ROVERS	4-3	Tabb, Burton, Rankin, Hargreaves	5621		9			2	5		3		11									1	13					10	14	7				12	6	8	4	
3	14	WREXHAM	1-0	O'Connor	5091		9			2	5		3		11									1	14					10	12	7	13				6	8	4	
4	21	Peterborough United	0-3		4868		9			2	5		3		11									1	14			12		10	13	7					6	8	4	
5	28	STOCKPORT COUNTY	3-0	Dobson, Salako, Burton	4643		9			2	5		3		11									1	14					10	12	7	13				6	8	4	
6	30	Bristol City	1-4	O'Connor	10296		9			2	5		3		11									1	8					10	14	13			6	7		12	4	
7	Sep 4	BOURNEMOUTH	2-1	Talbot, Rankin	5682						5		3		11		8							1	9					10	12	7			2			6	4	
8	11	Torquay United	2-2	Hargreaves, Sodje	3458		13				5		3		11		8							1	9					10		7			2		12	6	4	
9	18	PORT VALE	1-0	Salako (p)	5442		9						3		11		8			12				1	2					10	14	7			5		13	6	4	
10	25	Walsall	1-0	Salako (p)	5302		9						3		11	12								1	2					10		7			5		6	8	4	
11	Oct 2	OLDHAM ATHLETIC	2-0	Burton, Rankin	5818		9						3		11	13	12			14				1	2					10		7			5		6	8	4	
12	9	Barnsley	0-0		8453								3		11	9	8						13	1	2					10	12	7			5			6	4	
13	16	MK Dons	0-0		5924		9								11	14	8			12			3	1	2					10	13				5		6	7	4	
14	19	HARTLEPOOL UNITED	2-1	Burton, Rankin	4797		9								11	13	8			7				1	2					10	12	3			5		6		4	
15	23	BLACKPOOL	0-3		6722		9								6	12	8			7			3	1	2					10	14	11			5		13		4	
16	30	Tranmere Rovers	0-1		8740		9						3			8				7				1	2					10	12	11			5		13	6	4	
17	Nov 7	Huddersfield Town	1-1	Sodje	10810		9						3		11	12				13				1	2					10		7			5		6	8	4	
18	20	BRADFORD CITY	1-2	Rhodes	5909		9						3		11	13				14				1	2					10	12	7			5		6	8	4	
19	27	Hull City	0-2		15710								3		8	12				7			11	1	2		10	14			9	13			5		6		4	
20	Dec 7	LUTON TOWN	2-0	Burton, May	6393		9						3		11	13					10			1	2					14	12	7			5		6	8	4	
21	11	Sheffield Wed	2-1	Burton, Rhodes	21592		9						3		11						10		12	1	2					14	13	7			5		6	8	4	
22	18	COLCHESTER UNITED	1-0	Salako	5634		9		10				3		6					13				1	2					12	7	11			5			8	4	
23	26	TORQUAY UNITED	1-3	Sodje	6419		9		10				3							7	13			1	2					12	11	8			5		14	6	4	
24	28	Swindon Town	0-3		6875		9		10				3		11					7	13			1						8	12				5		2	6	4	
25	Jan 1	Bournemouth	2-3	Rankin 2	8072		9		12		5		3		11			6			10			1						8	14	7			2		13		4	
26	3	WALSALL	1-0	Broad (og)	5084		9						3		11			6		7	12			1						10	8				5		2		4	
27	15	Port Vale	1-0	Hutchinson	4230		9			2					11			6			10		3	1						7		12			5		13	8	4	
28	22	SWINDON TOWN	2-1	Burton, Hunt	5857		9			2					11		12	6			10			1								3			5		7	8	4	
29	25	BARNSLEY	1-1	Sodje	4835		9			2	5					10	14	6						1				13		7		11			3		8	12	4	
30	Feb 5	MK DONS	1-0	Hunt (p)	5077	1	9			2	5					10	6				7							12				11			3			8	4	
31	22	Hartlepool United	1-3	Rankin	4206		14			2						9	11	6			10			1				13	8	7		3			5		12		4	
32	26	SHEFFIELD WED	3-3	Burton, Peters, Hunt	8323	1	9			12							11	6							2			14	13	10		3			5		7	8	4	
33	Mar 5	Colchester United	1-0	Tabb	3066		9			12		13	3				11	6						1	2				10						5		7	8	4	
34	12	Doncaster Rovers	0-0		5525		9			13			11				12	6						1	2				14	10		3			5		7	8	4	
35	15	Oldham Athletic	2-0	SP Fitzgerald 2	4291		9			12		10	3				14	6						1	2				11	13					5		7	8	4	
36	19	CHESTERFIELD	2-2	Tabb, Burton	6097		9					10	3		11		13	6						1	2					7		12			5		8		4	
37	22	Blackpool	1-2	Pratley	5478		9			12		13	3		11			14						1	2				8	10					5		7	6	4	
38	28	PETERBOROUGH UTD.	0-0		6341					2		10					7	6						1	3			12	11	9					5		13	8	4	
39	Apr 2	Stockport County	2-1	Sodje, SP Fitzgerald	4408					2		10	3				7						14	1	9			13	11	12					5		6	8	4	
40	9	BRISTOL CITY	1-0	Sodje	6780		9					10	3	6		13								1	2				11	12					5		7	8	4	
41	12	TRANMERE ROVERS	1-0	Turner	6005		9					10	3	13		12								1	2				8	7		11			5		14	6	4	
42	16	Bradford City	1-4	Tabb	6743		9					10	3	6		14							12	1	2				8	7		11			5		13		4	
43	23	HUDDERSFIELD T	0-1		7703		9					12	3	6										1	2				11	10		13			5		7	8	4	
44	30	Luton Town	2-4	Burton, Sodje	9313		9					12	3	10		13		6						1	2				11	14		7			5			8	4	
45	May 3	Wrexham	2-1	Rankin, SP Fitzgerald	4374		9					13	3	12	11			6						1	2				14	10					5		7	8	4	
46	7	HULL CITY	2-1	Tabb	9604	1		8			5				11	9			12	7		14	3			2		10						4			6			13
					Apps	3	38	1	3	13	12	7	34	4	30	6	13	14	0	8	7	0	6	43	32	1	1	1	11	33	4	30	0	1	40	1	29	35	45	0
					Subs		2		1	5		5	1	2		13	6	1	1	6	3	1	4		5			8	3	8	18	5	2			1	11	2		1
					Goals		10			1		4			2		3	1			1				2			1	1	8	3	4		1	7		5	1	1	

Play Offs

No	Date	Opponent	Score	Scorers	Att	Bankole A	Burton DJ	Charles WDD	Claridge SE	Dobson MW	Fitzgerald SB	Fitzgerald SP	Frampton AJK	Gayle MA	Hargreaves C	Harrold MJ	Hunt S	Hutchinson ES	Ide CJ	Lawrence JH	May BS	Moleski GK	Myers AJ	Nelson SJ	O'Connor KP	Osborne KAJ	Pacquette RF	Peters RV	Pratley DA	Rankin I	Rhodes AG	Salako JA	Smith JM	Sobers JR	Sodje SO	Somner MJ	Tabb JA	Talbot SD	Turner MT	Watts RD
SF1	May 12	Sheffield Wednesday	0-1		28625		9						3	10	11			6						1	2				7	12					5		13	8	4	
SF2	16	SHEFFIELD WEDNESDAY	1-2	Frampton	10823		9					10	3	14	11			6						1					7	13		12			5		2	8	4	

F.A. Cup

No	Date	Opponent	Score	Scorers	Att	Bankole A	Burton DJ	Charles WDD	Claridge SE	Dobson MW	Fitzgerald SB	Fitzgerald SP	Frampton AJK	Gayle MA	Hargreaves C	Harrold MJ	Hunt S	Hutchinson ES	Ide CJ	Lawrence JH	May BS	Moleski GK	Myers AJ	Nelson SJ	O'Connor KP	Osborne KAJ	Pacquette RF	Peters RV	Pratley DA	Rankin I	Rhodes AG	Salako JA	Smith JM	Sobers JR	Sodje SO	Somner MJ	Tabb JA	Talbot SD	Turner MT	Watts RD
R1	Nov 12	Bristol City	1-1	Salako	10000		9						3		11					12				1	2					10	13	7			5		6	8	4	
rep	25	BRISTOL CITY	1-1	Frampton	3706								3		6	9				7				1	2					10	13	11			5		12	8	4	
R2	Dec 5	Hinckley United	0-0		2661								3		6	14				7	9			1	2					10	12	11			5		13	8	4	
rep	14	HINCKLEY UNITED	2-1	Talbot, Rhodes	4002		9								11	14		12			10		4	1	2					13	7	3			5		6	8		
R3	Jan 8	Luton Town	2-0	Tabb, Hargreaves	6861		9				5		3		11			6		2	10			1						7		13					12	8	4	
R4	29	HARTLEPOOL UNITED	0-0		8967		9			2			12				13	6			10			1						7		3			5		11	8	4	
rep	Feb 12	Hartlepool United	1-0	Rankin	7580		9			2					11		7	6			13			1						10		3			5		12	8	4	
R5	19	Southampton	2-2	Rankin, Sodje	24741		9			2			11			12	13	6			14			1						10		3			5		7	8	4	
rep	Mar 1	SOUTHAMPTON	1-3	Hutchinson	11720		9			2			11				14	6						1	13			12		10		3			5		7	8	4	

R1 replay won 4-3 on penalties a.e.t.

F.L. Cup (Carling Cup)

No	Date	Opponent	Score	Scorers	Att	Bankole A	Burton DJ	Charles WDD	Claridge SE	Dobson MW	Fitzgerald SB	Fitzgerald SP	Frampton AJK	Gayle MA	Hargreaves C	Harrold MJ	Hunt S	Hutchinson ES	Ide CJ	Lawrence JH	May BS	Moleski GK	Myers AJ	Nelson SJ	O'Connor KP	Osborne KAJ	Pacquette RF	Peters RV	Pratley DA	Rankin I	Rhodes AG	Salako JA	Smith JM	Sobers JR	Sodje SO	Somner MJ	Tabb JA	Talbot SD	Turner MT	Watts RD
R1	Aug 24	Ipswich Town	0-2		10190		9			2	5		3		11								4	1	8			10		13	7		6				14	12		

LDV Vans Trophy

No	Date	Opponent	Score	Scorers	Att	Bankole A	Burton DJ	Charles WDD	Claridge SE	Dobson MW	Fitzgerald SB	Fitzgerald SP	Frampton AJK	Gayle MA	Hargreaves C	Harrold MJ	Hunt S	Hutchinson ES	Ide CJ	Lawrence JH	May BS	Moleski GK	Myers AJ	Nelson SJ	O'Connor KP	Osborne KAJ	Pacquette RF	Peters RV	Pratley DA	Rankin I	Rhodes AG	Salako JA	Smith JM	Sobers JR	Sodje SO	Somner MJ	Tabb JA	Talbot SD	Turner MT	Watts RD
R1	Sep 28	MILTON KEYNES DONS	0-3		1979						5					9	8			7			3					10			11						6			

Also played: A Julian (1, subbed), S Hillier (2), J Palmer (4), J Lennie (12), L Muldowney (13), S Weight (14)

		Pl.	Home W	D	L	F	A	Away W	D	L	F	A	F. (Total)	A. (Total)	Pts
1	Luton Town	46	17	4	2	46	16	12	7	4	41	32	87	48	98
2	Hull City	46	16	5	2	42	17	10	3	10	38	36	80	53	86
3	Tranmere Rovers	46	14	5	4	43	23	8	8	7	30	32	73	55	79
4	**BRENTFORD**	**46**	**15**	**4**	**4**	**34**	**22**	**7**	**5**	**11**	**23**	**38**	**57**	**60**	**75**
5	Sheffield Wed.	46	10	6	7	34	28	9	9	5	43	31	77	59	72
6	Hartlepool United	46	15	3	5	51	30	6	5	12	25	36	76	66	71
7	Bristol City	46	9	8	6	42	25	9	8	6	32	32	74	57	70
8	Bournemouth	46	9	7	7	40	30	11	3	9	37	34	77	64	70
9	Huddersfield Town	46	12	6	5	42	28	8	4	11	32	37	74	65	70
10	Doncaster Rovers	46	10	11	2	35	20	6	7	10	30	40	65	60	66
11	Bradford City	46	9	6	8	40	35	8	8	7	24	27	64	62	65
12	Swindon Town	46	12	5	6	40	30	5	7	11	26	38	66	68	63
13	Barnsley	46	7	11	5	38	31	7	8	8	31	33	69	64	61
14	Walsall	46	11	7	5	40	28	5	5	13	25	41	65	69	60
15	Colchester United	46	8	6	9	27	23	6	11	6	33	27	60	50	59
16	Blackpool	46	8	7	8	28	30	7	5	11	26	29	54	59	57
17	Chesterfield	46	9	8	6	32	28	5	7	11	23	34	55	62	57
18	Port Vale	46	13	2	8	33	23	4	3	16	16	36	49	59	56
19	Oldham Athletic	46	10	5	8	42	34	4	5	14	18	39	60	73	52
20	Milton Keynes Dons	46	8	10	5	33	28	4	5	14	21	40	54	68	51
21	Torquay United	46	8	5	10	27	36	4	10	9	28	43	55	79	51
22	Wrexham	46	6	8	9	26	37	7	6	10	36	43	62	80	43
23	Peterborough Utd.	46	5	6	12	27	35	4	6	13	22	38	49	73	39
24	Stockport County	46	3	4	16	26	46	3	4	16	23	52	49	98	26

2004-05

Back: Lee, O'Connor, Rankin, Nelson, Julian, Burton, Rhodes, Smith
Middle: Griffin (Chief Scout), Whitehead (Goal.Coach), Doyle (Therapist), Tabb, Somner, Axbey ('No.100'), Bates ('No.13'), Sodje, Harrold, Taylor (Youth Manager), Quin (Youth Devt.), Hirons (Physio)
Front: Myers, Hutchinson, Fitzgerald, Dobson, Allen (Manager), Whitbread (Coach), Talbot, Hargreaves, Frampton, Salako
Seated: Morrison, Muldowney, Lennie, Palmer, Hillier.

2005-06

Back: Carter (Kit man), Gayle, Frampton, Bankole, Turner, Nelson, Sodje, Hutchinson, 'Old George' (Manager's Mate)
Middle: Griffin (Chief Scout), Quin (Head Youth Devt.), S.Fitzgerald Snr.(Youth Team Man.), Skulason, O'Connor, Tillen, Peters, Rhodes, Hirons (Physio), Sports (Sports Therapist), Andrews (No.'13')
Front: Campbell, Rankin, Owusu, Newman, Allen (Manager), Whitbread (Coach), Dobson, S.Fitzgerald Jnr., Tabb, Brooker.

2005/06

3rd in League One

No	Date	Opponent	Score	Scorers	Att	Bankole A	Brooker P	Campbell DJ	Charles D	Dobson MW	Fitzgerald SP	Frampton AJK	Gayle MA	Hutchinson ES	Keenan JJ	Lewis KJ	Mousinho J	Nelson SJ	Newman RA	O'Connor KP	Osborne KAJ	Owusu LM	Peters RV	Pratley DA	Rankin I	Rhodes AG	Skulason O-I	Smith J	Sodje SO	Tabb JA	Tillen SL	Turner MT	Willock C	Moleski GK	Ide CJ	Watts RD
1	Aug 6	SCUNTHORPE UNITED	2-0	Tabb, Campbell (p)	5952		8	14		12	13	3		6				1		2		9			10		7		5	11		4				
2	10	Chesterfield	3-1	Sodje, Rankin 2	4121		8	14				3		6	13			1		2		9			10		7		5	11	12	4				
3	15	Port Vale	0-1		4275		8	11		2	14	3		6	12			1		7		9			10				5		13	4				
4	20	TRANMERE ROVERS	2-0	Hutchinson, Tabb	5438		8	13		2	14	3		6	12			1		7		9			10				5	11		4				
5	27	Barnsley	1-1	Owusu	7462		8	13		7		3		6		12		1		2		9			10				5	11		4				
6	29	GILLINGHAM	1-1	Peters	6969			13		12		3		6		8		1		2		9	7		10				5	11		4				
7	Sep 3	Nottingham Forest	2-1	Frampton, Pratley	17234						9	3	8	6				1		2			12	7	10				5	11		4				
8	10	MK DONS	1-0	O'Connor (p)	5862			12			9	3	8	6				1		2			13	7	10				5	11		4				
9	17	Huddersfield Town	2-3	Rankin, Campbell	11622			12			9	3	6			8		1				13	14	7	10				5	11	2	4				
10	24	BRISTOL CITY	2-3	Sodje, Brooker	6413		13	14					6			8		1			2	9		7	10	12			5	11	3	4				
11	27	Walsall	0-0		4873		8	12				3	13			6		1				9		7	10	14			5	11	2	4				
12	Oct 1	ROTHERHAM UNITED	2-1	O'Connor (p), Rankin	5901		8					3				6		1		2		9		7	10	12			5	11		4				
13	9	Oldham Athletic	1-0	Fitzgerald	5089		8	12			13	3				6		1		2		9		7	10	11			5		14	4				
14	15	SWINDON TOWN	0-0		6969		8				12	3	13			6		1		2		9		7	10				5	11		4				
15	22	Blackpool	0-0		5041		8				13	5	14	12		6		1		2		9		7	10					11	3	4				
16	29	BOURNEMOUTH	0-2		6625		13	7				3		6		8		1	12	2		9			10				5	11	14	4				
17	Nov 12	Hartlepool United	2-1	Owusu, Campbell	4811		8	10		12		3		13				1	6	2		9		7					5	11		4				
18	19	OLDHAM ATHLETIC	3-3	Owusu, Campbell, Pratley	5450		8	10			14	3						1	6	2		9	13	7					5	11	12	4				
19	26	Scunthorpe United	3-1	Brooker, Pratley 2	4322		8	10				3		13				1	6	2		9		7	14				5	11	12	4				
20	Dec 6	YEOVIL TOWN	3-2	Jones (og), Turner, Tabb	5131		8	10				3		14				1	6	2		9		7	13				5	11	12	4				
21	10	CHESTERFIELD	1-1	O'Connor	5828		8	11	12				6	13				1	3	2		9	14	7	10				5			4				
22	17	Tranmere Rovers	4-1	O'Connor, Owusu, Tabb, Newman	6210		8						10	6		14	12	1	7	2		9	13						5	11	3	4				
23	26	SWANSEA CITY	2-1	O'Connor, Hutchinson	9903		8	7					10	6		11	13	1		2		9			12				5		3	4				
24	31	COLCHESTER UNITED	0-2		6397		8	10					12	6		14		1	7	2		9	13						5	11	3	4				
25	Jan 2	Bradford City	3-3	Sodje, Campbell 2 (1p)	7588			7	12					6			2	1	8			9			10				5	11	3	4				
26	14	Southend United	1-4	Campbell	10046		8	10				5	12	6			14	1	7	2		9			13					11	3	4				
27	17	NOTTM. FOREST	1-1	Campbell	7859	1	14	7			12	3	6						8	2		9			10				5	11	13	4				
28	21	HUDDERSFIELD T	2-0	Owusu, Campbell	7636	1	14	7				3		13				12	8	2		9			10				5	11	6	4				
29	Feb 4	WALSALL	5-0	O'Connor (p), Sodje, Brooker, Rankin, Newman	5645		8							14			12	1	6	2		9		7	10				5	11	3	4	13			
30	11	Bristol City	1-0	Owusu	10854								12				2	1	6	8		9	13	7					5	11	3	4	10			
31	14	SOUTHEND UNITED	2-0	Jupp (og), Gayle	7022							3	9					1	8	2		12		7	10				5	11	6	4				
32	25	PORT VALE	0-1		7542		8					3	9				2	1	6			12		7	10	13			5	11	14	4				
33	28	Doncaster Rovers	0-0		5250							3		6				1	8			9		7		12			5	11	2	4	10			
34	Mar 7	Yeovil Town	2-1	Rankin, Rhodes	5137		8						7	6				1	2			9		13	10	12			5	11	3	4				
35	11	BARNSLEY	3-1	Owusu 2 (1p), Newman	7352		8					3	13					1	6			9		14	10	7			5	11	2	4	12			
36	17	Swansea City	1-2	Frampton	13508		8					3						1	6			9		7	10	13			5	11	2	4	12			
37	21	Gillingham	2-3	Turner, Tabb	5745		8					3						1	6			9		13	10	7		2	5	11	12	4	14			
38	25	DONCASTER ROVERS	0-1		7323		8					5	10	6				1	7			9	14	13				2		11	3	4	12			
39	28	MK Dons	1-0	Owusu	5592		8					3		12				1	6			9		7		13		2	5	11		4	10			
40	Apr 1	Colchester United	1-1	Tabb	5635		8					3	7	12				1	6			9		14	13			2	5	11		4	10			
41	8	BRADFORD CITY	1-1	Owusu	6533		8					3						1	6			9		12	10	7		2	5	11	13	4	14			
42	15	Rotherham United	2-2	Owusu, Rankin	5242		8					3	12					1	6			9		7	10	14		2	5	11	13	4				
43	17	BLACKPOOL	1-1	Owusu (p)	7339							3				8		1	6			9		13	10	7			5	11	2	4	12			
44	22	Swindon Town	3-1	Brooker, Gayle, Willock	6845		8						10					1	6	2		9		7		12			5	11	3	4	13			
45	29	HARTLEPOOL UNITED	1-1	O'Connor	8725		8					3	10	13				1	6	2				7	14	12			5	11		4	9			
46	May 6	Bournemouth	2-2	Frampton, Sodje	9359							3	9					1	6	8				7	10	13		2	5	11	12	4				
					Apps	2	32	13	0	3	3	36	16	17	0	11	3	44	29	30	1	39	1	25	31	5	2	7	43	42	20	46	5			
					Subs		4	10	2	3	8		8	10	3	3	4	1	1			3	9	7	6	12					13		8			
					Goals		4	9			1	3	2	2					3	7		12	1	4	7	1			5	6		2	1			

Two own goals

Play Offs

No	Date	Opponent	Score	Scorers	Att	Bankole A	Brooker P	Campbell DJ	Charles D	Dobson MW	Fitzgerald SP	Frampton AJK	Gayle MA	Hutchinson ES	Keenan JJ	Lewis KJ	Mousinho J	Nelson SJ	Newman RA	O'Connor KP	Osborne KAJ	Owusu LM	Peters RV	Pratley DA	Rankin I	Rhodes AG	Skulason O-I	Smith J	Sodje SO	Tabb JA	Tillen SL	Turner MT	Willock C	Moleski GK	Ide CJ	Watts RD
SF1	May 11	Swansea City	1-1	Tabb	19060	12	13					5	9					1	6	8				7	10			2		11	3	4				
SF2	14	SWANSEA CITY	0-2		10652		12					3						1	6	8				7	10	9		2	5	11	13	4	14			

F.A. Cup

No	Date	Opponent	Score	Scorers	Att	Bankole A	Brooker P	Campbell DJ	Charles D	Dobson MW	Fitzgerald SP	Frampton AJK	Gayle MA	Hutchinson ES	Keenan JJ	Lewis KJ	Mousinho J	Nelson SJ	Newman RA	O'Connor KP	Osborne KAJ	Owusu LM	Peters RV	Pratley DA	Rankin I	Rhodes AG	Skulason O-I	Smith J	Sodje SO	Tabb JA	Tillen SL	Turner MT	Willock C	Moleski GK	Ide CJ	Watts RD
R1	Nov 5	Rochdale	1-0	O'Connor (p)	2928		8			13		3				6		1	12	2		9		7	10				5	11	14	4				
R2	Dec 3	Oldham Athletic	1-1	Sodje	4365		8	10				3		13				1	6	2		9		7					5	11	12	4				
rep	13	OLDHAM ATHLETIC	1-0	Owusu	3146		8	10										1	6	2		9	12	7	13				5	11	3	4				
R3	Jan 7	Stockport County	3-2	Owusu, Campbell, Rankin	4078		8	10				13	11	6				1	7	2		9			12				5		3	4				
R4	28	SUNDERLAND	2-1	Campbell 2	11698		12	7				3		13			2	1	8			9			10				5	11	6	4				
R5	Feb 18	Charlton Athletic	1-3	Rankin	22098		12					3	10					1	8	2		9	14	7	13				5	11	6	4				

F.L. Cup (Carling Cup)

No	Date	Opponent	Score	Scorers	Att	Bankole A	Brooker P	Campbell DJ	Charles D	Dobson MW	Fitzgerald SP	Frampton AJK	Gayle MA	Hutchinson ES	Keenan JJ	Lewis KJ	Mousinho J	Nelson SJ	Newman RA	O'Connor KP	Osborne KAJ	Owusu LM	Peters RV	Pratley DA	Rankin I	Rhodes AG	Skulason O-I	Smith J	Sodje SO	Tabb JA	Tillen SL	Turner MT	Willock C	Moleski GK	Ide CJ	Watts RD
R1	Aug 23	Cheltenham Town	0-5		2113		8	9			10		5		11			1		2	6		7							12	3	4				

LDV Vans Trophy

No	Date	Opponent	Score	Scorers	Att	Bankole A	Brooker P	Campbell DJ	Charles D	Dobson MW	Fitzgerald SP	Frampton AJK	Gayle MA	Hutchinson ES	Keenan JJ	Lewis KJ	Mousinho J	Nelson SJ	Newman RA	O'Connor KP	Osborne KAJ	Owusu LM	Peters RV	Pratley DA	Rankin I	Rhodes AG	Skulason O-I	Smith J	Sodje SO	Tabb JA	Tillen SL	Turner MT	Willock C	Moleski GK	Ide CJ	Watts RD
R1	Oct 18	OXFORD UNITED	1-1	Fitzgerald	1785	1			8	7	9		5	6			4		11		2		10								3			12	13	14

Lost 3-4 on penalties a.e.t.

		Pl.	Home W	D	L	F	A	Away W	D	L	F	A	F. (Total)	A.	Pts
1	Southend United	46	13	6	4	37	16	10	7	6	35	27	72	43	82
2	Colchester United	46	15	4	4	39	21	7	9	7	19	19	58	40	79
3	**BRENTFORD**	**46**	**10**	**8**	**5**	**35**	**23**	**10**	**8**	**5**	**37**	**29**	**72**	**52**	**76**
4	Huddersfield Town	46	13	6	4	40	25	6	10	7	32	34	72	59	73
5	Barnsley	46	11	11	1	37	19	7	7	9	25	25	62	44	72
6	Swansea City	46	11	9	3	42	23	7	8	8	36	32	78	55	71
7	Nottingham Forest	46	14	5	4	40	15	5	7	11	27	37	67	52	69
8	Doncaster Rovers	46	11	6	6	30	19	9	3	11	25	32	55	51	69
9	Bristol City	46	11	7	5	38	22	7	4	12	28	40	66	62	65
10	Oldham Athletic	46	12	4	7	32	24	6	7	10	26	36	58	60	65
11	Bradford City	46	8	9	6	28	25	6	10	7	23	24	51	49	61
12	Scunthorpe United	46	8	8	7	36	33	7	7	9	32	40	68	73	60
13	Port Vale	46	10	5	8	30	26	6	7	10	19	28	49	54	60
14	Gillingham	46	13	4	6	31	21	3	8	12	19	43	50	64	60
15	Yeovil Town	46	8	8	7	27	24	7	3	13	27	38	54	62	56
16	Chesterfield	46	6	7	10	31	37	8	7	8	32	36	63	73	56
17	Bournemouth	46	7	11	5	25	20	5	8	10	24	33	49	53	55
18	Tranmere Rovers	46	7	8	8	32	30	6	7	10	18	22	50	52	54
19	Blackpool	46	9	8	6	33	27	3	9	11	23	37	56	64	53
20	Rotherham United	46	7	9	7	31	26	5	7	11	21	36	52	62	52
21	Hartlepool United	46	6	10	7	28	30	5	7	11	16	29	44	59	50
22	Milton Keynes Dons	46	8	8	7	28	25	4	6	13	17	41	45	66	50
23	Swindon Town	46	9	5	9	31	31	2	10	11	15	34	46	65	48
24	Walsall	46	7	7	9	27	34	4	7	12	20	36	47	60	47

2006/07

24th in League One: Relegated

No	Date		Opponent	Score	Scorers	Att	Abbey N	Brooker P	Carder-Andrews	Charles D	Cox S	Dark L	Frampton A	Griffiths A	Heywood M	Ide C	Keith J	Leary M	Masters C	Montague R	Moore C	Mousinho J	Nelson S	O'Connor K	Onibuje F	Osborne K	Osei-Kuffour J	Owusu L	Partridge D	Peters R	Pinault T	Rhodes A	Richards G	Shipperley N	Skulason O	Taylor S	Tillen S	Tomlin G	Wijnhard C	Willock C	Wilson C	England J
1	Aug	5	BLACKPOOL	1-0	Skulason	6048		7		6			3		5				1					2			10				4	11			8		12	13		9		
2		8	Northampton Town	1-0	Moore	5707				6			3	12	5	13					9		1	2			10				4	14			8		11	7				
3		12	Brighton & Hove Albion	2-2	O'Connor, Moore	6745		12					3	6	5						9		1	2			10				4	14			8		11	7		13		
4		19	HUDDERSFIELD T	2-2	Osei-Kuffour 2	5709		7						6	5						11	12	1	2		13	10				4	14			8		3			9		
5		26	Scunthorpe United	1-1	Osei-Kuffour	3942		7		12				6	5						9	8	1	2			10				4	11					3	13				
6	Sep	2	BRADFORD CITY	2-1	O'Connor, Osei-Kuffour	5471		7		3				6	5						14	8	1	2		13	10				4	12					11			9		
7		9	Leyton Orient	1-1	Tillen	5420		7	14	12				6	5						13		1	8		2	10				4	11					3			9		
8		12	SWANSEA CITY	0-2		5392		7			8			6	5						9		1	2		13	10				4	11					3	14		12		
9		16	BOURNEMOUTH	0-0		6272		7			8			6	5						12		1	2		13	10				4	11					3	9				
10		23	Chesterfield	1-3	Griffiths	3877		7		12	8			6	5							14	1			2	10			13	4						3	11		9		
11		26	Millwall	1-1	Willock	7618		7		12	8			6	5							4	1			2	10			14							3	13	9	11		
12		30	YEOVIL TOWN	1-2	Osei-Kuffour	5770		7						6	5							8	1	2			10			14	4	12					3	13	9	11		
13	Oct	7	BRISTOL CITY	1-1	O'Connor (p)	6740		7					3	6	5						13		1	2			10			14	4	11			8		12		9			
14		14	Rotherham United	0-2		4722		7					3	6	5						12	14	1	2			10			13	4				8		11		9			
15		21	GILLINGHAM	2-2	Heywood, Willock	5759			7				3	4	5				1			14		2		6	10				12				8			11	9	13		
16		28	Oldham Athletic	0-3		4708			7				3	6	5				1					2		4	10				14				8		12	11	13	9		
17	Nov	4	Nottingham Forest	0-2		18003		7					3	6	5	9			1		12	4		2			10								8		11		13			
18		18	CREWE ALEXANDRA	0-4		4771		7		5			3	6					1		9	8		2	14		12				4						11	13	10			
19		24	Cheltenham Town	0-2		3646		12		3	13			6	5				1			7		2	14		10				4	11			8				9			
20	Dec	5	DONCASTER ROVERS	0-4		4296				12	7		6		5	13			1		9	8		2			10				4	11					3					
21		9	TRANMERE ROVERS	1-1	Ide	4878		12			7		3	6	5	11			1		9	8		2		4	10													13		
22		16	Port Vale	0-1		4166		12			7		3	6	5	11			1			8		4		2	10					13								9		
23		23	Carlisle United	0-2		6805					7		3	6	5	11			1		12	8		4		2	10			13										9		
24		26	MILLWALL	1-4	O'Connor (p)	6925					7		3	6	5	11			1		12	8		2		4	10													9		
25		30	CHESTERFIELD	2-1	Osei-Kuffour 2	4540	1	7		12	11		3	6	5							8		2		4	10										13			9		
26	Jan	1	Swansea City	0-2		12554	1	7		8	11		3	6								2		5		4	10			13	12						14			9		
27		6	Bournemouth	0-1		5782	1	12			13		3	6		7	11	8						2			10		5		4									9		
28		13	LEYTON ORIENT	2-2	Ide 2	6765	1	12					3	6		7	11	4				8		2			10		5	13										9		
29		20	Yeovil Town	0-1		5373	1	7					3	6		9	11	4				8					10		5	13										12	2	
30		27	CARLISLE UNITED	0-0		5381	1	12					3	6		7	11	4				8				2	10							9			5			13		
31	Feb	3	Blackpool	3-1	Frampton, Osei-Kuffour 2	6086	1		13				5	12		7	11					8				6	10				4			9			3				2	
32		10	BRIGHTON & HOVE ALB	1-0	Osei-Kuffour	7023	1						3			7	11	4				8		12			10						5	9			6				2	
33		17	Huddersfield Town	2-0	Ide, Osei-Kuffour	10520	1	12					5	14		7	11	4						2		6	10						8	9			3			13		
34		19	NORTHAMPTON T	0-1		5164	1	12					5	14		7	11					8		2		4	10						6	9			3			13		
35		24	Bradford City	1-1	O'Connor (p)	7627	1									7	11	4				8		2		5	10						6	9			3					
36	Mar	3	SCUNTHORPE UNITED	0-2		5645	1	7					5			11		4				8		2						12			6	9			3			10		
37		10	Bristol City	0-1		11826	1						5	6	12	7	13	4				8		2									3	9		10	11					
38		17	ROTHERHAM UNITED	0-1		4937	1	7					5		12	11	3	4				8		2				14					6	9		10	13					
39		25	OLDHAM ATHLETIC	2-2	Richards, Keith	4720							5	12		7	11	4				8	1	2			10	14					6	9		13	3					
40		31	Gillingham	1-2	Osei-Kuffour	6113							5			7	11	4				8	1	2			10	13					6	9		12	3					
41	Apr	7	CHELTENHAM TOWN	0-2		4831		13					5		12	7	11	8					1	2			10	9			4		6			14	3					
42		9	Crewe Alexandra	1-3	O'Connor (p)	4667		7		13			5		6		3	11				14	1	2			10	9			4					8				12		
43		14	NOTTM. FOREST	2-4	Pinault, Ide	6637		7		12			5	6		10	3	11		14		8	1	2				9			4									13		
44		21	Doncaster Rovers	0-3		8713		7		3		14		6		10		8		13			1	2		5		9		12	4						11					
45		28	PORT VALE	4-3	Ide 2, Keith (p), Charles	5125	1	7	13	5		2		6		9	11			14		8								12	4						3			10		
46	May	5	Tranmere Rovers	1-3	Willock	6529	1	7		5		2		6		10	3	11		14		8								12	4	13								9		
						Apps	16	24	2	9	11	2	32	32	25	24	17	17	11	0	8	29	19	38	0	17	38	4	3	0	24	8	10	11	10	3	28	6	7	18	3	
						Subs		10	3	8	2	1		5	3	2	1			4	8	5		1	2	4	1	3		13	3	7				3	6	6	2	10		
						Goals				1			1	1	1	7	2				2			6			12				1		1		1		1			3		

F.A. Cup

Rd	Date		Opponent	Score	Scorers	Att	Abbey N	Brooker P	Carder-Andrews	Charles D	Cox S	Dark L	Frampton A	Griffiths A	Heywood M	Ide C	Keith J	Leary M	Masters C	Montague R	Moore C	Mousinho J	Nelson S	O'Connor K	Onibuje F	Osborne K	Osei-Kuffour J	Owusu L	Partridge D	Peters R	Pinault T	Rhodes A	Richards G	Shipperley N	Skulason O	Taylor S	Tillen S	Tomlin G	Wijnhard C	Willock C	Wilson C	England J
R1	Nov	10	DONCASTER ROVERS	0-1		3607		7					5	6		10			1		14	4		2	11		9				12				8		3		13			

F.L. Cup (Carling Cup)

Rd	Date		Opponent	Score	Scorers	Att	Abbey N	Brooker P	Carder-Andrews	Charles D	Cox S	Dark L	Frampton A	Griffiths A	Heywood M	Ide C	Keith J	Leary M	Masters C	Montague R	Moore C	Mousinho J	Nelson S	O'Connor K	Onibuje F	Osborne K	Osei-Kuffour J	Owusu L	Partridge D	Peters R	Pinault T	Rhodes A	Richards G	Shipperley N	Skulason O	Taylor S	Tillen S	Tomlin G	Wijnhard C	Willock C	Wilson C	England J
R1	Aug	22	Swindon Town	2-2	O'Connor, Osei-Kuffour	5582		7		14				6	5	13					9	8	1	2		12	10				4	11					3					
R2	Sep	19	LUTON TOWN	0-3		3005		7		3	8				5						14	6	1			2	10				4						11	9		12		13

R1 won 4-3 on penalties a.e.t.

Johnstone's Paint Trophy

Rd	Date		Opponent	Score	Scorers	Att	Abbey N	Brooker P	Carder-Andrews	Charles D	Cox S	Dark L	Frampton A	Griffiths A	Heywood M	Ide C	Keith J	Leary M	Masters C	Montague R	Moore C	Mousinho J	Nelson S	O'Connor K	Onibuje F	Osborne K	Osei-Kuffour J	Owusu L	Partridge D	Peters R	Pinault T	Rhodes A	Richards G	Shipperley N	Skulason O	Taylor S	Tillen S	Tomlin G	Wijnhard C	Willock C	Wilson C	England J
R1	Oct	17	Northampton Town	0-0		2088		13	6				3		5				1		9	12		2		4	10			7					8		11	14				
R2		31	Nottingham Forest	1-2	Osei-Kuffour	2031		7					3		5	9			1			8		2			10			14	4				11	6	13	12				

R1 won 4-2 on penalties (no extra time)

		Pl.	Home W	D	L	F	A	Away W	D	L	F	A	F. (Total)	A.	Pts
1	Scunthorpe United	46	15	6	2	40	17	11	7	5	33	18	73	35	91
2	Bristol City	46	15	5	3	35	20	10	5	8	28	19	63	39	85
3	Blackpool	46	12	6	5	40	25	12	5	6	36	24	76	49	83
4	Nottingham Forest	46	14	5	4	37	17	9	8	6	28	24	65	41	82
5	Yeovil Town	46	14	3	6	22	12	9	7	7	33	27	55	39	79
6	Oldham Athletic	46	13	4	6	36	18	8	8	7	33	29	69	47	75
7	Swansea City	46	12	6	5	36	20	8	6	9	33	33	69	53	72
8	Carlisle United	46	12	5	6	35	24	7	6	10	19	31	54	55	68
9	Tranmere Rovers	46	13	5	5	33	22	5	8	10	25	31	58	53	67
10	Millwall	46	11	8	4	33	19	8	1	14	26	43	59	62	66
11	Doncaster Rovers	46	8	10	5	30	23	8	5	10	22	24	52	47	63
12	Port Vale	46	12	3	8	35	26	6	3	14	29	39	64	65	60
13	Crewe Alexandra	46	11	4	8	39	38	6	5	12	27	34	66	72	60
14	Northampton Town	46	8	5	10	27	28	7	9	7	21	23	48	51	59
15	Huddersfield Town	46	9	8	6	37	33	5	9	9	23	36	60	69	59
16	Gillingham	46	14	2	7	29	24	3	6	14	27	53	56	77	59
17	Cheltenham Town	46	8	6	9	25	27	7	3	13	24	34	49	61	54
18	Brighton & Hove A.	46	5	7	11	23	34	9	4	10	26	24	49	58	53
19	Bournemouth	46	10	5	8	28	27	3	8	12	22	37	50	64	52
20	Leyton Orient	46	6	10	7	30	32	6	5	12	31	45	61	77	51
21	Chesterfield	46	9	5	9	29	22	3	6	14	16	31	45	53	47
22	Bradford City	46	5	9	9	27	31	6	5	12	20	34	47	65	47
23	Rotherham United	46	8	4	11	37	39	5	5	13	21	36	58	75	38
24	**BRENTFORD**	**46**	**5**	**8**	**10**	**24**	**41**	**3**	**5**	**15**	**16**	**38**	**40**	**79**	**37**

2006-07

Back: Kuffour, Tomlin, Peters, Ide, Tillen, Willock, Owusu, Rhodes
Middle: Stannard (Goal.Coach), Fitzgerald (Coach), Osborne, Moore, Masters, Heywood, Nelson, Charles, Mousinho, Harling (Fitness Coach), Carter (Kit man)
Front: Pinault, Brooker, Griffin (Asst.Manager), O'Connor, Rosenior (Manager), Frampton, Mortimer (Coach), Griffiths, Skulason

2007-08 (August)

Back: Hutchinson (Physio), Carder Andrews, Heywood, Charles, Marsella (Goal.Coach), Osborne, Montague, Dark, Carter (Kit man)
Middle: Starosta, Ide, Thorpe, Masters, Brown, Connell, Mousinho, Basey
Front: Tillen, Pead, Mackie, Butcher (Manager), Scott (Assist. Man.), O'Connor, Poole, Peters.

2007/08

14th in League Two

No			Opponent	Res	Scorers	Att	Hamer	Starosta	Basey	Pettigrew	Mackie	Mousinho	O'Connor	Moore	Connell	Ide	Poole	Smith	Peters	Brooker	Tillen	Osborne	Thorpe	Heywood	Pead	Shakes	Brown S	Charles	Emanuel	Montague	Dickson	Sinclair	Masters	Sankofa	Elder	Stone	Parkes	Reid	Milsom	Brown W	Bennett
1	Aug	11	MANSFIELD TOWN	1-1	Connell	4909	1	2	3	4	5	6	7	8	9	10	11	12	13	14																					
2		18	Notts County	1-1	O'Connor	4670	1	2	3	4	5	6	7	8		10	11		12		13	9																			
3		25	BARNET	2-1	Mousinho, O'Connor (p)	4744	1	2	3	6	5	11	7	8		10	12		13			4	9																		
4	Sep	1	Bury	2-1	Poole, Shakes	2301	1	2	3	6		11	7	8		10	9					4		5	12	13															
5		9	Wycombe Wanderers	0-1		4711	1	2	3	6			7	8	12	10	9					4		5	13	11															
6		15	MILTON KEYNES DONS	0-3		4476	1	2	3	6		8	7			10	12	11	13			4	9	5		14															
7		22	Chester City	2-0	Moore, Thorpe	2453		2		4	5		6	8	10	13	11	12					9			7	1	3													
8		29	STOCKPORT COUNTY	1-3	Connell	4449		2		4	5		6	8	10	14	11					12	9		13	7	1	3													
9	Oct	2	DAGENHAM & REDBRIDGE	2-3	Mousinho, Thorpe	3662		2		4		12	6	8	9	10	11					13	5		7		1	3													
10		6	Hereford United	0-2		2942		12	3		5	6	2	8	10		11						9	4	7	13	1	14													
11		12	ROTHERHAM UNITED	1-1	Thorpe	3841		2	3		5	6	8	14	13	10	11						9	4		7	1	12													
12		20	Rochdale	1-1	Poole	2424		2		12	5		8		14	10	11	13					9	4	6	7	1	3													
13		27	LINCOLN CITY	1-0	Moore	4368		2		12	5		8	14	10	7	11						9	4	6		1		3	13											
14	Nov	3	Bradford City	2-1	Poole, Thorpe	###		2			5		7	8	10		11						9	4	6	14	1	13	3	12											
15		6	Macclesfield Town	0-1		1378		2			5		7	8	10		11						9	4	6	13	1	12	3												
16		17	DARLINGTON	0-2		4657		2			5		3	8	14	10	11						9	4	6	7	1	12			13										
17		24	Peterborough United	0-7		4865					5		2		14	7	11						9	4	6	12	1	3			8	10	13								
18	Dec	4	MORECAMBE	0-1		3155		2			5		7	8	13		11						9	4	12		1	3		10	6	14									
19		8	GRIMSBY TOWN	0-1		3999		2					8	12	9	7		6				4	14	5		13	1	3		10	11										
20		15	Wrexham	3-1	Connell 2, S Evans (og)	3811		2					8		9	7	12	6				4	10	5		13	1	3			11	14									
21		21	Milton Keynes Dons	1-1	Connell	8445		2					8	14	9	13	11	6				4	10	5	12	7	1				3										
22		26	WYCOMBE WANDERERS	1-3	Poole	5841		2					8		9	7	11	6				4	10	5			1	12			3	13									
23		29	CHESTER CITY	3-0	Connell, Poole, Montague	4323							8	13	9	7	11	6				4		5	2	12	1			10	3										
24	Jan	1	Dagenham & Redbridge	2-1	Poole 2	2353	1						8	12	9		11	6				4		5	2	7		13		10	3										
25		5	Shrewsbury Town	1-0	Osborne	5083	1					13	8	12	9		11	6				4		5	2	7				10	3										
26		12	CHESTERFIELD	2-1	Poole, Smith	4882	1					12	8		9		11	6				4	13	5	2	7				10	3										
27		29	NOTTS COUNTY	0-0		4332	1						8		9		11	6				4		5	2	7				10	3			12							
28	Feb	2	Mansfield Town	3-2	O'Connor, Connell, Elder	2511	1						8		10		11	6						5	2	7				12	3			4	9	13	14				
29		9	SHREWSBURY TOWN	1-1	Connell	5353	1								10		11	6						5	2	7					3			4	9	8		12			
30		12	Barnet	2-1	Poole 2 (1 p)	2522	1								10		11	6				12		5	2	7					3			4	9	8		13	14		
31		16	ACCRINGTON STANLEY	3-1	Connell, Poole, Heywood	4635	1								10		11					12		5	2	7					3			4	9	8		13	6		
32		23	Chesterfield	0-1		3728	1					12			10		11	6				4		5		7		13			3			2	9			14	8		
33		26	Accrington Stanley	0-1		1149	1					13			9		11	6				4			2	12					3			5	14			10	8	7	
34	Mar	1	Darlington	1-3	Reid	3508	1					13			10		11	6				4			2	12					3			5	9			14	8	7	
35		4	BURY	1-4	Poole (p)	3333	1					5			10		11	6				4				12					3			2	9			13	8	7	
36		8	MACCLESFIELD TOWN	1-0	Poole	3863									10		11	6				4			2	7	1				3				9	8					5
37		11	PETERBOROUGH UTD	1-2	Connell	4049						12			10		11	6				4			2	7	1				3				9	8					5
38		15	Morecambe	1-3	Elder	2180						8	14		10		11	6				4				7	1				3			2	9			12		13	5
39		22	WREXHAM	2-0	Shakes 2	4448						12	8		10		11	6				4			2	7	1				3				9						5
40		24	Grimsby Town	2-1	Connell, W Brown	4620						6	8		10		11					4			2	7	1				3				9			13		12	5
41		29	ROCHDALE	0-2		4896						6	8		10		11							4	2	7	1				3				9					12	5
42	Apr	5	Rotherham United	2-1	Connell, Elder	2979						13	8		12		11	6						4	2	10	1				3				9					7	5
43		12	BRADFORD CITY	2-2	Poole, Bennett	4336							8		10		11	6						4	2	12	1				3				9					7	5
44		19	Lincoln City	1-3	Elder	3699						2	8		10		11	6						4		12	1				3				9			13		7	5
45		26	HEREFORD UNITED	0-3		6246	1					13	8		9		11	6				4		12	2	10					3									7	5
46	May	3	Stockport County	0-1		6284	1					7	8		9		11	6				4		12		10		13			3			2						14	5
						Apps	20	20	8	9	14	13	36	13	35	16	42	26				25	17	30	27	25	26	8	3	7	30	1		10	16	5		1	5	7	11
						Subs		1		2		10	1	7	7	3	3	3	4	1	1	4	2	2	5	14		9		3	1	3	1	1	1	1	1	9	1	4	
						Goals						2	3	2	12		14	1				1	4	1		3				1					4			1		1	1

F.A. Cup

Rd			Opponent	Res	Scorers	Att	Hamer	Starosta	Basey	Pettigrew	Mackie	Mousinho	O'Connor	Moore	Connell	Ide	Poole	Smith	Peters	Brooker	Tillen	Osborne	Thorpe	Heywood	Pead	Shakes	Brown S	Charles	Emanuel	Montague	Dickson	Sinclair	Masters	Sankofa	Elder	Stone	Parkes	Reid	Milsom	Brown W	Bennett
R1	Nov	10	Luton Town	1-1	Ide	4167		2		4			3	8		10	11						9	5	6	7	1	12													
rep		27	LUTON TOWN	0-2		2643					5		2	8	10	7	11	13				12	9	4	6	14		3					1								

F.L. Cup (Carling Cup)

Rd			Opponent	Res	Scorers	Att	Hamer	Starosta	Basey	Pettigrew	Mackie	Mousinho	O'Connor	Moore	Connell	Ide	Poole	Smith	Peters	Brooker	Tillen	Osborne	Thorpe	Heywood	Pead	Shakes	Brown S	Charles	Emanuel	Montague	Dickson	Sinclair	Masters	Sankofa	Elder	Stone	Parkes	Reid	Milsom	Brown W	Bennett
R1	Aug	14	BRISTOL CITY	0-3		2213	1	2	3	4	5	6	7	8	9	10		12	14	11	13																				

Johnstone's Paint Trophy

Rd			Opponent	Res	Scorers	Att	Hamer	Starosta	Basey	Pettigrew	Mackie	Mousinho	O'Connor	Moore	Connell	Ide	Poole	Smith	Peters	Brooker	Tillen	Osborne	Thorpe	Heywood	Pead	Shakes	Brown S	Charles	Emanuel	Montague	Dickson	Sinclair	Masters	Sankofa	Elder	Stone	Parkes	Reid	Milsom	Brown W	Bennett
R1	Sep	4	Swindon Town	1-4	Shakes	3118			3	6			2	8	9	14	10	11	13			4		5	12	7	1														

		Pl.	Home W	D	L	F	A	Away W	D	L	F	A	F. (Total)	A.	Pts
1	Milton Keynes Dons	46	11	7	5	39	17	18	3	2	43	20	82	37	97
2	Peterborough Utd.	46	14	4	5	46	20	14	4	5	38	23	84	43	92
3	Hereford United	46	11	6	6	34	19	15	4	4	38	22	72	41	88
4	Stockport County	46	11	5	7	40	30	13	5	5	32	24	72	54	82
5	Rochdale	46	11	4	8	37	28	12	7	4	40	26	77	54	80
6	Darlington	46	11	7	5	36	22	11	5	7	31	18	67	40	78
7	Wycombe Wands	46	13	6	4	29	15	9	6	8	27	27	56	42	78
8	Chesterfield	46	9	8	6	42	29	10	4	9	34	27	76	56	69
9	Rotherham United	46	12	4	7	37	29	9	7	7	25	29	62	58	64
10	Bradford City	46	10	4	9	30	30	7	7	9	33	31	63	61	62
11	Morecambe	46	9	6	8	33	32	7	6	10	26	31	59	63	60
12	Barnet	46	10	6	7	37	30	6	6	11	19	33	56	63	60
13	Bury	46	8	6	9	30	30	8	5	10	28	31	58	61	59
14	**BRENTFORD**	**46**	**7**	**5**	**11**	**25**	**35**	**10**	**3**	**10**	**27**	**35**	**52**	**70**	**59**
15	Lincoln City	46	9	3	11	33	38	9	1	13	28	39	61	77	58
16	Grimsby Town	46	7	5	11	26	34	8	5	10	29	32	55	66	55
17	Accrington Stanley	46	7	1	15	20	39	9	2	12	29	44	49	83	51
18	Shrewsbury Town	46	9	6	8	31	22	3	8	12	25	43	56	65	50
19	Macclesfield Town	46	6	8	9	27	31	5	9	9	20	33	47	64	50
20	Dagenham & Red.	46	6	7	10	27	32	7	3	13	22	38	49	70	49
21	Notts County	46	8	5	10	19	23	2	13	8	18	30	37	53	48
22	Chester City	46	5	5	13	21	30	7	6	10	30	38	51	68	47
23	Mansfield Town	46	6	3	14	30	39	5	6	12	18	29	48	68	42
24	Wrexham	46	6	7	10	16	28	4	3	16	22	42	38	70	40

2007-08 (February)
Back: Charles, Stone, Osborne, Mousinho, Elder, Heywood, Reid
Middle: Carter (Kit man), Montague, Sankofa, Hamer, Brown, Shakes, O'Connor, Hutchinson (Physio), Marsella (Goal.Coach)
Front: Poole, Ide, Pead, Smith, Scott (Manager), Parkes, Dark, Dickson, Connell.

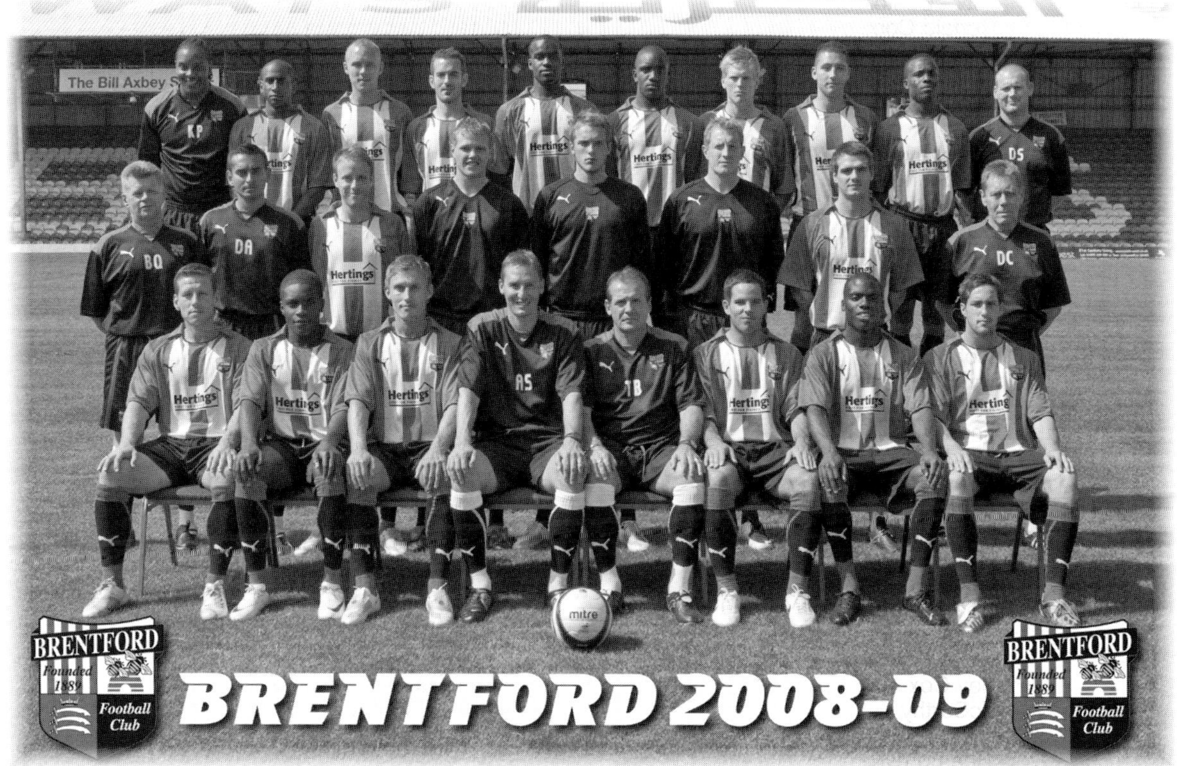

Back: Phillips (Youth Physio), Newton, Mills, O'Connor, Osborne, Elder, Connell, Montague, Bean, Sarll (Youth Manager)
Middle: Quin (Youth Devt.), Appanah(Physio), Poole, Seb Brown, Hamer, Simon Brown, Dickson, Carter (Kit Man),
Front: MacDonald, Ademola, Pead, Scott (Manager), Bullivant (Asst.Manager), Wood, Williams, Smith.

Dedications:

From the following supporters or by way of a dedication
a £10 donation from each has been given to a youth project at Brentford F.C.

For Graham a Wonderful Husband
You gave me passion for Life - Stephen Haynes
(Graham) Mr. Perfect. A Special Dad.
Miss You Graham -"The Family"
Joan and Alf Haynes
Pauline Young
"Dad". Daisy and Java Haynes
In Memory of Graham Haynes
Graham Happy Dog Memories Carole
(Graham) He Made Me Laugh - Maisie.
Graham Thanks for the Memories
Friend and Colleague greatly missed
Fondly Remembered by Reading Nightingales
Thanks Graham for Wonderful Memories
Thanks for Everything Sam Heckley
Graham Haynes - missed - David Barnett
David Barnett Life Supporter
Keith MacInnes Up The Bees
Mike Cabble Fan since 1943
John Hawkes
Malcolm Hobday
Deborah Hobday
Neil Hobday - Knightley
Chloe Knighley - Kay
Yvonne Enstone
Clive Soden
Arthur Richards. Bees until death
The Porter Family - Boston Manor
In Memory of Ronald Cooper
In Memory of Henry Cooper
Megan Taylor. Norwood Green Southall
Susan Taylor. Norwood Green Southall
Brentford Forever
Charlie Cooper. Always Remembered. Tony
Elizabeth Cable - Stung since 1976
Gary Pain. Farnborough Hampshire
Steven Cowen - Join Bees United
Ian Venner
Herbie Whitaker. Tom Guilfoyle Remembered
Bring on the Dancing Girls
Lee Emmerson - Brentford for Life
Ray Silver. Didcot
George, Geoff and Darren Vial
Emily and Gary Backler 2008
Gordan and Sandra - St. Margarets
Sharon Hurley and Junior Bee
Jim Walsh - Hayes Bees
Terry and Kimberley Atkins
Peter and Jean Atkins
Jeremy Clark - Hounslow West
Peter Clark (Deceased) - Heston
Richard, Rob, Joe, Sam Bartram
Lynne Morgan Lifelong Bees Supporter
Ben Wildman Bees Forever
Peter and Bradley Cox
Michael John McCarthy
Popsy from the Gray Bees
Emma Grey A Bee Forever
Gary Stenning follow follow 1889
Sarah, Callum, Conor, Emily, Josh
Brian Eyles
Bees Always Brian Moriarty
Paul Wust
Mark Croxford
Paulyboy and Dad
Rik Scales
Rod Scales
Bill Billings - Maidenhead Berks
Arran Matthews - Tylers Green
In Memory of Tom Twydell
John, Sarah, Matthew Pitt Mightybees
David Furlong
Derek Furlong
Kevin Furlong
Jamie Whale
Robert Whale
James Sexton supporting since 1937
Reginald, Ted, Malcolm. Brentford Forever
Jonathan Burchill, Harrow
Jamie Burchill
John Huggins
Lynda and Paul Londra
Ray Smith "Sixty Year Dedication"
Stuart and Ray Smith Slough
Gary Piggott Bees Fan Forever
Keith Piggott Brentford for Life
In Memory of Dick Harrison
Ian Gilding
Alan Gilding
John Stride From East Sheen
Matthew Stride From East Sheen
Martin Barrett
Paul, Emily, Joseph, Molly Bryce
Noreen Johnson formerly of Chiswick
Darren, Helen and Courtney Wells
To Simon From Annie
Kayden Jeffery
Paul Jeffery
Mary Jeffery
Peter Jeffery
Geoffrey Wheeler Son's James, Matthew
Phil Coffey - Dad and Grandad
Geoffrey Green
Andrea and Paul Haines
G.J. Chandler
David Ohl
Paul Reddick
Mick Cabble Bees Forever
Stick It Up Them Bees
Neil Plunkett - Brentford Forever
Since 1943 A Bee Stan King
"Dover" Jack Lahr Happy 21st
"Isleworth" Gary Lahr Happy 50th
Paul Merritt, Worcester Park
Malcolm Graham
Emily Turner, Young Brentford Fan
David Stallabrass Up the Bees
For Paul (Hiskett) from Dad
Robert Spenceley
Keep Supporting Us Alan
In memory of David Westbrook
Saul Westbrook
Juliette Westbrook
Hugh Westbrook
Maureen, Daniel and Fliss Lister
Matt and Claire Lister
I Love My Wife Too
Russell Barker
Dean, Gemma and Robbie Lefever
James Rudman Hounslow

John Barnjum Chiswick
In Memory of Fred Guyett
In Memory of Frank Thomas
In Memory of Harry Barnett
Alfie Mick Boulden, Bees Forever
Alan Winter - Twickenham
Paul and Georgie Thompson
Darryl Howell - True Supporter
Mark Bluck - Fairweather Fan
The Jeffs Family Alton Hants
Rob Winter Bees Forever
Les Charlie Varley Isleworth Middx
The Old Boy Heston Middx
Roy Bird RIP 1925 - 2007
Brian McDonough Up The Bees
Up The Bees Peter Franks
In Memory of George Sear
Dave Baxter Dedicated Lifelong Supporter
David Brown and Family, Hampton
Never Give Up, Graham Brooks
Carl Brooks
Tony Brooks 1924 - 1990
Joseph Snelling, Acton Green
George Snelling, Acton Green
Graham Hunt, Basingstoke
Memory of Frederick Charles Bond
Barry Linda and Ian Neighbour
Danny and Edna Neighbour RIP
Beeattidude GPG New Malden Twickenham
Dan Jervis New Malden
Peter Dray
In Memory of Tom Ward
David Cordery
Richard and Alison Evans
Tracy Woods
Roy and Rita Woods
Tracey Forrester
Danielle,Luke and Jordan Forrester
Tony Cooper, Dad and Gramps
P. Minkkinen, J. Finch, J. Hart
Elena, Olivia Niamh Love Grandad
Barry Mingard and Lewis Byrne
Steve Ramnarain
Asraf Din Ramnarain
Bruce Powell
Christina Powell
Victor Honhold, Chiswick, Deceased
Paul Honhold, Chiswick
Carlos (Joe) Joannides - Brentford
The English Family
Steve Hayes Bees Forever
Simon Marriott Balti Pie King
Barry Paul
David and Gary Taylor, Hounslow
Ken Powell, Lower Sunbury
Daniel Powell, Ashford
Jamie Powell, Ashford
The Roker Family
In Memory of Ken Boddie
In Memory of Christel Knowles
Arthur Gregory 1913 - 1991
Billy, Alfie Read Forever Brentford
Peter Page, Chesham
Christopher Page, Chesham
Frank, Susan and Sally Coumbe
Stephen Walter
Leighton Matthews (Slough) Clonmel, IE
Alan Matthews Slough
Paul Baston, Burgess Hill
Russell Owen Bee Forever
Kevin Fancourt, Dagenham
In Memory of Ronald Randall
In Memory of Gwendoline Randall
Lifetime Bees Supporter Geoffery Randall
Lifetime Bees Supporter Clifford Randall
Lifetime Bees Supporter Raymond Randal
Lifetime Bees Supporter Mary Renforth
David Sissons
For My Son Jacob Wellington
Peter Gilham
Adrienne Gilham
Graham Sandys, Wallington
Barr Boys Remember Good Times
Gary Paul
In Memory of Albert Godfrey
Brentford Till I Die Brian Godfrey
John Iain and Michael Habes
Dennis Smith, Egham
Top Fan John Davis, Charvil
Daniel Carroll,
Max Brentford Cox
William D. Carroll (Deceased)
Sheila Carroll
John “Daddy” Carroll
Ian Powell
Julian, Balqees, Joshua, Bethany Mann
James Malcolm
Clive Brooks
Owen Brooks
Carol Brooks Long Suffering Wife & Mother
My ‘Superbees’ Dad Gordon Cousins
Peter Miller Always Remembered
Eric Miller
Alan Rogers
Chris, James, Stephen Margaret Armstrong
Jason Clarridge Born A Bee
Andew Martin, Old Windsor
Phil Coates